palgrave macmillan law masters

family law

Series editor: **Marise Cremona**

Business Law   Stephen Judge
Company Law   Janet Dine and Marios Koutsias
Constitutional and Administrative Law   John Alder
Contract Law   Ewan McKendrick
Criminal Law   Jonathan Herring
Economic and Social Law of the European Union   Jo Shaw, Jo Hunt and Chloe Wallace
Employment Law   Deborah J. Lockton
Evidence   Raymond Emson
Family Law   Kate Standley
Intellectual Property Law   Tina Hart, Linda Fazzani and Simon Clark
Land Law   Joe Cursley, Mark Davys and Kate Green
Landlord and Tenant Law   Margaret Wilkie, Peter Luxton, Jill Morgan and Godfrey Cole
Law of the European Union   Jo Shaw
Legal Method   Ian McLeod
Legal Theory   Ian McLeod
Sports Law   Mark James
Torts   Alastair Mullis and Ken Oliphant
Trusts Law   Charlie Webb and Tim Akkouh

palgrave macmillan law masters

family law

kate standley

Senior Lecturer in Law at the
University of Essex

Seventh edition

Series Editor: Marise Cremona
Professor of European Law
European University Institute
Florence, Italy

palgrave
macmillan

This edition first published 2010 by PALGRAVE MACMILLAN

Palgrave Macmillan in the UK is an imprint of Macmillan Publishers Limited, registered in England, company number 785998, of Houndmills, Basingstoke, Hampshire RG21 6XS.

Palgrave Macmillan in the US is a division of St Martin's Press LLC, 175 Fifth Avenue, New York, NY 10010.

Palgrave Macmillan is the global academic imprint of the above companies and has companies and representatives throughout the world.

Palgrave® and Macmillan® are registered trademarks in the United States, the United Kingdom, Europe and other countries

ISBN 978–0–230–25159–5   paperback

This book is printed on paper suitable for recycling and made from fully managed and sustained forest sources. Logging, pulping and manufacturing processes are expected to conform to the environmental regulations of the country of origin.

A catalogue record for this book is available from the British Library.

10   9   8   7   6   5   4   3   2   1
19   18   17   16   15   14   13   12   11   10

Printed and bound in Great Britain by
CPI Antony Rowe, Chippenham and Eastbourne

Contents

Nearly two decades have passed since the first edition of *Family Law* was published in 1993. A great deal has happened in family law in England and Wales during that time. Civil partnership has been introduced, cohabitants have acquired more rights, and transsexual persons have gained new rights. More recent changes have included a new law of adoption, the introduction of special guardianship, increased protection for victims of domestic violence, protection for victims of forced marriages and improvements to the child protection system. Important decisions have been made by the courts, including, in particular, decisions on the courts' powers in respect of the allocation of property and finance on divorce. Major social changes have also taken place. Cohabitation has increased. The number of marriages is declining. Increasing numbers of families are step-families.

Family law continues to move forward at a pace. In the two years since the last edition there have been important legislative and case-law developments. Radical changes have been made to the child support system and the family courts have been opened up to the media. Changes in respect of facilitating and enforcing contact have come into force. There have been important decisions in the courts, for instance on pre-nuptial and post-nuptial agreements and on the burden of proof in care proceedings. A Cohabitation Bill was placed before Parliament at the end of 2008 but progressed no further. A further development was the opening of the new Supreme Court in 2009.

As far as the future is concerned, the Law Commission is currently conducting a project on the question of the enforceability of pre-nuptial and post-nuptial agreements and is considering the question of property rights on death; and the Government is proposing to introduce compulsory birth registration for unmarried fathers.

There have been calls for reform in some areas of family law. Giving the child a greater voice in proceedings for residence and contact has been, and continues to be, a 'hot topic' and so does reform of the law to give cohabitants property and financial rights on relationship breakdown. Another area of concern, and where criticism has been voiced, is in respect of the discretionary regime for adjusting property and financial matters on the breakdown of marriage and civil partnership. There have also been calls for reform of the law of divorce.

Despite the many changes in family law, my aim in writing this book remains the same as it was when I wrote the first edition, which is to provide a clear, comprehensive and up-to-date account of family law in England and Wales.

Finally, my thanks go to John, my husband, for his love, support and encouragement over the years; and for the many cups of coffee he has made which have stopped me falling asleep over my laptop.

Kate Standley

Table of cases

Table of statutes

Part I

Family law – an introduction

Chapter 1

Family law

1.1 Family law – changes and trends

Family law is an area of law which changes rapidly. There have been many important legislative and case-law developments in the last few years. Keeping up with the changes can be difficult. There are also rules of court, practice directions, government papers and other materials which have to be digested.

(a) Legislative developments

There have been major legislative developments in family law in the last 20 years. In the 1990s a particularly important development was the Children Act 1989, which came into force in October 1991 and made far-reaching changes to the civil law relating to children. In 1993 the Child Support Act 1991 moved child maintenance from the courts into the Child Support Agency. In the mid-1990s civil remedies for victims of domestic violence were made available to a wider class of family members by Part IV of the Family Law Act 1996. Also during the 1990s, there was an attempt to introduce a radically new divorce law, but this was eventually abandoned by the Government as the proposed reforms proved to be unworkable in practice.

In the first few years of the new millennium there were further important legislative developments. Of particular importance was the Human Rights Act 1998 which came into force in the year 2000. In 2003 new provisions were introduced to allow unmarried fathers to acquire parental responsibility by birth registration. Pension sharing on divorce was also introduced. In the last few years there have been changes to the law to give victims of domestic violence greater protection under new provisions introduced by the Domestic Violence, Crime and Victims Act 2004. New civil law remedies were introduced in 2008 by Part 4A of the Family Law Act 1996 to provide remedies for victims of forced marriage. An important development was the introduction of civil partnership by the Civil Partnership Act 2004. Transsexual persons have also been given the right, by the Gender Recognition Act 2004, to enter into a valid marriage in their newly acquired sex.

Important legislative changes have been made in the last few years to the law relating to children. Radical changes to adoption law have been made by the Adoption and Children Act 2002; and special guardianship has been introduced. The Children Act 2004 has, among other things, made changes to the structural framework governing the practice of child protection; and s.58 of that Act has placed restrictions on the use of corporal punishment on children by parents. Reforms have also been made to improve the facilitation and enforcement of contact on family breakdown; and radical changes to the child support system are currently in the process of being implemented. Changes to the law governing parenthood in cases of assisted reproduction have also recently been made by the Human Fertilisation and Embryology Act 2008.

(b) Case-law developments

There have been important case-law developments. These have included two decisions of the House of Lords (now the Supreme Court) dealing with the approach the courts must adopt in proceedings for property and financial orders on divorce (see 7.6). Other decisions of the House of Lords have dealt with the rights of transsexuals (see 2.7), the threshold conditions for making care and supervision orders (see 14.7), the power of the courts to enforce payment of child support (see 12.3), and the interface between the homelessness legislation and family proceedings (see 4.11). The House of Lords has also handed down some important decisions on the law governing international child abduction.

As a result of their obligations under the Human Rights Act 1998, courts have to exercise their powers in the light of the European Convention for the Protection of Human Rights and Fundamental Freedoms, and human rights arguments have been used in some cases. The law on the succession by a homosexual person to the tenancy of a deceased partner, for example, was extended by the House of Lords in order to bring the law into line with the Human Rights Act 1998 (see 4.15), and so was the law governing the rights of transsexuals (see 2.7).

(c) Current discussions

Current discussions in family law range across a wide range of issues. Thus, there are proposals to make it mandatory for unmarried fathers to be named on children's birth certificates in order to give them parental responsibility (see 9.4). There has been ongoing discussion about changing the law to allow children to have a greater voice in private family law proceedings (such as in residence and contact proceedings) (see 8.6). There have also been discussions and proposals about reforming the law to give cohabitants rights on family breakdown (see 3.4). The Law Commission (the Government's law reform body) is currently considering reform of the law governing inheritance and financial provision on death; and is also to consider whether the law should be changed to make pre-nuptial agreements legally binding (see 7.14).

(d) Demographic and social changes

There have been important demographic and social changes which impact on family law. Many people cohabit, fewer people marry and family breakdown is common. Increasing numbers of families are lone-parent families; and many children are brought up by a single parent. Many children are born outside marriage. There are also increasing numbers of elderly persons.

A particularly important change in family law has been the recognition given by legislators and courts to different forms of family living. The traditional family (married couple and children) is no longer the only family form, and families are also increasingly complex. There are homosexual families, step-families and multiple step-families. There are civil partnerships. The recognition by the Government of these increasingly complex family forms has resulted in an increasingly complex set of statutory provisions. The driving forces behind the changes which have taken place in family life are articulated by Mr Justice Munby in the following extract:

> ▶ **Mr Justice Munby, 'Families old and new – the family and Article 8' [2005]** *Child and Family Law Quarterly* **487**
>
> 'There have been very profound changes in family life in recent decades. They have been driven by four major developments. First, there have been enormous changes in the social and religious life of our country. The fact is that we live in a secular and pluralistic society. But we also live in a multi-cultural community of many faiths. …
>
> Secondly, there has been an increasing lack of interest in – in some instances a conscious rejection of – marriage as an institution. There is no lack of interest in family life (or at least in intimate relationships) but the figures demonstrate a striking decline in marriage. At the same time, it has never been easier for the married to be divorced. The truth is that, for all practical purposes, we permit divorce on demand.
>
> Thirdly, there has been a sea-change in society's attitudes towards same-sex unions. …
>
> Fourthly, there have been enormous advances in medical and in particular reproductive science so that reproduction is no longer confined to "natural" methods. …'

The following extract from the Green Paper, *Support for All*, lists some of the changes which have had an impact on family life:

> ▶ *Support For All*, **Department for Children, Schools and Families, Cm 7787, 2010, pp.5–6**
>
> 'The very significant economic, social and demographic changes seen in recent decades have had a pronounced effect on family forms, family life and public attitudes. For example:
>
> ▶ in 2008 64 per cent of children were living in families with married couples, 13 per cent with co-habiting couples and 23 per cent with a lone parent;
> ▶ most children still live in a married family and marriage remains the most common form of partnership in Britain today. However, marriage rates show an overall decline since their peak in the 1970s;
> ▶ divorce rates increased considerably between the 1950s and the mid-1980s but then levelled off. In recent years they have started to fall and in 2007 the divorce rate reached its lowest level since 1981;
> ▶ the numbers of step-families are growing;
> ▶ in general, women are having fewer children and doing so later in life;
> ▶ since the Second World War the proportion of children born outside marriage has increased very significantly, right across Europe;
> ▶ about ten per cent of the adult population in England and Wales was cohabiting in 2007; co-habitation covers a wide range of relationships, including a precursor to marriage and an alternative to it;
> ▶ there is greater acceptance and recognition of same sex relationships and this is reflected in the introduction of civil partnerships; and
> ▶ people are healthier than ever and living longer which means that many more grandparents now see their grandchildren grow up.'

In *Support for All* (above) the Government announced that it was to undertake a review of the family justice system and that it would report on the matter in 2011 (see paras. 4.29–4.37). The review would include, among other matters, consideration of what can be done to promote informed settlement and agreement of family law cases outside of the court system (see further at 1.4 below) The Government said that it was also considering removing the requirement that a grandparent needs leave of the court to apply for a contact order.

1.2 Openness and transparency in family proceedings

Changes have been made to allow the media, in certain circumstances, to attend some family proceedings. The Government's aim in allowing media attendance is to improve public confidence in the family justice system and to educate the public about the work and decisions of family courts. The aim is also to eliminate accusations of secrecy and bias. However, whether this aim will be achieved remains to be seen. According to Brophy ([2009] Fam Law 271) evidence from courts in Australia, Canada and New Zealand shows that, despite being open to the press and the public for many years, allegations of secrecy and bias continue to be made. (For the background to these changes, see *Family Justice in View*, Ministry of Justice, 2008. Cm 7502).

The new rules governing media access came into force on 27 April 2009. Under r.10.28 of the Family Proceedings Rules 1991 and r.16A of the Family Proceedings Courts (Children Act 1989) Rules 1991 media representatives can attend family proceedings, but the court has a discretion to remove them from all, or part, of the proceedings on a wide variety of grounds, for example to protect the welfare of a child. The media are not permitted to attend hearings which are conducted for the purpose of judicially assisted conciliation or negotiation (see r.10.28(1)); and there are restrictions on media access to court documents. The rules are supported by two *Practice Directions*, one for magistrates' family proceedings courts ([2009] 2 FLR 157), and the other for the High Court and county courts ([2009] 2 FLR 162).

Special restrictions apply to media attendance in cases involving children, in order to protect their privacy and anonymity (s.12 Administration of Justice Act 1960 and s.97 Children Act 1989). In *Re Child X (Residence and Contact; Rights of Media Attendance; FPR Rule 10.28(4))* [2009] EWHC 1728 (Fam), for example, Sir Mark Potter P held that the media should be excluded from residence and contact proceedings (involving a father who was a celebrity) because of concerns about the child's welfare if the media was admitted.

In July 2009 the Government announced that it was proposing to give the media greater access to family proceedings, including adoption proceedings; and that it was also proposing to amend s.12 of the Administration of Justice Act 1960 which limits the publication of information concerning children. Some judges and lawyers have expressed concern about these proposals (see [2009] Fam Law 780).

1.3 The discretionary nature of family law

A distinguishing feature of family law is its discretionary nature. Each case depends on its own facts. Judges have to reach conclusions based on the circumstances of each case. Sometimes this can involve a difficult balancing exercise. Judges have a wide discretion in particular in disputes about children on family breakdown and in proceedings about property and finance on divorce. It is important that judges have wide discretion in family matters, because family life is infinitely variable – no two cases are the same.

Discretion has advantages and disadvantages. Its main advantage is its flexibility. Its disadvantages are that it creates unpredictability and that it can be a time-consuming exercise which can increase the cost of litigation. There is also a risk of arbitrariness, as judges may reach different conclusions in cases which are factually similar.

In some areas of the law statutory checklists of factors are provided in order to help guide judges when exercising their discretion and in reaching their decisions. There are statutory checklists which must be taken into account in children's cases under the Children Act 1989 (see 10.3), in ancillary relief cases on divorce under the Matrimonial Causes Act 1973 (see 7.4), and in adoption cases under the Adoption and Children Act 2002 (see 15.4).

The discretionary nature of family law has an impact on appeals. Thus, because there may be several reasonable solutions to a family law dispute, the appeal courts are unwilling to overturn decisions made by the lower courts, unless the decision is wrong in law or plainly wrong on its facts (*G* v. *G (Minors) (Custody Appeal)* [1985] 1 WLR 647; and *Piglowska* v. *Piglowski* [1999] 1 WLR 1360, [1999] 2 FLR 763).

1.4   The importance of reaching agreement

Most private law family matters (such as those involving divorce, residence and contact) are settled by the parties themselves, and, despite the impression given by the number of reported cases, most cases do not go to court. Furthermore, if family lawyers are consulted, they work within a conciliatory framework.

Resolution (an association of family lawyers) encourages the use of alternative dispute resolution methods. Members of Resolution adhere to a Code of Practice which requires them to 'see the advantages of a constructive and non-confrontational approach as a way of resolving differences' (rule 2). The principles of the Code have been adopted by the Law Society as rules of good practice for family law solicitors generally (see the *Family Law Protocol*, 2nd edn., 2006, Appendix 2).

There is an increasing emphasis on the importance of reaching agreement in family law cases. In fact, recent changes to child support (see 12.3) place a greater emphasis on parents making their own agreements; and in the context of property and finance on divorce there is discussion about making pre-marital agreements binding (see 7.14). Agreement between the parties can be facilitated by the use of ADR (alternative dispute resolution) techniques such as mediation and collaborative law.

(a)   Mediation

Mediation is a form of alternative dispute resolution whereby a mediator helps the parties identify the issues in dispute with the aim of them reaching agreement. The mediator acts as an impartial third party. It is the parties themselves who make the decision. It is not imposed by the mediator, who merely acts as a facilitator. The process is confidential and non-coercive.

Mediation can take place out-of-court or in-court, and is available from independent mediation agencies, and from some law firms. In ancillary relief proceedings on divorce, the district judge performs a mediatory role, as the parties must attend a Financial Dispute Resolution Appointment where the judge will encourage the parties and their lawyers to reach a settlement (see 7.2).

The Law Society's *Family Law Protocol* requires solicitors at an early stage to explain to clients the benefits of mediation, to keep the suitability of mediation under review throughout the case and to encourage clients to go to mediation wherever appropriate. The *Protocol* states, however, that some cases are unsuitable for mediation (for instance, child protection, child abduction and domestic violence cases, and cases where emergency action is required).

The Family Mediation Council is the umbrella organisation for the following mediation bodies: National Family Mediation (NFM), the Family Mediators' Association (FMA), Resolution, the Alternative Dispute Resolution Group (ADRg), the Law Society, and the College of Mediators. (For websites, see the end of this chapter).

The Government is committed to promoting mediation and has established a Family Mediation Helpline and website to provide information and advice about mediation (www.familymediationhelpline.co.uk). However, despite Government attempts to promote mediation, it is not being extensively used. According to the National Audit Office (*Legal Aid and Mediation for People Involved in Family Breakdown*, 2007), only 20 per cent of persons funded by legal aid for family breakdown cases (excluding those involving domestic violence) chose to use mediation.

Despite its commitment to promoting mediation, the Government has no plans to make it compulsory as it is in some countries (for example, in Australia, New Zealand, Norway and some states in the USA and Canada). However, the Government may take more steps in the future to increase the use of mediation, as it has adopted the EU Directive 2008/52/EC of 21 May 2008 (Certain Aspects of Mediation in Civil and Commercial Matters), which creates an expectation that EU Member States will encourage mediation wherever possible. The directive has a three-year timetable for implementation.

In January 2010 the Government announced (see the Green Paper, *Support for All*, Cm 7787, Department for Children, Schools and Families, paras. 4.29–4.37) that it would be conducting a comprehensive review of the family justice system which would include considering how to promote mediation. The Government said that it proposed to promote mediation online and explore other means of promoting mediation, and that it would work with the Family Mediation Council to build on accreditation for mediators. In the Green Paper the Government said that it was interested in hearing views on the question of whether mediation should be made compulsory for parents who go to court to seek to resolve residence or contact disputes.

Mediation has many advantages over more formal legal mechanisms for settling the sensitive and emotional issues surrounding family matters. Reaching agreement by way of mediation is more likely to result in the parties making and maintaining cooperative relationships on divorce and family breakdown. It reduces conflict and encourages continuing contact between children and parents. Mediation also avoids the cost, trauma, uncertainty and delay of court proceedings, and helps improve communication between the parties thereby reducing conflict and bitterness. By making disputes less hostile, mediation may make things better for the parties' children. It may also empower the parties and make them better able to deal with disputes in the future.

However, mediation has some disadvantages. Thus, there is a danger that a mediator may put pressure on a party to reach an unsatisfactory agreement. Mediation may also work against a party's best interests because of a lack of legal knowledge. There may be difficulties where a party has made allegations of unreasonable behaviour or there is domestic violence. There is also a danger that mediation may not take sufficient account of the welfare needs of children. For these reasons, collaborative law may be a better solution.

(b) Collaborative family law

Collaborative law, like mediation, is a form of alternative dispute resolution used by some family lawyers which provides a way of resolving issues about finance and property and/or children on divorce or separation without the need to go to court. It was developed in North America during the 1990s and was first used in England and Wales in 2003. It is used only by clients who agree to use it after they have received legal advice about the other options available. With collaborative law, the clients and their lawyers sign a participation agreement in which they agree to a commitment to make a transparent search for fair solutions and not go to court. The clients and their lawyers then conduct round-table negotiations in order to find the best outcome. The process is transparent and written correspondence is actively discouraged. The clients set both the pace and scope of the negotiations, but with assistance from their lawyers. Parties can also seek the assistance of mediation and counselling. If a settlement is not reached, and either client decides to go to court, then each client must consult a new lawyer.

Collaborative law is being increasingly promoted. Resolution has trained many of its members as collaborative lawyers, who have formed themselves into 'PODs' (practice and organisational development groups), which act as support groups to enable lawyers to share experience and build trust with fellow lawyers with whom they work collaboratively. There has been judicial support for the use of collaborative law (for example, by Coleridge J in *S v. P (Settlement by Collaborative Process)* [2008] 2 FLR 2040, who held that collaboratively negotiated agreements needing consent orders could be taken to court with one day's notice).

Research conducted by Resolution between April and November 2008 (*Collaborative Law in England and Wales: Early Findings,* 2009) found that collaborative law was increasingly being used and successfully so. Disputes were settled more quickly and in cases involving cohabitants more generous settlements were reached than would have been possible if the law relating to cohabitants had been strictly applied.

1.5 The courts administering family law

(a) The courts

There are three tiers of court with jurisdiction to hear family cases: magistrates' family proceedings courts (FPCs); county courts; and the Family Division of the High Court. Some proceedings can be heard in any of these courts, but others must be heard in a particular court. For instance, divorce proceedings must be heard in a divorce county court, and child abduction and other cases with an international dimension must be heard in the High Court. Proceedings under the Children Act 1989 and applications for orders for protection against domestic violence under Part IV of the Family Law Act 1996 can generally be heard in any tier of court, although some cases must be heard only in the High Court.

(i) Family proceedings courts (FPCs)   These courts are staffed by lay magistrates who are specially trained in family work and who are assisted by the clerk of the court. Sometimes district judges sit with lay magistrates. Broadly speaking, all family matters except divorce, and cases which are complex (as defined by specified criteria), can be heard in FPCs. They have concurrent powers with the other family courts in private and public law proceedings under the Children Act 1989 and in adoption proceedings under the Adoption and Children Act 2002, but they cannot deal with divorce matters. Public law cases under the Children Act 1989 must start in the FPC, but may be transferred to the

county court to minimise delay, to consolidate with other family proceedings, or where the matter is exceptionally grave, complex or important. Private law proceedings can commence in any FPC or county court, but can be transferred laterally between courts, and vertically to the High Court in some circumstances.

(ii) County courts These courts deal with most family law matters. There are different types of county court. For instance, some county courts are designated as divorce county courts, where all actions for divorce, nullity and judicial separation must start. Some are family hearings centres which hear contested private family matters (such as applications for residence and contact orders, and domestic violence injunctions). Some county courts are adoption centres (specialised centres with jurisdiction to deal with adoptions); and some are care centres (with full jurisdiction in all private and public matters, such as care and supervision orders, divorce, and adoptions).

(iii) The Family Division of the High Court The Family Division of the High Court hears a wide range of different family law cases, including wardship cases, and cases with an international dimension. It also has an inherent parental type of jurisdiction (see 8.7), and it hears cases transferred from county courts or magistrates' family proceedings courts. These are usually complex and difficult cases requiring the expertise of the High Court. The President of the Family Division is the senior family law judge in England and Wales.

1.6 Cafcass

Cafcass (the Children and Family Court Advisory and Support Service) was established under s.11 Criminal Justice and Court Services Act 2000 to look after the best interests of children involved in family proceedings. The principal functions of Cafcass officers (in England) and Welsh family proceedings officers (in Wales) are: to safeguard and promote the welfare of children in family proceedings; to make provision for children to be represented; and to provide information, advice and other support for children and their families (s.12(1)).

One of Cafcass' main functions is to advise courts on issues such as residence and contact and on placing children in local authority care. It also performs an important reporting function in family proceedings, for instance in residence and contact disputes. Cafcass performs other important tasks, including facilitating contact on family breakdown and conducting risk assessments to establish whether children are at risk of abuse or domestic violence.

Cafcass provides the following officers for the family courts:

▶ *Children and Family Reporters* When parents cannot agree about residence and contact arrangements for children on family breakdown, the court will usually appoint a Children and Family Reporter who will meet and talk with the family and help and encourage parents to agree about arrangements for their children. The Children and Family Reporter may be asked by the court under s.7 Children Act 1989 to write a report explaining what enquiries have been made and making recommendations about arrangements for the children. The Children and Family Reporter is responsible for conveying the child's wishes and feelings to the court.

> *Children's Guardians* are responsible for investigating the case and safeguarding and promoting the child's welfare before the court in public law proceedings for care and supervision orders and emergency protection and child assessment orders under the Children Act 1989. They work in tandem with the lawyer who is representing the child. In some private law proceedings (such as for residence and contact) a Children's Guardian may also be appointed (see 8.6).
> *Reporting Officers* are responsible for ensuring that the required consents to adoption and to placements for adoption have been given.

1.7 Family law and the Human Rights Act 1998

The Human Rights Act (HRA) 1998 is relevant to family law, as family courts and public authorities must abide by its provisions. The Act came into force in October 2000. The effect of the Act is to weave the European Convention for the Protection of Human Rights and Fundamental Freedoms (the ECHR) into the fabric of UK law. The Act makes Convention rights directly enforceable in the UK. Thus, the HRA 1998 gives UK citizens the right to rely on the Convention in proceedings before the courts; and courts and public authorities must act in accordance with it. It remains open, however, for litigants to take claims to the European Court of Human Rights in Strasbourg, provided they have exhausted all their remedies in domestic law.

(a) The courts and the Human Rights Act 1998

When deciding any question which has arisen in connection with a Convention right the courts in the UK must 'take into account' the judgments, decisions and opinions of the European Court of Human Rights (s.2 HRA 1998). The courts, so far as it is possible, must also read and give effect to primary and secondary legislation in a way which is compatible with Convention rights (s.3). If the High Court, Court of Appeal or the Supreme Court (formerly the House of Lords) determines that a UK legislative provision is not compatible with the Convention, and cannot be read to make it compatible, then it may make a 'declaration of incompatibility' to that effect (s.4).

As courts are public authorities for the purposes of the HRA they must not act in a way which is incompatible with a Convention right (s.6). Thus in family cases, the court must ensure that it considers and upholds Convention rights, for otherwise it may be in breach of the Convention.

(b) Public authorities and the Human Rights Act 1998

It is unlawful for a public authority to act in a way which is incompatible with a Convention right, subject to some exceptions (s.6). There is no definition of 'public authority' in the Human Rights Act 1998, but the term includes Government departments, local authorities, the National Health Service, the police and any other body or person exercising a public function. Because of the obligations imposed on public authorities by the Act, the Convention is particularly important in public family law, for instance in child protection and adoption cases.

(c)   Asserting a Convention right

A victim of an unlawful act or proposed act of a public authority (because it is a breach of a Convention right) may bring free-standing court proceedings against the public authority under the Human Rights Act, or rely on a Convention right in any other legal proceedings (s.7). In practice, claims in family law are usually brought as supporting arguments in family proceedings, although challenges against local authorities in child protection cases are sometimes brought in judicial review proceedings (see 14.11). If an applicant proves that a public authority has acted in breach of a Convention right, the court may grant such relief or remedy or make such order within its powers as it considers just and appropriate, including awards of damages (s.8). Awards of damages under s.8 are usually low, however, because the court takes into account the levels of damages set by the European Court of Human Rights, which tend to be much less than those awarded under domestic law.

(d)   Convention rights

The following Convention rights are those most likely to impact on family law: the right to life (art. 2); the right not to be subjected to torture or to inhuman or degrading treatment (art. 3); the right to a fair trial (art. 6); the right to a private and family life (art. 8); the right to freedom of thought, conscience and religion (art. 9); the right to marry and found a family (art. 12); the right to an effective remedy (art. 13); and the right to enjoy Convention rights without discrimination (art. 14).

The Convention and decisions of the European Court of Human Rights have been raised in a wide variety of different family situations, for instance:

▷ Transsexuals have argued that the UK's failure to allow them to change their birth certificates and to marry in their newly acquired sex is a breach of their right to family life under art. 8 and the right to marry under art. 12 (see 2.7).

▷ Children and parents have argued that corporal punishment of children by parents and teachers is inhuman and degrading treatment under art. 3 (see 8.5).

▷ Unmarried fathers have argued that their lack of automatic parental responsibility is a breach of the right to family life under art. 8 and is thereby discriminatory under art. 14 (see 9.4).

▷ Parents have argued in child protection cases that local authorities have breached their right to family life under art. 8 and that the procedures have breached their right to a fair hearing under art. 6 (see 14.3).

▷ In contact cases and in relocation applications to take a child out of the UK, parents have argued that there has been a breach of their right to family life under art. 8 (see 11.8).

▷ In negligence cases involving children who have been harmed by local authority action or inaction, children have argued that striking out their claims in negligence is a breach of their right not to suffer inhuman and degrading treatment under art. 3 and a breach of their right to an effective remedy under art. 13 (see 14.11).

▷ In the child support context, it has been argued that the lack of an effective remedy in the courts for a person entitled to child support is a breach of their right to a fair trial under art. 6 (see 12.3).

(e)   The right to family life (article 8)

The right to family life in art. 8 ECHR is particularly relevant to family law:

Article 8 European Convention for the Protection of Human Rights

'1. Everyone has the right to respect for his private and family life, his home and his correspondence.
2. There shall be no interference by a public authority with the exercise of this right except such as is in accordance with the law and is necessary in a democratic society in the interests of national security, public safety or the economic well-being of the country, for the prevention of disorder or crime, for the protection of heath or morals, or for the protection of the rights and freedoms of others.'

The aim of art. 8 is to protect the individual against arbitrary interference by public authorities. In addition, national authorities have positive obligations to promote family life under art. 8.

The right to family life under art. 8 is not an absolute right (because of the exceptions laid down in art. 8(2)). Interference with the right is permitted, provided that the interference is lawful, necessary and proportionate. The right to family life is also subject to the rights and freedoms of others. For instance, the rights of a child might prevail over the rights of his or her parents where that is in the child's best interests. In respect of the right to family life, regard must be had to the fair balance that must be struck between the competing interests of the individual and the wider community; and States Parties enjoy a 'margin of appreciation' (see below).

What is 'family life' for the purposes of article 8?   There is no definition of 'family life' in the European Convention for the Protection of Human Rights. Whether or not there is a family life depends on the facts and circumstances of the case. However, the European Court of Human Rights (ECtHR) has made the following statements about 'family life' for the purposes of art. 8:

▶ The existence or non-existence of family life is a question of fact depending on the real existence of close personal ties (*Lebbink* v. *The Netherlands (Application No. 45582/99)* [2004] 2 FLR 463; and *K and T* v. *Finland* (2000) 31 EHRR 484, [2000] 2 FLR 793).
▶ The bond between natural parents and children is a strong indicator of the existence of family life, and that bond amounting to family life cannot be broken by subsequent events, save in exceptional circumstances (*Ahmut* v. *The Netherlands* (1997) 24 EHRR 62).
▶ Family life is not limited to relationships based on marriage or blood, or relationships recognised in law. It can include cohabitants (*Abduluziz, Cabales and Balkandali* v. *United Kingdom* (1995) 7 EHRR 471), even if they do not live together (*Kroon* v. *The Netherlands* (1995) 19 EHRR 263). It can include relationships between near relatives, such as between grandparents and grandchildren (*Marckx* v. *Belgium* (1979) 2 EHRR 330); and between nephew and uncle (*Boyle* v. *United Kingdom* (1995) 19 EHRR 179). It can also include the relationship between a foster-parent and foster-child (*Gaskin* v. *United Kingdom* (1990) 12 EHRR 36).

- When deciding whether a cohabitation relationship amounts to family life, the following factors are relevant: whether the couple live together; the length of their relationship; and whether they have demonstrated their commitment to each other by having children together or by any other means. A family life was found to exist, for instance, in *X, Y and Z* v. *United Kingdom* (1997) 24 EHRR 143, [1997] 2 FLR 892, where X, a female-to-male transsexual, and his female partner Y had a child (Z) by artificial insemination by donor, and X was involved throughout the process and acted as Z's father in every respect.
- As the ECtHR considers the Convention to be a 'living instrument' which must be interpreted in the light of societal changes (*Selmouni* v. *France* (2000) 29 EHRR 403), courts must adapt themselves to changing social conditions when interpreting family life (for example, the decline in marriage, the increase in cohabitation, the acceptance of same-sex relationships and developments in reproductive science).
- Family life can include the potential for family life, for instance the potential relationship which might have developed between an unmarried father and his child; or where the child is in the process of being adopted.
- For the purpose of art. 8, family life must be viewed in the context of the relevant social, religious and cultural setting.

When deciding whether family life exists, the ECtHR takes into account the relevant principles of international law, and interprets art. 8 so far as possible to be in harmony with those principles (including the principles in the UN Convention on the Rights of the Child 1989, see 8.2).

The European Court's approach to article 8

The European Court of Human Rights has laid down the following propositions in respect of art. 8:

- Although the main aim of art. 8 is to protect the individual against arbitrary action by public authorities (*Kroon* v. *The Netherlands* (1995) 19 EHRR 263), there are also positive obligations inherent in an effective 'respect' for family life under art. 8.
- As well as a substantive right to respect for family life, there is also a procedural right inherent within art. 8.
- In respect of the substantive and procedural rights under art. 8, regard must be had to the fair balance that has to be struck between the competing interests of the individual and of the community as a whole; and the State enjoys a certain margin of appreciation (see *Keegan* v. *Ireland* (1994) 18 EHRR 342).
- The right to family life is not an absolute right, but a qualified right. Under art. 8(2) State interference into family life is justifiable if: it is in accordance with the law; it is in pursuit of a legitimate aim; and it is necessary in a democratic society. Any intervention must be relevant and sufficient; must meet a pressing social need; and must be proportionate to that need (*Olsson* v. *Sweden (No. 1)* (1988) 11 EHRR 259).
- Under the principle of proportionality, the more serious the intervention into family life, the more compelling must be the justification (*Johansen* v. *Norway* (1997) 23 EHRR 33).
- In respect of a State's obligation to take positive measures, art. 8 includes an obligation on national authorities to take measures to reunite parents with their

children (*Ignaccola-Zenide* v. *Romania* (2001) 31 EHRR 7; and *Nuutinen* v. *Finland* *(Application No. 32842/96)* (2000) 34 EHRR 358, [2005] 2 FLR 596), unless it is contrary to the interests of those concerned, particularly the best interests of the child.

▶ When carrying out the balancing exercise under art. 8(2) between the interests of children and parents and/or the wider public, the court takes into account the paramountcy of the best interests of the child.

(f)   The margin of appreciation

Claims under the Convention have sometimes failed because the Court of Human Rights has recognised a 'margin of appreciation' in the State's decision-making process – in other words, a reasonable discretion is permitted within States to exercise their powers while remaining in compliance with the Convention. The margin of appreciation possessed by the UK meant that for many years transsexuals failed in their claims before the European Court of Human Rights (see 2.7). Where a common approach or practice in respect of a particular matter exists among the different Member States the margin of appreciation will be narrow, but where there are disparities of approach or practice the margin will be wider.

(g)   The principle of proportionality

The principle of proportionality is an important principle in the jurisprudence of the European Court of Human Rights, and which must be applied by courts and public authorities in the UK. This principle requires that any interference with a Convention right must be proportionate to the legitimate aim pursued. The principle of proportionality would be breached, for example, if a care order was made to protect a child from significant harm when an alternative remedy (such as a supervision order) would be adequate and appropriate (see 14.7).

(h)   Procedural fairness (article 6 ECHR)

Article 6 ECHR provides that in the determination of 'his civil rights and obligations' everyone is entitled to a fair hearing by an independent and impartial tribunal established by law. Article 6 is particularly relevant in child protection cases (see 14.3).

Summary

1   There have been many important legislative developments in family law, in particular the Children Act 1989, the Child Support Act 1991, the Adoption and Children Act 2002, the Civil Partnership Act 2004 and the Gender Recognition Act 2004.

2   There have been important case-law developments, in particular in respect of ancillary relief on divorce, the burden of proof in care proceedings, the rights of transsexuals, and the rights of same-sex partners to succeed to their deceased's partner's tenancy on death.

3   Current areas of concern and debate include, in particular, the vulnerability of cohabitants on relationship breakdown, giving children a voice in private family law proceedings (for residence and contact), reforming the law governing property and finance on divorce (including whether pre-nuptial agreements should be binding).

Summary cont'd

4 Demographic and social changes, in particular the decline of marriage and the rise of cohabitation, have had an impact on family law.

5 Family law has changed dramatically in the last few years to give 'non-traditional' families and other family members rights, in particular same-sex partners and transsexuals.

6 New legal provisions have been introduced to allow the media into court in certain circumstances, in order to make the family justice system more transparent.

7 In family law cases judges have considerable discretion. Cases turn on their own facts.

8 The settlement of family cases (by mediation and collaborative law, in particular) is encouraged, as going to court can increase bitterness and hostility and is costly and unpredictable. Reaching agreement is also better for the parties' children.

9 Family cases are heard in magistrates' family proceedings courts, county courts and the Family Division of the High Court.

10 The Children and Family Courts Advisory and Support Service (Cafcass) provides officers to assist the court in family cases, and also performs reporting functions. In the last few years it has been given additional responsibilities, including facilitating and enforcing conduct and conducting risk assessments to establish whether or not children are at risk of domestic violence.

11 The Human Rights Act 1998 came into force in October 2000. The effect of the Act is to weave the European Convention for the Protection of Human Rights and Fundamental Freedoms into the fabric of UK law. Of particular importance in family law cases is art. 8 (the right to family life). The right to family life under art. 8 is not an absolute right, but any interference with that right must be lawful, necessary and proportionate (see art. 8(2)).

Further reading and references

Booth and Kennedy, 'The "traditional family" and the law' [2005] Fam Law 482.

Choudhry and Herring, *European Human Rights and Family Law*, 2010, Hart Publishing.

Cretney, 'The family and the law – status or contract?' [2003] CFLQ 403.

Cretney, *Family Law in the Twentieth Century: A History*, 2003, Oxford University Press.

Douglas and Lowe (eds.), *The Continuing Evolution of Family Law*, 2009, Family Law.

Harris-Short, 'Family law and the Human Rights Act 1998: judicial restraint or revolution?' [2005] CFLQ 329.

Maclean (ed.), *Family Law and Family Values*, 2005, Hart Publishing.

Munby, The Honourable Mr Justice, 'Families old and new – the family and Article 8' [2005] CFLQ 487.

Munby, The Honourable Mr Justice, 'The family justice system' [2004] Fam Law 574.

Probert, ' "Family law" – a modern concept?' [2004] Fam Law 901.

Roberts, *Mediation in Family Disputes*, 2008, Ashgate.

Ryder, Honourable Mr Justice, 'The family courts of the future' [2008] Fam Law 854.

Wallbank, Choudhry and Herring (eds.), *Rights, Gender and Family Law*, 2009, Routledge-Cavendish.

Walsh, *Working in the Family Justice System: The Official Handbook of the Family Justice Council* (2nd edn), 2006, Family Law.

Westcott (ed.), *Family Mediation: Past, Present and Future*, 2004, Family Law.

Websites

Government services

Child Maintenance and Enforcement Commission: www.childmaintenance.org
Department for Children, Schools and Families: www.dcsf.gov.uk
Department for Work and Pensions: www.dwp.gov.uk
Department of Health: www.dh.gov.uk
Home Office: www.homeoffice.gov.uk
House of Lords' Debates: www.parliament.the-stationery-office.co.uk/pa/ld/ldhansrd.htm
Judiciary of England and Wales: www.judiciary.gov.uk
Law Commission: www.lawcom.gov.uk
Ministry of Justice: www.justice.gov.uk
UK National Statistics: www.statistics.gov.uk
United Kingdom Parliament: www.parliament.uk

Courts and law reports

British and Irish Legal Information Institute: www.bailii.org
European Court of Human Rights: www.echr.coe.int
Her Majesty's Courts Service: www.hmcourts-service.gov.uk
Incorporated Council of Law Reporting: www.lawreports.co.uk
Supreme Court: www.supremecourt.gov.uk

Other legal materials

Statute Law Database: www.statutelaw.gov.uk
UK Official Publications: www.ukop.co.uk

Other websites

Alternative Dispute Resolution Group (ADRg): www.adrgroup.co.uk
Cafcass (England): www.cafcass.gov.uk
Cafcass (Wales): www.wales.gov.uk/cafcasscymru
College of Mediators: www.collegeofmediators.co.uk
Family Justice Council: www.family-justice-council.org.uk
Family Mediation Council: www.familymediationcouncil.org.uk
Family Mediation Helpline: www.familymediationhelpline.co.uk
Family Mediators' Association (FMA): www.fmassoc.co.uk
Law Society, The: www.lawsoc.org.uk
Legal Services Commission: www.legalservices.gov.uk
National Family Mediation (NFM): www.nfm.org.uk
Resolution: www.resolution.org.uk

Websites cont'd

Abbreviations of law journals

CFLQ: *Child and Family Law Quarterly.*
Fam Law: *Family Law Journal.*
IFL: *International Family Law.*
IFLJ: *International Family Law Journal.*
IJLP&F: *International Journal of Law Policy and the Family.*
LQR: *Law Quarterly Review.*
LS: *Legal Studies.*
MLR: *Modern Law Review.*

Part II

Marriage, civil partnership and cohabitation

Chapter 2

Marriage and civil partnership

This chapter considers the status relationships of marriage and civil partnership and the legal consequences which attach to them. Cohabitation and its legal consequences are considered in Chapter 3.

2.1 Marriage

Marriage statistics in England and Wales for 2007
(published by the Office for National Statistics (www.statistics.gov.uk)).

▶ There were 231,450 marriages, the lowest number since 1895.
▶ 143,440 of these marriages were first marriage for both parties (62 per cent of all marriages).
▶ The average age at marriage was 36.4 years (for men) and 33.8 years (for women).
▶ The number of religious ceremonies fell by 4.5 per cent from 2006, to 77,490.
▶ Civil ceremonies accounted for 67 per cent of all ceremonies.
▶ 99,760 marriage ceremonies took place in approved premises (such as hotels, stately homes and historic buildings); and accounted for 43 per cent of all marriages and two-thirds of all civil marriages.

▶ **Sir Mark Potter P in *Wilkinson* v. *Kitzinger and Others* (No. 2) [2006] EWHC 2022 (Fam), [2007] 1 FLR 295**

'The common law definition of marriage is that stated by Lord Penzance in *Hyde* v. *Hyde* (1866): "The voluntary union for life of one man and one woman, to the exclusion of all others." ... As stated by Lord Nicholls of Birkenhead in *Bellinger* v. *Bellinger* (*Lord Chancellor Intervening*) [2003] UKHL 21, "Marriage is an institution, or a relationship, deeply embedded in the religious and social culture of this country. It is deeply embedded as a relationship between two persons of the opposite sex."'

Marriage is not a contract which can be created and terminated at the will of the parties. It is an arrangement in which the State has an interest. For this reason, there are legal rules governing its creation (see 2.2–2.5) and rules governing its dissolution (see Chapter 6). The legal effect of marriage is to give the parties various rights, obligations and privileges (see 2.9). Similar provisions apply in respect of the creation and dissolution of a civil partnership, and the rights and obligations of civil partners are similar to those of married couples (see 2.10).

(a) Marriage as a human right

Article 12 of the European Convention for the Protection of Human Rights

'Men and women of marriageable age have the right to marry and to found a family according to the national laws governing the exercise of this right.'

The right to marry in art. 12 of the European Convention for the Protection of Human Rights is a strong right, as there is no second paragraph in art. 12 (as there is for the right to family life in art. 8) permitting interferences with or limitations to the right to marry.

In *R (Baiai and Others)* v. *Secretary of State for the Home Department* [2008] UKHL 53, [2008] 2 FLR 1462 the House of Lords held that, although the right to marry under art. 12 is not an absolute right, it is a strong right; and, although it can be regulated by national laws both as to procedure and to substance, national laws must not deprive a person (or category of persons) of full legal capacity of the right to marry, or substantially interfere with their exercise of that right. In *R (Baiai)* challenges were made in respect of a legislative provision requiring persons subject to immigration control to obtain written permission of the Home Secretary to marry in the UK, unless they intended to enter into an Anglican marriage. The House of Lords held that the provision breached art. 12 ECHR (the right to marry) and art. 14 (discrimination in respect of an ECHR right).

The right to marry under art. 12 has resulted in successful challenges being brought before the European Court of Human Rights by transsexual persons (see 2.7).

2.2 Capacity to marry

To contract a valid marriage the parties must have the capacity to marry and must comply with the legal formalities governing the creation of a marriage, otherwise the marriage may be void.

Section 11 Matrimonial Causes Act (MCA) 1973 provides that the parties have capacity to marry if:

(a) they are not within the prohibited degrees of relationship;
(b) they are both over the age of 16;
(c) neither of them is already married; and
(d) one of them is male and the other female.

(a) Not within the prohibited degrees of relationship

A marriage is void if the parties are within the 'prohibited degrees of relationship' (s.11(a)(i)). Marriages between certain relatives related by blood or by marriage (affinity) are prohibited by the Marriage Act 1949, as amended by the Marriage (Prohibited Degrees of Relationship) Act 1986.

A person is prohibited from marrying the following blood relatives: parent; grandparent; child; grandchild; brother or sister; uncle or aunt; nephew or niece. There are fewer restrictions on marrying a relative who is not a blood relative but where the relationship is created by marriage. Thus a person can marry his or her: step-child; step-parent; step-grandparent; or parent-in-law. However, a person cannot marry a step-child unless both parties are aged 21 or over, and the step-child was not at any time before the age of 18 brought up by that person as a step-child. An adopted child is in the same degrees of prohibited relationships in respect of his or her birth-parents, but fewer restrictions apply to a relationship acquired by adoption (for example, a person can marry an adopted brother or sister).

'In-law' marriages   Restrictions on certain 'in-law' marriage were removed in 2007 as a result of the following decision of the European Court of Human Rights:

> ▶ *B and L v. United Kingdom (Application No. 36536/02)* [2006] 1 FLR 35
>
> A father-in-law and his daughter-in-law claimed that the bar on 'in-law' marriages was a breach of their fundamental right to marry under art. 12 ECHR. The daughter-in-law (L) wished to marry her father-in-law (B). She had previously been married to his son, but the marriage had broken down and she had developed a relationship with the father. The Superintendent Registrar refused to give her and B permission to marry, because B's son (L's former husband) was still alive. They took their case to the ECtHR, which allowed their claim, holding that the UK was in breach of art. 12. The prohibition was neither rational nor logical and served no useful purpose of public policy.

After the decision in *B and L* the Marriage Act 1949 (Remedial Order) 2007 was passed amending Sched. 1 to the Marriage Act 1949 to remove the restriction on a person marrying the parent of his/her former spouse and on a person marrying the former spouse of his/her child.

(b)   Over the age of 16

A marriage is void if either party is under the age of 16 (s.2 Marriage Act 1949). The consent of the following persons is needed if a party to the marriage is aged 16 or 17 (s.3 MA 1949): each parent with parental responsibility (or guardian); a special guardian; any person with whom the child lives (or is to live) under a residence order (if not the parent or guardian); a local authority if the child is in care (in addition to parental and guardian consent); and, if a residence order is no longer in force, but was in force immediately before the child attained the age of 16, the consent of the person(s) with whom the child lived under that order. If the child is a ward of court, the court's consent is required. Consent can be dispensed with if a person whose consent is needed is absent, inaccessible or suffers from a disability. If a person refuses to give consent, the court can give consent (but such applications are rare).

(c)   Not already married

A party to a marriage must not be already married, otherwise the marriage is void (s.11(b) MCA 1973). Marriage is 'the voluntary union for life of one man and one woman to the exclusion of all others' (Lord Penzance in *Hyde v. Hyde* (1866) LR 1 P& D 130). A spouse who remarries without an earlier marriage being terminated may commit the crime of bigamy. Where a spouse has disappeared and/or is thought to be dead, the other spouse can apply for a decree of presumption of death and dissolution of marriage, which, if granted, prevents the second marriage being bigamous even if the first spouse reappears (see 6.10).

(d)   Respectively male and female

The parties to a marriage must be respectively male and female, otherwise the marriage is void (s.11(c) MCA 1973). Same-sex marriages are not permitted in the UK, but same-sex partners can enter into a civil partnership (see 2.10). There have been changes to the law governing the rights of transsexuals to marry (see 2.7).

2.3 Preliminary formalities

In addition to having the capacity to marry, the parties must satisfy certain preliminary formalities before the marriage can take place. The purpose of these preliminaries is to establish that the required consents have been given and that there are no lawful impediments to the marriage taking place. The marriage ceremony itself must also comply with certain formalities, and the marriage must be registered.

Two systems of preliminary formalities exist, one for marriages which are not celebrated in the Church of England and one for Church of England marriages.

(a) Preliminaries for marriages not celebrated in the Church of England

Marriages which are not celebrated in the Church of England must be preceded by preliminary formalities for which the superintendent registrar of the relevant district is responsible under the Registration Act 1953. A marriage can be solemnised in a register office or in any venue that has been approved for the purpose of civil marriage, but only after the grant of: a superintendent registrar's certificate; or a Registrar-General's licence.

(i) A superintendent registrar's certificate Both parties must give notice of the marriage in prescribed form to the superintendent registrar in the district (or districts) in which each of them has resided for at least the previous seven days (s.27(1) MA 1949), and the register office where the ceremony is to take place (if this is different). Both parties must attend the register office in person to give notice. A fee must be paid. The notice must be accompanied by a declaration that there are no lawful impediments to the marriage, that the residence requirements have been satisfied and that the required consents have been given. Notice of the marriage is entered in a marriage notice book and is publicly displayed in the register officer. At the end of a 15-day period from giving notice, and provided there has been no objection to the marriage, the superintendent registrar issues a certificate, after which the marriage must be solemnised within three months from the date of entry of the notice in the marriage notice book (s.31 MA 1949). The Registrar-General has the power in exceptional circumstances to reduce the 15-day period (s.31(5A) MA 1949). Under the Marriage Act 1983 persons who are housebound due to illness or disability (which is likely to last for at least three months) or who are detained in prison or due to mental ill-health can marry on the authority of a superintendent registrar's certificate in the place where they are residing or are detained.

(ii) Registrar-General's licence This procedure is available only in exceptional circumstances, such as when a person is seriously ill and not expected to recover and cannot be moved to a place where the marriage can be solemnised. It authorises the solemnisation of marriage in a place other than a register office, an Anglican church or a place registered for worship (Marriage (Registrar-General's Licence) Act 1970).

(b) Church of England preliminaries

A Church of England marriage can be solemnised after the publication of banns or after the completion of one of the formalities above. Most marriages usually take place, however, after the publication of banns.

2.4 The marriage ceremony

(a) Formalities in respect of the marriage ceremony

The marriage ceremony must comply with certain formalities, which differ depending on whether the marriage is civil or religious.

(i) Civil marriages   Once the preliminary formalities have been satisfied (see above), the marriage can be solemnised in a register office or in 'approved premises' (a venue which has been approved for the purposes of conducting a civil marriage), or, in special cases, in the place where the person is housebound or detained. Under the Marriage Act 1994 'approved premises' are premises approved for marriage by local authorities in accordance with regulations laid down by the Secretary of State. Many hotels, stately homes, castles and other places are 'approved premises'. The ceremony, whether in a register office or approved premises, is public and secular, but may be followed by a religious ceremony in a church or chapel (s.46 MA 1949). It is the civil ceremony, however, which is legally binding. At the civil ceremony, the parties must declare that there are no lawful impediments to the marriage and they must exchange vows. The ceremony must be witnessed by at least two witnesses. Some registrars remind the parties of the solemn nature of the vows they are making.

(ii) Church of England marriages   After complying with the preliminary formalities (see above), the marriage is solemnised by a clergyman according to the rites of the Church of England in the presence of at least two witnesses.

(iii) Quaker and Jewish marriages   A Quaker or Jewish marriage cannot be solemnised until the civil preliminary formalities above have been satisfied. Quakers must also make special declarations when giving notice (s.47 MA 1949). Both parties to a Jewish marriage must profess to belong to the Jewish faith (s.26(1)(d) MA 1949). Quaker and Jewish marriages are celebrated according to their own religious rites, but they need not take place in a registered building, or in public, or before an authorised person. There are special rules for the registration of Quaker and Jewish marriages.

(iv) Other religious marriages   Other religious marriages can be solemnised after the parties have complied with the civil preliminary formalities above. The certificate will state where the ceremony is to be held, which will usually be a 'registered building' in the district where one of the parties resides. A 'registered building' is a building registered by the Registrar-General as 'a place of meeting for religious worship' (s.41 MA 1949). Some Sikh and Hindu temples and Muslim mosques are registered. If a marriage takes place in a building which is not registered for the purpose of marriage, the marriage may be void, or there may be no marriage at all (see over).

A non-Anglican religious marriage must be attended either by a registrar or an 'authorised person' and must take place in the presence of at least two witnesses and be open to the public. The ceremony can take any form, provided that during the ceremony the required declarations are made.

(b) Effect of non-compliance with formalities

Breach of the formality requirements can attract criminal sanctions. Giving a false declaration is an act of perjury. Sometimes it is necessary to determine whether a marriage is a void marriage or there was no marriage at all. In some circumstances, a marriage may be upheld under the common law presumption of marriage from long cohabitation.

(i) Void marriage or 'non-marriage'? A failure to comply with the required marriage formalities results in the marriage being void, or there being no marriage at all (a 'non-marriage'). The distinction is important, because in the case of a 'non-marriage' a decree of nullity cannot be granted so that it will not be possible to apply for property and finance orders in ancillary relief proceedings (see Chapter 7). This is because the court's power to make property and finance orders on nullity under Part II of the Matrimonial Causes Act 1973 is dependent on there being a decree. The following cases provide examples of void marriages and 'non-marriages':

▶ *Ghandi* v. *Patel* [2002] 1 FLR 603

A Hindu marriage ceremony conducted by a Brahmin priest in a London restaurant was held not to be a void marriage but a 'non-marriage' – there was no marriage at all.

▶ *Gereis* v. *Yagoub* [1997] 1 FLR 854

The marriage ceremony took place in a Coptic Orthodox Church not licensed for marriages and was conducted by a priest not licensed to conduct marriages. In nullity proceedings one of the parties submitted that a decree of nullity should not be granted as there was no marriage at all. The court rejected this submission, and held that the church ceremony bore all the hallmarks of an ordinary Christian marriage and that the marriage had been treated as a subsisting marriage by all those who had attended. There was a marriage, but it was void and a decree of nullity was granted under s.11(a)(iii) MCA 1973.

▶ *Alfonso-Brown* v. *Milwood* [2006] 642 (Fam), [2006] 2 FLR 265

A 'marriage' which had taken place in Ghana was held to be no marriage at all, as both parties lacked the necessary intent at the time of the ceremony and neither party had believed that the ceremony was anything other than an engagement ceremony.

▶ *B* v. *B* [2007] EWHC 2492 (Fam), [2008] 1 FLR 813

The parties went through a marriage ceremony in a hot air balloon in California, USA. They failed to obtain a marriage licence prior to the ceremony, but did so afterwards. When the marriage broke down, the wife sought a decree of nullity under ss.11–14 MCA 1973, but the husband sought to dismiss the petition on the basis that the marriage was a non-marriage, a sham orchestrated by both of them. Coleridge J (preferring the wife's evidence as to their intentions) held that she was entitled to seek a decree of nullity, as the circumstances of the case (fulfilment of local requirements as to capacity but failure to observe a technical preliminary formal requirement) were nowhere near the category of non-marriage disentitling the petitioner to a decree of nullity.

(ii) The common law presumption of marriage from long cohabitation A marriage which fails to comply with the required formalities may be upheld under the common law presumption of marriage from long cohabitation:

> ▶ *Chief Adjudication Officer v. Bath* **[2000] 1 FLR 8**
>
> The marriage was invalid because it had taken place in a Sikh temple not registered for marriages. As a result Mrs Bath was not entitled to a widow's pension. However the marriage was upheld as valid under the presumption of marriage from long cohabitation. The Court of Appeal said that the presumption can be rebutted, but only by positive, not merely clear, evidence, and that guilty knowledge by both parties was needed for a marriage to be void because of improper formalities under s.49 MA 1949.
>
> ▶ *Pazpena de Vire v. Pazpena de Vire* **[2001] 1 FLR 460**
>
> The parties had married by proxy in Uruguay. Neither party was present at the marriage ceremony. The couple came to live in England where they lived as husband and wife for 35 years. The wife petitioned for a decree of divorce, or alternatively for a decree of nullity on the ground that the marriage had been defective. The High Court held that there was a valid marriage by reason of the presumption of long cohabitation.
>
> (See also *A-M v. A-M (Divorce: Jurisdiction: Validity of Marriage)* [2001] 2 FLR 6.)

2.5 Void and voidable marriages – the law of nullity

The law of nullity is laid down in Part I of the Matrimonial Causes Act (MCA) 1973. This is the same Act of Parliament which governs divorces and judicial separations.

Nullity petitions are relatively uncommon when compared with divorces. Only 331 petitions for nullity of marriage were filed in the courts in 2008 (*Judicial and Court Statistics 2008*, Ministry of Justice, 2009, Cm 7697).

(i) Nullity compared with divorce Like divorce, an annulment is granted in two stages: decree nisi followed by a decree absolute (s.1(5)). Only on grant of decree absolute is the marriage annulled. On or after the grant of a decree, the court has jurisdiction, like it has on divorce, to make finance and property orders under Part II of the MCA 1973 (see Chapter 7). Unlike divorce, however, a decree of nullity can be sought at any time after marriage, there being no one-year bar as there is for divorce (s.3). The procedure for nullity is also different from that of divorce.

(ii) Procedure for nullity A nullity petition must include the same essential background information as a divorce petition and the petitioner must show that the court in England and Wales has jurisdiction to hear the petition. However, unlike divorce, nullity petitions (whether or not undefended) are heard in open court, with the parties giving oral evidence. There is nothing equivalent to the 'special procedure' for divorce which is essentially a 'paper exercise' with no requirement that either party attend court (see 6.6). The fact that nullity proceedings take place in open court can be distressing for the parties, and is particularly unsatisfactory in forced marriage cases (see 2.6). Responses to the Government's consultation document on the Family Procedure Rules (*Family Procedure Rules: A New Procedural Code for Family Proceedings*, CP 19/06) showed that a significant

majority of respondents supported a proposal that the courts should be able to make nullity orders without hearing oral evidence but with the court having a discretion to require a hearing.

A decree of nullity can be sought on the ground that the marriage is void or voidable.

(a)　Grounds on which a marriage is void

A void marriage is one that is void *ab initio* (right from the beginning). A decree of nullity is not technically necessary to dissolve a void marriage, but is useful because it gives the court jurisdiction to make finance and property orders equivalent to those which can be made on divorce (see Chapter 7). A third party may bring proceedings in respect of a void marriage. A void marriage is different from a 'non-marriage' (see above). A marriage is voidable on the following grounds:

Section 11 Matrimonial Causes Act 1973

'A marriage celebrated after 31st July 1971 shall be void on the following grounds only, that is to say –

(a) that it is not a valid marriage under the provisions of the Marriage Acts 1949 to 1986, that is to say where –
    (i)　the parties are within the prohibited degrees of relationship;
    (ii)　either party is under the age of sixteen; or
    (iii)　the parties have intermarried in disregard of certain requirements as to the formation of marriage;
(b) that at the time of the marriage either party was already lawfully married;
(c) that the parties are not respectively male and female;
(d) in the case of a polygamous marriage entered into outside England and Wales, that either party was at the time of the marriage domiciled in England and Wales.'

These grounds were considered in 2.4 above. For the purposes of s.11(a)(iii) not every breach of the formality requirements of the Marriage Acts necessarily invalidates a marriage. There are no 'bars' (statutory defences) for void marriages as there are for voidable marriages.

(b)　Grounds on which a marriage may be voidable

A voidable marriage is a marriage which is a valid and subsisting marriage until annulled by a decree of nullity (s.16 MCA 1973). A marriage is void on the following grounds:

Section 12 Matrimonial Causes Act 1973

'A marriage celebrated after 31st July 1971 shall be voidable on the following grounds only, that is to say –

(a) that the marriage has not been consummated owing to the incapacity of either party to consummate it;
(b) that the marriage has not been consummated owing to the wilful refusal of the respondent to consummate it;

(c) that either party to the marriage did not validly consent to it, whether in consequence of duress, mistake, unsoundness of mind or otherwise;

(d) that at the time of the marriage either party, though capable of giving a valid consent, was suffering (whether continuously or intermittently) from mental disorder within the meaning of the Mental Health Act 1983, of such a kind or to such an extent as to be unfitted for marriage;

(e) that at the time of the marriage the respondent was suffering from venereal disease in a communicable form;

(f) that at the time of the marriage the respondent was pregnant by some person other than the petitioner;

(g) that an interim gender recognition certificate under the Gender Recognition Act 2004 has, after the time of marriage, been issued to either party to the marriage;

(h) that the respondent is a person whose gender at the time of the marriage had become the acquired gender under the Gender Recognition Act 2004.'

(i) Non-consummation

Cases involving non-consummation sometimes arise in the context of certain religious marriages. With some religious marriages the civil ceremony takes place first, followed later by a religious ceremony. Only after the religious ceremony are the parties deemed to be married in the eyes of their religion. In some of the reported cases a decree of nullity has been sought because the religious ceremony has not taken place, and the marriage has not been consummated (see *Kaur* v. *Singh* [1972] 1 All ER 292; and *A* v. *J (Nullity)* [1989] 1 FLR 110).

Consummation   Consummation is the first act of intercourse after marriage. It must be 'ordinary and complete, not partial and imperfect' (Dr Lushington in *D-E* v. *A-G* (1845) 1 Rob Eccl 279 at 298). It takes place whether or not a condom is used (*Baxter* v. *Baxter* [1948] AC 274), and whether or not ejaculation takes place (*R* v. *R* [1952] 1 All ER 1194).

Incapacity to consummate (s.12(a))   The petition can be based on the petitioner's or respondent's incapacity to consummate. The inability must be permanent and incurable. Incapacity to consummate includes not just physical incapacity, but 'an invincible repugnance to the respondent due to a psychiatric or sexual aversion' (*Singh* v. *Singh* [1971] 2 WLR 963).

Wilful refusal to consummate (s.12(b))   To establish wilful refusal there must be 'a settled and definite decision come to without just excuse' and the whole history of the marriage must be looked at (Lord Jowitt LC in *Horton* v. *Horton* [1947] 2 All ER 871). Refusal can be express or inferred (for example, by refusing to go through a required religious ceremony). In *Kaur* v. *Singh* [1972] 1 All ER 292 a marriage was arranged between two Sikhs. The civil ceremony took place, but the husband refused to arrange the religious ceremony. The wife was granted a decree of nullity on the ground of her husband's wilful refusal to consummate the marriage.

Unlike incapacity to consummate, the petition cannot be brought on the basis of the *petitioner's* refusal to consummate (see s.11(b)). This means that a wife who has been forced into an arranged marriage, but who refuses to consummate the marriage, cannot petition on this ground; she must, instead, prove incapacity to consummate or duress.

Probert (2005) has argued that non-consumation as a ground for avoiding a marriage is a legacy of ecclesiastical law, and should be abolished in order to 'define marriage in a way that is relevant for the twenty-first century'.

(ii) Lack of consent (s.12(c))

A marriage is voidable if a party did not validly consent to the marriage, whether in consequence of duress, mistake, unsoundness of mind or otherwise.

Duress The test for establishing duress is subjective, in other words it depends on whether the particular petitioner was under duress. This rule was laid down in the following case where the Court of Appeal relaxed the earlier rule which required the petitioner to establish a threat of danger to life, limb or liberty.

> ▶ *Hirani* v. *Hirani* (1983) 4 FLR 232
>
> The petitioner (aged 19) had entered into an arranged marriage with a man she had never met – because her parents threatened to throw her out of the house if she did not go ahead with the ceremony. The Court of Appeal held, granting the decree of nullity, that there was no requirement that a threat to life, limb or liberty had to be proved. The test for duress was a subjective test. The question to be asked by the court was whether the particular petitioner, taking account of his or her personal qualities, had submitted to the duress. On the facts, it was held that the petitioner's will had been overborne, with the result that her consent to the marriage had been vitiated and she was entitled to a decree.

The test of duress in *Hirani* v. *Hirani* is relevant to the issue of forced marriages (2.6).

Mistake The mistake must be in respect of the identity of the other party (not as to his or her qualities); or there must be a mistake as to the nature of the ceremony (such as a party mistakenly believing that the ceremony was an engagement ceremony).

Lack of capacity to consent Lack of capacity to consent usually arises owing to mental disorder or mental illness, but it may also arise because of coercion in the context of a forced marriage. The test for capacity to marry is whether the person can understand the nature of the marriage contract, which means that he or she must be mentally capable of understanding the duties and responsibilities that normally attach to marriage (*per* Singleton LJ in *Re Estate of Park, Deceased, Park* v. *Park* [1954] P 112, and endorsed by Munby J in *Re E (An Alleged Patient); Sheffield City Council* v. *E and S* [2004] EWHC 2808 (Fam), [2005] 1 FLR 965).

The inherent jurisdiction of the High Court (see 8.7) can be invoked to protect a vulnerable adult who lacks the capacity to marry;

> ▶ *M* v. *B, A and S (By the Official Solicitor)* [2005] EWHC 1681 (Fam), [2006] 1 FLR 117
>
> The local authority was concerned that the parents of a young woman aged 23 (with a severe learning disability and who attended a special school) were organising an arranged marriage for her in Pakistan. The local authority therefore applied for declarations that the daughter lacked capacity to marry and that it was not in her best interests to leave the jurisdiction.

Sumner J made the declarations sought, and held that in appropriate circumstances the court has jurisdiction to grant an injunction restraining those persons responsible for an adult who lacks capacity from entering into a contract of marriage, if such an order is required to protect the adult's best interests.

▶ *X City Council* **v. MB, NB and Mab (By His Litigation Friend The Official Solicitor) [2006] EWHC 168 (Fam), [2006] 2 FLR 968**

A 25-year-old man who, as a result of autism, lacked capacity to marry was given protection by Munby J under the inherent jurisdiction of the High Court on the application of the local authority, in order to prevent him being taken abroad by his parents to be married in Pakistan.

(c)   Voidable marriages – statutory bars

Section 13 of the Matrimonial Causes Act 1973 lays down the following statutory bars to nullity petitions in cases of voidable marriage:

Approbation by the petitioner   The court cannot grant a decree on any ground in s.12 if the respondent proves that: the petitioner knew that he or she could have avoided the marriage, but whose conduct in relation to the respondent led the respondent reasonably to believe that the petitioner would not do so; and the court considers that it would be unjust to the respondent to grant the decree (s.13(1)).

Three-year bar   The court cannot grant a decree on ground (c), (d), (e), (f) or (h) of s.12 MCA 1973 (see p. 28–29 above) unless proceedings are instituted within three years of the marriage (s.13(2)). But the court can grant leave to apply after that three-year period if the petitioner has suffered from a mental disorder within the meaning of the Mental Health Act 1983 and it would in all the circumstances be just to grant leave (ss.13(4), (5)).

Six-month bar   A decree cannot be granted on ground (g) (issue of interim gender recognition certificate) unless proceedings were instituted within six months of the issue of the interim gender recognition certificate (s.13(2A)).

Ignorance   A decree cannot be granted on grounds (e), (f) and (h) unless the court is satisfied that the petitioner was ignorant of those facts at the time of the marriage (s.13(3)).

2.6   Forced marriages

Article 16(2) of the Universal Declaration of Human Rights

'Marriage shall be entered into only with the free and full consent of the intending spouses.'

Article 1 of the UN Convention on Consent to Marriage, Minimum Age for Marriage and Registration of Marriages

'No marriage shall be legally entered into without the full and free consent of both parties.'

(a) The problem of forced marriages

A forced marriage is one which is conducted without the valid consent of one or both of the parties and where duress is a factor. It is not the same as an arranged marriage, which is a marriage where the families of both spouses take a leading role in choosing a marriage partner, but where the choice of whether to accept the arrangement remains with the potential spouses. Forced marriages are sometimes used for immigration purposes, because by marriage a person acquires British citizenship and can gain entry into the UK. Forced marriages involve a wide range of behaviour, including emotional threats, imprisonment, violence, abduction and blackmail.

The courts are not opposed to arranged marriages, but they do not tolerate forced marriages. In *NS* v. *MI* [2006] EWHC 1646 (Fam), [2007] 1 FLR 444, where a decree of nullity was granted to the petitioner who had entered into a forced marriage, Munby J said that, while forced marriages were utterly unacceptable, arranged marriages were to be respected and supported. He said that 'the court must not hesitate to use every weapon in its protective arsenal if faced with what is, or appears to be, a case of forced marriage.' In *Re K; A Local Authority* v. *N and Others* [2005] EWHC 2956 (Fam), [2007] 1 FLR 399 Munby J described forced marriage as 'a gross abuse of human rights' and as 'a form of domestic violence that dehumanises people by denying them their right to choose how to live their lives'. It was, he said, 'an appalling practice'.

The problem of forced marriages has come to the fore in recent years. In order to help deal with the problem, the Foreign & Commonwealth Office has established the Forced Marriage Unit, which is responsible for developing government policy on forced marriages and for providing support and information for those persons at risk. It also runs a public helpline that provides advice and support to practitioners handling cases of forced marriage and to victims themselves.

The Forced Marriage Unit deals with about 400 cases each year (although the true number of forced marriage cases is likely to be far higher). The majority of cases involve families of Pakistani and Bangladeshi origin. Some cases involve children, some as young as 13. Most cases involve young women, but a small number involve the coercion of men. Figures published by the Forced Marriage Unit in July 2009 showed an increase in the numbers of people willing to come forward to seek protection. They showed that the majority of reportings to the Unit involved families of Pakistani (70 per cent) and Bangladeshi (11 per cent) origin, with smaller percentages of those of Indian, Middle Eastern, European and African origin. Victims in 14 per cent of cases were male. 33 per cent of all assistance cases involved under 18-year-olds and 14 per cent were under 16.

Various legal remedies are available to protect actual and potential forced marriage victims. Protection is available under the criminal law and the civil law. Family law also provides victims with remedies.

(b) The criminal law

The police take forced marriages very seriously and have policy guidelines for dealing with them. Under the criminal law, parents and other persons who force a person into marriage can be prosecuted for various offences (for example, kidnapping, false imprisonment, assault, or harassment), but there is no specific criminal offence of forcing someone to marry.

In September 2005 the Home Office and the Foreign & Commonwealth Office published a consultation paper (*Forced Marriage: A Wrong Not a Right*) in order to discuss whether a new criminal offence of forcing someone to marry should be introduced. But, after the consultation process had taken place, the idea was shelved by the Government, as the police, the Crown Prosecution Service and the Probation Service offered little support for the proposal. Although a new criminal offence of forcing someone to marry would have advantages (for example, it might create a change of culture, have a deterrent effect, make the law clear, and empower young people), these advantages were considered to be outweighed by certain disadvantages. Thus, the creation of a new criminal offence might drive forced marriages underground, isolate victims and cause racial segregation at a time of heightened racial tension. The Government favoured instead the introduction of new civil remedies for victims (which are now in force, see below). The Government has nonetheless recommended that the law be kept under review.

(c) Tort

Forcing someone to marry may be a tort (that of trespass to the person, false imprisonment or harassment) and give a victim a right to obtain damages and/or injunctive protection.

(d) Family law remedies

There are three family law 'remedies' available for victims of forced marriages: annulment; protection under the inherent jurisdiction of the High Court or in wardship; and forced marriage protection orders.

(i) Annulment   A person who enters into a forced marriage can have the marriage annulled on the ground of lack of consent to the marriage due to duress (see p. 30 above). The following case provides an example of the use of annulment in the case of a forced marriage:

> ▶ *P v. R (Forced Marriage: Annulment)* [2003] 1 FLR 661
>
> The petitioner, a 20-year-old girl, had been forced to enter into a marriage in Pakistan. Her brother threatened her with violence and she believed that if she did not go ahead with the marriage she would be unable to return to England. Her parents told her that it would bring shame and disgrace on the family if she did not go ahead with the marriage, and during the ceremony her mother forced her to nod by pushing her head forward three times. She signed the marriage certificate out of fear. On her return to England, she petitioned for a decree of nullity. Coleridge J held that she had not validly consented to the marriage, as her consent had been vitiated by force, both physical and emotional. Coleridge J said that public funding should be available in forced marriage cases, so that they could be transferred to the High Court and be investigated properly and fully in open court.

A petitioner alleging duress is required to give oral evidence in open court; but, where a petitioner is reluctant to give evidence (because her family is present), the court will do whatever it can to afford the petitioner protection (*per* Munby J in *NS* v. *MI* [2006] EWHC 1646 (Fam), [2007] 1 FLR 444). A Muslim petitioner will be required to remove her veil when giving evidence, but appropriate arrangements can be made (such as screens and a woman judge, if possible) to enable her to do so without breaching her religious principles (*per* Macur J in *Re S (Practice: Muslim Women Giving Evidence)* [2007] 2 FLR 461 where a young Muslim woman was granted a decree of nullity because she had entered into a forced marriage following a two-year campaign of family pressure).

(ii) The inherent jurisdiction or wardship The inherent jurisdiction of the High Court can be invoked to protect an adult who is being forced into marriage; or the wardship jurisdiction in the case of a person aged under 18 (see 8.7). The High Court has held that in exceptional circumstances a victim of a forced marriage can be made a ward of court even though the victim is not living in the UK. In the following cases the circumstances were considered to be sufficiently exceptional for wardship to be appropriate;

▶ *Re B; RB v. FB* [2008] EWHC 1436 (Fam) [2008] 2 FLR 1624

A 15-year-old Pakistani girl who was a British national living in Pakistan was made a ward of court on the basis that she was a British national who was in desperate need of help. She had approached the British High Commission in Islamabad for help after learning that it had been arranged for her to marry an older man. Hogg J held that, in the very dire and exceptional circumstances of the case, the tentacles of the court should stretch towards Pakistan to rescue the girl from the situation she found herself in, even though she had no connection with the UK other than the fact that her late father was British.

▶ *SB v. RB* [2008] EWHC 938 (Fam) [2008] 2 FLR 1588

An 11-year-old girl was made a ward of court because she had been forced to marry a 20-year-old man in Bangladesh. With the assistance of the Forced Marriage Unit she was subsequently returned to the UK and placed with an uncle and aunt. The marriage was subsequently declared void.

The inherent jurisdiction of the High Court was invoked in the following case. Although the person needing protection did not necessarily lack the mental capacity needed to enter into a valid marriage, Munby J held that it was sufficient that she was at risk of being forced into marriage.

▶ *Re SA (Vulnerable Adult With Capacity: Marriage)* [2005] EWHC 2942 (Fam), [2006] 1 FLR 867

The local authority feared that a 17-year-old girl (who was profoundly deaf, unable to speak, and who had the intellect of a 13- or 14-year-old) might be taken by her family to Pakistan for the purposes of an arranged marriage. Munby J made an order under the inherent jurisdiction of the High Court requiring the girl to be properly informed, in a manner she would understand, about any specific marriage prior to entering into it.

(iii) Forced marriage protection orders: Part 4A of the Family Law Act 1996 In November 2006 Lord Lester introduced a Private Member's Bill into the House of Lords, the Forced Marriage (Civil Protection) Bill, which received the Royal Assent in July 2007. The Forced Marriage (Civil Protection) Act 2007 inserted Part 4A into the Family Law Act 1996 which

gives the High Court and county courts jurisdiction to make forced marriage protection orders (s.63M). These provisions (which came into force on 25 November 2008) were introduced with the aim of providing greater protection for actual and potential victims of forced marriage; and to send out a strong message that forced marriages were not acceptable and would not be tolerated. The provisions were modelled on the remedies available to protect victims of domestic violence in Part IV of the Family Law Act 1996 (see Chapter 5).

The Government has published a guidance for persons dealing with forced marriage (*The Right to Choose: Multi-Agency Statutory Guidance for Dealing With Forced Marriage*, available at www.fco.gov.uk), setting out the responsibilities of the various agencies in England and Wales which deal with forced marriage cases. Part 2 of the *Guidance* is issued as statutory guidance under s.63Q(1) of Part 4A of the Family Law Act 1996.

Forced marriage protection orders: A forced marriage protection order (a FMPO) is an order which provides legal protection to actual or potential victims of forced marriages or of attempted forced marriages (s.63A(1)). A forced marriage is a marriage where a person has not given full and free consent (s.63A(4)). 'Force' includes not just physical coercion, but coercion by threats or other psychological means (s.63A(6)).

The court has wide powers to include in the order such prohibitions, restrictions or requirements or other such terms as are considered appropriate; and the terms of the order can relate to conduct outside and/or within England and Wales (ss.63B(1) and (2)). For example, an order could be made prohibiting a parent from taking an unwilling daughter outside England and Wales for the purpose of marriage; or prohibiting a family from contacting or molesting a daughter who has taken refuge from her family. To prevent a forced marriage occurring the court could, for example, require a passport to be handed over or order a person to reveal the whereabouts of a person.

Orders without notice (s.63D) The court can make a FMPO without notice. In other words, it can make an order where it is just and convenient to do so, even though the respondent has not been given notice of proceedings.

Undertakings (s.63E) In an appropriate case, the court can accept an undertaking from the respondent instead of making a FMPO; but it cannot do so if it would have attached a power of arrest (see over) to a FMPO, had it made an order. In other words, the court cannot accept an undertaking instead of making an order where the respondent has used or threatened violence.

Applicants An application for a FMPO can be made by: a person who needs protection; a relevant third party (as specified by order of the Lord Chancellor); or any other person who has leave of the court (s.63C(2)). Local authorities do not need leave as they are 'specified' third parties.

The court also has jurisdiction to make a FMPO of its own motion (that is, where no application has been made for one) (s.63C(1)).

Factors governing the exercise of discretion to make the order When deciding whether to exercise its powers to make a FMPO and, if so, in what manner, the court must consider all the circumstances of the case including the need to secure the health, safety and well-being of the person to be protected (s.63A(2)). In ascertaining well-being the court must, in particular, have regard to that person's wishes and feelings (so far as they are readily ascertainable) as the court considers appropriate in the light of the person's age and understanding (s.63A(3)).

Power of arrest (s.63H)   The court can attach a power of arrest to a FMPO (but not one made without notice), if it considers that the respondent has used or threatened violence against the person being protected or otherwise in connection with the matters being dealt with in the order. The effect of a power of arrest is to give a police constable the power to arrest without warrant a person whom he has reasonable cause for suspecting to be in breach of an order.

Duration, discharge and variation   The order can be made for a specified period or until varied or discharged (s.63F). The court has the power to vary or discharge an order (s.63G).

Breach   If the respondent breaches the order, it is not a criminal offence; but a constable may arrest a person whom he has reasonable cause to suspect is in breach or otherwise in contempt of the order. A respondent who breaches an order can be brought back to the original court for it to consider the alleged breach. Failure to comply with a FMPO, or an undertaking, is contempt of court, which can result in a fine or imprisonment.

2.7   Transsexuals and marriage

Transsexualism is a medically recognised gender identity disorder (gender dysphoria). Persons with this disorder may opt to have a gender reassignment, which involves hormonal treatment, and, in some cases, surgery. These treatments are available on the National Health Service. Advances in medical science and recognition of transsexualism as a genuine medical problem have resulted in the law having to grapple with the issue of what should be the legal effects of acquiring a reassigned sex. One question which has arisen is whether a transsexual person can enter into a valid marriage in his or her reassigned sex. The starting point in the development of the law was the case of *Corbett* v. *Corbett*:

> ▶ *Corbett* v. *Corbett (Otherwise Ashley)* [1971] P 83, [1970] 2 WLR 1306
>
> The petitioner, a man, petitioned for a decree of nullity on the ground that the marriage was void as the respondent was male. The respondent had been born male but had undergone gender reassignment surgery and hormone treatment and lived as a woman. Ormrod J held, granting the decree, that the marriage was void because both parties were male, as a person's biological sex was fixed at birth and could not be altered by a sex-change operation. Ormrod J held that the respondent was male by chromosomal, gonadal and genital criteria, and it was irrelevant that the respondent considered himself philosophically, psychologically and socially to be a woman.

The biological test laid down in *Corbett* was applied in subsequent cases, but transsexuals began to take their cases to the European Court of Human Rights. They claimed that they were discriminated against because the restricted biological approach to gender adopted in *Corbett* was applied to, and adversely affected, other areas of their lives.

(a) Transsexuals and human rights

▶ *Rees* v. *United Kingdom* (1986) 9 EHRR 56, [1987] 2 FLR 111

The applicant, a female-to-male transsexual, claimed that UK law violated art. 8 ECHR (the right to a private and family life) by failing to provide measures that would legally constitute him as a male and allow him full integration into social life. He argued that the discrepancy between his apparent and legal sex as stated on his birth certificate caused him embarrassment and humiliation whenever the certificate was required to be produced. He also argued that the UK was in breach of art. 12 (the right to marry and found a family) as he could not marry a woman. The ECtHR held by 12 votes to 3 that there had been no breach of art. 8, and unanimously that there had been no breach of art. 12. Although the ECtHR said that it was conscious of the distress suffered by transsexuals, this was an area of law where States enjoyed a wide margin of appreciation (a wide discretion). The ECtHR stressed the need, however, for appropriate legal measures to be kept under review, having regard to scientific and societal developments.

In *Cossey* v. *United Kingdom* [1991] 2 FLR 492 the ECtHR adopted the same reasoning as in *Rees* (above) and dismissed the claim by the male-to-female transsexual, but by a smaller majority. In *B* v. *France* [1992] 2 FLR 249, where the facts were different from *Rees* and *Cossey*, a French transsexual was successful before the ECtHR as it found that French bureaucracy had made the applicant's daily life unbearable. Despite the requirement in *Rees* that the law should be kept under review, in the following case the ECtHR took the same approach it had taken in *Cossey* and *Rees*:

▶ *Sheffield and Horsham* v. *UK* [1998] 2 FLR 928

The claimants, male-to-female transsexuals, argued that the UK was in breach of arts. 8 and 12 ECHR because of the difficulties and embarrassment they encountered, in particular in respect of their birth certificates and other records recording their original gender. Miss Horsham also wished to marry a male partner in the Netherlands but had been informed that her marriage would not be recognised in English law. The ECtHR held by 11 votes to 9 that there had been no violation of art. 8. It held that the applicants' cases were similar to *Rees* and *Cossey*, and there had been no scientific or legal developments which persuaded the court that it should depart from those decisions. The UK was still entitled to rely on a margin of appreciation to defend its refusal to recognise a post-operative transsexual's identity. The ECtHR held by 18 votes to 2 that there had been no violation of art. 12. It reiterated the principles in *Rees*, and held that the right to marry guaranteed by art. 12 referred to the traditional marriage between persons of the opposite biological sex. However, in the *Horsham* case, the ECtHR forcefully stressed the need for contracting States to keep this area under review, because of increasing social acceptance of transsexualism and growing recognition of the problems which post-operative transsexuals encountered.

The following case also involved a transsexual:

> ▶ *X, Y and Z* v. *United Kingdom* [1997] 2 FLR 892
>
> The female-to-male transsexual (X), whose female partner (Y) had had a child (Z) by artificial insemination by donor, was unable to be registered as the child's father as this was not permitted under English law because he was not a man, applying the biological test laid down in *Corbett* (above). He claimed violations of arts. 8 and 14, but his application failed. The ECtHR, while recognising that 'family life' for the purposes of art. 8 was not confined solely to families based on marriage, held that there was a wide margin of appreciation and that, where the community had interests in maintaining a coherent system of family law which prioritised the best interests of the child, it could be justifiably cautious about changing the law. It held that the applicant was not prevented from acting as the child's father in a social sense and could apply for a joint residence order with his partner, and thereby acquire parental responsibility for the child.

In the following case the ECtHR took a different approach to transsexuals, and it was this case that led to a change of the law in the UK:

> ▶ *Goodwin* v. *United Kingdom* (2002) 35 EHRR 18, [2002] 2 FLR 487
>
> The applicant, a male-to-female transsexual, claimed that the UK had violated arts. 8 and 12 ECHR because it failed to recognise the legal status of transsexual persons in respect of employment, social security, State pensions, car insurance and marriage.
>
> The ECtHR held, unanimously, that the UK was in breach of art. 8 (the right to family life) and art. 12 (the right to marry). It held as follows:
>
> In respect of art. 8, the unsatisfactory situation whereby post-operative transsexuals lived in an intermediate zone as not quite one gender or the other was no longer sustainable. The UK could no longer claim that the matter fell within their margin of appreciation. As there were no significant factors of public interest to weigh against the interest of the applicant in obtaining legal recognition of gender reassignment, the fair balance inherent in the Convention tilted in her favour. Accordingly there had been a breach of art. 8.
>
> In respect of art. 12, the term 'man and woman' in relation to the fundamental right to marry in art. 12 could not still be assumed to refer to a determination of gender by purely biological criteria. A test of gender based purely on biological factors (as laid down by Ormrod J in *Corbett*) was not appropriate to the current understanding of transsexualism, and could no longer be decisive in denying legal recognition to the change of gender of a post-operative transsexual. There were other important factors, such as the acceptance of the condition of gender identity disorder by the medical profession, the provision of treatment including surgery, and the assumption by transsexual people of the social role of the assigned gender. As the applicant had no possibility of marrying a man but yet lived as a woman, was in a relationship with a man and would wish to marry only a man, the very essence of her right to marry had been infringed and there was no justification for barring her from enjoying that right under the circumstances. Accordingly there had been a breach of art. 12.
>
> (In *I* v. *United Kingdom* [2002] 2 FLR 518, heard with *Goodwin*, the applicant was a male-to-female transsexual who had not been admitted to a nursing course because she had failed to show her birth certificate (which stated she was male). The UK government, as in *Goodwin*, raised the margin of appreciation defence, but the ECtHR, applying the same reasoning as in *Goodwin*, held that there were violations of arts. 8 and 12).

In *Goodwin*, the ECtHR was referred to *Re Kevin: Validity of Marriage of Transsexual* [2001] Fam CA 1074, a decision of the Australian Family Court, where Chisholm J had strongly criticised the reasoning in *Corbett* and had upheld the validity of a marriage between a woman and a female-to-male transsexual. Chisholm J said that sex was to be determined at the date of marriage, having regard to all relevant factors, including life experiences and self-perception.

Changing attitudes to transsexualism   As a result of the decisions in *Goodwin* and *I v. UK* (above), the UK was obliged to comply with its Convention obligations and decide whether to reform the law in order to permit the amendment of birth certificates and the recognition of gender change. After the decisions the Interdepartmental Working Group on Transsexual People (which had been set up by the Home Office in 1999) was reconvened in 2002, and the Government announced that it would introduce legislation to reflect the decisions in *Goodwin* and *I v. UK*, which would include not only changes in respect of birth certificates, inheritance provision and pension rights, but which would give transsexuals the right to marry a person of the opposite sex to their post-operative sex. Measures would also be introduced so that transsexuals would be better protected from constantly and unnecessarily having to reveal their history.

Subsequent to these developments, the House of Lords in the following case had to consider the legal position of transsexuals in the light of the obligations imposed by the Human Rights Act 1998:

> ▶ *Bellinger v. Bellinger (Lord Chancellor Intervening)* [2003] UKHL 21, [2003] 1 FLR 1043
>
> Mr Bellinger and Mrs Bellinger (a male-to-female transsexual) had married in 1981 and lived happily since then. Mrs Bellinger sought a declaration in the High Court under s.55 Family Law Act 1986 that the marriage was a valid and subsisting marriage. Johnson J in the High Court, and the Court of Appeal by a majority, refused to grant the declaration, applying the biological test of gender laid down in *Corbett v. Corbett* (see p. 36 above). Mrs Bellinger appealed to the House of Lords, arguing that the Court of Appeal's decision was incompatible with the ECHR and was therefore unlawful under s.7 HRA 1998. As the UK courts must take account of the judgments of the ECtHR when determining any question arising in connection with a Convention right (s.2(1) HRA 1998), the *Goodwin* case (above) became relevant to the appeal before the House of Lords. Under the HRA 1998 a court is a public authority (s.6(3)) and must act in accordance with the ECHR (s.6(1)), and, so far as it is possible to do so, primary legislation must be read and given effect to in a way which is compatible with Convention rights (s.3(1)). Under s.4 HRA 1998 the House of Lords also had the power to declare s.11(c) MCA 1973 (parties to a marriage must be male and female) incompatible with the ECHR.
>
> The House of Lords held, dismissing the appeal, that to allow the appeal would represent a major change in the law which was better dealt with by Parliament rather than by the courts, particularly as the Government had already said that it would introduce legislation on the matter. But it made a declaration under s.4 HRA 1998 that s.11(c) MCA 1973 was incompatible with arts. 8 and 12 ECHR.

After the decisions in *Goodwin* and *Bellinger*, the Government was put under pressure to consider reforming the law in order to improve the legal position of transsexuals. As a result the Gender Recognition Act 2004 was enacted.

(b)　The Gender Recognition Act 2004

The Gender Recognition Act (GRA) 2004 gives legal recognition in their acquired gender to transsexuals who can show that they have taken decisive steps towards living fully and permanently in their acquired gender. The Act came into force on 4 April 2005.

Under the GRA 2004 a transsexual person aged at least 18 can obtain a gender recognition certificate issued by the Gender Recognition Panel (s.1). If a full gender recognition certificate is issued, the person's gender becomes for all purposes the acquired gender (s.9). The practical effect of a gender recognition certificate is to provide a transsexual person with legal recognition in the acquired gender. Thus, he or she is entitled to a new birth certificate reflecting the acquired gender, and is able to enter into a valid marriage or valid civil partnership in his or her new gender.

Before issuing a certificate, the Gender Recognition Panel must be satisfied that the applicant (s.2): has, or has had, gender dysphoria; has lived in the acquired gender throughout the preceding two years; and intends to continue to live in the acquired gender until death. The Gender Recognition Panel can only issue an interim gender recognition certificate to a married applicant (s.4). If within six months of the issue of the interim certificate the marriage is ended, the applicant can seek a full certificate (s.5).

Parenthood　Section 12 GRA 2004 provides that, although a person is regarded as being of the acquired gender, that person retains their original status as father or mother of a child. This provision ensures the continuity of parental rights and responsibilities.

Annulling a marriage or civil partnership to a transsexual partner　A party to a marriage can have the marriage annulled under the Matrimonial Causes Act 1973 on the ground that it is voidable on the basis that one of the parties is seeking a certificate from the Gender Recognition Panel; or on the ground that he or she married a transsexual person in ignorance of that fact (s.12(h) MCA 1973 (see 2.5)). Proceedings must be instituted within three years of the marriage and the petitioner must have been ignorant of the facts at the time of marriage (ss.13(2) and (3) MCA 1973). The same rules apply to civil partnerships.

2.8　Recognition of an overseas marriage

(i) Recognition of an overseas marriage　A marriage contracted overseas (in other words, out of the jurisdiction of the UK) may be recognised as valid in England and Wales under the Family Law Act 1986 provided: each of the parties has the capacity to marry according to his or her place of domicile; and the formalities required by the law of the place where the marriage was celebrated were complied with. An overseas marriage celebrated by local custom may be recognised (see *McCabe* v. *McCabe* [1994] 1 FLR 410, where a marriage which had taken place in Ghana (involving a bottle of whisky and a sum of money) was upheld as valid). Special rules apply in certain cases, for instance where a party is serving in HM Forces (see Foreign Marriages Acts 1892–1947).

In the following two cases the marriages were held not to be valid under the Family Law Act 1986:

> ▶ *City of Westminster v. IC (By His Litigation Friend the Official Solicitor) and KC and NNC* [2008] EWHC 198, [2008] 2 FLR 267

A Muslim arranged marriage, which had taken place over the telephone between an autistic man (aged 26, but with the mental age of 3) and a woman in Bangladesh, was held to be invalid, even though it was agreed by all the parties that the marriage was valid under Shariah law and had taken place in Bangladesh. The Court of Appeal refused to recognise the marriage as being valid under English law, as both parties must have capacity to enter into a marriage according to the law of their respective domiciles. The Court of Appeal held that the man, due to his disability, lacked capacity and was therefore unable to give valid consent to the marriage. Wall LJ held that the marriage was not entitled to recognition in English law and there were powerful public policy grounds to that effect.

> ▶ *Hudson v. Leigh* [2009] EWHC 1306 (Fam), [2009] 2 FLR 1129

Bodey J made a declaration that a 'marriage' conducted in South Africa did not create a valid marriage because the formal requirements for a valid marriage had not been satisfied. Both parties, and the minister who had conducted the religious ceremony, did not, at the time of the ceremony, intend or believe it to be legally binding. Thus, while the ceremony had the trappings of marriage, it had fundamentally failed to effect a valid marriage.

(ii) A same-sex overseas marriage is not recognised in the UK   A same-sex marriage entered into legally overseas will not be recognised by the courts in England and Wales as being a valid marriage in the UK – although it may be recognised as a valid civil partnership. This is so, even though it is now possible for same-sex couples to enter into a civil partnership in the UK (see 2.10). In the following case, a lesbian couple unsuccessfully applied to have their Canadian marriage recognised in England and Wales:

> ▶ *Wilkinson v. Kitzinger and Others (No. 2)* [2006] EWHC 2022 (Fam), [2007] 1 FLR 295

Wilkinson (the petitioner) and Kitzinger (the respondent) were a lesbian couple living in England who had married in British Columbia, Canada. They wished their Canadian marriage to be regarded as a valid marriage in the UK. An application for a declaration as to marital status was made under s.55 Family Law Act 1986. They argued that ss.212–218 of the Civil Partnership Act 2004 (which treats an overseas marriage as a civil partnership) and s.11(c) Matrimonial Causes Act 1973 (parties to a marriage must be male and female) violated their human rights under the following articles of the European Convention for the Protection of Human Rights: art. 8 (right to family life); art. 12 (right to marry); and art. 14 (discrimination in respect of an ECHR right). In the alternative, they argued that the common law definition of marriage should be developed so as to recognise same-sex marriages; and they sought a declaration under s.4(2) Human Rights Act 1998 that the statutory provisions above were incompatible with arts. 8, 12 and 14 ECHR.

Sir Mark Potter P dismissed the petition as there had been no violation of the parties' human rights. There was no consensus, he said, about same-sex marriages in Europe, and the ECtHR had declared itself slow to trespass into this area. There was no breach of art. 8 because, according to the jurisprudence of the ECtHR, the right to family life did not extend to childless same-sex couples. There was no breach of art. 12 because Strasbourg jurisprudence referred to marriage in the traditional sense – as a marriage between a man and a woman. The 'living instrument' doctrine, by which the ECHR is to be interpreted in the light of present-day conditions, could not be applied to art. 12 to bring it within the scope of Convention issues which were plainly outside its contemplation. The difference in treatment of same-sex couples was reasonable, legitimate and proportionate. Parliament had enacted the CPA 2004 as a policy choice creating a legal status for same-sex partners, but at the same time demonstrating support for marriage. Sir Mark Potter P said that the CPA 2004 had accorded to same-sex partners all the advantages of civil marriage, save in name.

(For a discussion of *Wilkinson* v. *Kitzinger*, see Bamforth [2007] CFLQ 133).

2.9 The legal consequences of marriage

On marriage, the parties acquire a legal status from which various rights and duties flow.

(a) Separate legal personalities

Each spouse has a separate legal personality. This means that a husband and a wife can each own property solely (or jointly) and can bring proceedings in tort and contract separately against each other or against third parties (Law Reform (Married Women and Tortfeasors) Act 1935; s.1 Law Reform (Husband and Wife) Act 1962). They can also enter into contracts with each other.

As spouses have separate legal personalities, they can make unilateral decisions about their own medical treatment. This includes the right of a wife to abort a child born of the marriage. In *Paton* v. *British Pregnancy Advisory Service Trustees* [1979] QB 276 the husband applied for an injunction to prohibit the defendant carrying out an abortion on his wife, but his application failed.

(b) Financial obligations

Parties to a marriage have a mutual duty to maintain each other during the marriage (and in some circumstances after marriage), and they can obtain financial provision orders from the court against the other party if that party fails to provide such maintenance. In practice, however, applications during marriage are rare because any dispute is likely to arise in the context of divorce, when the divorce court has powers to determine the allocation of any finance or property in dispute (see Chapter 7). Spouses also have a duty to provide maintenance for any child of the family (see Chapter 12).

Married couples can apply for financial orders from the magistrates' family proceedings court, or the county court or the High Court under the following statutory provisions:

(i) An application for financial provision in the family proceedings court Under the Domestic Proceedings and Magistrates' Courts Act 1978 the family proceedings court has jurisdiction to make periodical payments and lump sum orders on the application of a spouse (or of its own motion) if the respondent spouse (s.1(1)): has failed to provide reasonable maintenance for the applicant; or has failed to provide, or to make proper contribution towards, reasonable maintenance for any child of the family; or has behaved in such a way that the applicant spouse cannot reasonably be expected to live with the respondent; or has deserted the applicant. Orders can be made in favour of the applicant

or to or for the benefit of a child, but most child maintenance cases are dealt with by the Child Maintenance and Enforcement Commission (see Chapter 12).

When considering whether to make an order and, if so, in what manner, the magistrates must have regard to all the circumstances of the case (including certain specified matters), but with first consideration being given to the welfare of any child of the family (s.3). The court must not dismiss the application or make a final order, however, until it has considered whether it should exercise any of its powers under the Children Act 1989 (s.8). The magistrates have the power to make consent orders (s.6), and can also make periodical payments orders where the parties have been living apart by agreement and one of the parties has been making periodical payments (s.7). Orders can be varied or revoked (s.20).

(ii) Financial provision in the county court or High Court   Under s.27 Matrimonial Causes Act 1973 the county court or High Court can make orders for periodical payments and lump sums where the applicant spouse proves that the other spouse has failed to provide reasonable maintenance for the applicant (s.27(1)(a)), or has failed to provide, or to make a proper contribution towards, reasonable maintenance for any child of the family (s.27(1)(b)). An order may be made in favour of the applicant and/or to or for the benefit of any child of the family, but most child support claims are dealt with by the Child Maintenance and Enforcement Commission (see Chapter 12). The statutory criteria laid down in s.25 Matrimonial Causes Act 1973 (see 7.4) govern the exercise of the court's discretion.

(iii) Agreements about maintenance   Married couples can enter into agreements about maintenance, but an agreement cannot be conclusive, as the court has the power to vary or revoke the terms of an agreement and can insert new terms. Also, any provision in an agreement prohibiting the right of one of the parties to apply to the court for an order for financial provision is void. Private maintenance agreements are not precluded by the child support legislation, but any provision in an agreement restricting the right of a person to apply for child support is void. (For pre-marital and post-marital agreements in the context of divorce, see 7.9).

(c)   The criminal law

For the purposes of giving evidence, the spouse of the accused is a competent witness for the prosecution, the accused and any co-accused, except where the spouses are jointly charged, when neither is competent to give evidence for the prosecution if either of them is liable to be convicted (s.80 Police and Criminal Evidence Act 1984). A person has the right to refuse to give evidence against a spouse except where the spouse is charged with personal violence against the other spouse or against a child under 16, or a sexual offence against a child under 16 (s.80). A husband can commit the crime of rape against his wife, as the common law rule that by marriage a wife impliedly consents to intercourse was overturned by the House of Lords in *R* v. *R* [1992] 1 AC 599, where Lord Keith said that marriage 'is in modern times regarded as a partnership of equals and no longer one in which the wife must be the subservient chattel of the husband'.

(d) Property rights

As each party to a marriage has a separate legal personality, each party may own property solely or jointly. During a marriage, the rules governing property ownership are the same as those which apply to other persons, with the exception of some special statutory provisions which apply only to spouses (see 4.2). The position is different, however, on divorce (see Chapter 7). Married persons, unlike cohabitants, also enjoy statutory rights of occupation of the family home ('home rights') under s.30 of Part IV of the Family Law Act 1996 (see 5.3).

Property rights on death   Each spouse is free to make a will leaving his or her property to whomsoever he or she wishes. On intestacy (that is, where there is no will) the surviving spouse succeeds to the estate of the deceased spouse (see 4.12). A surviving spouse can apply under the Inheritance (Provision for Family and Dependants) Act 1975 for reasonable provision from the other party's estate without having to prove dependency or that he or she was being maintained by the deceased party (see 4.13). Marriage automatically revokes an existing will unless it was made in contemplation of marriage (see 4.12).

(e) Children

Parents who are married have 'automatic' parental responsibility in law for their children (see 9.3). They can apply for residence and contact orders and other orders under the Children Act 1989 (see Chapters 10 and 11). Spouses have a duty to provide maintenance for any child of the family. They can apply for financial provision for a child under Sched. 1 to the Children Act 1989 and spouses can seek child support (see Chapter 12).

(f) Protection against domestic violence and harassment

Spouses (and former spouses) can seek remedies under Part IV of the Family Law Act 1996 and under the Protection from Harassment Act 1997 (see Chapter 5) to protect themselves and their children from violence in the home.

(g) Rights on the breakdown of a marriage

On marriage breakdown, a married person can petition for divorce, nullity or judicial separation under Part I of the Matrimonial Causes Act 1973 (see 2.5 above and Chapter 6); and can apply to the court under Part II of the 1973 Act for property and financial orders, including orders in respect of the matrimonial home and orders in respect of pension entitlement (see Chapter 7).

(h) Rights in respect of adoption

Married couples can jointly (and in some circumstances solely) apply to adopt a child. They also have rights in respect of giving consent to (or refusing to give consent to) the adoption of their child (see Chapter 15).

(i) Citizenship and immigration

Under the British Nationality Act 1981 a person who marries a British citizen does not automatically acquire British citizenship, but can apply for naturalisation under conditions which are more favourable than those which apply to other persons, including cohabitants. As far as children are concerned, a child born in the UK is a British citizen if either of his or her married parents is a British citizen. Under the Immigration Act 1971 a British citizen has the right to live in and to enter and leave the UK. Whether or not a non-British spouse of a British citizen is able to live in and enter and leave the UK is governed by the immigration rules, but a person may be refused permission to enter the UK if the marriage is a 'sham', in other words one entered into merely for the purpose of circumventing the immigration rules.

(j) Taxation; pensions

Transfers between parties to a marriage are exempt from inheritance tax, and a transfer between spouses does not give rise to a chargeable gain for the purpose of capital gains tax. A married person can benefit from a deceased spouse's pension rights.

2.10 Civil partnerships

Statistics on civil partnership for 2008 (www.statistics.gov.uk)

▶ 7,169 civil partnerships were registered in the UK, compared with 8,728 in 2007 (a drop of 18 per cent).
▶ 6,588 civil partnerships were registered in England and Wales.
▶ 189 civil partnership dissolutions were granted in the UK, compared to 42 in 2007. Most dissolutions involved female couples.

(a) Introduction

In some countries same-sex couples can enter into a valid marriage (for example, in the Netherlands, Canada, Belgium and Spain). In others they can enter into a registered civil partnership (for example, in Denmark, Sweden, Finland, Portugal, France and Germany). Some of these civil partnership schemes are also open to opposite-sex couples (such as in France). Under the Civil Partnership Act 2004 (which came into force on 5 December 2005) same-sex partners in the UK can register their partnership and by doing so acquire rights and obligations similar to those of married couples.

Before the Civil Partnership Act 2004 came into force various informal registration schemes were available in England and Wales enabling same-sex (and opposite-sex) couples to declare their partnership (for example, the London Partnership Register introduced in 2001). The disadvantage of these informal schemes, however, was that they created no legally recognised status and consequently had no legal effects.

Because of the disadvantages for same-sex couples compared with married couples, there was increasing discussion about implementing new laws to permit civil partnership registration. Discussion was fuelled largely by pressure from the gay community, in particular the gay pressure group Stonewall, who felt that same-sex couples suffered many disadvantages as a result of being treated as separate individuals rather than as a couple. Visiting a partner in hospital or organising a partner's funeral arrangements, for example, created difficulties because of confusion as to whether a partner was next-of-kin. Same-sex couples were also denied employment benefits and pension rights, and some found themselves unable to remain in their partner's home on death, or to succeed to their deceased partner's estate on intestacy. In fact, the House of Lords, before civil partnerships were introduced, had recognised that same-sex cohabitants were being discriminated against (see *Fitzpatrick* v. *Sterling Housing Association* [2001] AC 27, [2000] 1 FLR 271; and *Ghaidan* v. *Godin-Mendoza* [2004] UKHL 30, [2004] 2 FLR 600).

In December 2002 the Government announced that it proposed to introduce a same-sex partnership registration scheme, and in June 2003 the Women and Equality Unit of the Department of Trade and Industry published a consultation paper, *Civil Partnership: A Framework for the Legal Recognition of Same-Sex Couples*, setting out proposals for reform:

> **Civil Partnerships: A Framework for the Legal Recognition of Same-Sex Couples (June 2003), para. 1.2**
>
> 'Civil partnership registration would be an important equality measure for same-sex couples in England and Wales who are unable to marry each other. It would provide for the legal recognition of same-sex partners and give legitimacy to those in, or wishing to enter into, interdependent same-sex couple relationships which are intended to be permanent. Registration would provide a framework whereby same-sex couples could acknowledge their mutual responsibilities, manage their financial arrangements and achieve recognition as each other's partner. Committed same-sex relationships would be recognised and registered partners would gain rights and responsibilities which would reflect the significance of the roles they play in each other's lives. This in turn would encourage more stable family life.'

The Government was keen to emphasise, however, that civil partnership would not undermine the institution of marriage or offend religious beliefs;

> **Baroness Scotland QC introducing the second reading of the Civil Partnership Bill:**
>
> '[Civil partnership] offers a secular solution to the disadvantages which same-sex couples face in the way they are treated by our laws. ... This Bill does not undermine or weaken the importance of marriage and we do not propose to open civil partnership to opposite-sex couples. Civil partnership is aimed at same-sex couples who cannot marry. However, it is important for us to be clear that we continue to support marriage and recognise that it is the surest foundation for opposite-sex couples raising children.'

(b) The Civil Partnership Act 2004

The Civil Partnership Act 2004, which came into force in December 2005, enables same-sex partners to register their partnership and thereby acquire the status of civil partner. The effect of registration is to give civil partners various rights, responsibilities and obligations broadly analogous to those possessed by married couples. If the partnership breaks down, it can be dissolved in a procedure similar to that of divorce. Decrees of separation, nullity and presumption of death are also available, and the court has jurisdiction to make finance and property orders on civil partnership breakdown equivalent to those it can make on divorce. Civil partners have rights and responsibilities in respect of children, and provision is made in respect of residence and contact. They also have rights on death. Thus, the surviving civil partner can register the other partner's death, and can claim a survivor's pension. Civil partners are entitled to bereavement benefits and compensation for fatal accidents or criminal injuries. They also have rights to succeed to a tenancy on the death of their partner, and have rights of inheritance on intestacy like those of married couples. In respect of taxation, civil partners have the same rights as married couples.

Although the Government has been keen to stress that civil partnership is not 'gay marriage', there are in fact very few differences between civil partnership and marriage. As Sir Mark Potter P said in *Wilkinson* v. *Kitzinger* (see p. 41, above), the 2004 Act had accorded to same-sex partners all the advantages of civil marriage, save in name. There are differences, however, between civil partnership and marriage:

- persons who marry can opt for a religious or civil marriage, whereas civil partnership registration is exclusively civil;
- a civil partnership is registered when both civil partners sign the register, whereas a civil marriage is registered when the couple exchange vows;
- non-consummation and venereal disease are not available as grounds for voidability of a civil partnership, as they are in the case of marriage;
- with civil partnership, unlike divorce, there is no adultery ground for dissolution.

(i) Eligibility – who can enter into a civil partnership? Section 3(1) CPA 2004 provides that in order to be able to register a civil partnership: (a) both parties must be of the same sex; (b) either party must not already be a civil partner or lawfully married; (c) each party must be aged at least 16; and (d) the parties must not be within the prohibited degrees of relationship (as determined by s.3(2) and Part I of Schedule 1 to the Act). Where a party is aged under 18, parental (or guardian) consent is required (s.4(1)).

(ii) Formation of a civil partnership Local registration services are responsible for registration, a process which is similar to that for civil marriages. As with civil marriages, preliminary formalities must be satisfied. Thus, under s.8(1), each party must have lived in England and Wales for at least 7 days immediately before giving notice and each party must give the Register Office notice of their intention to register their partnership. Each party must make a declaration that there is no impediment to the formation of the partnership and that the residence requirement is satisfied (s.8(4)). Notice of the proposed registration must be published (s.10) and after a 15-day waiting period (ss.11 and 12), and in the absence of any objections (s.13), the registration authority in whose area registration of the partnership is to take place can issue a 'civil partnership schedule' (s.14). The 15-day waiting period can be reduced in special cases (such as where there is military posting or illness) (s.20). Special provision exists for housebound persons (s.18) and hospital patients or prisoners (s.19).

Once the preliminaries above are satisfied, registration can take place. Registration can only take place at the Register Office; it cannot take place in religious premises (s.6(1)). Registration is completed when each party has signed the civil registration document at the invitation of, and in the presence of, the civil partnership registrar; and in the presence of each other and two witnesses (s.2(1)). The civil partnership document must then be signed, in the presence of the civil partners and each other, by each of the two witnesses and the civil partnership registrar (s.2(4)). There must be no religious service at the registration (s.2(5)). There is no requirement that the parties make a verbal commitment to each other, as there is in the case of marriage.

(iii) Civil partnership agreements Civil partners can enter into a civil partnership agreement, which is the equivalent of an engagement to marry. The same rules which apply to engagements also apply to civil partnership agreements. Thus, a civil partnership agreement does not have contractual effect (s.73) and the same rules about rights in property apply on the termination of a civil partnership agreement as those which apply on the termination of an engagement (s.74). Thus, where a party to a civil partnership agreement makes a gift to the other party on the condition (express or implied) that it is to be returned if the agreement is terminated, he or she is not prevented from recovering the property merely because he or she was responsible for terminating the agreement (s.74(5)).

(iv) Legal consequences of civil partnership registration During the partnership, and on its breakdown, civil partners have the same rights and responsibilities as married couples (see also 2.9).

Financial provision Civil partners, like spouses, have a mutual duty to maintain each other, and a civil partner can apply against the other partner for financial provision in the magistrates' family proceedings courts during their relationship (s.72(3) and Sched. 6). They have the same rights as married couples with respect to giving evidence in criminal proceedings. Civil partners have the same pensions rights as married couples; and they are treated in the same way as married couples for all tax purposes (including inheritance tax and capital gains tax). In respect of state benefits, the income of a civil partner is taken into account when calculating entitlement to income-related benefits (such as income support) and tax credits.

Children and parenting A civil partner who is not the biological parent of a child can apply for parental responsibility for his/her civil partner's child either by agreement or by court order (see 9.5). New provisions have been introduced to allow lesbian civil partners to apply for parental responsibility (see 9.5) and to gain the status of parenthood where they have a child by means of assisted reproduction or surrogacy (see 9.9). Civil partners can apply for residence and contact orders (and other orders under s. 8 Children Act 1989) (see Chapter 10). Civil partners have a duty to provide maintenance for any child of the family; and they can apply for financial provision for a child in the same way as married couples (see Chapter 12). Civil partners can apply to adopt a child (see Chapter 15).

Property on death If one of the civil partners dies intestate (without making a will), then the surviving party is treated in the same way as a surviving spouse in respect of inheriting the deceased's estate (see 4.12). A civil partner is also entitled to inherit the tenancy belonging to his/her deceased civil partner in the same way as a surviving spouse (see 4.15).

Protection against domestic violence　Civil partners, like spouses and cohabitants, are entitled to seek legal protection against violence under Part IV of the Family Law Act 1996 (see Chapter 5).

(v) Dissolution of a civil partnership　Under ss.37–64 CPA 2004 county courts and the High Court have jurisdiction to make dissolution orders and nullity orders (see below), and separation and presumption of death orders. Dissolution is a court-based process like divorce, and, with the exception of adultery, the grounds for dissolution are the same as those for divorce. The applicant for a dissolution order must prove that the partnership has irretrievably broken down on the basis of one or more of the following facts (s.44(5)): (a) unreasonable behaviour; (b) two years' separation with consent to the dissolution; (c) five years' separation; and (d) desertion for at least two years. Like divorce, an application for dissolution cannot be made until one year has passed from the date of formation of the civil partnership (s.41). Attempts at reconciliation are permitted. For example, a period of up to six months' cohabitation can be disregarded when calculating periods of separation or desertion (s.42). Provision is also made for the refusal of a dissolution order in five-year separation cases and for the protection of respondents in separation cases (ss.47 and 48).

The terminology for dissolution, however, is different from that of divorce. Thus, there is no decree nisi or decree absolute, as there is for divorce, but instead a conditional order followed by a final order.

(vi) Nullity　The court has the power under ss.49 and 50 CPA 2004 to make nullity orders in respect of a void or voidable civil partnership.

Void partnerships　A partnership is void if (s.49): the parties were not eligible to register as civil partners (that is, they were within the prohibited degrees of relationship, either party was aged under 16, or aged 16 or 17 and the required consents had not been given); or there was non-compliance with formalities.

Voidable partnerships　A partnership is voidable if (s.50): there was lack of valid consent (because of duress or mistake); mental disorder; or pregnancy by a third party. These mirror the grounds for nullity in Part I of the Matrimonial Causes Act 1973, except for the non-inclusion of non-consummation and venereal disease. Certain bars exist in respect of voidable partnerships (s.51).

(vii) Ancillary relief on dissolution, nullity and separation　Under s.72 and Sched. 5 CPA 2004 the court has discretionary powers on or after making a dissolution order (or a nullity or separation order) to make finance and property orders similar to those which the court can make on divorce (see Chapter 7). Thus the courts can make periodical payments and lump sum orders, orders for the sale or transfer of property and pension orders. The court also has the power to make finance and property orders after the overseas dissolution, annulment or legal separation of a civil partnership (s.72(4) and Sched. 7).

(viii) Recognition of overseas civil partnerships, dissolutions, annulments and separations　Sections 233–238 CPA 2004 make provision for the recognition of overseas civil partnerships, and for the recognition of overseas civil partnership dissolutions, annulments and separations.

These are equivalent to the provisions governing the recognition of overseas marriages (see 2.8) and overseas divorces (see 6.9). However, overseas same-sex marriages are not recognised in the UK (see *Wilkinson* v. *Kitzinger* at p. 41, above).

Summary

1 The number of marriages in England and Wales has been declining.

2 Marriage is a human right under art. 12 of the European Convention for the Protection of Human Rights.

3 To contract a valid marriage the parties must have the capacity to marry and must comply with certain formalities. Failure to comply with these requirements can render the marriage void (s.11 Matrimonial Causes Act 1973).

4 Parties have the capacity to marry if they: are not within the prohibited degrees of relationship; are aged 16 or over; are not already married; and respectively male and female (s.11 MCA 1973).

5 Parties to a civil or religious marriage (other than a Church of England marriage) must obtain a superintendent registrar's certificate or Registrar-General's licence. Special provisions exists for housebound and detained persons.

6 A Church of England marriage can take place after the publication of banns, or the grant of a superintendent registrar's certificate or a Registrar-General's licence.

7 The marriage ceremony must be celebrated according to certain formalities. A civil ceremony takes place in the Register Office or approved premises. A religious marriage must take place in a church or other place registered for religious worship.

8 A decree of nullity can be sought under Part I of the Matrimonial Causes Act 1973 (MCA 1973) on the ground that a marriage is void (s.11) or voidable (s.12). There is no prohibition on seeking a decree during the first year of marriage (s.3), as there is for divorce.

9 In some circumstances a marriage is not void, but is no marriage at all as there was no semblance of a marriage.

10 In certain restricted circumstances a marriage may be upheld under the common law presumption of marriage from long cohabitation.

11 The grounds for a void marriage are laid down in s.11 MCA 1973.

12 The grounds for a voidable marriage are laid down in s.12 MCA 1973. Statutory bars (defences) in respect of voidable marriages are laid down in s.13 MCA 1973.

13 A decree of nullity gives the court jurisdiction to make orders for ancillary relief under Part II of the MCA 1973 (see Chapter 7).

14 A victim of a forced marriage can have the marriage annulled on the ground that it is voidable due to duress. There have also been other developments to protect actual or potential victims of forced marriage, including the introduction of forced marriage protection orders which the court can make under Part 4A of the Family Law Act 1996.

15 Important developments in the case-law of the European Court of Human Rights and the decision of the House of Lords in *Bellinger* v. *Bellinger* (2003) led to the enactment of the Gender Recognition Act 2004 which removes the discrimination transsexual persons suffer; and also allows a transsexual person who acquires a full gender recognition certificate to enter into a valid marriage or valid civil partnership in his or her acquired gender.

Summary cont'd

16 An overseas marriage is recognised as valid in England and Wales if each party has the capacity to marry according to his or her domicile, and the formalities of the place where the marriage was celebrated have been complied with.

17 An overseas same-sex marriage cannot be recognised in England and Wales as a valid UK marriage, but can be recognised as a valid civil partnership.

18 Married couples have separate legal personalities. They can own property separately and can bring actions in tort and contract against each other, and separately or jointly against third parties. Husbands and wives have a mutual duty to provide each other with financial support, and either party may apply for financial provision from the courts. Married persons enjoy certain tax advantages. Married parents both have parental responsibility. Married couples have rights and remedies under the criminal and civil law to protect themselves and their children against domestic violence.

19 The Civil Partnership Act 2004 permits same-sex partners to enter into a registered civil partnership, and thereby acquire rights, obligations and privileges which are virtually the same as those possessed by married couples.

Further reading and references

Auchmuty, 'What's so special about marriage? The impact of *Wilkinson* v. *Kitzinger*' [2008] CFLQ 475.

Bamforth, ' "The benefits of marriage in all but name?" Same-sex couples and the Civil Partnership Act 2004' [2007] CFLQ 133.

Barlow, Duncan, James and Park, *Cohabitation, Marriage and the Law: Social Change and Legal Reform in the 21st Century*, 2005, Hart Publishing.

Borkowsi, 'The presumption of marriage' [2002] CFLQ 251.

Cretney, *Same Sex Relationships: From 'Odious Crime' to 'Gay Marriage'*, 2006, Oxford University Press.

Gaffney-Rhys, '*M* v. *B, A and S (By the Official Solicitor)* – protecting vulnerable adults from being forced into marriage' [2006] CFLQ 445.

Gilmore, '*Bellinger* v. *Bellinger* – Not quite between the ears and the legs – transsexualism and marriage in the Lords' [2003] CFLQ 295.

Kirby, 'Equal treatment of same-sex couples in English family law?' [2007] Fam Law 413.

Probert, 'How would *Corbett* v. *Corbett* be decided today?' [2005] Fam Law 382.

Probert, '*Hyde* v. *Hyde*: defining or defending marriage?' [2007] CFLQ 322.

Probert, 'When are we married? Void, non-existent and presumed marriages' [2000] 22 *Legal Studies* 398.

Probert and Barlow, 'Displacing marriage – diversification and harmonisation within Europe' [2000] CFLQ 153.

Vallance-Webb, 'Forced marriage: a yielding of the lips not the mind' [2008] Fam Law 565.

Websites

Forced Marriage Unit (Foreign & Commonwealth Office): www.fco.gov.uk

3.1 Cohabitation

(a) Introduction

Many couples choose to cohabit rather than marry, and the numbers who choose to do so are increasing as the following statistics show:

> **Statistics on cohabitation**
>
> According to the 2001 Census, there were more than 2 million cohabiting couples in England and Wales (compared to more than 10 million married couples) which was a 67 per cent increase from the 1991 Census. The number of cohabiting couple households with dependent children doubled from the 1991 Census with more than 1.25 million children dependent on cohabitants.
>
> According to the Office for National Statistics, in 2006 14 per cent of the 17.1 million families living in the UK were cohabiting couple families (compared with 9 per cent in 1996). The number of opposite-sex cohabiting couples is projected to increase by almost two-thirds over the next 25 years.

A two-year study conducted by Barlow, Burgoyne, Clery and Smithson (2008) found that cohabitation is a popular choice of relationship in Britain, but that, despite the Government's Living Together Campaign (which aims to provide cohabitants with information about their legal rights and remedies), 53 per cent of the cohabitants surveyed believed, mistakenly, that 'common law marriage' gave them certain rights. Few cohabitants had taken steps to safeguard their legal position. Thus, only 15 per cent of those who owned their accommodation had a written agreement about their share of the ownership; and only 19 per cent had sought advice about their legal position. The research found that: few cohabitants made legal agreements; there was little support for the law to distinguish between financial remedies for married and cohabiting couples on death; and there was a widespread feeling that children of cohabitants should not be adversely affected by their parents' marital status on separation or death.

There has been increasing pressure for reform of the law to remove the injustices which some cohabitants can suffer in respect of finance and property, particularly on relationship breakdown (see 3.4).

(b) The problem of defining cohabitation for legal purposes

One of the difficulties for the law, whether it be judge-made or statute, is defining the terms 'cohabitation' or 'cohabitant' for the purposes of giving cohabitants legal rights and obligations. Unlike marriage and civil partnership there is no proof by registration of the status of cohabitant. In fact the parties themselves may have differing views as to whether or not they are cohabitants.

Statutory provisions giving cohabitants rights and obligations usually define cohabitation in terms of a quasi-marital relationship, and sometimes with a minimal duration and residence requirement. Thus, in order to apply for reasonable financial provision from a deceased cohabiting partner's estate under the Inheritance (Provision for Family and Dependants) Act 1975, a cohabitant must have lived in the same household as the deceased for at least two years as if he or she were the husband or wife (or civil partner) of the deceased (see 4.13). For the purposes of obtaining protection against domestic violence under Part IV of the Family Law Act 1996, however, the term 'cohabitant' is defined less restrictively, as there is no minimum duration requirement (see Chapter 5).

Defining cohabitation is important for determining eligibility for legal remedies, but how it should be defined raises certain policy issues. A definition of cohabitation giving a wide category of cohabitants the same legal rights and remedies as married couples (and civil partners) might undermine the institution of marriage; but it would also undermine the autonomy of cohabiting couples, some of whom may have made a conscious decision not to marry in order to avoid the rights and obligations which the State imposes on married couples and civil partners. How cohabitation is defined will be an important part of any discussions of reform.

(c) The vulnerability of cohabitants

Some cohabitants believe that there is something called a 'common law marriage,' which gives opposite-sex cohabitants quasi-marital rights (see Probert (2007) and Barlow *et al* (2008)). This is a myth. In fact, cohabitants can be in a disadvantageous position compared with married couples; and so can same-sex cohabitants who are not civil partners. Cohabitants are in an especially vulnerable position in respect of property entitlement on relationship breakdown and on the death of their partner. They can suffer disadvantages on relationship breakdown in respect of ownership and occupation of the family home, and in respect of other assets, such as pensions and investments. On the termination of a marriage (or civil partnership), the court has power under statute to adjust the parties' property and financial assets (see Chapter 7), but no such provision exists for cohabitants. Cohabitants must instead use the general rules of property law (see Chapter 4), and/or apply under Schedule 1 to the Children Act 1989 if they have children (see 10.12). Cohabitants are also vulnerable on the death of their partner. During their relationship cohabitants are also vulnerable as there is no legal obligation to provide financial support for each other. Married couples and civil partners, on the other hand, have mutual maintenance obligations and the courts have the power to make maintenance orders in their favour. Cohabitants also suffer tax disadvantages compared with married couples and civil partners.

Children of cohabiting couples can also be in a more vulnerable position than children whose parents are married, not only because cohabiting relationships are more prone to breakdown, but because the court has no power to oversee arrangements for children of cohabiting parents on family breakdown as it has when parents are married and divorcing. Children may also be vulnerable if one of their cohabiting parents loses a right to remain in the family home on relationship breakdown.

3.2 Cohabitants – rights and obligations

The position of cohabitants with regard to their legal rights and obligations is very different to that of married couples (and civil partners).

(i) Financial obligations Cohabitants, unlike married couples, have no mutual duty during their relationship, or on relationship breakdown, to provide each other with financial support. Consequently, they have no right to apply to the court for orders in respect of financial provision. However, cohabiting parents (whether or not they have parental responsibility) have a duty to maintain their children, and maintenance for children can be sought against a cohabiting parent by applying to the Child Maintenance and Enforcement Commission, and in some cases to the court (see Chapter 12). Cohabitants can also apply to the court for financial provision orders to or for the benefit of a child under Schedule 1 to the Children Act 1989 (see 10.12).

(ii) Property rights The property rights of cohabitants are determined by the law of property and the law of contract (see Chapter 4). With the exception of provisions for cohabitants to obtain occupation orders in respect of the home in the context of domestic violence (see 5.5), and transfers of a tenancy on the death of a partner (see 4.15), no special family law statutory provisions exist for cohabitants equivalent to those for married couples and civil partners whether during their relationship, on relationship breakdown or on death. Cohabitants must rely instead on equitable doctrines, such as trusts and proprietary estoppel, to establish interests. Cohabitants, unlike married couples and civil partners, have no statutory rights of occupation of the family home ('home rights'). However, if there are children, property orders can be sought to or for the benefit of a child under Schedule 1 to the Children Act 1989 (see 10.12).

The following case is often cited as the classic example of the injustices which a cohabitant can suffer on relationship breakdown, and is often referred to in discussions of reform:

> ▶ *Burns* v. *Burns* [1984] Ch 317
>
> The female cohabitant (she had taken her partner's name) cohabited with her partner for nearly 20 years. She brought up the children and looked after the home. On relationship breakdown, she brought a claim against her former partner (the owner of the home) arguing that she had an interest in the home under a trust. Her claim was dismissed by the Court of Appeal because there was no evidence of any intention that she was to have an interest. Looking after the home and bringing up the children were held to be insufficient evidence to enable the court to infer such an intention. While expressing considerable sympathy for her, the Court of Appeal felt that any change in the law was a matter for Parliament not the courts.

In *Hammond* v. *Mitchell* [1991] 1 WLR 1127, *sub nom H* v. *M (Property: Beneficial Interest)* [1992] 1 FLR 229, on the other hand, the female cohabitant was successful in obtaining an interest in the home under a trust on facts which were similar to those in *Burns*. This was because the court accepted her evidence that she and her partner had spoken about ownership of the home (even though briefly and many years earlier), and these words were held to be sufficient evidence of an inferred intention that she was to have a half-share. The different outcomes in *Burns* and *Hammond* v. *Mitchell* demonstrate the somewhat arbitrary nature of the law in this area.

(iii) Property rights on death   The surviving cohabitant has no right to inherit from a deceased partner's estate on intestacy. Instead any property goes to the deceased's children or parents. It is therefore particularly important for a cohabitant to make a will. However, a surviving cohabitant can apply under the Inheritance (Provision for Family and Dependants) Act 1975 (see 4.13) for reasonable financial provision out of the deceased cohabitant's estate, or claim a beneficial interest in the deceased cohabitant's property under a trust (see Chapter 4). On the death of a cohabitant partner, the surviving partner can succeed to the tenancy belonging to the deceased (see 4.15).

(iv) Property and finance on relationship breakdown   On relationship breakdown cohabitants have a duty to maintain their children, but there is no maintenance duty between the partners themselves. Furthermore, the courts have no powers, as they have on divorce, to adjust cohabitants' property entitlements according to their needs and resources. Cohabitants can therefore be in a vulnerable position on relationship breakdown in respect of property whether it be the family home, investments or pension provision.

(v) Cohabitants and children   Cohabiting parents have the same maintenance obligations to their children as married couples (see Chapter 12), whether or not the unmarried father has parental responsibility. Only a cohabiting mother has automatic parental responsibility in law for her children, but a cohabiting father may acquire it (see 9.3). Only the unmarried mother, not the father, has a duty to register the child's birth, but both parties can choose to do so jointly, whereupon the father will acquire parental responsibility. The Government is proposing to introduce compulsory joint birth registration for cohabiting couples (see 9.4).

A cohabiting parent can apply for section 8 orders under the Children Act 1989 (for example, residence and contact orders) (see Chapter 10). Eligibility to apply depends on the applicant being the biological parent of the child. It is not dependent on the applicant having parental responsibility.

Under the law of adoption (see Chapter 15) a cohabiting couple can make a joint application to adopt a child. However, an unmarried father without parental responsibility has no statutory right to consent to the adoption of his child.

(vi) Protection against violence   Cohabitants and former cohabitants (opposite-sex and same-sex) can apply for non-molestation orders and occupation orders under Part IV of the Family Law Act 1996 to protect themselves and their children against domestic violence (see Chapter 5).

(vii) British citizenship and immigration   Under the British Nationality Act 1981 it is more difficult for a non-British cohabitant partner of a British citizen to gain British citizenship by virtue of that partnership. It may also be more difficult to obtain permission to enter and remain in the UK. A child born to unmarried parents (on or after 1 July 2006) can take his or her nationality from the father, subject to proof of the relationship (s.9 Nationality, Immigration and Asylum Act 2002). A child born before that date to an unmarried British father and a non-British mother does not automatically gain British citizenship. The

parents will need to marry before the child's eighteenth birthday, thereby making the child 'legitimate' and giving the child an automatic right to citizenship; or apply for discretionary registration of the child as a British citizen.

(viii) Cohabitation contracts   Cohabitants can enter into a cohabitation contract to regulate their affairs (for example, to make arrangements about the allocation of property and other matters should their relationship break down). In practice, however, few do so. Cohabitation contracts were once considered to be contrary to public policy, as they undermined the sanctity of marriage. This is no longer the case, but cohabitation contracts remain open to challenge in the courts and may not be upheld, for instance if there is no intention to create legal relations, or there is duress, undue influence, misrepresentation or lack of independent legal advice. In *Sutton* v. *Mishcon de Reya and Gawor & Co* [2003] EWHC 3166 (Ch), [2004] 1 FLR 837 a cohabitation agreement was held not to be valid as it was an agreement about sexual relations rather than about property.

3.3   Homesharers

Some people who live together are not cohabitants but 'homesharers.' Such persons do not have the same family law rights as married couples, civil partners and cohabitants, except in respect of domestic violence when they can apply, in some circumstances, for protection against domestic violence under Part IV of the Family Law Act 1996 as associated persons living in the same household (see Chapter 5). 'Homesharers' can be particularly vulnerable in respect of property entitlement on the death of the other homesharer and they can suffer tax disadvantages, as the following case shows:

> ▶ *Burden and Burden* v. *United Kingdom (Application 13378/05)* **[2008] 2 FLR 787**
>
> Joyce and Sybil Burden, two unmarried sisters, aged 90 and 82 respectively, claimed that they were discriminated against in respect of inheritance tax under UK law because they did not have the same inheritance rights as same-sex couples, even though they had lived together for the whole of their adult lives and owned their home in joint names. On the death of one sister, the other would have to sell their house to pay the 40 per cent inheritance tax owed on its value. After their claim failed before the English courts they took their case to the European Court of Human Rights (ECtHR), arguing that UK inheritance tax laws discriminated against them under art. 14 of the European Convention for the Protection of Human Rights (ECHR) taken in conjunction with art. 1 of Protocol 1 ('Every natural or legal person is entitled to the peaceful enjoyment of his possessions'). They also argued that the Civil Partnership Act 2004 was discriminatory under the ECHR as it gave rights to same-sex, but not opposite-sex, couples.
>
> The ECtHR held by 15 votes to 2 that there had been no discrimination against the applicants and no violation of the ECHR. The UK had not exceeded the wide margin of appreciation afforded to it; and the difference of treatment for the purposes of the grant of inheritance tax exceptions was reasonably and objectively justified for the purpose of art. 14. Siblings could not be equated with married couples or civil partners for the purpose of inheritance tax obligations, even though they had lived together all their adult lives. Any workable tax system was bound to create marginal situations and individual cases of apparent hardship or injustice; and it was up to national authorities to decide how to strike the right balance between raising revenue and pursuing social policy objectives.

The Cohabitation Bill 2008–2009 (see p. 64 below) made provision for sibling homesharers and was supported by Joyce and Sybil Burden.

3.4 Reform of the law

(This section should be read in conjunction with Chapter 4 which deals with the law governing property ownership by cohabitants).

For many years there has been discussion about reforming the law to remove some of the injustices that cohabitants suffer. Discussions about reform have become more wide-ranging to include not just reforms relating to ownership of the family home, but also to provide cohabitants on relationship breakdown with financial provision. There has also been discussion about whether cohabitants should have the same rights as spouses or civil partners on the death of a partner.

(a) The need for reform

During the last 20 years or so there has been increasing dissatisfaction with the law governing the property rights of cohabitants on relationship breakdown and on the death of a cohabiting partner. There have been calls for reform from the Law Society, Resolution (the group of family lawyers), judges, lawyers and academics. The Law Commission has considered reform in respect of property and financial provision (see p. 62 below); and in 2009 it embarked on a project to consider reform of the law in respect of cohabitants and intestacy. According to the *2008 British Social Attitudes Report*, nearly 9 out of 10 people think that a cohabiting partner should have a right to financial provision on separation, if the relationship is long and/or includes children.

As long ago as 1984 in the case of *Burns* v. *Burns* [1984] Ch 317 (see p. 54 above) the Court of Appeal had drawn attention to the unfairness of the law but said that any reform of the law was a matter for Parliament, not the courts. Since 1984, changing social and economic conditions have, arguably, made reform even more pressing. As the law currently stands, cohabitants, unlike spouses and civil partners, are in a particularly disadvantageous position on relationship breakdown as the courts have no discretionary power to adjust their property interests. Instead, cohabitants must turn to the law of property, in particular the law of trusts. This is not only costly and time-consuming, but the law is sometimes insufficiently flexible to do justice between the parties and is complex and difficult to understand.

There are arguments for and against reforming the law to give cohabitants new rights and remedies:

Arguments in favour of reform

▶ The law should keep up to date with changing social conditions. Many couples choose to cohabit and many cohabitation relationships break down. 1 in 6 couples choose to cohabit, and this is predicted to rise to 1 in 4 by 2031 (Office for National Statistics).
▶ Cohabitants can suffer unfairness and injustice in respect of property, particularly on relationship breakdown.
▶ Children of cohabitants may be in a vulnerable position on relationship breakdown if the home belongs to one parent.

- Many cohabitants believe, mistakenly, that there is something called a 'common law marriage' whereby cohabitants acquire the same legal rights as married couples or civil partners after a period of cohabitation.
- The law has been reformed for same-sex cohabitants (by the Civil Partnership Act 2004), and so the law should be reformed for other cohabitants.
- Some cohabiting couples cannot marry for a variety of religious or practical reasons.
- The law of trusts is doctrinally unsatisfactory, difficult to understand and not designed to deal with cohabitation breakdown (see below at p. 59 and Chapter 4). Property entitlement should be determined by a family law, not a property law, regime.
- Bringing court proceedings is a costly, lengthy and difficult process.
- Many other countries (such as Scotland, Australia, New Zealand and Canada) have introduced reforms, and so England and Wales should do the same.

Arguments against reform

- Cohabitants can choose to marry (or enter into a civil partnership) and thereby acquire the rights that married couples and civil partners have.
- The social reality is that most cohabitants own their home jointly, and so very few cohabitants actually suffer any inequity and unfairness.
- Codification of the law would create its own set of problems.
- Reform of the law will be difficult (see p. 60 below).
- Reform will undermine the institution of marriage.
- Cohabitants may not wish to have an adjustive quasi-divorce regime forced upon them in respect of their property interests. That may be their reason for choosing not to marry.
- There is an increasing emphasis on party autonomy and settlement on divorce (with discussion about making pre-nuptial contracts binding); and so the same policy should be adopted in the context of cohabitation.

Some commentators have argued in favour of reform because cohabitants (and children) can suffer serious injustice. A research study conducted by Douglas, Pearce and Woodward found major instances of injustice caused by the current operation of the law of trusts:

> **Douglas, Pearce and Woodward, *A Failure of Trust: Resolving Property Issues on Cohabitation Breakdown* (2007), Cardiff University/University of Bristol Research Paper, Conclusion**
>
> 'Retrospective private ordering in cohabitation breakdown cases, set against a fog of uncertainty and complexity rather than the "shadow of the law", has led to a position where trusts law may now serve to perpetuate rather than redress injustice. Even if the parties reach some sort of rough and ready compromise, ignoring or sidestepping the "true" legal position, this comes at a cost, both actual and figurative. Whatever the fate of the Law Commission's (see p. 62 below) or other similar proposals, the present study has thus indicated that maintenance of the status quo is unarguable. However controversial it may be, reform of the current law to meet the legitimate interests of separating cohabitants is both justified and overdue.'

A former President of the Family Division, Baroness Butler-Sloss, has drawn attention to the problems which cohabitants may suffer:

> ▶ **Baroness Butler-Sloss in the House of Lords' debate on the Cohabitation Bill 2008**
> (*Hansard*, 13 March 2009)
>
> '[There are] very real problems on the ground. Lawyers recognise them and ... as a former
> family judge for 35 years ... there is a very real problem and I have met it in the cases I have
> tried. ... I have dealt with similar cases again and again. I should tell you what happens. A
> couple live together for, say, 17 years ... and the woman subordinates her career to the man.
> She takes some part-time work, she brings up their children and they live as if they are
> married but they do not get married. At the end of 17 years the man finds a younger woman
> ... and tells her to get out. When she says, "But I have a share of the house", he says, "The
> house is in my name. You have not put any money into it. You are out." ... She becomes a
> burden on the state.'

Drawbacks of the law of property   In addition to the arguments set out above, the law is open
to criticism, particularly in respect of acquiring an interest in the family home. The law is
complex and difficult to understand, but even more difficult to apply. As Carnwarth LJ
said in the Court of Appeal in *Stack* v. *Dowden* [2005] EWCA Civ 857, [2006] 1 FLR 254:

> 'To the detached observer, the result may seem like a witch's brew, into which various esoteric
> ingredients have been stirred over the years, and in which different ideas bubble to the surface at
> different times. They include implied trust, constructive trust, resulting trust, presumption of
> advancement, proprietary estoppel, unjust enrichment, and so on. These ideas are likely to mean
> nothing to laymen, and often little more to the lawyers who use them.'

Cohabitants may have to resort to the law of trusts to establish an interest in property
(for instance the family home, see 4.6), but the law of trusts has the following
disadvantages:

▶ The principles governing constructive trusts are based on intentions and
arrangements which are often vague and which may have arisen many years earlier.
For this reason, it may be difficult to establish any evidence of intention; and it is
possible that parties may be tempted to perjure themselves. In *Hammond* v. *Mitchell*
[1991] 1 WLR 1127 (where the female cohabitant successfully claimed a half-share in
the family home and a share of other property owned by the man) Waite J said that
'both parties were prone to exaggeration' and 'neither side had the monopoly of
truth'. Bailey-Harris, commenting on *Rowe* v. *Prance* [1999] 2 FLR 787 (where the
female cohabitant successfully claimed a half-share in a yacht owned by the man),
said that one is 'commonly left with the impression that the establishment of an
interest ... turns primarily on whose account of conversations is believed by the
judge' ([1999] Fam Law 623, at 624).

▶ A claimant is forced to trawl back through the relationship to find evidence of the
intention needed to establish a constructive trust, instead of being encouraged to look
at future needs and resources, which is the approach adopted on divorce and on
dissolution of a civil partnership.

▶ The requirement of a direct financial contribution to establish an interest under a
constructive trust (laid down by Lord Bridge in *Lloyds Bank plc* v. *Rosset* [1991] 1 AC
107, [1990] 2 FLR 155, at p. 58) means that some cohabitants are unable to acquire an
interest in the home even though they have spent many years contributing to its
upkeep and looking after the family. The courts are unwilling to adopt a more flexible

approach and accept evidence of an indirect contribution (such as looking after the children or paying for household goods).

▷ There is some judicial uncertainty about whether Lord Bridge's interpretation in *Lloyds Bank plc* v. *Rosset* of earlier authorities was correct, or whether it set the hurdle too high.

▷ Because of the vagueness of the relevant legal principles, unsatisfactory and unjust distinctions may be made. In *Hammond* v. *Mitchell* [1991] 1 WLR 1127 the female cohabitant was granted a half-share in the family home on the basis of a short conversation she had had with her partner many years earlier, but the female cohabitant in *Burns* v. *Burns* [1984] Ch 317 (see p. 54 above) failed to establish a beneficial interest in the home, despite her substantial contribution over many years to the household and family.

The drawbacks of the law were recognised by the Law Commission in its 2006 Consultation Paper (see further at p. 62, below):

▶ *Cohabitation: The Financial Consequences of Relationship Breakdown* (**Law Com No. 17, 2006**)

'The rules contained in the general law have proved to be relatively rigid and extremely difficult to apply, and their application can lead to what many would regard as unfairness between the parties. The formulation of a claim based on these rules is time-consuming and expensive, and the nature of the inquiry before the court into the history of the relationship results in a protracted hearing for those disputes that are not compromised. The inherent uncertainty of the underlying principles makes effective bargaining difficult to achieve as parties will find it hard to predict the outcome of contested litigation.'

(b) Reform – questions to be addressed

Any reform of the law governing the financial and property rights of cohabitants will have to address the following difficult questions:

▷ **Defining cohabitants**   Any reform will have to address the difficult issue of defining the term 'cohabitant.' Should there be a minimum duration requirement? Should there be evidence of financial dependency? Should there be a list of statutory factors to help define cohabitation? Should the birth of a child automatically result in a couple being deemed to be 'cohabitants'?

▷ **Remedies**   Should the remedies be the same as those which exist for married couples and civil partners on relationship breakdown? Should financial provision be restricted to lump sum orders, or should cohabitants (like divorcing couples) be entitled to periodical payments (maintenance), and, if so, for how long? Should cohabitants be entitled to property orders and to a share of their cohabiting partner's pension? However, if the remedies are too restricted, then, as Hess warns (see [2009] Fam Law 405) 'there is a real possibility of the court having regularly to conduct (simultaneously or at a different time) a detailed analysis of economic advantage and disadvantage as well as an old style Trusts of Land and Appointment of Trustees Act 1996 (TLATA) analysis.'

▶ *The exercise of discretion*   When deciding whether to grant a remedy what principles should govern the exercise of the court's discretion? Should there be a statutory list of factors equivalent to those for ancillary relief on divorce or on civil partnership dissolution?

▶ *Opting out*   Should cohabitants be given the right to opt out of any new scheme, and, if so, should there be any controls on this? Thus, should certain formalities have to be completed? Should there be a requirement of independent legal advice? Should future changes of circumstances (such as the birth of a child or loss of employment) vitiate the agreement? Should there be a right to have the agreement revoked if is likely to cause manifest injustice?

▶ *A limitation period*   Should there be a requirement that an application should be brought within so many years of relationship breakdown and/or separation? If so, how long should this be, and should it be extended at the discretion of the court in cases where there may be injustice and/or exceptional circumstances?

▶ *Property on death*   Should cohabitants on the death of a partner have the same or similar rights to those of married couples and civil partners?

(c) Proposals for reform

Proposals for reform of the law governing cohabitation have come not only from the Law Commission (the Government's reform body), but the Law Society and the Solicitors' Family Law Association (Resolution). At the end of 2008 a Cohabitation Bill was introduced into the House of Lords by Lord Lester QC (see further below).

(i) The Law Society's proposals   In 2002 the Law Society (*Cohabitation: The Case for Clear Law; Proposals for Reform*) published proposals for reform recommending that cohabitants (same-sex and opposite-sex) should be permitted to obtain court orders similar to those available for divorcing couples. Eligibility would be based on living together for at least two years in a relationship analogous to that of a married couple, or on whether the couple had children. A statutory checklist of factors (such as the existence of a sexual relationship, the provision of financial support, whether they had a child) would assist the court in determining whether the parties were cohabitants.

The court would have the power to make property adjustment orders and lump sum orders. Applications would be determined having regard to the principle that fair account should be taken of any economic advantage derived by either party from contributions by the other, and of any economic disadvantages suffered by either party in the interests of the other party or of the family. Cohabitants would also be allowed to apply for maintenance in limited circumstances (for example, to provide resources for training, retraining or to reflect capital payments which could not be made by way of a lump sum). Only in exceptional cases would maintenance orders last for more than four years.

The proposals included a range of other rights for cohabitants (in respect of transfers of tenancies, occupation of the home, succession, tax and immigration rights), but these rights would not be as great as those possessed by married couples. The Law Society recommended that the law relating to property disputes (for example, trusts) should continue to be available for cohabitants who, for whatever reason, were unable to invoke the remedies proposed.

(ii) The Solicitors' Family Law Association proposals   In 2000 the Solicitors' Family Law Association (Resolution) published *Fairness for Families* in which it recommended changes to the law similar to those above proposed by the Law Society. It recommended that cohabitants (opposite-sex and same-sex) should be able to apply for a financial relief order from the court if they had cohabited for at least two years and/or had children. The court would exercise its discretion by taking into account all the circumstances of the case with the aim of doing what was fair and reasonable between the parties, which would include taking into account the level and extent of their commitment to each other. There would be a presumption, however, that cohabitants should be self-supporting, where possible. The court would have the power to make lump sum orders and transfer of property orders, and also limited-term maintenance orders for up to three years from the date of separation.

(d)   Reform of the law – the work of the Law Commission

The Law Commission (the Government's law reform body) has spent many years addressing reform of the law to remove the injustices for cohabitants and other homesharers. As long ago as 1994 it announced that the law was unsatisfactory, arbitrary and unjust, and said that it would make proposals for reform. Its proposals were eagerly awaited, but it was not until 2002 that it published a discussion paper, *Sharing Homes*, with the aim of providing a framework for future debate (see below). The discussion paper, however, turned out to be a considerable disappointment, particularly for those who had been in favour of reforming the law for cohabitants rather than homesharers generally.

(i) The Law Commission's homesharers project   In *Sharing Homes: A Discussion Paper* (Law Com No. 278, 2002) the Law Commission discussed its findings in respect of its home-sharers' project, a project which was both narrow (as it concentrated solely on the home) and broad (as it concentrated on homesharers generally). In fact the breadth of the project was largely responsible for its failure.

In *Sharing Homes* the Law Commission chose a 'contribution-based' model for reform, which it applied to two hypothetical scenarios (one involving a son living at home with his parents who makes a financial contribution to the household budget; and the other a mother who cohabits for a long time with the father of their child but who makes no direct financial contribution to the purchase of the house). Applying the contribution-based model to these two scenarios, the Law Commission said that the son would acquire an interest in the home, but the female cohabitant would not. A contribution-based approach would therefore do nothing to improve the law for cohabitants, because it was insufficiently flexible to take account of different types of relationship. The Law Commission concluded that the basis for distinguishing between the different scenarios could not be expressed in a suitably principled or rational manner.

The Rt Hon Lord Justice Thorpe ([2002] Fam Law 891), commenting on *Sharing Homes*, said that the Law Commission should have taken a relationship-based, rather than a property-based, approach to the project. He criticised the Commission's approach as being cautious, and said that the responsibility for any Parliamentary reform should lie within the family justice system.

(ii) The Law Commission's cohabitation project   In 2005 it was announced that the Law Commission, at the request of the Government, was to conduct a two-year study with a

view to reforming the law in order to remove the disadvantages, in particular the financial hardships, which cohabitants and their children suffer on relationship breakdown and on death.

In 2006 the Law Commission published a Consultation Paper, *Cohabitation: The Financial Consequences of Relationship Breakdown* (Law Com No. 179, 2006) asking for responses to its suggested proposals for reforming the law relating to the property and financial consequences of cohabitation breakdown. This was followed in 2007 by the publication of a Report, *Cohabitation: The Financial Consequences of Relationship Breakdown* (Law Com No. 307), in which the Law Commission made recommendations for the introduction of a new scheme of remedies in England and Wales for cohabitants in respect of property on family breakdown and on death. Stuart Bridge, the Law Commissioner in charge of the project, stated ([2007] Fam Law 785) that the Law Commission considered that the scheme struck the 'right balance between protecting the vulnerable and respecting freedom of choice'.

Eligibility under the proposed scheme would depend on whether the couple had cohabited for a number of years (2–5 years was suggested); or on whether the parties had a child together. Cohabitants would be able to opt out of the scheme by making binding opt-out agreements, but these would be subject to safeguards (for example in respect of the formalities to be observed); and the court would have the power to set them aside where enforcement would cause manifest unfairness.

The remedies available would be similar to those the court can make for married couples on divorce: lump sum orders; property transfer orders; property settlement orders, orders for sale; and pension sharing orders. However, unlike divorce, periodical payments (maintenance) would not generally be available.

In order to obtain a remedy, a cohabitant would have to establish that he or she had made a financial or non-financial 'qualifying contribution' to the relationship which had given rise to certain enduring consequences at the point of separation. Thus, the applicant would have to prove that the respondent had retained a benefit (capital, income or earning capacity), or that he or she had suffered a continuing economic disadvantage, as a result of qualifying contributions made to the relationship. 'Economic disadvantage' would include present and future losses, including a diminution in current savings as a result of expenditure, or of earnings lost during the relationship, lost future earnings, or the future cost of paid child-care. A list of statutory factors would be applied by the court when exercising its powers, which would include considering the welfare of any child, the parties' financial needs and obligations, their financial resources and the conduct of each of the parties.

Other recommendations were made, including the promotion of mediation, a bar on eligible cohabitants using the law of property (trusts, estoppel and contract) to seek a remedy, and a bar on applications after the couple had separated for two years (but with a power to extend this limitation period in exceptional circumstances).

The Law Commission made no recommendations in respect of the law of intestacy, but recommended that the Inheritance (Provision for Family and Dependants) Act 1975 be amended so that cohabitants would be treated in the same way under that Act as spouses and civil partners

The proposals, however, were not taken further by the Government, for in March 2008 the Government announced that the proposals were to be shelved in order to see how similar reforms introduced in Scotland (by the Family Law (Scotland) Act 2006) would work before any changes were made in England and Wales. Resolution and the Family

Justice Council of England and Wales were critical of the Government's decision not to take the proposals forward, because of the unfairness and injustices that cohabitants can suffer.

(e) The Cohabitation Bill 2008–2009

At the end of 2008 Lord Lester of Herne Hill (a human rights lawyer) introduced the Cohabitation Bill 2008–2009 into Parliament, which was also promoted by Resolution (the group of family solicitors). The Bill had its second reading in the House of Lords in March 2009, but met with resistance from some members of the House of Lords and went no further.

Lord Lester of Herne Hill, commenting on the Cohabitation Bill

'Sensibly drafted legislation is urgently needed to tackle the vulnerability not only of unmarried cohabiting couples and their children but also co-dependent carers and siblings who live together. It is a scandal in modern Britain that existing law does almost nothing to prevent such people from losing their home or sliding into poverty if their relationship breaks down or their partner dies.'

The Cohabitation Bill was drawn up after a consultation paper (*Reforming the Law for People Who Live Together*) had been published in 2008 setting out two main options for reform: one similar to that proposed by the Law Commission being based on economic disadvantage (see p. 62 and 63 above); and the other a more discretionary scheme similar to that available on divorce under the Matrimonial Causes Act 1973 (see Chapter 7). However, it was the second option which was chosen and incorporated into the Bill.

In the Bill cohabitants were defined as persons who live together as a couple (opposite-sex or same-sex) for a continuous period of at least two years; or who live together as a couple and are the parents of a minor child or who have a joint residence order in respect of a child. (The two-year requirement was later amended to five after debate in the House of Lords).

Cohabitants would be able to opt out of the scheme by making an agreement in writing signed by both parties, provided they had each received independent legal advice. The court would have the power to vary or revoke such agreements if they were manifestly unfair due to circumstances at the time the agreement was made, or subsequently.

The court would have the power to make a wide range of 'financial settlement orders' similar to those that can be made on divorce, but with periodical payments orders being limited to a maximum of three years except in cases of exceptional hardship or where payments were needed to meet childcare costs.

When exercising its powers, the court would have to consider all the circumstances of the case and consider whether it would be just and equitable to make an order. The court would have to take into account a list of statutory factors, with the welfare of any child being the first consideration. The factors the court would have to take into account would include, for example, the parties' needs and resources, the duration of the relationship and the contributions of the parties to the welfare of any children. The court would also have to consider any economic advantage or disadvantage which either party has suffered, or would suffer. Unlike divorce, the court would be required to consider the nature of the commitment between the parties and the degree of dependency or independency, there would be no presumption of equal sharing, and any award would be limited to the party's reasonable needs. Also, unlike divorce, the court would not be able to take into account the parties' standard of living. However, the court would be required to apply a principle that the parties should be self-supporting as soon as was reasonably practicable (like the 'clean break principle' on divorce).

(f) Cohabitation reform: the future

A Private Member's Bill based on the Cohabitation Bill (above) was presented to Parliament by Mary Creah MP and had its second reading in the House of Commons in July 2009, but it went no further. At the time of writing there are no Government proposals to reform the law. However, developments like the Cohabitation Bill have raised awareness about reform, and it is possible that reform may take place at some time in the future, particularly as the law has been reformed in Scotland and in other countries (such as in Australia and New Zealand).

Summary

1 Many couples choose to cohabit; and the number who do so is predicted to increase.

2 Opposite-sex and same-sex cohabitants are given some protection under the law (for example, in respect of remedies against domestic violence), but they are vulnerable in particular in respect of property rights on relationship breakdown and on the death of their partner.

3 Cohabitants have no mutual maintenance duty to each other, unlike spouses and civil partners, but they have a maintenance obligation to their children. Only the unmarried mother has automatic parental responsibility but the unmarried father can acquire it.

4 Cohabitants can enter into cohabitation contracts, but these are open to challenge in the courts.

5 Homesharers (persons who are cohabiting but who are not a 'couple') may also suffer disadvantages (for example, in respect of inheritance tax).

6 There has been increasing concern about the lack of adequate legal remedies in respect of property and finance on cohabitation breakdown, and about the unfairness and injustice this can cause. As a result, there have been calls for reform to remove the perceived unfairness that exists. In July 2007 the Law Commission published a report making proposals for reform, but these were taken no further by the Government. At the end of 2008 Lord Lester presented a Bill, the Cohabitation Bill, to Parliament with the aim of giving cohabitants (and some home-sharers) greater legal protection; but the Bill went no further. There are currently no Government proposals to change the law.

Further reading and references

Bailey-Harris, 'Law and the unmarried couple – oppression or liberation?' [1996] CFLQ 137.

Barlow, Burgoyne, Clery and Smithson, *Cohabitation and the Law: Myths, Money and the Media*, 2008, *British Social Attitudes 24th Report*, Sage Publishing.

Barlow, Duncan, James and Park, *Cohabitation, Marriage and the Law: Social Change and Legal Reform in the 21st Century*, 2005, Hart Publishing.

Barton, 'Cohabitants, contracts and commissioners' [2007] Fam Law 407.

Bray, 'The financial rights of cohabiting couples' [2009] Fam Law 1151.

Bridge, 'Cohabitation: why legislative reform is necessary' [2007] Fam Law 911.

Bridge, 'Financial relief for cohabitants: eligibility, opt out and provision on death' [2007] Fam Law 1076.

Bridge, 'Financial relief for cohabitants: how the Law Commission's scheme would work' [2007] Fam Law 998.

Bridge, 'Money, marriage and cohabitation' [2006] Fam Law 641.

Burles, ' "Promises, promises" – *Burns* v. *Burns* 20 years on' [2003] Fam Law 834.

Douglas, Pearce and Woodward, 'Dealing with property issues on cohabitation breakdown' [2007] Fam Law 36.

Douglas, Pearce and Woodward, 'The Law Commission's cohabitation proposals: applying them in practice' [2008] Fam Law 351.

Douglas, Pearce and Woodward, *A Failure of Trust: Resolving Property Issues on Cohabitation Breakdown,* Cardiff Research Papers, No. 1 (July 2007) (available at www.law.cf.ac.uk/researchpapers/index).

Duncan, Barlow and James, 'Why don't they marry? Cohabitation, commitment and DIY marriage' [2005] CFLQ 383.

Fox, 'Reforming family property – comparisons, compromises and common dimensions' [2003] CFLQ 1.

Hess, 'The rights of cohabitants: when and how will the law be reformed?' [2009] Fam Law 405.

Kirby, 'Equal treatment of same-sex couples in English family law?' [2007] Fam Law 413.

Lewis, 'Marriage and cohabitation and the nature of commitment' [1999] CFLQ 355.

Miles, 'Property law v. family law: resolving the problems of family property' (2003) *Legal Studies* 624.

Pawlowski, 'Constructive trusts and improvements to property' [2009] Fam Law 680.

Pawlowski, 'Family home: doing justice to the parties' [2006] Fam Law 462.

Pawlowski, 'Sharing homes – legislation down under' [2003] Fam Law 336.

Probert and Barlow, 'Displacing marriage – diversification and harmonisation within Europe' [2000] CFLQ 153.

Probert, 'The Cohabitation Bill' [2009] Fam Law 150.

Probert, 'Common-law marriage: myths and misunderstandings' [2008] CFLQ 1.

Probert, 'Why couples still believe in common-law marriage' [2007] Fam Law 403.

Probert, 'Cohabitation: contributions and sacrifices' [2006] Fam Law 1060.

Probert, 'Trusts and the modern woman – establishing an interest in the family home' [2001] CFLQ 275.

Singer, 'What provision for unmarried couples should the law make when their relationships break down?' [2009] Fam Law 234.

Williams, Potter and Douglas, 'Cohabitation and intestacy: public opinion and law reform' [2008] CFLQ 499.

Websites

Law Commission: www.lawcom.gov.uk

OnePlusOne – Married or Not: www.oneplusone.org.uk/marriedornot

Resolution: www.resolution.org.uk

The Law Society: www.lawsoc.org.uk

The Living Together Campaign: www.advicenow.org.uk/livingtogether.

Part III
Family property

Chapter 4

Family property

4.1　Introduction

This chapter deals with the law governing family property, in particular ownership and occupation of the family home. It also deals with family property on death.

There has been discussion about reforming the law relating to the property ownership of cohabitants. This is dealt with in Chapter 3 on Cohabitation.

Property orders can be made for or to the benefit of children under s.15 and Schedule 1 to the Children Act 1989 (see 12.5).

During the relationship the rules governing the property rights of spouses, civil partners and cohabitants are similar; but on relationship breakdown the position is radically different. This is because, whereas the courts have wide discretionary powers to distribute the property and finances of married couples on divorce (and civil partners on dissolution) according to their needs and resources, there is no such provision for cohabiting couples. Instead, cohabiting couples (and other family members) must rely on the general principles of property law to determine any property or financial dispute which arises. A cohabitant who does not own property may find himself or herself in a vulnerable position on relationship breakdown, in particular in respect of ownership and occupation of the family home. Cohabitants are also in a vulnerable position on the death of their partner, for if there is no will they have no right to succeed to their deceased partner's estate. Because cohabitants (and their children) can be in a vulnerable position in respect of entitlement to property and financial provision, there have been calls for reform (see 3.4).

4.2　The property rights of married couples and civil partners

During a marriage and a civil partnership the general principles of property law and the law of contract apply to the ownership of property, but with the addition of some 'family law' statutes (see below).

(a)　Ownership of property during marriage and civil partnership

The following statutory provisions apply in respect of ownership of property and occupation of the home in the case of married couples and civil partners, but as married couples and civil partners are unlikely to litigate about property during the subsistence of their relationship, they have little relevance in practice.

(i) Separation of property　Each spouse or civil partner can own property separately. Thus, subject to any contrary intention, any property brought into the marriage or civil partnership belongs to that party; and so does any property acquired by either party during the marriage or civil partnership. Ownership depends on the law of contract.

(ii) Gifts to married couples and civil partners　A gift to a married couple or civil partners is presumed to be a gift to both of them, including a gift of financial assistance for the

purpose of acquiring a home (*Abbott* v. *Abbott* [2007] UKPC 53, [2008] 1 FLR 1457, applying *McHardy and Sons (A Firm)* v. *Warren and Another* [1994] 2 FLR 338 and *Midland Bank plc* v. *Cooke and Another* [1995] 2 FLR 915). This is subject to any contrary intention.

(iii) Improvements to property A spouse or civil partner can acquire a share, or an enlarged share, of property (or the proceeds of sale of such property) if he or she makes a substantial improvement in money or money's worth to that property, but subject to any intention to the contrary (s.37 Matrimonial Proceedings and Property Act 1970; s.65 Civil Partnership Act 2004).

(iv) Power of the court to declare property interests Under s.17 of the Married Women's Property Act 1882 the High Court and county courts have jurisdiction on the application of a spouse to make such order as they think fit as to the ownership or possession of any property. The court only has a power to declare property entitlement; it cannot create or adjust rights (*Pettitt* v. *Pettitt* [1970] AC 777). Having declared any interest, the court can order the sale of property and order that the proceeds of sale be divided in accordance with the parties' interests (s.7(7) Matrimonial Causes (Property and Maintenance) Act 1958). A former spouse can apply under s.17 within three years of termination of marriage (s.39 Matrimonial Proceedings and Property Act 1970). An application under s.17 can be made in respect of money or property that is not in possession (s.7(1) Matrimonial Causes (Property and Maintenance) Act 1958). Applications under s.17 are rare, but they were more common when divorce was less common.

The court has the same powers as those above in respect of applications by civil partners (ss.66–68 CPA 2004).

(v) Property bought by a wife from savings Section 1 of the Married Women's Property Act 1964 provides that any property bought by a wife with savings from housekeeping money given to her by her husband belongs to them both in equal shares. This provision is archaic and discriminatory. There have been proposals to repeal it (including a Parliamentary Bill in 2005), but it remains on the statute book.

(b)   Occupation of the home – 'home rights' of spouses and civil partners

A non-owning ('non-entitled') spouse or civil partner has a statutory right of occupation of the home ('home rights') by virtue of s.30 of Part IV of the Family Law Act 1996 (see further in Chapter 5). Thus a spouse or civil partner with no right of ownership in the home (under a contract, or trust or any enactment) has a right to occupy the home if the other spouse or civil partner has such a right (s.30(1)).

'Home rights' are: if in occupation, a right not to be evicted or excluded from the home by the other spouse or civil partner, except with leave of the court given by an order under s.33 of the Act; or, if not in occupation, a right with leave of the court so given to enter into and occupy the home (s.30(2)). 'Home rights' arise only in respect of a dwelling house which is (was, or was intended to be) the parties' matrimonial or civil partnership home (s.30(7)). A person with 'home rights' has other rights. Thus any payment or other thing done by that person in or towards satisfaction of any liability of the other party (the owner) in respect of rent, mortgage payments or other outgoings affecting the home is as good as if made or done by the owner (s.30(3)). Any mortgage payments by the party with 'home rights' may be treated as being made by the other party, but this does not affect any claim by the person with 'home rights' against the other party to an interest in the home by virtue of the payment (s.30(5)). Under Part IV of the Family Law Act 1996 spouses and civil partners have a right to take part in possession proceedings when the home is subject to a mortgage (ss.54–56), and the Act also makes provision for the transfer of tenancies on relationship breakdown (s.53 and Sched. 7).

A spouse or civil partner's 'home rights' are a charge on the other party's estate or interest (s.31). A charge is binding on a third party (for example, a purchaser or a mortgagee) if it has been protected by a notice on the register made under the Land Registration Act 2002 or any enactment replaced by that Act (s.30(10)).

4.3 The property rights of engaged couples

The Law Reform (Miscellaneous Provisions) Act 1970 provides that an engagement to marry is not a contract giving rise to legal rights and that no legal action (for breach of promise) can be brought against the person responsible for terminating the engagement (s.1). On termination of an engagement, any rule of law relating to the beneficial entitlement of spouses also applies to any property in which either or both parties had a beneficial interest during their engagement (s.2(1)). Thus, s.37 of the Matrimonial Proceedings and Property Act 1970 and s.17 of the Married Women's Property Act 1882 (see above) apply. An application under s.17 MWPA 1882 must be brought within three years of termination of the engagement (s.2(2)).

The fact that one party was responsible for terminating the engagement does not affect any express or implied arrangement in respect of the return of engagement gifts (s.3(1)). Ownership depends on the intention of the donor. In the absence of any intention, the court may infer that a gift from a relative belongs to the party to the engagement to whom the relative is related (by analogy with *Samson v. Samson* [1982] 1 WLR 252 where this rule was applied to wedding gifts).

An engagement ring is presumed to be an absolute gift (s.3(2)). Thus, it can be kept on the termination of an engagement unless there is an express or implied condition to the contrary (for instance, that it is a family heirloom).

Similar provisions also apply to civil partnerships agreements (see ss.73 and 74 of the Civil Partnership Act 2004).

4.4 The property rights of cohabitants

(a) Ownership of property

During a cohabiting relationship, and on cohabitation breakdown, the property rights of cohabitants (opposite-sex and same-sex) are governed by the general rules of property law. There are no special statutory provisions for cohabitants as there are for married couples, civil partners and engaged couples (see above). Cohabitants are in a particularly disadvantageous position on relationship breakdown, as there is no discretionary jurisdiction, as on divorce or dissolution of civil partnership, to adjust their property rights according to their needs and resources. A cohabitant is also in a vulnerable position where a deceased partner has made no will. For many years there has been discussion about reforming the law governing the property rights of cohabitants because of the perceived injustices they suffer (see 3.4).

A cohabitant (or former cohabitant) who wishes to claim a share, or an enlarged share, of property will have to turn to the law of equity (trusts and proprietary estoppel, see 4.7 and 4.8) to bring a claim. However, unlike disputes involving spouses on divorce (or civil partners on dissolution), claims by cohabitants are heard in the civil or chancery courts and from a property law, not a family law, perspective. Bringing a case is expensive and time-consuming, and the law of trusts is not entirely satisfactory for determining such disputes (see 3.4).

(b) Occupation of the home

A non-owning cohabitant, unlike a spouse or civil partner, has no statutory right of occupation of the home (see p. 72 above). Rights of occupation are instead dependent on a cohabitant having a right of ownership, a right under a tenancy, or having a licence to remain in occupation. Cohabitants and former cohabitants who are victims of domestic violence can, however, apply for an occupation order under Part IV of the Family Law Act 1996 which, if granted, will give the applicant a right of occupation for the duration of the order (see 5.5).

4.5 Ownership of property other than land

Family members may own a wide range of property other than land (for example, a pension, investments and household goods). Ownership of personal property (property other than land) depends on whether there is an interest under a contract or an interest in equity under a trust. As a general rule, title to the property passes to the purchaser, subject to there being a valid contract and no contrary intention (for instance, that the property is jointly owned or belongs to a third party). In the case of gifts of property, ownership passes to the recipient, provided the donor intended to transfer the gift and it was handed over.

(i) Acquiring a right of ownership   A person who has no right under a contract can claim an interest in personal property under an express, resulting or constructive trust.

▶ *Paul v. Constance* **[1977] 1 WLR 527**

The female claimant was held to have an interest by way of express trust in the bank account held in her cohabitant's sole name, as she had been authorised to draw on the account and he had told her on several occasions that the money in the account was as much hers as his.

▶ *Rowe v. Prance* **[1999] 2 FLR 787**

The female claimant was held to be entitled to a half-share in a valuable yacht owned by her former partner, with whom she had had a close relationship for 14 years. She had not contributed financially to its purchase, but her partner had referred to the yacht as 'our boat', had spoken of 'a share of the boat together' and had said 'your security is your interest in it'. The claimant had given up rented accommodation and put furniture in storage in order to move into the boat, which they intended to sail round the world together. The court accepted this evidence as sufficient to constitute the man as an express trustee of the boat, so that the claimant was entitled to a share.

However despite the successful outcome for the cohabitants in the two cases above, cohabitants should be wary of taking a case to court and should try to settle any dispute. Taking a case to court is costly, time-consuming and unpredictable. In *Hammond* v. *Mitchell* [1991] 1 WLR 1127, *sub nom H* v. *M (Property: Beneficial Interest)* [1992] 1 FLR 229 Waite J said that cohabitants on relationship breakdown should be encouraged to do their best to settle disputes about chattels on the understanding that in ordinary cases the court will divide them equally.

(ii) Bank accounts If a bank account is held in one person's name the money in the account belongs to that person (unless there is a contrary intention or another person has made a contribution to the fund). If a bank account is held in joint names the money in the account belongs to both parties as beneficial joint tenants of the whole fund (unless there is a contrary intention, such as that the account was put into joint names for the sake of convenience). As a general rule, any property bought with funds from a bank account belongs to the purchaser. However, where the parties have pooled their resources, the court may decide that the property belongs to them both.

4.6 Disputes about the family home

Disputes about property are often about the family home, as the home is not only a valuable asset but it also provides a roof over the family's head. Disputes about the family home (and about other property) may arise in the following situations:

- **On relationship breakdown** Spouses on divorce (and civil partners on dissolution) who cannot agree about ownership of the family home (and/or other property) can invoke the discretionary powers of the court on divorce or dissolution to settle their property disputes (see Chapter 7 and 2.10). Cohabitants, on the other hand, have to use the law of equity (see 4.7 and 4.8).
- **On death** If there is a will, then that determines the parties' property rights. Where there is no will, surviving spouses and civil partners have a statutory right to succeed to the deceased's estate (see 4.12). Cohabitants, on the other hand, have no rights of succession, but can bring a claim under the Inheritance (Provision for Family and Dependants) Act 1975 (see 4.13), or claim an interest in equity under a trust (see 4.7) or by way of proprietary estoppel (see 4.8).
- **Where the interests are not defined** Where there is no mention of the parties' respective interests on the transfer deed, the court may have to determine the matter (see p. 83).
- **Where a third party seeks possession** Where a third party (such as a purchaser, mortgagee or trustee in bankruptcy) seeks possession of the home, a spouse, civil partner, cohabitant (or other family member) may claim an interest in the home under a trust in order to defeat the claim to possession (see, for example, *Lloyds Bank plc* v. *Rosset* [1991] 1 AC 107, [1990] 2 FLR 155).

A claim to establish an interest in the home (other than on divorce or civil partnership dissolution) is usually brought under s.14 of the Trusts of Land and Appointment of Trustees Act 1996 (TLATA 1996). This is the mechanism which cohabitants use when bringing a claim to establish an interest in the home (see, for example, *Oxley* v. *Hiscock*

[2004] EWCA Civ 546, [2004] 2 FLR 669 where a cohabitant sought a declaration under s.14 TLATA 1996 that the proceeds of sale of the family home were held by her former cohabitant on trust for them both in equal shares). The High Court and the county court have jurisdiction to make declarations in respect of property rights, but the more usual practice is to use TLATA 1996.

4.7 Acquiring a right of ownership in the family home under a trust

There are two sorts of ownership in English law: ownership in law; and ownership in equity. Ownership in equity involves owning property as a beneficiary under a trust. A person can own property in law or in equity, or in both law and equity. Thus, for example, the male cohabitant may be the legal owner of the house, but he may also hold it on trust for himself and his female partner, the beneficiary, in equity. Many spouses and cohabitants, however, own their home jointly as co-owners both in law and in equity.

A person can claim a right of ownership in the family home under a trust, even if there is nothing in writing to that effect. This is because, although under s.53(1) of the Law of Property Act 1925 writing is required for the creation of interests in land and declarations of trusts of land, s.53(2) states that writing is not required for the creation of an implied, resulting or constructive trust in respect of land. Similar rules apply in respect of contracts for the sale of land. Thus, while s.2(1) of the Law of Property (Miscellaneous Provisions) Act 1989 requires contracts for the sale of land to be in writing, s.2(5) provides that writing is not required for the creation of an implied, resulting or constructive trust of land. As s.2(5), like s.53(2) of the Law of Property Act 1925, was intended to allow a range of equitable remedies, an interest in land can also be claimed under the equitable doctrine of proprietary estoppel (*per* Beldam LJ in *Yaxley* v. *Gotts and Gotts* [1999] 2 FLR 941, and see 4.8).

An interest in land, such as the family home, can be acquired under a resulting trust or a constructive trust. These two types of trust are distinct and different doctrines, each with their own body of case-law.

(a) Acquiring an interest in the home under a resulting trust

A resulting trust arises as a presumption of equity where a person makes a financial contribution to the purchase of property (the family home or other property). In the absence of a contrary intention (for example, that the contribution was a gift or a loan, or that other shares were intended) a person who contributes money to the purchase of property acquires an interest under a resulting trust proportionate to that contribution. Resulting trusts were claimed in the following cases:

> ▶ *Sekhon* v. *Alissa* **[1989] 2 FLR 94**
>
> The house had been bought in the name of the defendant daughter. She had contributed to the purchase price, but her mother had paid the balance. The mother claimed a share in the house under a resulting trust, arguing that, although it was bought in her daughter's name, it was purchased as a joint commercial venture and they both intended to own it in proportion to their respective financial contributions. The daughter attempted to rebut the presumption of resulting trust by arguing that her mother's financial contribution was intended as a gift or a

loan. The court had to decide what was the actual or presumed intention of the parties at the time of the conveyance. The question was whether the mother's financial contribution was a gift or an unsecured loan, or whether it was intended that she should have a beneficial interest in the property. The Court of Appeal held that the law presumed a resulting trust in the mother's favour, and on the facts the presumption was not rebutted by the daughter's allegation that the money was a gift or a loan.

▶ *Springette v. Defoe* [1992] 2 FLR 388

The parties, two elderly cohabitants, had bought their council house, but there was nothing in the registered transfer quantifying their respective beneficial interests. Each party had paid half the mortgage instalments, but the claimant, Miss Springette, had paid most of the balance of the purchase price. When the relationship broke down she issued an originating summons claiming that she was entitled to 75 per cent of the proceeds of sale, as this represented her contribution to the purchase. At first instance, the trial judge granted the parties an equal share of the beneficial interest, on the basis that it was their uncommunicated belief or intention that they were to share the property equally. The Court of Appeal allowed the claimant's appeal, holding that, as there was no discussion between the parties as to their respective beneficial interests, there was no evidence to rebut the presumption that the claimant was entitled to a 75 per cent share of the beneficial interest under a resulting trust.

Despite the successful use of a resulting trust in the cases above, cases are usually brought on the basis of a constructive trust (or proprietary estoppel). The demise of the resulting trust as a mechanism for claiming a share in the home is due, in part, to the fact that a claimant who establishes a resulting trust obtains only a share proportionate to his or her contribution to the purchase price. Furthermore, only a financial contribution to the initial purchase of property can give rise to an interest under a resulting trust, not contributions made after its purchase (see *Curley* v. *Parkes* [2004] EWCA Civ 1515). In fact the House of Lords has held that the constructive trust is the more appropriate tool of analysis in cases regarding ownership of the home (see *Stack* v. *Dowden* [2007] UKHL 17, [2007] 1 FLR 1858, see p. 84 below).

The presumption of advancement   Under this presumption, a transfer of property by a husband to his wife, or a father to his child, is presumed to belong to the wife, or child, absolutely. Although this presumption might be used to rebut the presumption of resulting trust (for example, by a wife arguing that her husband's contribution to the purchase of the home was an absolute gift) it is considered to be archaic and discriminatory. For this reason, it has little relevance today and is unlikely to be relied on. In *McGrath* v. *Wallis* [1995] 2 FLR 114 Nourse LJ said that in its application to a house acquired for joint occupation it was a judicial instrument of last resort which could be easily rebutted. A Parliamentary Bill in 2005 contained a clause abolishing the presumption, but it did not pass into law.

In *Laskar* v. *Laskar* [2008] EWCA Civ 347, [2008] 2 FLR 589, which involved a dispute between a mother and daughter about the size of their beneficial interests in a property of which they were joint legal owners, the Court of Appeal held that the presumption of advancement is a weak presumption rebuttable on comparatively slight evidence. It held that the presumption was even weaker in this case as the child was an adult who had managed her own affairs at the time of the transaction.

(b) Acquiring an interest in the home under a constructive trust

An interest in the family home (or other property) can be claimed under a constructive trust, or what is sometimes called a 'common intention constructive trust' (in order to distinguish it from another type of constructive trust which is used in the commercial context).

With a constructive trust, unlike a resulting trust, there is no need for any financial contribution to have been made to the purchase of property. Instead, the emphasis is on finding an express or implied agreement or intention that the non-owner is entitled to an interest. The court cannot, however, find a constructive trust merely to do justice in a case. In *Springette* v. *Defoe* [1992] 2 FLR 388 Dillon LJ said: '[T]he court does not as yet sit, as under a palm tree, to exercise a general discretion as to what the man in the street, on the general view of the case, might regard as fair'. The court cannot ascribe to parties intentions which they never had. It is also difficult to establish a constructive trust solely on the basis of conduct alone (*per* Sir John Chadwick LJ in *James* v. *Thomas* [2007] EWCA Civ 1212, [2008] 1 FLR 1598).

Despite *obiter dicta* by Lord Walker and Baroness Hale in *Stack* v. *Dowden* (2007) (see p. 84 below) that a broader approach should be taken to the question of finding a common intention in constructive trusts cases involving the family home, the courts have not shown themselves willing to adopt such an approach.

(i) A two-stage exercise   In a claim to a beneficial interest in the home under a constructive trust the court conducts a two-stage exercise. First it considers the evidence to establish whether or not the applicant can establish an interest under a constructive trust. If there is, then the court must consider all the circumstances of the case in order to decide what share of the beneficial interest the claimant should have.

The leading case on constructive trusts is *Lloyds Bank plc* v. *Rosset* in which Lord Bridge laid down the approach to be adopted by the courts:

▶ *Lloyds Bank plc* v. *Rosset* **[1991] 1 AC 107, [1990] 2 FLR 155**

The home had been purchased in the husband's sole name. His wife had helped to renovate it, but she had made no financial contribution to its purchase or renovation. Mr Rosset charged the house to Lloyds Bank as security for a loan, which Mrs Rosset knew nothing about. When Mr Rosset went into debt, Lloyds Bank claimed possession of the home and an order for sale. Mrs Rosset, by way of defence to the bank's claim, argued that she had a beneficial interest in the house under a constructive trust and that this interest coupled with her actual occupation gave her an overriding interest under s.70(1)(g) Land Registration Act 1925 which would defeat the bank's claims. (The 1925 Act has now been repealed and replaced by the Land Registration Act 2002).

The House of Lords held, dismissing her appeal, that her activities in relation to the renovation of the house were insufficient to justify the inference of a common intention that she was entitled to a beneficial interest under a constructive trust. Lord Bridge summarised and encapsulated the law as laid down in the two earlier House of Lords' decisions of *Pettitt* v. *Pettitt* [1970] AC 777 and *Gissing* v. *Gissing* [1971] AC 886, and referred also to the Court of Appeal decision in *Grant* v. *Edwards* [1986] Ch 638 (the leading case on detriment).

LORD BRIDGE: 'The first and fundamental question which must always be resolved is whether, independently of any inference to be drawn from the conduct of the parties in the course of sharing the house as their home and managing their joint affairs, there has at any time prior to acquisition, or exceptionally at some later date, been any agreement, arrangement or understanding reached between them that the property is to be shared beneficially. The finding of an agreement or arrangement to share in this sense can only, I think, be based on evidence of express discussions between the partners, however imperfectly remembered and however imprecise their terms may have been. Once a finding to this effect is made it will only be necessary for the partner entitled to the legal estate to show that he or she has acted to his or her detriment or significantly altered his or her position in reliance on the agreement in order to give rise to a constructive trust or proprietary estoppel.

In sharp contrast to this situation is the very different one where there is no evidence to support a finding of an agreement or an arrangement to share, however reasonable it might have been for the parties to reach such an agreement if they had applied their minds to the question, and where the court must rely entirely on the conduct of the parties both as the basis from which to infer a common intention to share the property beneficially and as the conduct relied on to give rise to a constructive trust. In this situation direct contributions to the purchase price by the partner who is not the legal owner, whether initially or by payment of mortgage instalments, will readily justify the inference necessary to the creation of a constructive trust. But, as I read the authorities, it is at least extremely doubtful whether anything less will do.'

Lord Bridge's words in *Rosset* have formed the template of analysis in subsequent cases. Thus, in order to establish a constructive trust, there must be evidence of a common intention and of detrimental reliance. A common intention can arise where there is an express or inferred agreement, arrangement or understanding that the property is to be shared beneficially. However, in a case involving an inference to share it will be difficult to establish a claim to a share if there has been no direct financial contribution to the purchase of the home, for, according to Lord Bridge, only a financial contribution will be sufficient to provide evidence of an inferred intention.

In *Oxley* v. *Hiscock* [2004] EWCA Civ 546, [2004] 2 FLR 669 Chadwick LJ usefully summarised the correct approach to be adopted in cases where a claim is made to a beneficial interest under a constructive trust:

'[T]he first question is whether there is evidence from which to infer a common intention, communicated by each to the other, that each shall have a beneficial share in the property. In many such cases ... there will have been some discussion between the parties at the time of the purchase which provides the answer to that question. Those are cases within the first of Lord Bridge's categories in *Lloyds Bank plc* v. *Rosset*. In other cases – where the evidence is that the matter was not discussed at all – an affirmative answer will readily be inferred from the fact that each has made a financial contribution. These are cases within Lord Bridge's second category. And, if the answer to the first question is that there was a common intention, communicated to each other, that each should have a beneficial share in the property, then the party who does not become the legal owner will be held to have acted to his or her detriment in making a financial contribution to the purchase in reliance on the common intention.'

(ii) Indirect financial contributions In *Rosset* Lord Bridge said that, on his reading of the authorities, he doubted whether anything less than a direct financial contribution to the purchase price would be sufficient to establish a share in the home where there was no express intention that the claimant should have a beneficial interest. Because of the ruling in *Rosset*, the courts have been unwilling to accept indirect contributions to the purchase of property as evidence from which to infer an intention to share. Thus indirect contributions (such as paying household bills or bringing up children) will not be accepted

as evidence to establish an interest under a constructive trust. It has been suggested, however, that judges should be more willing to do so (see further at p. 52 below).

(iii) Detrimental reliance In addition to proving a common intention (express or inferred), the claimant must also prove that he or she suffered some detriment as a result of relying on that intention. Detrimental reliance in most cases is usually fairly easily proved. Bringing up a family and running a home, for example, can be used as evidence of detriment. The more difficult hurdle is that of proving intention.

The act(s) of detrimental reliance must follow the common intention (see *Churchill* v. *Roach* [2004] 2 FLR 989, where the cohabitant's claim to property belonging to her deceased cohabitant's estate on the basis of a constructive trust failed, as the acts relied on as constituting detriment had occurred before the common intention was established).

(iv) Establishing the size of the beneficial interest Once the court finds that the claimant is entitled to a beneficial interest under a constructive trust, it must next determine the size of that interest. In *Midland Bank plc* v. *Cooke* [1995] 2 FLR 915 (see below) the Court of Appeal held that a 'broad brush' approach should be adopted by the court when deciding the size of the share. Thus, the court takes account of all the circumstances of the case, including financial and non-financial circumstances and the intentions of the parties. In *Oxley* v. *Hiscock* [2004] EWCA Civ 546, [2004] 2 FLR 669 Chadwick LJ adopted a broad test based on fairness.

Constructive trusts of the family home: examples from the case-law

▶ *Midland Bank plc* v. *Cooke* **[1995] 2 FLR 915**

The husband purchased the matrimonial home for £8,450, with £6,450 from a mortgage, £1,000 of his own savings and another £1,000 which was a wedding gift from his parents. His wife made no direct contribution to the purchase, except for the £500 which represented her half-share of the wedding gift, but she made considerable financial contributions to the upkeep of the house and to the household. She claimed a beneficial interest in the home. At first instance, the county court judge held that her beneficial interest in the house amounted to a sum equivalent to 6.47 per cent of the value of the property, representing her half-share of the wedding gift of £1,000. The Court of Appeal allowed her appeal, holding that, as she and her husband had agreed to share everything equally, including the house, she was entitled to half the beneficial interest. In respect of establishing the share of the beneficial interest, Waite LJ said that the court was permitted to undertake a survey of the whole course of dealing between the parties in respect of their ownership and occupation of the house and their sharing of its burdens and advantages.

▶ *Oxley* v. *Hiscock* **[2004] EWCA Civ 546, [2004] 2 FLR 669**

The female cohabitant applied under s.14 of the Trusts of Land and Appointment of Trustees Act 1996 for a declaration that the proceeds of sale were held by the man on trust for the parties in equal shares. Chadwick LJ conducted an extensive review of the authorities, and held, in respect of calculating the share of the beneficial interest, that each party 'is entitled to that share which the court considers fair having regard to the whole course of dealing between them in relation to the property'. Applying the broad-brush approach adopted in *Midland Bank* v. *Cooke* (above), the Court of Appeal held that a fair division of the sale of the property was 60 per cent to the man and 40 per cent to the woman, as equal division would have given insufficient weight to the disparity in the parties' financial contributions.

▶ *Cox* v. *Jones* **[2004] EWHC 1486 (Ch), [2004] 2 FLR 1010**

The claimant, a female cohabitant, had made no direct financial contribution to the purchase price of the property in dispute which was owned by her cohabitant partner. She had made no contribution to the mortgage repayments, but she had spent time renovating it. Mann J found that there was an express arrangement between the parties that she was to have a share of the house, and that she had acted to her detriment by putting her practice as a barrister to one side to spend her time and energy on renovating the property that was to be their home. Mann J granted her a 25 per cent share of the beneficial interest in the property, applying dicta of Chadwick LJ in *Oxley* v. *Hiscock* (2004) that her share of the interest in the house must be 'fair having regard to the whole course of dealing between them in relation to the property'.

▶ *Hyett* v. *Stanley* **[2003] EWCA Civ 942, [2004] 1 FLR 394**

The female cohabitant on the death of the male cohabitant was held to have a beneficial interest in the farm held in his name. The man's statement made in 1992 raised a clear inference that there was an understanding between him and the female applicant of a common intention that she was to have a beneficial interest in the farm. The detriment was assuming the risk of joint liability.

The following case was unusual in that it involved a dispute between a husband and wife, not cohabitants, about the ownership of property (as it was an appeal from Antigua where disputes about matrimonial property have to be decided under the ordinary law of property). Although the Privy Council adopted a flexible approach to ascertaining the size of the share of property, it is unlikely that such a flexible approach will be taken by the courts when deciding cases involving cohabitants. A flexible approach was adopted in *Abbott* because such an approach is adopted in ancillary relief cases on divorce in England and Wales (see Chapter 7). The Privy Council, however, make some important points about constructive trusts generally.

▶ *Abbott* v. *Abbott* **[2007] UKPC 53, [2008] 1 FLR 1457**

The matrimonial home in the husband's sole name was built on a plot of land in Antigua given by his mother when the parties married. The building was financed by a mortgage and a loan from the mother. All the money was paid into the couple's joint account from which the payments were made; and the wife was jointly and severally liable for the mortgage and the loan. The Court of Appeal (of England and Wales) held that there was no evidence to suggest that the mother had wished both spouses to share her gift of land, and held, applying Lord Bridge in *Rosset*, that the wife could only acquire an interest in the home by making direct contributions to the mortgage instalments, which gave her only an 8 per cent share. The wife appealed to the Privy Council *inter alia* in respect of her share in the matrimonial home.

The Privy Council allowed the appeal and awarded her a half-share in the matrimonial home, holding *inter alia* that:

▶ The constructive trust is generally the more appropriate tool of analysis in most matrimonial cases. The law had moved on from Lord Bridge's words in *Rosset*, which were themselves open to doubt in the light of *Gissing* v. *Gissing* [1971] AC 886; and the search is to ascertain the parties' actual or inferred shared intentions with respect to the property in the light of their whole course of conduct in relation to it (applying *Stack* v. *Dowden*, see p. 84 below).

> ▶ The inference that the wife was entitled to a half-share of the matrimonial home was supported by the behaviour of both parties until the breakdown of their marriage. They organised their finances entirely jointly and undertook joint liability for the repayment of the mortgage. This has always been a significant factor (applying *Hyett* v. *Stanley* [2003] EWCA Civ 942, [2004] 1 FLR 394).

(v) Should the courts take a broader approach in constructive trust cases? The question arises as to whether the courts in constructive trust cases should be more willing to infer intentions as to the existence of a beneficial interest. Should judges be willing to find evidence of intention not just from direct financial contributions but from indirect contributions (such as paying household bills, looking after the home and bringing up children). This question is particularly important for cohabitants, as there is no discretionary jurisdiction for cohabitants, as on divorce and civil partnership dissolution.

Although there have been some calls for the courts to adopt a broader and more flexible approach than that taken by Lord Bridge in *Rosset* and to take indirect contributions into account, the courts have been unwilling to do so because of the binding nature of *Rosset*. The Law Commission in its 2002 Report, *Sharing Homes* (see 3.4), and Lord Walker and Baroness Hale *obiter dicta* in *Stack* v. *Dowden* (2007) (see p. 84 below) have recommended such an approach. Baroness Hale, who gave the leading opinion in *Stack* v. *Dowden*, said that imputed intentions were acceptable. Her Ladyship said that in her view Lord Bridge in *Rosset* might have 'set the hurdle rather too high in certain respects'. Baroness Hale was also of the opinion that the resulting trust was no longer the appropriate tool of analysis in such cases and that 'many more factors than financial contributions may be relevant to divining the parties' true intentions'. These views were subsequently endorsed by the Privy Council in *Abbott* v. *Abbott* [2007] UKPC 53 [2008] 1 FLR 1457 (see p. 81 above) where Lord Walker, commenting on Lord Bridge's words in *Rosset*, said:

> 'Lord Bridge's extreme doubt "whether any less will do" was certainly consistent with many first instance and Court of Appeal decisions, but I respectfully doubt whether it took full account of the views (conflicting though they were) expressed in *Gissing* v. *Gissing* [1971] AC 886 [especially by Lord Reid … and Lord Diplock]. It has attracted some trenchant criticism from scholars as potentially productive of injustice. … Whether or not Lord Bridge's observation was justified in 1990, in my opinion the law has moved on, and your Lordships should move it a little more in the same direction.'

However, the more flexible approach recommended by Baroness Hale and Lord Walker in *Stack* v. *Dowden* has been held in subsequent cases to apply only to the question of the quantification of a beneficial interest, not to the question of whether a beneficial interest exists at all. Thus, in *Morris* v. *Morris* [2008] EWCA Civ 257 Gibson LJ said that Baroness Hale's *obiter dicta* in *Stack* v. *Dowden* were limited to the question of the quantification of beneficial interests; and that the authorities made it clear that 'a common intention constructive trust based solely on conduct will only be found in exceptional circumstances'.

Thus, despite the *obiter dicta* of Baroness Hale and Lords Walker in *Stack* v. *Dowden* and *Abbott* v. *Abbott* in 2007, the following case shows the courts continuing to use the principles laid down in *Rosset*. What was distinctive about the case, however, was that the male cohabitant owned the house *before* the female cohabitant moved in (it was a 'post-acquisition' case). It shows that, although discussions and conduct post-acquisition of the home can be considered by the court, an inference of an intention that both parties are beneficial owners is unlikely to be readily drawn from conduct alone in the absence of evidence of express agreement.

▶ *James* v. *Thomas* [2007] EWCA Civ 1212, [2008] 1 FLR 1598

The male cohabitant was the sole legal and beneficial owner of the property (which prior to him owning it had been owned by his family for about 20 years). Three years after he acquired the house the female claimant moved in and they lived together as cohabitants. She helped him with his business, but all the expenses for the house were paid from his bank account. When she moved in the claimant gave the defendant £5,000 to pay a tax bill, but it was unclear whether this was a gift or a loan. During the relationship various statements were made to the effect that the improvements to the property 'would benefit them both'. When their relationship ended the claimant claimed an interest in the property on the basis of a constructive trust or proprietary estoppel. Her claim failed at first instance, and so she appealed to the Court of Appeal.

The Court of Appeal dismissed her appeal. Sir John Chadwick held that a common intention to found a constructive trust can arise post-acquisition and that an intention can be inferred from the whole course of dealing between the parties. However, he held that, in the absence of an express post-acquisition agreement, the court would be slow to infer from conduct alone that the parties intended to vary beneficial interests established at the time of acquisition. The evidence was insufficient to establish a constructive trust expressly or by inference. It was also held that the claimant had not acted to her detriment in reliance on the assurances by the defendant.

SIR JOHN CHADWICK: 'Miss J's interest in the property (if any) must be determined by applying principles of law and equity which (however inadequate to meet the circumstances in which parties live together in the twenty-first century) must now be taken as well-established.'

The approach in *James* v. *Thomas* was applied in *Morris* v. *Morris* [2008] EWCA Civ 257 (another 'post-acquisition' case) where the Court of Appeal found no express or inferred common intention to share the property in dispute. Gibson LJ, referring to Sir John Chadwick in *James* v. *Thomas* held that, although a common intention could be inferred from conduct, the court would be slow to infer a subsequent common intention from conduct alone.

(For a commentary on *James* v. *Thomas* and *Morris* v. *Morris*, see Piska [2009] CFLQ 104, who states that, while they were correctly decided, the fact that both claimants received nothing seemed harsh).

(c) Joint owner cases

Where the parties are joint owners in law of the home, but there is no declaration of their beneficial interests (their interests in equity under a trust) *Stack* v. *Dowden* (below) establishes that beneficial ownership of the property should follow the legal ownership, unless there is a contrary intention, but that such an intention will arise only in very unusual circumstance. It also establishes that, in determining the parties' intentions, the court may consider a wide range of factors.

Although *Stack* v. *Dowden* was the first case to go to the House of Lords involving a dispute between cohabitants about ownership of the family home, it offers little hope for cohabitants who have no right of ownership in the home.

▶ *Stack* v. *Dowden* [2007] UKHL 17, [2007] AC 432, [2007] 1 FLR 1858

The parties had cohabited for 20 years. The family home was registered in their joint names but the transfer deed contained nothing about their interests in equity, as they had failed to draw up a declaration of trust. The purchase price other than the mortgage advance had been provided by Ms Dowden. When the relationship broke down, Mr Stack left the house and Ms Dowden remained there with the children. Mr Stack successfully sought an order for sale of the property and was granted a 50:50 division of the proceeds of sale. The Court of Appeal allowed Ms Dowden's appeal and held that she was entitled to 65 per cent of the proceeds of sale (as she had made a greater financial contribution to the purchase of the house), applying the fairness test laid down by Chadwick LJ in *Oxley* v. *Hiscock* (see p. 80, above). Mr Stack appealed to the House of Lords.

The House of Lords unanimously dismissed his appeal (Lord Neuberger dissenting as to reasoning) and held that, where a house is conveyed into joint names in the domestic consumer context, then *prima facie* joint and equal beneficial interests arise unless and until the contrary is proved. The burden was on the defendant to rebut the presumption by showing that equal beneficial shares were not intended. In the domestic context, factors other than financial contributions could be taken into account. Looking at the facts of the case, there were many factors to which the defendant could point to indicate that the intention of the parties was that the shares were not owned jointly in equity. For instance, when the property was bought, both parties knew that the defendant had paid more than the claimant, and they had kept their financial affairs separate. The defendant had therefore made good her case for a 65 per cent share.

BARONESS HALE: 'The search is to ascertain the parties' shared intentions, actual, inferred or imputed, with respect to the property in the light of their whole course of conduct in relation to it.'

Note: Changes to the Land Registry form were made in 1998, so that cases like *Stack* v. *Dowden* are much less likely to arise.

Stack v. *Dowden* was applied in *Fowler* v. *Barron* [2008] EWCA Civ 377, [2008] 2 FLR 831 where the cohabitant parties had put their property into joint names but had made no declaration of trust on the transfer document as to how their beneficial shares were to be held. The Court of Appeal ruled that the woman was entitled to a half-share in equity. The approach in *Stack* v. *Dowden* was held not to apply, however, in *Laskar* v. *Laskar* [2008] EWCA Civ 347, [2008] 2 FLR 589, which involved a dispute between a mother and daughter about the beneficial interest in the property which they had bought in joint names. The Court of Appeal held that, although the parties were mother and daughter and not in that sense in an arm's length commercial relationship, they had independent lives and the purchase was not for the purpose of providing a home for them both but was as an investment.

Stack v. *Dowden* was applied in the following case, which involved cohabiting parties:

> ▶ *Jones v. Kernott* [2009] EWHC 1713 (Ch)
>
> The cohabiting parties had bought the house as joint owners but 12 years after the relationship had broken down the male partner attempted to sever the joint tenancy. The court therefore had to establish the parties' respective ownerships of the beneficial interest. Since relationship breakdown the claimant had paid all the payments due under the mortgage endowment policy, and all the expenses associated with running and maintaining the house; and the defendant had made no contribution towards the children's maintenance, and the claimant had sought no contribution. Applying *Stack v. Dowden* and *Oxley v. Hiscock* and considering what would be 'fair and just' between the parties, taking account of 'the whole course of dealing' between them, it was held that the property should be divided 90:10 between Ms J and Mr K respectively. Nicholas Strauss QC (sitting as a High Court judge) held that, in the circumstances of the case, 'while the intention of the parties may well have been at the outset to provide them as a couple with a home … those intentions [had] altered significantly over the years'. He also said that, although it was not necessary in the circumstances of the case to take into account the fact that Mr K had not contributed to the maintenance of the children, he though that such a matter could legitimately be considered when assessing the appropriate quantification of beneficial shares, relying upon Baroness Hale's dicta in *Stack v. Dowden*.

Although *Jones v. Kernott* shows the court adopting a flexible approach to the question of beneficial ownership in a case involving cohabiting parties, it is an atypical case (because the man was attempting to sever the joint tenancy). It therefore offers little hope to non-owning cohabitants on relationship breakdown who have made no financial contribution to the purchase of the family home.

4.8 Acquiring an interest by way of proprietary estoppel

Proprietary estoppel can be used to claim an interest in the family home (and is often used as an alternative to a claim based on a constructive trust, see above).

Although the doctrines of constructive trust and proprietary estoppel are similar, in that they are both equitable doctrines providing relief against unconscionable conduct, the doctrines are separate and distinct. They have not been assimilated with each other. An important distinction between the two doctrines is in respect of the remedy available (see below). The existence of a constructive trust results in a right of ownership, whereas, if proprietary estoppel is established, the court merely has a discretion as to the remedy to be ordered to do justice in the case. Another difference is that a constructive trust is based on a shared intention, whereas this is not necessarily so with proprietary estoppel. In fact, despite a representation by the defendant, the claimant and the defendant may have perceived the matter quite differently.

Although the doctrines of proprietary estoppel and constructive trust are distinct and different doctrines, in *Q v. Q* [2008] EWHC 1874 (Fam), [2009] 1 FLR 935 Black J held that it is possible to satisfy the requirements of both doctrines in the same case.

The doctrine of proprietary estoppel was described by Balcombe LJ in *Wayling v. Jones* [1995] 2 FLR 1029, at 1031, as follows:

'Where one person (A) has acted to his detriment on the faith of a belief, which was known to and encouraged by another person (B), that he either has or is going to be given a right in or over B's property, B cannot insist on his strict legal rights if to do so would be inconsistent with A's belief.'

Thus there must be proof of an agreement or an expectation created or encouraged by one party upon which the other party has acted to his or her detriment. There must be a promise, and a sufficient link between the promise relied upon and the conduct which constitutes the detriment.

In *Gillett* v. *Holt and Another* [2000] 2 FLR 266 the Court of Appeal stated that, as proprietary estoppel is a flexible doctrine which is based on preventing unconscionable conduct, the facts must be looked at in the round. It held that detriment is not a narrow or technical concept but one which must be approached as part of a broad inquiry, and that reliance and detriment should not be treated as being divided into separate watertight compartments.

What constitutes an assurance for the purpose of establishing an estoppel?   In order to found an estoppel there must be a clear and unambiguous assurance given by the other party and relied on by the claimant. In *Thorner* v. *Major and Others* [2009] UKHL 18, [2009] 2 FLR 405 the House of Lords considered this requirement and held that the effect of the words or actions must be assessed in their context; and that it would be quite wrong to be unrealistically rigorous when applying the 'clear and unambiguous' test. It held that, if the statement relied on to found an estoppel was ambiguous, that ambiguity should not deprive a person who had reasonably relied on the assurance of all relief, although the relief should be limited to the least beneficial interpretation.

In *Negus* v. *Bahouse and Another* [2007] EWHC 2628 (Ch), [2008] 1 FLR 381 a cohabitant claimed, in an application made under s.14 of the Trusts of Land and Appointment of Trustees Act 1996, that she had an interest by way of proprietary estoppel in a flat where she had lived with her deceased partner. However, her claim failed, as the statements made by the deceased had been equivocal and were insufficient to amount to a specific agreement or understanding that she should have an interest. Nevertheless, it was held in the circumstances that the flat (plus a sum of £200,000) should be transferred to her under the Inheritance (Provision for Family and Dependants) Act 1975 (see 4.13).

What remedy to grant?   Once an estoppel is proved, the court must consider all the circumstances of the case and exercise its discretion to decide what remedy to grant. A claim based on estoppel may not be so advantageous as one based on a trust, because the claimant may not gain a right of ownership, but merely a licence to occupy the property or some financial compensation. Each case depends on its facts. Thus, for example, in *Gillett* v. *Holt* (above), a right to a freehold interest in the property in dispute was granted, but in *Matharu* v. *Matharu* [1994] 2 FLR 597 (where a father had bought a house which later became the matrimonial home of his son and daughter-in-law) the Court of Appeal overturned the trial judge's decision that the daughter-in-law should have a beneficial interest in the property and held instead that she merely had a licence to remain in the property.

Disadvantages of estoppel   Estoppel's main disadvantage compared with trusts is that the court may not necessarily grant the claimant a right of ownership. Another disadvantage of estoppel compared with trusts is that an estoppel arises only when the remedy is granted, whereas a beneficial interest under a trust arises when the claimant acted to his or her detriment on the basis of the common intention. Thus, interests under a trust arise earlier than they do with estoppel, which may be important if third party interests are involved.

4.9 A claim based on contract

An interest in property may be acquired under a contract, provided the legal requirements for creating a valid contract are satisfied. If a contract is for the sale or disposition of land it must be in writing (s.2 Law of Property (Miscellaneous Provisions) Act 1989), but this requirement does not prevent the creation of a resulting or constructive trust, or the creation of an interest by way of proprietary estoppel. The following cases are examples:

> ▶ *Tanner* v. *Tanner* [1975] 1 WLR 1341
>
> The claimant purchased a house for occupation by the defendant, his female partner, and their children. The defendant moved into the house, but when the relationship broke down the applicant sought possession on the basis that the defendant was only a bare licensee under a licence which he had revoked. The Court of Appeal held that there was an implied contractual licence under the terms of which the defendant was entitled to occupy the house while the children were of school age, or until some other circumstance arose which would make it unreasonable for her to remain in possession.
>
> ▶ *Layton* v. *Martin* [1986] 2 FLR 277
>
> The Court of Appeal held that there was no intention to create a legally enforceable contract, with the result that the claimant mistress failed in her claim against the deceased's estate even though she had accepted the man's offer that, if she were to live with him, he would give her emotional security, and also financial security on his death. Despite living with him for five years after he had made the offer, and for 13 years in total, her claim failed.

4.10 Tenancies

(a) Transferring a tenancy

Under s.53 and Sched. 7 of Part IV of the Family Law Act 1996, the High Court and the county court have jurisdiction to transfer tenancies on divorce, dissolution of a civil partnership, and on the breakdown of cohabitation. With civil partners courts can do so only where they have jurisdiction to make a property adjustment order under the Civil Partnership Act 2004. With cohabitants, they must merely have ceased living together as husband and wife – there is no mention of them ceasing to live in the same 'household.'

A tenancy is transferred by the court making 'a Part II order' which it has power to make whether a spouse, civil partner or cohabitant is solely or jointly entitled under a tenancy, provided the house was a matrimonial home in the case of a married couple, or, in the case of cohabitants, was a home in which the cohabiting couple lived together as husband and wife (para. 2 of Sched. 7 and s.62(1)). Paragraph 1 of Sched. 7 makes it clear that 'cohabitant' includes a former cohabitant. There is no requirement that cohabitants must have lived together for a minimum period, although the court is required to take into account the length of the relationship when deciding whether or not to order a transfer. These provisions also apply to civil partners, so that a tenancy of the civil partnership home can be transferred to one of the parties to the civil partnership, provided it was their home, and irrespective of whether they were solely or jointly entitled under the tenancy.

In determining whether to make a Part II order, and, if so, in what manner, the court must consider all the circumstances of the case including (see para. 5): the circumstances in which the tenancy was granted, or the circumstances in which either of them became tenant; the housing needs and housing resources of the parties and of any relevant child; their respective financial resources; the likely effect of any order (or no order) on the health, safety or well-being of the parties and of any relevant child; the conduct of the parties in relation to each other and otherwise; and the suitability of the parties as tenants.

Where the parties are cohabitants and only one of them is entitled to occupy the house under the tenancy, the court must also consider (see para. 5): the nature of their relationship; the length of time they have lived together as husband and wife; whether there are any children who are children of both parties or for whom both parties have or have had parental responsibility; and the length of time that has elapsed since the parties ceased to live together. Where the parties are council tenants, the housing policy of the local housing authority is a factor which the court can take into account (see *Jones* v. *Jones* [1997] 1 FLR 27).

Tenancies for the benefit of a child can be transferred under Schedule 1 to the Children Act 1989 (see 12.5).

(b) Succeeding to a tenancy on the death of a tenant

See 4.15

4.11 Homelessness and the family

Homelessness can arise in many different situations. A victim of domestic violence may be forced to leave the family home. A child leaving care may have no accommodation. A family relationship may break down and one of the parties may have to move out of the home.

Persons who are homeless can apply to their local housing authority for public sector housing. Housing authorities are responsible for managing, regulating and controlling housing vested in them, and have statutory duties and powers towards homeless persons under Part VII of the Housing Act 1996 (as amended by the Homelessness Act 2002). When exercising their duties and powers, local housing authorities must comply with the *Homelessness Code of Guidance for Local Authorities* (2006) (ss.169(1) and 182(1) Housing Act 1996). Housing authorities also have statutory duties to work jointly with other housing authorities, social services and other statutory, voluntary and private sector partners. Thus, for instance, if homelessness persists, any children in the family could be in need and the family could seek assistance from social services who have powers and duties under the Children Act 1989 (see further in Chapter 14).

The duties and powers of housing authorities vary depending on whether an applicant is homeless or intentionally homeless, and whether or not the applicant has a priority need. In some cases there is merely a duty to provide advice. In others there is a full housing duty to provide accommodation.

Housing and human rights As local housing authorities are public authorities under the Human Rights Act 1998 they must ensure that they exercise their powers and duties in line with the European Convention for the Protection of Human Rights (ECHR). For example, a failure on the part of a housing authority to provide suitable accommodation or the adoption of an unlawful homelessness allocation policy might constitute a breach of art. 8 ECHR (the right to family life). In *R (Morris)* v. *Westminster City Council* [2004] EWCH 2191 (Admin), for example, it was held that the local housing authority had breached the applicant mother's rights under art. 8 and art. 14 ECHR (right to enjoy a private and family life without discrimination) as it had refused to treat the mother as having a priority need.

In the following case the European Court of Human Rights (the ECtHR) held that the UK was in breach of art. 8 ECHR (the right to family life) in respect of the duties owed by local housing authorities (LHAs) and courts under the housing legislation, in particular in respect of procedural safeguards for those in need of housing. A decision by a LHA which deprives a person of accommodation must be lawful, necessary and proportionate otherwise it may breach art. 8. Loss of a home is regarded as an extreme form of interference with that right.

> ▶ *McCann* v. *United Kingdom (Application No 19009/04)* [2008] 2 FLR 899
>
> On marriage breakdown and in the context of the husband's violence, the wife, at the LHA's request, terminated the tenancy of the council house of which she and her husband were tenants (by signing a notice to quit); but she was not told that this would extinguish her husband's right to live in the house or his right to exchange it for another local authority property. After the LHA had successfully brought possession proceedings against the husband, he brought judicial review proceedings challenging the LHA's decision to obtain a notice to quit from his wife and its decision to issue possession proceedings. His claim failed, and so he took his case to the ECtHR claiming a violation of art. 8 ECHR (the right to respect for a person's private and family life, and home).
>
> The ECtHR held that there had been a breach of art. 8. The central question was whether the interference with the applicant's right under art. 8 was proportionate to the aim pursued and thus necessary in a democratic society. It held that the loss of one's home was a most extreme form of interference with art. 8. Any person at risk of an interference of that magnitude should in principle be able to have the proportionality of the measure determined by an independent tribunal in the light of the relevant principles under art. 8, notwithstanding that, under domestic law, the applicant's right of occupation has come to an end. The LHA did not appear, in the course of this procedure, to have given any consideration to the husband's right to respect for his home. Judicial review did not provide an adequate procedural safeguard (as required by art. 8) to assess the proportionality of the interference. It was immaterial whether the wife understood or intended the effects of the notice to quit. The husband was dispossessed of his home without any possibility to have the proportionality of the measure determined by an independent tribunal. It followed that, because of the lack of adequate procedural safeguards, there had been a violation of art. 8.

(a) Local housing authority duties

Under Part VII of the Housing Act 1996 local authority housing authorities (LHAs) must provide assistance for certain eligible persons (s.185) who are homeless or threatened with homelessness. Housing authorities have the following range of duties depending on the circumstances of the applicant:

- to make inquiries to establish whether an applicant who is homeless or threatened with homelessness is eligible for assistance and, if so, what duty is owed (s.184(1));
- to provide advice and information (s.179);

- ▷ to provide interim accommodation pending a decision as to a duty (if any) owed to an applicant if the local housing authority has reason to believe that the applicant may be homeless, eligible for assistance and has a priority need (s.188);
- ▷ to provide temporary housing, and advice and assistance to find long-term accommodation for an applicant who is homeless, eligible for assistance and who has a priority need, but who is intentionally homeless (s.190);
- ▷ to provide advice and assistance to an applicant who is homeless, eligible for assistance, but who has no priority need and who is intentionally homeless (s.190);
- ▷ to take reasonable steps to ensure that in the case of an applicant who is threatened with homelessness (but who is eligible for assistance, not threatened with homelessness intentionally, and has a priority need) that his accommodation does not cease to be available for his occupation (s.195), but, if there is no priority need or intentionality, the duty is merely to provide advice and assistance to help secure that the applicant's accommodation does not cease to be available for his occupation;
- ▷ to give advice and assistance with the power (not the duty) to secure accommodation for an applicant who is homeless, eligible for assistance, not intentionally homeless, but who has no priority need (s.192);
- ▷ to provide accommodation where the applicant is homeless, eligible for assistance, not intentionally homeless and has a priority need (s.193), unless the LHA refers the case to another LHA because of the local connection factor (see p. 91, below).

(b)   When is a person homeless?

A applicant is homeless if he or she has no accommodation available for his or her occupation in the UK or elsewhere which he or she (ss.175(1), (2)): is entitled to occupy; has an express or implied licence to occupy; occupies as a residence by virtue of any enactment or rule of law giving him or her the right to remain in occupation or restricting the right of another person to recover possession; or has occupation but cannot secure entry to it. A person is also homeless if the accommodation is a movable structure and there is no place where the applicant is entitled to place it and reside in it.

A person who has accommodation is treated as being homeless if it would not be reasonable for him or her to continue to occupy that accommodation (s.175(3)). Domestic (or other) violence may provide a reason for not continuing to occupy accommodation (see further below).

(c)   The full housing duty

The full or main housing duties in ss.193(2) and 195(2) (to secure suitable accommodation; or to take reasonable steps to prevent the loss of accommodation) are owed only to eligible persons who have a priority need for accommodation, and who are not intentionally homeless.

(i) Priority need   The categories of applicants who qualify as having a priority need have been extended over the years. Section 189(1) of Part VII of the Housing Act 1996 and the Homelessness (Priority Need for Accommodation) (England) Order 2002 provide that the following categories of applicant have a priority need for accommodation:

- a pregnant woman or a person with whom she resides or might reasonably be expected to reside;
- a person with whom dependent children reside or might reasonably be expected to reside;
- a person who is vulnerable as a result of old age, mental illness or handicap or physical disability or other special reason, or with whom such a person resides or might reasonably be expected to reside;
- a person aged 16 or 17 who is not a 'relevant child' or a child in need to whom a local authority owes a duty under s.20 of the Children Act 1989;
- a person under 21 who was (but is no longer) looked after, accommodated or fostered between the ages of 16 and 18 (except a person who is a 'relevant student');
- a person aged 21 or more who is vulnerable as a result of being looked after, accommodated or fostered (except a person who is a 'relevant student');
- persons who are vulnerable as a result of having been in HM's armed forces, or who have served a custodial sentence, or have been committed for contempt of court or any other kindred offences, or who have been remanded in custody;
- a person who is vulnerable as a result of ceasing to occupy accommodation because of violence from another person or threats of violence from another person which are likely to be carried out;
- a person who is vulnerable for any other special reason, or with whom such person resides or might reasonably be expected to reside;
- a person who is homeless or is threatened with homelessness as a result of an emergency such as flood, fire or other disaster.

(ii) Intentionality   A housing authority is under no duty to provide accommodation for a person who is intentionally homeless, in other words a person who deliberately does or fails to do anything in consequence of which he ceases to occupy accommodation that is available for his occupation and which it would have been reasonable for him to continue to occupy (s.191). Special rules apply in cases of domestic and other violence (see below). The *Guidance* states that a person who loses his home or who was obliged to sell it because of real financial difficulties (including because of family breakdown) should not be categorised as having made a deliberate act or omission for the purposes of s.191.

A LHA can satisfy the full housing duty by providing accommodation from its own stock or by arranging for it to be provided by a housing association or a landlord in the private sector. However, the duty to provide accommodation requires a LHA to provide 'suitable' accommodation (see *R* v. *Ealing London Borough Council ex parte Surdona* [1999] 1 FLR 650 where the duty to provide accommodation was not discharged by providing accommodation for a family in separate dwellings, as families should be able to live together as a unit).

(d)   Referral to another local housing authority – the local connection

Section 198 gives a housing authority the right to pass the housing duty on to another housing authority, if the applicant (or any person who might reasonably be expected to reside with the applicant) has no local connection with the authority to whom the application was made but has a local connection with the district of the other authority.

Referral to another housing authority is not permitted, however, where the applicant (or any person expected to reside with the applicant) will run the risk of violence or domestic violence in the district of the other housing authority (s.198).

(e)   Domestic violence and other violence

Certain applicants who leave the home as a result of actual or potential domestic or other violence are not treated as being intentionally homeless, as s.177(1) provides that it is not reasonable for a person to continue to occupy accommodation if it is probable that this will lead to domestic or other violence against: the applicant; a member of the applicant's family who normally resides with the applicant; or any other person who might reasonably be expected to live with the applicant.

Violence can be actual or threatened; but violence is only 'domestic' if the victim and perpetrator are 'associated persons' (s.177(1A)), as defined in s.178. The definition is the same as that used for associated persons in Part IV of the Family Law Act 1996 (the family law domestic violence legislation, see 5.6), but does not include a person in an intimate relationship (although such a person may be owed a housing duty as a person suffering from 'other violence').

The *Homelessness Code of Guidance* provides the following guidance in respect of violence, including domestic violence:

▶ Domestic violence (actual or threatened) is not confined to instances in the home but extends to violence outside the home (para. 8.19).

▶ The term 'violence' should not be given a restrictive meaning and 'domestic violence' should be understood to include threatening behaviour, violence or abuse (psychological, physical, sexual, financial or emotional) between persons who are, or who have been, intimate partners, family members or members of the same household, regardless of gender or sexuality (para. 8.21).

▶ An assessment of the likelihood of violence being carried out should not be based on whether there has been actual violence in the past; and must be based on the facts of the case and must be devoid of any value judgment about what an applicant should or should not do, or should or should not have done, to mitigate the risk of any violence (for example, to seek police help, or to apply for an injunction against the perpetrator) (para. 8.22).

▶ Inquiries into cases where violence is alleged need careful handling (para. 8.22).

▶ In cases involving violence, housing authorities may wish to inform applicants of the option of seeking an injunction, but should make it clear that there is no obligation on the applicant to do so (para. 8.23).

▶ Housing authorities should recognise that injunctions ordering a person not to molest, or enter the home of, an applicant may not be effective in deterring perpetrators from carrying out further violence or incursions, and applicants may not have confidence in their effectiveness. Consequently, applicants should not be expected to return home on the strength of an injunction (para. 8.23).

▶ Where there would be a probability of violence if the applicant continued to occupy his or her present accommodation, the housing authority must treat the applicant as homeless and should not expect him or her to remain in, or return to, the accommodation. In all cases involving violence, the safety of the applicant and his or her household should be the primary consideration at all stages of the decision-making as to whether or not the applicant remains in his or her own home (para. 8.24).

Referral to another housing authority (see above) is not permitted if there is a risk of violence or domestic violence to the applicant in the area of that other housing authority (s.198).

Women's refuges and homelessness   A victim of domestic violence who is living in a refuge is deemed not to be intentionally homeless. The House of Lords so held in *R (Aweys and Others)* v. *Birmingham City Council; Moran* v. *Manchester City Council* [2009] UKHL 36, where it held *inter alia* that it was not reasonable for a woman to live in a women's refuge indefinitely and that she therefore remained homeless for the purposes of the obligation owed by a local housing authority. The *Homelessness Code of Guidance* states that LHAs 'should recognise that placing an applicant in a refuge will generally be a temporary expedient only'; and that refuges 'should be used to provide accommodation for the minimum period necessary before alternative accommodation is secured elsewhere' (para. 16.27).

(f)   Homeless families with children

(i) The duty to dependent children   If there are dependent children an applicant has a priority need and the local housing authority has a duty to provide accommodation for the family, provided the applicant is eligible for assistance and is not intentionally homeless (see above).

The *Homelessness Code of Guidance* provides that, although there must be actual dependence on the applicant, the child need not be wholly and exclusively dependent on him; and, although there must be actual residence (or a reasonable expectation of residence) with some degree of permanence or regularity, the child need not be wholly and exclusively resident (or expected to reside wholly and exclusively) with the applicant. Dependent children need not necessarily be the applicant's own children, but there must be a parent–child relationship. The *Guidance* provides that the child does not need to have full-time residence with the applicant in order to qualify as a dependent child. It also provides that, if a shared residence order is in force (or an agreement about shared residence), it should not lead the local authority to conclude that it would be reasonable for the child to live with the other parent, rather than the applicant. Housing authorities are required to consider that, when parents separate, it is often in the best interests of the child to maintain a relationship with both parents.

(ii) Intentional homelessness   There is no duty to provide accommodation for intentionally homeless families with children, but they are entitled to advice and assistance and temporary accommodation. If homelessness continues, the children may be in need for the purposes of Part III of the Children Act 1989, and help can be sought from a local authority social services department. Housing authorities must have arrangements in place to ensure that social services are alerted as quickly as possible where the applicant has children aged under 18 and the housing authority considers the applicant may be

intentionally homeless (s.213A Housing Act 1996). If social services decide that the child's needs would best be met by helping the family to obtain accommodation, they can ask the housing authority for reasonable assistance in this matter and the housing authority must respond (s.27 Children Act 1989).

(iii) Housing applications by children are not permitted A child cannot apply for local authority housing if the child's parent has made an application and it has failed:

▶ *R v. Oldham Metropolitan Borough Council ex parte G and Related Appeals* **[1993] AC 509**

The father's application for housing had been rejected by the housing authority, because, although he had priority need, he was found to be intentionally homeless (he had deliberately failed to pay the mortgage). The father made a fresh application in the name of his 4-year-old son. The House of Lords held that the application had been properly rejected, as to allow such an application would render the intentional homelessness provisions redundant where there were dependent children.

(iv) The relationship between the housing legislation and the Children Act 1989 Local housing departments and local authority social services departments are required to work together when dealing with cases of homelessness involving children (see s.213A Housing Act 1996). However, there is no guarantee that a social services department will find housing for families where they do not qualify for housing under the housing legislation, as s.17(6) Children Act 1989 gives local authorities the power, not the duty, to provide accommodation (see the *Barnet* case below, and 14.6).

▶ *R v. Northavon District Council ex parte Smith* **[1994] 2 AC 402**

The father applied for housing from Northavon housing authority but was found to be homeless intentionally. He then applied to the local social services department (Avon) with a view to their performing their duty under s.17(6) of the Children Act 1989 to safeguard the welfare of his children by making cash payments to cover rent and deposits. Avon social services refused to do this, but invoked their power under s.27 of the Children Act 1989 and asked Northavon housing authority to help with the provision of housing. Northavon refused, on the basis that it had performed its duties under the housing legislation and that it would be a contradiction to offer the family housing in the light of the intentional homelessness decision. The father applied for judicial review to quash Northavon's decision but his application failed. The House of Lords held that there was a duty for the authorities to co-operate with each other, but that an action for judicial review was not the way to obtain that co-operation.

▶ *R (G) v. Barnet London Borough Council; R (W) v. Lambeth London Borough Council; R (A) v. Lambeth London Borough Council* **[2003] UKHL 57, [2004] 1 FLR 454**

The House of Lords held that local authority social services departments have no duty under Part III of the Children Act 1989 to provide accommodation for particular children in need, as this would subvert the provisions of the housing legislation (see 14.6).

Under s.13 of the Homelessness Act 2002 LHAs are required to refer homeless persons with dependent children (who are ineligible for homelessness assistance, or who are intentionally homeless) to social services, provided the person consents. If homelessness persists, any child in the family could be in need. In such cases, if social services decide the child's needs would be best met by helping the family to obtain accommodation, they can ask the LHA for reasonable assistance in this, and it must respond.

(vi) Housing homeless teenage children   In *R (G)* v. *Southwark London Borough Council* [2009] UKHL 26, [2009] 2 FLR 380 the House of Lords held that a local authority's children's services unit could not purport to have fulfilled its duties to look after a homeless child under the Children Act 1989 merely by referring the child to a homeless persons' unit under Part VII of the Housing Act 1996. Thus, social services working with children cannot 'pass the buck' by transferring their responsibilities to the local housing authority if a child or young person is a person to whom an accommodation duty is owed under s.20 of the Children Act 1989.

(vii) Housing and residence orders   The existence of a residence order in favour of an applicant for housing is a highly material consideration for a local housing authority when exercising its powers and duties under the Housing Act 1996, but it is not the only factor to be taken into account and will not be the determinative factor as to the allocation of housing.

(viii) Housing and shared residence orders   The following two cases involved shared residence orders made under the Children Act 1989 (see 11.4) and the duties of local housing authorities (LHAs). The first case involved the question of the allocation of housing, the second the question of whether a parent who was the subject of a shared residence order had a priority need:

▶ *R (Bibi)* v. *Camden London Borough Council* [2004] EWHC 2527 (Admin), [2005] 1 FLR 413

The parents had a 50/50 shared residence order in respect of their two children. The father had been given a three-bedroom house by Camden LBC, but the mother was offered only one-bedroom accommodation, on the basis that the children were not part of her household, and because of the acute shortage of three-bedroom accommodation in the borough, and the under-occupation which would result if both parents were granted three-bedroom accommodation. The mother successfully applied for judicial review. Davis J quashed the decision of the LHA, on the ground that it was flawed, as it failed to address the question of the position of the children with regard to the mother's own housing needs. There was no obvious basis for the conclusion that the children's main housing was with their father, and it was illogical that he was the primary-carer because he was working. The shortage of housing stock and the issue of under-occupation were relevant factors which could be taken into account, but, like the existence of the residence order, they could not be decisive. Davis J was keen to emphasise that his decision was very much dependent on the shared residence order providing for 50/50 sharing, and the fact that the order had been put into practice by the parents.

The following case dealt with the interface between the powers of LHAs under Part VII of the Housing Act 1996 and those of the family proceedings court under the Children Act 1989. The central question for the House of Lords was whether a shared residence order (where the children were to spend half their time with each parent) made the father 'a person with whom dependent children reside or might reasonably be expected to reside' thereby giving him a priority need for housing under the housing legislation. As a result of the ruling in the case, it is ultimately the decision of the LHA which prevails in cases where a shared residence order is in force. This may cast doubt on the decision in *R (Bibi)* (above).

> ▶ *Holmes-Moorhouse v. London Borough of Richmond-upon-Thames* [2009] UKHL 7, [2009] 1 FLR 904
>
> Before their separation the appellant father and the mother lived with their four children in council accommodation. By consent the judge in family proceedings made a shared residence order (see 11.4) (that the three younger children should spend alternate weeks and half of each school holiday with each parent); and an order that the father should leave the family home. The father's application for housing on the basis that he had a priority need as he had dependent children who might reasonably be expected to reside with him (s.189(1)(b) HA 1996) was rejected by the LHA on the basis that he was not in priority need (as the children would merely be staying, rather than residing with him). He challenged the decision. He failed at first instance but the Court of Appeal allowed his appeal. The LHA appealed to the House of Lords.
>
> The House of Lords allowed the LHA's appeal and restored the decision of the county court judge, holding *inter alia* that:
>
> ▶ A shared residence order did not oblige a LHA to regard a homeless parent as being in priority need on the ground that dependent children might reasonably be expected to reside with that parent. It was for the LHA under Part VII of the Housing Act 1996, not the family courts, to decide whether it was reasonable that a child who already had a home with a parent should also be able to reside with the other parent. The LHA could take into account the wishes of the parents and children and the court's opinion that shared residence would be in the interests of the children, but it was nonetheless entitled to decide that it was not reasonable to expect children who were not in any sense homeless to be able to live with both the mother and father in separate accommodation.
> ▶ In accordance with the *Homelessness Code of Guidance for Local Authorities* (2002), it would only be in exceptional circumstances that it would be reasonable to expect a child who had a home with one parent to be provided, under Part VII, with another so that he could reside with the other parent as well.
> ▶ The LHA's reviewing officer had therefore been entitled to conclude that, in the context of the duty of the authority to make provision for the homeless, the children could not reasonably be expected to live with the father as well as the mother.
>
> Baroness Hale was of the opinion that the shared residence order should not have been made. Her Ladyship said that orders made by the family court were meant to provide practical solutions to the practical problems faced by separating families and were not meant to be aspirational statements of what would be best in some ideal world and which had little prospect of realisation. It was one thing to make a shared residence order when each parent had a home to offer the children, but another thing entirely when the other parent had no accommodation at all. Family courts could not conjure up resources where none existed and could not order or put pressure on public agencies to do so.
>
> Both Lord Hoffman and Baroness Hale emphasised the different roles played by family courts and local housing authorities and the fact that decisions under Part VII of the Housing Act 1996 must have regard to wider considerations than the welfare of the relevant children (for instance the limited availability of public housing stock). Both Lord Hoffman and Baroness Hale were of the opinion that only in exceptional circumstances would it be reasonable to expect that, when a child has a home with one parent, the other parent would also be provided with housing under Part VII of the Housing Act 1996.

4.12   The devolution of property on death

(a)   Making a will

There is complete freedom of testamentary disposition in England and Wales. In other words, any adult person of sound mind may make a will disposing of his or her property to whomsoever he or she chooses. Thus, it is perfectly lawful, for example, for a spouse to make a will leaving his or her property to someone other than the other spouse.

A will is valid if it is made in writing and signed by the person making it in the presence of at least two witnesses, each of whom must attest and sign the will, or acknowledge the signature of the person making it (ss.7 and 9 Wills Act 1837). A will is revoked by the testator's (or testatrix's) marriage or civil partnership, unless it was made in contemplation of marriage or civil partnership to a particular person and the testator (testatrix) did not intend the will to be revoked (ss.18 and 18B Wills Act 1837). In the case of divorce or nullity, or dissolution or annulment of a civil partnership, then subject to any contrary intention in the will, any legacies and gifts to a former spouse or former civil partner lapse. However, a former spouse or former civil partner may still make a claim for reasonable financial provision from the deceased's estate under the Inheritance (Provision for Family and Dependants) Act 1975 (see 14.13).

According to research (*Intestacy and Family Provision Claims on Death*, Law Commission, 2009), although there is strong support for freedom of testamentary disposition, about one-third of those who die each year do so without having made a will. The Law Commission (as part of its Tenth Programme of Law Reform) is examining intestacy and the operation of the Inheritance (Provision for Family and Dependants) Act 1975. A Consultation Paper (*Intestacy and Family Provision Claims on Death*, Consultation Paper No. 191) was published in October 2009; and a report and draft Bill are expected to be published in late 2011.

One of the questions the Law Commissions is considering is whether the surviving spouse of the intestate should be allowed to take the whole estate. (For a discussion of spousal entitlement on intestacy by the Law Commissioner in charge of the project, see Cooke [2009] CFLQ 423.)

(b)   Devolution of property on the intestacy of spouses and civil partners

If a spouse or civil partner dies intestate (without making a will), the surviving spouse or civil partner's inheritance depends on the size of the estate and whether or not the deceased left children or other relatives. In outline, the estate (after the payment of debts and expenses) is distributed or held on trust according to the following rules laid down in the Administration of Estates Act 1925 (as amended):

- *If there is a surviving spouse/civil partner, and children* The spouse/civil partner inherits the personal chattels, the first £250,000 and a life interest in half of what is left. The children of the deceased share between them half of what is left straight away (if they are 18 or over), and the other half when the surviving parent dies.
- *If there is a surviving spouse/civil partner, and relatives but no children* The spouse/civil partner inherits the personal chattels, the first £450,000 and half of what

is left. The parents of the deceased, or if the parents have died, the brothers and sisters or their descendants, share the other half of what is left.

▶ *If there is a surviving spouse/civil partner, but no other relatives* The surviving spouse / civil partner inherits everything.

▶ *If there are children, but no surviving spouse/civil partner* The children share everything equally.

▶ *If there is no spouse/civil partner or children* Everything passes to the next available group of relatives.

▶ *If there are no available relatives* Everything goes to the State.

Rights in the family home   Where the family home was owned by the spouses or civil partners as beneficial joint tenants, it devolves to the surviving spouse or civil partner. Where it was owned by them as tenants in common, the deceased's share forms part of his or her estate and passes according to the will or according to the laws of intestacy. On intestacy, however, the Intestates' Estates Act 1952 allows a surviving spouse or civil partner in certain circumstances to retain the home.

(c)   Cohabitants on intestacy

Where a cohabitant dies without making a will there are no provisions equivalent to those above. Thus, the surviving cohabitant has no automatic right to succeed to the deceased's estate whatever the length of the relationship. Instead, the estate passes to the children, or otherwise to the parent(s) of the deceased. This is with the exception of any property which was jointly owned by the parties as joint tenants (such as the home or a bank account), when ownership passes to the survivor. As cohabitants are in a vulnerable position on intestacy, it is important for cohabitants to make a will. A cohabitant can, however, make a claim for reasonable financial provision against the deceased partner's estate under the Inheritance (Provision for Family and Dependants) Act 1975 (see below); or make a claim by way of a trust (see 4.7) or proprietary estoppel (see 4.8).

The Law Commission has provisionally proposed that couples who have had a child together or who have lived together continuously as a couple for at least five years, should have the same rights on intestacy as spouses (*Intestacy and Family Provision Claims on Death*, Consultation Paper 191, 2009).

4.13   The Inheritance (Provision for Family and Dependants) Act 1975

(a)   Introduction

Under the Inheritance (Provision for Family and Dependants) Act 1975 the court can make financial provision orders for certain family members and dependants out of a deceased person's estate where the deceased has failed under his or her will or under the laws of intestacy (or both) to make reasonable financial provision for the applicant. The Act applies if the deceased was domiciled in England and Wales at the time of death (s.1(1)). An application must be brought within six months of the date on which probate or letters of administration were taken out, or otherwise with the permission of the court (s.4).

The Act is concerned with dependency; it is not concerned with deciding how the assets should be fairly divided (*per* Goff LJ in *Re Coventry (Deceased)* [1980] Ch 461). In *Jelley*

v. *Iliffe and Others* [1981] Fam 128 Stephenson LJ said that the purpose of the Act is to remedy 'wherever reasonably possible, the injustice of one who has been put by a deceased person in a position of dependency upon him, being deprived of any financial support, either by accident or by design of the deceased, after his death'.

A two-stage exercise   When considering an application, the court adopts a two-stage exercise. First (under s.3) it has to make an objective assessment of the facts to establish whether or not the deceased made reasonable financial provision for the applicant. If the answer is 'no', then the court must next consider to what extent (if at all) it should exercise its powers to make financial provision under the Act. The first part of the exercise involves a value judgment, the second a question of discretion. When conducting the two-stage exercise the court must take into account a range of factors laid down in ss.2 and 3 of the Act (see p. 104 below). If the court decides to make an order it has a wide discretion under s.2 as to the nature of the order(s) it can make.

When conducting the two-stage exercise, the court draws a distinction between spouses (and civil partners) and other applicants. Spouses and civil partners are treated much more favourably than other applicants under the Act.

(b)   Applicants

(i) Applications by spouses and civil partners (and former spouses and civil partners)   The spouse or civil partner of the deceased can apply for reasonable financial provision (s.1(1)(a)), including someone who in good faith entered into a void marriage or void civil partnership (ss.25(4) and 25(4A)). This includes a former spouse or a former civil partner, provided that that person has not entered into a subsequent marriage or civil partnership (s.1(1)(b)). The court must consider the applicant's age, the duration of the marriage or civil partnership, and the applicant's contribution to the welfare of the family, including any contribution made by looking after the home or caring for the family (s.3(2)).

The divorce/dissolution comparison   In addition to the above factors, the court must take into account the award the applicant spouse (civil partner) might have expected to receive had the marriage (civil partnership) been terminated by divorce (dissolution) not death (s.3(2)). In *Fielden and Another* v. *Cunliffe* [2005] EWCA Civ 1508, [2006] 1 FLR 745 the Court of Appeal held that there was no reason why the principles laid down by the House of Lords in *White* v. *White* [2001] 1 AC 596, [2000] 2 FLR 981 (see 7.6) should not be applied to a claim by a spouse under the 1975 Act, but that caution was necessary when considering the *White* cross-check of equality. This was because a deceased spouse is free to bequeath his or her estate to whomsoever he or she pleases and the only statutory obligation under the 1975 Act is to make *reasonable* financial provision for the surviving spouse, to which the concept of equality may bear little relation (*per* Wall LJ). Thus, in *Fielden* v. *Cunliffe*, the Court of Appeal allowed the executors' appeal and reduced the amount of financial provision awarded to the surviving spouse from £800,000 to £600,000, as the judge had wrongly applied the principle in *White* (having presumed a starting point of a 50:50 split of the estate).

However, each case depends on its facts; and the Court of Appeal has stated that the 'hypothetical divorce' approach in s.3(2) is only one of the factors for the court to consider, and is subject to the overriding consideration of what is reasonable in all the circumstances (*Re Krubert (Deceased)* [1997] 1 FLR 42).

In *Barron* v. *Woodhead* [2008] EWHC 810 (Ch), [2009] 1 FLR 747 which involved a successful claim by a husband for reasonable financial provision against his deceased wife's estate (the bulk of which she had left to her children), it was held that considerations of conduct under s 3(1)(g) of the 1975 Act should be approached in a similar way to conduct under s 25(2)(g) of the Matrimonial Causes Act 1973. Thus, the threshold for establishing conduct was very high.

(For another case involving a claim by a spouse, see *Baker* v. *Baker* [2008] EWHC 977 (Ch), [2008] 2 FLR 1956).

Awards are not limited to maintenance   Spouses and civil partners are in a better position than cohabitants (see below) as a claim by a spouse or civil partner is not limited to maintenance (s.1(2)(a)).

Provisions relating to divorce, nullity, separation and dissolution of a civil partnership   Where an applicant spouse has applied for ancillary relief under s.23 or s.24 of the Matrimonial Causes Act 1973 (whether or not those proceedings have been determined by the date of death), the court can under the 1975 Act (but only within 12 months of the decree of divorce) treat the application as if the decree of divorce (or nullity) had not been made absolute (s.14). Similar provisions also apply to judicial separation (ss.14(1), (2)) and to dissolution, nullity and separation in respect of a civil partnership (s.14A).

As part of the 'clean break' policy on divorce (see 7.5), the divorce court on or after the grant of a decree nisi of divorce can on the application of either spouse make an order (where just to do so) prohibiting the other spouse from making an application under the 1975 Act on the applicant's death (s.15 I(PFD)A 1975). This power can also be exercised in the case of a decree of nullity, judicial separation or presumption of death. The court has the same powers in respect of a civil partnership order (s.15ZA I(PFD)A 1975). This rule also applies to ancillary relief orders made after an overseas divorce or civil partnership dissolution (including overseas annulments and separations) (ss.15A and 15B).

If an applicant spouse or civil partner is entitled to secured periodical payments (under Part II MCA 1973 or Sched. 5 CPA 2004), the court may, on application, vary or discharge the periodical payments order or revive the operation of any provision thereof which has been suspended under s.31 MCA 1973 or Part 2 of Sched. 5 CPA 2004 (s.16).

A maintenance agreement between the applicant and the deceased providing for maintenance on and after death can be varied or revoked (s.17). The court can in certain circumstances set aside a disposition made by the deceased within six years of death with the intention of defeating an application under the 1975 Act (s.10). Where a contract was made by the deceased without full valuable consideration with the intention of defeating an application for financial provision under the 1975 Act, the court can direct the personal representatives not to pass or transfer the whole or part of any money or property involved (s.11).

(ii) Applications by cohabitants   The surviving cohabitant (opposite-sex or same-sex) of the deceased can apply (s.1(1)(ba)). An application is sometimes made by a cohabitant who has failed to establish an interest under a trust or by way of proprietary estoppel (see, for example, *Negus* v. *Bahouse* [2007] EWHC 2628 (Ch), [2008] 1 FLR 381; and *Webster* v.

Webster [2008] EWHC 31(Ch), [2009] 1 FLR 1240 where both claims were successful under the 1975 Act).

A 'cohabitant' is defined in the Act as a person who was living in the same household as the deceased during the whole period of two years ending immediately before the date of the deceased's death, and was living as the husband or wife or civil partner of the deceased (ss.1(1A) and 1(1B)). As this definition does not include a former cohabitant, a former cohabitant will have to apply under s.1(1)(e) (see p. 102) as a person being maintained by the deceased.

Whether the applicant and the deceased were living together in the same household is a question of fact. In *Re Watson (Deceased)* [1999] 1 FLR 878 Neuberger J held that, when considering the definition of cohabitant, the court should 'ask itself whether, in the opinion of a reasonable person with normal perceptions, it could be said that the two people in question were living together as husband and wife'.

Occasional periods of separation may be permitted (see *Gully* v. *Dix* [2004] EWCA Civ 139, [2004] 1 FLR 918 where the applicant was held to be a cohabitant even though she had separated from the deceased for the last three months of his life, due to his intolerable behaviour). But each case depends on its own facts. In the following two cases the applicants were held not to be cohabitants for the purposes of the Act: *Churchill* v. *Roach* [2004] 2 FLR 989 (the applicant had not lived with the deceased for the full two-year period); and *Baynes* v. *Hedger* [2008] EWHC 1587 (Ch), [2009] 2 FLR 767 (the applicant had not been living in the same household as the deceased as the parties had had two separate houses and two separate economies).

Maintenance provision only Cohabitants are in a disadvantageous position compared with spouses and civil partners as the court is limited to making orders for their maintenance, although 'maintenance' may be interpreted flexibly (as it was in *Webster* v. *Webster* [2008] EWHC 31(Ch), [2009] 1 FLR 1240 where the court ordered the home to be transferred to the applicant whose partner had died suddenly at the age of 54 without making a will).

Bailey-Harris and Wilson (2003) have questioned whether the different treatment of cohabitants breaches arts. 8 and 14 of the European Convention on Human Rights.

(iii) Applications by children of the deceased and those treated as children of the deceased Marital and non-marital children, and adopted children, can apply (s.1(1)(c)) whether born before or after the deceased's death (s.25(1)) and whether or not they are minors or adult children of the deceased.

A person who is not included under s.1(1)(c) but who was, in the case of any marriage or civil partnership to which the deceased was at any time a party, treated by the deceased as a child of the family in relation to that marriage or civil partnership can also apply (s.1(1)(d)). This might include, for instance, a step-child or foster-child, whether or not a minor.

Adult children Applicants who are adult children of the deceased can apply, but they may find it difficult to succeed in an application, particularly if they are young and able-bodied, are in employment and are capable of maintaining themselves (see, for example, *Re Jennings (Deceased)* [1994] Ch 286, *sub nom Re Jennings (Deceased), Harlow* v. *National Westminster Bank plc and Others* [1994] 1 FLR 536). But each case depends on its own facts; and in *Re Abram (Deceased)* [1996] 2 FLR 379 the adult son successfully claimed against his deceased mother's estate, as he had worked for her in the family business for many years and for long hours and had received only a minimal wage. In *Garland v. Morris* [2007] EWHC 2 (Ch), [2007] 2 FLR 528, on the other hand, an adult daughter's claim against her deceased father's estate was dismissed, as she had failed to establish that it was unreasonable in all the circumstances for her father to make provision for her (she had neither spoken to nor met her father at any time in the 15 years preceding his death, and had made no real effort to do so; and she had received all of her mother's estate).

At one time the court took the view that an adult child had to prove special circumstances, or that the deceased had a moral obligation to him or her, in order to succeed. However, the courts no longer adopt such a restricted approach. In *Re Hancock (Deceased)* [1998] 2 FLR 346 the Court of Appeal held that, although the presence of special circumstances or a moral obligation may be relevant factors, particularly where the applicant is in employment or possessed of earning capacity, their absence does not necessarily preclude a successful claim. In *Espinosa v. Bourke* [1999] 1 FLR 747 the Court of Appeal allowed the 55-year-old daughter's appeal as the judge had erred in elevating moral obligation to a threshold requirement.

The existence of a moral obligation may still be determinative, however, as it was in *Re Pearce (Deceased)* [1998] 2 FLR 705 where the 29-year-old son succeeded in his claim against his deceased father's estate, as his father was held to have a moral obligation to him. The son had done substantial work on his father's farm, and his father had made representations that he would inherit it.

(iv) Persons being maintained by the deceased Any person who is not included in the categories above, but who was being maintained either wholly or partly by the deceased immediately before his or her death, can apply (s.1(1)(e)). Thus persons such as relatives, friends and carers can apply, and so can cohabitants who do not come within the definition in s.1(1)(ba) (above), provided that the applicant can prove that he or she was being maintained, wholly or partly, by the deceased. (For instance, in *Bouette v. Rose* [2000] 1 FLR 363 a mother brought a successful claim against the estate of her deceased daughter).

Section 1(3) provides that a claimant is only to be regarded as having been maintained by the deceased if the deceased, otherwise than for full valuable consideration, was making a substantial contribution in money or in money's worth towards the applicant's reasonable needs. An application can therefore be struck out on the ground that there was no dependency. In order to decide whether there was dependency, the court balances what the deceased was contributing against what the applicant was contributing, and, if the applicant made a greater or equal contribution, the claim is struck out (*per* Stephenson LJ in *Jelley v. Iliffe and Others* [1981] Fam 128). Although dependency is a question of fact, the court will look at the problem in the round and apply a common-sense sort of approach, avoiding fine balancing distinctions (*per* Butler-Sloss LJ in *Bishop v. Plumley* [1991] 1 All ER 236).

When considering a claim under this section the court is required (by s.3(4)) to have regard to the extent to which and the basis upon which the deceased had assumed responsibility for the maintenance for the applicant and to the length of time for which the deceased had discharged that responsibility However, the assumption of responsibility does not have to be express.

In *Baynes* v. *Hedger* [2009] EWCA Civ 374, [2009] 2 FLR 767 a goddaughter failed in her claim against her deceased godmother's estate as the Court of Appeal held that she had failed to bring herself within s.1(1)(e)) as: there had been no failure to make reasonable financial provision; the godmother had not assumed responsibility for her; and the payment of money by the godmother to enable the applicant goddaughter to pay off her debts did not constitute maintenance.

(c) 'Reasonable financial provision'

All applicants must prove that the deceased's will or the law of intestacy (or both, if there is partial intestacy) failed to make 'reasonable financial provision' for him/her (s.1(1)). The test is not whether reasonable provision has been made, but the more rigorous test of whether the failure to make provision was unreasonable (Judge Roger Cooke in *Re Abram (Deceased)* [1996] 2 FLR 379). However, spouses and civil partners are treated more generously than other applicants, as 'reasonable financial provision' for them means 'such financial provision as it would be reasonable in all the circumstances of the case for a husband or wife or civil partner to receive, whether or not that provision is required for his or her maintenance' (ss.1(2)(a) and (aa)). With other applicants, 'reasonable financial provision' means such financial provision as it would be reasonable in all the circumstances of the case for the applicant to receive for his or her maintenance (s.1(2)(b)).

Maintenance   With applicants other than spouses and civil partners reasonable financial provision is limited to what it would be reasonable to provide for the applicant's maintenance. 'Maintenance' is not defined in the Act. What constitutes 'maintenance' depends on the facts of the case, but it may be construed broadly (see, for example, *Rees* v. *Newbery and the Institute of Cancer Research* [1998] 1 FLR 1041 where the provision of accommodation by the deceased for 10 years at less than a market rent was held to be 'maintenance'). In *Re Coventry (Deceased)* [1980] Ch 461 Goff LJ said:

> 'What is proper maintenance must in all cases depend upon all the facts and circumstances of the particular case being considered at the time, but I think it is clear on the one hand that one must not put too limited a meaning on it; it does not mean just enough to enable a person to get by; on the other hand, it does not mean anything which may be regarded as reasonably desirable for his general benefit or welfare.'

(d) Orders that can be made

The court has the power to make a wide range of orders, which include (s.2): periodical payments; a lump sum (which can be paid in instalments); a transfer of property; a settlement of property; acquisition of property and its transfer to the applicant or for the settlement of the applicant; and a variation of an ante-nuptial or post-nuptial settlement. The court can make an interim order if immediate financial assistance is needed (s.5). Periodical payments orders can be varied, discharged, suspended or revived (s.6). A periodical payments order made in favour of a former spouse or former civil partner, or a spouse or civil partner subject to a decree or order of judicial separation (where separation was continuing at death), ceases to be effective on that person's remarriage or civil partnership, except in respect of any arrears due (s.19(1)).

(e) The exercise of discretion – matters to be taken into account

When deciding whether or not the deceased made reasonable financial provision for the applicant, and in what manner to exercise its powers, the court must have regard to the following matters laid down in s.3(1):

'(a) the financial resources and financial needs which the applicant has or is likely to have in the foreseeable future;
(b) the financial resources and financial needs which any other applicant ... has or is likely to have in the foreseeable future;
(c) the financial resources and financial needs which any beneficiary of the estate of the deceased has or is likely to have in the foreseeable future;
(d) any obligations and responsibilities which the deceased had towards any applicant ... or towards any beneficiary of the estate of the deceased;
(e) the size and nature of the net estate of the deceased;
(f) any physical or mental disability of any applicant ... or any beneficiary of the estate of the deceased;
(g) any other matter, including the conduct of the applicant or any other person, which in the circumstances of the case the court may consider relevant.'

The weight given to each factor depends on the circumstances of each case. For example, where an application is brought by an adult child against a deceased parent, needs and resources under s.3(1)(a) and obligations and responsibilities under s.3(1)(d) are likely to be crucial (see, for example, *Espinosa v. Bourke* [1999] 1 FLR 747).

In addition to the matters in s.3(1) above, the court must take into account other factors as follows:

(i) Applications by cohabitants The court must have regard to the applicant's age, the duration of the cohabitation and the contribution which the applicant made to the welfare of the deceased's family, including any contribution made by looking after the home or caring for the family (s.3(2A)).

(ii) Applications by children or persons treated like children The court must consider the manner in which the applicant was, or might be expected to be, educated or trained (s.3(3)). The court must also consider whether the deceased had assumed any responsibility for the applicant's maintenance (and, if so, its extent, basis and duration, and whether the deceased did so knowing that the applicant was not his own child), as well as the liability of any other person to maintain the applicant (s.3(3)).

(iii) Applications by persons being maintained by the deceased The court must consider the extent, basis and duration of the deceased's responsibility for maintenance (s.3(4)). Thus there must be an assumption of responsibility on the part of the deceased.

(f) Reform of the law

The Law Commission is examining reform of the Inheritance (Provision for Family and Dependants) Act 1975 (*Intestacy and Family Provisions Claims on Death*, 2009, Consultation

Paper 191) in order to establish, among other issues, whether a wider range of family members should be entitled to bring a claim under the Act, and whether changes are needed so that adult children have a greater prospect of success. It proposes that any person treated as a child of the deceased should be able to bring a claim; and it is seeking to clarify the position of those who claim as dependants of the deceased. It is also considering reforms to the orders that can be made.

4.14 Making a claim on death by way of a trust or proprietary estoppel

A person can claim an interest in a deceased person's estate by arguing that he or she has an interest in equity under a trust (see 4.7.) or by way of proprietary estoppel (see 4.8).

Thus, for example, in *Hyett* v. *Stanley* [2003] EWCA Civ 942, [2004] 1 FLR 394 a cohabitant was held to be entitled to an interest in her deceased partner's estate under a constructive trust arising as a result of a statement he had made during his lifetime. On the other hand, in *Negus* v. *Bahouse and Another* [2007] EWHC 2628 (Ch), [2008] 1 FLR 381 a cohabitant was held to have no beneficial interest by way of proprietary estoppel in a flat in which she had lived in with her deceased partner but she was instead granted an award under the Inheritance (Provision for Family and Dependants) Act 1975 (see above).

4.15 Succession to a tenancy on death

Succession to a tenancy on death is governed by Sched. 1 to the Rent Act 1977 (statutory tenancies), and by s.17 Housing Act 1988 (assured tenancies). Under these Acts a spouse, civil partner and a surviving cohabitant (opposite-sex or same-sex who had lived in a settled relationship with the deceased) can apply for a transfer of the deceased's tenancy on his or her death.

Under para. 2 of Sched. 1 to the Rent Act 1977 a spouse (or civil partner) or a cohabitant (living as a husband or wife, or as a civil partner of the deceased) can succeed to the deceased spouse's or cohabitant's tenancy. Under para. 3(1) a family member of the deceased tenant can succeed to the tenancy. A person who succeeds to a tenancy under para. 2 is in a better position than a family member who succeeds under para. 3 because he or she succeeds to a statutory tenancy, whereas a family member succeeds only to an assured tenancy. Statutory tenants are in a better position because they enjoy security of tenure and may register a fair rent for the property, whereas assured tenants are subject to a different form of security of tenure and may be charged a market, rather than a fair, rent.

Until amendments were made to the Rent Act 1977 and the Housing Act 1988, only spouses and heterosexual cohabitants could succeed to a deceased partner's tenancy under the Rent Act 1977 and s.17 Housing Act 1988. However, the following two cases heard by the House of Lords led to a change in the law, the second decision being influenced by the European Convention for the Protection of Human Rights as a result of the coming into force of the Human Rights Act 1998 (see 1.7):

▶ *Fitzpatrick v. Sterling Housing Association* [2001] AC 27, [2000] 1 FLR 271

The House of Lords held by a majority of 3 to 2 that a surviving same-sex cohabitant could succeed to the tenancy of the deceased tenant, on the basis that he or she could be construed as a member of the deceased tenant's 'family' under para. 3(1) of Sched. 1 to the Rent Act 1977. It unanimously held that the surviving homosexual partner could not be construed as a 'spouse' of the deceased under para. 2(2), because he could not be regarded as 'living with the original tenant as his or her husband or wife'.

▶ *Ghaidan v. Godin-Mendoza* [2004] UKHL 30, [2004] 2 FLR 600

Mr Godin-Mendoza had lived in a long, close and loving and monogamous homosexual relationship with his deceased partner, who was the protected tenant of a flat owned by Mr Ghaidan, the landlord. Mr Ghaidan brought possession proceedings, and Mr Godin-Mendoza claimed by way of defence that he was entitled to succeed to the tenancy under Sched. 1 to the Rent Act 1977. At first instance, the judge held that he could only succeed to a tenancy under para. 3(1), applying *Fitzpatrick* (above), but the Court of Appeal allowed his appeal, holding that there had been a breach of art. 14 of the European Convention for the Protection of Human Rights (discrimination) in conjunction with art. 8 (right to family life), and that the court had a duty under s.3 Human Rights Act 1998 to give effect to the Rent Act in a way which was compliant with the ECHR. The landlord, Mr Ghaidan, appealed.

The House of Lords dismissed the appeal (Lord Millett dissenting), holding that same-sex cohabitants are in the same position as married couples when it comes to security of tenure. It held that para. 2(2) of Sched. 1 to the Rent Act 1977, when construed with reference to s.3 Human Rights Act 1998, violated the surviving partner's right under art. 14 ECHR taken together with art. 8. It held that it was possible under s.3 Human Rights Act 1998 (which provides that primary and subordinate legislation must be read and given effect in a way which is compatible with the ECHR) to read para. 2(2) in a way which was compatible with the ECHR, in other words as though the survivor of a homosexual relationship was the surviving spouse of the defendant.

Summary

1 During a marriage or civil partnership the parties have the same property rights as cohabitants and other persons, with the exception of certain special statutory provisions which exist for married couples and civil partners. Who owns what therefore depends on the general principles of property law (contract and trusts).

2 On divorce or civil partnership dissolution, the courts have wide discretionary powers to adjust the parties' property rights irrespective of who owns what; and the law of trusts has no role to play.

3 Cohabitants are in a particularly vulnerable position on relationship breakdown and on death.

4 Married couples and civil partners with no right of ownership in the home have 'home rights' under s.30 of Part IV of the Family Law Act 1996, which are rights to remain in occupation of the home, and to enter in and occupy the home. 'Home rights' are binding on third parties if the home right is registered as a notice on the land register.

5 Special statutory provisions apply in respect of the property rights of engaged couples and civil partners who have entered into a civil partnership agreement.

6 There are no special statutory provisions for cohabitants in respect of property rights. They must rely on the general rules of property, in particular the equitable doctrines of resulting and constructive trusts, and proprietary estoppel.

Summary cont'd

7 For spouses, civil partners, cohabitants and other family members, ownership of personal property (property other than land) depends on the law of contract and trusts. As a general rule, property passes to the purchaser. Rights in personal property can be acquired expressly or impliedly (under a trust, estoppel or contract) and in many cases without written formalities.

8 Funds in a bank account presumptively belong to the party or parties in whose name the account is held, but the presumption can be displaced by proof of a contrary intention.

9 As far as the family home is concerned, trusts in respect of land and contracts for the sale of land must be in writing (s.53 Law of Property Act 1925; and s.2 Law of Property (Miscellaneous Provisions) Act 1989). However, interests in land can be acquired under resulting or constructive trusts, or under the doctrine of proprietary estoppel without the requirement of writing (s.53(2) Law of Property Act 1925; and s.2(5) Law of Property (Miscellaneous Provisions) Act 1989).

10 Orders for the sale and possession of land, and declarations of trusts in respect of land, can be sought under s.14 Trusts of Land and Appointment of Trustees Act 1996.

11 A presumption of resulting trust gives a claimant a share of the beneficial interest in property proportionate to his or her financial contribution, subject to any contrary intention.

12 A constructive trust arises where there is an express or implied agreement, arrangement or understanding that the claimant has an interest in property and the claimant has acted to his or her detriment on the basis of that agreement, arrangement or understanding.

13 An interest in the family home (and any other property) can be acquired under the doctrine of proprietary estoppel where the claimant has acted to his detriment on the basis of a belief encouraged by the other party that he is to have an interest in the property in question and it would be inequitable to deny the claimant an interest.

14 Tenancies can be transferred between married partners, civil partners and cohabitants (including former spouses, civil partners and cohabitants) under s.53 and Sched. 7 of Part IV of the Family Law Act 1996.

15 Under Part VII of the Housing Act 1996 local housing authorities have powers and duties in respect of persons who are homeless. A full housing duty is owed to persons who are eligible for assistance, and who have priority need and who are not intentionally homeless. In other cases, there is only an obligation to provide advice or assistance. Domestic violence is taken seriously by local housing authorities, and victims of violence, or of threatened violence, are not treated as being intentionally homeless if they leave the home.

16 Any adult person of sound mind can make a will leaving his or her property on death to whomsoever he or she chooses. A will is valid if it is made in writing and signed by the testator in the presence of two witnesses who must attest the will (ss.7 and 9 Wills Act 1837). A will is revoked by marriage or civil partnership, unless made in contemplation of a particular marriage or civil partnership.

17 Where a spouse or civil partner has not made a will, his or her property passes under the rules of intestacy which are laid down in the Administration of Estates Act 1925, as amended.

18 A cohabitant has no right to succeed to a deceased's partner's estate on his or her intestacy. It is therefore particularly important for cohabitants to make a will.

19 Under the Inheritance (Provision for Family and Dependants) Act 1975 certain family members and other dependants (including spouses, civil partners, former spouses, former civil partners and cohabitants) can apply for financial relief out of the deceased's estate where the deceased has failed to make reasonable financial provision either under the will or under the law of intestacy (or both).

Summary cont'd

20 The Law Commission as part of its Tenth Programme of Law reform is considering reform of the law governing intestacy and the Inheritance (Provision for Family and Dependants) Act 1975.

21 Under the Rent Act 1977 and s.17 Housing Act 1988 the deceased's tenancy can on death be transferred to a surviving spouse, or civil partner, or a surviving opposite-sex or same-sex cohabiting partner.

Further reading and references

Battersby, 'Ownership of the family home: *Stack* v. *Dowden* in the House of Lords' [2008] CFLQ 255.

Cooke, 'Wives, widows and wicked step-mothers: a brief examination of spousal entitlement on intestacy' [2009] CFLQ 423.

Cownie and Bradney, 'Divided justice, different voices: inheritance and family provision' (2003) *Legal Studies* 566.

Mee, 'The limits of proprietary estoppel: *Thorner* v. *Major'* [2009] CFLQ 367.

Piska, 'A common intention or a rare bird? Proprietary interests, personal claims and services rendered by lovers post-acquisition: *James* v. *Thomas*: *Morris* v. *Morris*' [2009] CFLQ 104.

Probert, 'Cohabitation and joint ownership: the implications of *Stack* v. *Dowden*' [2007] Fam Law 924.

Wilson and Bailey-Harris, 'Family provision: the adult child and moral obligation' [2005] Fam Law 555.

(See also the reading at the end of Chapter 3.)

Chapter 5

Domestic violence and occupation of the family home

The legislation

Part IV of the Family Law Act 1996 Provides civil remedies for protection against domestic violence and makes provision in respect of occupation of the family home.

Protection from Harassment Act 1997 Creates two criminal offences of harassment and gives the court power to grant injunctions restraining a defendant from pursuing any course of conduct which amounts to harassment.

Domestic Violence, Crime and Victims Act 2004 Has amended the two Acts above to give greater protection to victims of domestic violence in respect of both the criminal and the civil law.

5.1 Introduction

The Government is committed to fighting domestic violence and to giving support to its victims. In furtherance of its aims, the Domestic Violence, Crime and Victims Act 2004 was enacted to improve the protection available for victims (see over). As part of its drive to fight domestic violence, the Government has funded a number of initiatives, including a National Domestic Violence Helpline. It has also recognised the importance of adopting multi-agency and inter-agency approaches for tackling domestic violence, involving not just the courts, but the police, housing authorities and other agencies. Women's Aid, an organisation which campaigns for domestic violence reform, provides advice and information about domestic violence (www.womensaid.org.uk).

Statistics on domestic violence It is difficult to make accurate assessments of the number of people who experience domestic violence (because of a lack of standardised data and because many cases go unreported). As the Home Affairs Select Committee Report (*Domestic Violence, Forced Marriage and 'Honour' Based Violence*, HC 263-I, 2008) states, only a small proportion of victims come into contact with the statutory authorities dealing with domestic violence. However, it has been suggested that 1 in 4 women and 1 in 6 men will experience domestic violence at some point in their life-time, but with the vast majority of serious and recurring violence being perpetuated by men. According to the Home Office, 1 in 5 of all reported violent crimes are related to domestic abuse, while every year 1 in 6 of all murders in the UK are domestic violence-related homicides.

What is domestic violence? Domestic violence – violence in the home – can take many forms. It includes not just physical assault, but psychological and emotional molestation or harassment, and may also involve pestering, nagging, making nuisance telephone calls and intimidation. The Government defines domestic violence as:

'any incident of threatening behaviour, violence or abuse (psychological, physical, sexual, financial or emotional) between adults who are or have been intimate partners or family members, regardless of gender or sexuality.'

The causes of domestic violence are various, but alcohol and drugs often play a significant part.

Housing problems   Violence can create housing problems. Some victims will seek temporary accommodation in a refuge (see www.refuge.org.uk). It may be necessary for some victims to apply to their local housing authority for public sector housing (see 4.11). Some victims may end up divorcing (or dissolving their civil partnership), whereupon the court has jurisdiction to adjudicate on any dispute about ownership and occupation of the home (see Chapter 7 and 2.10). In some cases, the court will provide injunctive protection, and remove the perpetrator from the home and allow the victim back in (see 5.5 below).

Children and domestic violence   The civil and the criminal law provide protection for children who witness or suffer domestic violence. Sometimes local authority intervention will be needed (see Chapter 14). As violence in the home can be damaging to children who witness it, the word 'harm' in the Children Act 1989 has been amended to include 'impairment suffered from seeing or hearing the ill-treatment of another'. In the last few years there has been increasing recognition of the problem of domestic violence for children when their parents' relationship breaks down; and steps have been taken to give better protection to children in residence and contact cases where there is actual or potential violence in the home (see 11.5).

Specialist domestic violence courts   Specialist domestic violence courts have been established in some parts of England and Wales, with the aim of bringing more perpetrators of domestic violence to justice and to ensure that victims and their families are given support. The government has set a target of having a total of 128 special courts in place by 2011. These courts, which are part of the magistrates' family proceedings courts, deal with criminal prosecutions and have specially trained magistrates and other staff to deal with domestic violence. Cases are fast-tracked through the courts in order to eliminate distress. A multi-agency approach is adopted bringing together police, prosecutors, court staff, probation officers and specialist support services. Specialist support is also provided for victims by Independent Domestic Violence Advisors who are responsible for ensuring that the safety of the victim is co-ordinated across the criminal justice system and for giving expert advice on accessing essential services, such as victim and witness agencies, housing, health, counselling and child care.

The Domestic Violence, Crime and Victims Act 2004   The Domestic Violence, Crime and Victims Act (DVCVA) 2004 has amended the civil and the criminal law relating to domestic violence in order to give greater protection to victims. Amendments have been made to Part IV of the Family Law Act 1996 to extend the class of persons who can apply for remedies, and to make breach of a non-molestation order a criminal offence (see further at p. 114 below). The DVCVA 2004 has also amended the Protection from Harassment Act 1997, in particular to give the court power to make restraining orders not just for criminal harassment but for any criminal offence (see 5.8.) The Act also makes changes to the criminal law (see over).

5.2 Domestic violence – the criminal law

Domestic violence is a serious and frequently reported crime which the police treat as seriously as any other crime. Police forces are required to draw up clear policy statements about intervention in domestic violence cases and to have special domestic violence units. Police forces are also required to support victims of domestic violence by, for instance, finding temporary accommodation for them, and keeping them informed about the case. Police forces are involved in local domestic violence initiatives, including Domestic Violence Forums; and police domestic violence units work closely with solicitors, Women's Aid and other organisations. They also have powers and duties where children are suffering, or at risk of suffering, violence.

The police have a wide range of powers in respect of domestic violence. Under the common law the police can enter premises to prevent or deal with breaches of the peace, and they have a power of arrest in such circumstances. Under s.17 of the Police and Criminal Evidence Act 1984 a constable can enter premises to arrest or to save life or limb or to prevent serious damage to property. A perpetrator of violence can be prosecuted for: common assault (s.39 Criminal Justice Act 1998); assault occasioning actual bodily harm (s.47 Offences Against the Person Act 1861); rape (s.1(1) Sexual Offences Act 1956); indecent assault (ss.14 and 15 Sexual Offences Act 1956); affray (s.3(1) Public Order Act 1986); criminal damage (s.1(1) Criminal Damage Act 1971); and harassment (s.2 Protection from Harassment Act 1997). Under s.51 of the Criminal Justice and Public Order Act 1994 it is an offence to intimidate a witness or to harm, or threaten to harm, a witness. Offences can also be committed under the Telecommunications Act 1984, which prohibits the sending of grossly offensive, indecent, obscene or menacing communications, and under the Malicious Communications Act 1988, which prohibits the sending of indecent or grossly offensive letters which are intended to create distress or anxiety. Victims of domestic violence may be entitled to compensation under the Criminal Injuries Compensation Scheme.

The Domestic Violence Crime and Victims Act (DVCVA) 2004 has created a new criminal offence of causing or allowing the death of a child or a vulnerable adult (s.5) This offence is limited to cases where the victim has died of an unlawful act; and applies only where a member of a household (including a frequent visitor to the household) has frequent contact with the victim, and can therefore be reasonably expected both to have been aware of any risk to the victim, and to have had a duty to protect the victim from harm. The member of the household must have failed to take reasonable steps to protect the victim; and the victim must have been at significant risk of serious physical harm. Only a person over 16 may be guilty of the offence, unless he or she is the mother or father of the victim (s.5(3)). Section 10(1) of the DVCVA 2004 has also made common assault an arrestable offence under Schedule 1 to the Police and Criminal Evidence Act 1984, so that the police have the power to arrest a person on suspicion of assault and/or battery without an arrest warrant.

In September 2009 the Government announced proposals to give the police new powers to issue domestic violence protection orders ('go' orders) in order to bar perpetrators of domestic violence from the home for up to two weeks, with the aim of enabling victims to escape from the violence and have a breathing space in which to consider their options. Breach would be contempt of court, punishable by imprisonment. These proposals have been welcomed by Refuge and Women's Aid.

ASBOs and domestic violence   An ASBO (an anti-social behaviour order) is a civil law order, but, as breach of an ASBO is a criminal offence and as they are sometimes sought by the police, they are considered here under the heading of criminal remedies.

ASBOs (which are available under the Crime and Disorder Act 1998) are not generally used in cases of domestic violence but may be made where the domestic violence occurs in the public domain and thereby has an effect on other members of the public. This is what happened in *R (Rabess)* v. *Commissioner of the Police for the Metropolis* [2007] EWHC 2008 (Admin), where an ASBO was made against a cohabiting couple in order to prohibit them from using abusive, insulting, threatening or intimidating language or behaviour towards each other and from using or threatening violence against each other. The defendant's argument that his and his partner's right to privacy had been breached under art. 8 of the European Convention for the Protection of Human Rights (the right to a private and family life) was rejected because the court held that, while the couple were entitled to a private life, the exercise of that right had to be balanced against the rights of others (those of the members of the community affected by the domestic violence) and those rights prevailed. (For a case-note on *R (Rabess)*, see Burton [2008] CFLQ 95).

Drawbacks of the criminal law   Although police intervention may be required in domestic violence cases, recourse to the criminal law can be a rather heavy-handed instrument in family disputes. In fact, some victims, having contacted the police, do not wish criminal proceedings to be brought because they fear that they may lose their partner, their home, their financial stability and even their children. Punishing a violent partner may also have a disastrous emotional and financial impact on a family. There may also be evidential difficulties proving violence. Victims may be unwilling to co-operate with the police and may withdraw their evidence, because of feelings of disloyalty, or because prosecution and possible conviction will ruin any chance of reconciliation, or because they fear further violence. However, the police are now much more proactive in domestic violence cases, and prosecutions may be brought even where the victim does not wish the prosecution to proceed. In many cases, however, civil remedies may provide a better solution than criminal proceedings.

5.3   Civil remedies under Part IV of the Family Law Act 1996

Under Part IV of the Family Law Act 1996 magistrates' family proceedings courts, county courts and the Family Division of the High Court have jurisdiction to grant the following two remedies for victims of domestic violence:

A Non-Molestation Order   This is an order containing a provision prohibiting the respondent from molesting another person who is associated with the respondent; and/or a provision prohibiting the respondent from molesting a relevant child (s.42(1)).

An Occupation Order   This is an order made under ss.33, 35, 36, 37 or 38 of Part IV of the Family Law Act 1996 regulating, prohibiting, and governing the occupation of the family home.

Part IV of the Family Law Act 1996 was enacted because the family remedies providing protection against domestic violence before the Act came into force were unnecessarily complex, confusing and lacked integration. Different orders were available in the magistrates' court and the county court with different criteria applying; and they were available only to married couples and opposite-sex cohabitants. Other family members and former married couples and cohabitants were not included, even though persons whose relationship had broken down were particularly vulnerable to violence.

According to Government statistics (*Judicial Statistics 2008*, Ministry of Justice, 2009, Cm 7697), in 2008 there were 17,141 applications to the county court for non-molestation orders (an increase of 3 per cent on 2007); and 7,738 applications for occupation orders (a decrease of 7 per cent on 2007).

5.4 Non-molestation orders

Under Part IV of the Family Law Act 1996 magistrates' family proceedings courts, county courts and the Family Division of the High Court can make a non-molestation order prohibiting the respondent from molesting another person who is associated with the respondent and/or from molesting a relevant child (s.42(1)).

(i) Applicants The applicant must be 'associated' with the respondent, and the child must be a 'relevant child' (see definitions at 5.6 below). The court can make the order on an application, or of its own motion (in any family proceedings) (s.42(2)), or when it is considering whether to make an occupation order (s.42(4A)). A child can apply for a non-molestation order, but a child under 16 needs leave of the court to apply, which the court can grant only if the child has sufficient understanding to make the application (s.43).

(ii) What is 'molestation'? 'Molestation' is not defined in the Act, but is interpreted on a case-by-case basis by the courts. It has been widely interpreted to include not just violence, but pestering, harassment and threatening behaviour. In *C v. C (Non-Molestation Order: Jurisdiction)* [1998] Fam 70, [1998] 1 FLR 554 Stephen Brown P held that there 'has to be some conduct which clearly harasses and affects the applicant to such a degree that the intervention of the court is called for'.

(iii) Criteria for making a non-molestation order When deciding whether to make a non-molestation order, and, if so, in what manner, the court must have regard to all the circumstances of the case, including the need to secure the health, safety and well-being of the applicant and of any relevant child (s.42(5)).

(iv) Orders without notice (ex parte *orders*) As urgent action is often needed in domestic violence cases, the court, where just and convenient to do so, may make an *ex parte* order (one without the respondent being given notice of the proceedings) (s.45(1)). When deciding whether to make such an order, the court must consider all the circumstances of the case, including (s.45(2)): the risk of significant harm to the applicant or any relevant child by the respondent if an order is not immediately made; and the likelihood of the applicant being deterred or prevented from pursuing the application if an order is not

immediately made. The court must also consider: whether there is reason to believe that the respondent is aware of the proceedings but is deliberately avoiding service; and whether the applicant or relevant child will be seriously prejudiced by a delay in effecting service of proceedings or in effecting substituted service.

If an *ex parte* non-molestation order is made, the court must give the respondent an opportunity to make representations relating to the order at a full hearing, as soon as is just and convenient (s.45(3)).

(v) Terms and duration of the order   A non-molestation order can refer to molestation in general and/or to particular acts of molestation (s.48(6)). It can be made for a specified period or until further order (s.48(7)). Although the aim of the order is to give the parties a temporary breathing space, in *Re B-J (Power of Arrest)* [2000] 2 FLR 443 the Court of Appeal held that an order can be made for an indefinite period in appropriate circumstances.

(vi) Undertakings   Instead of making a non-molestation order the court may accept an undertaking (a promise to the court) from any party to the proceedings (s.46(1)). An undertaking is enforceable as if it were a court order (s.46(4)). However, the court cannot accept an undertaking if it appears that the respondent has used or threatened violence against the applicant or a relevant child, and a non-molestation order is needed so that any breach can be punishable as a criminal offence under s.42A (s.46(3A)). The advantage of an undertaking is that it carries less stigma than a court order, as the court does not make findings of fact about the respondent's behaviour.

(vii) Variation and discharge   A non-molestation order may be varied or discharged on the application of the respondent or by the applicant for the order (s.49).

(viii) Breach   Breach of a non-molestation order is a criminal offence (s.42A(1)). The effect of making breach a criminal offence is that it automatically becomes an arrestable offence (under s.24(1) Police and Criminal Evidence Act 1984).

The criminal offence of breaching a non-molestation order was introduced in 2007 as part of the Government's programme to give greater protection to victims of domestic violence. Prior to that date, breach of a non-molestation order was dealt with by civil proceedings for contempt of court. In contempt proceedings the courts had become increasingly willing to impose prison sentences (and longer ones) for breaches of non-molestation orders (and occupation orders), in order to send out a clear message that domestic violence would not be tolerated. In *Nicholls* v. *Nicholls* [2008] EWCA Civ 121, for example, an alcoholic mother, who had repeatedly breached the terms of a non-molestation order, was sentenced to 12 months' imprisonment.

Under s.42A a person is guilty of an offence if, without reasonable excuse, he or she does anything that he or she is prohibited from doing under the terms of a non-molestation order. If the order was made without notice (see above), there is no criminal offence unless the person was aware of the existence of the order (s.42A(2)). To prevent double jeopardy, a person convicted of the offence cannot be punished for contempt of court, and *vice versa* (ss.42A(3), (4)). A person found guilty of an offence can be fined or imprisoned for up to 5 years (s.42A(5)).

Concern has been expressed about breach of a non-molestation now being a criminal offence, as it may deter victims from seeking an order for fear of being involved in criminal proceedings (see Bessant (2005) and Platt, HHJ (2008)). There is also some evidence that the police are issuing cautions for breaches of non-molestation orders, rather than bringing charges (*Domestic Violence, Forced Marriage and 'Honour' Based Violence*, HC 263-I, 2008), but the Government has said that this is wholly inappropriate and dangerous in cases of domestic violence and that it must not continue.

5.5   Occupation orders

There may come a point where a victim of domestic violence is no longer able to tolerate living under the same roof as the perpetrator and decides to leave home and seek alternative accommodation with a relative or friend or in a refuge. A victim of domestic violence can apply for an occupation order under Part IV of the Family Law Act 1996. Such orders, however, are not routinely made, and they are a temporary, not permanent, remedy. In the longer term, a victim may end up applying for divorce.

Under ss.33 and 35–38 of Part IV of the Family Law Act 1996 magistrates' family proceedings courts, county courts and the High Court can make occupation orders (s.39). They can be made by the court on an application, or of the court's own motion in any family proceedings (ss.39(1), (2)) (for a definition of family proceedings, see 5.6). An occupation order does not affect a person's claim to any legal or equitable interest in the home in any subsequent proceedings (including subsequent proceedings under Part IV) (s.39(4)). If a respondent is ordered to leave the home immediately, or within a specified time, his or her rights of ownership in the home are not affected.

Variation and discharge   An occupation order may be varied or discharged on an application by the respondent or by the person who made the application (see s.49).

Categories of applicant   Part IV of the Family Law Act 1996 creates two categories of applicant: entitled and unentitled. The court's powers are much wider for entitled applicants.

> *An 'entitled' applicant* is a person who has a right to occupy the home by virtue of a beneficial estate or interest or contract; or by virtue of any enactment giving him the right to remain in occupation; or who has 'home rights' under s.30 of the Act (see 4.2) (s.30(1)).
>
> *A 'non-entitled' applicant* is a person who has no right to occupy the home by virtue of a beneficial estate, interest, contract, or enactment, or by having 'home rights.'

Different sections of the Act apply, depending on the party's status and whether or not he or she has a property entitlement. The basic scheme of the Act is as follows:

APPLICANT	RESPONDENT	THE APPLICATION IS MADE UNDER
Entitled Applicant	Entitled/Unentitled Person Associated with the Applicant	Section 33
Unentitled Former Spouse/ Former Civil Partner	Entitled Former Spouse/Former Civil Partner	Section 35
Unentitled Cohabitant/ Former Cohabitant	Entitled Cohabitant/Former Cohabitant	Section 36
Unentitled Spouse/Civil Partner or Former Spouse/ Former Civil Partner	Unentitled Spouse/Civil Partner or Former Spouse/Former Civil Partner	Section 37
Unentitled Cohabitant/ Former Cohabitant	Unentitled Cohabitant/Former Cohabitant	Section 38

Applications by children   A child aged under 16 can apply for an occupation order but only with leave of the court, which it can grant only if the child has sufficient understanding to make the proposed application (s.43). Applications by children are rare in practice. With occupation orders there is the added difficulty that a child cannot hold a legal estate in land. But a child may have a beneficial interest in land under a trust and thereby possess an entitlement to property.

(a)   'Entitled' applicants (s.33)

(i) 'Entitled' applicants   An entitled person (see above) can apply for an occupation order under s.33(1)(a) where he or she is 'associated' with the respondent and where the house is, was or was intended to be the home of both parties (s.33(1)(b)).

   'Associated person' includes a wide range of persons (see 5.6), not just spouses, civil partners and cohabitants, but family members, engaged couples, and persons living in the same household.

(ii) Powers of the court   The occupation order may (s.33(3)):

▶ enforce the applicant's entitlement to remain in occupation as against the respondent;
▶ require the respondent to permit the applicant to enter and remain in the home, or part of it;
▶ regulate the occupation of the home by either or both parties;
▶ if the respondent has a right to occupy the home (other than by way of having s.30 'home rights', see 4.2), prohibit, suspend or restrict the respondent's exercise of that right;
▶ if the respondent has s.30 home rights in relation to the home, and the applicant is the other spouse or civil partner, restrict or terminate those rights;
▶ require the respondent to leave the home, or part of it;
▶ exclude the respondent from a defined area in which the home is included.

Other powers   The order may declare that the applicant is an entitled person (s.33(4)). If the applicant has 'home rights' and the respondent is the applicant's spouse or civil partner, the court where just and reasonable to do so can, when making an order during the subsistence of a marriage or civil partnership, include a provision in the order that those rights are not to be brought to an end by the death of the other spouse or civil partner or by the termination of the marriage or civil partnership (ss.33(5), (8)).

(iii) How the court exercises its powers   In exercising its powers above and, if so, in what manner, the court must first apply the 'balance of harm test' in s.33(7). Thus the court must weigh the respective harm that may be caused to either party and any relevant child and decide where the balance lies. If the applicant or any relevant child is likely to suffer significant harm which is greater than that which the respondent or any relevant child is likely to suffer, then the court *must* make an occupation order. If, having applied the balance of harm test, the balance does not lie in favour of making the order (because the respondent or any relevant child is likely to suffer significant harm which is as great or greater than that of the applicant or any relevant child), then the court must conduct the s.33(6) discretionary exercise (see below).

In relation to an adult, 'harm' (see s.63(1)) means ill-treatment (whether or not physical) and impairment to health (whether physical or mental). In relation to a child, 'harm' has the same meaning, but also includes development (physical, intellectual, emotional, social or behavioural); and ill-treatment also includes sexual abuse. Where the question of whether the harm suffered by the child is significant turns on the child's health or development, the court must compare his health or development with that which could reasonably be expected of a similar child (s.63(3)).

The balance of harm test was applied in the following cases:

▶ *Chalmers v. Johns* [1999] 1 FLR 392

The relationship of the parties (cohabitants) had always been tempestuous. There had been acts of violence by each party against the other, resulting in minor injuries. Alcohol use, particularly by the mother, had been responsible for much of this. The mother left the family home with the daughter (aged 7) and moved into temporary council accommodation. She applied for an occupation order under s.33 (as she was a joint tenant of the home with the respondent). Applying the balance of harm test, the judge made an interim order on the basis that the mother and child were likely to suffer significant harm attributable to the father if the order were not made. The father appealed.

The Court of Appeal allowed the appeal, as the judge had incorrectly applied the statutory provisions. The mother and child were not likely to suffer significant harm attributable to the conduct of the father if the order were not made. There was no real risk of violence or any other harm befalling the child. The case was one in which the court should exercise its discretion by considering all the circumstances of the case and the prescribed matters in s.33(6). Occupation orders which overrode proprietary rights (the father was a joint tenant) were justified only in exceptional circumstances. The fact that the final hearing was to take place very shortly weighed against making such a draconian order at an interlocutory hearing, particularly as there was no evidence that any further domestic disharmony could not be managed by the imposition of injunctive orders. The trial judge had not clearly focused upon the alternative nature of the adjoining subsections of s.33(6) and s.33(7), but had treated them as if they were both simultaneously applicable to the facts of the case. Had she directed herself more closely to the statutory language, she would have seen that this was a case which came nowhere near s.33(7).

▶ *B v. B (Occupation Order)* [1999] 1 FLR 715

The wife left the matrimonial home, where she and her husband lived as council tenants, taking with her their baby daughter, and leaving her husband there with his 6-year-old son from a previous marriage. She was granted an occupation order. The husband appealed. The Court of Appeal allowed his appeal, as the balance of harm test had not been satisfied, as the husband's child would suffer more harm if an order was made than the wife and their baby daughter would suffer if an order was not made. While the husband's behaviour fully justified the order being made, his position as a full-time carer of his son had to be considered. If an order were to be made, his 6-year-old son would be placed in unsuitable temporary council accommodation and he would have to change schools. The Court of Appeal stressed, however, that each case turns on its facts, and that it did not intend to give out the message that other fathers in the same position as the husband could expect to remain in occupation.

▶ *G v. G (Occupation Order: Conduct)* [2000] 2 FLR 36

The wife's application for an occupation order was refused by the trial judge who held that, as the husband's conduct had been unintentional, the likelihood of harm could not be attributed to him. The wife appealed. The Court of Appeal held that the important factor, when applying the balance of harm test, was the effect of the conduct upon the applicant or child, not the intention of the respondent. Lack of intent might be a relevant consideration, but it did not mean that harm could not be attributed to the respondent's conduct without lack of intention. The judge had therefore erred in law in considering that the harm likely to be suffered by the children could not be attributed to the husband because it was not intentional. However, having concluded that the making of an order was not mandatory under s.33(7) on the facts, the judge had correctly proceeded to consider whether to make an order under s.33(6) in the exercise of his discretion. Even though criticisms could be made of the judge, his conclusion was in broad terms tenable. It was not a case where the applicant had suffered violence at the hands of her husband; and occupation orders excluding a person from their house were draconian orders to be used only in exceptional circumstances.

▶ *Banks v. Banks* [1999] 1 FLR 726

The wife, aged 79, suffered from manic-depression and dementia, and her verbal and physical abuse were a potential threat to her husband. The husband sought an occupation order to exclude her from the matrimonial home. Judge Geddes in the county court refused to make an occupation order because the harm to the wife if the order was made would be significantly greater than the harm to the husband if it was not. A final decision on the parties' occupation rights could be made in the divorce proceedings. He also refused to make a non-molestation order because her behaviour was a symptom of her mental condition and not something over which she was capable of control.

The discretionary exercise under s. 33(6)   If, applying the balance of harm test, the balance is not in favour of making the order (because the applicant and any relevant child will not suffer greater harm than the respondent if an order is not made), then the court must conduct the discretionary exercise under s.33(6), which requires the court when deciding whether or not to exercise its powers (see p. 116 above), and, if so, in what manner, to have regard to all the circumstances including:

'(a) the housing needs and housing resources of each of the parties and of any relevant child;
 (b) the financial resources of each of the parties;
 (c) the likely effect of any order, or of any decision by the court not to exercise any of the powers under s.33(3), on the health, safety or well-being of the parties and of any relevant child; and
 (d) the conduct of the parties in relation to each other and otherwise.'

(iv) Duration of the order The order may be made for a specified period, or until the occurrence of a specified event, or until further order (s.33(10)). There is no time-limit on the duration of the order, as there is for non-entitled applicants.

(b) Non-entitled applicants

A non-entitled applicant is a person who has no property right (see p. 115 above). Non-entitled applicants must apply under ss.35–38 of the Act. Each section of the Act applies to a particular sort of relationship (see the chart on p. 116 above).

(i) Non-entitled former spouse/former civil partner v. entitled former spouse/former civil partner (section 35) A non-entitled former spouse/former civil partner can apply against an entitled former spouse/former civil partner provided the house is, has been or is intended to be the matrimonial or civil partnership home of the parties (ss.35(1), (2)).

Powers of the court and how they are exercised Where the applicant is in occupation of the home, the order *must* give the applicant the right not to be evicted or excluded from the home or any part of it by the respondent for a specified period and must prohibit the respondent from evicting or excluding the applicant during that period (s.35(3)). If the applicant is not in occupation, the court *must* give the applicant the right to enter into and occupy the home for a specified period; and require the respondent to permit the exercise of that right (s.35(4)). When exercising its powers to decide whether to make an order containing any of these mandatory provisions, and, if so, in what manner, the court must have regard to all the circumstances, including the following (s.35(6)):

'(a) the housing needs and housing resources of each of the parties and of any relevant child;
(b) the financial resources of each of the parties;
(c) the likely effect of any order, or of any decision by the court not to exercise any of the powers under s.33(3), on the health, safety or well being of the parties and of any relevant child;
(d) the conduct of the parties in relation to each other and otherwise;
(e) the length of time that has elapsed since the parties ceased to live together;
(f) the length of time that has elapsed since the marriage or civil partnership was dissolved or annulled; and
(g) the existence of any pending proceedings between the parties for: an order under s.23A or s.24 Matrimonial Causes Act 1973 (property adjustment orders in connection with divorce proceedings); a property adjustment order under Part 2 of Sched. 5 to the Civil Partnership Act 2004; an order under para. 1(2)(d) or (e) of Sched. 1 to the Children Act 1989 (orders for financial relief against parents); or an order relating to the legal or beneficial ownership of the home.'

An order *may* (s.35(5)): regulate the occupation of the home or part of it; prohibit, suspend or restrict the respondent's right to occupy it; require the respondent to leave the home or part of it; or exclude the respondent from a defined area in which the home is included. When deciding whether to exercise its power to include one or more of these provisions and, if so, in what manner, the court must have regard to all the circumstances including the matters mentioned in s.33(6)(a)–(d) (see p. 120 above). However, if, applying the balance of harm test (in s.35(8)), the court decides that the applicant or any relevant child is likely to suffer significant harm attributable to the respondent's conduct which is as great or greater than the harm which is likely to be suffered by the respondent and any relevant child if a s.35(5) provision is included in the order, then the court *must* include one or more of the s.35(5) provisions in the order.

Duration   The order must be limited to a specified period not exceeding six months, but can be extended on one or more occasions for a further specified period not exceeding six months (s.35(10)). While the order is in force an applicant is treated as possessing home rights and ss.30(3)–(6) apply (s.35(13)) (see 4.2). An order cannot be made after the death of either party; and an order ceases to be effective on either party's death (s.35(9)).

(ii) Non-entitled cohabitant/former cohabitant v. entitled cohabitant/former cohabitant (section 36)   A cohabitant/former cohabitant with no right to occupy the home (or who has an equitable interest in the home or its proceeds of sale but in whom the legal estate is not vested) can apply for an occupation order against the entitled cohabitant/former cohabitant, provided the house is the home which they cohabit (have cohabited or intend to cohabit) (ss.36(1), (2)). The parties can be opposite-sex or same-sex cohabitants/former cohabitants.

Powers of the court and how they are exercised   Where the applicant is in occupation of the home, the order *must* give the applicant the right not to be evicted or excluded from the home or any part of it by the respondent for a specified period and prohibit the respondent from evicting or excluding the applicant during that period (s.36(3)). If the applicant is not in occupation, it *must* give the applicant the right to enter into and occupy the home for a specified period; and require the respondent to permit the exercise of that right (s.36(4)). When deciding whether to make an order containing these s.36(3) and (4) provisions, and, if so, in what manner, the court must have regard to all the circumstances of the case, including (s.36(6)):

'(a)   the housing needs and housing resources of each of the parties and of any relevant child;
(b)   the financial resources of each of the parties;
(c)   the likely effect of any order, or of any decision by the court not to exercise any of the powers under s.33(3), on the health, safety or well-being of the parties and of any relevant child;
(d)   the conduct of the parties in relation to each other and otherwise;
(e)   the nature of the parties' relationship and in particular the level of commitment involved in it;
(f)   the length of time during which they have cohabited;
(g)   whether there are or have been any children who are children of both parties or for whom both parties have or have had parental responsibility;
(h)   the length of time that has elapsed since the parties ceased to live together; and
(i)   the existence of any pending proceedings for an order under para. 1(2)(d) or (e) of Sched. 1 to the Children Act 1989 (orders for financial relief against parents); or relating to the legal or beneficial interest of the dwelling-house.'

The court *may* make an occupation order in order to (s.36(5)): regulate the occupation of the home or part of it; prohibit, suspend or restrict the respondent's right to occupy it; require the respondent to leave the home or part of it; or exclude the respondent from a defined area in which the home is included. When considering whether to make a s.36(5) provision and, if so, in what manner, s.36(7) requires the court to consider all the circumstances including those in s.36(6)(a)–(d) (see p. 120 above) and ask the questions mentioned in s.36(8). In other words, the court must ask whether the applicant or any relevant child is likely to suffer significant harm which is greater than that of the respondent or any relevant child if a s.36(5) provision is not included in the order. If the balance of harm lies in favour of the applicant and any relevant child there is no obligation, however, to make an order as there is in cases of entitled applicants (see p. 117 above); the court *may* make the order.

Duration   The order must be limited so as to have effect for a specified period not exceeding six months, but may be extended on one occasion for a further specified period not exceeding six months (s.36(10)). An order cannot be made after the death of either party and ceases to have effect on either party's death (s.36(9)).

(iii) Neither spouse/civil partner of former spouse/former civil partner is entitled to occupy (section 37)   Where a spouse or civil partner (or former spouse or former civil partner) occupies the matrimonial home or civil partnership home but neither of the parties is entitled to remain in occupation, either party may apply against the other for an occupation order under s.37 (ss.37(1), (2); s.37(1A)). The order may (s.37(3)): require the respondent to permit the applicant to enter and remain in the home or part of it; regulate the occupation of the home by either or both parties; require the respondent to leave the home or part of it; or exclude the respondent from a defined area in which the house is included (s.37(4)). When exercising its powers, the factors in s.33(6) (see p. 118 above) and the balance of harm test in s.33(7) (see p. 117 above) apply, as they apply to the exercise by the court of its powers under s.33(3) (s.37(4)).

Duration   The order is limited to six months, but may be extended on one or more occasion by a further specified period not exceeding six months (s.37(5)).

(iv) Neither cohabitant/former cohabitant is entitled to occupy (section 38)   Where both cohabitants or both former cohabitants (opposite-sex or same-sex) occupy a house which is the home where they live or have lived together as husband and wife or as civil partners, but neither party is entitled, either party may apply against the other for an occupation order (ss.38(1), (2)). The provisions which the order may contain are the same as those for a s.37 order (see above) (s.38(3)). In deciding whether to exercise its powers to include such a provision, and if so in what manner, s.38(4) requires the court to consider all the circumstances of the case and factors s.38(4)(a) to (d) (which are the same as those in s.33(6)(a)–(d) (see above)); and to apply the balance of harm test laid down in s.38(5). Thus the court must ask whether the applicant or relevant child is likely to suffer significant harm which if greater than that of the respondent or a relevant child if a s.38(3) provision is not included in the order. There is no obligation, however, to make a s.38(3) provision even if the balance leans in favour of doing so – the balance of harm test is merely part of the discretionary exercise.

Duration   The order is limited to a specified period not exceeding six months, but can be extended on one occasion by a further specified period of up to six months (s.38(6)).

(c)   Occupation orders: other powers

(i) Undertakings, orders without notice, and enforcement   The rules for undertakings, orders without notice, and enforcement are the same as those for non-molestation orders (see pp. 113 and 114 above), except that the restriction on accepting an undertaking (s.46(3A), see p. 114) does not apply to an occupation order.

(ii) Attaching a power of arrest Under s.47, the court can attach a power of arrest to an occupation order. The power differs depending on whether the occupation order is made with or without notice (*ex parte*).

If the order is made on notice and it appears to the court that the respondent has used or threatened violence against the applicant or a relevant child, it *must* attach a power of arrest to one or more provisions of the order, unless it is satisfied that the applicant or any child will otherwise be adequately protected (ss.47(1), (2)). Although it is usually preferable for a power of arrest to have effect for the same period as the order, it can be made to have effect for a shorter period than the other provisions in the order (see *Re B-J (Power of Arrest)* [2000] 2 FLR 443).

If the order is made without notice (*ex parte*), the court *may* attach a power of arrest to one or more provisions of the order, but only if the respondent has used or threatened violence against the applicant or a relevant child, and there is a risk that the applicant or child will suffer significant harm as a result of the respondent's conduct if the power of arrest is not attached to those provisions immediately (s.47(3)). A power of arrest can be imposed which is to have effect for a shorter period than the other provisions of the order (s.47(4)). The court can vary or discharge a power of arrest attached to an order without notice, whether or not an application for variation or discharge has been made (s.49(4)).

The effect of a power of arrest is to permit a constable to arrest, without a warrant, a person whom he has reasonable cause to suspect is in breach of any provision in an order to which the power of arrest is attached (s.47(6)). The respondent must be brought before a judge or justice of the peace within 24 hours, and, if the matter is not disposed of, the respondent may be remanded in custody or on bail (s.45(7)). A power of arrest can be attached even though the respondent is a minor (see *Re H (Respondent Under 18: Power of Arrest)* [2001] 1 FLR 641 where the Court of Appeal upheld an occupation order, which had been made with a power of arrest attached, ordering a 17-year-old boy, who had been violent and abusive to his parents, to leave the home and not return and not enter or attempt to enter it).

(iii) Ancillary powers (section 40) On or after making an occupation order under s.33, s.35 or s.36 (but not s.37 or s.38, in other words where neither party is entitled) the court has various ancillary powers (s.40(1)). It can impose repair and maintenance obligations, require a party to pay the rent, mortgage or other outgoings, and impose obligations in respect of the furniture or other contents of the house (for example, grant the use or possession of furniture or other contents, and order a party to take reasonable care of them). It can also require a party to keep the house, furniture and any other contents secure. When deciding whether and, if so, how to exercise these powers, the court must consider all the circumstances of the case, including the parties' financial needs and resources, and their present and future financial obligations, including their financial obligations to each other and any relevant child (s.40(2)). Ancillary orders are effective only for the duration of the occupation order (s.40(3)). In *Nwogbe v. Nwogbe* [2000] 2 FLR 744 the Court of Appeal drew attention to the fact that the court has no statutory power to enforce any ancillary obligation imposed in an order under s.40 (here the husband had defaulted on the requirement in the occupation order that he pay the rent and other expenses relating to the property).

(iv) Restrictions on the powers of magistrates   The magistrates' family proceedings court cannot hear an application or make an occupation order where the proceedings involve a disputed question about a party's right to occupy the home, unless it is not necessary to determine that question in order to deal with the application or to make the order (s.59(1)). The magistrates' court can also decline jurisdiction if it considers the case can be dealt with more conveniently by another court (s.59(2)).

(d) Breach of an occupation order

Breach of an occupation order is not a criminal offence as it is in the case of a non-molestation order (see p. 114). Instead, civil proceedings for contempt of court will have to be brought and, if contempt is proved, the contemnor will be ordered to pay a fine and/or serve a prison sentence. The courts have been increasingly willing to impose prison sentences (and longer ones) where there is breach. In *H v. O (Contempt of Court: Sentencing)* [2004] EWCA Civ 1691, [2005] 2 FLR 329 the Court of Appeal said that Parliament and society generally now regarded domestic violence and other violence associated with harassment and molestation as demanding rather more deterrent punishment than formerly.

The Court of Appeal has held that, as the Human Rights Act 1998 and the European Convention for the Protection of Human Rights (see 1.7) apply to committal proceedings, the family tribunal must take the greatest possible care to ensure that the applicable evidential and procedural rules are properly obeyed (see *Hammerton* v. *Hammerton* [2007] EWCA Civ 248, [2007] 2 FLR 1133).

5.6 Definitions

Section 62 of Part IV of the Family Law Act 1996 is important because it defines who can apply under the Act, and defines other terms.

(i) 'Cohabitants' and 'former cohabitants'   Cohabitants (and former cohabitants) include opposite-sex and same-sex cohabitants. Cohabitants are defined as two persons who are neither married to each other nor are civil partners of each other but who are living together as husband and wife or as if they were civil partners; but it does not include cohabitants who have subsequently married each other or become civil partners of each other (s.62(1)). As the court favours a purposive approach when construing the Act (in order to bring victims under the protective umbrella of the Act) the term 'cohabitant' can include persons who maintain separate households (see *G* v. *F (Non-Molestation Order: Jurisdiction)* [2000] 2 FLR 233, where Wall J held that the woman was associated with the respondent for the purposes of obtaining a non-molestation order, even though she only spent four or five nights of the week with him, there were no children and the relationship was unstable).

(ii) 'Relevant child'   A relevant child is: any child who is living with, or who might reasonably be expected to live with, either party to the proceedings; any child in relation to whom an order under the Adoption and Children Act 2002 or the Children Act 1989 is in question in the proceedings; and any other child whose interests the court considers relevant (s.62(2)). This broad definition highlights the importance of protecting *any* child

from domestic violence. Thus, the child need not be related to the applicant, nor be a child of the family.

(iii) 'Associated' persons   An applicant for a non-molestation order must be 'associated' with the respondent, and so must an entitled applicant for an occupation order who is not a spouse, civil partner or cohabitant (or a former spouse, civil partner or cohabitant). Associated persons are widely defined as (s.62(3)):

- spouses, or former spouses;
- civil partners, or former civil partners;
- cohabitants, or former cohabitants (opposite-sex or same-sex);
- persons who live, or have lived, in the same household, otherwise than merely by reason of one of them being the other's employee, tenant, lodger or boarder;
- relatives (see further below);
- engaged, or formerly engaged, couples;
- parties to a civil partnership agreement (whether or not that agreement has been terminated);
- persons who have, or have had, an intimate personal relationship with each other which is or was of significant duration;
- in relation to any child, both parties are a parent of the child or have or have had parental responsibility for the child (s.62(4));
- parties to the same family proceedings (see definition below) other than proceedings under Part IV FLA 1996.

(iv) A 'relative'   A 'relative' in relation to a person is (s.63(1)):

- the father, mother, step-father, step-mother, son, daughter, step-son, step-daughter, grandmother, grandfather, grandson or granddaughter of that person or of that person's spouse or former spouse, civil partner or former civil partner; or
- the brother, sister, uncle, aunt, niece or nephew (whether of the full blood or of the half blood or by marriage or civil partnership) of that person or of that person's spouse or former spouse, civil partner or former civil partner, and includes, in relation to a person who is cohabiting or has cohabited with another person, any person who would be any of the above relatives if the parties were married to each other or were civil partners of each other.

(v) Adopted children   If a child has been adopted, or an adoption agency has power to place the child for adoption by parental consent or by placement order (see Chapter 15), two persons are associated if: one of them is the natural parent of the child (or a parent of such a natural parent); and the other is the child or any person who has become a parent of the child under an adoption order or has applied for an adoption order, or is any person with whom the child has at any time been placed for adoption (ss.62(5), (7))

(vi) Engagements and civil partnership agreements   Written evidence of an engagement or civil partnership is needed, unless the court is satisfied that the engagement is evidenced by an engagement ring or an engagement ceremony; or by a gift by one party to the agreement as a token of the agreement or a civil partnership ceremony (s.44). If the

engagement or agreement has been terminated, an application for a non-molestation or occupation order must be brought within three years of termination (ss.33(2), 42(4)).

(vii) 'Family proceedings' 'Family proceedings' means any proceedings under (ss.63(1), (2)):

- the inherent jurisdiction of the High Court in relation to children;
- Part IV of the Family Law Act 1996;
- Part 4A of the Family Law Act 1996;
- the Matrimonial Causes Act 1973;
- the Domestic Proceedings and Magistrates' Courts Act 1978;
- Part III of the Matrimonial and Family Proceedings Act 1984;
- Parts I, II and IV of the Children Act 1989;
- s.54 Human Fertilisation and Embryology Act 2008;
- the Adoption and Children Act 2002;
- Schedules 5 to 7 to the Civil Partnership Act 2004.

5.7 Injunctions ancillary to legal proceedings

County courts and the High Court have jurisdiction (under s.38 of the County Courts Act 1984 and s.37 of the Supreme Court Act 1981) to grant injunctions ancillary to civil proceedings where it appears to the court to be just and convenient to do so. These powers may be useful if a victim of domestic violence does not come within the definition of associated person (see p. 124 above). However, the court can grant an injunction ancillary to civil proceedings only if the applicant has a legal or equitable right which is capable of being protected, such as a cause of action in tort or a proprietary interest. The House of Lords has held that it is not sufficient if another member of the family has such a right (*Hunter v. Canary Wharf Ltd* [1997] AC 655, [1997] 2 FLR 342).

Injunctions relating to domestic violence under the courts' general powers are rare (because of the statutory protection provided by the Family Law Act 1996 and the Protection from Harassment Act 1997), but an injunction was granted in *Tameside Metropolitan Borough Council v. M (Injunctive Relief: County Courts: Jurisdiction)* [2001] Fam Law 856 where social workers (who were working on a case where they had been threatened with violence by the children's parents) were granted injunctive protection as the local authority had a statutory right to be protected by virtue of the care order, and as it was necessary to do so in order for it to be able to implement its care plan. The local authority's alternative application for injunctive relief under the Protection from Harassment Act 1997 was dismissed, as the local authority was held not to be a 'person' for the purposes of that Act.

5.8 The Protection from Harassment Act 1997

The Protection from Harassment Act 1997 was enacted primarily to provide protection from harassment and other similar conduct arising in the context of 'stalking' (the obsessive harassment of one person by another), but it is sometimes used by victims of domestic violence. The Act creates criminal offences, and also provides civil remedies (injunctions and damages). It has been amended by the Domestic Violence, Crime and Victims Act 2004.

Under the Protection from Harassment Act 1997 there is no restriction on who can apply, whereas the parties must be 'associated' persons under Part IV of the Family Law Act 1996. Remedies under the 1996 Act specifically relate to occupation of the home, whereas those under the Protection from Harassment Act do not. Orders can be made without notice under the Family Law Act, but not under the Protection from Harassment Act. Applications under the Family Law Act are family proceedings, but those under the Protection from Harassment Act are not. Damages can be awarded under the Protection from Harassment Act but not under the Family Law Act.

Section 1(1) of the Protection from Harassment Act 1997 prohibits harassment by providing that a person must not pursue a course of conduct which amounts to harassment of another, and which that person knows or ought to know amounts to harassment of another. There is no definition of 'harassment' in the Act, but s.7(2) provides that references to harassing a person include alarming the person or causing the person distress. The Act may therefore be used to prosecute persons for acts other than stalking. In order for there to be harassment there must be 'a course of conduct' – a single incident is not sufficient. The Court of Appeal has held that, because the Act was passed to protect persons from stalking (an act performed by persons with an obsessive nature), a person who suffers from a mental illness can be convicted of harassment (see *R* v. *Colohan* [2001] EWCA Civ 1251 where the defendant was convicted, despite his defence that his schizophrenia took him outside the Act on the basis that he did not have the necessary mental state).

Course of conduct   In order for there to be harassment there must be a 'course of conduct', which s.7(3) defines as 'conduct on at least two occasions'. As 'conduct' can include speech (s.7(4)), verbal violence can constitute harassment. Course of conduct was considered in the following case:

▶ *R* v. *Hills* [2001] 1 FLR 580

After the woman left the defendant he was charged with harassment under the 1997 Act. The course of conduct consisted of various assaults during a seven-month period, but centred on two separate and individual assaults which took place approximately six months apart. The defendant was convicted but appealed against his conviction. The Court of Appeal allowed his appeal, holding that a course of conduct requires proof of a cogent link between the two (or more) incidents constituting harassment. As the case centred on two separate and individual incidents, the necessary cogent link between the two assaults had not been established. The case was held to be far from the stalking type of offence for which the 1997 Act was intended. The Court of Appeal held that, where a couple were frequently coming back together and having sexual intercourse, it was unrealistic to think that the behaviour fell within the stalking category. The Court of Appeal applied *Lau* v. *Director of Public Prosecutions* [2000] 1 FLR 799, which concerned two incidents between a girlfriend and a boyfriend, and where it was held that, although two incidents could be enough to establish harassment, the fewer the occasions and the wider they were spread the less likely it would be that a finding of harassment could reasonably be made for the purposes of the Act.

(a)   Criminal offences

The Act creates two levels of criminal offence, each of which must involve a 'course of conduct' (ss.1, 2(1) and 7(3)). The s.2 offence is where a person pursues a course of conduct which amounts to harassment of another, and which he knows or ought to know amounts to harassment of the other (s.2(1)). A person who is found guilty of this offence is liable to a fine or imprisonment for up to six months (s.2(2)). The other offence is the s.4 aggravated indictable offence of harassment, that of causing another person to fear on at least two occasions that violence will be used against him (s.4(1)). The s.4 offence carries stricter penalties.

Defences Both criminal offences are subject to statutory defences (ss.1(3) and 7(3)): that the course of conduct was pursued for the purpose of preventing or detecting crime; or that the pursuit of the course of conduct was reasonable (see ss.1(3) and 4(3)).

Restraining orders (s.5) The criminal court has power to make restraining orders (injunctive-style orders) under s.5 of the PHA 1997. Before 30 September 2009 the criminal court could impose a restraining order only on an offender convicted of harassment under the Act, but, as a result of new provisions inserted into the PHA 1997 (by the Domestic Violence Crime and Victims Act 2004), the criminal courts can now make a restraining order on conviction of *any* offence (such as an assault). The court also has the power (under s.5A) to make a restraining order where a person has been acquitted of harassment if it believes that such an order is necessary to protect a named person from harassment by the defendant in the future. The aim of these new wider powers is to give victims immediate protection and to save them having to bring a separate civil action.

A restraining order may have effect for a specified period or until further order (s.5(3)). Breach of the order without reasonable excuse is a criminal offence (s.5(5)), which can result in a fine or imprisonment (for up to five years) (s.5(6)).

(b) Civil remedies

The Protection from Harassment Act 1997 also provides civil remedies. Section 3 creates a statutory tort of harassment by providing that a person who is, or may be, the victim of harassment, as prohibited by s.1 of the Act, can bring a claim in civil proceedings against the person responsible for the harassment (s.3(1)). Damages can be awarded, including damages for anxiety caused by the harassment and for any financial loss resulting from the harassment (s.3(2)). Damages can be awarded without the need to seek an injunction (see *Singh* v. *Bhakar and Bhakar* [2007] 1 FLR 889 where a young Sikh girl, who had suffered harassment by her mother-in-law after she joined her husband in his extended family home, obtained damages under s.3 for the depression caused by the maltreatment).

If the High Court or a county court grants an injunction restraining the defendant from pursuing any conduct which amounts to harassment, and the complainant considers that the defendant has done anything which is prohibited by the injunction, the complainant may apply for the issue of a warrant for the arrest of the defendant (s.3(3)). Breach of an injunction restraining the defendant from pursuing any conduct which amounts to harassment is a criminal offence (s.3(6)); and is not punishable as a contempt of court (s.3(7)).

In an application for a civil remedy under s.3 the standard of proof is the civil standard of proof (on the balance of probabilities); and the court must make sure that it exercises its powers in compliance *inter alia* with art. 8 of the European Convention for the Protection of Human Rights (Tugendhat J in *Hipgrave and Hipgrave* v. *Jones* [2004] EWHC 2901 (QB), [2005] 2 FLR 174).

Summary

1 Violence in the home is a serious problem.

2 The Government is committed to tackling domestic violence and providing protection and support for victims. The Domestic Violence, Crime and Victims Act 2004 was enacted to make changes to the civil and criminal law in order to give greater protection to victims and their families.

3 The criminal law provides protection for victims of domestic violence, and the police treat domestic violence as a serious crime.

4 The civil law provides remedies for victims of domestic violence. Under Part IV of the Family Law Act 1996 magistrates' courts, county courts and the High Court have jurisdiction to make occupation orders and non-molestation orders for a wide class of applicants, including spouses, former spouses, civil partners, former civil partners, cohabitants (opposite-sex and same-sex), former cohabitants, family members and other persons who come within the definition of 'associated persons'.

5 In respect of occupation orders made under Part IV of the Family Law Act 1996, the court makes a distinction between 'entitled persons' (those with a right of occupation) and 'non-entitled persons' (those with no such right). Entitled applicants are treated more 'generously' under the Act.

6 The court can accept undertakings from respondents, in some circumstances, under Part IV of the Family Law Act 1996.

7 Orders can be made without notice under Part IV of the Family Law Act 1996.

8 County courts (under s.38 County Courts Act 1984) and the High Court (under s.37 Supreme Court Act 1981) have jurisdiction to grant injunctions ancillary to other proceedings where it is just and convenient to do so, but the applicant must have a right in law or in equity which is capable of being protected.

9 The Protection from Harassment Act 1997 makes provision for two types of criminal offence of harassment. It also creates a tort of harassment. Restraining orders are available under the Act.

Further reading and references

Bessant, 'Enforcing non-molestation orders in the civil and criminal courts' [2005] Fam Law 640.

Burton, *Legal Responses to Domestic Violence*, 2008, Routledge.

Burton, '*R (Rabess)* v. *Commissioner of the Police for the Metropolis* – "Scream Quietly or the Neighbours will Hear": Domestic violence, "nuisance neighbours" and the public/private dichotomy revisited' [2008] CFLQ 95.

Burton, '*Lomas* v. *Parle* – coherent and effective remedies for victims of domestic violence: time for an integrated domestic violence court?' [2004] CFLQ 317.

Hayes, 'Criminal trials where a child is the victim: extra protection for children or a missed opportunity?' [2005] CFLQ 307.

Platt, HHJ, 'The Domestic Violence, Crime and Victims Act 2004 Part I: Is it working?' [2008] Fam Law 642.

Reece, 'The end of domestic violence' (2006) 69(5) *Modern Law Review* 770.

Websites

Crime Reduction Website: www.crimereduction.homeoffice.gov.uk
Home Office: www.homeoffice.gov.uk
Refuge: www.refuge.org.uk
Women and Equality Unit: www.womenandequalityunit.gov.uk
Women's Aid: www.womensaid.org.uk

Divorce and its consequences

Chapter 6

Divorce

This chapter deals first with the development of divorce law, and then with the current law governing the obtaining of a divorce. Financial and property matters on divorce are dealt with in Chapter 7. Residence and contact arrangements for children are dealt with in Chapter 11 and financial provision for children in Chapter 12.

The key legislation

Matrimonial Causes Act 1973 Part I makes provision in respect of the grounds for divorce. Part II makes provision in respect of finance and property on divorce (see Chapter 7).

Family Law Act 1986, Part II makes provision in respect of the recognition of foreign divorces.

Family Proceedings Rules 1991 lays down the procedural rules governing divorce proceedings, and proceedings for property and finance on divorce.

Statistics on divorce for 2007 in England and Wales

These figures were published in August 2008 by the Office for National Statistics (www.statistics.gov.uk).

- There were 128,534 divorces, a drop of 3 per cent compared with 132,562 in 2006. This was the lowest number of divorces since 1976 (when there were 126,694).
- There were 11.9 divorces per 1,000 married men and women (compared with 12.2 in 2006).
- The average duration of marriage was 11.7 years (compared with 11.6 years in 2006).
- 1 in 5 men and women had had a previous marriage ending in divorce (compared with only 1 in 10 men and women in 1980).
- Men and women in their late twenties had the highest divorce rates of all five-year age groups (26.6 divorces per 1,000 married men aged 25–29; and 26.9 divorces per 1,000 married women aged 25–29).
- 68 per cent of divorces were granted to wives (and for 54 per cent of those divorces the fact proved was unreasonable behaviour). For 33 per cent of divorces granted to the husband, the fact proved was the wife's unreasonable behaviour.
- 51 per cent of divorcing couples had at least one child under 16.
- The average age at divorce was 41.2 years (for women) and 43.7 years (for men) (compared to 40.9 years and 43.4 years respectively in 2006).

6.1 The development of divorce law

(a) The grounds for divorce

Until the mid-nineteenth century the ordinary courts had no jurisdiction to grant decrees of divorce, although the ecclesiastical courts could annul marriages and grant a limited sort of divorce which relieved the spouses of the legal obligation to live together, but did not terminate the marriage. The Christian idea of marriage as an indissoluble life-long union prevailed. Anyone who wished to divorce could only do so by private Act of

Parliament, which was a complex, lengthy and expensive procedure available only to a few.

In order to remedy the inadequacies of the Act of Parliament procedure, the Matrimonial Causes Act 1857 was passed permitting judicial divorce on the ground of adultery by the respondent – a ground which was acceptable to the Church because of biblical precedent. In addition to adultery, the petitioner had to prove that there was no collusion, condonation or connivance between the parties. However, divorce was more difficult for wives, as, unlike husbands, they had to prove 'aggravated adultery' (adultery plus an additional factor, such as incest, cruelty, bigamy, sodomy or desertion). However, after considerable pressure for reform by the female emancipation movement, aggravated adultery was abolished by the Matrimonial Causes Act 1923.

The Matrimonial Causes Act 1937 added further grounds: cruelty; desertion for a continuous period of at least three years; and incurable insanity. In response to concerns that this more liberal divorce law would undermine the institution of marriage, the 1937 Act introduced an absolute bar on divorce in the first three years of marriage, unless the petitioner could prove exceptional hardship or that the respondent had shown exceptional depravity. The aim of the three-year bar was to deter trial marriages and hasty divorces. Condonation, connivance and collusion remained as bars.

At the end of the Second World War, there was a sharp increase in the number of people wishing to divorce, and a growing dissatisfaction with the law. It seemed wrong to have to prove a matrimonial offence, thereby apportioning blame, when both spouses might be responsible for marriage breakdown. It seemed wrong for a restrictive divorce law to perpetuate a dead marriage which had completely broken down. It was also easy to abuse the system, for example by fabricating adultery. In response to dissatisfaction with the law, a Royal Commission, the Morton Commission, was established to look at divorce, and in its *Report* in 1956 (Cmd. 9678) it recommended the retention of the matrimonial offence doctrine as the basis for a good divorce law. This was a considerable set-back for the proponents of reform, and it was not until the 1960s with the publication of two reports, one by the Church of England and the other by the Law Commission, that proposals for change began to be made. In 1963 the Archbishop of Canterbury appointed a Committee to study divorce, which in its report (*Putting Asunder*, 1966) recommended that the doctrine of the matrimonial offence be abolished and be replaced by a principle of irretrievable breakdown of marriage, which would be proved by holding an inquest into the causes of breakdown. Shortly after the publication of *Putting Asunder*, the Law Commission published a Report (*Reform of the Grounds of Divorce: The Field of Choice*, Cmnd. 3123, 1966) in which it stated that the objectives of a good divorce law should be:

'To buttress, rather than to undermine the stability of marriage; and when, regrettably a marriage has irretrievably broken down, to enable the empty legal shell to be destroyed with the maximum fairness, and the minimum bitterness, distress and humiliation.'

The Law Commission concluded that a divorce law based on a matrimonial offence failed to satisfy these objectives, and, while it agreed with the Archbishop's Committee that irretrievable breakdown should be the sole ground for divorce, it rejected the Committee's proposal that breakdown should be established by holding an inquest into its causes, as this would be distressing for the parties, expensive, time-consuming and essentially untriable. The Law Commission proposed instead that breakdown should be established on proof of one or more of five facts, three of which would be based on the old matrimonial offences, and the other two on periods of separation. The five facts proposed were: adultery plus intolerability; unreasonable behaviour; desertion for a period of at least two years; two-years' separation with consent to the divorce; and five-years' separation. The Law Commission also recommended that a new divorce law should incorporate certain policy objectives. It should encourage reconciliation, prevent injustice to economically vulnerable spouses and protect children. It also recommended that the three-year bar on divorce should be replaced with a one-year bar as the three-year bar prolonged poor marriages, encouraged allegations of exceptional hardship or depravity which were difficult to adjudicate, and caused hostility and bitterness between the parties. It also caused duplication of proceedings, as an unhappily married spouse would petition for a decree of judicial separation followed not long afterwards by a petition for divorce. The Law Commission recommended a one-year bar, as it felt that to have no bar at all would undermine the sanctity of marriage.

The Law Commission's recommendations were eventually enacted in the Divorce Reform Act 1969, which came into force on 1 January 1971 (but which was later re-enacted as Part I of the Matrimonial Causes Act 1973). Except for certain amendments (notably the 'clean-break' provisions introduced by the Matrimonial and Family Proceedings Act 1984) the reforms introduced by the Divorce Reform Act 1969 remain the law today. We therefore have a hybrid law of divorce made up of fault and no-fault grounds. The retention of fault means that the matrimonial offence doctrine remains, and in fact is particularly prevalent, as many divorces are sought on the basis of the fault grounds of adultery or unreasonable behaviour – as these enable a petitioner to obtain a 'quick' divorce. The Law Commission's belief that most couples would use the separation grounds has not been realised in practice.

Since the introduction of the current grounds for divorce (in 1971), there has been increasing dissatisfaction with the law; and in 2000 a radically new form of divorce was to have been introduced, but this was abandoned because it was found to be unworkable in practice.

(b) Divorce procedure

Changes to divorce procedure took place over the years. Initially, because divorce was considered a serious matter, proceedings were heard only in London and only by senior judges. At one time, divorces were heard in open court with the petitioner giving oral evidence to prove the ground alleged. However, it became increasingly recognised that hearing divorces in open court was not only distressing for the parties, as they would have their intimate marital details exposed in public, but it was also unnecessarily expensive and time-consuming. Divorce was failing to achieve one of its major policy aims, namely the burial of a dead marriage with the minimum of distress and humiliation.

With the huge increase in the divorce rate, particularly after the introduction of the more liberal grounds for divorce by the Divorce Reform Act 1969, the courts became overloaded, even though most undefended divorces were taking as little as ten minutes to be heard. Eventually, a new divorce procedure, the 'special procedure', was introduced with the aim of achieving simplicity, speed and economy. It was introduced in 1973 for childless couples divorcing with consent, but was extended in 1975 to all childless couples, except those petitioning on the basis of unreasonable behaviour. In 1977 it was extended to all undefended divorces.

All undefended divorces today are therefore dealt with by what is largely a 'paper exercise'. Thus the judge examines the papers to establish whether the fact alleged in the petition is proved, whether the marriage has irretrievably broken down and whether there is any reason for not granting the divorce. A list of petitioners who satisfy the judge is drawn up and is read out in open court by the judge's clerk, after which the judge pronounces decree nisi of divorce on block. This judicial pronouncement is the last vestige of the public hearing of divorce. If a divorce is undefended neither party need attend court. Defended divorces, on the other hand, which are virtually non-existent, are still required to be heard in open court with the parties giving oral evidence.

6.2 An attempt at reform

In the late 1980s, as a result of increasing dissatisfaction with divorce law, proposals for reform were made. Although these proposals were enacted in Parts I, II and III of the Family Law Act 1996, they were never implemented because the government concluded that they were unworkable in practice. Since then there has been no attempt to reform the law.

(a) The background to the proposed reforms

In the 1980s the Booth Committee looked at divorce procedure and made recommendations for reform which included joint applications for divorce, a system of initial hearings in which the parties would be able to reach a settlement or identify areas of dispute, and changes of terminology to make the law more understandable. These proposals were not implemented.

Concerns about the ground for divorce led to proposals for reform by the Law Commission (see *Facing the Future: A Discussion Paper on the Ground for Divorce*, Law Com No. 170, 1988; *Family Law: The Ground for Divorce*, Law Com No. 192, 1990; and *Looking to the Future: Mediation and the Ground for Divorce* Cm 2424, 1993; *Looking to the Future: Mediation and the Ground for Divorce. The Government's Proposals*, Cm 2799, 1995).

The Law Commission was of the view that, although the 1969 reforms were a considerable improvement on the previous law, a major aim of those reforms – to move away from fault – had not been achieved in practice, as most divorces were being sought on the basis of adultery and unreasonable behaviour. It concluded that divorce law was not working well for various reasons. It allowed a divorce to be obtained too quickly and easily without the parties being required to consider the consequences. It did nothing to save marriages. It could make things worse for children. It was unjust and exacerbated bitterness and hostility. It was confusing, misleading, open to abuse, discriminatory and it also distorted the parties' bargaining positions.

Having identified the weaknesses in the law, the Law Commission made proposals for reform which it claimed would introduce a truly, and not artificially, no-fault divorce which would encourage the parties to reach agreement and consider and face up to the consequences of marital breakdown. Having discussed various options for reform, the Law Commission concluded that a no-fault model was best. After discussing the advantages and disadvantages of different no-fault models (divorce on proof of marriage breakdown, separation, or divorce by mutual consent, or by unilateral demand), it recommended the retention of irretrievable breakdown as the ground for divorce, but with divorce available at the end of a period of time. The Commission claimed that divorce over a period of time would encourage the parties to co-operate and consider the practical consequences of divorce; and would reinforce the idea that divorce is a process and not an event. It would also fit well with mediation.

(b)   The proposed reform – 'divorce over a period of time'

'Divorce over a period of time,' which was enacted as Part II of the Family Law Act 1996, emphasised that divorce is a process, not an event, and introduced no-fault divorce. It required couples, in most cases, to have sorted out ancillary matters (finance, property and children) before being able to obtain a divorce. Parties were to be given more information about divorce, and greater emphasis was to be placed on mediation.

Irretrievable breakdown would be the sole ground for divorce, which would be proved if: the applicant(s) had made a statement of marriage breakdown; a required period for reflection and consideration had passed; and one or both parties had declared that, having reflected on the breakdown and having considered arrangements for their future, their marriage could not be saved. A series of steps would have to be taken in order to obtain a divorce. An applicant would first have to attend an 'information meeting' at which information about divorce would be given, and marriage counselling provided, if needed. At least three months later, one or both of the parties would have to send a 'statement of marital breakdown' to the court which would then have the power to make directions requiring the parties to attend a meeting at which mediation would be explained, and to make interim ancillary relief orders and interim orders under the Children Act 1989. Once the statement of marital breakdown was lodged with the court, a period for reflection and consideration (9 months in some cases, 15 in others) would have to pass during which the applicant(s) would be required to spend time reflecting on whether their marriage could be saved and, if not, then on making arrangements in respect of ancillary relief and the welfare of any children. At the end of that period, an application for a 'divorce order' could be made, which the court could grant if it was satisfied that: the marriage had irretrievably broken down; the information meeting requirements had been complied with; arrangements for the future had been made; there was no order preventing divorce; and the requirements in respect of the welfare of the children had been satisfied.

The court would be able to make 'orders preventing divorce' where divorce would result in substantial financial or other hardship to the other party, or to a child of the family.

(c)   The decision not to introduce the reforms

'Divorce over a period of time' was due to come into force on 1 January 1999, but implementation was suspended until 2000 until after the Government had received the results of a pilot scheme to see how the information meetings would work in practice. However, the results of the pilot scheme turned out to be disappointing. Only 7 per cent of those attending information meetings were diverted into mediation and very few couples attended the meetings together. The information meetings had failed to achieve the Government's stated objectives of saving saveable marriages and encouraging mediation. Because the proposals had failed to fulfil the policy objectives in Part I of the

Act of saving saveable marriages and, where they had broken down, bringing them to an end with the minimum of distress to the parties and any children, the reforms were never introduced and Parts 1 and II of the Family Law Act were eventually repealed.

The Government's decision not to implement the reforms was greeted with considerable relief by those who thought the proposals were inherently flawed – as they were unnecessarily complicated and unworkable in practice. One of the main criticisms was that the reforms placed impractical and impossible demands on divorcing couples. Couples in the throes of marriage breakdown would have found it difficult, and in some cases impossible, to make arrangements for the future. Cretney (1995) thought that the Government seemed 'curiously naive' about what was likely to happen during the period of reflection. He said that some couples would not spend time considering whether their marriage could be saved or making arrangements for the future, but would instead spend time conceiving children, or exploiting their emotional or financial advantage or brooding on their grievances. Freeman (1997) was critical of the length of the divorce process because he thought it would create 'more conflict, more tension, more domestic violence, unnecessary abortions and more children who [would] experience their parents' divorce while still of pre-school years'. Eekelaar (1999) criticised the need for information meetings, and considered them a form of 'social engineering'. The Solicitors' Family Law Association (now called Resolution) considered the new law to be cumbersome and confusing, and said it would create delay and uncertainty, which were contrary to the best interests of divorcing couples and their children.

Thus, despite more than a decade-long attempt at reform, the new divorce law never came to fruition; and there are no current proposals to reform the law. In Scotland, however, where divorce law is similar to that in England and Wales, a simple change to the law has been made, so that the five-year separation ground has been reduced to two, and the two-year separation with consent ground reduced to one. The aim of this change was to encourage the use of the separation grounds, and thereby lessen the acrimony and conflict which may be associated with fault-based divorces, and to allow parents and children to move on.

Major milestones in the development of divorce law	
1857	The Matrimonial Causes Act 1857 introduces judicial divorce by establishing the Court for Divorce and Matrimonial Causes with jurisdiction to grant decrees of divorce, nullity and judicial separation. Adultery is the sole ground for divorce, but women must prove 'aggravated adultery' (adultery plus cruelty, bigamy, sodomy or desertion).
1923	The Matrimonial Causes Act 1923 abolishes aggravated adultery in order to equalise the position of women with men.
1937	The Matrimonial Causes Act 1937 introduces additional grounds, so that a divorce can be obtained on the ground of: adultery; cruelty; desertion for a continuous period of at least three years; or incurable insanity. A bar on divorce in the first three years of marriage is introduced.
January 1st 1971	The Divorce Reform Act 1969 comes into force introducing irretrievable breakdown as the sole ground for divorce, but which must be established by proof of: adultery; unreasonable behaviour; two-years' separation with consent to the divorce; desertion; or five-years' separation. The three-year bar on divorce is reduced to one. The Divorce Reform Act is later re-enacted as Part I of the Matrimonial Causes Act 1973 (which is the law which applies today).

Major milestones in the development of divorce law	
1973	The 'special procedure' (administrative divorce) is introduced for undefended divorces by childless couples who are divorcing with consent. It is extended in 1977 to all undefended divorces.
January1st 1999	A new law of divorce ('divorce over a period of time') is due to come into force under Parts I, II and III of the Family Law Act 1996, but its implementation is suspended so that the Government can conduct a pilot study to see how the information meetings work in practice.
2000	The proposed new divorce law is abandoned.

6.3 The current law of divorce: introduction

The law of divorce is laid down in the Matrimonial Causes Act (MCA) 1973, Part I of which deals with obtaining a divorce (or an annulment or judicial separation), and Part II with finance and property orders on divorce (annulment or judicial separation) (see Chapter 7). Procedural rules governing divorce are found in the Family Proceedings Rules 1991.

An undefended divorce is obtained by means of what is essentially an administrative paper exercise. It can be granted in a matter of weeks without the need, in most cases, for either party to attend court. Sorting out ancillary matters (property, finance and children), if the parties cannot reach agreement, takes much longer. Obtaining a divorce is a two-stage process; decree nisi followed by decree absolute. Only on the grant of the decree absolute is the marriage terminated. The procedure for defended divorces is different, but divorces are rarely defended. The parties to a divorce are called the 'petitioner' and the 'respondent'.

Jurisdiction The jurisdictional rules for hearing a petition for divorce (or for nullity or judicial separation) in the courts in England and Wales are laid down in s.5 of the Domicile and Matrimonial Proceedings Act 1973; and, for divorces involving Member States of the EU, in Council Regulation (EC) (No. 2201/2003) Concerning Jurisdiction and the Recognition and Enforcement of Judgments in Matrimonial Matters and in Matters of Parental Responsibility (Brussels II Revised). The rules are complex, but in general terms the courts in England and Wales have jurisdiction to grant a divorce if either spouse is domiciled in England or Wales when the proceedings are begun, or is habitually resident in England or Wales throughout the period of one year ending with the date on which proceedings are begun.

In *Mark* v. *Mark* [2005] UKHL 42, [2005] 2 FLR 1193 the House of Lords held that, for the purpose of jurisdiction to entertain a divorce petition under s.5(2) of the Domicile and Matrimonial Proceedings Act 1973, residence in England and Wales need not be lawful residence. Thus a person can be habitually resident or domiciled in England and Wales even if his or her presence in the UK is a criminal offence under the Immigration Act 1971.

Difficulties can occur when a couple move out of the jurisdiction of the UK to another country. Thus, for example, in *Munro* v. *Munro* [2007] EWHC 3315 (Fam), [2008] 1 FLR 1613 Bennett J had to decide whether the wife should be allowed to petition for divorce in England and Wales even though she and her husband had moved to Spain shortly after marrying in England. The husband argued that, as his wife had acquired domicile in

Spain, the divorce should be heard in Spain. Applying Brussels II Revised (see above), Bennett J said that cogent evidence was required to prove that by unequivocal intentions and acts either party had abandoned his or her English domicile of origin and acquired a Spanish domicile of choice; and he held on the facts that the English, not the Spanish, court had jurisdiction.

Staying divorce proceedings   The Domicile and Matrimonial Proceedings Act 1973 gives the divorce courts in England and Wales the power to stay divorce proceedings where divorce proceedings are pending in another country (see, for example, *S v. S (Divorce: Staying Proceedings)* [1997] 2 FLR 100 where the English High Court granted the husband's application for a stay of proceedings, as the court in New York was the more appropriate forum for the divorce).

The 'one-year bar' on divorce   Divorce proceedings cannot be commenced within the first year of marriage (s.3(1) MCA 1973). This is an absolute bar – there is no discretion to waive it. Despite the one-year bar, a petitioner can base the divorce petition on matters which happened during the first year of marriage (s.3(2)). A decree of nullity or of judicial separation, on the other hand, can be sought during the first year of marriage.

Encouraging reconciliation   As part of the policy objective of divorce law to encourage the saving of saveable marriages, certain provisions in Part I of the MCA 1973 aim to encourage reconciliation. Thus, the court can adjourn divorce proceedings at any stage if there is a reasonable possibility of a reconciliation between the parties (s.6(2)), and certain periods of resumed cohabitation are ignored when establishing whether or not the marriage has irretrievably broken down.

6.4   The ground for divorce and the five facts

Under Part I of the Matrimonial Causes Act 1973 there is only one ground for divorce: irretrievable breakdown of the marriage (s.1(1)). To establish irretrievable breakdown, the petitioner must prove one or more of the following five 'facts' which in common parlance are referred to as the 'grounds' for divorce:

The five facts for divorce

Section 1(2) of the Matrimonial Causes Act 1973 requires the petitioner to prove to the court that:

'(a) the respondent has committed adultery and the petitioner finds it intolerable to live with the respondent;

(b) the respondent has behaved in such a way that the petitioner cannot reasonably be expected to live with the respondent;

(c) the respondent has deserted the petitioner for a continuous period of at least two years immediately preceding the presentation of the petition;

(d) the parties to the marriage have lived apart for a continuous period of at least two years immediately preceding the presentation of the petition … and the respondent consents to a decree being granted; or

(e) the parties to the marriage have lived apart for a continuous period of at least five years immediately preceding the presentation of the petition.'

If a fact is proved, the court must grant a decree nisi of divorce unless it is satisfied that the marriage has not irretrievably broken down (s.1(4)). The court must be satisfied *both* of irretrievable breakdown and at least one fact. This requirement was described by the Law Commission, when discussing reform (see 6.2 above), as being illogical (see, for example, *Richards* v. *Richards* [1972] 1 WLR 1073 and *Buffery* v. *Buffery* [1988] 2 FLR 365 where in each case the Court of Appeal found that irretrievable breakdown of marriage had been established, but not unreasonable behaviour).

(a)   Adultery (s.1(2)(a))

Adultery involves an act of voluntary heterosexual intercourse between two people who are not married to each other, but at least one of whom is married. Adultery is usually proved by the respondent acknowledging adultery on the Acknowledgment of Service form.

In addition to proving adultery, the petitioner must prove that he or she finds it intolerable to live with the respondent (s.1(2)(a)). This requirement was added to buttress the stability of marriage (a policy aim of the law), so that an act of adultery would be insufficient on its own to end a marriage. Adultery and intolerability are two separate and unrelated facts; and so the tolerability need not relate to the adultery (*Cleary* v. *Cleary* [1974] 1 WLR 73). The test of intolerability is subjective, namely whether the petitioner finds it intolerable to live with the respondent, not whether a reasonable petitioner would so find it.

As part of the policy objective of divorce law to encourage reconciliation, a petition based on adultery cannot be heard if the parties have lived together for more than six months (in one period, or more than one period, aggregated) after the petitioner discovered the adultery (s.2(1)); but a period (or aggregated periods) of living together not exceeding six months is disregarded when determining the question of intolerability (s.2(2)).

(b)   Unreasonable behaviour (s.1(2)(b))

The petitioner must prove that the respondent has behaved in such a way that the petitioner cannot reasonably be expected to live with the respondent. Although this fact is referred to as 'unreasonable behaviour', this is a misnomer because, under s.1(2)(b), it is the effect of the respondent's behaviour on the petitioner which is relevant, not whether the respondent's behaviour is unreasonable.

In *Livingstone-Stallard* v. *Livingstone-Stallard* [1974] Fam 47 Dunn J adopted the following test for establishing unreasonable behaviour:

'Would any right-thinking person come to the conclusion that this husband has behaved in such a way that this wife cannot reasonably be expected to live with him, taking into account the whole of the circumstances and the characters and personalities of the parties?'

This test was approved by the Court of Appeal in *O'Neill* v. *O'Neill* [1975] 1 WLR 1118, and endorsed by the Court of Appeal in *Buffery* v. *Buffery* [1988] 2 FLR 365.

Divorces are granted for a wide range of behaviour, including both acts and omissions. In *O'Neill* v. *O'Neill* (above), for example, the petitioner stated that her husband had a withdrawn personality, had doubted the paternity of their children, and had spent two years 'improving' the matrimonial home, which included mixing cement on the living-room floor and leaving the lavatory door off for about eight months.

Some behaviour, however, may be too trivial and a decree may be refused, as it was in *Buffery* v. *Buffery* (above) where the wife alleged that her husband was insensitive, never took her out, and that they had nothing to talk about and nothing in common after their children had grown up and left home. Her petition was dismissed, as her husband's behaviour was found to be insufficient to satisfy the behaviour ground. An accumulation of trivial incidents may, however, constitute unreasonable behaviour as they did in *Livingstone-Stallard* v. *Livingstone-Stallard* (above), where Dunn J held that the wife 'was subjected to a constant atmosphere of criticism, disapproval and boorish behaviour on the part of her husband'. However, as each case depends on its own facts, an accumulation of various minor matters will not necessarily result in a decree being granted. In *Butterworth* v. *Butterworth* [1997] 2 FLR 336, for example, the decree of divorce was set aside by the Court of Appeal as the petition was severely defective. The husband had denied the wife's allegations that he was a violent, possessive, sexually demanding and jealous alcoholic who had stopped her going to church. The Court of Appeal stressed that English divorce law still gave the respondent the right to oppose a divorce, and to have the allegations in the petition properly proved. The Court of Appeal held that the court had not applied the correct test for unreasonable behaviour, or anything like it.

Sometimes the court will have to decide whether to grant a divorce where the behaviour is not the respondent's fault, for example where the respondent is mentally or physically ill. Whether a divorce will be granted will depend on the circumstances of the case, and, although the court will be cognisant of the fact that marriage entails a commitment which includes caring for a sick spouse, it is likely to be sympathetic to the plight of a petitioner and the fact that illness can place severe strains on a marriage. A divorce may therefore be granted even though a respondent is not responsible for his or her own 'behaviour' (as it was, for example, in *Katz* v. *Katz* [1972] 1 WLR 955 where the petitioner's husband suffered from manic-depression).

The parties can live together for up to six months (in one period or more than one period, aggregated) after the last instance of behaviour alleged without losing the right to petition for divorce; and the court must ignore this period when determining whether the petitioner can reasonably be expected to live with the respondent (s.2(3)).

(c) Desertion (s.1(2)(c))

The respondent must have deserted the petitioner for a continuous period of at least two years immediately preceding the presentation of the petition. To prove desertion there must be: factual separation; an intention by the respondent to desert; no consent by the petitioner to the desertion; and no just cause to desert. Constructive desertion is also possible (in other words where a spouse's behaviour is so bad that the other spouse is forced to leave the home). To encourage reconciliation, a period of up to six months' resumed cohabitation does not prevent the desertion from being continuous (s.2(5)). Divorces based on desertion are rare.

(d) Two-years' separation with consent to the divorce (s.1(2)(d))

The parties must have lived apart for a continuous period of at least two years immediately preceding the presentation of the petition, and the respondent must consent to the decree being granted. The respondent must have the capacity to consent and must be given such information as will enable him or her to understand the effect of a decree being granted (s.2(7)). The usual way in which notice of consent is given is by the respondent signifying to that effect on the Acknowledgement of Service form. Consent may be withdrawn at any time before decree nisi, whereupon the proceedings must be stayed. At any time before decree absolute the respondent can apply to have the decree nisi rescinded if he or she had been misled by the petitioner in respect of any matter which he/she took into account in deciding whether to give consent (s.10(1)). The respondent can ask for the decree absolute to be postponed in certain circumstances (see 6.5 below).

The parties must be living in separate households for separation to be established (s.2(6)). This is a question of fact. However, as 'household' does not mean 'house', separation is possible even if the parties are living under the same roof (see, for example, *Fuller* v. *Fuller* [1973] 1 WLR 730, where a decree was granted even though the husband lived as a lodger with his wife and her new male friend).

When calculating separation, no account is taken of a period of up to six months (in one period or several aggregated) during which the parties resumed living together, but there must still be an aggregated period of actual separation for at least two years (s.2(5)). If the period of resumed cohabitation is more than six months, the two-year period of separation starts to run again.

(e) Five-years' separation (s.1(2)(e))

The parties must have lived apart for a continuous period of at least five years immediately preceding the presentation of the petition. The petitioner must establish factual separation, but there can be separation even though the spouses live under the same roof. To protect the respondent, the court can delay decree absolute or refuse decree nisi (see 6.5 below). A reconciliation period of up to six months can be ignored, provided the parties have separated for an aggregated period of at least five years, but, if the reconciliation is for more than six months, then the five-year period begins to run again (s.2(5)). In practice, few spouses petition for divorce on this fact because most petitioners do not wish to wait for five years to obtain a divorce.

6.5 Protection for respondents

Sections 10 and 5 of the Matrimonial Causes Act 1973 provide protection for respondents who are being divorced on the basis of two or five years' separation. The aim of these provisions is to protect 'innocent' spouses, in other words those who have committed no matrimonial offence.

(a) Section 10 Matrimonial Causes Act 1973

Under s.10(2) a respondent to a divorce based on two or five years' separation can ask the court to consider whether his or her financial situation after divorce will be satisfactory. If such an application is made, the court may refuse to grant the decree absolute unless it is satisfied: that the petitioner should not be required to make financial provision for the respondent; or that the provision made or to be made by the petitioner is reasonable and fair, or the best that can be made in the circumstances (s.10(3)). The court may, however, grant a decree absolute in any event if it is desirable to do so without delay, and it has obtained a satisfactory undertaking from the petitioner that he or she will make such financial provision as the court may approve (s.10(4)).

Few applications are made under s.10, but an application may be useful as a tactical manoeuvre to put pressure on a petitioner to sort out the parties' financial position, for instance where there may be a problem enforcing an ancillary relief order (see, for example, *Garcia* v. *Garcia* [1992] 1 FLR 256 where an application under s.10 was used to enforce maintenance payments for a child where the petitioner had failed to keep up with those payments under a Spanish separation agreement).

Section 10 applications were sometimes used to provide protection for respondents (particularly wives) who would be losing pension entitlements as a result of divorce (see, for example, *Jackson* v. *Jackson* [1993] 2 FLR 848), but, as the divorce court now has wide powers in respect of pensions (see 7.8), there is no longer any need to use s.10 for this purpose.

(b)   Section 5 Matrimonial Causes Act 1973

Under s.5 a respondent to a divorce based on five years' separation has a complete defence to divorce. The aim of s.5 is to safeguard the position of 'innocent' spouses who do not wish to be divorced. In practice it is rarely invoked, and even if it is, rarely succeeds. Under s.5, the court has the power to rescind a decree nisi if the respondent proves that he or she will suffer grave financial or other hardship if the divorce is granted; and that it would be wrong in all the circumstances to grant the divorce. The alleged hardship must arise as a result of the dissolution of the marriage. Hardship can include the loss of the chance of acquiring a benefit which the respondent might acquire if the marriage were not dissolved (s.5(3)) (for example, loss of a right to succeed under the other spouse's will or intestacy). Most of the reported cases have been in relation to pension rights (see, for example *Archer* v. *Archer* [1999] 1 FLR 327), but because of changes to the law on pensions on divorce (see 7.8) this is no longer necessary. 'Other hardship' for the purposes of s.5 could include, for instance, religious or social hardship that a respondent might suffer as a result of ostracism in the community because of religious or social attitudes to divorce.

Defences under s.5 are extremely rare, and even rarer now that pension provision on divorce has been improved (see 7.8). Even where pleaded, the defence may not be successful (see, for example, *K* v. *K (Financial Relief: Widow's Pension)* [1997] 1 FLR 35). In most cases the court will consider it best to end the marriage, despite the possibility of the respondent suffering hardship.

6.6   Divorce procedure

Divorce procedure differs according to whether a divorce is undefended or defended. In practice, virtually all divorces are undefended – because of the expense and futility of defending a divorce. The rules of procedure are laid down in the Family Proceedings Rules (FPR) 1991.

(a)   Undefended divorce

An undefended divorce is obtained by way of what is essentially a paper exercise. There is usually no need for the parties, or their legal representatives (if any), to attend court.

The petition is the central document in divorce proceedings, as it informs the respondent and the court of the basis on which the petitioner is seeking a divorce and of the orders that he or she will be seeking as part of the divorce. To commence divorce proceedings, the petitioner (the spouse seeking the divorce) must present a petition to a divorce county court (in London, the Divorce Registry) alleging that the marriage has irretrievably broken down and alleging at least one of the five facts (see p. 140 above). The petition cannot be presented to the court until one year has expired from the date of the marriage (s.3(1)); but anything that happened during that one-year period (such as unreasonable behaviour or adultery) can be used as evidence in the divorce proceedings (s.3(2)).

The petition must contain specified information (see r.2.3 FPR 1991), for example the names and addresses of the parties and any children under 16 or in full-time education, the occupations of the parties and details of the marriage. It must also contain a statement that the marriage has irretrievably broken down, the fact(s) relied on and brief particulars of such fact(s). It must conclude with a prayer for dissolution of the marriage, any claim for costs, and a prayer setting out any ancillary relief claimed (property and/or financial orders) and any child support maintenance claimed. The petition must contain the names and addresses of the parties.

The petition is sent to the court with the following documents: the marriage certificate; the Statement of Arrangements for the Children (see 11.3); certified copies of any court orders; and any certificate in respect of public funding. If a solicitor is acting in the divorce proceedings, the solicitor must also file with the court a reconciliation certificate stating whether or not he or she has discussed with the petitioner the possibility of a reconciliation and has given details of persons qualified to help to effect a reconciliation (r.2.6(3) FPR 1991). A solicitor is not obliged to discuss reconciliation with the client (s.6(1) MCA1973). A court fee must be paid when the petition is filed.

(i) Obtaining a decree nisi   Once the petition and other documents have been filed in the court, a copy of the petition is served on the respondent accompanied by a Notice of Proceedings (explaining the effect of the petition and informing the respondent of the procedure involved) and an Acknowledgement of Service.

The Acknowledgment of Service is a question-and-answer form which the respondent (or solicitor) must complete, sign and return to the court within seven days of receiving the divorce papers, failing which a further copy of the petition may be served upon the respondent personally. In the Acknowledgement of Service the respondent must state whether the petition has been received, whether he or she intends to defend the divorce, whether consent to the divorce is given if sought on the basis of two-years' separation with consent, and also whether he or she intends to apply for ancillary relief and/or for orders in respect of the children.

Once the Acknowledgement of Service has been returned to the court and the respondent does not wish to defend, the petitioner (or solicitor) must file a written request for 'directions for trial' together with a written statement and questionnaire in specified form, sworn by the petitioner providing evidence of the fact(s) relied on. The district judge gives 'directions for trial' by entering the cause in the special procedure list and thereafter considers the evidence filed by the petitioner for procedural regularity and to establish whether there is sufficient evidence to prove the fact alleged. The district judge may request further information or evidence, if needed. If satisfied that the fact is proved and that the marriage has irretrievably broken down, the district judge files a certificate to that effect and a date, time and place are fixed for the judge to pronounce decree nisi. Both parties receive a certificate and notice of the date and place for the pronouncement of decree nisi, which takes place in open court, but which neither the parties nor their legal representatives need attend. The process of pronouncement is a mere formality. The decrees are listed together in batches and collectively read out by the clerk of the court before the judge or district judge (or by the judge or district judge) who pronounces the decree nisi orally or by nodding.

Where there are children of the family aged under 16, or over 16 which the court directs should be included (for instance, because of disability), the court must consider the proposed arrangements for the children before granting a decree nisi of divorce (s.41 MCA 1973) (see 11.3).

A decree nisi may be rescinded by the court if both spouses are of sound mind and consent to this (and with advice, where appropriate) (*per* Singer J in *S* v. *S* (*Rescission of Decree Nisi: Pension Sharing Provision*) [2002] 1 FLR 457, where both parties wished to rescind the decree nisi in order to be subject to the new pension provisions on divorce).

(ii) Decree absolute   The grant of decree nisi (see above) does not terminate the marriage. It is only terminated on the grant of the decree absolute, which is automatically granted on the application of the petitioner, who can apply for it six weeks or more after decree nisi. A fee must be paid. If the petitioner fails to apply for decree absolute, the respondent may apply after three months have passed from the earliest date on which the petitioner could apply (s.9(2)). But in these circumstances the court cannot grant the respondent the decree absolute without a hearing by a judge or district judge (r.2.50 FPR 1991). These rules are strict. If a decree absolute is obtained in breach of the rules, the divorce is void (see *Dennis* v. *Dennis* [2000] 2 FLR 231).

If there are children, the divorce cannot be made absolute until the district judge has considered whether the court should exercise any of its powers under s.41 MCA 1973 (see 11.3). Where a divorce is sought on either of the separation grounds, a decree absolute can be refused where a respondent has not been satisfactorily financially provided for by the petitioner (see 6.5 above).

The purpose of the gap between decree nisi and decree absolute is to enable a respondent to appeal, and for the Queen's Proctor and other persons to intervene to show just cause why a decree should not be made absolute (s.8 MCA 1973). Intervention by the Queen's Proctor was much more of a possibility under the old divorce law where a decree absolute could be refused if the parties had colluded. Intervention by the Queen's Proctor is now rare (but see *Bhaijii* v. *Chauhan (Queen's Proctor Intervening)* [2003] 2 FLR 485 where the Queen's Proctor opposed the grant of decrees absolute where bogus allegations of behaviour had been made to obtain divorces in respect of five marriages which had been entered into solely for the purpose of circumventing the immigration rules).

(b)   Defended divorce

Defended divorce proceedings begin in the same way as an undefended divorce, but the respondent in the Acknowledgement of Service indicates an intention to defend. Provided various notice requirements have been satisfied (see r.10 FPR 1991), there is an exchange of pleadings and the hearing takes place in open court with oral evidence being given and cross-examination of both parties. (For a rare case involving a defended divorce, see *Hadjimilitis (Tsavliris)* v. *Tsavliris (Divorce: Irretrievable Breakdown)* [2003] 1 FLR 81.)

6.7   Effects of divorce

Once a decree absolute of divorce has been granted, the marriage is dissolved and each party is free to remarry. A decree absolute has other legal consequences. Financial provision and property adjustment orders made under Part II of the Matrimonial Causes Act 1973 in favour of the parties to the marriage take effect, and orders for settlement or variation of a settlement can take effect in respect of any child of the family. All other orders for children take effect as soon as they are made. Divorce also has an effect on a will made by either party to the marriage (see 4.2). Social security and pension rights and taxation are affected, and both parties lose rights under certain matrimonial legislation, in particular rights of occupation of the home ('home rights', see 4.2). However, as far as children are concerned, each parent retains parental responsibility and the obligation to provide children with financial support continues (see Chapter 12). Disputes about residence and contact can be settled by way of mediation or by an application to the court (see Chapter 11).

6.8   The future of divorce

> ▶ **Stephen Cretney,** *Family Law in the Twentieth Century*, **2003, p. 391**
>
> 'English divorce law is in a state of confusion. The theory of the law remains that divorce is a matter in which the State has a vital interest, and that it is only allowed if the marriage can be demonstrated to have irretrievably broken down. But the practical reality is very different: divorce is readily and quickly available if both parties agree, and even if one of them is reluctant he or she will, faced with a divorce petition, almost always accept the inevitable: there is no point in denying that the marriage has broken down if one party firmly asserts it has.'

After the Government's decision not to implement the divorce reforms in Part II of the Family Law Act 1996 (see 6.2), judges, practitioners and academics continued to voice concerns that divorce law was unsatisfactory. A former President of the Family Division (the Rt Hon Dame Elizabeth Butler-Sloss) described obtaining a divorce on the basis of unreasonable behaviour as a 'hypocritical charade' and said that there was a need to introduce a truly no-fault divorce. In July 2001, the Lord Chancellor's Advisory Board on Family Law in its final report regretted the missed opportunity to reform divorce, and urged that serious consideration be given to replacing the current adversarial and partly fault-based divorce regime. It said that the serious defects in the current law identified by the Law Commission still remained. In particular, allegations of adultery and unreasonable behaviour caused unnecessary conflict between the parties, and their distress and anger impacted on children.

Allegations of fault seem contrary to the promotion of the settlement culture which exists in respect of ancillary relief proceedings and arrangements for children on divorce. There is also a risk that some parties may be 'steam-rollered' into divorce, because a divorce can be obtained so quickly. As Kay (2004) states:

'Over two-thirds of divorces granted in England and Wales in 2002 were based on facts that clearly have connotations of blame and guilt, and where proceedings can be commenced in haste, without thought for the consequences of the breakdown and the legal ending of marriage. Taken as a whole, these statistics make a compelling case for reform.'

Kay also points out that, although divorce law is acknowledged to be unsatisfactory, it has nevertheless been replicated in virtually the same form for civil partners under the Civil Partnership Act 2004.

The possibility of introducing a purely administrative divorce has been considered. Cretney, for instance, asked ([2002] Fam Law 900):

'Should we not accept that the routine processing of marriage breakdown is no longer a judicial function and that it should accordingly be removed altogether from the courts and the judicial system, leaving them with more time to deal with the problems that do require their expertise and procedures? If we believe that respect for the law and the legal system is important, and that the 1996 reforms would have made the law even more complex and difficult to understand, should we not begin to ask whether there is not a simpler and better alternative?'

With the increasing emphasis on mediation and settlement, divorce by mutual consent would seem to be a good idea (although this option for reform was dismissed, somewhat cursorily, by the Law Commission when it was discussing divorce reform (in its 1988 Discussion Paper), on the basis that it would undermine the institution of marriage).

Resolution's proposals   Resolution (the organisation of family lawyers) has campaigned for many years for no-fault divorce to be introduced – because the current law of divorce does not sit well with the non-confrontational approach adopted and promoted in the rest of the family justice system. It has called for reform to be put back on the agenda (see [2007] Fam Law 1053). A more recent statement by Resolution (see Shepherd [2009] Fam Law 122) proposed that both divorce and civil partnership dissolution should be reformed; and it made proposals for reform. Thus, it recommended, *inter alia*, that the divorce process should be commenced by one party (or both) filing a statement of marital breakdown, after which there would be a waiting period of six months before one party (or both) could file a declaration that the marriage had broken down and the divorce could be finalised. There would be power to shorten the six-month waiting period in exceptional circumstances. There would be no requirement for the parties to separate, but, if they had separated, then that period of separation could be deducted from the waiting period. It recommended that there should be no extension to the waiting period where there were minor children or one party objected. Shepherd [2009] discussing Resolution's proposals said that 'ending the blame game should be right at the top of the list of priorities for all of us working with those who are having to come to terms with relationship breakdown'.

However, despite these calls for reform by Resolution, and others, there are currently no Government proposals to reform the law.

6.9   Recognition of an overseas divorce

Part II of the Family Law Act 1986 lays down rules for the recognition in the UK of divorces (and annulments and separations) obtained overseas. The Act makes a distinction between divorces obtained in judicial or other proceedings and those otherwise obtained. Recognition is much broader for divorces obtained in proceedings. An overseas divorce granted in proceedings is recognised in the UK if it is effective under the law of the country where it was obtained, and at the commencement of those proceedings either party was habitually resident or domiciled in that country or was a national of that country (s.46(1)). An overseas divorce obtained otherwise than in proceedings is recognised in the UK if it is effective in the country where it was obtained and at the date it was obtained one or both parties were domiciled there, or one party was domiciled there and the other party was domiciled in a country which recognised the divorce, and in any case neither party was habitually resident in the UK for one year immediately preceding the divorce (s.46(2)).

The English courts have a discretion to refuse recognition of an overseas divorce whether or not it was obtained in proceedings. Thus, for example, it may under s.51(3) refuse to recognise an overseas divorce if reasonable steps have not been taken for giving notice of the proceedings to a party to the marriage (see *Duhur-Johnson* v. *Duhur-Johnson (Attorney-General Intervening)* [2005] 2 FLR 1042 where a Nigerian divorce was refused recognition as a valid overseas divorce because the husband had not taken reasonable steps to give notice of the divorce proceedings to his wife).

An overseas divorce may not be recognised in England and Wales where recognition would be manifestly contrary to public policy (s.52). However, it may be difficult to argue that a divorce should not be recognised on public policy grounds (*per* Thorpe LJ in *Eroglu* v. *Eroglu* [1994] 2 FLR 287, where the wife's claim that her Turkish divorce should not be recognised in England and Wales was dismissed, despite her claim that it had been obtained by fraud). In *H* v. *H (The Queen's Proctor Intervening)(Validity of Japanese Divorce)* [2006] EWHC 2989 (Fam), [2007] 1 FLR 1318 a Japanese divorce by agreement (a Kyogi rikon) was recognised as a valid divorce, as there was no reason to refuse recognition on the grounds of public policy.

Recognition of divorces within the EU Special rules apply to the recognition of divorces within the European Union. Council Regulation (EC) (No. 2201/2003) Concerning Jurisdiction and the Recognition and Enforcement of Judgments in Matrimonial Matters and in Matters of Parental Responsibility (Brussels II Revised) applies (see, for example, *D* v. *D (Nature of Recognition of Overseas Divorce)* [2005] EWHC 3342 (Fam), [2006] 2 FLR 825 where Bodey J made a declaration that the Greek divorce was recognised in England and Wales under Brussels II, which had the effect of dissolving the parties' marital status).

Is a talaq a valid overseas divorce? A talaq is a unilateral Islamic divorce whereby the husband can divorce his wife by merely uttering the words 'I divorce you' three times without being in the presence of another person and without the wife's consent. Whether a talaq will be recognised in England and Wales depends on the circumstances of the case. If the talaq is obtained in England it will not be recognised as a valid divorce, as divorces obtained in England and Wales other than by court proceedings are not recognised. Thus, in *Sulaiman* v. *Juffali* [2002] 1 FLR 479 a talaq pronounced in England, but subsequently registered in Saudi Arabia, was held not to be a valid divorce within the meaning of s.45(1) of the Family Law Act 1986, as it was not obtained in Saudi Arabia. Even though the talaq had complied with all the formalities required by Sharia law in Saudi Arabia, it had clearly been obtained in England other than in a court, and thus fell foul of the FLA 1986.

Whether the court in England and Wales will recognise a talaq validly made *outside* the UK depends on the circumstances of the case, and is a matter for the discretion of the court. However, a talaq is likely to be upheld unless the court considers there are public policy reasons for not doing so. In the following cases talaqs declared overseas were recognised as valid divorces in England and Wales:

▶ *H v. H (Talaq Divorce)* [2007] EWHC 2945, [2008] 2 FLR 857

A talaq divorce validly announced in Pakistan was upheld by Sumner J in the English High Court. Sumner J said that it was important that marriages and divorces recognised in one country should be recognised in another unless there were good reasons for not doing so, especially when there were, as in this case, close links between the two countries and many people moved freely between them. There were no good reasons for refusing to recognise the talaq divorce in the circumstances of the case.

▶ *El Fadl v. El Fadl* [2000] 1 FLR 175

A talaq divorce registered with the Sharia court in Lebanon was recognised by the English High Court, and the wife's petition for an English divorce dismissed. Recognition of the talaq was not held to be contrary to public policy, even though such a divorce might offend English sensibilities.

6.10 Other decrees

Under Part I of the Matrimonial Causes Act 1973 the court has jurisdiction to grant decrees of nullity (see Chapter 2), decrees of judicial separation and decrees of presumption of death.

(a) Decree of judicial separation

Divorce county courts and the High Court have jurisdiction to grant a decree of judicial separation under s.17 of the Matrimonial Causes Act 1973, provided the petitioner can prove one of the five facts in s.1(2) MCA 1973 (see p. 140 above). There is no need to prove irretrievable breakdown of marriage. The effect of a decree of judicial separation is not to dissolve the marriage but merely to terminate the obligation of the petitioner to continue living with the respondent (s.18(1)) (although the spouses are not obliged to separate).

Where a decree of judicial separation is in force and separation is continuing, the surviving spouse is not entitled to succeed to the deceased spouse's property on his or her intestacy, but judicial separation does not affect a will (s.18(2)).

On the grant of a decree, the court has jurisdiction to make orders for ancillary relief under Part II of the Matrimonial Causes Act 1973 (see Chapter 7). Divorce is not precluded by a previous judicial separation and the divorce court can treat the decree of judicial separation as proof of one or more of the five facts alleged for divorce (s.4).

Decrees are rarely sought, but a decree may be useful for a spouse who does not wish to divorce or who is precluded from divorcing (for instance, for religious reasons) or who cannot divorce because one year of marriage has not elapsed. In 2008 there were only 421 petitions filed for judicial separation, a decrease of 16 per cent compared with 2007 (*Judicial and Court Statistics 2008*, Ministry of Justice, 2009, Cm 7697).

(b) Decree of presumption of death

Where a spouse is missing and thought to be dead, the other spouse can petition for a decree of presumption of death and dissolution of marriage under s.19 Matrimonial Causes Act 1973. If a decree is granted, the petitioner can contract a valid new marriage, which remains valid, even if the spouse who is presumed dead subsequently reappears. The court will grant a decree if it is satisfied that reasonable grounds exist for supposing the petitioner's spouse is dead. A spouse is presumed dead if he or she has not been seen for a continuous period of at least seven years. The petitioner must, however, have made reasonable enquiries to establish whether the other spouse is alive.

Summary

1 Although divorce is common in England and Wales, the numbers of divorces have been dropping.

2 Judicial divorce in England and Wales was introduced by the Matrimonial Causes Act 1857, with the sole ground being adultery.

3 The Matrimonial Causes Act 1937 extended the grounds for divorce to: adultery; cruelty, three-years' desertion and incurable insanity. It also introduced a bar on divorce in the first three years of marriage.

4 The Divorce Reform Act 1969 introduced new grounds for divorce, which were later re-enacted in Part I of the Matrimonial Causes Act 1973 and which remain the law today.

5 All divorces were once heard in open court, but in the 1970s the special procedure (an administrative form of divorce) was introduced for all undefended divorces.

6 The current law of divorce is found in Part I of the Matrimonial Causes Act 1973. There is one ground for divorce (irretrievable breakdown of marriage (s.1(1))), which is established on proof of one or more of the following five facts (s.1(2)): (a) adultery; (b) unreasonable behaviour; (c) desertion for a period of at least two years; (d) two-years' separation with consent to the divorce; and (e) five-years' separation. There must be proof of both irretrievable breakdown and at least one fact.

7 Divorce is not possible within the first year of marriage (s.3(1)).

8 Under s.10 MCA 1973 a respondent to a two-year or five-year separation divorce can ask the court to delay decree absolute until it is satisfied about financial arrangements made by the petitioner for the respondent.

9 Section 5 provides a complete defence to divorce for a respondent to a petition brought on the basis of five-years' separation, if the respondent can prove that the dissolution of the marriage will cause him or her grave financial or other hardship, and it would be wrong to grant the divorce.

10 Undefended divorces are dealt with under what is an essentially administrative procedure. They are commenced by the petitioner presenting a petition to a divorce county court (or the Principal Registry in London). There is usually no need to attend court. The other party is called the 'respondent'. Divorce involves a two-stage process: decree nisi followed by decree absolute. Only after decree absolute is the marriage terminated. Defended divorces, which are rare, are heard in open court.

11 As a result of dissatisfaction with the law, Parts I and II of the Family Law Act 1996 were enacted introducing a new form of divorce – 'divorce over a period of time'. However, the reforms were not implemented because of Government concerns that the changes might not work in practice and might not achieve their stated objectives.

Summary cont'd

12 Although it is generally agreed that divorce law is unsatisfactory, there are currently no Government proposals to reform the law.

13 Part II of the Family Law Act 1986 lays down rules for the recognition in the UK of divorces obtained overseas. Overseas divorces are more likely to be recognised if they were obtained in court proceedings.

14 Under s.17 Matrimonial Causes Act 1973 the court has jurisdiction to grant a decree of judicial separation if one of the five facts in s.1(2) is proved. Under s.19 it has jurisdiction to grant a decree of presumption of death.

Further reading and references

Cretney, 'Marriage, divorce and the courts' [2002] Fam Law 900.

Cretney, 'The Divorce White Paper – some reflections' [1995] Fam Law 302.

Deech, 'Divorce – a disaster?' [2009] Fam Law 1048.

Haskey, 'Divorce trends in England and Wales' [2008] Fam Law 1133.

Hasson, 'Setting a standard or reflecting reality? The "role" of divorce law, and the case of the Family Law Act 1996' [2003] IJLP&F 338.

Kay, 'Whose divorce is it anyway? – the human rights aspect' [2004] Fam Law 892.

Shepherd, 'Ending the blame game: getting no fault divorce back on the agenda' [2009] Fam Law 122.

Chapter 7
Finance and property on divorce

The legislation

Part II of the Matrimonial Causes Act 1973 makes provision in respect of the powers of the courts to determine disputes about property and finance on divorce (and on nullity and judicial separation).

Part III of the Matrimonial and Family Proceedings Act 1984 lays down the rules governing the powers of the courts in England and Wales to hear applications for finance and property orders after an overseas divorce (or annulment).

Family Proceedings Rules 1991 lays down the rules of procedure relating to applications for finance and property on divorce (and on nullity and judicial separation).

7.1 Introduction

On marriage breakdown it will usually be necessary for the divorcing couple to distribute and reallocate their property and financial assets, whether it be the family home, a pension, investments or other assets. Most couples will sort out matters themselves, but some will end up taking their case to court by bringing proceedings for ancillary relief on divorce. The distribution of finance and property on divorce by the court is referred to as 'ancillary relief', because the relief is ancillary to the petition for divorce. Obtaining a divorce and sorting out ancillary matters involve separate court proceedings. A decree of divorce can be obtained in a short time, a matter of weeks, but disputes about property and finance can take much longer.

A settlement culture   Despite the impression given by the number of reported cases, most couples do not litigate about property and finance but reach agreement with or without the assistance of a lawyer, and/or without resorting to mediation or collaborative law (see 1.4). If legal advice is sought, solicitors adopt a conciliatory approach. Resolution (the organisation of family solicitors) encourages solicitors to adopt a conciliatory approach in order to reduce the cost, unpredictability and trauma of going to court. It has a *Code of Practice* which is based on encouraging settlement. Solicitors who deal with divorce matters are required to follow the Law Society's *Family Law Protocol*, a set of guidelines which aim to make the process less confrontational. Solicitors are required to adopt conciliatory approaches and to encourage the parties to put the interests of their children first. However, despite the emphasis on settlement and an increasing move towards greater recognition of private agreements, the parties are not completely free to make their own arrangements, as the court has the power to scrutinise an agreement and, if necessary, overturn it.

Despite the emphasis on settlement, some couples spend vast sums of money on legal costs, particularly where there are substantial assets to fight over. In *Moore* v. *Moore* [2007] EWCA Civ 361, [2007] 2 FLR 339, for example, the parties spent £1.5 million on legal fees primarily to decide whether the English or Spanish courts would hear their application for ancillary relief. In *A* v. *A (No. 2) (Ancillary Relief: Costs)* [2007] EWHC 1810 (Fam), [2008] 1 FLR 1428 the costs amounted to 41.5 per cent of the matrimonial assets, and the wife ended up spending over 50 per cent of her final award on costs. Judges now have wider powers, however, to control the proceedings with the aim of reducing costs and encouraging the parties to reach agreement.

A wide range of different family situations   The courts exercise their discretion over a wide spectrum of family life. In *Dart* v. *Dart* [1996] 2 FLR 286 Butler-Sloss LJ said that the Matrimonial Causes Act 1973 'provides the jurisdiction for all applications for ancillary relief from the poverty-stricken to the multi-millionaire'. If the parties are wealthy, orders in respect of vast sums of money may be made. At the opposite end of the spectrum, on the other hand, the court may have to consider finance and property issues in the context of State benefits and local authority housing. In low-income cases 'the assessment of the needs of the parties will lean heavily in favour of the children and the parent with whom they live' (*per* Butler-Sloss LJ in *Dart* v. *Dart*). In *B* v. *B (Financial Provision: Welfare of Child and Conduct)* [2001] EWCA Civ 2308, [2002] 1 FLR 555, for example, the parties' sole asset of £124,000, which represented the proceeds of sale of the matrimonial home, was ordered to be transferred to the wife because of the need to rehouse her and the child.

Judicial discretion   The system governing disputes about matrimonial assets on divorce in England and Wales is based on judicial discretion. There is no community of property regime as there is in some European countries, whereby each spouse on marital breakdown is entitled to a fixed share of the matrimonial assets, subject to any agreement to the contrary. Under Part II of the Matrimonial Causes Act 1973 the court has wide discretionary powers to redistribute matrimonial assets, subject to the application of the statutory guidelines and the 'clean break' provisions laid down in the MCA 1973. The courts must also apply the guidelines laid down in the case-law. However the outcome of each case depends on its own particular facts.

A discretion-based system has the advantage of flexibility, in that the judge can tailor the order(s) to fit the facts of the case, but it can create uncertainty and unpredictability, and can involve the court in a time-consuming and expensive exercise. It is also difficult for lawyers to advise their clients with certainty as to what the outcome is likely to be.

7.2   Procedure in ancillary relief proceedings

The rules of procedure are laid down in the Family Proceedings Rules 1991 (FPR 1991), as amended. These rules aim to reduce delay and costs by facilitating settlement and allowing the court to have control over the conduct of proceedings. The Law Society's *Family Law Protocol* provides guidance on the conduct of ancillary relief with the emphasis being on settling disputes justly and speedily, safeguarding the interests of children and ensuring that costs are not out of proportion to the assets available.

The spouse who applies for ancillary relief is called the 'applicant' and the other spouse the 'respondent'. Cases are heard by a district judge in the divorce county court seized of the divorce petition; but complex or serious cases can be referred to the judge or transferred to the High Court. Except for maintenance pending suit and any order to or for the benefit of a child of the family, orders do not take effect until decree absolute.

The parties must attend a First Appointment, followed by a Financial Dispute Resolution hearing at which the district judge will help the parties reach agreement. If agreement cannot be reached, the case will proceed to a full hearing.

Media attendance   Media representatives are permitted to attend ancillary relief proceedings, unless the judge decides to exclude them or the rules provide otherwise (for instance where the proceedings involve conciliation or negotiation) (r.10.28 FPR 1991). In *Spencer* v. *Spencer* [2009] EWHC 1529 (Fam) Earl Spencer (the brother of Princess Diana) and his wife applied to exclude the media from their ancillary relief proceedings on the basis of their art. 8 ECHR rights to a private and family life. Munby J refused their application, holding that the issue of whether the media should be excluded was not simply a question of balancing the parties' art. 8 ECHR rights as against the media's art. 10 ECHR rights (the right to freedom of speech), but that important rights under art. 6 ECHR (the right to a fair trial) concerning the promotion of the administration of justice were also involved. (After the decision the parties decided to settle the case by negotiation and a consent order was made, which is confidential and is not read out in open court).

A duty of full and frank disclosure   Both parties have a duty to make full and frank disclosure of all their assets, documents and other relevant up-to-date information, for without this the court will be unable to exercise its discretion fairly and justly. The Law Society's *Family Law Protocol* emphasises this, and so do the courts. Failure to make full and frank disclosure is a serious matter and can result in an order being set aside (see 7.12). A costs penalty can be imposed on a dishonest party. (For a case where there was serious non-disclosure and other grave misconduct, see *Al-Khatib* v. *Masry* [2002] EWCH 108 (Fam), [2002] 1 FLR 1053).

The overriding objective   The district judge is required to engage in active case management to ensure that couples co operate in the conduct of proceedings, so as to further the overriding objective which is that cases must be dealt with justly (r.2.51 Family Proceedings Rules 1991). In furtherance of this objective, the district judge must: so far as is practicable, deal with the case in such a way as to ensure that the parties are on an equal footing and to save expense; deal with the case in a way which is proportionate to the amount of money involved, the importance and complexity of the issues, and the financial position of each party; and ensure that the case is dealt with expeditiously and fairly.

To further the overriding objective that cases be dealt with justly, the district judge must engage in active case management, which includes: encouraging the parties to co-operate and to mediate; identifying issues; regulating disclosure; helping the parties to settle; and fixing timetables. The parties themselves are required to help the court to further the overriding objective.

The First Appointment   The aim of the First Appointment is to define the issues and make directions (if needed), so that the parties can reach agreement, if possible. Both parties must attend, unless the court orders otherwise. The district judge has various powers, such as to: direct that further documents be produced; give directions about the valuation of assets; order that the case be adjourned for out-of-court mediation or private negotiation; and to make an interim order. The district judge must direct that the case be referred to a Financial Dispute Resolution Appointment (FDR), unless it is not appropriate in the circumstances. The district judge may treat the First Appointment as an FDR appointment.

The Financial Dispute Resolution (FDR) appointment   Both parties must attend the FDR appointment, unless the court orders otherwise. The aim of the FDR appointment is for discussion, negotiation and conciliation to take place. The emphasis is on encouraging the parties to settle, and they must use their best endeavours to reach agreement. If agreement is not possible, the case proceeds to a final hearing.

In *Rose* v. *Rose* [2002] EWCA Civ 208, [2002] 1 FLR 978 the Court of Appeal held that, although the FDR appointment can take many forms, depending on the style and practice of the judge, the judicial evaluation of the appointment should never be superficial or ill-considered. It held that the FDR appointment is an invaluable tool for dispelling unreasonable expectations, but that in a finely balanced case it is no substitute for a trial and should not be used to discourage either party to go to trial where the case can only be resolved in such a way. In *S* v. *S (Ancillary Relief: Importance of FDR)* [2007] EWHC 1975 (Fam), [2008] 1 FLR 944 Baron J held, *inter alia*, that the FDR procedure must be undertaken in an effective way in every case, because it gives the parties the opportunity to settle the litigation, to air the issues and to have neutral judicial evaluation at a time before costs have denuded assets.

The final hearing   The hearing usually takes place before the district judge in chambers, but the district judge can refer the case to a judge.

Staying divorce proceedings to allow the case to be heard in another jurisdiction   In an international case, the court can stay the proceedings if it considers it more appropriate for the matter to be determined outside England and Wales. In *Bentinck* v. *Bentinck* [2007] EWCA Civ 175, [2007] 2 FLR 1, for instance, the Court of Appeal stayed the English proceedings to allow the Swiss court to determine, in accordance with Swiss law, the issue of which jurisdiction was first seised. In *Ella* v. *Ella* [2007] EWCA Civ 99, [2007] 2 FLR 35 the Court of Appeal held that the existence of a pre-nuptial agreement conferring jurisdiction on the Israeli court was a major factor in the decision of the English court to stay divorce proceedings in England and Wales in what otherwise looked like a 'London' case.

7.3   Orders that can be granted

Under Part II of the Matrimonial Causes Act 1973 the court can make the following orders:

(a) **maintenance pending suit (s.22);**
(b) **financial provision orders (s.23):** periodical payments orders; lump sum orders; pension attachment orders;
(c) **property adjustment orders (s.24):** transfer of property; settlement of property; and variation of a settlement;
(d) **pension sharing orders (s.24B).**

According to Government statistics (*Judicial and Court Statistics 2008*, Ministry of Justice, 2009, Cm 7697), in 2008 almost 29,600 property adjustment orders and 30,200 lump sum orders were made. The majority of orders (70 per cent) were not contested. A further 23 per cent of orders were made by consent after initially being contested.

(a) Maintenance pending suit (s.22)

This is interim maintenance which terminates when the divorce suit is determined (or earlier if the court so orders). The court is required to exercise its discretion to make such order as is 'reasonable' (s.22). Although the exercise of discretion is not governed by the factors in s.25 (see 7.4), the court performs a similar exercise. The court has a wide discretion and in an appropriate case may make a substantial order (see, for example, *M* v. *M (Maintenance Pending Suit)* [2002] EWHC 317 (Fam), [2002] 2 FLR 123 where the wife was awarded £330,000 per annum maintenance pending suit). In *A* v. *A (Maintenance Pending Suit: Provision of Legal Fees)* [2001] 1 FLR 377 Holman J, referring to the non-discrimination principle in *White* v. *White* (see 7.6), held that maintenance pending suit need not be restricted to daily living expenses, but can, depending on the circumstances, include a sum to fund the costs of the proceedings. In *A* v. *A* there had been a long marriage, and complex issues involving bigamy and polygamy. Holman J warned, however, that the courts should be cautious about including a costs element in maintenance pending suit. In *G* v. *G (Maintenance Pending Suit: Costs)* [2003] 2 FLR 7 maintenance pending suit also included a sum for legal costs.

(b) Financial provision orders (s.23)

The following orders can be made in favour of a spouse and to or for the benefit of any child of the family aged under 18, or a 'child' over 18 who is undergoing education or training or who has special circumstances (such as a disability) (ss.23(1), 29(1), (3)).

(i) A periodical payments order (maintenance)   A periodical payments order can be ordered in favour of a spouse and/or to or for the benefit of any child of the family. (But most child maintenance disputes are dealt with by the Child Maintenance and Enforcement Commission (see Chapter 12), not the courts). Periodical payments can be secured or unsecured. If unsecured, payment is made from unsecured income. If secured, capital assets or other property are charged as security for payment. Periodical payments made in favour of a spouse terminate if that spouse remarries (s.28(1)), but they do not terminate on cohabitation, even if it is settled and long-term. In *Atkinson* v. *Atkinson* [1988] Ch 93 the Court of Appeal refused to equate long-term or settled cohabitation with remarriage after divorce, because of the difficulty of making qualitative judgments about what constituted settled cohabitation. In *Fleming* v. *Fleming* [2003] EWCA Civ 1841, [2004] 1 FLR 667 the Court of Appeal reaffirmed the rule in *Atkinson*, notwithstanding the fact of social changes in respect of cohabitation.

(ii) A lump sum order   A lump sum order (a capital sum) can be made in favour of a spouse and to or for the benefit of any child of the family (s.23(1)). It can be made to enable liabilities and expenses reasonably incurred by a spouse or a child prior to the application to be met (ss.23(3)(a), (b)). It can be ordered to be paid in instalments (s.23(3)(c)), and can incur interest (s.23(6)).

The advantage of a lump sum is that it can be used to affect a clean break between the parties (see 7.5). Sometimes a lump sum will be ordered to represent 'capitalised maintenance' (a sum which can be invested to provide an income). The '*Duxbury* calculation' is sometimes used as a guide to calculate capitalised maintenance needs by taking account of certain variables (such as inflation, life expectancy, income tax, capital growth and income from investments); but the court retains an overriding discretion, despite a *Duxbury* calculation.

A lump sum made in favour of a spouse is a final order which cannot be varied in variation proceedings under s.31 MCA 1973, except in exceptional circumstances (see *Westbury* v. *Sampson* [2001] EWCA Civ 4807, [2002] 1 FLR 166). Only one lump sum order can be made (the plural reference to 'lump sums' in s.23(1)(c) is merely to allow payment by instalments).

A lump sum order made in favour of a child, unlike one made in favour of a spouse, is not a final order, as the court's power to make orders for children is 'exercisable from time to time' (s.23(4)). In practice, however, lump sums in favour of children are rarely made, except in 'big money' cases.

Adjourning an application where a capital sum will become available in the future   To avoid the potential injustice caused by the finality of lump sum orders, the court can adjourn proceedings in order to do justice where there is a real possibility of capital from a specific source becoming available in the near future, for instance an inheritance (see *MT* v. *MT (Financial Provision: Lump Sum)* [1992] 1 FLR 363), or a pension. In *D* v. *D (Lump Sum Order: Adjournment of Application)* [2001] 1 FLR 633, however, Connell J said that the discretion to adjourn should be exercised rarely.

(c)   Property adjustment orders (s.24)

(i) A transfer of property order (s.24(1)(a))   This order directs a spouse to transfer specified property to the other spouse and/or to or for the benefit of a child of the family. Any property can be transferred, but the order is often used to transfer the matrimonial home. The transferee may be given a charge over the house for a fixed amount or a percentage of the value which is to be realised at a later date, or may be ordered to pay the transferor a lump sum representing the latter's share in the matrimonial home. A transfer of property is a useful way of effecting a 'clean break' (see 7.5). For example, a spouse could be ordered to transfer investments to the other spouse so that he or she can live on the income; or be ordered to transfer the matrimonial home to the other spouse with that spouse agreeing to forego any claim for maintenance.

(ii) A settlement of property order (s.24(1)(b))   This order directs a spouse to settle property for the benefit of the other spouse and/or any child of the family. Under a settlement, property is held on trust for certain persons who have an interest in the property. Settlement of property orders are rarely made. However, a settlement of property order is sometimes made to give the children a roof over their heads during their dependency but to enable the house to be transferred back to the owner once the children become independent (this order is known as a '*Mesher* order', see 7.7).

(iii) A variation of settlement (ante-nuptial or post-nuptial) order (ss.24(1)(c), (d)) This order can be made for the benefit of the parties and/or any child of the family. Such orders are rare.

(iv) Order for the sale of property (s.24A) The court can make an order for the sale of property (or proceeds of the sale of property) in which one spouse has, or both spouses have, a beneficial interest. But it can do so only if it has made a secured periodical payments, or lump sum or property adjustment order. The power to order sale is a useful enforcement mechanism where there is, or is likely to be, non-compliance with an order. For example, the court could order that property belonging to a spouse who has failed to pay a lump sum be sold and that the proceeds of sale be paid to the spouse who should have received it (s.24A(2)(a)). The court can defer sale until a specified event has occurred or until a specified period of time has expired (s.24A(4)). It can also order that property be offered for sale to a specified person or persons (s.24A(2)(b)). A third party with an interest in the property in dispute (such as a mortgagee) must be allowed to make representations to the court, and the third party's interest must be included as one of the circumstances of the case when the court performs its discretionary exercise (s.24A(6)).

Property adjustment orders and bankruptcy In the following case, which arose in the context of bankruptcy, the Court of Appeal held that a property adjustment order made following contested proceedings or by consent was made for consideration in money or in money's worth, and for that reason could not be set aside as a transaction at an undervalue under s.339 of the Insolvency Act 1986:

▶ *Hill v. Haines* **[2007] EWCA Civ 1284**

On divorce the husband was ordered to transfer the home to the wife. One month after the order for transfer became effective, a bankruptcy order was made against the former husband on his own petition. The trustees in bankruptcy applied to the county court for a declaration that the transfer of the home on divorce was a transaction at an undervalue under s.339 of the Insolvency Act 1986 and was therefore void. At first instance the district judge held that it was not a transaction at an undervalue as there was consideration for the transfer consisting of the satisfaction or partial satisfaction of the wife's claims for ancillary relief. The decision of the district judge was overturned in the Chancery Division, but the Court of Appeal unanimously allowed the wife's appeal, holding that there had been no transaction at an undervalue under s.339 of the 1986 Act. The Court of Appeal held that Parliament could not have intended that a court order of this type (one of the most commonly made in matrimonial proceedings) could be capable of automatic nullification on the suit of a trustee in bankruptcy of the husband against whom a bankruptcy order was subsequently made on his own petition. The Court of Appeal upheld the reasoning of the district judge and restored the original order.

(d) Pension orders

See 7.8.

7.4 The exercise of discretion: The section 25 factors

> ▶ **Lord Nicholls in *Miller* v. *Miller; McFarlane* v. *McFarlane* [2006] UKHL 24, [2006] 1 FLR 1186**
>
> 'The 1973 Act gives only limited guidance on how the courts should exercise their statutory powers. Primary consideration must be given to the welfare of any children of the family. The court must consider the feasibility of a 'clean break'. Beyond this the courts are largely left to get on with it for themselves. The courts are told simply that they must have regard to all the circumstances of the case.
>
> Of itself this direction leads nowhere. Implicitly the courts must exercise their powers so as to achieve an outcome which is fair between the parties. But an important aspect of fairness is that like cases should be treated alike. So, perforce, if there is to be an acceptable degree of consistency of decision from one case to the next, the courts must themselves articulate, if only in the broadest fashion, what are the applicable if unspoken principles guiding the court's approach.
>
> This is not to usurp the legislative function. Rather, it is to perform a necessary judicial function in the absence of parliamentary guidance. As Lord Cooke of Thorndon said in *White* v. *White* (2001), there is no reason to suppose that in prescribing relevant considerations the legislature had any intention of excluding the development of general judicial practice.'
>
> ▶ **Baroness Hale in *Miller* v. *Miller; McFarlane* v. *McFarlane* [2006] UKHL 24, [2006] 1 FLR 1186**
>
> 'There is much to be said for the flexibility and sensitivity of the English law of ancillary relief. It avoids the straitjacket of rigid rules which can apply harshly or unfairly in an individual case. But it should not be too flexible. It must try to achieve some consistency and predictability. This is not only to secure that so far as possible like cases are treated alike but also to enable and encourage the parties to negotiate their own solutions as quickly and cheaply as possible.'

The court in ancillary relief proceedings has wide discretionary powers. Property law principles, such as the laws of trusts, are not relevant and will not be investigated by the court except where there is a genuine third-party interest in any property.

In addition to applying the s.25 factors (see below) and considering whether to effect a clean break (see 7.5) the courts must apply the principles laid down by the House of Lords in *White* v. *White* [2001] 1 AC 596, [2000] 2 FLR 981 and *Miller* v. *Miller; McFarlane* v. *McFarlane* [2006] UKHL 24, [2006] 1 FLR 1186 (see 7.6).

The section 25 factors

When exercising its powers to make orders under Part II of the Matrimonial Causes Act 1973, and, if so, in what manner, the court must take into account the welfare of the child (s.25(1)) and a statutory list of factors (s.25(2)):

> **Section 25(1)** 'It shall be the duty of the court in deciding whether to exercise its powers, … and, if so, in what manner, to have regard to all the circumstances of the case, first consideration being given to the welfare while a minor of any child of the family who has not attained the age of eighteen.'
>
> **Section 25(2)** 'As regards the exercise of the powers of the court in relation to a party to the marriage, the court shall in particular have regard to the following matters –

(a)   The income, earning capacity, property and other financial resources which each of the parties to the marriage has or is likely to have in the foreseeable future, including in the case of earning capacity any increase in that capacity which it would in the opinion of the court be reasonable to expect a party to the marriage to take steps to acquire.
(b)   The financial needs, obligations and responsibilities which each of the parties to the marriage has or is likely to have in the foreseeable future.
(c)   The standard of living enjoyed by the family before the breakdown of marriage.
(d)   The age of each party to the marriage and the duration of the marriage.
(e)   Any physical or mental disability of either of the parties to the marriage.
(f)   The contribution which each of the parties has made or is likely in the foreseeable future to make to the welfare of the family, including any contribution by looking after the home or caring for the family.
(g)   The conduct of each of the parties, if that conduct is such that it would in the opinion of the court be inequitable to disregard it.
(h)   In the case of proceedings for divorce or nullity of marriage, the value to each of the parties to the marriage of any benefit which by reason of the dissolution or annulment of the marriage, that party will lose the chance of acquiring.'

The list of factors in s.25(2) is not arranged in any hierarchy (no one factor is more important than another); and the weight or importance attached to these factors depends upon the facts of the particular case. In practice, however, financial needs and financial resources are often particularly important. The factors in s.25(2) are not exclusive – other factors can be taken into account, as s.25(1) refers to 'all the circumstances of the case'. Cultural factors can be taken into account (see *A v. T (Ancillary Relief: Cultural Factors)* [2004] EWHC 471 (Fam), [2004] 1 FLR 977 where the spouses were Iranian Muslims bound by Sharia law, and where the High Court considered how the matter would be dealt with in Iran).

The factors in s.25(2) are as follows:

(a)   *'The income, earning capacity, property and other financial resources which each of the parties to the marriage has or is likely to have in the foreseeable future, including in the case of earning capacity any increase in that capacity which it would in the opinion of the court be reasonable to expect a party to the marriage to take steps to acquire.'*
The court, in the exercise of its discretion, can take into account a wide range of resources, such as business profits, interest on investments, insurance policies, pension rights, welfare benefits and damages for personal injury. In an appropriate case, the court may impute a notional earning capacity, or infer that unidentified resources are available from a spouse's expenditure or style of living. Future earning potential is an important consideration when the court is deciding whether to effect a clean break between the parties (see 7.5). As future financial resources must be considered, the court may postpone making an order if financial resources are likely to be available in the relatively near future, for instance a pension, an inheritance, or assets tied up in a business which are realisable at a later date.

Obligations to a new partner   The court can take into account the fact that a former spouse is living with a new partner, as this may affect the parties' financial resources and financial needs under s.25(2)(a). Thus, in *Atkinson* v. *Atkinson (No. 2)* [1996] 1 FLR 51 the wife's periodical payments were reduced when she began to cohabit with a new partner after the original order had been made. However, each case depends on its facts. In *Duxbury* v. *Duxbury* [1987] 1 FLR 7 the wife's cohabitation was ignored in calculating capitalised maintenance (her husband was a millionaire).

Inherited assets As Lord Nicholls confirmed in the House of Lords in *White* v. *White* (2000) (see 7.6), inherited assets stand on a different footing from other assets acquired during marriage, and fairness generally requires that a spouse should be allowed to keep inherited property, unless the other party's financial needs cannot otherwise be satisfied. Whether inherited assets can be invaded therefore depends on the circumstances of the case. In some cases inherited property may count for little, but in others it may be of the greatest significance. Thus, for example, in *H* v. *H (Financial Provision: Special Contribution)* [2002] 2 FLR 1021 inherited assets were quarantined from the pool of assets to be divided, but in *Norris* v. *Norris* [2002] EWHC 2996 (Fam), [2003] 1 FLR 1142 and *GW* v. *RW (Financial Provision: Departure from Equality)* [2003] 2 FLR 108 they were taken into account as being part of the pool of assets to be divided. Fairness may require that different types of inheritance be treated differently. In *P* v. *P (Inherited Property)* [2004] EWHC 1364 (Fam), [2005] 1 FLR 576 Munby J held that the bulk of the matrimonial assets (a farm which had been in the husband's family for generations) should, in the circumstances of the case, be treated differently from a case involving a pecuniary inheritance.

Each case depends on its own facts and other s.25 factors (such as the parties' needs and the length of the marriage) may result in an inheritance being counted as part of the assets to be divided on divorce. Thus in *S* v. *S* [2007] EWHC 1975 (Fam), [2008] EWCA Civ 543, for example, the wife's inherited assets were treated as part of the pool of assets to be divided because they had become amalgamated with other assets during the 20-year marriage. Baron J held that the district judge had been plainly wrong to ring-fence the wife's inherited assets, as all the assets which had come into the marriage had to be available to cover the parties' requirements. Baron J held that, as time went by in a marriage, all assets became amalgamated.

(b) *'The financial needs, obligations and responsibilities which each of the parties to the marriage has or is likely to have in the foreseeable future.'*
Financial needs can include, for example, the provision of accommodation and general living expenses. If there are children, the financial needs of the parent with whom the children are to live may be greater than those of the other parent, particularly if the primary-carer is not working. Obligations and responsibilities to a new partner or a new family may be taken into account.

It was held in *White* v. *White* (2000) (see further at 7.6) that an award can be made which exceeds a party's financial needs as the general principle which applies in ancillary relief cases is fairness without discrimination. This may be possible in 'big money' cases, but in practice most cases are still needs-based and involve courts having to make decisions where there are often insufficient assets to be distributed between the parties on divorce.

Obligations to a second family Obligations to a second family can be taken into account, depending on the facts of the case and applying all the s.25 criteria. As far as the principle of equality laid down in *White* v. *White* is concerned (see 7.6), different approaches have been taken in the case-law In *S* v. *S (Financial Provision: Departing from Equality)* [2001] 2

FLR 246 it was held that obligations to a second family could justify a departure from equality, whereas in *H-J* v. *H-J (Financial Provision: Equality)* [2002] 1 FLR 415 Coleridge J held that such an approach would normally be wrong in principle.

(c) *'The standard of living enjoyed by the family before the breakdown of marriage.'*
Although the court must take this factor into account, in practice it is often not possible for the parties to enjoy the same standard of living after divorce as they did before it, unless there are substantial assets available for distribution.

(d) *'The age of each party to the marriage and the duration of the marriage.'*
The needs and resources of a couple whose marriage has been of short duration (and possibly childless) are likely to differ from those who are divorcing after a long marriage.

The duration of the marriage will be an important consideration when the court is considering whether assets such as inheritances or investments accrued before marriage should be part of the pool of assets available for distribution on divorce. Thus, the longer the marriage the less likely the court is to categorise different types of property as 'matrimonial' or 'non-matrimonial' (see *Miller* v. *Miller* at 7.6).

However, each case depends on its facts, and other factors, in addition to the length of the marriage, will be relevant to the question of whether assets are 'matrimonial' or not. For example in *Foster* v. *Foster* [2003] EWCA Civ 565, [2003] 2 FLR 299, even though the marriage had lasted only three years, the husband and wife were awarded 39 per cent and 61 per cent of the assets respectively, taking into account the fact that the wife had contributed more income. In *GW* v. *RW (Financial Provision: Departure From Equality)* [2003] EWHC 611 (Fam), [2003] 2 FLR 108, after a 12-year marriage, the wife was awarded 40 per cent of the assets, as the facts justified a departure from equality (the husband had brought capital assets into the marriage and had a developed career, high earnings and a high earning capacity).

Pre-marital cohabitation At one time the courts were unwilling to take pre-marital cohabitation into account when calculating the duration of a marriage, because they considered that marital obligations and needs began on marriage, not before (*Foley* v. *Foley* [1981] 2 All ER 857). This approach has now changed (as social attitudes to cohabitation have changed) and the court may in the exercise of its discretion decide to take a settled and committed period of pre-marital cohabitation into account when calculating the duration of a marriage, particularly where cohabitation has seamlessly and immediately preceded the marriage (see, for example, *Co* v. *Co (Ancillary Relief: Pre-Marriage Cohabitation)* [2004] EWHC 287 (Fam), [2004] 1 FLR 1095; and *C* v. *C* [2007] EWHC 2033 (Fam), [2009] 1 FLR 8 where Moylan J took into account generally the couple's period of pre-marital cohabitation of approximately four years).

(e) *'Any physical or mental disability of either of the parties to the marriage.'*

(f) *'The contribution which each of the parties has made or is likely in the foreseeable future to make to the welfare of the family, including any contribution by looking after the home or caring for the family.'*
Under s.25(5) the court can take into account both financial and non-financial contributions to the home and caring for the family. The court will not favour the

'breadwinner' over the 'homemaker' as this would be contrary to the need for fairness and non-discrimination expounded by the House of Lords in *White* v. *White* (see 7.6). In *Lambert* v. *Lambert* [2002] EWCA Civ 1685, [2003] 1 FLR 139 Thorpe LJ said that there must be an end to the sterile suggestion that the breadwinner's contribution was more important than that of the homemaker.

(g) *'The conduct of each of the parties, if that conduct is such that it would in the opinion of the court be inequitable to disregard it.'*

Only conduct of an extreme or exceptional kind is taken into account, as to do otherwise would contradict one of the policy aims of divorce law which is not to apportion blame. In *Wachtel* v. *Wachtel* [1973] Fam 72 Lord Denning MR said that conduct must be 'obvious and gross'. The s.25 exercise is essentially a financial, not a moral, exercise. In *Miller* v. *Miller* (2006) (see 7.6) the House of Lords held that the lower court had been wrong to take into account the husband's alleged responsibility for the marriage breakdown (he had left his wife for another woman), given that it was conduct which fell far short of 'conduct which it would be inequitable to disregard' under s.25(2)(g).

As the case-law shows, only extreme types of conduct will be taken into account, such as: malicious persecution by a schizophrenic spouse (*J (HD)* v. *J (AM) (Financial Provision: Variation)* [1980] 1 WLR 124); alcoholism causing disagreeable behaviour and neglect of the home (*K* v. *K (Conduct)* [1990] 2 FLR 225); inciting a spouse's murder (*Evans* v. *Evans* [1989] 1 FLR 351); assisting a spouse's suicide (*K* v. *K (Financial Provision: Conduct)* [1988] 1 FLR 469); stabbing a spouse (*H* v. *H (Financial Provision: Conduct)* [1994] 2 FLR 801); and violently attacking the wife in the matrimonial home in front of the children (*H* v. *H (Financial Relief: Attempted Murder as Conduct)* [2005] EWHC 2911 (Fam), [2006] 1 FLR 990). An accumulation of serious misconduct, such as failing to make full and frank disclosure, dissipating matrimonial assets and abducting a child might constitute conduct for the purposes of s.25(2)(g) (as it did in *Al-Khatib* v. *Masry* [2002] EWHC 108 (Fam), [2002] 1 FLR 1053).

However, each case depends on its facts, and even when conduct is serious the court in the exercise of its discretion can discount that conduct and take other factors into account, as it did in *A* v. *A (Financial Provision: Conduct)* [1995] 1 FLR 345 where, even though the depressed and suicidal husband had assaulted his wife with a knife, which constituted conduct which it would be inequitable to disregard, other s.25 factors were taken into account.

If the court considers that the conduct is sufficiently serious to be taken into account, it does not necessarily mean that the 'guilty' party will receive nothing. In *Clark* v. *Clark* [1999] 2 FLR 498 the wife had married a husband 36 years her senior. She had refused to consummate the marriage and had induced him to buy property, most of which was transferred into her name. She relegated him to a caravan in their garden and later made him a virtual prisoner in his own home. The court considered that this was conduct which it was inequitable to disregard, but nevertheless made an order in her favour. In *H* v. *H (Financial Provision: Conduct)* [1998] 1 FLR 971, where the husband's conduct was held to be too inequitable to ignore (he had transferred money for three years into a Swiss bank account), Singer J said that the approach to be taken was not to fix a sum as a 'penalty', but to carry out an evaluation based on all the relevant factors taken in the round.

Domestic violence Unless the violence is extremely severe it will not be taken into account as conduct under s.25(2)(g). Inglis ([2003] Fam Law 181) has argued, however, that the courts should consider changing their approach and treat domestic violence as conduct which it is inequitable to disregard, as the 'message received by litigants is that most domestic violence is unimportant' and this approach is unsustainable today when there is a greater recognition of the harm caused to adults and children by domestic violence.

Non-disclosure   A failure to make full and frank disclosure (or any other misconduct in respect of the process of the case) will be taken into account, but may only affect costs (see *Tavoulareas* v. *Tavoulareas* [1998] 2 FLR 418; and *Young* v. *Young* [1998] 2 FLR 1131), but in a serious case it may be taken into account when assessing the substantive order. Depending on the circumstances, however, the court may decide to exercise its discretion and dismiss the application.

Bigamy   Although bigamy is a criminal offence and a ground for nullity under s.11 Matrimonial Causes Act 1973 (see 2.5), a party to a bigamous marriage is not necessarily barred from applying for ancillary relief, even though it is the general policy of the law not to allow a person to profit from his or her own crime. It depends on the particular circumstances of the case. Thus, in *Whiston* v. *Whiston* [1995] 2 FLR 268 a bigamist was barred from seeking ancillary relief on grounds of public policy, but in *Rampal* v. *Rampal (No. 2)* [2001] EWCA Civ 989, [2001] 2 FLR 1179 a bigamist was allowed to pursue a claim, on the basis that he had been much less culpable than the bigamist in *Whiston*. In *Ben Hashem* v. *Al Shayif* [2008] EWCH 2380 (Fam), [2009] 1 FLR 115 Munby J held that the wife was entitled to ancillary relief (and awarded her more than £7 million), even though the marriage was bigamous, as both parties were aware that the husband was married to another woman and the impact of the bigamy was marginal in that neither party had been deceived as to the status of the marriage.

(h)   *'In the case of proceedings for divorce or nullity of marriage, the value to each of the parties to the marriage of any benefit which by reason of the dissolution or annulment of the marriage, that party will lose the chance of acquiring.'*
On divorce a spouse may lose certain property rights and interests, such as the benefit of a pension, the surrender value of an insurance policy, future business profits, or the right to succeed to the other spouse's estate. The court can take these and other lost benefits into account. It might, for example, decide to increase an order for financial provision to compensate for the loss of future benefits, or make a deferred lump sum order, or in an exceptional case adjourn proceedings. Pensions on divorce are governed by special rules (see 7.5).

7.5   The 'clean break'

A major policy aim of the law governing ancillary relief on divorce is that a divorced spouse cannot expect a 'meal ticket' for life. For this reason the court is required to determine cases in such a way as to effect, where possible, a 'clean break' between the parties. The 'clean break' provisions were inserted into Part II of the Matrimonial Causes Act 1973 by Part II of the Matrimonial and Family Proceedings Act 1984 after the Law Commission in its *Report on the Financial Consequences of Divorce* (Law Com No. 112) had recommended that greater weight should be given to the possibility of spouses becoming financially self-sufficient on divorce. The clean break was introduced to encourage the parties to put the past behind them and to begin a new life which would not be overshadowed by the relationship which had broken down (*per* Lord Scarman in *Minton v. Minton* [1979] AC 593).

> ▶ **Baroness Hale in *Miller* v. *Miller; McFarlane* v. *McFarlane* [2006] UKHL 24, [2006] 1 FLR 1186**
>
> 'Section 25A is a powerful encouragement towards securing the court's objective by way of lump sum and capital adjustment (which now includes pension sharing) rather than by continuing periodical payments. This is good practical sense. Periodical payments are a continuing source of stress for both parties. They are also insecure. With the best will in the world, the paying party may fall on hard times and be unable to keep up with them. Nor is the best will in the world always evident between formerly married people. It is also the logical consequence of the retreat from the principle of the life-long obligation. Independent finances and self-sufficiency are the aims. Nevertheless, section 25A does not tell us what the outcome of the exercise required by section 25 should be. It is mainly directed at how that outcome should be put into effect.'

The court encourages the parties to go their separate ways after divorce, provided it is fair in the circumstances. Thus, under s.25A(1), when exercising its powers to make finance and property orders in favour of a spouse, the court must consider 'whether it would be appropriate so to exercise those powers that the financial obligations of each party towards the other will be terminated as soon after' the divorce as the court 'considers just and reasonable'. However, there is no presumption that a clean break must be ordered. Each case depends on its own facts. The court's duty to consider whether to effect a clean break, however, is subject to the overarching objective of fairness laid down by the House of Lords in *White* v. *White* (see 7.6).

The court can effect a clean break between the parties in an application for periodical payments in the following ways:

- ▶ by dismissing the application;
- ▶ by dismissing the application with a direction that the applicant shall not make any further application (s.25A(3));
- ▶ by making a limited term periodical payments order (s.25A(2));
- ▶ by making a limited term periodical payments order with a direction that no application can be made in variation proceedings for an extension of that term (s.28(1A));
- ▶ by ordering a lump sum representing capitalised periodical payments as a means of discharging a party's liability to make further periodical payments (ss.31(7A) and (7B)).

The court also has a duty to consider a clean break in s.31 variation proceedings, when the court can make a limited term order 'to enable the party in whose favour the order was made to adjust without undue hardship to the termination of those payments' (s.31(7)).

Depending on the circumstances, the court may decide to make a nominal periodical payments order (such as for £10 per annum), so that there is an order in place which can be varied if circumstances change in the future. It can do this even though it seems to be contrary to the aim of the clean break principle (see *Whiting* v. *Whiting* [1988] 1 WLR 565 where a nominal order was upheld by the Court of Appeal even though the wife had qualified as a teacher and had a steady job).

Despite the court's duty to consider a clean break, it may be unwilling to effect one where it makes unrealistic expectations of a spouse's capacity for economic independence (see *M* v. *M (Financial Provision)* [1987] 2 FLR 1 where the wife was aged 47 and had genuinely failed to find employment and had lost the chance of a secure future which her husband's pension would have provided). In cases where there is ill-health, the court may also be unwilling to order a clean break (see *Purba* v. *Purba* [2000] 1 FLR 444).

7.6 The discretionary exercise – *White* v. *White* and *Miller* v. *Miller*

There have been two important cases heard by the House of Lords on the question of how the courts should exercise their discretion in ancillary relief cases on divorce. The first was *White* v. *White* [2001] 1 AC 596, [2000] 2 FLR 981. The second was *Miller* v. *Miller; McFarlane* v. *McFarlane* [2006] UKHL 24, [2006] 1 FLR 1186. Both cases were 'big money' cases, but the principles laid down in them apply to all ancillary relief cases.

(a) *White* v. *White* (2000)

Before the important decision of the House of Lords in *White* v. *White* [2001] 1 AC 596, [2000] 2 FLR 981 the Court of Appeal had adopted a 'reasonable requirements' approach in 'big money' cases, whereby the main breadwinner (usually the husband) would be ordered to pay an amount which was sufficient to satisfy the other spouse's reasonable requirements even though he could afford to pay more. This approach resulted in many wives receiving a substantially smaller proportion of the matrimonial assets than their husband.

In the late 1990s, however, the Court of Appeal began to question whether the 'reasonable requirements' approach in 'big money' cases was the proper approach as it might be causing injustice. Thus, in *Dart* v. *Dart* [1996] 2 FLR 286, for example, where the wife was awarded a mere £4 million of her husband's £400 million fortune, Butler-Sloss LJ wondered whether the courts might have given too much weight to reasonable requirements over the other s.25 criteria. But the Court of Appeal held that any challenge to the reasonable requirements approach should be made by Parliament, not the courts.

The reasonable requirements approach was also reinforced by the courts' endorsement of the '*Duxbury* formula' (which was based on calculating income needs) and by the courts' acceptance of the 'millionaire's defence', whereby a wealthy spouse (usually the husband) was not obliged to disclose details of property and financial assets if there was sufficient money available to satisfy the other spouse's reasonable needs (see *Thyssen-Bornemisza* v. *Thyssen-Bornemisza (No. 2)* [1985] FLR 1069). Although the reasonable requirements approach was considered to be unsatisfactory – because it discriminated against wives, and prioritised needs when there was no hierarchy in the list of s.25 factors (see 7.4) – it was not until the decision of the House of Lords in *White* v. *White* that the reasonable needs or reasonable requirements approach was overturned.

▶ *White* v. *White* [2001] 1 AC 596, [2000] 2 FLR 981

After 33 years of marriage the wife obtained a divorce and sought enough capital to set herself up independently in farming, arguing that her equal contribution to the parties' farming business throughout their long marriage justified her claim to an equal share of the assets. Her husband argued that she should only be given enough to satisfy her reasonable needs or requirements, applying the approach adopted in earlier decisions of the Court of Appeal. Their overall assets were assessed at approximately £4.6 million. They had three adult children who were independent.

At first instance, the judge adopted a reasonable needs approach and, on the basis that it was impractical for the wife to continue farming, awarded her one-fifth of their joint assets and ordered that the farming business remain with the husband. The Court of Appeal allowed the wife's appeal and increased her award to £1.5 million. Butler-Sloss LJ said that cases where a wife was an equal business partner were in a wholly different category from other 'big money' cases such as *Dart* v. *Dart* (see above) and *Conran* v. *Conran* [1997] 2 FLR 615 where the origin of the wealth was clearly on one side and the emphasis was rightly on contribution, not entitlement. The Court of Appeal also held that it was not the function of the judge to criticise the wife's plans to carry on farming. Both parties appealed to the House of Lords.

The House of Lords held, dismissing the appeals, that, although the judge had been mistaken in regarding reasonable requirements as the determinant factor, the award made by the Court of Appeal was within the ambit of reasonable discretion. The House of Lords, with Lord Nicholls giving the leading opinion, laid down the following statements of principle:

▶ The objective implicit in s.25 is to achieve a fair outcome in financial arrangements on divorce, giving first consideration to the welfare of any children.
▶ Fairness requires the court to take into account all the circumstances of the case. In seeking to achieve a fair outcome, there is no place for discrimination between husband and wife in their respective roles. Fairness requires that their division of labour should not prejudice or advantage either party when considering their contributions to the welfare of the family under s.25(2)(f). If each in their different spheres contributed equally to the family, then in principle it matters not who earned the money and built up the assets. There should be no bias in favour of the money-earner as against the homemaker and the child-carer.
▶ Before making an order for division of assets, a judge should check his tentative views against the yardstick of equality of division. As a general rule, equality should be departed from only if, and to the extent that, there is good reason for doing so. The need to consider and articulate reasons for doing so will help the parties and the court to focus on the need to ensure the absence of discrimination.
▶ Section 25(2) does not rank the matters listed therein in any hierarchy and other matters may also be important. Financial need is only one of the several factors to be taken into account in determining a fair outcome. When considering s.25(2)(b), confusion will be avoided by courts ceasing to employ the expression 'reasonable requirements' and returning to the statutory language of 'needs', which preserves the necessary degree of flexibility.

Lord Nicholls, who laid down the propositions above, dismissed, however, the idea that there should be a presumption of equality, as this would be an impermissible judicial gloss on s.25, and the introduction of such a presumption was a matter for Parliament.

In *White* the 'reasonable requirements' approach was therefore rejected and replaced by 'a yardstick of equality of division' in order to ensure fairness and abolish discrimination. *White* recognised that marriage is a partnership of equals and that the homemaker should not be discriminated as against the breadwinner. Discrimination was the antithesis of fairness. This was a principle of universal application which was to be applied to all cases, whether 'big money' ones or not. In *Miller* v. *Miller* (see p. 171, below), however, Lord Nicholls, who gave the leading opinion in *White*, said that the yardstick of equality was 'to be applied as an aid, not a rule'.

Reaction to White   The decision in *White* provoked considerable comment from lawyers and academics. Duckworth and Hodson (2001) thought that the decision would increase the impetus for recognising formal agreements between spouses, especially pre-marital contracts. Eekelaar ([2001] Fam Law 30) thought that the equality of sharing approach might deter people from marrying. But he was also of the view that the decision in *White* was no great advance in the law because the House of Lords had provided no suggestions as to what sorts of reasons might justify departing from equality. Cretney ([2001] Fam Law 3) thought that the House of Lords had gone too far. He thought it might have been a 'trifle rash' in overturning the settled practice of the courts, particularly in a case which was highly untypical of other 'big money' cases (both parties were in business together). He also questioned whether such a change of approach should have been decided by the House of Lords at all, but instead should have been a matter for Parliament. Cretney also stated ([2003] CFLQ 303) that the preference in *White* for equal division 'was expressed in such a muted and – let us use plain English – confused way that it became difficult to predict how cases would be decided'. He said that the 'result must have been … hugely to increase the expense, uncertainty and consequent destructive emotional stress of resolving the consequences of marriage breakdown'. In *Charman* v. *Charman (No. 4)* [2007] EWCA Civ 503, [2007] 1 FLR 1246 (see p. 173) Sir Mark Potter P said that the decision in *White* had undoubtedly not resolved 'the problems faced by practitioners in advising clients or by clients in deciding upon what terms to compromise'.

Another criticism that might be made is that, although the House of Lords in *White* (and in *Piglowska* v. *Piglowska* [1999] 1 WLR 1360, [1999] 2 FLR 763) had emphasised the importance of applying the statute (particularly the s.25 factors), *White* introduced a yardstick of equality which had no basis in the statute. Furthermore, as the non-discrimination principle laid down in *White* is derived from s.25(2)(f) of the statutory guidelines, the House of Lords appeared to have elevated that factor, when it had stressed in *Piglowska* v. *Piglowski* that there was no hierarchy in the s.25 factors. Although the House of Lords in *White* said that no gloss must be put on needs in s.25 (as to whether they are reasonable or not), it imposed fairness and equality as glosses on the s.25 factors. The relationship between s.25 and the principles enunciated in *White* is therefore left rather unclear. Perhaps any 'glosses' on s.25 would have been better left to Parliament. It is also unsatisfactory that the principles propounded by Lord Nicholls in *White* (equality, fairness and discrimination) arose in an atypical ancillary relief case, one in which both parties to the marriage were involved as partners in a family business.

The case-law after White v. White: *special contribution*   After *White* v. *White* the courts began to order more equal divisions of matrimonial assets, at least in 'big money' cases, as *White* had removed the requirement laid down in the earlier case-law that awards should be limited to reasonable needs. As a result, husbands began to argue that their special business contribution justified a departure from the yardstick of equality laid down in *White*. In other words, they began to argue that, as they had been responsible for the accumulation of matrimonial assets, they were entitled to more than half of those assets on divorce. This argument was sometimes successful. Thus, in *Cowan* v. *Cowan* [2001] EWCA Civ 679, [2001] 2 FLR 192 the wife (after a long marriage) was awarded only a 38 per cent share of the assets (worth over £11 million) on the basis that equal division would not be fair in the circumstances, in particular because of the husband's special business talent and the great wealth which he had thereby produced. The Court of Appeal so held even though its approach seemed to contradict the non-discrimination principle laid down in *White*.

After *Cowan* v. *Cowan* courts began to take into account special contributions by husbands as a justification for departing from equality, but this began to create difficulties. Not only did it lead to detailed evidence of contribution being put forward – which increased the length and cost of litigation and was contrary to the policy objective of encouraging agreement – but the courts began to adopt different approaches to contribution. Some judges accepted special contribution as a justification for departing from equality of division of matrimonial assets, but others began to express concerns about such an approach. Coleridge J, in particular, expressed concern. In *H-J* v. *H-J (Financial Provision: Equality)* [2002] 1 FLR 415 Coleridge J awarded the wife 50 per cent of the assets on the basis that there was nothing special about the husband's contributions and that to hold otherwise would drive a wedge into the heart of the principles underlying *White*. In *G* v. *G (Financial Provision: Equal Division)* [2002] EWHC 1339 (Fam), [2002] 2 FLR 1143 Coleridge J expressed disquiet about the growing forensic practice of routinely arguing special contribution in 'big money' cases, which, he said, invited recrimination and was not conducive to settlement.

The difficulties created by *Cowan* (of allowing arguments based on special contribution to justify a departure from equality) were eventually addressed by the Court of Appeal in the following case, where it endeavoured to confine the doctrine of exceptional or special contribution, endorsed by the Court of Appeal in *Cowan*, within narrow bounds. The Court of Appeal recognised that domestic contribution is just as special as business contribution.

▶ *Lambert* v. *Lambert* [2002] EWCA Civ 1685, [2003] 1 FLR 139

The parties had been married for 23 years. Their matrimonial assets were worth £20.2 million, and two years after their separation the sale of shares in the husband's business had produced more than £26 million. The husband argued that he had made an exceptional business contribution in generating the family fortune. His wife claimed 50 per cent of the assets arguing that she had been the principal homemaker and parent during the marriage, and that she had played a significant role in the husband's business. Connell J, applying *Cowan* (see above), awarded her 37.5 per cent of the assets, on the basis that her contribution had been modest, in fact merely 'ornamental' whereas the husband's contribution to the welfare of the family, by creating such a substantial fortune, had been 'really special' or 'exceptional'. The wife appealed, arguing *inter alia* that the judge had fallen into the trap of gender discrimination by concluding that the husband's contribution as a money maker was special and therefore greater than her contribution, and that this justified a departure from equality. She argued, on the other hand, that there had been insufficient consideration of her needs. The husband argued that the Court of Appeal should be slow to interfere with the exercise of judicial discretion.

The Court of Appeal allowed the wife's appeal and awarded her 50 per cent of the assets. Thorpe LJ said that there 'must be an end to the sterile assertion that the breadwinner's contribution weighs heavier than the homemaker's'. However, Thorpe LJ said that he did not consider that the decision of Coleridge J in *H-J* v. *H-J* (see above) had created a presumption of equality. He said that it was possible for the court to order unequal division, even where the parties' contributions had been equal, because other s.25(2) factors might prevail and because of the overarching need to achieve fairness.

THORPE LJ: '[I]f the decision of this court in *Cowan* has indeed opened what Coleridge J described as a forensic Pandora's box, then it is important that we should endeavour to close and lock the lid. ... However, for the present, given the infinite variety of fact and circumstance, I propose to mark time on a cautious acknowledgement that special contributions remain a legitimate possibility but only in exceptional circumstances.'

After *Lambert* the courts took a variety of approaches to the division of matrimonial assets. Thus, for example, in *Norris* v. *Norris* [2002] EWHC 2996 (Fam), [2003] 1 FLR 1142 the wife claimed more than half the assets on the basis that she had made an exceptional contribution (primary carer of the child, domestic contribution and financial contribution from her inherited wealth), but Bennett J found to the contrary, applying *Lambert*. In *L* v. *L (Financial Provision: Contributions)* [2002] FLR 642 the wife claimed she had played a pivotal role in the success of the business, but Connell J found to the contrary and awarded her only 37 per cent of the matrimonial assets because of her husband's special contribution. In *Parra* v. *Parra* [2002] EWCA Civ 1886, [2003] 1 FLR 942 the wife was awarded 54 per cent of the assets in the special circumstances of the case (they were joint owners of a business and the matrimonial home had been bought by their joint efforts). The Court of Appeal held that the parties had effectively opted for a regime of community of property. Thorpe LJ stated that the outcome of ancillary relief cases depended on the exercise of judgment using a broad-brush approach which obviated the need to investigate minute detail and findings on minor issues in dispute. He suggested that the introduction of a 'no order' principle into the s.25 statutory guidelines (like that in s.1(5) of the Children Act 1989) might contribute to the elimination of unnecessary litigation.

(b) *Miller v. Miller; McFarlane v. McFarlane (2006)*

In *Miller* v. *Miller* (heard with *McFarlane* v. *McFarlane*) the House of Lords had the opportunity once again to consider 'the most intractable of problems: how to achieve fairness in the division of property following a divorce' (*per* Lord Nicholls in *Miller*), but this time in the light of the principles it had laid down in *White* v. *White* (above). It also had the opportunity (in *McFarlane*) to consider for the first time whether the principles in *White* should apply to the power of the court to order periodical payments on divorce. In *Miller* the House of Lords also made important statements about conduct and special contribution.

In *Miller* the wife argued that her husband's conduct in ending the marriage should cancel out his argument that the short duration of the marriage should reduce her entitlement to ancillary relief.

▶ *Miller v. Miller; McFarlane v. McFarlane* [2006] UKHL 24, [2006] 1 FLR 1186

In the *Miller* appeal the husband (aged 41) and wife (aged 36) had been married for less than three years, and had no children. At the time of the marriage the husband was an exceptionally successful businessman earning about £1 million a year, and the wife earned £85,000 a year. The matrimonial home was purchased by the husband for £1.8 million and he subsequently bought a second property in joint names in the South of France. During the marriage the husband acquired shares in a new firm which subsequently proved to be extremely valuable. The wife gave up work to concentrate on furnishing their two homes. The husband left his wife for another woman, whom he subsequently married. Singer J in the High Court held that the award should not be limited to putting the wife 'back on her feet', but should recognise that the husband had, by marriage, despite its short duration, given her a reasonable and legitimate expectation that she would be able to leave the marriage significantly better off in terms of accommodation and spendable income than when she had entered it. Singer J therefore ordered the husband to transfer the matrimonial home (worth £2.3 million) to his wife and to pay her a lump sum of £2.7 million. The husband appealed to the Court of Appeal, which held, dismissing the appeal, that the judge had been entitled to take into account the husband's responsibility for the breakdown of the marriage and the wife's legitimate expectation of a higher standard of living. The husband appealed to the House of Lords.

The House of Lords, dismissing the husband's appeal and applying the principles in *White* (see p. 168, above), held *inter alia* that:

In ancillary relief cases the redistribution of resources from one party to the other following divorce was justified on the basis of the following three principles:

▶ the needs (generously interpreted) generated by the relationship between the parties;
▶ compensation for relationship-generated disadvantage; and
▶ the sharing of the fruits of the matrimonial partnership.

These principles, each of which looked at factors linked to the parties' relationship, rather than to extrinsic unrelated factors, could guide a court in making an award. Any, or all of them, might justify redistribution of resources, but the court must be careful to avoid double counting. Which of the three would be considered first depended on the circumstances of the case. In general it could be assumed that the marital partnership did not stay alive for the purpose of sharing future resources unless this was justified by needs and compensation. The ultimate object was to give each party an equal start on the road to independent living.

The House of Lords held that, in the circumstances of the case, the needs generated by the relationship were comparatively small, as was the need for compensation, but the wife was entitled to some share of the assets, including the considerable increase in the husband's wealth during the marriage. Had the yardstick of equality been applied to all the assets which had accrued during the marriage, the wife would have obtained more. But here there were reasons to depart from the yardstick of equality, either on the basis that the substantial growth was attributable to contacts and capacities that the husband brought to the marriage, or on the basis that the assets were business assets generated solely by the husband during a short marriage.

The House of Lords also considered: the role of conduct in ancillary relief cases; the role of special contribution; the distinction between matrimonial and non-matrimonial property; and whether periodical payment can be made to afford compensation as well as to meet financial needs (see further below).

Thus in *Miller* the House of Lords held that the following three principles should be applied by the courts when deciding how to distribute resources from one party to the other in ancillary relief cases: needs (generously interpreted); compensation; and sharing.

(According to Deech [2009] Fam Law 1140, Mr Miller is taking the Government to the European Court of Human Rights on the ground that the divorce laws in England and Wales are so uncertain that they infringed his human rights).

In the following case, heard after *Miller* v. *Miller*, the Court of Appeal considered and applied the principles laid down in *White* and *Miller*. It dealt, in particular, with the issue of special contribution (see pp. 169–171), but also considered the *White* yardstick of equality or, what was described in *Miller*, as the equal sharing principle.

> ▶ *Charman* v. *Charman (No. 4)* [2007] EWCA Civ 503, [2007] 1 FLR 1246
>
> The parties (both aged 54) had been married for almost 28 years. Before the birth of their first child, the wife had given up work to look after their two children (now adult). Their very substantial assets had been generated solely during the marriage as a result of the husband working in the insurance industry. The assets amounted to about £131 million, and there was a separate trust for the children worth at least £30 million. It also included a trust set up by the husband which held £68 million. The wife conceded that the husband had made a special contribution in the generation of the fortune and sought 45 per cent of the matrimonial assets. The husband offered her £20 million. At first instance Coleridge J awarded her £48 million, representing 36.5 per cent of the assets, basing his departure from equality both on special contribution by the husband and on the greater risks inherent in the assets remaining with the husband.
>
> The husband appealed to the Court of Appeal arguing, *inter alia*, that Coleridge J had made insufficient allowance for his special contribution which merited an increased share. He also argued that the methodology adopted was flawed as Coleridge J had incorrectly started with a premise of equality and then factored in the special contribution as a discount, instead of starting with the s.25 exercise and then considering whether there should be a discount for his special contribution. He also argued that the offshore trusts should not have been treated as his financial resources as they were intended for the benefit of future generations.
>
> The Court of Appeal, led by Sir Mark Potter, President of the Family Division, dismissed the appeal; and the husband's application for leave to appeal to the House of Lords was refused. The Court of Appeal held that:
>
> ▶ Special contribution has survived *Miller/McFarlane* but the bar is set very high. Special contribution can include non-financial contributions, although it has not tended to do so in practice.
> ▶ The section 25 criteria 'rule the day'; and the three strands of need (generously interpreted), compensation and sharing are actually collected from s.25.
> ▶ The *White* 'yardstick of equality' has developed into the 'equal sharing principle' or 'the sharing entitlement'. The equal sharing principle is no longer postponed to the end of the statutory exercise. Thus, the property should be shared equally unless there is good reason to do otherwise. Departure is not from the principle but takes part within the principle. The principle of equal sharing, in general, applies to all the parties' property, but to the extent that it is non-matrimonial property, there is a better reason to depart from equality.
> ▶ Need (generously interpreted), compensation and sharing must be applied taking into account the size and nature of all the resources.
> ▶ Need requires a consideration of: the financial needs, obligations and responsibilities of the parties; the standard of living enjoyed by the family; the age of each party; and of any physical or mental disability of either party.
> ▶ Compensation relates to prospective financial disadvantage which one party to the marriage faces as a result of decisions which the parties took for the benefit of the family during the marriage (for example, in sacrificing or not pursuing a career). It can also refer to a disadvantage arising from the termination of the marriage (for example, loss of pension rights).

> ▶ Sharing is dictated by reference to the contributions of each party to the welfare of the family. Where appropriate, conduct can be taken into account.
> ▶ If there is a conflict between the distributive principles then this must be resolved by deciding what is fair.

A yardstick of equality or a principle of equal sharing? In *White* v. *White* the House of Lords introduced the idea of a 'yardstick of equality', but in *Miller* the term 'yardstick of equality' was referred to as 'the equal sharing principle' and to 'sharing entitlement' which, as Sir Mark Potter P in *Charman* v. *Charman (No 4)* (above) recognised, created more than a yardstick for use as a check. In *White* the House of Lords held that the judge must conduct the s.25 exercise and then test his or her tentative view against the yardstick of equality; but in *Miller* the House of Lords treated the yardstick of equality as 'the equal sharing principle' and appeared to adopt an approach where the starting point is equality of sharing rather than equality being a yardstick to check a tentative calculation once it has been made. In other words, *Miller* seemed to create a presumption of equal sharing. Thus, the two approaches (in *White* and *Miller*) appear to be quite different; and could produce significantly different results.

In cases after *Charman (No. 4)* (above) the approach of the courts was that the *Miller* sharing principle should be determined first and the outcome checked against the parties' needs. In other words, property should be shared equally unless there was good reason to the contrary. However, in the following case in which Hughes and Wall LJJ gave the leading judgments, and with whom Sir Mark Potter P concurred, the Court of Appeal re-introduced the yardstick of equality approach (adopted in *White*) as a cross-check to the court's fair and non-discriminatory approach, thereby rejecting the idea that there was an overriding principle of equality. The Court of Appeal held that there was no rule that equal division was the starting point; but that the starting point was the financial position of the parties and s.25 MCA 1973 (see 7.4).

> ▶ *B* v. *B (Ancillary Relief)* **[2008] EWCA Civ 284, [2008] 2 FLR 1627**
>
> The spouses had cohabited for 3 years and were married for a further 15. The wife purchased the matrimonial home from her inherited assets, and also a car wash business. The district judge held that there was no reason to depart from equality; and so the wife appealed to the Court of Appeal.
>
> The Court of Appeal, allowing her appeal, and exercising the discretion afresh, held that, in the unusual circumstances of the case, to divide the assets equally did not lead to a fair result.
>
> The Court of Appeal said that there was no rule that equal division was the starting point in ancillary relief cases; on the contrary, the starting point was the financial position of the parties and s.25 MCA 1973. In all cases the objective was fairness. The yardstick of equality was to be applied to every outcome, and departed from only if and to the extent that there was a good reason for doing so. One reason for departing from equality was where the assets were an inheritance.

In *B* v. *B* the Court of Appeal said that the application of the yardstick of equality is to underline the importance of not treating financial contributions differently from other contributions, and to underline the essential fairness of equal division in many cases of shared matrimonial life. It said that there would often be good reason to depart from the yardstick of equal division. The commonest reason for doing so, it said, was where there was need (especially housing need where children were to be provided for) and a disparity of future financial resources, especially earning capacity. In *B* v. *B* the reason for departing from equality was the fact that the assets were a product, not of the spouses' efforts, but of one spouse's inheritance.

B v. *B* therefore indicates that the yardstick of equal division is *not* a sharing principle, but a tool to be used as a check at the *end* of the s.25 exercise, rather than as a principle of sharing operating within the s.25 discretionary exercise. These fine and difficult distinctions (as to whether or not equal sharing is a yardstick to check the results of the discretionary exercise or a presumption which governs the discretionary exercise) have muddied, rather than clarified, the law; and, as a result, have made it more difficult for lawyers to advise their clients. Reaction to the needs, sharing and compensation 'formula' has also not been positive (see further at p. 201 below). As a result, there have been calls for reform of the law (see 7.14).

(c) How the court conducts the discretionary exercise after *White* and *Miller*

After the decisions of the House of Lords in *White* v. *White* (see p. 168) and *Miller* v. *Miller* (see p. 172), the court in ancillary relief proceedings must conduct the s.25 exercise, but also exercise its discretion by taking into account the principle of fairness without discrimination (laid down in *White*) and the 'strands' of needs (generously construed), compensation and sharing (laid down in *Miller*). It must then test its tentative conclusions against the 'yardstick of equality' (laid down in *White*).

The trend in the case-law following *White* and *Miller* has been to emphasise the wide discretion of the courts and their duty to apply the s.25 factors in order to achieve a fair result. The following propositions can be extracted from the case-law following *White* and *Miller*:

- **The section 25 factors prevail** The courts post-*Miller* have been keen to emphasise that the three 'strands' (of needs, compensation and sharing) have not supplanted the requirement that courts must apply the factors in s.25 of the MCA 1973. Thus, for example, in *H* v. *H* [2008] EWHC 935 (Fam), [2008] 2 FLR 2092 Moylan J said that the pivotal factor in every ancillary relief case is to ensure that the order is fair and for all the relevant factors in s.25 to be considered. Only afterwards, would there be a consideration of needs, compensation and sharing, if these are relevant at all to the facts of the case.
- **Special contribution** This can be taken into account as a reason for departing from equality but only in exceptional circumstances, for otherwise the principles of fairness and non-discrimination may be jeopardised. In *Miller* the House of Lords approved the words of Thorpe LJ in *Lambert* (see p. 170 above), who had acknowledged that 'special contribution remains a legitimate possibility but only in exceptional circumstances'. Even where there is evidence of special contribution, departing from equality must nevertheless be kept within narrow bounds. In *Miller* the House of Lords held that the question of contribution should be approached in much the same way as conduct. In other words, it should be regarded as a factor leading to a

departure from equality of division only in wholly exceptional cases when it would be inequitable to disregard it. In *Charman* v. *Charman (No. 4)* (2007) (see p. 173 above) the Court of Appeal (with Sir Mark Potter P giving the leading judgment) held that special contribution had survived *Miller* but that the bar is set very high; and that 'special contribution' could include not just financial, but non-financial, contributions.

▷ *The courts should adopt a flexible, not formulaic, approach* The courts have emphasised that a flexible, not formulaic, approach should be adopted in ancillary relief cases in order to do what is fair in the circumstances (see, for example, *C* v. *C* [2007] EWHC 2033 (Fam), [2009] 1 FLR 8).

▷ *The three strands of needs, sharing and compensation are not to be elevated into separate 'heads of claim'* In *CR* v. *CR* [2007] EWHC 3206 (Fam), [2008] 1 FLR 323 Bodey J said that it was important that the three 'strands' should not become elevated into separate 'heads of claim' or 'loss' independent of the MCA 1973, for, if such an approach were to gain a momentum, there would be a real danger of double-counting, against which the House of Lords in *Miller* had warned (see also Coleridge J in *RP* v. *RP* [2006] EWHC 3409 (Fam), [2007] 1 FLR 2105).

▷ *What constitutes matrimonial property and valuations of matrimonial property must be viewed broadly* In *CR* v. *CR* (above) Bodey J held that, although matrimonial property must now, post *Miller*, be identified, the court must strive to take as broad a view as possible of what constitutes matrimonial property. In *H* v. *H* [2008] EWHC 935 (Fam), [2008] 2 FLR 2092 Moylan J said that, in approaching valuation issues in respect of matrimonial property, the court must avoid over-artificial constructs of marital and non-marital property which could lead to an unduly formulaic approach. The valuation exercise was an art, not a science. The court was not engaged in a detailed accounting exercise, but in a broad analysis in the exercise of its jurisdiction under the 1973 Act. The purpose of valuations was to assist the court in testing the fairness of the proposed outcome, not to ensure mathematical/accounting accuracy.

▷ *Compensation should not be treated separately from the strands of needs and sharing; and is a feature of the concept of fairness, rather than a separate head of claim* In *RP* v. *RP* [2006] EWHC 3409 (Fam), [2007] 1 FLR 2105 Coleridge J warned against the introduction of an approach post-*Miller* and *White* which separated out and quantified the element of compensation, rather than treating it as one of the strands in the overall requirement of fairness in the assessment of the parties' joint contribution to the marriage. Coleridge J was of the view that compensation might be taking on too significant a role; and he doubted whether it was necessary to seek to distinguish the compensation element of a division. The three distributive principles were not akin to heads of claim in a personal injury claim. He felt that it was unnecessary to focus too heavily on compensation as it was not a new concept and it was generally accepted that, where a wife had given up work to look after the children, then both parties should be entitled to a full share of the fruits of their combined and equal contribution. Coleridge J's warning was endorsed by Sir Mark Potter, President of the Family Division, in *VB* v. *JP* [2008] EWHC 112 (Fam), [2008] 1 FLR 742 where he laid down guidance as to the approach the courts should take in cases where there was a claim for compensation for relationship-generated disadvantage. Sir Mark Potter P said that compensation was to be regarded as a feature of the concept of fairness rather than as a head of claim in its own right.

- *Compensation may not always be a factor*   Compensation may not necessarily be a factor to be considered (for example, where there is not enough money available to compensate the other party). In *Miller/McFarlane* the House of Lords described Mrs McFarlane's case as a 'paradigm case' for an award of compensation. In many cases compensation is unlikely to be a relevant factor; and may not be relevant even in a 'big money' case (as it was held not to be in *McCartney* v. *Mills McCartney* (see below).

- *Sometimes only one strand may apply*   In the following case it was held that needs (generously interpreted), not compensation and sharing, was the only relevant strand that applied in the circumstances of the case:

▶ *McCartney* v. *Mills McCartney* [2008] EWHC 401 (Fam), [2008] 1 FLR 1508

The parties had separated after less than four years of marriage; and the vast bulk of the husband's enormous wealth had been made before they had met. The wife (who had a modest career in modelling and public speaking) sought a settlement of £125 million, but was prepared to accept £50 million. The parties had one child. The wife claimed she was entitled to compensation for the loss of her career opportunity and also argued that the husband's conduct should be taken into account.

Bennett J ordered the husband to pay the wife a lump sum of £16.5 million, with periodical payments for the child of £35,000 per annum plus expenses for a nanny of up to £30,000 per annum and school fees. He held that the compensation principle was not in any way engaged (as the wife had exaggerated her case). Fairness required that the wife's needs (generously interpreted) were the dominant factor under the s.25 exercise. Any other way of looking at the case would be manifestly unfair. The sharing principle did not apply as the marriage had been short and the husband's wealth had been accumulated before they had met (unlike in Mrs Miller's case in *Miller* v. *Miller* where the husband's shares had grown very substantially in value during the marriage).

(d)   Matrimonial and non-matrimonial property and short and long marriages

In exercising their discretion in ancillary relief cases the courts may sometimes be required (particularly in 'big money' cases) to consider whether or not to ring-fence certain assets from the pool of assets and treat them as non-matrimonial assets. Depending on the facts of the case, property acquired before marriage and inheritances and gifts received during marriage may be deemed not to be part of the pool of assets to be divided by the court on divorce. The length of the marriage will be an important factor, as property (such as an inheritance owned by one of the spouses) may become part of the pool of assets to be distributed at the end of a long marriage, but not at the end of a short one (unless the parties' needs require those assets to be treated as such). However, in *Miller* v. *Miller* there were conflicting opinions about matrimonial and non-matrimonial property.

In the following case the husband argued that a large proportion, if not most, of his fortune had been acquired prior to the marriage (of 17 years). It is not a 'leading' case but it provides an example of how the courts approach a 'big money' case where one party argues that there are 'non-matrimonial' assets.

▶ *C v. C* [2007] EWHC 2033 (Fam), [2009] 1 FLR 8

The 17-year marriage was preceded by a relationship of approximately 4 years. In ancillary relief proceedings the wife sought half the assets (valued at £22 million), arguing that the bulk of those assets had been built up during their relationship. The husband, a property developer, argued that the wife's entitlement should be limited to her needs (generously construed), on the basis that a large proportion, if not most, of his fortune had been acquired prior to their relationship.

Moylan J, awarding the wife 40 per cent of the assets, held that:

▶ It was not the intention of the House of Lords in *Miller* v. *Miller*; *McFarlane* v. *McFarlane* (see p. 172 above) that the parties, after a long marriage, should have to conduct a financial account of the sources of family wealth. It was not a requirement that the court should identify matrimonial and non-matrimonial property. A formulaic approach should be resisted, as potentially productive of injustice. A flexible approach was required, to ensure that the court's focus remained on achieving a result which was fair. The correct approach was to consider the s.25 factors and then to consider the principles of needs and sharing (neither party having raised the issue of compensation).

▶ Parties were not to be encouraged to expect courts, many years later, to enter into an extensive investigation of their pre-marital relationship. In this case, taking a broad assessment, the parties had maintained separate homes until shortly before marriage, and there was no clearly defined 'start date' for the relationship prior to marriage. Nevertheless, the parties' pre–marriage relationship would be taken fully into account as one of the circumstances of the case.

▶ After a long marriage/relationship it would be foolish to require parties to produce a detailed account of their financial affairs at the commencement of the marriage/relationship, and that could not have been intended by the House of Lords. In this case the court would not attempt to arrive at a precise view of the husband's wealth at various dates, but instead would make a broad assessment and conclude that he had significant resources by the time the parties' relationship developed.

▶ This was not a case in which the wife's award should be confined to her needs, as such an award would not be fair. This was a case in which the sharing principle subsumed needs.

▶ After a long marriage, factors of substance had to justify a departure from an equal division of assets. In this case, the substantial wealth of the husband prior to the commencement of the parties' relationship justified a departure from equality. The extent of departure in any particular case was not to be calculated according to a formula or clear mathematics.

However, even though a marriage is a long one, the court must always take into account the source of the assets even if it decides to discount it. Thus, although Baroness Hale in *Miller* had said that the 'importance of the source of the assets will diminish over time', in *Vaughan* v. *Vaughan* [2007] EWCA Civ 1085, [2008] 1 FLR 1108 Wilson LJ held that, despite the long marriage (of nearly 20 years), the judge in the lower court had not properly taken into account the fact that the husband had bought the matrimonial home in his sole name (free of mortgage) three years prior to the marriage.

'Big money' cases involving short marriages are likely to be dealt with on the basis of the applicant's needs (generously interpreted), as the decision of Bennett J in *McCartney* v. *Mills McCartney* [2008] EWHC 401 (Fam), [2008] 1 FLR 1508 above shows. In *McCartney* Bennett J found that the needs of the wife were the dominant factor in the case, and that the sharing principle was subsumed within the wife's needs.

(e)   Big money cases and periodical payments

Although *White* v. *White* involved a lump sum, the House of Lords held in the *McFarlane* appeal in *Miller/McFarlane* that the overriding objective of fairness laid down in *White* v. *White* could also apply to periodical payments in an exceptional case. In *McFarlane* the facts were exceptional as there was a huge surplus of available income after the needs of the parties had been met:

> ▶ *Miller* v. *Miller; McFarlane* v. *McFarlane* [2006] UKHL 24, [2006] 1 FLR 1186
>
> In the *McFarlane* case the parties had been married for 16 years. Both were qualified professionals and, until shortly before the birth of their second child, earned similar sums of money. The wife gave up her highly-paid career to care for the family, while the husband continued his professional career, with his annual salary increasing considerably from year to year (and which stood at £750,000 per annum by the time of the hearing). The family had insufficient capital available to achieve a clean break, but the husband earned substantially more than would be needed to meet his own and the wife's budgeted household expenditure. The district judge made a periodical payments order of £250,000 per year (on the basis that fairness required the wife to have a share of her husband's future earnings). This was reduced to £180,000 by the High Court; but the Court of Appeal allowed the wife's appeal in part, restoring the award to £250,000, but limiting the term to 5 years. The Court of Appeal held that in exceptional cases, and on the basis of term rather than joint lives orders, periodical payments could be used to accumulate capital. The wife appealed.
>
> The House of Lords held, upholding the £250,000 award but removing the 5-year term, that a periodical payments order could be made to afford compensation as well as to meet financial needs. However, a clean break was not to be achieved at the expense of a fair result. Thus, if a claimant was owed compensation and capital assets were not available, the social desirability of a clean break would not be sufficient reason for depriving a claimant of that compensation. There was no reason to limit periodical payments to a fixed term in the interests solely of achieving a clean break.
>
> The House held that the case was a paradigm case for an award of compensation in respect of the significant future economic disparity sustained by the wife, arising from the way the parties had conducted their marriage.
>
> *Note*: In *McFarlane* v. *McFarlane* [2009] EWHC 891 (Fam), after a change of circumstances (Mr McFarlane's earnings had risen to over £1 million per annum), Mrs McFarlane obtained (in variation proceedings) a 40 per cent increase in periodical payments for herself and the three children.

Cooke ([2004] Fam Law 906) was critical of the decision in *McFarlane* for extending the principles in *White* to income, as it perpetuated 'dependency and perhaps animosity'.

7.7   The family home on divorce

The future of the family home on divorce will be important, not just because of its financial value but because it provides accommodation for the family. The provision of accommodation will be a primary consideration for the court when deciding how to distribute the matrimonial assets, and the provision of a home for any children will be particularly important. However, although the housing needs of both parties must be taken into account, the outcome in the case will depend on all the circumstances, as the following two cases show:

▶ *M* v. *B* [1998] 1 FLR 53

The Court of Appeal allowed the husband's appeal, as the judge had failed to take into account the importance of the parent who was not the primary carer having a home of his own where the children could enjoy contact. The wife should have a cheaper house so that her husband would also have enough to buy a property of his own where the children could visit him. Thorpe LJ said that 'it is one of the paramount considerations, in applying the section 25 criteria, to endeavour to stretch what is available to cover the need of each for a home, particularly where there are young children involved'.

▶ *Piglowska* v. *Piglowski* [1999] 1 WLR 1360, [1999] 2 FLR 763

The question for the House of Lords, like that in *M* v. *B* (above), was whether the wife should have a cheaper house so that her husband could buy himself a house in England, even though he had accommodation in Poland. Lord Hoffman said that to treat *M* v. *B* as a case laying down the rule that both spouses invariably have a right to purchase accommodation was a misuse of authority and he distinguished *M* v. *B* on the basis that the children in *Piglowska* were adults, so that there was no question of the husband needing a home to receive them. The House of Lords warned against treating earlier cases as binding precedents and restored the order of the trial judge which had given particular weight to the wife's need to stay in the matrimonial home (s.22(2)(b)) and the fact that she not only looked after the home and cared for the family but had made a substantially greater financial contribution to the matrimonial assets (s.25(2)(f)).

When deciding what should happen to the home on divorce the court has various options available, depending on the facts. It might, for example, order one spouse to transfer the house, or his or her share of the house, to the other spouse with or without the other spouse making any compensating payment. It might order a transfer but make it subject to a charge in favour of the transferor, representing the value of the transferor's interest in the home which will be realised on sale at a later date. The house might be transferred for the purpose of effecting a clean break (for instance by being transferred to the wife with her forbearing to claim periodical payments).

A Mesher order This is an order made under s.24(1)(b) MCA 1973 whereby the house is settled on trust for one or both of the spouses in certain shares, but with sale postponed until a future event, such as until the children have reached a particular age or have finished full-time education, or until the death, remarriage or cohabitation of the other spouse. *Mesher* orders were once popular with the courts, but they have become less popular because of their drawbacks. One drawback is that some spouses (usually wives) may find that they have insufficient funds from the eventual proceeds of sale to rehouse themselves.

Another drawback is that children often continue to need accommodation after the event triggering sale has occurred, although it is possible for the court to take this into account, as it did in *Sawden* v. *Sawden* [2004] EWCA Civ 339, where the Court of Appeal inserted another condition into the *Mesher* order whereby the children could remain indefinitely in the home, if they wished, without their father enforcing sale and claiming his 45 per cent of the proceeds of sale. Another disadvantage of *Mesher* orders is that they are contrary to the clean break as, until sale, the parties are tied together as joint owners, thereby restricting their chances of financial self-sufficiency.

Despite their drawbacks, the Court of Appeal in *Clutton* v. *Clutton* [1991] 1 WLR 359 said that a *Mesher* order might be appropriate where the family assets were sufficient to provide both parties with a roof over their heads if the matrimonial home were sold at a later date, but where the interest of the parties required the children to stay in the matrimonial home. However, Lloyd LJ stressed that, where there were any doubts about a wife's eventual ability to rehouse herself, then a *Mesher* order should not be made. The Court of Appeal held that a '*Martin* order' did not suffer from the same disadvantage. (A *Martin* order is an order giving one spouse a right to occupy the house until that party's death, remarriage or cohabitation, after which the proceeds of sale are divided in certain shares). In *B v. B (Mesher Order)* [2002] EWHC 3106 (Fam), [2003] 2 FLR 285 a *Mesher* order was held not to be appropriate in the circumstances (because of the wife's inability to generate capital at the date of the suggested *Mesher* triggering event and because it would impose a significant financial burden on her).

An order for sale   Under s.24A MCA 1973 the court can order that the matrimonial home be sold, but this power is only ancillary to the court's power to make a financial provision or property adjustment order. Thus, for example, the court could order sale of the home so that one of the parties receives a lump sum from the proceeds of sale.

If the house is in joint names the signatures of both parties will be required for sale. However, if it is in the name of one spouse, and there is a danger that the sole owner may sell it before the divorce court has exercised its powers, the non-owner spouse should register his or her 'home rights' (see 4.2). Where the house has been sold to defeat a claim to ancillary relief on divorce, an application can be made under s.37 MCA 1973 to have the transaction set aside (see 7.11).

Tenancies of the home   Section 53 and Sched. 7 to the Family Law Act 1996 make provision for the transfer of tenancies on divorce. A tenancy can also be transferred under s.24 MCA 1973.

7.8   Pensions on divorce

A pension can be a valuable financial asset. Loss of a pension as a result of divorce can therefore be a substantial loss. Although pension entitlement is something which the divorce courts have always been able to take into account as part of the s.25 discretionary exercise (see 7.4), amendments to the Matrimonial Causes Act 1973 have improved the pension position on divorce. The following options are available in respect of pension entitlement on divorce:

(i) 'Off setting'   To compensate for loss of a pension, or reduced entitlement to a pension, the court in the exercise of its s.25 discretionary powers can make compensatory adjustments in respect of the division of matrimonial assets other than the pension. For example the court might order that the matrimonial home be transferred to the wife and/or a larger lump sum be paid in order to compensate for the husband's pension. In this way, rights under a pension scheme are left untouched but their value is taken into account by giving a party an appropriately enlarged share of the other party's assets. Off-setting may be useful where pension assets are inaccessible (for example, where they are held outside the jurisdiction). Off-setting can only be used, however, if there are sufficient assets available to compensate for the loss of pension entitlement. If this is not the case then the other options below will have to be considered. Off-setting has the advantage of

creating a clean break between the parties, for, unlike pension attachment, there will be no need for the parties to have contact with each other in the future.

(ii) Pension attachment orders ('earmarking) Pension attachment orders can be made under ss.25B–25D MCA 1973. Pension attachment involves a pension being 'earmarked' for the other party. If an order is made, then once the pension becomes payable the person responsible for the pension arrangement (the trustee or managers of the fund) must pay part of the pension income and/or lump sum available under the pension arrangement to the other party to the marriage (s.25B(4)). An attachment order must be expressed in percentage terms (s.25B(5)). A pension attachment order can be varied during the payer's lifetime and terminates on the payee's death or remarriage.

The main advantage of pension-attachment is that the payment is more likely to represent the actual value of the pension at the time when the pension becomes payable. However, pension attachment orders have several disadvantages. Thus, they undermine the policy of the clean break (as the parties remain financially tied to each other, and either party may apply for variation). It may be difficult for the court to force the pension holder to continue to make payments to the pension fund or to retire by a specified age. It may also be difficult for the court to predict the value of the pension and the needs of the parties when the pension becomes payable. Pension attachment may also create uncertainty and insecurity as to when payments are to take effect and how long they will last. Problems may also occur on remarriage or death, because, if the applicant remarries, income payments terminate; and, if the respondent dies, the pension attachment order terminates. Because of these disadvantages, pension sharing orders provide a better solution; and are therefore much more commonly used in practice.

(iii) Pension sharing orders Pension sharing was introduced in 2000. The divorce court has power under s.24 MCA 1973 to make a pension sharing order, which is an order which enables pension benefits to be irrevocably split at the time of divorce, forming two separate pensions, so that one can be allocated to the other spouse to invest as he or she thinks appropriate. The pension sharing order will specify the percentage value to be transferred (s.21A(1)). An order can be made in respect of a pension which is already being paid. The provisions do not apply to the basic State retirement pension. The s.25 guidelines apply when the court is deciding whether to make a pension sharing order and, if so, in what manner.

Pension sharing orders have various advantages over offsetting and pension attachment. One advantage is that a clean break can be effected, because the pension fund is split at the time of divorce. Another is that the order allows the pension assets to be kept separate from other assets on divorce and avoids the problems involved in offsetting assets fairly in order to compensate for loss of a pension. The disadvantages relate to the fact that there will be a charge for the administration of the pension sharing order and there may be difficulties involved in actuarial calculation.

(iv) The exercise of discretion in respect of a pension The court's powers in respect of pension arrangements are governed by the factors in s.25 Matrimonial Causes Act 1973 (see 7.4), and the objective of the court is to achieve a fair result which does not discriminate against either spouse (applying *White* v. *White* and *Miller* v. *Miller*, see 7.6). In exercising its powers, the court has considerable discretion as to whether or not to make an order, and, if so, in

what manner. Section s.25B(1) expressly requires the court when conducting its s.25(2) exercise to have regard to: any benefits under a pension arrangement which a party to the marriage has or is likely to have; and any benefits under a pension arrangement ,which by reason of the divorce (or annulment), a party to the marriage will lose the chance of acquiring. When considering any benefits under a pension arrangement, there is no requirement that the courts take into consideration only those benefits which will be available in the foreseeable future (s.25B(1)). A pension can also be taken into account under s.25(2)(a) as a 'financial resource' which a party has or is likely to have in the future. If retirement is reasonably imminent, the court may decide to adjourn the proceedings.

7.9   Agreements about property and finance on separation and divorce

Divorcing couples are encouraged to reach agreement about ancillary matters on divorce whether they be in respect of property, finance or children. The Code of Practice of Resolution (the group of family solicitors) and the Law Society's *Family Law Protocol* require solicitors to encourage the parties to reach amicable agreements, rather than to engage in hostile, unpredictable and emotionally stressful litigation. Many couples reach agreement of their own accord, but others may do so with the assistance of mediators and/or lawyers. Collaborative law is also being increasingly used (see 1.4). Most couples, in fact, do not go to court to litigate about financial and property matters on divorce, but make their own arrangements.

Some couples may wish to enter into a more formal agreement, which they can do in the following ways: by applying for a consent order; by making a post-marital agreement; and / or by making a pre-marital agreement. Each of these three forms of agreement are addressed below, but it is pre-marital agreements ('pre-nups') which are most controversial, and which the Government's law reform body, the Law Commission, is to look at with a view to reform.

(a)   Consent orders

Agreements about finance and property on divorce can be incorporated into a consent order, which the court has jurisdiction to make under s.33A of the Matrimonial Causes Act 1973. Consent orders encourage settlement and reduce the cost of litigation. However, they can contain only those orders which the court has power to make under Part II of the 1973 Act. In order to enable the court to exercise its discretionary powers, the parties must provide the court with prescribed information, such as the duration of the marriage, the ages of the parties and children, an estimate of the approximate value of their capital resources, accommodation arrangements for themselves and their children, and whether either party has remarried or intends to marry or cohabit (s.33A). Failure to provide this information can result in an order being set aside (see 7.12). Although consent orders are based on an agreement, they are not treated as ordinary contracts. General contract principles do not determine the outcome of a case. It is the consent order itself which determines the rights and duties of the parties, not the agreement which the parties make before the order is made (*Xydhias* v. *Xydhias* [1999] 1 FLR 683).

When considering whether to make a consent order, the court does not just 'rubber-stamp' the proposed agreement. It considers all the circumstances and applies the s.25 factors, the clean break provisions and the approaches laid down in the case-law. However, the court will usually approve the agreement, as the fact that it has been drawn up and agreed to by the parties, usually with legal advice, is *prima facie* proof of its reasonableness. The terms of a consent order can be varied in variation proceedings, but only in respect of periodical payments (see p. 194 below). Consent orders may be set aside in some circumstances, for example if there has been non-disclosure (see p. 199, below).

(b) Post-marital (post-nuptial) agreements

Married couples can enter into agreements about finance and property, including agreements about what is to happen to any property and finance should their marriage break down (see ss.34–36 MCA 1973). However, although they can do this, such agreements are not automatically binding, because the divorce court retains a supervisory role in respect of such agreements. Thus, the court has power under s.35(2) to vary, revoke or insert new terms into an agreement if the terms of the agreement (or omission of terms) do not allow for a change of circumstances; or where there is no provision in the agreement for proper financial arrangements with respect to any child of the family. Furthermore, any provision in an agreement restricting the right of either party to apply to the court for ancillary relief is void (s.34(1)).

Before the decision in *MacLeod* v. *MacLeod* [2008] UKPC 64, [2009] 1 FLR 641 (see further below), although married couples could (and still can) enter into maintenance and separation agreements about finance and property under ss.34–36 of the Matrimonial Causes Act 1973, these provisions were held not to be applicable to post-marital agreements because s.34(1)(b) provides that financial arrangements shall be binding 'unless they are void or unenforceable for any other reason'; and one such reason was the rule laid down in *Hyman* v. *Hyman* [1929] AC 601 that any agreement made in contemplation of marital breakdown was contrary to public policy. However, in *MacLeod* the Privy Council rejected this rule of public policy on the ground that the rule on which it had been founded (namely that a husband and wife have an enforceable duty to live together) no longer existed. There was no longer an enforceable rule that a married couple had a duty to live together. The rule had been abolished by the Matrimonial Proceedings and Property Act 1970 at the same time as the Law Reform (Miscellaneous Provisions) Act 1970 had abolished all the common law actions against third parties who interfered between husband and wife.

The Privy Council in *MacLeod*, however, affirmed the importance of *Edgar* v. *Edgar* (see below) because it is still open to the divorce court to set aside an agreement (post-marital or pre-marital) where the agreement is unfairly entered into or fails to make sufficient provision where there has been a change of circumstances. Although private agreements have the advantages of promoting amicable settlement and avoiding the uncertainty and cost of litigation, *Edgar* v. *Edgar* shows that a post-separation agreement can have serious disadvantages.

▶ *Edgar* v. *Edgar* [1980] 1 WLR 1410, (1981) 2 FLR 19

The parties entered into a separation agreement in which the husband, a multi-millionaire, agreed to pay his wife a lump sum of £100,000 and in which she agreed to seek no further provision. She entered into the agreement despite her solicitor's advice that she would obtain a better settlement in divorce proceedings. Later in ancillary relief proceedings on divorce she was granted a lump sum of £760,000. The husband appealed to the Court of Appeal.

The Court of Appeal held, allowing his appeal and setting the order aside, that the wife was bound by the terms of the original agreement. There was no evidence that she had been exploited. She had received legal advice and there had been no adverse conduct by her husband during negotiations leading up to the agreement. A large disparity between the sum agreed and the sum that she might have been awarded in divorce proceedings was insufficient on its own for the court to ignore the agreement. The court acknowledged that it had a duty to exercise its discretionary powers under s.25, but Ormrod LJ held that it was an important general principle that 'formal agreements, properly and faithfully arrived at with competent legal advice' should not be displaced unless there were 'good and substantial grounds' for concluding that an injustice would be done by holding the parties to the terms of their agreement. Ormrod LJ said that 'good and substantial grounds' included whether there was pressure from one side, exploitation of a dominant position, inadequate knowledge, bad legal advice or an unforeseen change of circumstances. His Lordship said that 'the existence of a freely negotiated bargain entered into at the instance of one of the parties and affording him or her everything for which he or she has stipulated must be a most important element of conduct which cannot lightly be ignored'.

ORMROD LJ. 'To decide what weight should be given, in order to reach a just result, to a prior agreement not to claim a lump sum, regard must be had to the conduct of both parties, leading up to the prior agreement, and to their subsequent conduct, in consequence of it. It is not necessary in this connection to think in formal legal terms, such as misrepresentation or estoppel; all the circumstances as they affect each of two human beings must be considered in the complex relationship of marriage. So, the circumstances surrounding the making of the agreement are relevant. Undue pressure by one side, exploitation of a dominant position to secure an unreasonable advantage, inadequate knowledge, possibly bad legal advice, an important change of circumstances, unforeseen or overlooked at the time of making the agreement, are all relevant to the question of justice between the parties. Important too is the general proposition that, formal agreements, properly and fairly arrived at with competent legal advice, should not be displaced unless there are good and substantial grounds for concluding that an injustice will be done by holding the parties to the terms of their agreement. There may well be other considerations which affect the justice of this case; the above list is not intended to be an exclusive catalogue.'

Ormrod LJ went on to say that whilst in many cases there is a disparity of bargaining power, the crucial question is 'whether [the husband] exploited it in a way which was unfair to the wife, so as to induce her to act to her disadvantage'.

Baroness Hale in *MacLeod* (see further below) explicitly endorsed Ormrod LJ's analysis above, stating that, although the courts 'must be alive to the risk of unfair exploitation of superior strength', 'the fact that the agreement is not what a court would have done cannot be enough to have it set aside'.

Edgar v. *Edgar* therefore emphasised the important policy objective of achieving finality; and the undesirability of opening up arrangements which have already been settled by the parties. As a result of the decision, a spouse will not be permitted to resile from an agreement without good reason, but each case will be depend on its own facts. Thus, for example, in *G* v. *G (Financial Provision: Separation Agreement)* [2004] 1 FLR 1011 the agreement was upheld (even though it had been drawn up without legal advice and at a time when emotional pressures were high and judgment was likely to be clouded), as both parties had previous experience of marital breakdown and had from the outset of their marriage elected to regulate their affairs contractually).

The following decision of the Privy Council is the leading case on post-marital agreements. It involved an appeal from the Isle of Man, but, because the Manx legislation governing matrimonial law has its equivalent in the Matrimonial Causes Act 1973, the decision is also relevant to the law in England and Wales. Although decisions of the Privy Council are not binding on the courts in England and Wales (but are only persuasive), the decision is likely to be followed by the courts in England and Wales because members of the Privy Council are also members of the Supreme Court (formerly the House of Lords).

The case is also relevant to pre-marital agreements, as Baroness Hale made important statements about such agreements (see further below).

> ▶ *MacLeod* v. *MacLeod* [2008] UKPC 64, [2009] 1 FLR 641
>
> The parties, an American couple, had entered into a pre-nuptial agreement in the USA on the day of their marriage. Each had received separate legal advice and had disclosed their resources. The husband was worth about £7 million as a result of business and property development. The pre-nuptial agreement provided for each spouse to retain the property that each of them had brought into the marriage and to share any jointly owned property. It was also agreed that the husband would pay the wife a lump sum dependent on the number of years the marriage lasted. A year later the parties moved to the Isle of Man where they made a home and raised their five children. After about eight years of marriage they made a post-nuptial agreement confirming the pre-nuptial agreement but making some substantial variations. Each party was separately represented during the negotiations (which lasted about 14 months). Under the terms of the agreement the wife would *inter alia* receive a lump sum to invest, a monthly allowance, and the husband's half-share in a property. The financial needs of the children were to be dealt with separately. On divorce, the wife sought financial relief, and argued that the court should disregard both the pre-nuptial and the post-nuptial agreements. The husband, on the other hand, argued that all agreements, whether pre-nuptial or post-nuptial should be valid and binding. He accepted the rule of public policy laid down in *Hyman* v. *Hyman* [1929] AC 601 and confirmed by s.34(1)(a) MCA 1973 Act (that such agreements could not oust the jurisdiction of the court to make orders containing financial arrangements), but he argued that such agreements should be 'presumptively dispositive' of claims to such an order. The judge held that the agreement should be taken into account, but that, as it did not provide enough money to enable the wife to buy the children a house of a comparable size, he awarded her £1.25 million, and rejected the husband's argument that any such housing provision should be by way of trust until the children no longer needed to be accommodated. The husband appealed to the Privy Council arguing that any capital funding for the children should be provided by way of trust (until the youngest child reached the age of 23).
>
> The Board of the Privy Council held (with Baroness Hale giving judgment for the Board), allowing the husband's appeal, that:
>
> Although it was not open to the Board to reverse the long-standing rule that pre-nuptial agreements were contrary to public policy and thus not valid or binding in a contractual sense, post-nuptial agreements were very different from pre-nuptial agreements. Thus, there was nothing to stop a married couple from entering into a separation agreement which would then be governed by ss.49–51 of the Manx Matrimonial Proceedings Act 2003 (the equivalent of ss.34–36 of the Matrimonial Causes Act 1973 in England and Wales). There was nothing to limit those provisions to people who had already separated or who were on the point of separating. This meant that those provisions could apply to post-nuptial agreements in just the same way as they did to any other agreement. In particular, they could be varied in either

of the circumstances of s.50(2) of the Manx Act, namely (i) where there had been a change in the circumstances in the light of which any financial arrangements had been made or omitted; and/or (ii) where the agreement did not contain proper financial arrangements with respect to any child of the family.

Applying these conclusions to the facts, Baroness Hale held, allowing the husband's appeal, that the post-nuptial agreement was a valid and enforceable agreement, not only with respect to the arrangements made for the time when the parties were together, but also with respect to the arrangements made for them to live separately. However, the latter arrangements were subject to the court's powers of variation, and the provisions which purported to oust the jurisdiction of the court (whether on divorce or during the marriage) were void. However, on the basis of the facts of the case, there had been no change of circumstances to justify a variation of the financial arrangements for the wife under the agreement. As the agreement had not purported to contain financial arrangements for the children, the judge had been right to make provision for them. However, the housing provision for the children should have been on the basis of a trust, not as a lump sum to the wife. The appeal would be allowed, and an appropriate trust deed should be drafted. The case was remitted to the High Court for an appropriate trust deed to be drafted if it could not be agreed.

BARONESS HALE: 'Post-nuptial agreements ... are very different from pre-nuptial agreements. The couple are now married. They have undertaken towards one another the obligations and responsibilities of the married state. ... There is nothing to stop a couple entering into contractual financial arrangements ... as this couple did as part of their 2002 agreement.'

The effect of the decision in *MacLeod* (with its rejection of the *Hyman* (1929) rule of public policy, see p. 184 above) is that post-marital agreements are now more likely to be upheld (and without the need for new legislation). The position with pre-marital agreements, however, is quite different (see below), because the Privy Council held that any change to the law governing pre-marital agreements was a matter for Parliament, not the courts.

The effect of *MacLeod* therefore is that ss.34–36 MCA 1973 (which are the equivalent of ss.49–51 of the Manx Matrimonial Proceedings Act 2003) apply to post-marital agreements made in contemplation of marital breakdown just as they do to other agreements. Thus post-nuptial agreements can be varied in the light of changes of circumstances. In fact changes of circumstance (such as the birth of a child) are the key benchmark for determining whether or not the agreement should be upheld by the court. For this reason, the closer the making of the post-marital agreement is to the actual separation of the parties, then the more likely it is that it will be upheld. For this reason, a post-marital agreement needs to be updated, particularly where there has been a change of circumstances (such as the birth of a child) in order to ensure that the divorce court will uphold it.

(c) Pre-marital (pre-nuptial) agreements

A pre-marital (pre-nuptial) agreement is an agreement entered into by a man and woman on contemplation of marriage which deals with the financial arrangements that they are to make should their marriage end in divorce.

Pre-marital agreements are treated differently from post-marital agreements (see above). In *MacLeod* v. *MacLeod* [2008] UKPC 64, [2009] 1 FLR 641 (above) the Privy Council reviewed the law on the validity and effect of separation and maintenance agreements. In respect of *pre-marital* agreements the Privy Council upheld the long-standing rule that pre-marital agreements are not valid or binding in the contractual sense; and stated that it was more appropriate for Parliament, rather than the courts, to decide if the time had come for pre-marital agreements to be regarded as binding under the law of England and Wales. In respect of *post-marital* agreements (separation agreements), however, Baroness Hale said that the position was different; and they could be treated as binding (without the need for new legislation), subject to certain controls (see above).

Thus, despite the decision in *MacLeod* about the validity of *post-marital* agreements, the policy arguments against making *pre-marital* agreements binding on the courts still exist (because *MacLeod* did not reject them). One such policy argument is that parties cannot oust the jurisdiction of the court or limit the broad discretionary powers of the court once its jurisdiction is invoked (see *Hyman* v. *Hyman* [1929] AC 601). For many years, pre-marital agreements, for reasons of public policy, carried little weight, but over the years the courts have shown themselves more willing to uphold them.

Pre-marital agreements about marital property and finance, while not binding, are taken into account by the divorce court in ancillary relief proceedings under the Matrimonial Causes Act 1973, either as a relevant circumstance under s.25(1) or as a matter of conduct under s.25(2)(g). Other circumstances of the case are taken into account, not just the existence of the agreement. The weight given to an agreement will depend on the facts of the case. However, as the court is required to apply the factors in s.25 (see 7.4) and the objectives in ancillary relief cases are fairness and non-discrimination (see 7.6), the court may decide in the exercise of its discretion not to uphold the terms of the agreement and may make an order which is not the same as the terms of the agreement. It might be unfair and discriminatory, for instance, to uphold an agreement which fails to make provision for a child of the family. The divorce court will also consider the circumstances surrounding the making of the agreement, in order to see whether it was fairly entered into, and may decide not to uphold it, applying the principles in *Edgar* v. *Edgar* (see p. 185 above). A pre-marital agreement is more likely to be accepted as binding by the divorce court where the marriage has been relatively short and where there are no children, provided there has been full disclosure and the parties have received independent and competent legal advice. An agreement which is validly drawn up and binding in another jurisdiction is also more likely to be binding (see *Radmacher* v. *Granatino* [2009] EWCA Civ, [2009] 2 FLR 1181 p. 190 below).

At one time there was considerable judicial reluctance to uphold pre-marital agreements for reasons of public policy. In 1995, for instance, Thorpe J (as he was then) had stated in *F* v. *F (Ancillary Relief: Substantial Assets)* [1995] 2 FLR 45 (where the parties were German and the husband had sought to rely on ante-nuptial contracts drawn up in Germany) that such agreements were of 'very limited significance' in England and Wales. Accordingly Thorpe J refused to attach any significant weight to the German contracts, even though they might be strictly enforced against the wife in Germany. (In *Rachmacher* v. *Granatino* (see p. 190 below), Thorpe LJ speaking of his judgment in *F* v. *F* said that he would not now be so dismissive). In recent years, however, there has been a change of attitude, and the benefits of such agreements have been increasingly recognised as an important part of the settlement culture. However, they are not necessarily binding, as the court has the ultimate say and will take the agreement into account when conducting its discretionary exercise.

The principles in *Edgar* v. *Edgar* (see p. 185 above) are still relevant to the validity of pre-marital agreements (and post-marital agreements), for example: whether the parties understood the agreement; whether they had independent legal advice; whether there was any pressure to sign the agreement; whether there was full disclosure; whether there was any misrepresentation; whether the agreement was made very close to the marriage; and whether there was any abuse of a dominant position. In *X* v. *X (Y and Z Intervening)* [2002] 1 FLR 508, where the wife was held to the agreement (because she had willingly entered into it with the benefit of expert advice) Munby J listed the following rules which apply to such agreements:

- The court must apply the s.25 criteria and reach a just and fair result; but the fact that the parties have entered into an agreement is a very important factor in considering what is a fair and just outcome between the parties.
- The court will not lightly allow parties to depart from an agreement; and a formal agreement, properly arrived at with competent legal advice, should as a matter of general policy be upheld by the court unless there are good and substantial grounds for concluding that an injustice would be done by holding the parties to it. Thus, unless contrary to public policy or subject to some vitiating feature such as lack of legal advice, duress or change of circumstances, the agreement should be upheld.
- The mere fact that one party might have done better by going to court is not of itself generally a ground for permitting that party to resile from an agreement. The court must nonetheless have regard to all the circumstances, including, in particular, the circumstances surrounding the making of the agreement, the extent to which the parties attached importance to it, and the extent to which the parties have acted upon it. The relevant circumstances are not limited to the purely financial aspects of the agreement, but social, personal, religious and cultural considerations can also be taken into account.

The following cases involving pre-marital (pre-nuptial) agreements provide examples of the courts' approach:

- *M* v. *M (Pre-nuptial Agreement)* [2002] 1 FLR 654

The parties had entered into a pre-nuptial agreement in Canada, which the wife had signed contrary to legal advice that it was not in her best interests. She applied for ancillary relief in the English courts. Connell J awarded her a lump sum which was £600,000 greater than amount agreed upon in the agreement, plus child maintenance and school fees. Although the husband was worth £7.5 million and the wife had sought £1.3 million by way of ancillary relief, Connell J allowed the existence of the agreement to affect the amount of the award, holding that it did not matter whether the court treated the agreement as a circumstance of the case, or as conduct which it would be inequitable to disregard under s.25(2)(g) MCA 1973. He said that under either approach, the court's duty was to look at the agreement and decide in the particular circumstances what weight to give it. Connell J held that it would have been unjust to the husband to ignore the existence of the agreement and its terms, as it would have been to the wife to hold her strictly to its terms.

- *K* v. *K (Ancillary Relief: Pre-nuptial Agreement)* [2003] 1 FLR 120

The existence of a pre-nuptial agreement signed the day before marriage but with independent legal advice was taken into account as one of the circumstances of the case under s.25 and as conduct which it would be inequitable to disregard under s.25(2)(g). The parties understood the agreement. They had been properly advised. There was no pressure to sign. They knew there was soon to be a child. There was no unforeseen change of circumstances which would make it unfair to hold one party to the agreement, and there was no injustice to the other party. However, the court gave the wife an award which was higher than that agreed upon in the agreement, because of the wife's enormous contribution to the upbringing of the child, and because under s.25(1) the child's welfare required him to have a home to live in with his mother and for there to be sufficient income to provide for his and his mother's maintenance. The child was entitled to be brought up in circumstances that bore some sort of relationship to the father's current resources and standard of living.

A pre-nuptial agreement made abroad The court is more likely to uphold an agreement, or give it greater weight, if one or both of the parties has come from a jurisdiction where pre-nuptial agreements are commonplace and enforceable (for example, in Europe or some states of the USA), as the following case shows:

▶ *Radmacher v. Granatino* [2009] EWCA Civ, [2009] 2 FLR 1181

The wife (a German heiress said to be worth in excess of £100 million) and her French husband married in London in 1998 and had two children. Three months before the marriage they entered into a pre-nuptial contract which was signed in Germany (and which would have been binding both in Germany and France), the terms of which provided for no financial provision to be made to either spouse in the event of divorce. The parties divorced in England and the husband claimed ancillary relief, basing his claim on needs, and not compensation and sharing. The wife argued that the pre-nuptial contract was binding.

Baron J refused to recognise and enforce the pre-nuptial contract as it was defective under English law as: the husband had received no independent legal advice; the contract deprived him of all claims even in a situation of need, which was manifestly unfair; there had been no disclosure by the wife; there were no negotiations; and there was no provision for the two children of the marriage. But as the contract would have been binding in both Germany and France (the wife and husband's respective home countries), Baron held that it would not be right to ignore it and, in assessing the husband's needs, awarded him a lump sum of £5.56 million with a further £504,000 paid by the wife to provide a home for him in Germany to have contact with the two children, and periodical payments for the children of £70,000 per annum. The wife appealed to the Court of Appeal.

The Court of Appeal (with Thorpe LJ giving the leading judgment) allowed the wife's appeal, holding that, although Baron J had correctly held that pre-nuptial settlements were not binding *per se* but were a factor to be taken into account, she had not taken into account certain factors, including *inter alia* that: the execution of a contract providing for the property regime of the intended marriage would have been standard practice in both France and Germany and that under the national law of both husband and wife the prenuptial contract would have been binding; and the fact that the husband had clearly had the opportunity to seek independent advice during the development of the contract, but had chosen not to do so.

The Court of Appeal held, that where an agreement is binding in the parties' own countries, and there was no evidence of duress, misrepresentation or a lack of opportunities to take legal advice etc, then the court would give the agreement substantial weight in the s.25 discretionary exercise. There was no good reason not to hold the husband to the agreement.

Thorpe LJ said that, if this case had been heard in Germany or France, the husband would have had no claims whatsoever, and yet in the High Court in England he had claimed approximately £5 million. Thorpe LJ said that his opinion was based on the following foundations:

▶ that any provision in the agreement that seeks to oust the jurisdiction of the court will always be void but severable:

▶ any contract will be voidable if it breaches proper safeguards or was vitiated under general principles of contract law;

▶ any contract would be subject to the review of a judge exercising his duty under s.25 if asserted to be manifestly unfair to one of the contracting parties

Thorpe LJ said it seemed to be increasingly unrealistic to hold such contracts void; and to do so reflected the laws and morals of earlier generations. It did not sufficiently recognise the rights of autonomous adults to govern their future financial relationship by agreement in an age when marriage is not generally regarded as a sacrament and divorce is a statistical commonplace. As a society Thorpe LJ said that we should be seeking to reduce, not maintain, rules of law that divide us from the majority of the member states of Europe. We are in danger of isolation in the wider common law world if we do not give greater force and effect to ante-nuptial contracts. He said that, pending statutory reform, the judge in future cases broadly in line with this case should give due weight to the marital property regime into which the parties had freely entered.

Wilson LJ said that, although it was good practice for both parties to take independent legal advice when entering into a pre-nuptial agreement, the husband's lack of legal advice did not justify a decision to discount the agreement in the circumstances of the case. Wilson LJ said that in some cases (for example where there was duress or a party genuinely did not know what they were signing) then lack of independent legal advice might still be fatal. Wilson LJ also said that good practice required there to be a reasonable level of disclosure of the resources available to each of the parties. Deliberate non-disclosure or misrepresentation might lead to the court having a lack of confidence about the agreement. But if one party chose not to pursue detailed or any disclosure then this might not of itself be fatal to the agreement.

(*Note:* The husband was subsequently given leave to appeal to the Supreme Court).

The effect of *Radmacher* v. *Granatino* is that, as the courts must give 'due weight to the marital property regime into which the parties freely entered' (*per* Thorpe LJ above), then it is likely that more pre-marital agreements made in a foreign jurisdiction will be upheld by the courts. In *Radmacher*, the Court of Appeal also called for the law on pre-nuptial contracts to be reformed (see further at 7.14).

Crossley v. *Crossley* *and agreement*   Although a pre-marital agreement is not necessarily binding in England and Wales and is one of the circumstances of the case to be considered when the court is carrying out its s.25 discretionary exercise, Thorpe LJ in *Crossley* v. *Crossley* [2007 EWCA Civ 1491, [2008] 1 FLR 1467, with whom Keene and Wall LJJ agreed, held that in an appropriate case (one where the judge has identified the case as one in which the agreement is the dominant consideration in the s.25 exercise) a judge in the exercise of his or her discretion can require a party to ancillary relief proceedings to show good cause why the pre-nuptial agreement should not govern the division of assets on divorce. In *Crossley* Thorpe LJ therefore sanctioned the use of a shorter procedure, as the terms of the agreement were ones which could be upheld. In *Crossley* the parties had divorced after a short childless marriage, a substantial part of which they had spent living apart. They each possessed substantial independent wealth. The pre-nuptial agreement provided that each of them should walk away from the marriage with what he or she had brought in and that neither party should apply for any order for financial provision. Thorpe LJ said: 'All these cases are fact dependent, ... but if ever there is to be a paradigm case in which the court will look to the prenuptial agreement as not simply one of the peripheral factors in the case but as a factor of magnetic importance, it seems to me that this is just such a case'.

(See also *S* v. *S (Ancillary Relief)* [2008] EWHC 2038 (Fam), [2009] 1 FLR 254, which was held by Eleanor King J to be one of the types of cases identified in *Crossley* where the agreement was of such magnetic importance that the just cause procedure could be used).

Reforming the law   There have been calls from judges, lawyers and academics for the law to be reformed so that pre-marital contracts are binding. Reform is discussed at 7.14 in the context of reform of the law on ancillary relief generally.

7.10   Enforcing ancillary relief orders

Ancillary relief orders can be enforced in various ways. Remedies for enforcement available in the High Court and county courts differ from those in the magistrates' family proceedings courts.

(a)   Enforcing orders for payment of money

Enforcement procedures for enforcing orders for payment of money include:

- *Judgment summons* The spouse wishing to enforce the order can apply for a judgment summons which requires the other party to attend before a judge to be examined as to his or her means. At the hearing, the judge will make such order as he thinks fit in relation to the arrears or outstanding payment. Committal to prison can be exercised but only for dishonesty or contempt of court; and only if the court, applying the criminal burden of proof, is satisfied that the defaulter has, or has had, the means to pay.
- *An order for sale under s.24A Matrimonial Causes Act 1973* can be made to enforce a lump sum payment. The order can direct that the proceeds of sale, or part of them, be used to pay the lump sum.
- *Execution against goods* A writ of *fieri facias* (in the High Court) or a warrant of execution (in the county court) can be made authorising the sheriff (in the High Court) or the bailiff (in the county court) to seize sufficient of the other spouse's goods to pay the debt (excluding basic goods for domestic needs).
- *A garnishee order* directing a sum of money to be paid (for example a spouse's bank or building society may be ordered to pay a sum owed to the other spouse directly).
- *A charging order* imposing a charge over one of the defaulting party's property assets (for example, shares or a house) may be ordered so that priority is gained over the property charged, and an order is then sought that the property be sold so that the debt can be paid out of the proceeds of sale.
- *Appointment of receiver* to receive rents, profits and other proceeds of property belonging to the defaulting spouse, or of a business carried on by that spouse. This is an exceptional remedy.
- *A writ of sequestration* preventing the defaulting spouse from dealing with property until the default has been made good.

- *An attachment of earnings order* ordering that payments from the defaulter's earnings be paid to the collecting officer of the court (see the Attachment of Earnings Act 1971, as amended).
- *Registration in the family proceedings court* A periodical payments order made by the High Court or county court can be registered in the magistrates' family proceedings court, whereupon it can be enforced as a magistrates' court order under the Magistrates' Courts Act 1980 (for example by warrant of distress, attachment of earnings, a fine or imprisonment).
- *Committal* The court has the power to commit a defaulting party to prison for failing to obey a court order.

(b) Enforcing property adjustment orders

Where a spouse fails to co-operate in completing the required formalities for the transfer of the matrimonial home to the other spouse, an application can be made to the court for an order that, unless the transfer is completed within a specified time, then the document(s) will be executed by a district judge or judge. In the case of a s.24A order for sale, if a party refuses to vacate the matrimonial home, an application can be made to the court for an order ordering that spouse to give up possession, so that the sale can proceed.

7.11 Protecting matrimonial property pending ancillary relief proceedings

There are two orders which can be used to protect matrimonial property pending ancillary relief proceedings: a freezing order; and a seek and search order. However, as these orders are considered to be draconian orders, they are granted only as a last resort and only in exceptional circumstances. Where there is a danger that a party may leave the jurisdiction before a claim for ancillary relief has been settled, a writ *ne exeat regno* can be sought which directs the tipstaff, an officer of the court, to arrest the respondent and bring him or her before a judge. The respondent's passport may also be seized. However, these orders are rarely sought, and rarely made.

(i) A freezing order Sometimes a spouse may dispose, or attempt to dispose, of matrimonial assets in order to defeat a claim to ancillary relief, for example by selling them, giving them away, or sending them out of the UK. In order to protect property pending a hearing for ancillary relief, the court can make a 'freezing order' under s.37 of the Matrimonial Causes Act 1973 or under the High Court's inherent jurisdiction. The applicant must have a good arguable case and show that there is a real risk that the respondent will seek to defeat or thwart the case by disposing of his or her assets unless restrained from doing so by the court. Overseas assets can be frozen, unless there will be problems enforcing the order in a foreign court. The order does not usually freeze all the defendant's property assets, but only the maximum amount of property likely to be awarded in the divorce proceedings.

(ii) A search and seize order This order allows a named person to enter premises to search for and seize documents which might be useful as evidence in ancillary relief proceedings. It can be granted only by the High Court. The aim of the order is to ensure that the

respondent does not dispose of evidence which may be useful at the ancillary relief hearing. Strict rules apply to the grant of an order and to the way in which the entry and search powers can be exercised.

7.12 Challenging an order for ancillary relief

An order for ancillary relief in divorce can be challenged by: (a) asking for a rehearing; (b) applying for variation under s.31 Matrimonial Causes Act 1973; (c) appealing, which may require an application for leave to appeal out of time; or (d) applying to have the order set aside.

(a) A rehearing

Where a party considers that there was something fundamentally wrong with the way in which the case was heard (for example, there was non-disclosure or misrepresentation), an application can be made for a rehearing. Sometimes an appeal court will order a rehearing because the order is fundamentally flawed.

(b) Variation

Under s.31 of the Matrimonial Causes Act 1973 the court has wide powers to vary or discharge certain orders (whether or not made by consent) or temporarily to suspend and revive any provision contained therein (s.31(1)). The most common applications for variation are in respect of periodical payments orders by payees who wish to have payments increased, and by payers who wish to have them reduced. Only the following orders can be varied (s.32(2)):

- maintenance pending suit or interim maintenance;
- periodical payments (secured or unsecured);
- an order providing for the payment of a lump sum by instalments;
- any deferred order made by virtue of s.23(1)(c) (lump sum) which includes a provision made by virtue of s.25B(4) or s.25C (provision in respect of pension rights);
- an order for the sale of property under s.24A;
- a s.24B pension sharing order made before decree absolute.

Lump sum orders and property adjustment orders cannot be varied. They are 'once and for all' orders. The reason for the final nature of these orders is to create certainty, so that the parties can make plans for the future without worrying about whether an order will be overturned. Lump sum orders and property adjustment orders can, however, be appealed against or set aside (see below).

How the court exercises its variation powers   When exercising its variation powers the court must consider all the circumstances of the case, but must give first consideration to the welfare of any child of the family aged under 18, and any changes of circumstance, including any change in any of the matters to which the court was required to have regard when making the original order (s.31(7)). The court must also consider whether to effect a clean break. In other words, it must consider whether it is appropriate to vary a periodical payments order so that payments will be made for a limited term sufficient to enable the payee to adjust without undue hardship to the termination of those payments (s.31(7)(a)). For the purpose of effecting a clean break, the court can make a compensating lump sum or property adjustment order under s.31(7B) (see below). The court has various powers. It can remit payment of all or part of any arrears due under any periodical payments order, including maintenance pending suit and interim maintenance (s.31(2A)). Where a periodical payments order is for a limited term, it can extend the term, unless the original order prohibited it (s.28(1A)). The court has a wide discretion in variation proceedings.

The principles laid down by the House of Lords in *Miller* (2006) (see p. 172) apply in variation applications. Sir Mark Potter P so held in *VB* v. *JP* [2008] EWHC 112 (Fam), [2008] 1 FLR 742, which dealt with a variation application under s.31(7) by a former wife for an upward variation of periodical payments; and where the payments were increased on appeal on the basis that she was entitled to an element of compensation for loss of earning capacity applying *Miller*. In other words, relationship-generated disadvantage was taken into account in the circumstances of the case. In *North* v. *North* [2007] EWCA Civ 760, [2008] 1 FLR 158 Thorpe LJ said that in any application under s.31 MCA 1973 the applicant's needs were likely to be the dominant or magnetic factor, but that it did not follow that the respondent would inevitably be held responsible for any established needs.

Cohabitation and variation   The fact that a former spouse is cohabiting with a new partner may be taken into account in variation proceedings, and may result in a reduction, or termination, of periodical payments. In *K* v. *K (Periodical Payments: Cohabitation)* [2005] EWHC 2886 (Fam), [2006] 2 FLR 468 Coleridge J held that the law should keep up with changing social conditions and treat cohabitation after divorce as a relevant factor; and that the court could place considerable weight on cohabitation as a factor in the case. The wife's settled cohabitation for three years had resulted in a reduction in her dependency on her former husband and constituted a relevant circumstance under s.31(7)(b). He said that there was no reason today why the court should not order termination of periodical payments after a certain period of cohabitation. Coleridge J concluded by saying, however, that this was 'a troubling and messy area of the law' and that the current legislation 'enacted against an utterly different social fabric [was] not adequate to deal with it'.

Achieving a clean break   In order to effect a clean break in variation proceedings, the court has power under s.31(7B) (on discharging a periodical payments order in favour of a party to a marriage, or on varying such an order so that payments are to be made for a fixed period) to substitute the periodical payments for one or more of the following orders as a means of effecting a variation: a lump sum order; a property adjustment order; a pension sharing order; and a direction that the person in whose favour the original order discharged or varied was made is not entitled to make any further application for a periodical payments order or an extension of the period to which the original order is limited by any variation made by the court. Thus, s.31(7B) allows a clean break to be achieved in variation proceedings which was not possible when the original order was made. In exercising its powers to capitalise periodical payments, Baron J in *Lauder* v. *Lauder* [2007] EWHC 1227 (Fam), [2007] 2 FLR 802 said that 'the proper approach in this type of application is to apply the precise terms of the statute in the light of the factual matrix and give proper consideration to the recent guidance given by the House of Lords in the case of *Miller'*.

(c) Appeals and permission to appeal out of time

Appeals are only allowed if there has been some procedural irregularity, or the judge has taken into account irrelevant matters or ignored relevant matters, or has otherwise reached a conclusion which is plainly wrong (*G* v. *G* [1985] 1 WLR 647). The policy of this high hurdle is not only to promote finality in litigation but to recognise that in discretionary judicial decision-making it is possible for different, but reasonable, decisions to be arrived at.

If the date for lodging the appeal has passed, an application for leave to appeal out of time will be required. Appeals out of time are often combined with an application to set aside the original order (see p. 199 below). As the courts are unwilling to reopen litigation unless it is really necessary (because it increases costs and extends the duration of the conflict), leave to appeal out of time is not easily obtained, because of the need for certainty and finality in litigation and to prevent a flood of appeals being taken before the courts. For these reasons, leave to appeal out of time will not be granted unless the principles laid down in the following case are satisfied:

▶ *Barder* v. *Barder* [1988] AC 20, *sub nom Barder* v. *Barder (Caluori Intervening)* [1987] 2 FLR 480

A consent order was made in full and final settlement, in which the husband agreed to transfer his half-share in the matrimonial home to his wife. Four weeks after the order was made, but outside the time-limit for lodging an appeal, the wife killed the children and committed suicide. The husband sought leave to appeal out of time against the order (it could not be varied under s.31 as it was a property order), arguing that the basis on which the order had been made had been fundamentally altered by the unforeseen change of circumstances – the death of his wife and children.

The House of Lords held that he should be granted leave to appeal out of time and that the order should be set aside. Lord Brandon said, however, that leave to appeal should be granted only where the following four conditions were satisfied:

▶ the new events relied on had invalidated the fundamental basis or assumption on which the original order had been made, so that, if leave to appeal were granted, the appeal would be certain or very likely to succeed;
▶ the new events had occurred within a relatively short time of the original order being made – probably less than a year;
▶ the application for leave to appeal had been made promptly; and
▶ the grant of leave would not prejudice third parties who had acquired in good faith and for valuable consideration an interest in the property subject to the order.

Thus, there must be a material change of circumstances which has undermined or invalidated the basis of the order. Not every application will result in permission to appeal being granted and an order being set aside. The *Barder* principles are strict, in order to ensure that the courts are not swamped by meritless applications.

The supervening event must be an unforeseeable event   In *Barder* (above) it was held that the supervening event must be unforeseen. In *Maskell* v. *Maskell* [2001] EWCA Civ 858, [2003] 1 FLR 1138 the Court of Appeal held, for instance, that becoming unemployed two months after an order for ancillary relief was made was not a *Barder* event – as it was foreseeable. Foreseeability of the event was also fatal to the claim in *S* v. *S* (*Ancillary Relief: Consent Order*) [2002] EWHC 223 (Fam), [2002] 1 FLR 922 where the wife applied to have a consent order set aside six months after it had been made, because the House of Lords had given its decision in *White* v. *White* and she thought she would have obtained a better settlement on divorce if the propositions laid down in that case had been applied. However, Bracewell J said that she and her legal advisers should have known that the decision of the House of Lords was foreseeable and that its impact was unavoidable. Bracewell J said that there were public policy arguments against setting aside a consent order on the basis of a change in the law, as this would lead to the floodgates opening.

Examples of situations where appeals out of time have been brought

Appeals out of time are claimed in a wide range of situations, for instance where there is unforeseen death or serious illness (*Amey* v. *Amey* [1992] 2 FLR 89; *Reid* v. *Reid* [2003] EWHC 2878 (Fam), [2004] 1 FLR 736); or misrepresentation (*Ritchie* v. *Ritchie* [1996] 1 FLR 898). However, appeals out of time are often brought because of fluctuations in property valuations and where a former spouse is alleged to have unexpectedly remarried or cohabited after divorce.

Changes in property valuations   A change in respect of a property valuation (upward or downward) or a misrepresentation as to valuation is sometimes used as a ground for an appeal out of time, but the court may decide, as it did in the following cases, that it does not constitute a '*Barder* event'.

▶ *B* v. *B* [2007] EWHC 2472 (Fam), [2008] 1 FLR 1279

The parties obtained a valuation of the matrimonial home (of £1.25 million) but the husband renovated the property and subsequently sold it for £1.6 million. The wife applied for leave to appeal out of time on the basis that: there had been an error in the valuation of the matrimonial home; her husband had misrepresented its value; and there had been a supervening *Barder* event by reason of an unforeseen and unforeseeable increase in its value.

Sir Mark Potter P dismissed her application. There was no reason to suppose that the valuation had been wrong. Valuation on a rising market was an inexact science, and where a property was improved prior to sale, the price could increase well out of proportion to the costs of refurbishment. There had been no misrepresentation by the husband invalidating the fundamental assumption on which the order had been made. Furthermore, none of the *Barder* conditions were satisfied, in particular as the subsequent event was a foreseeable event.

▶ *Walkden* v. *Walkden* [2009] EWCA Civ 627

The parties negotiated an agreement in respect of ancillary relief which was eventually approved in the form of a consent order (on the basis that the husband's share of a timber company was £800,000). Later, when the husband sold his share of the company for more than £3.7 million, the wife applied for leave to appeal and/or to set aside the consent order on the basis of a new event, or of material non-disclosure. When the trial judge granted her leave to appeal, the husband appealed to the Court of Appeal.

The Court of Appeal, allowing the husband's appeal, held that mistake as to value did not fall within the *Barder* principles. The *Barder* principles did not apply as there had been no consensus as to the value of the husband's shares. There had been no dramatic and unexpected turnaround in the company's performance, nor could it be said that the sale of the shares had been either unforeseen or unforeseeable.

In *Cornick* v. *Cornick* [1994] 2 FLR 530 (where the wife applied to set aside an order on the basis of a dramatic upward, not downward, change in share prices) Hale J (as she was then) said that the case-law did not 'suggest that the natural processes of price fluctuation, whether in houses, shares or other property, and however dramatic' provided grounds for setting an order aside. Hale J said that, only where there had been a misvaluation or mistake at the trial, might an order be set aside. The fact that an order was unfair was an insufficient ground on its own.

Hale J's dicta in *Cornick* were applied by Thorpe LJ in *Myerson* v. *Myerson (No. 2)* [2009] EWCA Civ 282, [2009] 2 FLR 147 where the husband (a victim of the dramatic global economic downturn, the 'credit crunch') failed in his claim to appeal out of time. Had he done so, it would have opened the floodgates to many other claimants, which was something that Thorpe LJ took note of in the case. In *Myerson (No 2)* the Court of Appeal warned that anyone contemplating an attempt to reopen an existing ancillary relief order on the grounds of a subsequently encountered financial eclipse should be well advised to heed the warning that a natural price fluctuation, however dramatic, was not sufficient.

(For another case on valuation, see *S* v. *S (Ancillary Relief: Application to Set Aside Order)* [2009] EWHC 2377 (Fam) where Singer J held that the subsequent sale of property far in excess of its original valuation did not provide sufficient grounds for allowing the original order to be set aside on the basis of misrepresentation or non-disclosure, mistake and/or a *Barder* event, as there was no evidence that, if a higher valuation had been known, the court would have made a materially different order).

Unexpected remarriage or cohabitation   In some cases unexpected marriage or cohabitation has been held to be a *Barder* event (see, for example, *Wells* v. *Wells* [1992] 2 FLR 66; and *Williams* v. *Lindley* [2005] EWCA Civ 103, [2005] 2 FLR 710 where the wife became engaged within one month of a lump sum being ordered in her favour). However, each case depends on its own facts; and in *Dixon* v. *Marchant* [2008] EWCA Civ 11, [2008] 1 FLR 655 the Court of Appeal (Wall LJ dissenting) refused to accept the husband's argument that his former wife's remarriage (7 months after a consent order had been made) was a *Barder* event, as there was no evidence to indicate that the wife had been fettering her right to marry and the risk of remarriage was something the husband had to accept. The Court of Appeal distinguished *Wells* v. *Wells* and *Williams v. Lindley* (above). Wall LJ, on the other hand, said that there was a fundamental, albeit tacit, assumption that the wife would not marry within the *Barder* time-frame.

How the court exercises its powers once permission to appeal has been granted
In *Smith* v. *Smith (Smith and Others Intervening)* [1991] 2 FLR 432, [1992] Fam 62 the Court of Appeal stated that the correct approach was to start the s.25 exercise from the beginning and consider what order should be made on the basis of the new facts. In *Smith* a lump

sum order had been made in favour of a wife, which represented half the family assets, but six months later she committed suicide leaving her whole estate, including the lump sum, to her daughter. Applying the s.25 guidelines to the new facts (that she would have had only a few months to live), Butler-Sloss LJ reduced the lump sum.

(d)   Setting the original order aside

An application can be made to set aside an order which has been made on an improper basis (for example, because of non-disclosure, fraud, duress or misrepresentation, or where changes of circumstances have occurred which were unforeseen when the original order was made). An application to set an order aside will often be made in conjunction with an appeal out of time (see above). However, because of the need for finality in litigation, the courts will not usually set aside an order unless the circumstances are exceptional.

Applications are sometimes made where there has been a failure to disclose information which is required by the rules of court. This occurred in the following case, which lays down the approach to be adopted by the court in applications to set aside:

> ▶ *Jenkins* v. *Livesey (Formerly Jenkins)* [1985] AC 424, *sub nom Livesey (Formerly Jenkins)* v. *Jenkins* [1985] 1 FLR 813
>
> A clean break consent order was made, in which the parties agreed that the husband would transfer to his wife his half-share in the matrimonial home, on her foregoing all claims to ancillary relief. Three weeks after the house had been transferred, the wife remarried and two months later put the house up for sale. The husband appealed out of time, asking for the consent order to be set aside on the grounds of misrepresentation and non-disclosure.
>
> The House of Lords allowed his appeal and held that parties who wished the court to exercise its discretionary powers under Part II of the 1973 Act were under a duty in contested or consent proceedings to make full and frank disclosure of all material matters, so that the court could exercise its discretion properly. However, because of the importance of encouraging a clean break, orders should not be lightly set aside. They should only be set aside if the failure to make full and frank disclosure led the court to make an order which was substantially different from the one it would have made had there been full and frank disclosure. As the wife's engagement was a material circumstance directly relevant to the parties' agreement about ancillary relief, she was under a duty to disclose it before the agreement was put into effect by means of the consent order. Her failure to disclose the engagement invalidated the order. The order was set aside, and the case remitted for a rehearing.
>
> The House of Lords stressed that non-disclosure of itself is not a sufficient ground for an order to be set aside. Like applications for appeals out of time, where the policy objective of finality is also upheld, the circumstances must be such that a fundamentally different order would have been made had the circumstances been known.

Thus, in *Jenkins* v. *Livesey (formerly Jenkins)* the House of Lords held that not every breach of the duty of full and frank disclosure would result in an ancillary relief consent order subsequently being set aside. It has to be shown that the absence of disclosure had led the court to make an order which was substantially different from that which would have been made had full disclosure been made.

In *Harris* v. *Manahan* [1997] 1 FLR 205 the Court of Appeal had to consider whether a consent order could be set aside because a party had received bad legal advice. The Court of Appeal held that the requirements of public policy that there be finality in litigation also required, save in the most exceptional cases of the cruellest injustice, that bad legal advice should not be a ground for interfering with a consent order. The rationale for such an approach was that, once an agreement has been embodied in a consent order, the source of the obligation becomes the court's order rather than the agreement made by the parties (*De Lasala* v. *De Lasala* [1979] 2 All ER 1146). However, where any agreement about property and finance has not been embodied in a consent order, then the court may take into account the quality of any legal advice.

In *I* v. *I (Ancillary Relief: Disclosure)* [2008] EWHC 1167 (Fam), [2009] 1 FLR 201, although there had been non-disclosure on the part of the husband (by not disclosing his intention to change his employment), Charles J refused to set aside the order as disclosure would have made no difference to the terms of the order.

7.13 Applications for ancillary relief after a foreign divorce

Under Part III of the Matrimonial and Family Proceedings Act 1984 a person who has divorced outside England and Wales can apply for ancillary relief in the courts in England and Wales, provided the court grants leave to apply, which it can only do if there is a substantial ground for making the application (s.13). The purpose of Part III of the 1984 Act is to remit hardship in the exceptional case where serious injustice would otherwise be done. Its purpose is not to encourage or condone 'forum shopping', in other words choosing to bring a case in the courts in England and Wales because they will provide a better outcome in the case. Once leave has been granted, the court can apply its ancillary relief powers under Part II of the Matrimonial Causes Act 1973.

Granting leave to apply   Under s.16 of the 1984 Act the court, when deciding whether to grant leave, must consider whether England and Wales is the appropriate venue for the application (s.16(1)) and must have regard to a number of specified matters (s.16(2)), such as: the connection that the parties have with England and Wales, the country where they were divorced and any other country; and any financial benefit the applicant or child of the family has received or is likely to receive by agreement or by operation of law in another country. Consideration of these matters in s.16 acts as a threshold (or filter) to prevent unmeritorious applications and to avoid the abuse of the purpose of the provision (*per* Coleridge J in *M* v. *L (Financial Relief After Overseas Divorce)* [2003] EWHC 328 (Fam), [2003] 2 FLR 425).

Because of the need for finality in litigation and the importance of the principle of comity (respect for the courts and laws of other countries), leave will only be granted in exceptional cases, for instance where a spouse has suffered serious injustice in the foreign forum. Thus, as the purpose of the 1984 Act is 'to remit hardships which have been experienced in the past in the presence of a failure in a foreign jurisdiction to afford appropriate financial relief' (*per* Purchas LJ in *Holmes* v. *Holmes* [1989] Fam 47), the courts have used their leave powers sparingly. Leave was refused, for instance, in *Hewitson* v. *Hewitson* [1995] 1 FLR 241, as a court of competent jurisdiction in California had made the consent order, which had been negotiated by lawyers, and was designed to be comprehensive and final. The wife who sought leave was not therefore entitled to 'two bites of the cherry'. However, in *A* v. *S (Financial Relief After Overseas UK Divorce and Financial Proceedings)* [2002] EWHC 1157 (Fam), [2003] 1 FLR 531, where the court in

Texas, USA, had awarded the wife practically nothing on the basis of the doctrine of community of property, Bodey J took a generous approach, and, while recognising the need for caution when an overseas court had already ruled on the matter, nonetheless granted leave in order to do justice between the parties.

The substantive application   Once leave has been granted, ss.17 and 18 provide that the court can exercise its ancillary relief powers under Part II of the Matrimonial Causes Act 1973 having regard to the s.25 factors (see 7.4). The overriding principle of fairness laid down in *White* v. *White* and endorsed in *Miller* v. *Miller* also applies (see 7.6).

In the following case, the Court of Appeal, for the first time, reviewed a substantive order under Part III of the Matrimonial and Family Proceedings Act 1984, as opposed to considering the grant of leave to apply. The case addresses the question of whether a spouse, who has been disappointed by the financial relief granted by a court in an overseas jurisdiction, can have a 'second bite of the cherry' by bringing a claim for ancillary relief in England and Wales.

▶ *Agbaje* v. *Agbaje* [2009] EWCA Civ 1, [2009] 1 FLR 987

The parties, a Nigerian couple, had spent most of their 33-year marriage in Nigeria but had acquired British citizenship and spent some time living in England. After their separation, the wife made her home in England. When the husband began divorce proceedings in Nigeria, the wife subsequently filed for divorce in England and also cross-petitioned for judicial separation in Nigeria. In the Nigerian proceedings she sought maintenance and property settlement orders (there was no jurisdiction to transfer property). The Nigerian court declined to stay its proceedings, and granted a divorce and awarded her a life interest in the matrimonial home (worth £83,000) and a lump sum of £21,000 as maintenance for life. The husband retained assets worth £616,000, including two London properties. The wife applied for financial relief in the English courts under Part III of the Matrimonial and Family Proceedings Act 1984. She was granted leave on the ground that, if leave were refused, she would suffer real hardship. In the substantive application, Coleridge J finding that the parties had a real connection with England and holding that it was appropriate for the English court to make an order, awarded the wife £275,000 from the sale of the English property on condition that she transferred her interest in the Nigerian property to her husband.

The Court of Appeal allowed the husband's appeal on the basis that Coleridge J had failed to address the issue of comity (respect for the law and courts of the other jurisdiction) and to explain why the case was an exceptional case which justified the wife having a 'second bite of the cherry'. It held that the parties' connection with Nigeria was more significant than with England; and Nigeria was the appropriate forum for resolving the wife's claims. Serious injustice had not been done to her by the Nigerian court. Although it was plain that she would suffer real hardship in England and Wales, comity commanded respect for the overseas order.

(The Supreme Court unanimously allowed her appeal, see [2010] UKSC 13).

7.14   Reforming the law on ancillary relief

(a)   Criticisms of the law

There has been considerable criticism of the law on ancillary relief, not just in respect of the statutory provisions, but in respect of the decisions of the House of Lords, particularly that in *Miller* v. *Miller*; *McFarlane* v. *McFarlane* [2006] UKHL 24, [2006] 1 FLR 1186 (see p. 172);

and as a result there have been calls for reform from judges, lawyers and academics. Even the senior family judge in England and Wales, Sir Mark Potter, President of the Family Division, has called for reform. Resolution (the group of family lawyers) has also called for reform (see [2007] Fam Law 203).

Much of the criticism relates to the uncertainties created by a discretionary system for dealing with ancillary relief on divorce, which, although it has the advantage of flexibility, remains difficult to apply and difficult for outcomes to be predicted.

There have been strong criticisms of the decision of the House of Lords in *Miller* (2006) which laid down the three 'strands' of needs, compensation and sharing which are to be applied in ancillary relief cases (see 7.6). Criticism has come not only from judges, but also from lawyers and academics. *White* and *Miller* have been criticised for adding obfuscation rather than clarity to the law. For instance, when is special contribution to be taken into account? What is 'matrimonial property'? To what extent will the length of a marriage affect whether an inheritance, for example, is to be part of the matrimonial assets to be divided? What is the starting point in ancillary relief cases? Does equality apply as a yardstick to test the conclusion which has been tentatively reached by a judge after conducting the s.25 exercise, or is there a principle of equality which acts as a starting point in ancillary relief cases?

In *RP* v. *RP* [2006] EWHC 3409 (Fam), [2007] 1 FLR 2105 Coleridge J was strongly critical of the decision in *Miller*. He said that although *Miller* was a 'high profile case' which had sent 'seismic reverberations throughout the whole [family justice] system', the case had created 'very real uncertainty as to outcome' and, as a result, the 'consensual disposal of individual cases in this huge and, sadly, ever growing area of litigation' had become 'that much harder to achieve and that much more costly'. Coleridge J said that 'considerable confusion' still existed. In particular, Coleridge J said that the word 'compensation' did not appear in the statute, and that 'talk of "compensation"' in respect of the circumstances of the case in *RP* had 'added nothing except confusion and the real risk of double counting'.

Sir Mark Potter P, the leading family law judge in England and Wales, has also been critical of the law. In *Charman* v. *Charman (No. 4)* [2008] EWCA Civ 503, [2007] 1 FLR 1246 Sir Mark Potter was of the opinion that the decision in *White* v. *White* had undoubtedly not resolved 'the problems faced by practitioners in advising clients, or by clients in deciding upon what terms to compromise'.

As two of the three strands laid down in *Miller* (compensation and sharing) are not mentioned in the list of statutory factors in s.25 MCA 1973, the House of Lords may also be criticised for introducing changes to the law by means of judicial law-making when it is Parliament's responsibility to change the law. In *MacLeod* v. *MacLeod* (see p. 186) on the other hand, the Privy Council was reluctant to change the law in the context of pre-nuptial agreements (see Geffin [2009] Fam Law 412). As Stephen Cretney said (see *Family Law in the Twentieth Century*, 2003) the decision in *White* (and also *Miller/McFarlane*) 'may come close to the imposition by the judiciary of the community of property neither Parliament nor any official advisory body had ever accepted as the basis of English matrimonial law'.

Elizabeth Cooke (the current Law Commissioner responsible for family law reform), commenting on *Miller* (see [2007] CFLQ 98), said that crucial issues of principle were left unresolved by the House of Lords in *White*, and that *Miller* had left the operation of s.25 MCA 1973 the subject of considerable uncertainty. She said that, as divorce is common, then the principles which apply to ancillary relief ought to be clear enough to be applied without recourse to litigation, and so that the parties can work matters out for themselves or with the help of a mediator or lawyer. Harris ([2008] Fam Law 1096) has also criticised *Miller* for failing to increase the predictability of the law.

Determining what is, or is not, matrimonial property (for the purpose of distributing property in ancillary proceedings on divorce) remains uncertain and unpredictable. As Cooke (above) says, although 'the concept of non-matrimonial property is firmly embedded in law and practice … we do not know how it is defined'. In Europe, on the other hand, community of property regimes define the term 'matrimonial property'.

Determining the question of special contribution is also difficult to predict. What sorts of contribution are 'special' and how will other factors, such as the duration of the marriage, impact on the issue? As Coleridge J said, '[f]rom the summit of the mountain, the House of Lords has pronounced some of the principles which underlie the "special contribution" issue', but '[t]hey are silent on how to apply them' (see *Charman* v. *Charman (No 2)* [2006] EWHC 1879 (Fam), [2007] 1 FLR 593).

There has also been concern about the trend since the decision in *White* to give wives greater shares of property on divorce in big money cases. For example, at a public lecture in 2009 Baroness Deech called for an end to the idea that women deserve half of their husband's wealth on divorce. She said that '[t]he notion that a wife should get half of the joint assets of a couple after even a short, childless marriage has crept up on us without any parliamentary legislation to this effect' (see [2009] Fam Law 1140).

There has also been criticism of the fact that pre-marital agreements are not binding, but are subject to the overriding discretion of the court (see p. 187).

These uncertainties and difficulties in the law have been seen by some commentators as sufficiently serious to justify reform of the law.

(b) Discussion of reform

Discussion of reform of ancillary relief has focused on three main options: making pre-marital agreements binding; introducing a presumptive 50:50 split of matrimonial assets; and introducing a set of policy objectives to help govern the exercise of judicial discretion. These three options for reform were considered as long ago as 1991 by the Family Law Committee of the Law Society (see *Memorandum: Capital Provision on Divorce*, Law Society, 1991), but the proposals were not taken forward.

At the end of the 1990s there was renewed discussion of reform when the Government considered these three options for reform in its consultation paper, *Supporting Families*, (Home Office, 1998). These discussions were taken further by the Lord Chancellor's Ancillary Relief Advisory Group (chaired by the Rt Hon Lord Justice Thorpe), but the group concluded that there was a need for research and wide consultation, which would encompass both social and public policy issues (see the *Report of the Lord Chancellor's Advisory Group on Ancillary Relief*, July 1998). Some of the Advisory Group, however, urged the retention of the status quo.

In July 2003 the Family Law Committee of the Law Society published a report (*Financial Provision on Divorce: Clarity and Fairness – Proposals for Reform*) in which it recommended *inter alia* that s.25 Matrimonial Causes Act 1973 should have a series of guidelines for the sharing of assets incorporated into it. The Family Law Committee was of the view, however, that pre-marital contracts should not be given binding status. Instead the courts should continue to consider them as the factors to be taken into account, because of the risks involved in not doing so.

The Law Commission announced in June 2008 that it would not be considering (as part of its Tenth Programme of Law Reform) the factors governing ancillary relief proceedings in s.25 MCA and the reform of ancillary relief generally, but would instead be limiting its examination to agreements about finance and property, because issues concerning marriage and civil partnership were becoming increasingly politicised, and because a project conducted in the current climate, no matter how closely it focused on legal issues would inevitably have to engage with highly controversial socio-political debate.

(c) Reform: pre-marital agreements

Changing the law to make pre-marital agreements binding is one reform that has been proposed; and the role of 'contractual dealing' and the autonomy of the parties has been gaining increasingly in importance (*per* Thorpe LJ in *Crossley* v. *Crossley* [2007 EWCA Civ 1491, [2008] 1 FLR 1467).

As the law currently stands, couples are free to make pre-marital agreements about what should happen in respect of financial provision should their relationship break down; but these agreements are not binding as the divorce court has a discretion to decide whether the terms of the agreement should be binding in the circumstances of the case (see p. 187 above). However, although the courts have been increasingly willing to accept such agreements as binding, particularly if they have been made in a foreign jurisdiction (see *Radmacher* v. *Granatino* (1990) at p. 190), or where the marriage has been short and childless (see *Crossley* v. *Crossley* (2008), at p. 191), they have been unwilling to radically change the law. In *MacLeod* v. *MacLeod* [2008] UKPC 64, [2009] 1 FLR 641 Baroness Hale, giving judgment for the Board of the Privy Council, held that the difficult issue of the validity and effect of pre-nuptial agreements was more appropriate to legislative rather than judicial development.

In *Radmacher* v. *Granatino* [2009] EWCA Civ, [2009] 2 FLR 1181 (see p. 90) Thorpe LJ argued that the law should be changed to make pre-marital agreements binding:

> 'Due respect for adult autonomy suggests that, subject of course to proper safeguards, a carefully fashioned contract should be available as an alternative to the stress, anxieties and expense of a submission to the width of the judicial discretion. ... In so far as the rule that such contracts are void survives, it seems to me to be increasingly unrealistic. It reflects the laws and morals of earlier generations. It does not sufficiently recognise the rights of autonomous adults to govern their future financial relationship by agreement in an age when marriage is not generally regarded as a sacrament and divorce is a statistical commonplace. As a society we should be seeking to reduce and not to maintain rules of law that divide us from the majority of the member states of Europe. Europe apart, we are in danger of isolation in the wider common law world if we do not give greater force and effect to ante-nuptial contracts.'

In *Charman* v. *Charman (No 4)* [2007] EWCA Civ 503, [2007] 1 FLR 1246 (see p. 173), Sir Mark Potter P also expressed the view that consideration should be given to making pre-nuptial agreements binding in order to remove the difficulty of harmonising the law with the law in other Members States of the European Union where property agreements are upheld. Thorpe LJ made a similar plea in *Crossley* v. *Crossley* [2007 EWCA Civ 1491, [2008] 1 FLR 1467 (see p. 191).

Discussion about making pre-marital contracts is not new. In 1998 the government mooted the possibility of legislative reform to make pre-marital agreements binding, subject to certain safeguards (for example, if there was a child of the family) (*Supporting Families*, 1998, Home Office), but these proposals were taken no further.

In 2004, Resolution (the group of family lawyers) recommended that the s.25 factors (see 7.4) should be amended to give the court a duty to treat pre-marital agreements as legally binding, subject to the overriding safeguard of significant injustice to either party or to any minor child of the family (*A More Certain Future – Recognition of Pre-Marital Agreements in England and Wales*).

In July 2007 the Pre-Nuptial Agreement Bill was introduced into the House of Commons by Quentin Davies MP as a private member's bill to provide for the enforceability of pre-nuptial agreements, but this was not taken forward. The most recent development, however, is that the Law Commission, the Government's reform body, is to consider reform (see over).

There are arguments for and against making pre-marital agreements legally binding, which can be summarised as follows:

Arguments for making pre-marital agreements legally binding

- It would remove some of the uncertainty and unpredictability created by the current discretionary and alleged unsatisfactory nature of the law governing ancillary relief (see above), as the parties, not the courts, would be responsible for regulating their own financial and property matters on divorce.
- It would reduce the need for costly, time consuming and unpredictable litigation.
- It would respect the autonomy of the parties to choose how to regulate their own affairs.
- It would bring the law in England and Wales into line with Europe and other countries where marital agreements are binding.
- It would bring the law into line with the increasing emphasis on settlement and agreement on divorce.
- It might encourage more people to get married, as there may be people (particularly if they have been married before) who decide not to marry because they do not wish the courts to deal with their property in ancillary relief proceedings on divorce, should their marriage break down.

Arguments against making pre-marital agreements legally binding

- Making them binding may be unjust and unfair, particularly where unforeseen events happen in the marriage which are not catered for in the agreement (for instance the birth of children, ill-health, loss of a job, or receipt of a windfall).
- There may be problems drafting agreements, and lawyers may risk having negligence claims brought against them for failing to draft them appropriately.
- There may be problems of non-disclosure, duress, mistake and inequality of bargaining power.
- The birth of children may cause particular problems, because, although it may be appropriate for a spouse to contract out of any financial obligation to the other spouse, the parental obligation to support and maintain children cannot be terminated by agreement.
- Although greater use of agreements will reduce lawyers' and court time spent in respect of ancillary relief, cases are likely to be brought attacking such agreements on various grounds (such as duress, non-disclosure, incapacity and hardship).
- It may be difficult to draft legislation to protect against injustice and unfairness; and any new legislation may lead to greater complexity.

The Law Commission's programme   The Law Commission, the Government's reform body, is currently examining the status and enforceability of marital property and finance agreements made before or during marriage (and civil partnership). When announcing its programme of reform in 2008 it said that the legal recognition of marital property agreements as binding is of great social importance, and the fact that pre-nuptial agreements are not currently binding may deter some people from marrying or from entering into a civil partnership. It was of the view that a project on marital property agreements 'could reduce the impact of some of the most heavily criticised elements of the law of ancillary relief' and that they had 'the potential to offer couples a means of ensuring more certain outcomes on divorce'. It said that the issue might be of particular importance to couples who had experienced divorce and who wished to protect their assets, however extensive, from a future claim for ancillary relief; and for those who had entered into marital property agreements in jurisdictions in which such agreements were enforceable. The Law Commission's project began in September 2009 and it aims to produce a report and a draft parliamentary Bill by September 2012.

What will discussion of reform have to consider?

Although reform making pre-marital agreements binding would not be a panacea for solving all the problems in the current discretionary system of ancillary relief, there are strong arguments for making them binding and encouraging their use. However, discussion of reform will have to consider such matters as the following:

▷ *Formalities*   Should there be any particular formalities? Should there be a prescribed form? Should there be a compulsory requirement that the parties must seek independent legal advice? Should there be any limitation periods, for instance in respect of the time between the agreement and the marriage?

▷ *What about circumstances surrounding the making of the agreement?*   Should agreements be set aside on the basis of, for example, duress, lack of consent, non-disclosure, misrepresentation and mistake? Should they be set aside if they are manifestly unfair? Should they be set aside if there is no independent legal advice?

▷ *What about changes of circumstances during the marriage?*   Should they be open to scrutiny after they have been made? Should they be set aside if there is a change of circumstances, for instance the birth of a child, loss of employment or illness?

(d)   Reform: a 50:50 split of matrimonial assets

Equal division of matrimonial assets (subject to any agreement to the contrary) is common throughout Europe. Some states in the USA also have such arrangements on divorce; and in New Zealand, too, if a marriage has lasted more than three years, then the matrimonial assets are shared equally between the spouses unless extraordinary circumstances render equality repugnant to justice.

While a 50:50 split has certain advantages, in particular that it creates certainty, it does have drawbacks. One drawback is that, while such a split might create a fairer and more equitable result for middle and upper income families, it would be likely to create hardship for poorer families, because such a split would give many parties insufficient funds to rehouse themselves. This would cause hardship for children and injustice for the parties.

The possibility of introducing a 50:50 split has been discussed from time to time over the years, but although there have been no proposals to change the law, there has been a move towards equality of division of assets in 'big money' cases. In fact, Cretney went so far as saying that: 'English law now has, by virtue of judicial decision rather than legislation, a matrimonial regime of community of property' ([2003] CFLQ 403). Cooke ([2007] CFLQ 98) claimed that community of property was part of the thinking behind the yardstick of equality idea laid down by the House of Lords in *White* v. *White* (see p. 168).

(e) Reform: a set of general principles

Another possible reform that has been mooted is that the Matrimonial Causes Act 1973 should be amended to include a set of general principles which must be applied in addition to the s.25 factors. Although s.25 contains a list of factors to be taken into account, there is no express articulation of the principles and policies which govern the distribution of assets on divorce, other than that the child's welfare is the court's first consideration. There is no mention of any policy of fairness or whether marriage is a partnership of equals or whether there should be no discrimination between husbands and wives. The House of Lords in *Miller* v. *Miller* (see p. 172) laid down three 'principles' of needs, compensation and sharing, but has been criticised for adding what appears to be a gloss to the MCA 1973 by means of judicial law-making when such important changes to the law should have been done by Parliament.

Scotland has a discretionary system for allocating finance and property on divorce similar to that in England and Wales, but Scottish legislation lays down a set of general principles which courts must take into account when exercising their discretion. The introduction of a similar set of principles in England and Wales has been mooted from time to time. In 1998 the Government in its discussion paper, *Supporting Families* (Home Office, at para. 4.49), suggested the following set of general principles which the court could apply:

1. Seek first to promote the welfare of children by meeting their housing needs and those of their primary-carer.
2. Take into account any written agreement about financial arrangements.
3. Divide any surplus so as to achieve a fair result, recognising that fairness will generally require the value of the assets to be divided equally between the parties.
4. Try to determine financial relationships at the earliest date practicable.

The Lord Chancellor's Advisory Group on Ancillary Relief, which reported in 1998, said that it would not be appropriate to adopt the set of principles used in Scotland, but it was in unanimous agreement that there was a strong case for codifying in legislation the principles that are applied by the courts in England and Wales (*Report of the Lord Chancellor's Advisory Group on Ancillary Relief*, 1998).

Eekelaar (1998) has suggested a set of principles. The first would give priority to providing accommodation for the parties and children. After that, all property would be subject to a presumption of equal sharing, provided the parties had lived together for a minimum specified duration, and (unless the circumstances are exceptional) had brought up at least one child during that period. If the parties had lived together for less than the set period (he suggests 15 years), then the assets should not be divided 50:50, but in other proportions (perhaps 10:90 after 3 years, 20:80 after 6, 30:70 after 9, and 40:60

after 12). He said that such an approach could be used not just for divorcing couples, but also for cohabiting couples on relationship breakdown, at least for cohabitants who had children.

However, it must be questioned whether a set of principles will actually improve the law. The three strands of needs (generously construed), sharing and compensation enunciated in *Miller* v. *Miller* (see p. 172) have done little to stem the criticism emanating from lawyers, judges and academics about the unsatisfactory nature of the law in terms of certainty and predictability. In fact, the principles in *Miller* have been criticised for obfuscating rather than clarifying the law.

(f) Reform: the future

Despite discussions about reform, there is no consensus as to what the nature of any reform should be, except for the fact that there is some support for making pre-marital agreements binding, and the Law Commission is currently looking at this. While some commentators believe that clear rules may reduce litigation and encourage agreement, others believe that there is no firm evidence that clearer rules make agreement easier. Some believe that the unpredictability of the present system may actually encourage agreement and settlement (see Davis, Cretney and Collins, 1994). Harris (2008) makes the same point by referring to the following 'paradox' in *Miller* v. *Miller*:

> '[The paradox is] that in failing to achieve greater certainty the judges have both secured a powerful incentive for parties to negotiate rather than litigate (which incentive would be weakened if the law were more certain) and, further, have reduced the incentive for parties to incur costs and prolong cases by haggling over detailed facts.'

Harris states that the 'assertion that greater certainty in the law encourages, speeds up and reduces the cost of settlements, while uncertainty has the opposite effect, may be as open to question as it is trite'.

What is clear from discussions of reform, however, is that it will be extremely difficult to reform the law in order to produce a fair, just and effective system for adjusting finance and property matters on relationship breakdown which is both predictable and also flexible enough to deal with the infinite variety of family circumstances. Reforms of child support have been riddled with the same problems (see Chapter 12). Furthermore, in *Miller* v. *Miller* Baroness Hale spoke of the need for flexibility but for the law not to be 'too flexible'. This is the source of the difficulty. Rigid rules have their advantages and disadvantages. Flexibility has its advantages and disadvantages. But so too does a compromise which exists somewhere between the two extremes.

However, despite the difficulty of deciding on the nature of any reforms, practitioners and judges clearly believe that reform is needed. Resolution (the organisation of family law solicitors) has called for a fundamental reform of the rules of ancillary relief ([2007] Fam Law 203), and Nicholas Mostyn QC has strongly criticised the law for its continuing uncertainty ([2007] Fam Law 573).

Another way forward is to encourage couples to settle their own affairs. Hodson ([2007] Fam Law 57), in the wake of *Miller* v. *Miller*, suggested that one possible way forward is to adopt a formulaic approach in ancillary relief cases, not to replace the law and not to produce binding outcomes – but 'to help cases along the road to a settlement'. Another possibility is that of introducing statutory arbitration in ancillary relief cases. Thorpe LJ ([2008] Fam Law 27) has suggested that any debate about future legislative reform should consider 'the introduction of binding arbitration to enable couples, for whom compromise proves elusive, to embrace arbitration as an alternative route to a binding non-consensual outcome'. This, his Lordship claimed, would give parties 'some choice of the adjudication process and avoid the risk of lengthy delays in litigation'.

Summary

1   The emphasis in respect of finance and property on divorce is on settlement, with court proceedings being brought only in the last resort.

2   If the parties cannot reach agreement, financial provision and property adjustment orders can be sought on divorce (and on nullity or judicial separation) in ancillary relief proceedings under Part II of the Matrimonial Causes Act 1973. Orders can be made for a spouse and/or to or for the benefit of a child of the family, although child maintenance must be sought in most cases from the Child Maintenance and Enforcement Commission.

3   The procedure for ancillary relief applications is laid down in the Family Proceedings Rules 1991. The emphasis is on reaching agreement, saving cost and reducing delay. The district judge must 'actively manage' the case to achieve these aims. Both parties must personally attend a First Appointment (unless the court orders otherwise). At this hearing the district judge will define the issues, recommend the parties to mediation, and set an appointment for the next hearing. The parties will then be encouraged to settle their dispute at a Financial Dispute Resolution appointment. If the parties are unable to settle their differences, the case will proceed to a contested hearing.

4   There is a duty of full and frank disclosure.

5   The court in ancillary relief proceedings can make the following orders: maintenance pending suit (s.22), periodical payments orders (s.23); lump sum orders (s.23); property adjustment orders (s.24); orders for the sale of property (s.24A); and orders in respect of pensions (ss.25B–D).

6   The court must apply the s.25 guidelines when considering whether to make an order, and, if so, in what manner.

7   The House of Lords in *White* v. *White* (2000), a 'big money' case, said that the overarching objective in ancillary relief cases is that of fairness, and that there must be no discrimination between husbands and wives.

8   The House of Lords in *Miller* v. *Miller* (2006) endorsed the principles laid down in *White* v. *White*, and identified three guiding general principles which apply in ancillary relief cases: needs; compensation; and sharing.

9   The court must apply the clean break provisions when making orders in favour of spouses in original proceedings (s.25A) and in variation proceedings (s.31(7)).

10 Various orders may be made in respect of the matrimonial home. Tenancies can be transferred under s.24 Matrimonial Causes Act 1973 or under s.53 and Sched. 7 of the Family Law Act 1996.

11 Pensions can be taken into account by: 'offsetting'; making a pension attachment order; or making a pension sharing order.

Summary cont'd

12 Private agreements may be made on divorce. The court has jurisdiction to make consent orders (a court order incorporating an agreement in respect of periodical payments, lump sum and property adjustment). The parties can enter into a pre-marital or post-marital agreement, but there is a clear distinction between these orders. In *MacLeod* v. *MacLeod* (2008) the Privy Council held that post-marital agreements can be upheld (as they are no longer contrary to public policy), provided the terms of the agreement are fair and the circumstances surrounding the making of the agreement were fair. The Privy Council said that any change to the law on pre-marital agreements, on the other hand, was not a matter for the courts, but for Parliament.

13 Orders can be enforced in various ways.

14 A 'freezing order' can be granted under s.37 of the Matrimonial Causes Act 1973 or under the High Court's inherent jurisdiction to protect matrimonial assets pending the outcome of ancillary relief proceedings. A 'seek and search order' can be granted by the High Court to gain entry to premises to take out and copy evidence relevant to ancillary relief proceedings. These orders are granted only in exceptional circumstances because of their draconian nature.

15 An order for ancillary relief can be challenged in the following ways: by asking for a rehearing; by applying to have the order varied under s.31; by appealing against the order, which may require an application for permission to appeal out of time; or by applying to have the order set aside.

16 Applications for appeals out of time and applications to set orders aside are granted only in exceptional circumstances, because of the policy objective of finality in litigation. The court will not grant permission to appeal out of time unless the *Barder* principles are satisfied. An application to set aside an order will only be granted if the order is fundamentally unsound (such as for non-disclosure, fraud, mistake).

17 An application for permission to seek ancillary relief in the courts in England and Wales after a foreign divorce can be sought under Part III of the Matrimonial and Family Proceedings Act 1984.

18 The law on ancillary relief has been criticised because the discretionary jurisdiction creates uncertainty and unpredictability; and because the decisions of the House of Lords in *White* v. *White* (2000) and in *Miller* v. *Miller* (2006) have not helped to resolve these problems. Reforms have been discussed, in particular a presumption in favour of a 50:50 split of matrimonial property, making pre-nuptial agreements enforceable, and introducing a set of policy guidelines to govern the exercise of judicial discretion. There are no Government proposals to change the law, although the Law Commission is considering the law on marital agreements.

Further reading and references

Bailey-Harris, '*Lambert* v. *Lambert* – towards the recognition of marriage as a partnership of equals' [2003] CFLQ 417.

Barton, 'Domestic partnership contracts: sliced bread or a slice of bread?' [2008] Fam Law 900.

Bird, '*Miller* v. *Miller*: Guidance or confusion?' [2005] Fam Law 874.

Burrows, 'Enforceability of Family Agreements' [2008] Fam Law 235.

Cooke, '*White* v. *White* – a new yardstick for the marriage partnership' [2001] CFLQ 81.

Cooke, '*Miller/McFarlane*: law in search of discrimination' [2007] CFLQ 98.

Cretney, 'Community of property imposed by judicial decision' (2003) LQR 349.

Cretney, 'Private ordering and divorce – how far can we go?' [2003] Fam Law 399.

Davis, Cretney and Collins, *Simple Quarrels*, 1994, Clarendon Press.

Further reading and references cont'd

Davis, Pearce, Bird, Woodward and Wallace, 'Ancillary relief outcomes' [2000] CFLQ 43.

Deech, Baroness, 'What is a woman worth?' [2009] Fam Law 1140.

Douglas and Perry, 'How parents cope financially on separation and divorce – implications for the future of ancillary relief' [2001] CFLQ 67.

Duckworth and Hodson, '*White* v. *White* – bringing s.25 back to the people' [2001] Fam Law 24.

Eekelaar, 'Should s.25 be reformed?' [1998] Fam Law 469.

Eekelaar, 'Asset distribution on divorce – the durational element' (2001) LQR 552.

Eekelaar, 'Back to basics and forward into the unknown' [2001] Fam Law 30.

Eekelaar, 'Asset distribution on divorce – time and property' [2003] Fam Law 828.

Eekelaar, '*Miller* v. *Miller*. The descent into chaos' [2005] Fam Law 870.

Eekelaar, 'Property and financial settlement on divorce – sharing and compensation' [2006] Fam Law 754.

George, Harris and Herring, 'Pre-nuptial agreements: for better or for worse?' [2009] Fam Law 934.

Greensmith, 'Let's play ancillary relief' [2007] Fam Law 203.

Geffin, 'The judiciary: shifting the constitutional boundary and usurping Parliament's role' [2008] Fam Law 550.

Geffin, '*Miller/McFarlane* and *MacLeod* – the duality of law-making' [2009] Fam Law 412.

Harris, 'The *Miller* paradoxes' [2008] Fam Law 1096.

Harper and Alhadeff, '*Crossley* v. *Crossley*. Are pre-nuptial agreements now binding in England?' [2008] Fam Law 334.

Hodson, 'Financial provision: a formula will do nicely, sir' [2007] Fam Law 57.

Meehan, 'Analyse this: *Radmacher* v. *Granatino*' [2009] Fam Law 305.

Miles, '*Charman* v. *Charman (No 4)* – making sense of need, compensation and equal sharing after *Miller/McFarlane*' [2008] CFLQ 378.

Miles, '*Radmacher* v. *Granatino*: Upping the ante-nuptial agreement' [2009] CFLQ 513.

Miles and Probert (eds.), *Sharing Lives, Dividing Assets*, 2009, Hart Publishing

Morley, 'Enforceable prenuptial agreements: their time has come' [2006] Fam Law 772.

Ouazzani, 'Ancillary relief and the public/private divide' [2009] Fam Law 842.

Sharpe QC, 'Pre-Nuptial Agreements: A Rethink Required' [2008] Fam Law 741.

Thorpe, The Rt Hon Lord Justice, 'London – the divorce capital of the world' [2009] Fam Law 21.

Thorpe, The Rt Hon Lord Justice, 'Statutory arbitration in ancillary relief' [2008] Fam Law 27.

Warshaw and Brunsdon, 'The meaning of *MacLeod*' [2009] Fam Law 305.

Websites

The Law Society: www.lawsociety.org.uk
Resolution: www.resolution.org.uk

(For mediation websites, see Chapter 1).

Part V
Children and parents

Chapter 8

Children

This chapter considers children's rights and the protection of children under the wardship and inherent jurisdictions of the High Court. It considers, in particular, children's autonomy rights, the corporal punishment of children and children's right to participate in court proceedings.

8.1 Introduction

(a) Children's rights

During the twentieth century there was an increasing recognition and acceptance of the fact that children have rights. A major impetus for this was the children's liberationist movement in the USA in the 1960s and 1970s, which generated debate about the extent to which children should have rights. The children's liberationists took the view that children had the right to enjoy certain freedoms, in particular the right to be free to make decisions about themselves. Radical liberationists took the view that children had the right to enjoy the same freedoms as adults, but others took a more moderate view and argued that children have a right not to be forced into adulthood, and have rights to be protected and cared for. To give children too much autonomy might undermine and inhibit parental authority and have adverse repercussions for children.

Some theorists have preferred not to talk about rights, because of theoretical difficulties in doing so. Thus, under the 'will theory' it has been argued that children cannot have rights, because they do not have the necessary competence, or will, to make decisions. Children need adults to champion their rights. Some theorists have preferred not to talk about rights, but about children's 'interests' (for instance, Eekelaar, 1986), or to view children's rights in terms of the obligations adults owe them (for instance O'Neill, in Alston *et al*, 1992).

Some writers on children's rights and interests have attempted to classify them. Freeman (1983), for example, proposed four categories of rights: welfare rights; protective rights; rights grounded in social justice; and rights based on autonomy. Eekelaar (1986), who preferred to talk about 'interests', suggested that children have three types of interests: basic; developmental; and autonomy interests. Basic and developmental interests, he said, would prevail over autonomy interests where this was necessary to protect a child.

One of the dilemmas in the context of children's rights is the extent to which children should have rights of self-determination or autonomy. While some advocates of children's rights have argued in favour of greater autonomy for children, the law must strike a balance between recognising that children have greater rights of self-determination as they near adulthood, while also recognising that they need the protection of the law.

(b) Children's Commissioners

England and Wales each has a Children's Commissioner to act as a champion for children. The powers and duties of the English Commissioner are laid down in Part I of the Children Act 2004 and those of the Welsh Commissioner in the Care Standards Act 2000. However, whereas the Welsh Commissioner has a duty to 'to safeguard and promote the *rights* and welfare of children' (s.72A CSA Act 2000), the general function of the English Commissioner is merely to promote 'awareness of the views and *interests* of children in England' (s.2(1) CA 2004). The fact that there is no mention of the word 'rights' in the statutory provisions governing the role of the English Commissioner has been criticised by some commentators on children's rights (see Clucas [2005] Fam Law 290; and Fortin [2006] Fam Law 757).

The UK Children's Commissioners have a statutory responsibility for promoting the UN Convention on the Rights of the Child (see 8.2). Consequently, in June 2008 they submitted a joint report to the UN Committee on the Rights of the Child to show how the UK was failing to uphold the Convention. The worst injustices they identified were in respect of youth justice, immigration, the use of restraints in institutions and child poverty.

8.2 The UN Convention on the Rights of the Child 1989

The UN Convention on the Rights of the Child 1989 (the UNCRC) was created with the aim of encouraging governments worldwide to recognise the importance of children in society and to recognise that children have rights. It is the most ratified UN convention (with the USA and Somalia being the only UN members who have not ratified it). It covers the social, economic and civil rights of children and young people, as well as their protection from abuse, discrimination, exploitation, abduction and armed conflict.

Although the UK has ratified the UNCRC, it does not have the same force as the European Convention for the Protection of Human Rights (ECHR) (see 1.7) because it has not been incorporated into UK law and no court exists under the UNCRC to enforce it. The ECHR, in contrast, has been incorporated into the law of the UK by the Human Rights Act 1998 and persons can take cases to the European Court of Human Rights in Strasbourg. However, despite these drawbacks, the UNCRC is referred to by judges and lawyers in cases heard in the courts in England and Wales, and by judges in the European Court of Rights; and is also of persuasive value in legal argument before the courts in England and Wales. Furthermore, the UN Committee on the Rights of the Child monitors the implementation of the Convention in Member States. The UK Government also takes the UNCRC into account when considering new policies relating to children. The UNCRC has become increasingly recognised partly as a result of the Human Rights Act 1998, which has created a more rights-based culture in the UK.

The following articles of the UNCRC lay down key principles:

Article 2(1)

'States Parties shall respect and ensure the rights set forth in the present Convention to each child within their jurisdiction without discrimination of any kind, irrespective of the child's or his or her parent's or legal guardian's race, colour, sex, language, religion, political or other opinion, national, ethnic or social origin, property, disability, birth or other status.'

> ### Article 3(1)
>
> 'In actions concerning children, whether undertaken by public or private social welfare institutions, courts of law, administrative authorities or legislative bodies, the best interests of the child shall be a primary consideration.'
>
> ### Article 6
>
> '1. States Parties recognise that every child has the inherent right to life.
> 2. States Parties shall ensure to the maximum extent possible the survival and development of the child.'

Under the UNCRC children also have rights, *inter alia*: to freedom of expression (art. 13); to freedom of association and freedom of peaceful assembly (art. 15); to a private and family life (art. 16); to freedom of thought, conscience and religion (art. 14); to education (art. 28); to enjoy minority rights (art. 30); to rest and leisure (art. 31); to an adequate standard of living (art. 27); to protection against economic exploitation (art. 32); and to social security benefits (art. 26).

Children also have a right to contact with both parents on a regular basis, except when a court decides that it is contrary to the child's best interests (art. 9). States Parties must also protect children from all forms of abuse, neglect, maltreatment, exploitation and sexual abuse while in the care of their parents or other persons (art. 19). Children must be protected against: drugs (art. 33); sexual exploitation (art. 34); other forms of exploitation (art. 36); abduction (art. 35); and cruel, inhuman or degrading treatment or punishment (art. 37). The UNCRC also lays down rights for refugee children (art. 22) and disabled children (art. 23), and rights to health care and medical provision for children (art. 24).

The UNCRC recognises the importance of the family unit, and the importance of parents in the upbringing of their children. It provides that respect must be afforded to the responsibilities, rights and duties of parents, members of the extended family or community and others who are legally responsible for children (art. 5). It also recognises the importance of both parents having common responsibilities for the upbringing and development of their children, and having the primary responsibility for bringing them up (art. 18). Parents and others responsible for children must ensure that the child's living conditions are the best that can be secured in the circumstances (art. 27(2)), and States Parties must take all appropriate measures to recover maintenance for children from parents having financial responsibility (art. 27(4)).

The UN Committee on the Rights of the Child   The UN Committee on the Rights of the Child is responsible for monitoring the implementation of the UNCRC in Member States (see arts. 43 and 44). It does so by responding, by way of report, to periodical reports submitted by Member States about children's rights in their State. This reporting mechanism puts pressure on Member States to change their law when the UN Committee's Report (which is put into the public domain) criticises them for failing to promote the rights and best interests of children. In July 2007 the UK Government submitted its consolidated third and fourth Report to the UN Committee, whose responses to the Report were published in October 2008. In its Report on the UK, the UN Committee expressed concerns about a wide range of children's issues in the UK, including the treatment of young offenders in the youth justice system, child poverty, bullying and exclusion in schools, and the fact that the UK still permitted corporal punishment of children by their parents.

8.3 Children and the European Convention for the Protection of Human Rights

Children have rights under the European Convention for the Protection of Human Rights (ECHR) (see 1.7), even though it makes no express provision for, or reference to, children. Despite concerns (for example, by Herring (1999) and Fortin (1999)) about the impact of the ECHR on the welfare of children, and the possibility of tensions between the rights of parents and those of children, particularly in respect of the right to family life under art. 8, the European Court of Human Rights (ECtHR) has recognised that children have rights under the Convention and that their best interests are paramount and can prevail over parental interests. In *Hoppe* v. *Germany (Application No. 28422/95)* [2003] 1 FLR 384 the ECtHR made clear its acceptance of the primacy of the child's interests where a balance is required to be struck between competing Convention rights. In *Johansen* v. *Norway* (1997) 23 EHRR 33 it held that 'particular weight should be attached to the best interests of the child ... which may override those of the parent'. In *Scott* v. *UK* [2000] 1 FLR 958, which concerned the question of whether a mother's art. 8 rights had been breached by a local authority who had applied to free her child for adoption, the ECtHR stated that 'consideration of what is in the best interests of the child is always of crucial importance'. In *Keegan* v. *Ireland* (1994) 18 EHRR 342 the ECtHR held that a right to family life exists between a child and his parents 'even if at the time of his or her birth the parents are no longer cohabiting or if their relationship had then ended'.

The European Convention has played a greater role for children in England and Wales as a result of the coming into force of the Human Rights Act 1998 (see 1.7). Human rights are used in legal argument and by judges when making their decisions. However, Fortin claims that human rights arguments are not being used enough in children's cases, largely due to the primacy of the welfare principle in English law ([2006] 69 *Modern Law Review* 299).

8.4 The autonomy of children – the *Gillick* case

Gillick v. *West Norfolk and Wisbech Health Authority* [1986] AC 112 was an important case for two main reasons. First, it gave greater recognition to the rights of children to make decisions for themselves without parental interference. Secondly, it emphasised that it is better to talk about parental responsibilities, rather than parental rights. Children's autonomy rights have been considered by the courts mainly in the context of consent to medical treatment but in *Re Roddy (A Child) (Identification: Restriction on Publication)* (2003) (see p. 222 below) they were considered in the context of the right to freedom of expression.

▶ *Gillick* v. *West Norfolk and Wisbech Health Authority* **[1986] AC 112**

A Department of Health and Social Security (DHSS) circular was sent to doctors advising them that they would not be acting unlawfully if in exceptional circumstances they prescribed contraceptives to girls under the age of 16 without first obtaining parental consent, provided they did so in good faith. Mrs Gillick, an ardent Roman Catholic with teenage daughters, brought an action against the DHSS and her local hospital authority seeking a declaration that the circular was illegal on two grounds. First, it enabled doctors to break the criminal law by causing or encouraging unlawful sexual intercourse under the Sexual Offences Act 1956. Secondly, the circular was inconsistent with her parental rights. Mrs Gillick was successful in the Court of Appeal. The defendants appealed to the House of Lords.

The House of Lords held, allowing the appeal, that:

(i) There was no rule of absolute parental authority over a child until a fixed age, but that parental authority dwindled as the child grew older and became more independent. The law recognised parental rights only in so far as they were needed for the child's protection, so that it was more appropriate to talk of duties and responsibilities than rights. Parental rights, if any, yielded to the right of the child to make his or her own decisions if of sufficient understanding and intelligence. Consequently a girl under 16 did not merely by reason of her age lack legal capacity to consent to contraceptive treatment.

(ii) Neither had any offence under the Sexual Offences Act 1956 been committed, as the *bona fide* exercise of a doctor's clinical judgment negated the necessary *mens rea* (mental element).

LORD SCARMAN: 'The underlying principle of the law was exposed by Blackstone [in his *Commentaries on the Laws of England*] and can be seen to have been acknowledged in the case-law. It is that parental right yields to the child's right to make his own decisions when he reaches a sufficient understanding and intelligence to be capable of making up his own mind on the matter requiring decision.'

Gillick was applied and upheld in the following case, despite the applicant's argument that, with the coming into force of the Human Rights Act 1998, *Gillick* could no longer be considered good law. The case focused on the question of medical confidentiality between doctors and children:

▶ *R (Axon)* v. *Secretary of State for Health* [2006] EWHC 37 (Admin), [2006] 2 FLR 206

The applicant, the mother of teenage daughters, applied in judicial review proceedings for the following declarations: (i) that a doctor is under no obligation to keep confidential the advice or treatment he proposes to give a young person aged under 16 in respect of contraception, sexually transmitted infections and abortion, and should therefore not provide such advice and treatment without a parent's knowledge unless to do so might prejudice the child's physical or mental health so that it was in the child's best interests not to do so; and (ii) that the Department of Health's *Best Practice Guidance for Doctors and Other Health Professionals on the Provision of Advice and Treatment to Young People Under 16 on Contraception, Sexual and Reproductive Health* (2004) was unlawful because it violated parents' rights under art. 8 of the European Convention for the Protection of Human Rights (ECHR).

Silber J dismissed the application, holding that the *Gillick* case (see above) was determinative of these issues. There was no different rule on waiving confidentiality when abortion advice or treatment was being discussed from when contraceptive advice or other treatment was under consideration. Silber J held that the very basis and nature of the information which a medical professional received relating to the sexual and reproductive health of any patient of whatever age deserved the highest degree of confidentiality. The proposed limitation on the young person's right to confidentiality might well be inconsistent with the current trend towards a 'keener appreciation of the autonomy of the child and the child's consequential right to participate in the decision making-process'. The guidelines laid down in *Gillick* did not infringe parental rights under the ECHR. Not only did a young person

> have his or her own right to respect for family life, and a significant and compelling right to confidentiality of health information under the ECHR which would compete with, and potentially override, any right to parental authority, but also the right to parental authority dwindled as a child matured. The 2004 *Guidance* was not unlawful. *Gillick* did not establish as a matter of law that a medical professional should regard it as an exceptional practice, or unusual, to offer contraceptive advice or abortion advice or treatment to young people without first involving a parent.
>
> Silber J stated, however, that nothing in his judgment was intended to encourage young people to seek or to obtain advice or treatment on sexual matters without first informing their parents and discussing matters with them.

In *Axon* the challenge to *Gillick* on the basis of human rights therefore failed and *Gillick* remains a landmark decision in the development of children's rights. It was a landmark case because it brought about a recognition that children, particularly those of sufficient age and understanding, should have a greater say in decisions concerning them.

The impact of Gillick *on the Children Act 1989* The recognition in *Gillick* that children have a voice that should be heard was also reflected in the drafting of the Children Act 1989. Thus, in s.8 order proceedings (see 10.4) and in care and supervision proceedings (see 14.7) the court must have regard to the ascertainable wishes and feelings of the child concerned (considered in the light of his age and understanding) (s.1(3)(a)). A child can apply for s.8 orders, with leave of the court (s.10(8)); and a child with sufficient understanding to make an informed decision can refuse to consent to a medical or psychiatric examination, or other assessment (s.38(6)).

However, although *Gillick* had an impact on the content of the Children Act 1989, and the views and wishes of children of sufficient intelligence and understanding are given greater recognition, a child does not necessarily have the final say. It is always open to the court to overrule or discount a child's wishes. Furthermore, although there are many references to the child's welfare in the Children Act 1989, nowhere is there any reference to children's 'rights'. A child is not necessarily a party to family proceedings; and the child's consent is not needed in respect of removal from the UK or for a change of surname.

Gillick *– its progeny* Although *Gillick* was hailed as a landmark case for children's rights, it did not give children absolute rights. In fact, the House of Lords in *Gillick* stressed that, as far as contraception was concerned, only in exceptional cases would there be no parental involvement. As subsequent case-law has shown, the scope of children's autonomy rights depends on all the circumstances of the case. The wishes of a '*Gillick* competent' child (a child who is mature and intelligent enough to make an informed decision) can be overridden. The child's welfare is the court's paramount consideration, and '*Gillick* competence' is only one of the circumstances of the case. Thus, the outcome of a case depends not just on whether a child is *Gillick* competent, but on the nature and seriousness of the decision to be taken.

(a) Autonomy rights and medical treatment

The issues of autonomy rights of children and *Gillick* competency have been considered in several reported cases where children have *refused* to consent to medical treatment (*Gillick* was about consent). In these cases the courts have overridden the wishes of the child and authorised the treatment, even though the child concerned was mature enough to make an informed decision, and even though s.8 of the Family Law Reform Act 1969 provides that 16 and 17-year-olds can give valid consent to medical or dental treatment.

▶ *Re R (A Minor) (Wardship: Medical Treatment)* **[1992] Fam 11**

R, a girl aged 15 who had a serious mental illness, had been placed in an adolescent psychiatric unit. The local authority applied in wardship (see 8.7) for her to be given psychiatric treatment without her consent.

The Court of Appeal allowed the application, holding that she was not *Gillick* competent as her mental state fluctuated from day to day, but, even if she had been, the court would still have had the power to override her refusal. Lord Donaldson MR was also of the opinion that a *Gillick* competent child's refusal to have treatment could be overridden if a person with parental responsibility gave consent. The Court of Appeal held that a *Gillick* competent child could consent to medical treatment, but where such a child refused to give consent, then consent could be given by someone else with parental responsibility, including the court.

▶ *Re W (A Minor) (Medical Treatment: Court's Jurisdiction)* **[1993] Fam 64, [1993] 1 FLR 1**

W, a 16-year-old girl, suffered from anorexia nervosa. Her condition was rapidly deteriorating, but she refused treatment. The local authority applied to the court under its inherent jurisdiction (see 8.7) for it to authorise medical treatment for the girl, despite her refusal.

The Court of Appeal held, authorising the treatment, that the court has jurisdiction to override a *Gillick* competent child's refusal to consent to medical treatment, despite the provisions of s.8 Family Law Reform Act 1969 (which allows 16 and 17-year-olds to give valid consent to surgical, medical and dental treatment), as the court under its inherent *parens patriae* jurisdiction had theoretically limitless powers extending beyond the powers of natural parents. Nolan LJ said: 'In general terms the present state of the law is that an individual who has reached the age of 18 is free to do with his life what he wishes, but it is the duty of the court to ensure so far as it can that children survive to attain that age'.

▶ *South Glamorgan County Council v. W and B* **[1993] 1 FLR 574**

An interim care order had been made in respect of a severely disturbed 15-year-old girl with a direction under s.38(6) Children Act 1989 that she receive a psychiatric examination and assessment. When she refused to consent to the examination and assessment, the court under its inherent jurisdiction overrode her wishes and gave the local authority permission to take the necessary steps for her to be treated and assessed. The court so decided, despite the fact that s.38(6) expressly states that a child of sufficient understanding to make an informed decision can refuse to submit to the examination or other assessment, and notwithstanding the fact that she was *Gillick* competent. The court had the power to override the wishes of a mature minor in respect of medical treatment, despite statutory provisions in the Children Act 1989 to the contrary.

In *Re M (Medical Treatment: Consent)* [1999] 2 FLR 1097 Johnson J, following *Re W* (above), authorised that a 15-year-old girl should undergo an urgent heart transplant operation, despite her refusal to give consent.

In several cases the High Court has authorised the treatment of children who were refusing to undergo life-saving medical treatment because of their religious beliefs (they were Jehovah's Witnesses) (see, for example, *Re E (A Minor) (Wardship: Medical Treatment)* [1993] 1 FLR 386; and *Re P (Medical Treatment: Best Interests)* [2003] EWHC 2327 (Fam), [2004] 2 FLR 1117).

The cases therefore show that the *Gillick* competency principle is limited. A child does not have an absolute power of veto over medical treatment, as the court can always intervene to override the child's wishes. Thus, while children may have greater rights of self-determination than they used to have, they do not have absolute autonomy. Furthermore, the cases show that refusing treatment is treated quite differently from consenting to it. *Gillick* was about consent.

What if the child is nearly an adult? In *Re P (Medical Treatment: Best Interests)* [2003] EWHC 2327 (Fam), [2004] 2 FLR 1117 Johnson J held, *obiter dicta*, that where a child is nearly an adult the court will give very careful consideration to the child's wishes about medical treatment; and that there could be cases where the refusal of a child approaching 18 would be determinative. Nonetheless, in this case Johnson J granted the hospital leave to administer blood or blood treatments to a Jehovah's Witness (aged nearly 17) who objected, as did his parents, to the doctors using medical treatment involving blood or blood products.

(b) Autonomy rights and human rights

In the following two cases the court had to consider the autonomy of children in the context of their human rights, as it did in the *Axon* case (see p. 219 above). In both cases, teenage girls claimed that their human rights under the European Convention for the Protection of Human Rights (the ECHR) had been breached.

▶ *Re Roddy (A Child) (Identification: Restriction on Publication)* [2003] EWHC 2927 (Fam), [2004] 2 FLR 949

Angela Roddy (aged 16 at the time of the hearing) had given birth to a baby at the age of 12; and she had been in care of the local authority. Her baby was adopted despite her refusal to consent to adoption. On her reaching 16, the care order was discharged, on her application, and she wished to publish an account of her experiences in a national newspaper. The local authority applied to prevent publication, but Munby J refused the application, holding that she should be permitted to publish her story subject to conditions imposed to preserve the anonymity of the father and baby.

Munby J, referring to *Gillick* (see p. 218 above), held that the same principles which applied in other areas of adolescent decision-making also applied to the question of whether a minor could exercise her right to freedom of expression under art. 10 ECHR and choose to waive her right to privacy under art. 8. He held that it was the court's duty to defend the right of the child (who had sufficient understanding to make an informed decision) to make his or her own choice.

▶ *R (On the Application of Begum)* v. *Headteacher and Governors of Denbigh High School* [2006] UKHL 15

The claimant, a Muslim girl, claimed that her school had breached her right to freedom of religion under art. 9 ECHR because she had been excluded from school for wearing a jilbab (a form of Muslim dress which covers the arms and legs) rather than the shalwar kameez (tunic and trousers) which was permitted by her school. She also claimed that the school had breached her right to education under Art. 2 of Protocol 1 to the ECHR because she had been excluded from school. Her claim failed at first instance, but she was successful in the Court of Appeal. However, the House of Lords unanimously allowed the school's appeal, with the majority holding that her art. 9 right had not been breached. Lord Nicholls and Baroness Hale, on the other hand, held that her art. 9 right had been breached but that the breach was proportionate and justifiable on the facts (in particular, because the school had taken thorough steps to ensure that its school uniform policy did not offend the religious beliefs of Muslim children who attended the school, and those of their families).

8.5 The corporal punishment of children

Article 37 UN Convention on the Rights of the Child 1989

'No child shall be subject to cruel, inhuman and degrading treatment or punishment.'

Article 3 European Convention for the Protection of Human Rights

'No one shall be subject to inhuman or degrading treatment.'

Corporal punishment of children by their parents is permitted in limited circumstances, but it is outlawed in schools. Childminders are also prohibited from using any form of corporal punishment in respect of children in their care.

(a) Corporal punishment of children by parents

The development of society's attitude to the corporal punishment of children shows how differently children are treated today. At one time it was acceptable for parents to beat their children. Today, however, parents may commit a criminal offence if they use corporal punishment.

Physical chastisement of a child can constitute significant harm for the purposes of the Children Act 1989 and result in a local authority applying for a care or supervision order in respect of the child under s.31 CA 1989 (see 14.7), but the court may decide that the harm is not significant enough, as it did in the following two cases:

▶ *Re F (Interim Care Order)* [2007] EWCA Civ 516, [2007] 2 FLR 891

The Court of Appeal ordered that a child with attention deficit hyperactivity disorder who had been struck with a belt be placed in the care of the local authority with a view to adoption; but it refused to make final care orders in respect of the two younger siblings because the corporal punishment was not serious enough to justify their permanent removal from their parents.

▶ *Re MA (Children) (Care Proceedings: Threshold Criteria)* [2009] EWCA Civ 853

The Court of Appeal upheld a decision of the High Court to dismiss care proceedings in respect of three siblings, after the girl had said she had been kicked and slapped by her parents. The statutory threshold for a care order had not been crossed as the children had not suffered significant harm. Wall LJ held that the harm was insufficient to justify the intervention of the State and disturb the autonomy of the parents. Hallett LJ, agreeing with Wall LJ, said that reasonable physical chastisement of children by parents was not yet unlawful in England and Wales, and that slaps and kicks can vary enormously in their seriousness.

The corporal punishment of children by parents is not completely outlawed, as the defence of reasonable chastisement can be used in certain restricted circumstances. The defence of reasonable chastisement was laid down in the case of *R* v. *Hopley* (1860) 2 F&F 202 where Cockburn CJ held that the beating of a boy aged 13 by a teacher (which was supported by the parent) was 'reasonable' even though the boy later died.

In many European countries, however, there is a total ban on parents using corporal punishment. Sweden, for instance, imposed a ban in 1979, and other countries have outlawed it (for example, Austria, Croatia, Cyprus, Denmark, Finland, Germany, Iceland, Latvia, Norway, Romania and Ukraine). Over the years there has been increasing pressure to outlaw it in the UK, in particular by organisations such as End All Corporal Punishment of Children, and the National Society for the Prevention of Cruelty to Children (NSPCC). The UN Committee on the Rights of the Child in its three Reports on the UK has been critical of the UK for continuing to permit parents to inflict corporal punishment on their children.

Pressure to change the law   At the end of the 1990s the UK Government came under increasing pressure to change the law because of the following decision by the European Court of Human Rights:

▶   *A* v. *United Kingdom (Human Rights: Punishment of Child)* **[1998] 2 FLR 959**

The applicant, a boy aged 9, was beaten with a garden cane on a number of occasions by his step-father. The step-father was charged with assault occasioning actual bodily harm (under s.47 Offences Against the Persons Act 1861), but was acquitted because, although it was not disputed by the defence that the step-father had caned the boy on a number of occasions, the jury accepted his defence of 'reasonable chastisement' (see above). The applicant claimed before the European Court for the Protection of Human Rights (ECtHR) that the UK was in breach of art. 3 ECHR (the right not to be subjected to torture or to suffer inhuman or degrading treatment or punishment) and art. 8 (the right to a private and family life).

The ECtHR unanimously held that the UK was in breach of art. 3, because the reasonable chastisement defence did not give a child sufficient protection. It said that the ill-treatment must attain a minimum level of severity in order to fall within art. 3. On the facts, the step-father's ill-treatment of the child had reached that level taking into account the age of the child and the severity of the treatment. It held that the following factors were particularly important when establishing whether punishment was sufficiently severe to constitute ill-treatment for the purposes of art. 3: the nature and context of the defendant's treatment; its duration; its physical and mental effects in relation to the age and personal characteristics of the victim; and the reasons given by the defendant for administering the punishment.

Having concluded that there was a breach of art. 3, it held that there was no need to consider art. 8. The applicant was awarded £10,000 by way of damages.

As a result of the decision in *A* v. *UK*, the UK Government was obliged to consider the law with a view to reform, but it was not obliged to impose a complete ban on corporal punishment by parents, as the breach of art. 3 in *A* v. *UK* related to the degree of severity of the step-father's ill-treatment and to the unsatisfactory nature of the reasonable chastisement defence. The step-father's use of corporal punishment was not of itself a breach of art. 3.

In January 2000 the Government published a consultation document (*Protecting Children, Supporting Parents: A Consultation Document on the Physical Punishment of Children,* Department of Health) in which it said that, while harmful and degrading treatment of children could never be justified, it did not consider the right way forward was to make all physical punishment by parents unlawful. It said that there was 'a common-sense distinction between the sort of mild physical rebuke which occurs in families, and which most loving parents consider acceptable, and the beating of a child' (para. 1(5)). The Government said that it was considering introducing a statutory definition of the defence of 'reasonable chastisement' based on the criteria laid down in *A* v. *UK* (nature of the treatment, its context, duration etc), but this became unnecessary because, with the coming into force of the Human Rights Act 1998 (in October 2000), the courts in the UK were obliged to take account of the ruling in *A* v. *UK* in any event (under s.2(2) HRA 1998). In fact, before the HRA 1998 had come into force, the decision in *A* v. *UK* had been applied in *R* v. *H (Reasonable Chastisement)* [2001] EWCA Civ 1024, [2001] 2 FLR 431, where the Court of Appeal had held that, when juries are considering the reasonableness or otherwise of reasonable chastisement, they must be instructed by the judge to consider the criteria laid down in *A* v. *UK*.

In November 2001 the Government published its conclusions on the responses to its consultation document (above) (*An Analysis of Responses to Protecting Children, Supporting Parents: A Consultation Document on the Physical Punishment of Children*); and concluded (at para. 76) that it did not believe that 'any further change to the law at this time would command widespread public support or that it would be capable of consistent enforcement'. It said that the guidance issued by the Court of Appeal in *R* v. *H* (above) was sufficient to provide the protection guaranteed by art. 3 ECHR. It did say, however, that it intended to keep the defence of reasonable chastisement under review.

The Government's refusal to change the law did not command widespread support, and further pressure was put on the Government to change the law. At the end of 2004 renewed attempts were made to prohibit parents from using corporal punishment but proposals for an absolute ban were defeated in the House of Commons. However, a last-minute amendment to the Children Bill 2004 by Lord Lester of Herne Hill was accepted by the Government, which resulted in the enactment of s.58 of the Children Act 2004.

Section 58 Children Act 2004 This provision does not outlaw all forms of corporal punishment, as parents (and adults *in loco parentis*) can still continue to raise the defence of reasonable chastisement when charged with the offences of common assault or battery against a child (under s.39 of the Criminal Justice Act 1998). However, s.58 has removed the availability of the reasonable chastisement defence where the accused is charged with wounding, causing grievous bodily harm, assault occasioning actual bodily harm, or cruelty to a person under the age of 16. As a result, a defendant like the step-father in *A v. UK* (see above) would no longer be able to raise the defence.

When s.58 was going through Parliament, the Government promised to conduct a review of s.58 after it had been in force for two years. The Government kept to its promise, and published the results of its review in October 2007 (*Review of Section 58 of the Children Act 2006*, Cm 7232, Department for Children, Schools and Families). On the basis of its findings, the Government concluded that it did not intend to change the law to outlaw corporal punishment completely. It considered that, through the enactment of s.58, it had met its international obligations under the UN Convention on the Rights of the Child and the European Convention for the Protection of Human Rights. The Government found, as part of its review, that parents were using corporal punishment less, but that 52 per cent of parents (compared with 88 per cent in 1998) still favoured retaining the right to do so. The Government noted, and accepted, however, that there appeared to be a lack of understanding about what the law did and did not allow. It said that it would do more to help with positive parenting; and also ask the Crown Prosecution Service and the police to monitor the situation with regard to the use of reasonable punishment.

Should corporal punishment by parents be outlawed completely?   Despite the restrictions imposed by s.58 on parental punishment of children, many organisations believe corporal punishment should be outlawed completely (for example the NSPCC, Save the Children, 11 Million, and the Children's Rights Alliance). The UN Committee on the Rights of the Child (see 8.2) has also recommended its complete abolition.

Various arguments can be put forward in favour of imposing a complete ban. One is that condoning corporal punishment creates a culture of abuse which can lead to children being harmed – in some cases very seriously. It can also be argued that the current law creates confusion for parents, advisers and prosecutors, because of the difficulty of distinguishing common assault and battery from the other criminal offences for which there is no defence of reasonable punishment available. Another argument in favour of a complete ban is that the current law breaches children's human rights under the European Convention for the Protection of Human Rights. On the basis that adults do not suffer the same treatment, it can be argued that children are being discriminated against under art. 14 in respect of their art. 3 right not to suffer inhuman and degrading treatment, and their art. 8 right to a private and family life.

(b)   Corporal punishment in schools

Corporal punishment of children is banned in all schools (by s.548 Education Act 1996). It was banned first of all in State schools (s.47 Education (No. 2) Act 1986), and later in independent schools. Thus the use of physical force or punishment by a teacher on a schoolchild can give rise to criminal or civil liability, and there is no defence of reasonable chastisement. However, a teacher can in certain limited circumstances use reasonable restraint on a schoolchild (s.550A Education Act 1996).

The following case was highly influential in leading to the abolition of corporal punishment in State schools:

▶ *Campbell and Cosans* v. *UK* (1982) 4 EHRR 293

Two mothers from Scotland claimed that the use of corporal punishment in State schools breached their son's rights not to suffer inhuman and degrading treatment under art. 3 ECHR.

The ECtHR found no breach of art. 3 – as the boys had not been punished or threatened with punishment – but held that there had been a breach of art. 2 of Protocol 1 to the ECHR, which provides that '[n]o person shall be denied the right to education', and that 'the State shall respect the right of parents to ensure such education and teaching in conformity with their own religious and philosophical convictions'. The ECtHR held that Jeffrey Cosan's right to education had been breached as he had been suspended from school for nearly a year, because his parents objected to corporal punishment. And both applicants' rights had been breached, because corporal punishment was not in conformity with their philosophical convictions.

In *Costello-Roberts* v. *UK* (1993) 19 EHRR 112 the applicant boy claimed that the corporal punishment he had suffered at his independent school breached arts. 3, 8 and 13 of the European Convention for the Protection of Human Rights. His claim failed, but in September 1999 corporal punishment in independent schools was eventually abolished.

In the following case parents and teachers at Christian schools objected on religious grounds to the abolition of corporal punishment in schools:

▶ *R (Williamson)* v. *Secretary of State for Education and Employment and Others* [2005] UKHL 15, [2005] 2 FLR 374

Headteachers, teachers and parents at certain Christian independent schools claimed in judicial review proceedings that the ban on corporal punishment in schools breached their rights to freedom of religion under the European Convention for the Protection of Human Rights. They claimed that it was a tenet of their fundamental Christian belief that parents (and teachers) should be able to administer physical punishment to children. They wished teachers to be able to administer reasonable chastisement because they believed it was conducive to the moral well-being of children. They claimed that s.548 of the Education Act 1996 did not completely abolish the use of corporal punishment in independent schools, and that, if it did so, it was a breach of art. 9(1) (right to freedom of religion) and art. 2 of Protocol No. 1 ECHR, which provides that '[n]o person shall be denied the right to education' and that 'the State shall respect the right of parents to ensure such education and teaching in conformity with their own religious and philosophical convictions'. Their application was rejected at first instance. Their appeal was dismissed by the Court of Appeal, and so they appealed to the House of Lords.

The House of Lords held, dismissing their appeal, that there was no breach of the ECHR. Section 548 of the Education Act 1996 did not breach their rights to freedom of religion under art. 9(1) because the ban complied with art. 9(2), which permits freedom of religion to be limited by law where 'necessary in a democratic society … for the protection of the rights and freedoms of others'. The statutory ban pursued a legitimate aim (to protect children from physical violence) and the means used to achieve that aim were appropriate and not disproportionate.

8.6 Children as parties in family proceedings

Article 12 United Nations Convention on the Rights of the Child 1989

'1. States Parties should assure to the child who is capable of forming his or her own views the right to express those views freely in all matters affecting the child, the views of the child being given due weight in accordance with the age and maturity of the child.

2. For this purpose, the child shall in particular be provided the opportunity to be heard in any judicial and administrative proceedings affecting the child, either directly, or through a representative or an appropriate body, in a manner consistent with the procedural rules of national law.'

The rules for representation of children in private law family proceedings differ from those which apply in public law proceedings. In private law proceedings the child can be represented through a Children's Guardian or instruct a solicitor without such person but only if the judge so decides. In other words, involving the child is a matter for the court's discretion. In public law proceedings, on the other hand the child automatically becomes a party to the proceedings, and is represented through a Children's Guardian.

(a) Private law

(i) Making an application to the court   A child can apply for a s.8 order under the Children Act 1989 (such as for residence or contact), but only with leave of the court, which can be granted if the court considers that the child has sufficient understanding to make the application (s.10(8) CA 1989). Although the test of sufficient understanding is that of *Gillick* competence (see p. 218), only older teenagers are likely to be held to have the required sufficiency of understanding (see, for example, *Re C (Residence: Child's Application for Leave)* [1995] 1 FLR 927). In practice very few applications are brought by children.

Children can also bring proceedings under the inherent jurisdiction of the court (see 8.7) with a next friend or Children's Guardian, or can apply during such proceedings to discharge the next friend or Guardian.

(ii) Rights of representation for children   The usual way in which the voice of the child is conveyed to the court in private law proceedings (such as for residence and contact) is by means of a welfare report prepared by the Child and Family Reporter (a Cafcass officer, see 1.6). Children do not have party status, or the legal representation that accompanies it, unless the court makes an order under r. 9 of the Family Proceedings Rules 1991. If the court considers it is in the child's best interests to be made a party to family proceedings, it can in the exercise of its discretion appoint a Children's Guardian (an officer of Cafcass) to take part in the proceedings on the child's behalf (r.9.5 FPR 1991). The guardian will work in tandem with the lawyer acting for the child. Macdonald ([2009] Fam Law 40) has argued that there should be a *duty*, rather than a discretion, under r.9.5 to appoint a guardian, unless the court is satisfied that such an appointment is not necessary to safeguard the child's interests.

(iii) Separate representation of children   In recent years there has been growing concern that children in private family proceedings (particularly for residence and contact) are not being given sufficient opportunity to instruct their own solicitor without having to do so via a Children's Guardian (see above). Thus, although under r.9.2A(4) FPR 1991 the child can ask the court for leave to remove the Children's Guardian (so that the child can instruct the lawyer directly), in practice this rarely happens, even though the rules provide that the court *must* give leave if it considers the child has sufficient understanding to participate in the proceedings without a Guardian (r.9.2A(6) FPR 1991).

The *President's Direction (Representation of Children in Family Proceedings Pursuant to Family Proceedings Rules 1991, Rule 9.5)* [2004] 1 FLR 1188 provides that making a child party to proceedings is a step to be taken only in cases involving an issue of significant difficulty. For this reason, it states that separate representation will occur in only a minority of cases. Before making a child a party, it states that the court should consider whether an alternative might be better. The *Direction* states that the court might be justified in making an order for a child to be a party, and have separation representation, where, for example: there is an intractable residence or contact dispute; the child has interests which are not capable of being represented by any of the adult parties; the child's views cannot be adequately met by a report to the court; an older child is opposing a proposed course of action; or there are complex medical, mental health or other issues which necessitate separate representation of the child. The *Direction* also draws attention to the fact that granting separate representation to a child may cause delay.

The following important case concerned children having the right to instruct their own lawyer in private family law proceedings:

> ▶ *Mabon v. Mabon and Others* **[2005] EWCA Civ 634, [2005] 2 FLR 1011**
>
> Three teenage boys (aged 13, 15 and 17), who were living with their father on the breakdown of their parents' relationship, wished to be separately represented in court proceedings involving a residence dispute between their parents. The boys had three younger siblings, who were living with the mother, but the mother sought residence orders against the father in respect of all six children. A Cafcass officer filed a report and was appointed Guardian of all six children. During the trial, however, the three oldest boys contacted a solicitor. At the residence hearing the boys' solicitor applied under r.9.2A FRP 1991 (see above) for them to be separately represented, but the application was refused. The boys appealed to the Court of Appeal.
>
> The Court of Appeal unanimously allowed their appeal, holding that the judge had been plainly wrong. Thorpe LJ said that it was unthinkable to exclude young men from knowledge of and participation in legal proceedings that affected them so fundamentally. He said that, in the case of articulate teenagers, courts must accept that the right to freedom of expression and participation in family life outweighed the paternalistic judgment of welfare, and that the case provided a timely opportunity to recognise the growing acknowledgment of the autonomy and consequential rights of children. Thorpe LJ said that in individual cases trial judges must equally acknowledge this shift of approach when they made a proportionate judgment of the sufficiency of the child's understanding.

(*Mabon* v. *Mabon* was applied in *Re C (Abduction: Separate Representation of Children)* [2008] EWHC 517 (Fam), [2008] 2 FLR 6 where the children were granted separate representation in a case brought under the Hague Convention on Abduction, see 13.4).

In most cases, however, unlike the approach adopted in *Mabon*, the court will usually consider that the child's views and best interests will be sufficiently safeguarded by asking for a welfare report (under s.7 Children Act 1989). Participating in court proceedings can be a harrowing and traumatic experience for some children. Not only are they exposed to the risk of having to make choices about their parents, but they are also open to being manipulated by one parent, or both. The courts are keen to ensure that children are protected from the potentially harmful effect of being involved in adversarial litigation. Allowing children to participate in family proceedings, such as contact and residence, can also add to the delay and cost of the trial. In the following case a different approach was taken from that in *Mabon*:

> ▶ *Re N (Contact: Minor Seeking Leave to Defend and Removal of Guardian)* [2003] 1 FLR 652
>
> Coleridge J held that an 11-year-old boy who wished to defend the contact proceedings did not have sufficient understanding to participate and give instructions on his own behalf without a Guardian. Complex issues were involved against a background of a long and stormy contact dispute. The child would not be able to understand the issues involved. Consequently he did not have sufficient understanding to participate. Coleridge J held that the test of competence was 'not whether the child was capable of articulating instructions but whether the child was of sufficient understanding to participate as party in the proceedings, in the sense of being able to cope with all the ramifications of the proceedings and giving considered instructions of sufficient objectivity'.

Whybrow (2004), commenting on *Re N*, said that the test of competence was set high and 'would render many adults incapable of conducting their family litigation, let alone children'.

The Court of Appeal has held that there is no objection to a service such as the National Youth Advocacy Service (www.nyas.org.uk) representing a child in private law proceedings, such as in a contact dispute (see *Re H (National Youth Advocacy Service)* [2006] EWCA Civ 896, [2007 1 FLR 1028).

(iv) Is the voice of the child being heard sufficiently in family proceedings? Despite the fact that art. 12(2) of the UN Convention on the Rights of the Child 1989 requires a child to be given the opportunity to be heard in legal proceedings either directly or indirectly (see p. 228 above) and s.1(3)(a) of the Children Act 1989 requires the court to have regard to 'the ascertainable wishes and feelings of the child concerned (considered in the light of his age and understanding)' (see 10.3), there has been concern that children are not being listened to enough in private law proceedings; and that judges should be more willing to allow them to be separately represented by their own lawyer (see, for example, Macdonald [2008] Fam Law 648; [2009] Fam Law 40). In *Mabon* v. *Mabon* (see above) Thorpe LJ said that 'in the twenty-first century, there is a keener appreciation of the autonomy of the child and the child's consequential right to participate in decision-making processes that fundamentally affect his family life'. Furthermore, in *Re D (A Child) (Abduction: Rights of Custody)* [2006] UKHL 51, [2007] 1 FLR 961 Baroness Hale drew attention to the growing importance of listening to the views of children:

'[T]here is now a growing understanding of the importance of listening to children in children's cases. It is the child, more than anyone else, who will have to live with what the court decides. Those who do listen to children understand that they often have a point of view which is quite distinct from that of the person looking after them. They are quite capable of being moral actors in their own right. Just as the adults may have to do what the court decides whether they like it or not, so may the child. But that is no more reason for failing to hear what the child has to say than it is for refusing to hear the parent's views.'

In the last few years, there has been a growing interest and increased debate about reforming the law governing the voice of the child in family proceedings, something which has been promoted in part by the Family Justice Council (see [2008] Fam Law 431), and the views of Sir Mark Potter, President of the Family Division. However, although there is considerable support for the idea that children should be more involved in family proceedings, the difficult question concerns the extent to which they should be involved. For some children it may be distressing to hear the details of their parents' case in court. As Thorpe LJ warned in *Mabon* (see above), if direct participation in proceedings 'would pose an obvious risk of harm to the child, arising out of the continuing proceedings, and, if the child is incapable of comprehending that risk, then the judge is entitled to find that sufficient understanding has not been demonstrated'. Thorpe LJ said, however, that judges also have to be 'equally alive to the risk of emotional harm that might arise from denying the child knowledge of and participation in the continuing proceedings'.

(v) A breach of human rights?   Refusing to allow a child to participate in family proceedings, with or without a guardian, might, depending on the circumstances of the case, be a breach of one or more of the following rights in the European Convention for the Protection of Human Rights: art. 6 (the right to a fair trial); art. 8 (the right to family life); art. 10 (the right to freedom of expression); and art. 12 (the right to an effective remedy). In *Re A (Contact: Separate Representation)* [2001] 1 FLR 715 Butler-Sloss P recognised that there were cases where children needed to be separately represented, and cases where she suspected that the voices of children had not always been sufficiently heard. She said that the courts' attitude to separate representation needed to change as a result of arts. 6 and 8 of the ECHR. However, although the European Court of Human Rights has not ruled on the need for separate representation in children's cases, in two cases brought against Germany involving contact disputes it was critical of the German courts' failure to hear the children's views (see *Elsholz v. Germany* [2000] 2 FLR 486; *Sahin v. Germany* [2002] 1 FLR 119).

In respect of the child's right to be heard in legal proceedings under art. 12(2) of the UNCRC (see p. 228 above), the UN Committee on the Rights of the Child has expressed concern about the failure of the UK courts to allow children to be represented in private law proceedings.

(vi) Are some children's voices being heard at all?   There is concern not just about whether separate representation should be more widely available for children in private family proceedings, but whether children's voices are being sufficiently heard at all. The wishes and feelings of the child may be overlooked by parents who are involved in a difficult conflict, and in some cases the court may decide not to commission a welfare report (under s.7 Children Act 1989). There have also been concerns that Cafcass officers may not be listening to children enough because of time constraints arising as a result of the under-staffing and under-resourcing of Cafcass.

(vii) Separate representation of children – reform   Although s.122 Adoption and Children Act 2002 amended the Children Act 1989 to allow rules of court to be drawn up to allow children to have separate representation in s.8 order proceedings under the Children Act 1989 (s.41(6A)), these rules have not been made but merely discussed. The Government has consulted on the question of allowing separate representation of children in private law proceedings. In its *Consultation Paper, Separate Representation of Children* (CP/20/06, 2006) it said that its aim in reforming the law would be to create a cultural change in respect of the availability of separate representation for children and to create greater consistency in its use between different courts. However, it said that only a small proportion of s.8 proceedings would be suitable for separate representation. The responses to the consultation were published in July 2007 in *Separate Representation of Children: Summary of Responses to a Consultation Paper*, CP(R)20/06, in which the Government said that it proposed to extend jurisdiction for deciding whether a child should be made a party to family proceedings to all levels of court. It also proposed that children would be provided with information during the course of proceedings to help them cope with associated anxieties and uncertainties; and that, subject to agreement with the judiciary, children who wished to speak to a judge or magistrate should be able to do so.

These proposals have not been introduced. However, Sir Mark Potter, President of the Family Division, reported that in 2008–2009 there was a more than a 30 per cent increase (on 2007–2008) in the ordering of separate representation of children under r.9.5 FPR 1991 (see [2009] Fam Law 466).

(viii) Should judges interview children?   In the last few years there has been discussion about whether judges should have the right to interview children in order to discover their views. In New Zealand, for instance, the courts have adopted the practice of interviewing children but with carefully written guidelines governing the practice ([2008] Fam Law 809). Sir Mark Potter, President of the Family Division, is in favour of judicial interviews of children in some cases ([2008] Fam Law 809; and [2008] IJFL 140); and has supported Wilson LJ's view ([2007] Fam Law 808) that it should become the norm for a judge when concluding family proceedings to offer a child who lacks a Guardian the opportunity for a face-to-face meeting with the judge. No reforms, however, have been introduced.

(b) Public law cases

In public law proceedings (such as for care and supervision orders) the system of representation for children operates with a Children's Guardian (an officer of Cafcass) and a solicitor acting side by side. Thus, children involved in public law proceedings are made a party to the proceedings. This has been so since the mid-1970s when the practice of using guardians *ad litem* to put forward the voice of the child was introduced as a result of the recommendations made in the wake of the Maria Colwell Inquiry in 1974.

8.7 Protection for children in wardship and under the inherent jurisdiction

(a) Introduction

The inherent jurisdiction, of which wardship is a part, is an ancient jurisdiction deriving from the right and duty of the Crown as *parens patriae* (parent or protector of the realm) to take care of persons who are unable to care for themselves, which includes not just children, but also incapacitated adults (for instance in the context of marriage, see 2.2). Only the High Court has jurisdiction in wardship and under the inherent jurisdiction.

(i) Applications by local authorities   Before the Children Act 1989 came into force, local authorities preferred using wardship to take a child into care, even though there were statutory provisions for obtaining and making care orders. However, the Children Act 1989 changed that practice, so that a local authority can no longer use the inherent jurisdiction to: place a child in its care or under its supervision (s.100(2)(a)); accommodate a child in care (s.100(2)(b)); make a child a ward of court (s.100(2)(c)); or give it power to determine a question about any aspect of parental responsibility for a child (s.100(2)(d)).

However, a local authority is not totally precluded from invoking the inherent jurisdiction, as it can, in circumstances other than those prohibited above, ask the High Court to give it leave to invoke it (s.100(3) CA 1989). The High Court can grant leave if it is satisfied that: the result which is wanted cannot be achieved by any other order; and there is reasonable cause to believe that the child will suffer significant harm if the inherent jurisdiction is not exercised (s.100(4)). Local authorities have sometimes successfully invoked the inherent jurisdiction in cases where children need medical treatment (see p. 221). Hospitals and health authorities sometimes invoke the jurisdiction in difficult medical cases in order to ask the court to authorise or terminate the medical treatment of a child.

(ii) Applications by private individuals   Although there is no express prohibition in the Children Act 1989 against private individuals invoking the inherent jurisdiction, including wardship, it is now rarely invoked, as the Children Act 1989 has two orders (the s.8 specific issue and prohibited steps orders, see 10.7 and 10.8) which are similar to the High Court's inherent powers. As a result, in private law cases, as in local authority cases, the inherent jurisdiction, including wardship, now exists only as a residual jurisdiction providing a safety net for complex and difficult cases (for example, difficult medical cases involving children (see p. 221); some international child abduction cases (see 13.10); and some forced marriage cases (see 2.6)).

(iii) Section 8 orders   As proceedings under the inherent jurisdiction (and in wardship) are 'family proceedings' for the purpose of the Children Act 1989, the High Court can make any s.8 order in the proceedings (see 10.4), except where the child is in care, when only a residence order can be made (s.9(1)). As a s.8 order cannot be made in favour of a local authority on an application by a local authority when a child is in care (ss.9(1) and (2)), a local authority which wishes to resolve a question about a child in care (such as in respect of medical treatment) must apply for leave to invoke the inherent jurisdiction (see above).

(b)　Wardship

Wardship is part of the inherent jurisdiction of the High Court. The essence of wardship is that, once a child is made a ward of court, the situation is frozen and the court stands *in loco parentis* for the child. As the court has parental responsibility for the child, any major step in the child's life requires the court's prior consent. Thus, for example, a ward cannot marry, be adopted, leave the jurisdiction, or receive serious medical treatment without the court's consent. It is this supervisory role of the court which distinguishes wardship from the inherent jurisdiction. Wardship is also useful in urgent situations, for the High Court acquires powers in respect of the child automatically on the issue of the initial application. For this reason wardship is useful in abduction cases (see 13.10). It has also been used in forced marriage cases, even where the young person concerned is residing outside the jurisdiction (see 2.6).

The governing principle in wardship proceedings is that the welfare of the child is the court's paramount consideration (s.1(1) CA 1989). Provided the High Court has jurisdiction to make the child a ward of court, it can exercise a wide range of powers. Under the Children Act 1989 it can: make any s.8 order; make a s.37 direction that a local authority make enquiries about a child; appoint a guardian for the child; and make orders for financial provision under Sched. 1. It also has the power to grant injunctions.

Although the wardship jurisdiction is theoretically limitless, in some situations the court will refuse to exercise it (for instance, where wardship will undermine a statutory power; and in immigration and asylum cases) (see below). Inappropriate uses of wardship are therefore not permitted.

(c)　The inherent jurisdiction

The High Court has a general inherent power to protect children (and incapacitated adults) which is independent of the wardship jurisdiction. The inherent jurisdiction is sometimes used to obtain the court's permission to allow or refuse medical treatment, for example: to arrange medical treatment for a 16-year-old anorexic girl in care (*Re W (A Minor) (Medical Treatment: Court's Jurisdiction)* [1993] Fam 64); to give blood transfusions to a child whose parents object to treatment on religious grounds (*Re O (A Minor) (Medical Treatment)* [1993] 2 FLR 149); and to obtain guidance on the treatment of a severely handicapped child (*Re J (A Minor) (Medical Treatment)* [1992] 2 FLR 165).

The inherent jurisdiction is also sometimes used in forced marriage cases (see 2.6); and in abduction cases (see 13.10). It has also been be used in the case of vulnerable adults, in other words where a person lacks mental capacity (see, for example, *A Local Authority* v. *E* [2007] EWHC 2396 (Fam), [2008] 1 FLR 978, which involved a 19-year-old woman with a severe learning difficulty who had been made the subject of a care order at the age of 15).

The inherent jurisdiction has sometimes been used to fill in gaps in the law in order to protect the best interests of children, as it was in *Re D (Unborn Baby)* [2009] EWHC 446 (Fam), [2009] 2 FLR 313 where Munby J made an order under the inherent jurisdiction in respect of an unborn baby, because the Children Act 1989 and the wardship jurisdiction could not be invoked in respect of an unborn child. In this case the local authority successfully applied for an anticipatory declaration under the inherent jurisdiction declaring that it could lawfully remove a baby at birth from her mother because there was a serious and likely risk that the mother would seriously harm the child. The inherent jurisdiction was also invoked in *Re C (Abduction: Separate Representation of Children)* [2008] EWHC 517 (Fam), [2008] 2 FLR 6, where the child concerned was too old to come within the jurisdiction of the Hague Convention on Abduction (see 13.5).

(d) Limits on the use of wardship and the inherent jurisdiction

In addition to the restrictions placed on local authorities (see p. 233 above), the High Court may refuse to exercise the jurisdiction or refuse to make a child a ward of court even though wardship and the inherent jurisdiction are theoretically limitless. The following cases provide examples:

> ▶ *S v. S* **[2007] EWHC 2640 (Fam), [2009] 1 FLR 241**
>
> The mother of the child was resisting deportation as a failed asylum seeker. The mother's cousin began wardship proceedings in respect of the child, but Munby J dismissed the application, holding that the High Court cannot, even in the exercise of its inherent jurisdiction, make orders which in any way impinge upon or prevent the Secretary of State exercising powers lawfully conferred by statute in the context of immigration and asylum (following *R v. Secretary of State for the Home Department ex parte T* [1995] 1 FLR 293; and *Re A (Care Proceedings: Asylum Seekers)* [2003] EWHC 1086 (Fam), [2003] 2 FLR 921). Munby J held that, in the circumstances of the case, the wardship proceedings were not serving any useful or permissible purpose.
>
> ▶ *Re F (In Utero)* **[1998] Fam 122**
>
> The High Court refused to make an unborn child a ward of court, as this would place an unjustifiable fetter on the rights of the child's mother.
>
> ▶ *R (Anton) v. Secretary of State for the Home Department; Re Anton* **[2004] EWHC 273/2731 (Admin/Fam) [2005] 2 FLR 818**
>
> The High Court refused to make an injunction in wardship to prevent a child leaving the UK where the child and his family were subject to immigration control. Munby J held that the fact that the child was a ward of court could not limit or confine the exercise of the Secretary of State's powers.
>
> ▶ *Re X (A Minor) (Wardship: Jurisdiction)* **[1975] Fam 47**
>
> An application was made to ward a child for the purpose of prohibiting the publication of a book which contained references to the salacious behaviour of her deceased father which might harm her if the book came to her knowledge. Jurisdiction was refused on the ground that freedom of speech and freedom of publication prevailed over the child's welfare.

(e) Protecting children from media intrusion and harmful publication

Applications to the High Court in wardship or under its inherent jurisdiction can be made to obtain an injunction to protect a child from harmful media attention and exposure (see, for example, *Re Z (A Minor) (Freedom of Publication)* [1996] 1 FLR 191, [1997] Fam 1; and *Nottingham City Council v. October Films Ltd* [1999] 2 FLR 347). But jurisdiction may be refused on the ground that freedom of speech prevails, as the following case shows:

> ▶ *R (Mrs)* v. *Central Independent Television plc* **[1994] Fam**
>
> A child was made a ward of court, on the application of her mother, in order to prevent a television programme being broadcast which discussed the child's father's conviction and imprisonment for indecency. The decision of the High Court was overturned by the Court of Appeal. Waite LJ stated that no child, simply by virtue of being a child, is entitled to a right of privacy or confidentiality. As the programme had nothing to do with the care or upbringing of the child, there was nothing to put in the balance against the freedom to publish.

The Human Rights Act 1998 gives particular priority to the right to freedom of speech under art. 10 of the ECHR (see s.12(4)) and the High Court in children's cases must weigh this in the balance when considering the child's art. 8 right to a private and family life, and the child's welfare.

The following decision of the House of Lords is the leading case on preventing publication in order to protect a child:

> ▶ *Re S (Identification: Restriction on Publication)* **[2004] UKHL 47, [2005] 1 FLR 591**
>
> The guardian of an eight-year-old child obtained an injunction under the inherent jurisdiction to restrain publication of the identity of the child's mother who had been charged with the murder of the child's older brother. The judge in the High Court (on the application of the newspaper) modified the injunction so that the newspaper could, in reports of the criminal trial, publish the identity of the mother and the deceased brother and reproduce their photographs. This decision was upheld by the Court of Appeal. The child appealed to the House of Lords, arguing that his right to respect for his private and family life under art. 8 ECHR meant that he was entitled to protection against harmful publicity concerning his family.
>
> The House of Lords unanimously dismissed his appeal, holding that cases decided before the Human Rights Act 1998 on the existence and scope of the High Court's inherent jurisdiction to restrain publicity no longer need to be considered. The foundation to restrain publicity now derives from rights under the European Convention for the Protection of Human Rights (ECHR). However, the case-law on the inherent jurisdiction is not wholly irrelevant, as it might remain of some interest in regard to the ultimate balancing exercise to be carried out under the provisions of the ECHR. Article 8 was engaged in the case, but the child would not be involved in the trial as a witness or otherwise. The impact of the trial on the child would be indirect. Competing rights of freedom of the press under art. 10 were also engaged but were not outweighed by the rights of the child under art. 8. Given the weight traditionally given to the importance of open reporting of criminal proceedings, it had been important for the judge, in carrying out the exercise required by the ECHR, to begin by acknowledging the force of the argument under art. 10 before considering whether the right of the child under art. 8 was sufficient to outweigh it.
>
> The House of Lords referred to the UN Convention on the Rights of the Child, which protects the privacy of children directly involved in criminal proceedings, but not children indirectly affected by criminal trials.

(For a case involving wardship and restricting publication, see *Re Stedman* [2009] EWHC 935 (Fam); [2009] 2 FLR 852; and for a case involving autonomy of the child and freedom to publish, see *Re Roddy* at p. 222).

Summary

1 It is recognised that children have rights and that parents have responsibilities.

2 Children have greater rights of self-determination than they once had, partly as a result of the decision of the House of Lords in *Gillick* (1986).

3 Various theories of children's rights have been put forward, but some theorists have argued that 'rights talk' is not appropriate in the context of children.

4 The UN Convention on the Rights of the Child 1989 (the UNCRC) has been ratified by the UK but it is not part of English law and does not have its own court. Enforcing its provisions is therefore difficult. However, arguments based on the UNCRC can be used persuasively in court, and judges refer to it in their decisions. Government policy-makers also take it into account.

5 In the *Gillick* case the House of Lords said that, where necessary, doctors could prescribe contraceptives to children under the age of 16 without parental consent.

6 Section 8 Family Law Reform Act 1969 allows children aged 16 and 17 to give valid consent to medical and dental treatment.

7 Cases since *Gillick* have shown that children's rights are not absolute, and that children cannot have the final say about medical treatment (and other matters), particularly if a course of action, or inaction, is contrary to their welfare.

8 *Gillick* was also important for emphasising that parents have responsibilities, not rights.

9 Parents are not prohibited from using corporal punishment on their children, but s.58 Children Act 2004 has outlawed the defence of reasonable punishment for all criminal charges except common assault or battery. Some proponents of children's rights are in favour of an outright ban.

10 Corporal punishment is outlawed in all schools.

11 A child cannot bring private law proceedings other than through a next friend (for example, a parent, guardian, relative or friend) or a Children's Guardian. A child can apply for a s.8 order under the Children Act 1989 with leave of the court (s.10(8) CA 1989). In private law proceedings a Children's Guardian may be appointed, who will instruct a solicitor on behalf of the child, but under the Family Proceedings Rules 1991 the court can, on the application of the child, dismiss the Guardian so that the child can instruct the solicitor on his own. In public law proceedings the child has automatic rights of representation under s.41 CA 1989. There is concern that the voice of the child is not being sufficiently heard in private family law proceedings, in particular for residence and contact orders.

12 The High Court has an inherent jurisdiction (which includes wardship) to protect children. This is a parental type of jurisdiction. The welfare of the child is the court's paramount consideration in such cases (s.1(1) CA 1989). The High Court's powers are not invoked as much as they once were (following changes introduced by the Children Act 1989). Thus, there are restrictions on local authorities using the inherent jurisdiction and wardship, but local authorities sometimes invoke them in difficult medical cases involving children. Wardship is useful in difficult and complex cases where urgent action is needed (such as in international child abduction cases). The High Court may refuse to exercise its jurisdiction where other interests prevail over the child's welfare, for instance under the immigration rules or where there is a need to uphold freedom of speech.

Further reading and references

Alston, Parker and Seymour (eds.), *Children, Rights and the Law*, 1992, Clarendon Press.

Bainham, 'Can we protect children and protect their rights?' [2002] Fam Law 279.

Bainham, *Children: The Modern Law* (3rd edn), 2005, Family Law.

Bainham, 'Is legitimacy legitimate?' [2009] Fam Law 673.

Barton, '*A* v. *UK* – The thirty thousand pound caning – An "English vice" in Europe' [1999] CFLQ 63.

Barton, 'Hitting your children: common assault or common sense?' [2008] Fam Law 65.

Brazier and Bridge, 'Coercion or caring – Analysing adolescent autonomy' (1996) *Legal Studies* 84.

Bridge, 'Religion, culture and conviction – The medical treatment of young children' [1999] CFLQ 1.

Bridgeman, Keating and Lind (eds.), *Responsibility, Law and the Family*, 2008, Ashgate.

Clucas, 'The Children's Commissioner for England: the way forward?' [2005] Fam Law 290.

Crichton, District Judge, 'Listening to children' [2006] Fam Law 849.

Edwards, 'Imaging Islam … of meaning and metaphor symbolising the jilbab – *R (Begum)* v. *Headteacher and Governors of Denbigh High School*' [2007] CFLQ 247.

Eekelaar, 'The emergence of children's rights' (1986) 6 OJLS 161.

Eekelaar, 'The importance of thinking that children have rights' (1992) 6 IJLF.

Eekelaar, 'The interests of the child and the child's wishes: the role of dynamic self-determinism' (1994) 8 IJLF 42.

Family Justice Council, 'Enhancing the participation of children and young people in family proceedings: starting the debate' [2008] Fam Law 431.

Fenwick, 'Clashing rights, the welfare of the child and the Human Rights Act' (2004) 67(6) *Modern Law Review* 889.

Fortin, 'The HRA's impact on litigation involving children and their families' [1999] CFLQ 237.

Fortin, 'Rights brought home for children' (1999) 62 *Modern Law Review* 350.

Fortin, *Children's Rights and the Developing Law* (3rd edn), 2009, Cambridge University Press.

Fortin, 'Accommodating children's rights in a post HRA era' [2006] 69 *Modern Law Review* 299.

Fortin, 'Children's rights – substance or spin?' [2006] Fam Law 757.

Fortin, 'Children's representation through the looking glass' [2007] Fam Law 500.

Freeman, *The Rights and Wrongs of Children*, 1993, Frances Pinter.

Freeman, 'Disputing children', chapter 20 in Katz, Eekelaar and Maclean (eds.), Cross Currents, 2000, Oxford University Press.

Hagger, *Parental Responsibility, Young Children and Healthcare Law*, 2007, Cambridge University Press.

Herring, 'The Human Rights Act and the welfare principle in family law – conflicting or complementary?' [1999] CFLQ 223.

Hunter, 'Close encounters of a judicial kind: "hearing" children's "voices" in family law proceedings' [2007] CFLQ 283.

Huxtable, '*Re M (Medical Treatment: Consent)* – time to remove the "flak jacket" ' [2000] CFLQ 83.

Levy, 'Do children have human rights?' [2002] Fam Law 204.

Loughrey, 'Can you keep a secret? Children, human rights, and the law of medical confidentiality' [2008] CFLQ 312.

Macdonald, 'Bringing rights home for children: arguing the UNCRC' [2009] Fam Law 1073.

Macdonald, 'The voice of the child – still a faint cry?' [2008] Fam Law 648.

Macdonald, 'The child's voice in private law: loud enough?' [2009] Fam Law 40.

Further reading and references cont'd

Masson, 'Paternalism, participation, and placation: young people's experience of representation in child participation proceedings in England and Wales', in Dewar and Parker (eds.), *Family Law: Processes; Practices, Pressures*, 2003, Hart Publishing.

Murch with Keehan, *The Voice of the Child in Private Law Proceedings*, 2003, Family Law.

Parkinson and Cashmore, *The Voice of the Child in Family Disputes*, 2008, Oxford University Press.

Potter, Sir Mark P, 'Voice of the child: children's "rights" in family proceedings' [2008] *International Journal of Family Law* 140.

Taylor, 'Reversing the retreat from *Gillick*? *R (Axon) v. Secretary of State for Health*' [2007] CFLQ 81.

Wall, Rt Hon Lord Justice, 'Separate representation of children' [2007] Fam Law 124.

Walsh, 'Enhancing the participation of children and young people in family proceedings: starting the debate' [2008] Fam Law 431.

Whybrow, 'Children, guardians and rule 9.5' [2004] Fam Law 504.

Williams, 'Effective government structures for children?: The UK's four Children's Commissioners' [2005] CFLQ 37.

Williams, 'Voices in the wilderness: hearing children in financial applications' [2008] Fam Law 135.

Wilson, Sir Nicholas, 'The ears of the child in family proceedings' [2007] Fam Law 808.

Websites

Association of Lawyers for Children: www.alc.org.uk

Children are Unbeatable! Alliance: www.childrenareunbeatable.org.uk

Children's Commissioner (for England): www.11million.org.uk

Children's Commissioner (for Wales): www.childcom.org.uk

Children's Legal Centre: www.childrenslegalcentre.com

Children's Rights Alliance for England: www.crae.org.uk

Department for Children, Schools and Families: www.dcsf.gov.uk

End All Corporal Punishment of Children: www.endcorporalpunishment.org

Every Child Matters: www.everychildmatters.gov.uk

National Youth Advocacy Service: www.nyas.net

NSPCC: www.nspcc.org.uk

United Nations Convention on the Rights of the Child: www.unicef.org/crc

Article 5 United Nations Convention on the Rights of the Child 1989

'States Parties shall respect the responsibilities, rights and duties of parents.'

Article 18(1) United Nations Convention on the Rights of the Child 1989

'States Parties shall use their best efforts to ensure recognition of the principle that both parents have common responsibilities for the upbringing and development of the child, and that parents or guardians have the primary responsibility for the upbringing and development of the child.'

9.1 Introduction

(a) Who is a parent?

Most children are brought up by parents with whom they have a biological link, but some are brought up by step-parents, foster-parents (see below) or guardians (see 9.8). Some children have adoptive parents (see Chapter 15); or special guardians (see 15.14) who act as 'parents'.

The word 'parent' is not defined in the Children Act 1989 (see Chapter 10). In *Re G (Children)* [2006] UKHL 43, [2006] 2 FLR 629 (below) Baroness Hale considered the meaning of the term 'parent'; and said that parents could be classified as 'legal' and/or 'natural' parents, and that a person could be, or could become, a natural parent in one of three ways: by genetic parenthood (where the parent provides the gametes which produce the child); by gestational parenthood (where the parent conceives and bears the child); or by 'social and psychological parenthood'. Baroness Hale said that in the great majority of cases the child's mother would combine all three types of natural parenthood, and the father would combine two.

The importance of the biological bond between parent and child   In the following case the House of Lords considered the importance of the biological bond (the 'blood tie') between parent and child, while also acknowledging the importance of social and psychological parenting:

▶ *Re G (Children)* [2006] UKHL 43, [2006] 2 FLR 629

CG and CW were a lesbian couple who had two daughters (full sisters) by artificial insemination (by an unknown donor). CG was the children's genetic and gestational mother. When their relationship broke down CW applied for contact and shared residence. A shared residence order was made at first instance with CG being granted a 70 per cent share. CG moved to Cornwall in breach of a court order requiring the children to live in Leicester. Bracewell J therefore made an order changing the children's primary place of residence to that of CW, as she had no confidence that CG would promote the 'essential close relationship' with CW and her family. CG's appeal to the Court of Appeal was dismissed and so she appealed to the House of Lords on the basis, *inter alia*, that it was wrong for the courts below to have attached no significance to the fact that she was the children's genetic and gestational mother.

The House of Lords unanimously overturned the decision of the Court of Appeal and reversed the children's living arrangements so that their primary home was once more with CG, the biological mother. It held that it was contrary to the welfare of the children to remove them from their biological mother.

BARONESS HALE: 'I am driven to the conclusion that the courts below have allowed the unusual context of this case to distract them from principles which are of universal application. First, the fact that CG is the natural mother of these children in every sense of that term, while raising no presumption in her favour, is undoubtedly an important and significant factor in determining what will be best for them now and in the future. Yet nowhere is that factor explored in the judgment below. Secondly, while it may well be in the best interests of children to change their living arrangements if one of their parents is frustrating their relationship with the other parent who is able to offer them a good and loving home, this is unlikely to be in their best interests while that relationship is in fact being maintained in accordance with the court's order.'

LORD NICHOLLS: 'I decry any tendency to diminish the significance of this factor. A child should not be removed from the primary care of his or her biological parents without compelling reason.'

(For a discussion of *Re G (Children)*, see Diduck [2007] CFLQ 458).

However, despite the ruling in *Re G* above (about the importance of the biological bond between parent and child) any decision is subject to the overriding principle that the welfare of the child is the court's paramount consideration. The Supreme Court so held in *Re B (A Child)(Residence)* [2009] UKSC 5 where a grandmother succeeded in her appeal against the decision of the Court of Appeal which had held that her grandson (whom she had cared for during the three years since his birth) should live with his father.

Step-parents Many children are brought up by step-parents. A step-parent is not a biological parent but a parent created by marriage or civil partnership. Step-parents have legal obligations towards their step-children, including the duty to provide financial support. Step-parents can obtain parental responsibility (see 9.5). In respect of their step-child, they can apply for: s.8 orders under the Children Act 1989 (see 10.5); special guardianship (see 15.4); and they can apply to adopt their step-child (see Chapter 15).

Foster-parents Foster-parent are persons who act *in loco parentis* for a child on a fairly settled basis. There are two types of foster-parent: those who care for children under a private fostering arrangement; and those who look after children in local authority care. Although foster-parents do not have parental responsibility they can acquire it by means of a s.8 residence order (see 10.5) or special guardianship (see 15.14). In some cases, they may decide to apply to adopt the child in their care (see Chapter 15). Even though they may have no parental responsibility, they have an obligation to care for the child, as they have a delegated form of parental responsibility under s.3(5) of the Children Act 1989. Because they have no parental responsibility, foster-parents have no right to change a child's first name (*Re D, L and LA (Care: Change of Forename)* [2003] 1 FLR 339).

(b) The importance of parents

The Government recognises the importance of parents and is keen to support them. In its Consultation Document (*Supporting Families*, 1998, Home Office) the Government said that good parenting benefits us all and that all parents need support, advice and guidance on how to bring up their children (paras. 1.1 and 1.2). The Government has introduced various support initiatives for parents, for instance the Family and Parenting Institute; and has also funded various parenting projects.

The parental presumption   The courts also recognise the importance of parents by upholding the principle that it is usually in a child's best interests to be brought up by his or her natural parents. In *Re KD (A Minor) (Ward: Termination of Access)* [1988] AC 806 Lord Templeman said:

> '[T]he best person to bring up a child is the natural parent. It matters not whether the parent is wise or foolish, rich or poor, educated or illiterate, provided the child's moral and physical health are not endangered.'

The presumption in favour of parents is also enshrined in the Children Act 1989, which is based on a policy of minimum State intervention into family life.

Human rights and parents   The importance of parents is also recognised in the decisions of the European Court of Human Rights which, by virtue of the Human Rights Act 1998 (see 1.7), must be taken into account by the courts in England and Wales.

In *Kosmopolou* v. *Greece (Application No. 60457/00)* [2004] 1 FLR 800 the ECtHR held that the bond between a child and his marital parents amounts to a right to family life under art. 8, and that this right arises from the moment of the child's birth and cannot be broken by subsequent events, other than in exceptional circumstances. The ECtHR held that the mutual enjoyment of parent and child of each other's company constitutes a fundamental element of family life, even if the relationship between the parents has broken down; and that any interference must be justified under art. 8(2), applying the principle of proportionality and the principle of the best interests of the child.

Courts and public authorities in the UK must abide by the provisions of the European Convention for the Protection of Human Rights, as a result of their obligations under the Human Rights Act 1998 (see 1.7), and must therefore do their best to foster co-operation between parents in order to maintain the bond between parent and child (see also *Johansen* v. *Norway* (1997) 23 EHRR 33; and *K and T* v. *Finland* (2001) 36 EHRR 255, [2001] 2 FLR 707). Thus, for instance, the failure of a court in England and Wales to enforce a contact order, or the failure of social services to allow a parent to have contact with a child in care, might amount to a breach of a parent's and a child's right to family life under art. 8 ECHR, with the possibility of liability to pay damages by way of compensation.

The importance of parents is also recognised in arts. 5 and 8 of the UN Convention on the Rights of the Child 1989 (see 8.2).

9.2 Parentage

(a) Establishing parentage

Sometimes it may be necessary to establish a child's parentage. Usually it is paternity that needs to be established. Thus, for example, a man may need to prove that he is the father so that he can seek an order under the Children Act 1989 (for example, a parental responsibility order, or a contact or residence order). A mother may need to prove paternity so that the father can be required to pay child support maintenance. Parentage may need to be proved for the purpose of amending a birth certificate, for establishing inheritance rights or for acquiring British nationality or citizenship.

(i) Presumptions of parentage Certain presumptions exist in respect of parentage. Under the presumption of legitimacy a child born to a married woman is presumed to be the child of the married couple. This presumption applies to any child conceived or born during marriage, or born within the normal gestation period if the marriage is terminated by death or divorce. Under the presumption of birth registration the entry of a man's name as the child's father on the birth register is *prima facie* evidence that he is the father (s.10 Births and Deaths Registration Act 1953).

Presumptions, however, have little relevance today, as parentage can be established with almost 100 per cent certainty by DNA profiling. In fact the Court of Appeal has held (see over) that legal presumptions should not be relied on when scientific tests can be carried out.

(ii) Directing a scientific test Provisions governing the use of scientific tests for determining parentage in civil proceedings are laid down in ss.20–25 of the Family Law Reform Act 1969. Special provisions exist under the Child Support Act 1991 for determining parentage for child support purposes.

Section 20(1) Family Law Reform Act 1969

'In any civil proceedings in which the parentage of any person falls to be determined, the court may, either of its own motion or on an application by any party to the proceedings, give a direction –

(a) for the use of scientific tests to ascertain whether such tests show that a party to the proceedings is or is not the father or mother of that person; and

(b) for the taking, within a period specified in the direction, of bodily samples from all or any of the following, namely, that person, any party who is alleged to be the father or mother of that person and any other party to the proceedings;

and the court may at any time revoke or vary a direction previously given by it under this subsection.'

'Bodily sample' means a sample of bodily fluid or bodily tissue taken for the purpose of scientific tests (s.25). The scientific test must be carried out by an accredited body (s.20(1A)); and the result reported to the court (s.20(2)). The court can draw such inferences as appear proper in the circumstances if a person fails to comply with any step required for the purpose of giving effect to a s.20 direction for scientific testing (s.23(1)).

In *Re F (Children) (DNA Evidence)* [2007] EWHC 3235 (Fam), [2008] 1 FLR 348 it was held that any order for DNA testing made by the family courts must be made, and specify that it is being made, pursuant to the Family Law Reform Act 1969 (and not under any other statutory provision or under the inherent jurisdiction).

Consents are required (s.21) Adults and children (aged 16 or over) must give their consent to a bodily sample being taken (s.21(1)). The consent of a child (aged 16 or over) is as effective as if he were of full age; no other person's consent is needed (s.21(2)). Where the child is under 16 the person with care and control of the child must give consent to a bodily sample being taken from the child; but if consent is not forthcoming the court can give consent, provided it is in the child's best interests (s.21(3)).

The approach of the courts In the following case the Court of Appeal outlined the principles which apply in cases on establishing parentage:

▶ *Re H and A (Paternity: Blood Tests)* [2002] EWCA Civ 383, [2002] 1 FLR 1145

The applicant applied for contact with, and parental responsibility for, twins who were living with their mother and her husband. The applicant believed that he was their father, as he had had a sexual relationship with the mother. When the mother challenged his claim to paternity he applied for a blood sample to be taken from the twins with the court's consent (under s.23(1)(b) FLRA 1969). The judge refused the application, because of the possible disastrous disintegrative effects upon the mother's family unit if the applicant was proved to be the father. The father appealed.

The Court of Appeal allowed his appeal and remitted the case for a retrial, as there had been fundamental flaws in the judge's assessment of the individual factors which had to be brought into the essential balancing exercise. Thorpe LJ held that it was necessary to introduce into the balancing exercise the advantages of establishing scientific fact against the risks of perpetuating a state of uncertainty that bred rumour and gossip. The judge had also fallen into error in calculating the real chance of the applicant being the father as 1 per cent instead of 50 per cent, and that factor had tainted the judge's conclusion that the test offered no advantage to the applicant. The judge had also erred in finding that to order the test would drive the mother's husband from the family. The Court of Appeal also doubted whether the judge had given sufficient weight to the importance of certainty.

The Court of Appeal held that the following two principles applied to cases on establishing parentage: that the interests of justice are best served by the ascertainment of the truth; and that the court should be provided with the best available science and not be confined to such unsatisfactory alternatives as presumptions and inferences.

Thus, in parentage cases, the interests of justice and the child's right to know the truth are important considerations, but these considerations are subject to the child's welfare being the paramount consideration.

The child's rights and best interests A child has a right to know his true identity, and this is recognised in the UN Convention on the Rights of the Child. Article 7(1) provides that a child has 'as far as possible, the right to know and be cared for by his parents', and art. 8(1) provides that States Parties must 'respect the right of the child to preserve his or her identity, including … family relations'. If a child is illegally deprived of some or all of the elements of his identity States Parties must 'provide assistance and protection with a view to speedily re-establishing his or her identity' (art. 8(2)). In *Re H (Paternity: Blood Tests)* [2001] 2 FLR 65 Ward LJ, referring to art. 7(1) UNCRC, stated that 'every child has a right to know the truth unless his welfare clearly justifies the cover-up'.

The right to family life in art. 8 of the European Convention for the Protection of Human Rights may also provide a justification for the truth to be known:

> ▶ *Re T (Paternity: Ordering Blood Tests)* [2001] 2 FLR 1190
>
> The applicant, who believed he had fathered a child during a sexual relationship with a friend's wife, wanted blood tests to be taken for DNA sampling to prove his paternity as a preliminary to applying for parental responsibility and contact. He relied on the right to family life in art. 8 ECHR. Bodey J ordered the tests to be taken, as it was in the child's best interests to be sure about his father's identity, and suspicions about the child's identity were already in the public domain. Bodey J balanced the rights of the adults and the child under art. 8, but held that the child's right to know his true identity carried most weight. Any interference with the mother and her husband's rights to family life under art. 8 was proportionate to the legitimate aim of providing such knowledge to the child.

(Fortin ((2006) MLR 299) has stated that *Re T* (above) showed 'a rare willingness' on the part of the courts to articulate the various ECHR rights enjoyed by *all* the parties, including the child).

In *Re F (Children) (Paternity: Jurisdiction)* [2007] EWCA Civ 873, [2008] 1 FLR 225 a s.8 specific issue order (see 10.8) ordering that the children be informed of their paternity was upheld by the Court of Appeal.

Refusing to direct a scientific test   Although the court will often direct a scientific test, because it is usually in the child's best interests to know the truth, the court may decide to refuse to do so where it is contrary to a child's best interests.

In the following cases, for example, the court refused to order a scientific test: *Re F (A Minor) (Blood Tests: Parental Rights)* [1993] 1 FLR 598 (as the test would destabilise the child); *Re K (Specific Issue Order)* [1999] 2 FLR 280 (as the mother had an obsessional hatred of the applicant and the truth would cause the child emotional disruption); *Re D (Paternity)* [2006] EWHC 3545 (Fam), [2007] 2 FLR 26 (as it was in the best interests of the child (a boy aged 11 who was not *Gillick* competent) due to the turbulence in his life and his strong resistance to scientific testing); and in *Re J (Paternity: Welfare of Child)* [2006] EWHC 2837 (Fam), [2007] 1 FLR 1064 (as the undoubted advantage of the child learning the truth was outweighed by the impact that the process of revealing the child's paternity would have on the child's mother and family upon whom the child was dependent).

Fortin has argued ([2009] CFLQ 336) that, although the idea of children having a right to know their origins appears to be reasonable, there are risks involved. She claims that the importance of the biological tie between child and parent may be being applied in paternity cases when it is not necessarily in a child's best interests to know his or her parent. She states that the human right of a child to know his or her parents is not an absolute right; and that when 'dealing with applications from putative fathers, it is arguable that the domestic courts are extending a child's right to know beyond its appropriate boundaries'.

Paternity fraud Where a person fraudulently assures another person that he or she is the child's parent, but knows this is not so, then that person may be liable under the tort of deceit to pay damages to the wronged person. In *A* v. *B (Damages: Paternity)* [2007] EWHC 1246 (QBD) the claimant was successful in obtaining damages against the defendant mother who had repeatedly and fraudulently assured him that he was the child's biological father, with the result that he had provided maintenance for the mother and child for several years. Such claims, however, are rare.

(b) Declarations of parentage

A declaration of parentage may be required, for instance to impose (or deny) a child support obligation; or for the purpose of establishing citizenship, nationality or inheritance rights; or to amend a birth certificate.

Under s.55A of the Family Law Act 1986 a person domiciled in England and Wales, or habitually resident in England and Wales for at least one year, can apply to a magistrates' family proceedings court, county court or the High Court for a declaration of parentage (or non-parentage). An applicant seeking a declaration that he is the parent of a named person, or that a named person is his parent, has an unqualified right to apply (s.55A(4)). Other applicants must prove a sufficient personal interest in the determination of the application before the court can hear their case (s.55A(3)).

The court can refuse to hear an application which is not in the child's best interests (s.55A(3)). If it refuses to hear an application it can order that a further application may not be made without leave of the court (s.55A(6)).

The child's involvement in proceedings A failure to involve a child in proceedings for a declaration of status may be a breach of the child's rights under the European Convention for the Protection of Human Rights (ECHR):

▶ *Re L (Family Proceedings Court) (Appeal: Jurisdiction)* **[2003] EWHC 1682 (Fam), [2005] 1 FLR 210**

A girl (aged 15) who had learned that her parentage was in doubt, applied for permission to appeal a declaration of parentage which had been made under s.55A of the Family Law Act 1986 for the purposes of child support (see s.20 Child Support Act 1991). She alleged breaches of her rights under art. 6 ECHR (right to a fair trial) and art. 8 ECHR (right to family life), as the declaration affecting her status had been made without reference to her or her mother. She had not been a party to proceedings, had not been given notice of proceedings, and had not been given the opportunity to be heard or to make representations.

Munby J held that it was not disputed that she was fully entitled to invoke what she correctly described as a basic and fundamental human right. Information about one's biological father went to the very heart of a person's identity (*per* Scott Baker J in *Rose* v. *Secretary of State for Health and Human Fertilisation and Embryology Authority* [2002] EWHC 1593 (Admin), [2002] 2 FLR 962). As her human rights had been infringed the decision could not stand. She had not been given a fair hearing or a fair trial (art. 6), and the declaration breached her rights under art. 8. She was entitled to have the order made by the family proceedings court set aside.

Adoption – declaration of parentage A declaration of parentage may be useful in the context of adoption, as it was in *M* v. *W (Declaration of Parentage)* [2006] EWHC 2341 (Fam), [2007]

2 FLR 270 where the petitioner, an adopted adult, applied for a declaration of parentage in respect of his natural father who had died in Australia and with whom he had never had any contact. Hogg J, granting the declaration, drew attention to the importance of adopted persons knowing about their background and said that the declaration would be of assistance to the petitioner, and his children, in relation to medical conditions or genetic make-up. Furthermore, the declaration would not affect the validity of the adoption order.

(c) Declarations of legitimacy or legitimation

Under s.56 of the Family Law Act 1986 a person may apply to the High Court or a county court for a declaration in respect of legitimacy or legitimation. An application under this provision can be made only by a child. The court can make a declaration that: the applicant is the legitimate child of his or her parents; or that the applicant has (or has not) become a legitimated person.

9.3 Parental responsibility

The law governing parental responsibility is laid down in the Children Act 1989. 'Parental responsibility', not 'parental rights', is the term used in the Act to describe parental interests in children. 'Responsibility' not 'rights' was adopted in order to reflect the idea that children are persons to whom duties are owed rather than persons over whom power is wielded. The emphasis on parental responsibility, not rights, arose partly as a result of the influence of the *Gillick* case (see 8.4) where Lord Scarman had said that parental rights are derived from parental duty.

Parents without parental responsibility can have legal rights and obligations Parents have legal rights and obligations even though they may have no parental responsibility in law. Of particular importance is the parental duty to provide financial support, which arises whether or not a parent has parental responsibility. Parents without parental responsibility also have succession rights; and they can apply for orders under the Children Act 1989 (e.g. residence, contact and parental responsibility orders) (see Chapter 10).

(a) Who has parental responsibility?

More than one person can have parental responsibility for a particular child (s.2(5) CA 1989); and parental responsibility does not terminate when another person acquires it (s.2(6)), except in the case of adoption (which involves a complete transfer of parental responsibility to the adopters, see Chapter 15). Parental responsibility is not lost when a child goes into local authority care. It also continues after divorce, dissolution of a civil partnership, or if parents separate. It terminates on the child reaching the age of majority, and on adoption, and in some circumstances by court order.

(i) 'Automatic' parental responsibility Some persons have 'automatic' parental responsibility, in other words there is no need for them to apply for it because statutory provisions provide that they have it. Over the years, the law governing who has parental

responsibility (and who can acquire it) has become more complex because of changes to the law governing step-parents, civil partners, and persons who become parents as a result of assisted reproduction. Recent changes to the law by the Human Fertilisation and Embryology Act 2008 (see further at 9.9) have made the law even more complex.

The following persons have parental responsibility 'automatically' for the child, in other words without the need to apply for it:

- *Married Parents* (s.2(1) CA 1989).
- *An Unmarried Mother* (s.2(2) CA 1989), but the father can acquire it (see 9.4).
- *A Mother and Her Civil Partner Who is a Parent by Virtue of Section 42 HFEA 2008* (s.2(1A)(a) CA 1989) (see 9.9).
- *The Mother and Her Female Partner Who is a Parent by Virtue of Section 43 HFEA 2008* (s.2(1A)(b) CA 1989) (see 9.9).
- *A Mother Who is Parent by Virtue of Section 43 HFEA 2008* (s.2(2A) CA 1989) (a mother who has a child by assisted reproduction) (see 9.9)
- *Parents Whose Marriage is Void,* provided that at the time of the child's conception, or at the time of the marriage (if later), either or both of them reasonably believed that the marriage was valid (s.1 Legitimacy Act 1976).
- *Parents Who Marry After the Child's Birth* are treated as if they were married to each other at the time of the birth (s.2 Legitimacy Act 1976), and therefore have parental responsibility.

(ii) Persons who can acquire parental responsibility   The Children Act 1989 makes provision for the following persons to acquire parental responsibility (see further at 9.4 and 9.5):

- *An Unmarried Father* (s.4 CA 1989) (see below).
- *A Step-Parent (Whether by Marriage or Civil Partnership)* (s.4A CA 1989) (see 9.5).
- *A Female Non-Biological Parent in a Same-Sex Female Relationship* (s.4ZA CA 1989) (see 9.5 and 9.9).

Other persons   Parental responsibility can be acquired by other persons, for instance by means of a residence order (10.5), a special guardianship order (15.14), or an adoption order (Chapter 15). Local authorities have a limited kind of parental responsibility when a child is in care (Chapter 14). The court has parental responsibility when a child is a ward of court (8.7).

(b)   The exercise of parental responsibility

(i) Parental responsibility can be exercised jointly and severally   Persons with parental responsibility can act independently of each other in meeting their responsibility for their child, unless the law requires otherwise. However, the following decisions concerning the child require the consent of *both* parents with parental responsibility (and of other persons with parental responsibility):

- *removing the child from the UK* (see 11.8 and 13.3);
- *consenting to the child's adoption* (although consent can be dispensed with, see 15.9);

- *deciding about the child's education*;
- *changing the child's surname* (see 11.7);
- *consent to serious or irreversible medical treatment* (such as sterilisation, circumcision and immunisation, see p. 260);
- *consenting to the child's marriage (if aged 16 or 17)*.

If consent is not forthcoming, the court's consent can be obtained by applying for a specific issue order under s.8 of the Children Act 1989 (see 10.8) or by invoking the wardship or inherent jurisdiction of the High Court (see 8.7).

Parents are prohibited from exercising parental responsibility in a way which is incompatible with a court order made under the Children Act 1989 (s.2(8)). Where persons who share parental responsibility cannot agree on a particular course of action an application can be made for a s.8 order (see 10.4), or in some cases in wardship or under the inherent jurisdiction (see 8.7).

A person without parental responsibility who has care of a child may (subject to the provisions of the CA 1989) 'do what is reasonable in all the circumstances of the case for the purpose of safeguarding or promoting the child's welfare' (s.3(5)). This provision enables, for example, a doctor to act without parental or judicial consent in an emergency. As Munby J said in *R (G)* v. *Nottingham City Council* [2008] EWHC 152 (Admin), [2008] 1 FLR 1660, doctors and midwives do not have to stand idly by waiting for a court order if a premature baby desperately needs to be put in a special unit or placed on a ventilator.

(ii) Parental responsibility is not transferable   A person with parental responsibility cannot surrender or transfer any of that responsibility, but may arrange for some or all of it to be met by one or more persons acting on his or her behalf (s.2(9)), including another person with parental responsibility (s.2(10)). Thus it is lawfully permissible to place the child with a person acting *in loco parentis* (for example a childminder or babysitter) or with someone else with parental responsibility. However, as a person with parental responsibility cannot escape liability under the criminal or civil law by delegating responsibility to another person (s.2(11)), the onus is on parents to make proper arrangements for their children.

9.4   Unmarried fathers and parental responsibility

(a)   Unmarried fathers do not have 'automatic' parental responsibility

An unmarried father has no parental responsibility automatically arising as a result of his being the child's natural parent (s.2(2)). Subject to a court order to the contrary, he therefore has no legal right to consent: to his child's adoption; to his child leaving the UK; to a change of his child's surname; or to a decision about his child's education or medical treatment.

Unmarried fathers were not given 'automatic' parental responsibility by the Children Act 1989 because the Government considered that it might be detrimental to some unmarried mothers and children. The reasoning behind this was explained by Balcombe LJ in *Re H (Illegitimate Child: Father: Parental Rights) (No. 2)* [1991] 1 FLR 214:

'The position of the natural father can be infinitely variable; at one end of the spectrum his connection with the child may be only the single act of intercourse (possibly even rape) which led to conception; at the other end of the spectrum he may have played a full part in the child's life from birth onwards, only the formality of marriage to the mother being absent. Considerable social evils might have resulted if the father at the bottom of the spectrum had been automatically granted full parental rights and duties.'

A similar view was taken by the European Court of Human Rights in *McMichael* v. *United Kingdom (Application No. 16424/90)* (1995) 20 EHRR 205 where it held that, compared with married fathers, unmarried fathers inevitably vary in their commitment and interest in, or even knowledge of, their children. However, it held, as a general rule, unmarried fathers who had established family life with their children could claim rights of contact and custody equal to those of married fathers.

Since the implementation of the Children Act 1989 there has been increasing criticism of the fact that unmarried fathers do not have 'automatic' parental responsibility. Unmarried fathers may be unaware of their lack of parental responsibility. Lack of parental responsibility can cause problems for unmarried fathers in some areas of the law, for instance in child abduction cases and adoption cases. However, the European Court of Human Rights has held that the lack of automatic parental responsibility for unmarried fathers is not necessarily a breach of the European Convention for the Protection of Human Rights (ECHR):

> ▶ *B* v. *UK* [2000] 1 FLR 1
>
> An unmarried father without parental responsibility complained that his inability to obtain a declaration that his child had been unlawfully removed from the UK (because he had no custody rights) was a breach of his right to family life under art. 8 ECHR and was therefore discriminatory under art. 14 ECHR.
>
> The ECtHR dismissed his claim and held that unmarried fathers in the UK are not discriminated against because they have no automatic parental responsibility. It held that, as the relationship between unmarried fathers and their children varies from ignorance and indifference to a close stable relationship indistinguishable from the conventional family-based unit, the UK Government had an objective and reasonable justification for the difference in treatment between married and unmarried fathers with regard to the automatic acquisition of parental rights.

As a result of concern about the lack of automatic parental responsibility for unmarried fathers and the injustices it could create, the law was changed in December 2003 to give unmarried fathers parental responsibility if they are registered on the child's birth certificate with the mother (see over). The Government is currently proposing to introduce compulsory joint birth registration for unmarried fathers, subject to certain exceptions and safeguards (see over).

(b) The unmarried father – acquiring parental responsibility

An unmarried father can acquire parental responsibility by:

- ▶ becoming registered as the father jointly with the mother on the child's birth certificate (see over);
- ▶ making a parental responsibility agreement with the mother (see over);
- ▶ obtaining a parental responsibility order from the court (see over);

- obtaining a residence order in respect of his child (see 10.5);
- becoming the child's guardian on the mother's death (see 9.8);
- adopting the child (see Chapter 15);
- obtaining a special guardianship order (see 15.14); or
- marrying the mother (s.1 Legitimacy Act 1976).

Once a father has acquired parental responsibility he has the same rights as a married father, except that his parental responsibility can be terminated by the court (see p. 253). In this respect, unmarried fathers are still discriminated against.

(i) Acquiring parental responsibility by birth registration   Under ss.4(1)(a) and 4(1A) Children Act 1989 an unmarried father has parental responsibility for his child if he is registered with the child's mother on the child's birth certificate (under ss.10(1)(a)–(c) and 10A(1) of the Births and Deaths Registration Act 1953). These provisions came into force in December 2003. An unmarried father who is not so registered can acquire parental responsibility by other means (see below). Acquiring parental responsibility by birth registration is not permanent, however, as it can be terminated by court order (see p. 253).

Compulsory birth registration   New provisions are contained in s.56 and Schedule 6 of the Welfare Reform Act 2009 (see p. 257) to make it compulsory for *both* unmarried parents to register the child's birth unless the registrar deems it impossible, impractical or unreasonable. This will result in more unmarried fathers having parental responsibility. One of the aims of this new measure is to promote the involvement of both unmarried parents in the child's upbringing. Section 56 and Schedule 6 are not currently in force. (For the background to these proposals, see the White Paper, *Joint Birth Registration: Recording Responsibility*, Cm 7293, 2008).

(ii) Acquiring parental responsibility by agreement with the child's mother   Under s.4(1)(b) CA 1989 an unmarried father can enter into a parental responsibility agreement with the mother and thereby acquire parental responsibility for his child. The agreement is made on a prescribed form (available at HM Courts' Service) which must be signed by both parties, witnessed and then registered in the Principal Registry of the Family Division. There is no judicial scrutiny of the agreement, but parental responsibility acquired in this way can be revoked by court order (see p. 253 below). A local authority has no power to stop a mother of a child in care entering into a parental responsibility agreement with the child's father (*Re X (Parental Responsibility Agreement: Children in Care)* [2000] 1 FLR 517).

(iii) Acquiring parental responsibility by parental responsibility order   An unmarried father can apply to the court under s.4(1)(c) CA 1989 for an order giving him parental responsibility. When considering whether to grant the order the child's welfare is the court's paramount consideration (see s.1(1)). The other welfare principles apply, but not the welfare checklist (see 10.3).
    In 2008, there were 9,280 applications for parental responsibility orders made in the courts, with 7,072 orders being made (*Judicial and Court Statistics 2008*, Cm 7697, 2009, Ministry of Justice).

The approach of the courts In *Re H (Minors) (Local Authority: Parental Rights) (No. 3)* [1991] Fam 151 Balcombe LJ held that the following factors are important when the court is considering whether to make a parental responsibility order: the degree of commitment which the father has shown towards the child; the degree of attachment which exists between the father and the child; and the father's reasons or motivation for applying for the order. However, although these factors have been applied in subsequent cases (see, for example, *Re CB (A Minor) (Parental Responsibility Order)* [1993] 1 FLR 920; and *Re G (A Minor) (Parental Responsibility Order)* [1994] 1 FLR 504), the Court of Appeal has stressed that they are only a starting point and that other factors can be taken into account (see *Re H (Parental Responsibility)* [1998] 1 FLR 855).

As the court recognises the important status conferred by the order, it will usually make the order unless it is clearly contrary to the child's welfare. Thus, parental responsibility orders have been made even where there is acrimony between the parents (*Re P (A Minor) (Parental Responsibility Order)* [1994] 1 FLR 578); or where parental responsibility cannot be exercised (*Re H (A Minor) (Parental Responsibility)* [1993] 1 FLR 484). Failure to provide maintenance may not of itself provide a reason for refusing an order (*Re H (Parental Responsibility: Maintenance)* [1996] 1 FLR 867). In *Re S (Parental Responsibility)* [1995] 2 FLR 648 the Court of Appeal stressed that, as a parental responsibility order granted an important status, it was wrong to place an undue and false emphasis on the rights, duties and powers comprised in parental responsibility, because any abuse of its exercise could be controlled by making a s.8 order under the Children Act 1989 (see 10.4).

Despite the willingness of the courts to make parental responsibility orders, in exceptional cases they may be refused, as they were, for example, in the following cases:

▶ *Re M (Contact: Parental Responsibility)* [2001] 2 FLR 342

The child had multiple handicaps and special needs. To give the father parental responsibility would place stress on the mother and undermine her ability to care for the child, even though the father was committed to the child and his motivation for applying was for the recognition of his status as the child's father.

▶ *Re H (Parental Responsibility)* [1998] 1 FLR 855

The father had injured the child, and the child of a former partner, and had displayed cruel behaviour with an element of sadism.

▶ *Re P (Parental Responsibility)* [1998] 2 FLR 96

The father was found to be in possession of obscene photographs of young children.

▶ *M v. M (Parental Responsibility)* [1999] 2 FLR 737

The father was held to be incapable of exercising parental responsibility because he had suffered serious head injuries in a motorcycle accident, and Wilson J took the view that the motivation factor (see above) required a father to be capable of reason.

▶ *Re B (Role of Biological Father)* [2007] EWHC 1952, [2008] 1 FLR 1015

Hedley J refused to grant a parental responsibility order to a father whose child had been born as a result of him donating his sperm to his sister who was living in a lesbian civil partnership. Although the father had fulfilled the three essential conditions needed before a court could make a parental responsibility order (commitment, attachment and motivation, see above), such an order would be wholly contrary to the best interests of the child, applying the welfare principle in s.1(1) of the Children Act 1989.

(c) Termination and revocation of parental responsibility

Parental responsibility agreements and parental responsibility orders terminate when the child reaches 18, unless terminated earlier by court order (ss.91(7), (8) CA 1989).

A person who has acquired parental responsibility under s.4(1) CA 1989 (by birth registration, parental responsibility agreement or court order) can lose it only by court order (s.4(2A)). The court can revoke a parental responsibility order under s.4(2A) on the application of any person with parental responsibility for the child; or on the application of the child (with leave of the court) (s.4(3)). The court can grant leave to a child but only if the child has sufficient understanding to make the proposed application (s.4(4)).

In revocation applications the child's welfare is the court's paramount consideration (s.1(1)). Parental responsibility will only be revoked in exceptional circumstances, as the following cases show:

> ▶ *Re P (Terminating Parental Responsibility)* [1995] 1 FLR 1048
>
> The child had suffered severe non-accidental injuries as a very young baby which were subsequently attributed to the father. Singer J terminated the father's parental responsibility, but said that parental responsibility should not be terminated except on strong grounds, as there was a strong presumption in favour of its continuance. Here the father had shown no attachment or commitment to the child. Singer J was keen to stress, however, that an application for termination of parental responsibility should not be used as a weapon by a dissatisfied unmarried mother.
>
> ▶ *Re F (Indirect Contact)* [2006] EWCA Civ 1426, [2007] 1 FLR 1015
>
> The father's parental responsibility was revoked on an application by the mother as the father had a history of serious and uncontrollable violence. He had breached court orders, had served prison sentences for breach and for harassment of the mother's parents; and the mother and child had been given new identities to protect them. Indirect contact was ordered, via Cafcass Legal, despite the removal of parental responsibility.

Although revocation of the father's parental responsibility in the above cases seemed an appropriate response in the circumstances, the law continues, arguably, to discriminate against unmarried fathers, because it would not have been possible for a *married* father in the same position as the fathers above to have had his parental responsibility revoked. In *Re M (A Minor) (Care Order: Threshold Conditions)* [1994] 2 AC 424, for example, the married father had murdered the mother in the presence of the children, but there was no question of him losing his parental responsibility.

9.5 Step-parents and other persons – acquiring parental responsibility

Step-parents

(a) Under s.4A of the Children Act 1989 a step-parent (whether by marriage or civil partnership) can acquire parental responsibility for a step-child by parental responsibility agreement or parental responsibility order. Alternative ways of acquiring parental responsibility are by means of a special guardianship order (see 15.14), a residence order (see 10.5), or adoption (see Chapter 15).

(i) Parental responsibility agreement   Under s.4A(1)(a) the child's parent(s) with parental responsibility may enter into a parental responsibility agreement with the step-parent to provide for the step-parent to have parental responsibility for the child. This involves filling in a prescribed form (s.4A(2)). The agreement takes effect once it has been received and recorded at the Principal Registry of the Family Division.

(ii) Parental responsibility order   Under s.4A(1)(b) the court may, on the application of the step-parent, order that the step-parent shall have parental responsibility for the child. The welfare of the child is the court's paramount consideration (under s.1(1) CA 1989) and the other principles in s.1 will apply, except for the welfare checklist (see 10.3).

(iii) Termination of parental responsibility   A step-parent's parental responsibility (whether acquired by agreement or court order) can be terminated by the court on the application of any person with parental responsibility, or, with leave of the court, the child (s.4A(3)). The court can grant leave to the child to apply for termination of the order, provided it is satisfied that the child has sufficient understanding to make the proposed application (s.4A(4)).

(b)   The female non-biological parent in a same-sex female relationship

A female non-biological parent in a same-sex female relationship can acquire parental responsibility in relation to the child by registering the birth jointly, or by way of a parental responsibility agreement or parental responsibility order (s.4ZA CA 1989, as inserted by the Human Fertilisation and Embryology Act 2008). Parental responsibility acquired in any of these ways can be terminated by court order (s.4ZA(5)).

(c)   Other persons

Persons other than those above can acquire parental responsibility by obtaining a residence order (see 10.5), or a special guardianship order (see 15.14), or by adoption (see Chapter 15).

In *Re A (Joint Residence: Parental Responsibility)* [2008] EWCA Civ 867, [2008] 2 FLR 1593 an unmarried man acquired parental responsibility by way of a *joint* (not shared) residence order made in his and the mother's favour, because he was unable to apply for a parental responsibility order (he had been at the child's birth and had lived with the child and the mother for two years before the relationship broke down, but it had subsequently transpired that he was not the biological father). The trial judge made a joint residence order under s.12(2) CA 1989 to confer parental responsibility on him, as this was the only way in which he could obtain parental responsibility. The decision was upheld by the Court of Appeal as being a legitimate means by which parental responsibility could be acquired by a person who could not otherwise apply for it.

9.6   Parental responsibility and parental rights

Parental responsibility is defined in s.3(1) of the Children Act 1989 as:

> 'all the rights, duties, powers, responsibilities and authority which by law a parent of a child has in relation to the child and his property.'

This definition is not very helpful, however, as it does not define the precise nature and scope of parental responsibility. This must be deduced from statute and case-law.

(a)   What rights do parents have?

Despite the emphasis on parental responsibility in the Children Act 1989, parents do possess parental rights. They have a right, for instance, to bring proceedings under the Children Act 1989, and a right to challenge a local authority's decision to institute care and supervision proceedings. In fact s.3(1) above mentions the word 'rights', and in the *Gillick* case (see 8.4) Lord Scarman, while recognising that 'responsibility' was a more appropriate term than 'rights', nevertheless stated that parental rights clearly exist but that the law had never treated such rights as 'sovereign or beyond review and control'.

Parental rights include the following rights (but subject, in some circumstances, to the parent having parental responsibility for the child):

- to physical possession of the child;
- to contact with the child;
- to decide on the child's education;
- to choose the child's religion;
- to consent to the child's medical treatment;
- to consent to the child's marriage or civil partnership;
- to choose the child's surname and register the child's birth;
- to consent to the child's adoption;
- to discipline the child;
- to administer the child's property and enter into contracts on the child's behalf;
- to appoint a guardian for the child;
- to bring legal proceeding in respect of the child.

Parents also have duties to their children, in particular a duty to provide maintenance (see Chapter 12). Some of the rights above are also duties. For example, a parent has both a right and a duty to register the child's birth. Unmarried fathers have some, but not all, of the rights above (see p. 248).

Parental rights are not absolute   Parents' rights are not absolute. They are subject to the principle that the child's welfare is the court's paramount consideration. Parental wishes can therefore be overridden by the court. In *Re Z (A Minor) (Freedom of Publication)* [1996] 1 FLR 191, [1997] Fam 1 Sir Thomas Bingham MR said that if the court's judgment 'is in accord with that of the devoted and responsible parent, well and good. If not, then it is the duty of the court … to give effect to its own judgment'.

Thus, the court can restrain a parent from doing any act which might adversely affect the child's welfare. In adoption law parental consent to adoption can be dispensed with if this is in the child's best interests (see 15.9). In proceedings for residence, contact and other orders under the Children Act 1989 parental wishes are not paramount – the child's welfare prevails. In the context of medical treatment for the child, parental wishes can be overridden (see p. 258 below). Children who suffer significant harm can be taken into the care of the local authority, whereupon parental responsibility is not removed from the parents, but the local authority is 'in the driving seat' (see Chapter 14).

(b) Important parental rights

The following parental rights are particularly important:

(i) A right to the physical possession of the child   The criminal and civil law relating to child abduction (see Chapter 14), and the restriction in s.13 of the Children Act 1989 on removing a child out of the UK (when the child is subject to a residence order) show that parents have a right to physical possession of their child. This is also emphasised by the fact that under the Children Act 1989 a parent can ask a local authority to hand the child back if the child is not subject to a care or emergency protection order. The right to physical possession also includes the right to decide where the child lives. Thus, for example, when a child is accommodated in local authority care under a voluntary arrangement a local authority cannot place the child in accommodation against parental wishes (see *R* v. *Tameside Metropolitan Borough Council ex parte J* [2000] 1 FLR 942). The right to physical possession also includes the right to decide on travel and emigration, although this right is subject to certain controls and safeguards (see 11.8).

(ii) A right to have contact with the child   The s.8 contact order and the presumption of reasonable contact when a child is in local authority care show that parents have a right to contact with their child. But this right is not an absolute or fundamental right. It is always subject, like all parental rights, to the welfare of the child; and can be terminated by the court. However, the law encourages parent–child contact, as contact is generally considered to be beneficial for the child. Although the law encourages contact, the case-law and the UN Convention on the Rights of the Child emphasise that contact is a right of the child. For this reason contact is also a parental duty.

(iii) A right to decide on education   Parents have a legal duty to ensure that a child aged between five and 16 receives efficient, full-time education (suitable to the child's age, ability and aptitude, and to any special needs) either by regular attendance at school or otherwise (s.7 Education Act 1996). The words 'or otherwise' mean that parents can lawfully educate their children at home, provided it is an efficient and suitable education. A parent who fails to comply with this duty can be prosecuted. Parents have a right to express a preference as to which school the child shall attend and the admissions authority must comply with that preference, subject to certain exceptions (s.86(1) School Standards and Framework Act 1998). Parents have a right of appeal against a refusal of a place at a chosen school, and have a right to be provided with information about the school, such as the curriculum, discipline, school policy and so on. A parent also has a right to withdraw a child from religious education and from some sex education classes.

(iv) A right to choose the child's religion   Parents have a right to choose the child's religion (if any), at least until the child becomes '*Gillick* competent' (see 8.4). Parents have the right to choose to remove their child from religious instruction and school assemblies. The importance of religion is also reflected in statutory provisions relating to fostering and adoption placements, as the local authority and adoption agency must take into consideration the child's religious beliefs and background. However, parental wishes are not absolute, and in some circumstances the best interests of the child, not the religious wishes of parents, will prevail, for instance in the context of medical treatment (see 9.7 below) and in respect corporal punishment in schools (see p. 227).

(v) A right to consent to medical treatment   (See 9.7 below.)

(vi) A right to consent to the child's marriage or civil partnership   Where a child is aged over 16 but under 18 the child's parents and other persons with parental responsibility must give their consent to the marriage or civil partnership, although failure to do so is unlikely to invalidate it.

(vii) A right to choose the child's surname and to register the child's birth   A child by convention takes the father's surname, although this is not compulsory. A parent can choose any surname for the child. Where a residence order is in force the child's surname cannot be changed without the *written* consent of all those with parental responsibility, or otherwise with permission of the court (see s.13(1) Children Act 1989).

Parents have a statutory duty to register the child's birth. Under the Births and Deaths Registration Act 1953, if the mother and father are married either parent can register the child's birth. If they are not married, only the unmarried mother has a duty to register the birth, and the registrar is not permitted to enter the name of any person as the child's father in the register, unless: both parents attend together and make a joint request to register the birth; or one of them makes a request to register the child's birth and provides a statutory declaration acknowledging paternity. If both unmarried parents are registered on the birth certificate the father has parental responsibility for the child with the mother (see p. 251 above). If a child is legitimated by the parents' subsequent marriage, the parents must re-register the child's birth (s.9 Legitimacy Act 1976).

Compulsory birth registration   The Government is proposing to change the law to make it compulsory for unmarried fathers to be jointly named on the child's birth certificate with the mother, with the aim of making unmarried fathers acknowledge their responsibilities to their children and to promote the welfare of children (see the White Paper, *Joint Birth Registration: Recording Responsibility*, Cm 7293, June 2008). Birth registration will not be mandatory if registration is: impossible (e.g. where the father's identity is not known); impracticable (e.g. where the father's whereabouts are not known); or unreasonable (e.g. where the child is conceived by rape, or where joint registration would not be in the mother and/or child's best interests). The new provisions are laid down in s.54 and Schedule 6 to the Welfare Reform Act 2009, but they are not currently in force.

Wallbank ([2009] CFLQ 267) is critical of the assumption that child welfare is best served by having two parents with parental responsibility for the child. She says that the White Paper conflates fathers' and children's interests and the assumption that it will make the father responsible for their child does not necessarily follow on from birth registration. She says: 'It is highly questionable as to whether any form of meaningful parental responsibility will necessarily ensue as a result'.

Since 1 September 2009 (as a result of amendments made to the Births and Deaths Regulations 1987 by the Human Fertilisation and Embryology Act 2008), female couples have been able to register the birth of their child conceived as a result of fertility treatment, and with both female parents' names being included on the birth certificate. These provisions apply only to female couples who had fertility treatment on or after April 6 2009.

(viii) A right to consent to the child's adoption   Under the adoption legislation parents have a right to consent to their child's adoption, although consent may be dispensed with on certain grounds (see Chapter 15).

(ix) A right to discipline the child and to administer reasonable punishment   A parent has a right and a duty to discipline a child, but must inflict only reasonable punishment otherwise he or she may be guilty of a criminal offence. The law has been reformed so that the defence of reasonable punishment is now available only for minor assaults on children (see 8.5).

(x) Other rights   Parents have other rights. Thus, they can administer the child's property and enter into contracts on the child's behalf. They have a right to appoint a guardian for the child (see 9.8). They also have rights to apply for court orders in respect of their children (see Chapter 10); and have a right to apply for child support (see Chapter 12).

9.7   Parents and children – medical treatment

The *Gillick* case (see 8.4) did not remove the right and duty of parents to consent to their child's medical treatment. In fact the Department of Health and Social Security circular, which was the object of Mrs Gillick's wrath, stated that doctors should act on the presumption that parents should be consulted before contraceptives were prescribed. If a child is a mature minor (that is '*Gillick* competent'), parental consent to medical treatment may not be needed; and young persons aged 16 or 17 have a statutory right to give valid consent to medical, dental or other treatment under s.8 Family Law Reform Act 1969. However, the court has the power to override the wishes of a child (of whatever age and maturity), and also the wishes of a parent, if it considers the medical treatment, or the withdrawal of medical treatment, is in the best interests of the child.

(a)   Disputes between parents and doctors about medical treatment of a child

Although a failure to obtain parental consent could result in a medical practitioner being liable for assault under the civil and criminal law, parental rights in medical matters are not absolute as they can be overridden by the court. Where there is a dispute between the medical profession and parents the court will be asked to intervene. The usual procedure is for the hospital or National Health Service Trust to seek a declaration from the High Court under its inherent jurisdiction (see 8.7). Another option, which is less often used, is to apply for a s.8 specific issue order under the Children Act 1989, which requires leave to apply (see 10.8) if the applicant is not the child's parent or guardian.

If doctors treat (or fail to treat) a child in defiance of parental wishes, this may be a breach of the parents' and child's rights to family life under art. 8 of the European Convention for the Protection of Human Rights. In *Glass* v. *United Kingdom (Application No. 61827/00)* [2004] 1 FLR 1019 (where doctors, in contravention of the mother's wishes, stopped giving medical treatment to her child who was severely mentally and physically disabled) the European Court of Human Rights held that the UK was in breach of art. 8, and awarded the mother and child damages. The ECtHR held that the NHS Trust should have sought the intervention of the court before deciding to withdraw medical treatment in contravention of the mother's wishes.

(b) The governing principles in disputes between doctors and parents

The following principles are applied by the court in cases where parents are in dispute with the medical profession:

- The best interests of the child test applies, which includes emotional and other factors.
- The matter is to be decided by the application of an objective approach or test.
- Each case depends on its own specific facts.
- There is a very strong presumption in favour of prolonging life, but there is no obligation on the medical profession to give treatment which would be futile. In *Re J (A Minor) (Wardship: Medical Treatment)* [1991] Fam 33, [1991] 1 FLR 366 Lord Donaldson MR said that account had to be taken of the pain and suffering and quality of life which the child will experience if life is prolonged, and the pain and suffering involved in the proposed treatment.

Thus, the court has to conduct a balancing exercise and weigh up the advantages and disadvantages of giving, or withholding, medical treatment in order to decide what is in the child's best interests. While the courts accord great respect to parental wishes, and they are usually put into the balancing exercise, parental wishes never prevail over the best interests of the child (but for a rare case where they seemed to do so, see *Re T (Wardship: Medical Treatment)* [1997] 1 FLR 502, below).

There are many reported cases involving disputes between parents and the medical profession about the medical treatment of children. The following are some examples:

▶ *Re C (HIV Test)* [1999] 2 FLR 1004

A specific issue order was granted under s.8 of the Children Act 1989 on the application of the local authority, so that an HIV test could be carried out on a baby, despite the mother and father's refusal to consent to the test.

▶ *Re B (A Minor) (Wardship: Medical Treatment)* [1990] 3 All ER 927

A baby born with Down's syndrome was ordered to have a life-saving operation to remove an intestinal blockage where the parents refused to consent to the operation.

▶ *A National Health Service Trust* v. *D* [2000] 2 FLR 677

A declaration was granted that the child need not be ventilated, and this was held not to breach art. 2 (right to life) and art. 3 (the right not to suffer inhuman and degrading treatment) under the ECHR.

▶ *Re R (A Minor) (Blood Transfusion)* [1993] 2 FLR 757

A specific issue order was granted on the application of a local authority ordering that a child with leukaemia be given medical treatment (including blood transfusions) despite the parents' religious objections as they were Jehovah's Witnesses.

▶ *Re A (Conjoined Twins: Medical Treatment)* [2001] 1 FLR 1

Conjoined twins were ordered to be separated despite their parents' wishes to the contrary, and the fact that separation would inevitably lead to the death of the weaker twin.

▶ *Portsmouth NHS Trust* v. *Wyatt and Wyatt, Southampton NHS Trust Intervening* [2004] EWHC 2247 (Fam), [2005] 1 FLR 21

Hedley J made declarations that further aggressive treatment to prolong the life of a seriously ill one-year-old child was not in her best interests, despite her parents' wishes to the contrary (but see *Portsmouth NHS Trust* v. *Wyatt and Wyatt, Southampton NHS Trust Intervening* [2005] EWHC 693 (Fam), [2005] 2 FLR 480 where the restriction was lifted as the child showed signs of improvement). (See also *Wyatt* v. *Portsmouth NHS Trust* [2005] EWCA Civ 1181, [2006] 1 FLR 554).

▶ *Re T (Wardship: Medical Treatment)* [1997] 1 FLR 502

The parents (medical professionals) refused to give consent to their child having a life-saving liver transplant, as they did not wish to care for the child. The court under its inherent jurisdiction, applying the welfare principle, refused to overrule the parents' refusal to consent.

▶ *NHS Trust* v. *A* [2007] EWHC 1696 (Fam), [2008] 1 FLR 70

The parents of a 6-month-old child refused to consent to the child having a life-saving bone marrow transplant on religious grounds, and because they did not want her to suffer further. The doctors and the child's guardian were in favour of the treatment. Holman J granted the declaration sought by the NHS Trust, holding that the question of whether the court should consent to the treatment in the face of disagreement was to be decided by the application of an objective test based on the best interests of the child, where best interests were considered in the widest sense.

(c)   Seriously invasive medical treatment

Where the medical treatment of a child is seriously invasive the court's consent may be needed. For instance, sterilisation of a child usually requires the prior sanction of the High Court under its inherent or wardship jurisdiction (although an application by way of specific issue order was permitted in *Re HG (Specific Issue Order: Sterilisation)* [1993] 1 FLR 587).

In *Re B (A Minor) (Wardship: Sterilisation)* [1988] AC 199 the House of Lords authorised the sterilisation of a mentally retarded 17-year-old girl child under the wardship jurisdiction. In *Re D (A Minor) (Wardship: Sterilisation)* [1976] Fam 185, on the other hand, sterilisation was refused, because the court felt that the girl might be able to give informed consent to the operation at a later date. Consent of the court is not required, however, where sterilisation is needed for therapeutic reasons, such as cancer of the womb (see, for example, *Re E (A Minor) (Wardship: Medical Treatment)* [1993] 1 FLR 386).

(d)   Where parents cannot agree about medical treatment

The consent of the court may be needed in respect of certain types of medical treatment of a child where the child's parents cannot agree between themselves about the treatment.

This is so even though s.2(7) of the Children Act 1989 provides that each parent with parental responsibility can act independently of the other. Medical treatment, such as circumcision and immunisation, may, for example, need the court's consent if the child's parents cannot agree about the treatment. The following cases are examples:

> ▶ *Re J (Specific Issue Orders: Child's Religious Upbringing and Circumcision)* [2000] 1 FLR 571
>
> A Muslim father applied for a specific issue order so that his son (aged 5) could be circumcised, as the mother, a Christian, objected to it. The Court of Appeal held that a parental dispute about circumcision is one of the exceptional cases where a disagreement between those who possess parental responsibility must be determined by the courts. The father's application was refused, as the best interests of the child prevailed over the parents' religious beliefs and wishes.
>
> (See also *Re S (Specific Issue Order: Religion: Circumcision)* [2004] EWHC 1282 (Fam), [2005] 1 FLR 236 where a Muslim mother's application for a specific issue order authorising her son's circumcision (which the Hindu father had objected to) was refused, as the child might be able to make his own informed choice about circumcision when he was older).
>
> ▶ *Re C (Welfare of Child: Immunisation)* [2003] EWCA Civ 1148, [2003] 2 FLR 1095
>
> Fathers, who had parental responsibility and contact rights, were granted specific issue orders ordering that their daughters be immunised with the MMR vaccine, despite the mothers' opposition. Immunisation was held to be in the girls' best interests, applying the welfare principle in s.1(1) of the Children Act 1989. It was not a breach of the mothers' right to family life under art. 8 ECHR, because art. 8(2) allowed a court to interfere with the rights of parents and children in order to protect the health of a child.

(e)   Disputes between parents and children about medical treatment

See 8.4.

9.8   Appointing a guardian for a child

(a)   Appointing a guardian for the child

The aim of guardianship is to ensure that an appropriate person can exercise parental responsibility for a child when a parent dies. Appointment of a guardian is governed by ss.5 and 6 of the Children Act 1989. Under s.5 a guardian can be appointed by a parent, guardian or special guardian of the child; or by the court.

(i) Appointment by parent, guardian or special guardian (s.5) A parent with parental responsibility, a guardian, or a special guardian can appoint a guardian for the child. Two or more persons may do so jointly. The appointment must be: made in writing, and be dated and signed by the person making the appointment; or if made in a will which is not signed by the testator, be signed at the direction of the testator in accordance with s.9 of the Wills Act 1837; or in any other case be signed at the direction of the person making it in his presence or in the presence of two witnesses who must each attest the signature.

Revocation, disclaimer and termination of appointment (s.6)   An appointment of a guardian can be revoked by a later appointment or by a written instrument revoking the appointment. An appointment (excluding one made in a will or codicil) can be revoked by the instrument being destroyed, provided it is the appointer's intention to revoke the appointment. An appointment made in a will or codicil is revoked if the will or codicil is revoked.

A person appointed a guardian (other than by the court) can disclaim the appointment by an instrument in writing signed by him and made within a reasonable time of his first knowing that the appointment has taken effect. An appointment made by an individual (not the court) is revoked if the person appointed is the spouse or civil partner of the appointer and the marriage or civil partnership is terminated by divorce or dissolution.

Any appointment of a guardian (by an individual or by the court) can be terminated by court order on: the application of any person with parental responsibility for the child (including a local authority); or on the application of the child concerned, with leave of the court; or by the court of its own motion in any family proceedings if it considers that the appointment should be brought to an end.

(ii) Appointment by the court (s.5)   The court can order that an applicant be appointed as a guardian of a child if: the child has no person with parental responsibility; or a residence order has been made with respect to the child in favour of a parent, guardian, or special guardian, who has died while the order was in force; or where there is no residence order and the child's only last surviving special guardian has died. The court cannot appoint a guardian if a residence order was also made in favour of a surviving parent of the child. The court can also appoint a guardian under s.5 of its own motion in any family proceedings (see 10.9), in other words without any application for appointment having been made.

When exercising its powers to decide whether to appoint a guardian the child's welfare is the court's paramount consideration and the 'no-delay' (s.1(2)) and the 'no-order' provisions (s.1(5)) apply (see 10.3). As proceedings for the appointment of a guardian are family proceedings (see s.8(4)) the court can instead of, or in addition to, appointing a guardian, make a s.8 order under the Children Act 1989 (see 10.10).

Termination of court order (s.6)   A court order appointing a guardian can be terminated by the court: on the application of any person with parental responsibility for the child (including a local authority); or on the application of the child concerned, with leave of the court; or by the court of its own motion in any family proceedings.

(b)   Effects of guardianship

Appointment of a guardian under s.5 takes effect on the appointer's death provided: the child concerned has no parent with parental responsibility; or where immediately before death the appointer had a residence order in his/her favour (but not a shared residence order) with respect to the child or he/she was the child's only (or last surviving) special guardian. If on the appointer's death the child concerned has a parent with parental responsibility for him, and there is no residence order in favour of the appointer, the appointment takes effect when the child no longer has a parent with parental responsibility.

A guardian has parental responsibility for the child (see 9.6). He must therefore ensure that the child is cared for and provided for, and that the child is educated. A guardian also has the right to apply for orders under the Children Act 1989 (see Chapter 10); and to consent to adoption (see Chapter 15). However, as a guardian, unlike a parent or step-parent, has no legal duty to provide financial support for the child (as this might deter people from becoming guardians), an application cannot be made against a guardian for child support maintenance and orders for financial relief. A guardian has no right to succeed to the child's estate on the child's intestacy, and a child cannot acquire British nationality under the British Nationality Act 1981 by virtue of the guardian being resident or settled in the UK.

9.9 Parenthood – assisted reproduction

Assisted reproduction is governed by two Acts of Parliament: the Human Fertilisation and Embryology Acts 1990 and 2008. The 2008 Act was enacted primarily as a response to the technological and scientific developments which have occurred since the implementation of the 1990 Act. The 2008 Act is relevant to family lawyers because it makes changes to the law governing parenthood.

The legal provisions governing parenthood and assisted reproduction are laid down in Part 2 of the Human Fertilisation and Embryology Act 2008 (HFEA 2008). These came into force on 6 April 2009. They extend the rules on parenthood to include lesbian couples (whether or not they are civil partners). These provisions apply only when the woman receiving the treatment conceived on or after 6 April 2009. They are not retrospective.

(a) Who is the child's mother?

The woman who is carrying (or has carried) a child as a result of the placing in her of an embryo or of sperm and eggs, and no other woman, is treated as the mother of the child (s.33(1) HFEA 2008). This rules applies whether or not the woman was in the UK or elsewhere at the time of the placing in her of the embryo or the sperm and eggs (s.33(3)).

(b) Who is the child's 'father' or 'other parent'?

The rules differ depending on the status of the couple's relationship.

(i) Married couples   The husband is automatically recognised as the legal father of a child born as a result of his wife having fertility treatment, unless the husband did not consent to the treatment (s.35(1) HFEA 2008). This rule applies, whether or not the wife was in the UK or elsewhere at the time of the treatment (s.35(2)).

(ii) Unmarried couples   Under ss.36 and 37 HFEA 2008, where the woman has a child as a result of insemination in a UK licensed clinic and the couple have in place, at the time of the transfer of the sperm or embryo which results in conception, current notices of the man stating that he consents to being treated as the father of any child resulting from the assisted reproduction, then he is the legal parent of the child. The parties must not be within the degrees of prohibited relationship with each other (s.37(1)(e)).

(iii) Lesbian couples who are civil partners If the child was conceived before 6 April 2009, the non-birth mother in a lesbian civil partnership has no 'automatic' recognition as a parent and has no 'automatic' parental responsibility. If she wishes to acquire parental responsibility she will have to do so by means of a parental responsibility agreement or parental responsibility order, or by a residence order, a special guardianship order, or an adoption order.

If the child is conceived on or after 6 April 2009, s.42 HFEA 2008 provides that, where a female civil partner gives birth to a child conceived as a result of donor insemination (whether the woman was in the UK or elsewhere) she is the mother of the child; and her civil partner will automatically be the other parent in law unless that person did not consent to the treatment. In other words, the legal position is the same as for married couples above. If the civil partner did not consent, she may acquire parental responsibility in relation to the child in the ways listed above.

(iv) Lesbian couples who are not civil partners Sections 43 and 44 HFEA 2008 make provision in respect of lesbian couples who are not civil partners. The law is the same as that for lesbian civil partners (see above), except that the mother's lesbian partner will be the other parent in law of the child only if the child was conceived at a licensed clinic in the UK. If the child was conceived outside the UK or at home, or the partner did not consent to the treatment, she can acquire parental responsibility in one of the ways listed above.

(c) Deceased persons

Sections 39 and 40 HFEA 2008 enable a man to be registered on the child's birth certificate as the father of a child conceived after his death using his sperm or using an embryo created with his sperm before his death. It also enables a man to be registered as the father of a child conceived after his death using an embryo created using donor sperm before his death. The provisions apply to unmarried and cohabiting fathers. Registration of the child does not confer upon the child any legal status or rights as a consequence of the registration. The father must give written consent to registration of his name on the birth register.

Section 46 HFEA 2008 lays down similar provisions in respect of a deceased lesbian partner (whether or not that partnership had been registered as a civil partnership).

(d) Consent and assisted reproduction

Consent is an essential requirement in the law governing assisted reproduction, not just for the purpose of acquiring parenthood (see above), but also for the purpose of whether a woman can receive any fertility treatment at all. The issue of consent was considered in the following case in respect of s. 12 HFEA 1990, which required the genetic parent's consent to *in vitro* fertilisation (IVF). The same approach is likely to be taken under HFEA 2008.

▶ *Evans* v. *Amicus Healthcare Ltd; Hadley* v. *Midland Fertility Services Ltd* [2003] EWHC 2161 (Fam), [2004] 1 FLR 67

In each appeal the claimant had undergone IVF treatment with her respective partner, but after the relationships broke down the male partner in each case withdrew his consent to IVF treatment and to storage of the embryos, and wished them to perish. The claimants argued that the court had the power to override the withdrawal of consent and to permit the embryos to be used. Each claimant sought an injunction to restore the man's consent, and a declaration of incompatibility under the Human Rights Act 1998 arguing that the relevant provisions in the HFEA 1990 were in breach of the European Convention for the Protection of Human Rights (ECHR).

Wall J held that the court had no power to override the unconditional statutory right of either party to withdraw or vary consent to the use of embryos in connection with IVF treatment at any time before implantation in the woman. Where consent had originally been given for treatment together with a named partner it was neither effective nor valid once the parties had ceased to be together. The HFEA 1990 did not breach the claimants' right to family life under art. 8 ECHR. As the HFEA 1990 was enacted with sound policy reasons for requiring treatment to be consensual throughout, any interference by the State was both lawful and proportionate. There was no breach of art. 12 (right to marry and found a family) and art. 14 (discrimination in respect of a Convention right). Nor was there a breach of art. 2 (right to life), as an embryo is not a person in English law.

Note: Ms Evans (who had received IVF treatment prior to surgical removal of her ovaries due to a pre-cancerous condition but whose partner subsequently refused to consent to their use when their relationship broke down) sought leave to appeal to the Court of Appeal, but it upheld the decision of Wall J and refused leave to appeal (see [2004] EWCA (Civ) 727). She subsequently applied to the European Court of Human Rights (*Evans* v. *United Kingdom* (*Application No 6339/05*) [2007] 1 FLR 1990) claiming that the requirement of the father's consent to the continued storage and implantation of the fertilised eggs was in breach of her rights under arts. 8 and 14 ECHR, and the rights of the embryos under art. 2. However, the ECtHR held by a majority of 13-4 that there had been no breach of her human rights or those of the embryo.

In the following case it was held that, where a man and a woman separate before a successful implantation takes place, even though it started out as a 'joint enterprise,' the man may not be the legal father of the child. The case related to s.28(3) HFEA 1990, but the same approach is likely to be taken under HFEA 2008.

▶ *Re R (IVF: Paternity of Child)* [2005] UKHL 33, [2005] 2 FLR 843

The mother and her unmarried partner sought fertility treatment involving donor sperm. The man signed the prescribed documents acknowledging that he intended to become the legal father of any child born as a result of the treatment. An implantation was successful, but the mother failed to inform the clinic after the pregnancy was confirmed that she had separated from her partner. Her former partner obtained a declaration of paternity but the Court of Appeal allowed the mother's appeal. The man appealed to the House of Lords.

The House of Lords dismissed his appeal, and held that, in conferring the relationship of parent and child on people who were related neither by blood nor marriage, the rules must be applied very strictly. If the 'joint' enterprise of fertility treatment had ended by the time the successful treatment had begun (because by that stage the couple had separated), the man was not the legal father of the resulting child.

9.10 Surrogacy

(a) Introduction

Some couples may resort to surrogacy to have a child. Under a surrogacy arrangement a surrogate mother acts as a birth mother for the commissioning parent(s) and agrees to hand the child over soon after birth (see, for example, *Re C (A Minor) (Wardship: Surrogacy)* [1985] FLR 846; and *Re P (Minors) (Wardship: Surrogacy)* [1987] 2 FLR 421).

The practice of surrogacy is governed by the Surrogacy Arrangements Act 1985. Under the Act a surrogate mother is defined as a woman who carries a child in pursuance of an arrangement made before she began to carry the child, and with a view to any such child being handed over to, and parental responsibility being met (so far as practicable) by, another person or persons (s.1(2)). If surrogacy takes place in a licensed clinic it has the advantage of ensuring that any man who goes for treatment with the woman is treated as the father under s.28(3), whether or not he provides sperm.

Under the Surrogacy Arrangements Act 1985 surrogacy arrangements between private individuals are permitted (s.2(2)), but it is a criminal offence to set up a surrogacy agency commercially and to advertise and to negotiate a surrogacy arrangement for money (s.2(1)). However, payment of money in respect of a surrogacy arrangement may in appropriate circumstances be authorised retrospectively by the court (see *Re X and Y (Foreign Surrogacy)* [2008] EWHC 3030, [2009] 1 FLR 733, below).

Surrogacy can cause problems, however, as it did, for example, in *Re P (Surrogacy: Residence)* [2008] 1 FLR 177 where the surrogate mother, who had entered into surrogacy agreements involving two different commissioning fathers, failed to hand the children over at birth.

In the following case McFarlane J laid down some principles in respect of surrogacy which should be borne in mind in future cases. He also expressed concern about the fact that surrogacy agencies, such as COTS (Childlessness Overcome Through Surrogacy), which was involved in the case, were not covered by any statutory or regulatory provision. Given that COTS was unaware of the domicile requirements to apply for a parental order under s.30 of the Human Fertilisation and Embryology Act 1990 (see below) and had not realised that it was unlawful to take a child abroad for an adoption, McFarlane J said that it had to be asked whether some form of inspection or authorisation should be required in order to improve the quality of advice offered to couples who sought to have a child through surrogacy.

▶ *Re G (Surrogacy: Foreign Domicile)* [2007] EWHC 2814 (Fam), [2008] 1 FLR 1047

A surrogacy arrangement was entered into whereby an English surrogate mother agreed to give birth to a surrogate child for a married couple living in Turkey. The child was conceived using the egg of the surrogate mother and the Turkish husband's sperm. The surrogate mother's estranged husband had not given written consent to the insemination due to lack of communication between the couple. The Turkish parents came to England and (as a precursor to returning to Turkey where they would apply to adopt the child) they applied for a s.30 parental order under HFEA 1990. However, as they had failed to satisfy the domicile requirements in s.30(3)(b) of the 1990 Act (because of the short time they had spent in the UK), McFarlane J instead made an order under s.84 of the Adoption and Children Act 2002, which confers parental responsibility on a prospective adopter.

In respect of the issue of consent to insemination by the estranged husband of the surrogate mother, McFarlane J held that, pursuant to s.28 of the 1990 Act, the common law position applied and that the father was to be treated for all purposes as the child's father. The fact that there had been no written consent did not necessarily mean that the father had not consented for the purposes of s.28(2). The term 'consent' was not confined to the narrow meaning argued for by COTS. It was necessary for the court to look more widely than simply at whether the husband had signed the form at the clinic. McFarlane J listed the principles which should be borne in mind in trying to ensure that lessons were learned for the future:

▶ Non-commercial surrogacy arrangements where neither of the commissioning parents is domiciled in the UK are to be discouraged; as it is not open to them to apply for a parental order under s.30 (see below).
▶ Surrogacy agencies must ensure they are fully familiar with the basic legal requirements.
▶ Any application for a parental order under s.30 involving an international element should be transferred to a nominated inter-country adoption county court or the High Court.
▶ Any court hearing an application for a parental order under s.30 must ensure that the qualifying conditions required of the applicants are met.
▶ Where a surrogate mother is married, but separated from her husband, all reasonable attempts should be made before the surrogacy process begins, in order to establish whether or not her husband consented to the proposed arrangement.
▶ The court can make orders as to costs, as costs should not be borne by the British taxpayer in such cases.

(For a discussion of *Re G (Surrogacy: Foreign Domicile)* [2007] EWHC 2814 (Fam), [2008] 1 FLR 1047, see Howe [2008] Fam Law 61).

(b) Surrogacy and parenthood

The rules on parenthood are the same as those which apply in non-surrogacy cases (see above). However although the surrogate mother is the legal mother of the child, the commissioning parents can apply for a parental order (see below) to transfer parenthood to them.

(c) Surrogacy-parental orders

As the law currently stands, only *married* couples can apply for a parental order where they have entered into a surrogacy arrangement; but new provisions governing parental orders, which will give civil partner couples and other couples the right to apply, are due to come into force in 2010, whereupon s.30 HFEA 1990 will be replaced by s.54 HFEA 2008 (see below).

In the case of a surrogacy arrangement, commissioning *married* parents (the couple who arranged for the surrogate mother to carry the child for them) can apply to the court under s.30(1) Human Fertilisation and Embryology Act 1990 for a 'parental order' which transfers parenthood from the surrogate mother (and her husband or partner if she has one) to the commissioning parents. Where an application is made to the court for a parental order, an officer of Cafcass (see 1.6) is appointed by the court to investigate the case. On issuing the parental order, the court notifies the General

Register Office of Births, which re-registers the birth, and the new birth record supersedes the original.

As s.30 proceedings for a parental order are family proceedings for the purposes of the Children Act 1989 (s.30(8)(a)) the court may make any s.8 order under the Children Act 1989 in those proceedings, either on an application or of its own motion.

Conditions and requirements   The court can make a parental order in respect of a child of a married couple where one parent is the genetic parent (s.30(1)), but only if the following conditions and requirements are satisfied:

▷ The application must be made within six months of the child's birth (s.30(2)).
▷ At the time of the application and of the making of the order the child's home must be with the applicants, and one or both parties must be domiciled in a part of the UK or in the Channel Islands or in the Isle of Man (s.30(3)) (see *Re G (Surrogacy: Foreign Domicile)* [2007] EWHC 2814 (Fam), [2008] 1 FLR 1047, above).
▷ At the time of making the order each spouse must have attained the age of 18 (s.30(4)).
▷ The court must be satisfied that the child's genetic father (whether or not the husband) and the woman who carried the child have freely, and with full understanding of what is involved, agreed unconditionally to the making of the order (s.30(5)). Agreement is not required if they cannot be found or are incapable of giving agreement; and the agreement of the mother who carried the child is ineffective if given less than six weeks after the child's birth (s.30(6)).
▷ The court must be satisfied that no money or other benefit (other than expenses reasonably incurred) has been given or received by either of the applicants in respect of the making of the order or the surrogacy arrangement (or in consideration of the making of the order, any surrogacy agreement, the handing over of the child or the making of any arrangement with a view to making the order), unless the money or other benefit has been authorised by the court (s.30(7)).

Authorising payments   The court can authorise payments even though they are prohibited by s.30(7). Thus, in *Re C (Application by Mr and Mrs X Under s.30 of the Human Fertilisation and Embryology Act 1990)* [2002] EWHC 157 (Fam), [2002] 1 FLR 909 £12,000 paid to the surrogate mother by the commissioning parents (because they did not wish her to work during pregnancy) was authorised by Wall J as being expenses reasonably incurred under s.30(7). *Re C* was applied by Hedley J in the following case:

▶ *Re X and Y (Foreign Surrogacy)* [2008] EWHC 3030 (Fam), [2009] 1 FLR 733

A married couple from the UK had entered into a surrogacy agreement with a married woman in the Ukraine who had produced twins for them (by embryos conceived with donor eggs and fertilised by the husband's sperm). The expenses paid for the arrangement were contrary to s.30(7). They UK parents applied for a parental order under s.30 HFEA 1990.

Hedley J granted the s.30 parental order, despite the unauthorised payments, on the basis that retrospective authorisation of those payments was legally possible. Earlier case-law had established that three questions had to be asked when considering whether payments should be authorised: was the sum paid disproportionate to reasonable expenses; were the applicants acting in good faith and without 'moral taint' in their dealings with the surrogate mother; and were the applicants a party to any attempt to defraud the authorities? On the facts Hedley J held that the three questions were satisfied and that he was satisfied that the welfare of the children required that they be regarded as life-long members of the applicants' family and that the payments should be authorised under s.30(7). Hedley J held that the granting of a parental order would not be an affront to public policy, even though it was difficult to determine whether the surrogacy payments were 'disproportionate' to reasonable expenses.

The new law on parental orders   Section 54 of the Human Fertilisation and Embryology Act 2008 will replace s.30 of HFEA 1990 and enable not just married couples, but civil partners and other couples, to apply for a parental order where the child is born under a surrogacy arrangement. This new provision is due to come into force in April 2010.

The court can make a parental order only on the application of a couple (*not* a single person) providing for a child to be treated in law as the child of the applicants if (s.54(1): the child has been carried by a woman who is not one of the applicants, as a result of the placing in her of an embryo or sperm of eggs or her artificial insemination; the gametes of at least one of the applicants were used to bring about the creation of the embryo; and the conditions in ss.54(2)–(8) are satisfied (see below).

Applicants: The following 'couples' can apply (s.54(2)): married couples; civil partners; and two persons who are living in an enduring family relationship (and who are not within the prohibited degrees of relationship with each other).

Conditions and requirements that must be satisfied: The requirements that must be satisfied, in addition to the need for the applicants to be a couple (s.54(2)) are laid down in ss.54(3)–(8) HFEA 2008. These are the same as the requirements laid down for s.30 orders under s.30 HFEA 1990 (see p. 268 above); and the same case-law will apply.

Summary

1   The biological bond between parent and child is an important bond, but this is always subject to the overriding principle that the welfare of the child is the court's paramount consideration.

2   It is a judge-made presumption of law that the best person to bring up a child is the child's natural parent. This approach is also enshrined in the Children Act 1989 (see Chapter 10).

3   A child born of married parents is presumed to be the child of the husband. Legal presumptions about parentage are not very relevant today because parentage can be proved virtually conclusively by DNA profiling. The court has held that scientific tests, not legal presumptions, should be used to prove parentage.

4   The court can direct that a scientific test take place to establish parentage (s.20 Family Law Reform Act 1969). The consent of the child is needed (if aged 16 and over), or the consent of the person with the care and control of the child if the child is aged under 16. If consent is not forthcoming the court can give consent. Although the courts have held that it is normally in the best interests of the child to know his or her origins, and for the truth to come out, this is subject to the overriding principle that the child's welfare is the court's paramount consideration.

5   The court can grant a declaration of parentage under s.55 Family Law Act 1986.

6 Married parents and unmarried mothers have 'automatic' parental responsibility for their child (ss.2 and 3 Children Act 1989); and so does a lesbian mother whether or not she is a civil partner (s.2(2A) CA 1989).

7 The unmarried father has no 'automatic' parental responsibility (s.2(2) CA 1989), but can acquire it under s.4 of the Children Act 1989 by making an agreement with the mother on a prescribed form, or by obtaining a parental responsibility order, or by being registered on the child's birth certificate with the mother. The Government is proposing to introduce compulsory joint birth registration in the case of unmarried fathers, but subject to certain restrictions and safeguards (see s.56 and Schedule 6 to the Welfare Reform Act 2009, which is not currently in force).

8 A step-parent and the lesbian partner of a child's mother can acquire parental responsibility by parental responsibility agreement, parental responsibility order, or birth registration (s.4ZA CA 1989 and s.4AZ CA 1989 respectively).

9 Other ways in which parental responsibility can be acquired are by: a residence order (see 10.5); special guardianship (see 15.15); or by adoption (see Chapter 15).

10 Parents have certain rights and duties at common law and under statute, but parental rights are not absolute.

11 Disputes between parents and doctors about medical treatment of a child can be decided by the High Court under its inherent jurisdiction or in wardship; or by making an application for a s.8 specific issue order under the Children Act 1989. The best interests of the child are paramount in these cases, and parental wishes, while respected by the courts, do not prevail. Serious and irreversible operations on the child (such as sterilisation and circumcision) may need the consent of the court. Disputes between parents about medical treatment can be decided by making an application for a specific issue order under s.8 Children Act 1989, or by making an application under the High Court's inherent or wardship jurisdiction. Where a parent wishes to prevent the other parent deciding on medical treatment an application can be made for a s.8 prohibited steps order.

12 A guardian can be appointed for a child (see ss.5 and 6 of the Children Act 1989).

13 Some couples may decide to have a child by way of assisted reproduction or by way of a surrogacy arrangement. The Human Fertilisation and Embryology Acts 1990 and 2008 govern assisted reproduction. Under the Surrogacy Arrangements Act 1985 it is a criminal offence to make surrogacy arrangements on a commercial basis.

14 Married commissioning parents of a surrogacy arrangement and married parents of a child conceived by assisted reproduction can apply for a parental order under s.30 of the Human Fertilisation and Embryology Act 1990 (HFEA 1990), which is an order for a child to be treated in law as a child of the parents' marriage. In 2010, s.30 will be replaced by s.54 HFEA 2008 which will extend eligibility to apply for a parental order to civil partners and to two persons who are living in an enduring family relationship.

Further reading and references

Bridge, 'Religion, culture and conviction: the medical treatment of children' [1999] CFLQ 217.

Diduck ' "If only we can find the appropriate terms to use the issue will be solved": law, identity and parenthood' [2007] CFLQ 458.

Downie, '*Re C (HIV Test)* – the limits of parental autonomy' [2000] CFLQ 197.

Eekelaar, 'Are parents morally obliged to care for their children?' (1991) OJLS 340.

Further reading and references cont'd

Eekelaar, 'Parental responsibility: State of nature or nature of the state?' (1991) JSWFL 37.

Eekelaar, 'Rethinking parental responsibility' [2001] Fam Law 428.

Fortin, 'Accommodating children's rights in a post Human Rights Act era' (2006) *Modern Law Review* 299.

Fortin, 'Children's rights to know their origins – too far, too fast?' [2009] CFLQ 336.

Lind, '*Evans* v. *United Kingdom* – judgment of Solomon: power, gender and procreation' [2006] CFLQ 576.

Probert, Gilmore and Herring (eds.), *Responsible Parents and Parental Responsibility*, 2009, Hart Publishing.

Howe, 'International surrogacy: a cautionary tale' [2008] Fam Law 61.

Maidment, 'Parental responsibility – Is there a duty to consult?' [2001] Fam Law 518.

Pedain, 'Doctors, parents and the courts: legitimising restrictions on the continued provision of lifespan maximising treatments for severely handicapped, non-dying babies' [2005] CFLQ 535.

Sheldon, '*Evans* v. *Amicus Healthcare; Hadley* v. *Midland Fertility Services*: Revealing cracks in the twin pillars' [2004] CFLQ 437.

Wallbank, '"Bodies in the shadows": joint birth registration, parental responsibility and social class' [2009] CFLQ 267.

Websites

Advice Now: www.advicenow.org.uk

Families Need Fathers: www.fnf.org.uk

Family and Parenting Institute: www.familyandparenting.org

Human Fertilisation and Embryology Authority: www.hfea.gov.uk

Parentline Plus: www.parentlineplus.org.uk

Chapter 10

The Children Act 1989

The Children Act 1989

The Children Act 1989 contains both private and public law provisions relating to children. Private law governs the relationships between private individuals, usually parents, and includes rules on parental responsibility, guardianship and residence and contact. Public law, on the other hand, is the law governing State intervention into family life by local authority social services departments who have duties and powers to provide for children in need and to protect children who are suffering, or who are at risk of suffering, significant harm. The Act came into force in 1991, but there have been many subsequent amendments.

The *Children Act 1989 Guidance and Regulations: Volume 1 – Court Orders* (Department for Children, Schools and Families, 2008) is a guide published by the Government for use primarily by local authorities. It replaces the volume which was published in 1991.

(i) Influences on the Act and its principles and policies   The Children Act 1989 was an important Act not only because it consolidated much of the civil law relating to children, but because it introduced new principles and policies. Government reports and public inquiries relating to the management of child abuse by social workers and other agencies had a considerable influence on the Act. Of particular importance was *The Report of the Inquiry into Child Abuse in Cleveland* 1987 (Cm 412, 1988), which severely criticised the over-zealous intervention of local authority social services in children's cases in Cleveland in the North East of England. The *Report* had an important influence on the public law provisions of the Act, in particular in respect of emergency protection of children and the importance of promoting inter-agency co-operation.

The *Gillick* case (see 8.4) also had an impact on the Children Act 1989, by giving children of sufficient age and understanding the right to bring proceedings and to have their views taken into account by the court. The Act also introduced the concept of 'parental responsibility', not rights, (partly as a result of *Gillick*), in order to stress the positive ongoing nature of parental involvement in bringing up children and to remove the adversarial undertones of the word 'rights'.

An important policy in the Act is that of minimum State intervention. Thus, under the no-order provision in s.1(5), courts must decide whether or not an order is really necessary in the circumstances. The aim of the Act is to restrict intervention into family life by courts and local authorities unless really necessary for the child's welfare.

Another aim of the Act is to provide a flexible court structure and a flexible range of orders available in all family proceedings involving children (and which can be made on an application to the court or by the court of its own motion). Applications under the Act can be brought in magistrates' family proceedings courts, county courts and the High Court, but cases can be transferred between these courts if the matter is urgent or serious, or where proceedings should be consolidated.

(ii) Strengths and weaknesses   The Children Act 1989 has generally been considered to be a 'successful' Act (and this was recognised by the inquiry which followed the tragic

death of Victoria Climbié, see 14.5), but it has been criticised by some commentators for not putting children's interests sufficiently to the fore (see Freeman, 1998) and for failing to include any reference to children's rights (see Fortin, 2006). A major problem with proceedings under the Act, however, is that of delay. Delays can be particularly long in child protection cases, but steps have been taken to resolve the problem (see Chapter 14).

(iii) Human rights   The Children Act 1989 must be construed and applied by courts and public authorities in a way which complies with the European Convention for the Protection of Human Rights as a result of the obligations courts and other public authorities have under the Human Rights Act 1998 (see 1.7).

(iv) Amendments to the Act   New provisions have been inserted into the Children Act 1989 over the years. Thus, the Act has been amended to allow unmarried fathers to acquire parental responsibility by birth registration (see 9.4); and step-parents to acquire parental responsibility for a step-child (see 9.5). New provisions on special guardianship have been inserted into the Act (see 15.14); and in respect of facilitation and enforcement of contact (see 11.6). In 2009 changes were made extending the duration of residence orders (see 10.5); and new provisions were inserted into the Act governing the parental responsibility of a female civil partner who has had a child by assisted reproduction (see 9.5). Amendments have also been made to the public law provisions of the Act, for instance in respect of provisions concerning children leaving care (see further in Chapter 14).

10.2   An overview of the Act

Parts I to V of the Children Act 1989 are the parts most relevant to family lawyers. Part XII ('Miscellaneous and General') is also important because it includes provisions, about the effect and duration of orders (s.91), privacy for children in certain proceedings (s.97), restrictions on the use of the wardship jurisdiction (s.100), and the interpretation section of the Act (s.105). The following schedules are also important: Schedule 1 (Financial Provision for Children); Schedule 2 (Local Authority Support for Children and Families); and Schedule 3 (Supervision Orders).

The main provisions of the Children Act 1989 are as follows:

Children Act 1989

Part I Introductory

Welfare principle and other principles applicable in proceedings under the Act (s.1). Parental responsibility (ss.2–4A). Appointment of guardians for children (ss.5 and 6). Welfare reports (s.7).

Part II Orders with respect to children in family proceedings

Section 8 orders (residence, contact, specific issue and prohibited steps), and the powers of the court in respect of these orders (ss.9–14), including new provisions in relation to contact (for example contact activity directions and conditions) (ss.11A–P). Special guardianship orders (ss.14A–G). Orders for financial relief for children (s.15 and Schedule 1). Family assistance orders (s.16). Risk assessments (s.16A).

Part III Local authority support for children and families

Local authority services for children in need, their families and others (ss.17–19). Payments and vouchers in respect of children in need (ss.17A and B). Provision of accommodation for children in need (ss.20 and 21). The duties of local authorities in relation to children looked after by them (ss.22 and 23). Advice and assistance for children (s.24). Advice and assistance for children and young persons who have left care (ss.23A–E, ss.24A–D). Secure accommodation (s.25). Independent reviewing officers (ss.25A–C). Case reviews (s.26). Co-operation between local authorities (s.27). Advocacy services for children (s.27A). Consultation with local education authorities (s.28). Recoupment of cost of providing services (s.29).

Part IV Care and supervision

Care orders, supervision orders and education supervision orders (ss.31–40). Care plans (s.31A).

Part V Protection of children

Child assessment orders (s.43). Emergency protection orders (ss.44–45). Police removal of children (s.46). Local authority duty to investigate (s.47). Power to assist in discovery of children who may be in need of emergency protection (s.48).

10.3 The welfare principles

Important principles are laid down in s.1 of the Children Act 1989 which apply to most court applications involving children, whether brought by private individuals or by public authorities. These principles are as follows:

(a) The welfare principle (s.1(1))

The paramountcy of the child's welfare is the governing principle in children's cases.

Section 1(1) Children Act 1989

'When a court determines any question with respect to—

(a) the upbringing of a child; or
(b) the administration of a child's property or the application of any income arising from it,

the child's welfare shall be the court's paramount consideration.'

The child's welfare is the paramount consideration in private law proceedings (such as for residence and contact orders) and in public law proceedings (such as for care and supervision orders). The Children Act 1989 does not expressly require the welfare principle to be applied in applications for leave to apply for a s.8 order (see 10.4) or in applications for financial relief for children under s.15 and Sched. 1 (see 12.5), but in practice the court will consider the child's welfare as part of its statutory obligation to consider all the circumstances of the case.

The paramountcy of the child's welfare is enshrined in art. 3(1) of the UN Convention on the Rights of the Child 1989, and is recognised by the European Court of Human Rights even though there is no express reference to children in the European Convention for the Protection of Human Rights (see 1.7).

(b)　The 'welfare checklist' (s.1(3))

Section 1(3) contains a list of factors (a 'welfare checklist') which imposes some structure on the broad exercise of judicial discretion in the application of the welfare principle above. The court must have regard to the checklist when deciding whether to make, vary or discharge a s.8 order in contested proceedings (s.1(4)(a)), or to make, vary or discharge a special guardianship order, or a care or supervision order (s.1(4)(b)). Thus, the checklist must be applied in private law proceedings and also in public law proceedings involving local authorities (except in emergency protection proceedings – as to apply the checklist would inhibit emergency action).

Section 1(3) Children Act 1989

'… a court shall have regard in particular to—
(a) the ascertainable wishes and feelings of the child concerned (considered in the light of his age and understanding);
(b) his physical, emotional and educational needs;
(c) the likely effect on him of any change in his circumstances;
(d) his age, sex, background and any characteristics of his which the court considers relevant;
(e) any harm which he has suffered or is at risk of suffering;
(f) how capable each of his parents, and any other person in relation to whom the court considers the question to be relevant, is of meeting his needs;
(g) the range of powers available to the court under this Act in the proceedings in question.'

'*Harm*' in s.1(3)(e) has the same meaning as it has in s.31 of the Act (see 14.7); and also includes harm caused by seeing or hearing the ill treatment of another person. Witnessing or hearing domestic violence can therefore constitute harm.

The list is not exclusive – other factors may be taken into account – and the factors are not listed in any hierarchy of importance. Furthermore, as the Act does not refer to s.1(3) as a 'checklist', a judge is not required 'to read out the seven items in s.1(3) and pronounce his conclusion on each' (*per* Staughton LJ in *H v. H (Residence Order: Leave to Remove from Jurisdiction)* [1995] 1 FLR 529). In *B v. B (Residence Order: Reasons for Decision)* [1997] 2 FLR 602, Holman J held that, although it is not always necessary or appropriate for a judge to go through the checklist item by item, it does represent an extremely useful and important discipline for judges to ensure that all the relevant factors and circumstances are considered and balanced. In *Re G (Children)* [2006] UKHL 43, [2006] 2 FLR 629 Lord Nicholls said that in a 'difficult or finely balanced case it is a great help to address each of the factors in the list, along with any others which may be relevant, so as to ensure that no particular feature of the case is given more weight than it should properly bear'.

A failure to consider one or more of the factors in the checklist may provide a successful ground for an appeal, but not necessarily so (see *Re S and Others (Residence)* [2008] EWCA Civ 653, [2008] 2 FLR 1377 where, although Thorpe LJ said that the trial judge's token reference to the checklist had been perfunctory, her decision had not been plainly wrong).

(c)   The 'minimum intervention principle' (s.1(5))

This principle was introduced as part of the general policy of the Children Act 1989 to place the primary responsibility for children on their parents.

Section 1(5) Children Act 1989

'Where a court is considering whether or not to make one or more orders under this Act with respect to a child, it shall not make the order or any of the orders unless it considers that doing so would be better for the child than making no order at all.'

The aim of s.1(5) is to discourage courts making unnecessary orders and to ensure that orders are made only if they will positively improve the child's welfare. Sometimes an order may exacerbate problems and increase hostility between parents, with harmful repercussions for the child.

Section 1(5) has been interpreted by some commentators and judges as creating a presumption in favour of making no order, and for this reason has been referred to as the 'no-order' principle. However, in *Re G (Children) (Residence Order: No Order Principle)* [2005] All ER 399 the Court of Appeal held that this is an incorrect interpretation, as it is perfectly clear that s.1(5) does *not* create a presumption either way. It merely requires the court to ask whether making an order would be better for a child than making no order at all. The district judge's decision not to make a residence order was therefore wrong in law because he had wrongly considered that s.1(5) raised a legal presumption against making an order.

(d)   The 'no-delay' principle (s.1(2))

The Children Act 1989 recognises that delay is harmful for a child:

Section 1(2) Children Act 1989

'In any proceedings in which any question with respect to the upbringing of a child arises, the court shall have regard to the general principle that any delay in determining the question is likely to prejudice the welfare of the child.'

To avoid delay, the progress of cases is determined by the court, which must draw up a timetable for s.8 order proceedings (s.11) and for care and supervision proceedings (s.32). The court can give directions and the rules of court make provision to avoid delay. Children's issues must be determined as soon as possible so that minimum disruption is caused to the child's life and the child is not left in limbo. Despite attempts to reduce delay, it continues to be a problem, particularly in child protection cases.

10.4   Section 8 orders

Section 8 of the Children Act 1989 makes provision for the following orders which can be used in a wide range of different situations involving children:

- **Residence Order** (determining with whom the child should live);
- **Contact Order** (determining with whom the child should visit or stay);
- **Prohibited Steps Order** (preventing an action in respect of parental responsibility being taken);
- **Specific Issue Order** (determining an issue arising in respect of parental responsibility).

According to *Judicial and Court Statistics 2008* (Ministry of Justice, Cm 7697, 2009), in 2008 in England and Wales the numbers of applications for s.8 orders were: residence orders (38,080); contact orders (40,900); prohibited steps orders (14,570); and specific issue orders (8,560).

Applicable principles   When considering whether to make, vary or discharge any s.8 order, the court must apply the welfare principle and the welfare checklist; and the other provisions in s.1 of the Act (namely the no-delay and no-order provisions) (see above).

Applicants   Some persons have an 'automatic' right to apply for a s.8 order, but others, including children, need the court's leave (permission) to apply (see p. 282). Restrictions exist in respect of applications by local authorities (see below).

General provisions   The court can: make interim s.8 orders (s.11(3)); attach directions and conditions to a s.8 order (s.11(7)); and grant a s.8 order without the other party being given notice of the proceedings (if urgent action is needed).

Restrictions   Section 9 lays down the following restrictions which apply to s.8 orders:

- A court cannot make any s.8 order (other than a residence order) with respect to a child who is in local authority care (s.9(1)).
- A local authority cannot apply for a residence or contact order and no court shall make such an order in favour of a local authority (s.9(2)). This prohibition is to prevent local authorities using s.8 orders instead of the care or supervision order provisions in Part IV of the Act.
- A local authority foster-parent (or a person who was a foster-parent at any time during the previous six months) cannot apply for leave to apply for a s.8 order with respect to a foster-child unless the foster-parent has the consent of the local authority; or is the relative of the child; or the foster-child has lived with the foster-parent for at least one year preceding the application (s.9(3)).
- A court cannot make a specific issue order or a prohibited steps order with a view to achieving a result which could be achieved by making a residence or contact order; or in any way which is denied to the High Court (by s.100(2)) in the exercise of its inherent jurisdiction with respect to children (s.9(5)).
- Unless the circumstances are exceptional, a court cannot make a specific issue order, contact order or prohibited steps order to last after the child has reached the age of 16 (s.9(6)).
- Unless the circumstances are exceptional, a court cannot make any s.8 order if the child has already reached the age of 16 (s.9(7)).

10.5 Residence orders

> **A residence order** is an order 'settling the arrangements to be made as to the person with whom the child is to live' (s.8(1)).

(For residence orders on family breakdown, see 11.4).

Residence orders were introduced by the Children Act 1989 to replace custody orders, with the aim of removing the claim right implicit in, and the adversarial undertones of, the term 'custody'. The emphasis on residence rather than custody was to reinforce the fact that both parents have a continuing role to play in relation to a child. With a residence order it is a question of where the child should live, rather than to whom the child belongs.

In addition to the general provisions and restrictions applicable to s.8 orders (see above), the following provisions specifically apply to residence orders:

▷ The court can make a 'shared' residence order in favour of two or more persons who live in different households (s.11(4)) (see 11.4).
▷ If a residence order is made there are restrictions on changing the child's surname and taking the child out of the UK (ss.13(1) and (2)).
▷ If under a residence order the child is to live with one of two parents who each has parental responsibility for him the order ceases to be effective if the parents live together for a continuous period of more than six months (s.11(5)).
▷ The court can impose conditions on residence orders (s.11(7)).

Local authorities and residence orders   A residence order is the only s.8 order that can be made in respect of a child in local authority care (s.9(1)), for otherwise a local authority's statutory powers would be undermined. However, a residence order cannot be applied for by, or be made in favour of, a local authority (s.9(2)), as this would allow a local authority to gain parental responsibility for a child by means other than a care order.

Residence orders and parental responsibility   A residence order does not affect the parental responsibility of any other person who possesses such responsibility. Thus, parental responsibility is retained and continues whether or not a residence order is made.

If a residence order is made in favour of an unmarried father without parental responsibility, the court must also make an order under s.4 (see 9.4) giving him that responsibility (s.12(1)). Where a residence order is made in favour of a female civil partner who is a parent of a child by virtue of assisted reproduction or artificial insemination, but who does not have parental responsibility, then the court must make an order under s.4ZA giving her that responsibility (s.12(1A)) (see 9.5)

Where the court makes a residence order in favour of any person who is not the parent or guardian of the child concerned, then that person has parental responsibility for the child while the residence order is in force (s.12(2)). But a person who acquires parental responsibility in this manner does not have a right to agree, or refuse to agree, to the making of an adoption order; or to appoint a guardian (s.12(3)).

10.6   Contact orders

> **A contact order** is an order 'requiring the person with whom the child lives, or is to live, to allow the child to visit or stay with the person named in the order, or for that person and the child otherwise to have contact with each other' (s.8(1)).

The Children Act 1989 introduced the term 'contact' to replace that of 'access' in order to stress the importance of children maintaining links with their parents and other family members on family breakdown. (For contact orders on family breakdown, see 11.5).

The welfare principles and general provisions and restrictions which apply to s.8 orders (see above) also apply to contact orders. In respect of local authorities, a contact order cannot be made in respect of a child in care and cannot be applied for by, or be made in favour of, a local authority (ss.9(1) and (2)). Contact in care is governed by s.34 of the Children Act (see 14.8). A s.8 contact order ceases to be effective if the parents live together for a continuous period of more than six months (s.11(6)).

New provisions governing the enforcement and facilitation of contact were brought into force on 8 December 2008 (see 11.6). There have also been developments in respect of contact and domestic violence (see p. 303).

10.7   Prohibited steps orders

> **A prohibited steps order** is an order 'that no step which could be taken by a parent in meeting his parental responsibility for a child, and which is of a kind specified in the order, shall be taken by any person without the consent of the court' (s.8(1)).

The prohibited steps order, and the specific issue order (see over), give the court powers similar to those which, before the Children Act 1989, were available only to the High Court under its inherent jurisdiction and in wardship (see 8.7).

A prohibited steps order is a flexible injunctive type of order which can be used in a wide range of circumstances, for example to prohibit a parent taking a child out of the UK or from making a unilateral decision about the child's medical treatment or education, or from changing the child's surname. In *Re G (Parental Responsibility: Education)* [1994] 2 FLR 964, for example, a mother applied for a prohibited steps order to prevent her husband from sending their son away to boarding school, but her application was refused.

In addition to the general provisions and restrictions which apply to s.8 orders (see p. 277 above), a prohibited steps order cannot be made to achieve the same result which could be achieved by making a residence or contact order, and cannot be made in any way which is denied to the High Court (by s.100(2)) in the exercise of its inherent jurisdiction with respect to children (s.9(5)).

As a prohibited steps order is an order prohibiting 'a step which could be taken by a parent in meeting his parental responsibility' for a child, it cannot be used to restrict anything other than some aspect of parental responsibility. For example, it cannot be used to restrict publicity about a child, since this is not within the scope of parental responsibility (this must be dealt with by the High Court under its inherent jurisdiction); or to prohibit a parent from occupying the family home (see *Nottinghamshire County Council* v. *P* [1993] 2 FLR 134, [1994] Fam 18; and *Re D (Prohibited Steps Order)* [1996] 2 FLR 273).

10.8 Specific issue orders

> **A specific issue order** is an order 'giving directions for the purpose of determining a specific question which has arisen, or which may arise, in connection with any aspect of parental responsibility for a child' (s.8(1)).

This order can be made to settle any dispute which has arisen, or which may arise, in respect of the exercise of parental responsibility. It can be used, for example, to settle a dispute arising in respect of a child's education or medical treatment, or a decision to move a child abroad, or to change a child's surname. A specific issue order (like a prohibited steps order) gives the court powers similar to those of the High Court under its inherent and wardship jurisdictions (see 8.7). In addition to the general provisions and restrictions which apply to s.8 orders (see p. 277 above), a specific issue order, like a prohibited steps order, cannot be made to achieve the same result which could be achieved by making a residence or contact order, and cannot be made in any way denied to the High Court (by s.100(2)) in the exercise of its inherent jurisdiction with respect to children (s.9(5)).

Specific issue orders have been sought by parents in a wide range of situations, for example:

> ▶ **To obtain permission for a child to be sterilised** (*Re HG (Specific Issue Order: Sterilisation)* [1993] 1 FLR 587).
> ▶ **To require a child to be brought up in the Muslim religion and be circumcised** (*Re J (Specific Issue Orders: Child's Religious Upbringing and Circumcision)* [2000] 1 FLR 571; *Re S (Specific Issue Order: Religion: Circumcision)* [2004] EWHC 1282 (Fam), [2005] 1 FLR 236).
> ▶ **To require a child to be informed about his paternity and the existence of his father** (*Re K (Specific Issue Order)* [1999] 2 FLR 280).
> ▶ **To resolve a parental dispute about a child's education** (*Re A (Specific Issue Order: Parental Dispute)* [2001] 1 FLR 121; and *M* v. *H (Educational Welfare)* [2008] EWHC 324 (Fam), [2008] 1 FLR 1400).

In respect of local authorities, a specific issue order cannot be made in respect of a child in local authority care (s.9(1)). A local authority will instead have to seek leave to invoke the court's inherent jurisdiction to decide a particular matter (ss.100(2)–(5)) (see 8.7). A specific issue order cannot be made to deem a child to be in need for the purposes of Part III of the Children Act 1989 (see 14.6), as this is not an 'aspect of parental responsibility' for the purposes of the order – the appropriate remedy is judicial review (see *Re J (Specific Issue Order: Leave to Apply)* [1995] 1 FLR 669).

10.9 Power of the court to make section 8 orders in family proceedings of its own motion

In any family proceedings in which a question arises with respect to the welfare of any child, the court may make a s.8 order with respect to the child if (s.10(1)): a person is entitled to apply for a s.8 order with respect to the child; or a person has been given leave of the court to make the application; or the court considers that the order should be made even though no such application has been made.

'Family proceedings' are defined in ss.8(3), (4) as being proceedings under the following (but not including an application for leave under s.100(3) CA 1989):

- the inherent jurisdiction of the High Court in relation to children;
- Parts I, II and IV of the Children Act 1989;
- the Matrimonial Causes Act 1973;
- Schedule 5 to the Civil Partnership Act 2004;
- the Adoption and Children Act 2002;
- the Domestic Proceedings and Magistrates' Courts Act 1978;
- Schedule 6 to the Civil Partnership Act 2004;
- Part III of the Matrimonial and Family Proceedings Act 1984;
- the Family Law Act 1996;
- ss.11 and 12 of the Crime and Disorder Act 1998.

Thus s.8 orders can be made in a wide range of proceedings involving children, for example in divorce proceedings, adoption proceedings, and proceedings for non-molestation orders and occupation orders in domestic violence cases.

10.10 Power of the court to make section 8 orders in family proceedings on the application of certain persons

In addition to having the power to make a s.8 order of its own motion in any family proceedings (see above), the court may make an order with respect to a child on the application of persons who are entitled to apply or of persons who have been granted leave to do so by the court (s.10(2)).

(a) Persons entitled to apply without leave of the court

(i) Any s.8 order The following persons are entitled to apply for any s.8 order (s.10(4)): a parent, guardian, or special guardian of the child (s.10(4)(a)); a step-parent who has parental responsibility for the child under s.4A (s.10(4)(aa)); and a person in whose favour a residence order is in force with respect to the child (s.10(4)(b)).

(ii) Residence or contact order The following persons are entitled to apply for a residence or contact order (s.10(5)): any party to a marriage or civil partnership (whether or not subsisting) in relation to whom the child is a child of the family (ss.10(5)(a), (aa)); any person with whom the child has lived for at least three years, which period need not be continuous but must not have begun more than five years before, or have ended more

than three months before, applying for the order (ss.10(5)(b), (10)); any person who has the consent of each person in whose favour a residence order was made; any person who has the consent of the local authority when a child is in care; and any other person who has the consent of each person (if any) who has parental responsibility for the child (s.10(5)(c)).

An application for a residence order can be made in respect of a child who is the subject of a special guardianship order, but only with leave of the court to apply (s.10(7A)).

(iii) Residence order (local authority foster-parents and relatives)   A local authority foster-parent is entitled to apply (without leave) for a residence order with respect to the child if the child has lived with him/her for a period of at least one year immediately preceding the application (s.10(5A)). The same rule applies to a relative of a child (s.10(5B)).

(b)   Applications where leave of the court is needed

Some persons need leave (permission) of the court to apply for a s.8 order.

(i) Children – leave to apply   A child needs leave of the court to apply for a s.8 order, which the court may grant only if it is satisfied that the child has sufficient understanding to make the proposed application (s.10(8)). The court can take into account the likelihood of the proposed application succeeding, and, on that basis, refuse leave even if the child has sufficiency of understanding (*per* Booth J in *Re SC (A Minor) (Leave to Seek a Residence Order)* [1994] 1 FLR 96; and Johnson J in *Re H (Residence Order: Child's Application for Leave)* [2000] 1 FLR 780). Leave applications by children are heard in the High Court (*Practice Direction (Children Act 1989: Applications by Children)* [1993] 1 FLR 668).

There has been conflicting judicial opinion as to whether the child's welfare is paramount in leave applications; but in *Re C (Residence) (Child's Application for Leave)* [1995] 1 FLR 927 Stuart-White J considered these divergent views and concluded that the child's welfare is an important, but not a paramount, consideration; and this approach was subsequently adopted by Johnson J in *Re H (Residence Order: Child's Application for Leave)* (above).

(ii) Other persons – leave to apply   In leave applications by persons other than children the court must, when deciding whether or not to grant leave, have particular regard to (s.10(9)): the nature of the proposed application; the applicant's connection with the child; any risk of the proposed application disrupting the child's life to such an extent that he would be harmed by it; and (where the child is being looked after by a local authority) the local authority's plans for the child's future and the wishes and feelings of the child's parents.

The welfare principle does not apply to a leave application (*Re A and W (Minors) (Residence Order: Leave to Apply)* [1992] Fam 182, [1992] 2 FLR 154). The application will be refused if it is frivolous or vexatious, or otherwise an abuse of the court. The case must disclose a real prospect of success, and there must be a serious issue to be tried and a good arguable case (*per* Wall J in *Re M (Minors) (Contact: Leave to Apply)* [1995] 2 FLR 98). Leave was granted, for example, in: *G v. F (Contact and Shared Residence: Applications for Leave)* [1998] 2 FLR 799 (to allow a lesbian couple to apply for contact and shared residence orders); *Re J (Leave to Issue Application for Residence Order)* [2003] 1 FLR 114 (to allow a grandmother to apply for a residence order); and in *Re H (Leave to Apply for Residence Order)* [2008] EWCA Civ 503, [2008] 2 FLR 848 (to allow a married couple to apply for a residence order after they had been adjudged to be too old to apply for an adoption order in respect of a child whose half-sibling they were already legally bringing up).

10.11   Jurisdiction to make section 8 orders

Jurisdiction to make s.8 orders is governed by the Family Law Act 1986. The court has jurisdiction if on the date of the application the child is habitually resident in England and Wales, or is present in England and Wales and is not habitually resident in any other part of the UK (s.2(2)). Habitual residence is not defined in the 1986 Act – case-law principles apply. The court may refuse jurisdiction where public policy considerations prevail over the child's welfare (for example in immigration cases, see *Re M (A Minor) (Immigration: Residence Order)* [1993] 2 FLR 858). The court can refuse to hear an application if the matter has already been determined in proceedings outside England and Wales (s.5(1) Family Law Act 1986) and may, on application, stay the proceedings if proceedings relating to the same matters are continuing outside England and Wales, or if it would be more appropriate for those matters to be dealt with outside England and Wales (s.5(2)) (see, for example, *Re F (Residence Order: Jurisdiction)* [1995] 2 FLR 518; and *Re S (Jurisdiction to Stay Application)* [1995] 1 FLR 1093).

In cases involving Member States of the European Union the above jurisdictional rules are subject to the rules laid down in Council Regulation (EC) No 2201/2003 Concerning Jurisdiction and the Recognition and Enforcement of Judgments in Matrimonial Matters and in Matters of Parental Responsibility (Brussels II Revised). The principal rule is that the courts of a Member State have jurisdiction in respect of a child who is habitually resident in that state (art. 8).

10.12   Other orders under the Children Act 1989

A wide range of orders other than s.8 orders can be made by the courts under the Children Act 1989.

(a)   Part I orders

Parental responsibility orders   The court can make a parental responsibility order giving the following persons parental responsibility: an unmarried father (s.4, see 9.4); the second female parent where the mother has had a child by assisted reproduction or artificial insemination (s.4ZA, see 9.5); and a step-parent (s.4A, see 9.5).

Order appointing a guardian of a child (s.5)   The court can appoint a person to be a guardian of a child (see 9.8).

Order for a welfare report (s.7)   When considering any question with respect to a child under the Children Act 1989, the court may request a report from a Cafcass officer (see 1.6) or from a local authority officer (or such other person as the authority considers appropriate) on such matters relating to the child as are required to be dealt with in the report (s.7(1)).

(b) Part II orders (orders with respect to children in family proceedings)

Part II makes provision in respect of the following orders:

(i) Section 8 orders (see 10.4–10.8 above).

(ii) Contact activity directions and conditions etc (ss.11A–P) The family courts have new powers to improve the facilitation and enforcement of contact orders (see 11.6).

(iii) Special guardianship orders (ss.14A–G) A special guardianship order is an order giving a person parental responsibility for a child which, while the order remains in force, can be exercised to the exclusion of the parental responsibility of any other person (apart from another special guardian). Special guardianship orders are sometimes used as an alternative to adoption (see 15.14).

(iv) Orders for financial relief (s.15 and Schedule 1) The family courts have jurisdiction to make finance and property orders for children under Schedule 1 (see 12.5).

(v) Family assistance orders (s.16) Under s.16 the court in family proceedings can make a family assistance order which is an order requiring a Cafcass officer or a Welsh family proceedings officer or an officer of the local authority to assist, advise and befriend any person named in the order (s.16(1)).

The following persons can be named in the order: any parent, guardian or special guardian of the child; any person with whom the child is living or in whose favour a contact order is in force with respect to the child; and the child (s.16(2)). An order cannot be made without the consent of all those persons named in the order (other than the child) (s.16(3)). The order may direct the person(s) named in the order to take such steps as may be so specified with a view to enabling the officer concerned to be kept informed of the address of any person named in the order and to be allowed to visit any such person (s.16(4)). The order can be made to last for up to 12 months (s.16(5)). An order cannot be made against a local authority officer unless the local authority agrees and the child concerned lives (or will live) in its area (s.16(7)).

If the court makes a family assistance order which is to be in force at the same time as a section 8 order (see 10.4 above) with respect to a child, the order may direct the officer concerned to report to the court on such matters relating to the s.8 order as the court may require (including whether the s.8 order should be varied or discharged) (s.16(6)).

Section 16 has been amended to make family assistance orders useful for the purpose of facilitating contact (see 11.6). Thus, if the court makes a family assistance order with respect to a child which is to be in force at the same time as a contact order, the order may direct the officer concerned to give advice and assistance as regards establishing, improving and maintaining contact to such of the persons named in the order as may be specified (s.16(4A)).

The *Practice Direction: Family Assistance Orders: Consultation (3/9/07)* [2007] 2 FLR 626 provides that, before making an order, the court must obtain the opinion (oral or written) of a Cafcass officer (or Welsh family proceedings officer) as to whether it is in the best interests of the child for an order to be made; and, if so, how the order should operate and for what period. The *Practice Direction* also provides that, before making an order, the court must give any person whom it proposes to name in the order the opportunity to comment on any opinion given by that officer.

(c)   Part IV orders (care and supervision)

(i) Care and supervision orders (s.31)   Where a child is suffering, or is likely to suffer, significant harm the court can, if certain threshold criteria are satisfied and the child's welfare requires it, make a care order placing the child in the care of a local authority, or a supervision order placing the child under the supervision of a local authority officer or probation officer (s.35) (see 14.7).

(ii) Order for contact with a child in care (s.34)   Where a child is in local authority care the authority must allow parents and certain other persons reasonable contact with the child, and the court can make orders in respect of such contact, including the termination of contact (see 14.8).

(iii) Education supervision order (s.36)   Where a child of compulsory school age is not being properly educated the court can, on the application of a local education authority, make an education supervision order in favour of that authority (see, for example, *Essex County Council* v. *B* [1993] 1 FLR 866). These orders are rarely made.

(iv) Order that a local authority investigate the child's circumstances (s.37)   Where in any family proceedings a question arises in respect of the child's welfare and it may be appropriate for a care or supervision order to be made, the court may direct that a local authority undertake an investigation into the child's circumstances (s.37(1)). The Court of Appeal has held that it is for the courts, not local authorities, to determine whether the requirements for making a s.37 order are satisfied and whether directions should be made under s.37 (see *K* v. *A Local Authority* [2008] EWCA Civ 103, *sub nom Lambeth LBC* v. *TK and KK* [2008] 1 FLR 1229).

(d)   Part V orders (protection of children)

(i) Child assessment order (s.43)   Where there is reasonable cause to suspect that a child is suffering, or is likely to suffer, significant harm and an assessment of the child's health and development or of the way in which the child is being treated is needed the court can make a child assessment order (see p. 410).

(ii) Emergency protection order (s.44)   Where there is reasonable cause to believe that a child is likely to suffer significant harm the court can in certain circumstances make an emergency protection order, which authorises the removal from, or retention of the child in, certain accommodation (see p. 411).

(e)   A section 91(14) order restricting an application to the court

Under s.91(14) CA 1989, when disposing of any application under the Children Act 1989, the court (whether or not it decides to make an order) can order that no application for an order under the Children Act of any specified kind may be made with respect to the child by any person named in the order without the court's permission.

The aim of a s.91(14) order is to prevent unnecessary and disruptive court applications which may be detrimental to the child's best interests. It gives the court power to restrict persons making repeated and unreasonable applications to the court. However, an order does not impose an absolute bar on applying to the court, as it can be lifted by the court where the applicant can show a need for renewed judicial investigation into the matter (see, for example, *Re A (Application for Leave)* [1998] 1 FLR 1). Because of the human rights implications of prohibiting access to the courts, there are strict controls on the exercise of the courts' power to make a s.91(14) order (see below).

The most common use of this order is in the context of protracted contact disputes (see, for example, *Re F (Restrictions on Applications)* [2005] EWCA Civ 499, [2005] 2 FLR 950 where a s.91(14) order lasting two and a half years was imposed on a father who wished to apply for contact, but against whom the mother had obtained injunctive protection against domestic violence).

The approach of the courts   The courts are greatly aware of the severity of making a s.91(14) order, and will only do so if there is a clear evidential basis for making it. In *B v. B (Residence Order: Restricting Applications)* [1997] 1 FLR 139 the Court of Appeal held that the power must be exercised with great care as it represents a substantial interference with the principle of public policy that all citizens enjoy a right of unrestricted access to the courts.

In *Re P (A Minor) (Residence Order: Child's Welfare)* [2000] Fam 15, *sub nom Re P (Section 91(14) Guidelines) (Residence and Religious Heritage)* [1999] 2 FLR 573 the Court of Appeal laid down the following guidelines governing the exercise of the court's discretion to make a s.91(14) order restricting an application to the court:

▶ When exercising the power to make a s.91(14) order the court must weigh in the balance all the relevant circumstances; and apply the principle in s.1(1) CA 1989 that the child's welfare is the court's paramount consideration.

▶ As making an order under s.91(14) is a statutory intrusion into a party's right to bring court proceedings and to be heard in matters affecting the child, the power must be used with great care and sparingly, and is the exception and not the rule. It is a useful weapon of last resort in cases of repeated and unreasonable applications.

▶ The order can be made in the absence of a request from any of the parties, subject to the rule of natural justice that parties should be given an opportunity to be heard on this point.

▶ The order can be imposed with or without limitation of time (but this is the exception rather than the rule, see *Re S (Permission to Seek Relief)* [2006] EWCA Civ 1190, [2007] 1 FLR 482).

▶ The degree of restriction in the order must be proportionate to the harm it is intended to avoid; and for this reason the court must carefully consider the extent of the restriction and specify, where appropriate, the type of application to be restrained and the duration of the order. (In *Re B (Section 91(14) Order: Duration)* [2003] EWCA Civ 1966, [2004] 1 FLR 871 an order imposed for the duration of the child's minority (to prevent any further contact applications by the father) was reduced to two years, on the basis that the court should never abandon any endeavours to right the wrongs within the family dynamics).

▶ It is undesirable in other than the most exceptional cases to make the order without notice (*ex parte*) (see *Re S (Permission to Seek Relief)* [2006] EWCA Civ 1190, [2007] 1 FLR 482).

(For cases where appeals against the making of a s.91(14) direction were allowed by the Court of Appeal on the ground that the lower court had failed to apply the above guidelines appropriately, see, for example: *Re G (Residence: Restriction on Further Applications)* [2008] EWCA Civ 1468, [2009] 1 FLR 1229; *Re C (Contact Order: Variation)* [2008] EWCA Civ 1389, [2009] 1 FLR 869; and *Re C (Litigant in Person: s.91(14) Order)* [2009] EWCA Civ 674).

Human rights   As a result of their obligations under the Human Rights Act 1998 (see 1.7) the courts must ensure that making a s.91(14) order does not infringe a person's rights under the European Convention for the Protection of Human Rights, in particular art. 6 (the right of access to the court) and art. 8 (the right to family life). In *Re P (A Minor) (Residence Order: Child's Welfare* (see above), although the Court of Appeal held that making a s.91(14) order did not breach art. 6 ECHR (at it was only a partial restriction on disallowing claims before the court), it ruled that, because of the severity of making an order, the court should specify what type of court applications are restricted and for how long.

Summary

1 The Children Act 1989 (CA 1989) contains much of the civil law, private and public, relating to children.

2 The following welfare principles are laid down in s.1 of the Children Act 1989: the welfare principle (s.1(1)); the no-delay principle (s.1(2)); the 'welfare checklist' (s.1(3)); and the minimum intervention principle (s.1(5)). The welfare checklist must be applied in contested s.8 order proceedings, special guardianship proceedings and in care and supervision proceedings, under Part IV of the Act (s.1(4)).

3 The court can make the following s.8 orders: residence order; contact order; prohibited steps order; and specific issue order.

4 Section 8 orders can be made on application or by the court of its own motion in any family proceedings. Some persons have an automatic right to apply but other persons, including the child, need leave of the court (s.10). The court has jurisdiction to make s.8 orders if the child is habitually resident or present in England and Wales and is not habitually resident in any other part of the UK (s.2 Family Law Act 1986). Special rules apply in cases involving Member States of the European Union.

5 Under Part I of the CA 1989 the court can make the following private law orders: parental responsibility orders (s.4 and s.4A); orders appointing a guardian (s.5). It can also order a welfare report (s.7).

6 Under Part II of the CA 1989, in addition to s.8 orders (see above), the court can make: special guardianship orders (ss.14A–G); orders for financial relief (s.15 and Sched. 1); and family assistance orders (s.16). The provisions governing family assistance orders (see s.16) have been amended so that an order can be usefully used in difficult contact cases. New provisions have been introduced in respect of facilitating and enforcing contact (see ss.11A–11P). Cafcass officers and Welsh family proceedings officers have a duty under Part II of the Act to conduct risk assessments of children (s.16A).

Summary cont'd

7　The court can make a range of public law orders, in particular care and supervision orders (see Part IV of the Children Act 1989), and orders for the emergency protection of children (see Part V).

8　The court can also make the following: an order that a local authority investigate the child's circumstances (s.37); and a s.91(14) order restricting an application to the court under the Children Act 1989.

Further reading and references

Bailey-Harris, Barron and Pearce, 'The settlement culture and the use of the "no order" principle under the Children Act 1989' [1999] CFLQ 53.

Children Act 1989 Guidance and Regulations: Volume 1 – Court Orders (Department for Children, Schools and Families, 2008), available on the Every Child Matters website (see below).

Eekelaar, 'Beyond the welfare principle' [2002] CFLQ 237.

Fortin, 'Children's rights – substance or spin?' [2006] Fam Law 757.

Freeman, 'The next Children's Act' [1998] Fam Law 341.

Websites

Every Child Matters: www.everychildmatters.gov.uk

Chapter 11

Children on family breakdown

Introduction

This chapter deals with the law governing residence and contact disputes when parental relationships break down, whether the parents are married, civil partners or cohabitants. The law is laid down in the Children Act 1989 (see also Chapter 10). On divorce or parental separation, parents continue to have parental responsibility (see 9.3). Parents also have a duty, whether or not they have parental responsibility, to provide financial provision for their children on and after relationship breakdown. If a parent refuses to provide financial support, or insufficient support, an application can be made to the Child Maintenance and Enforcement Commission and in some circumstances to the court; and applications can be made to the court for lump sum orders and property orders to or for the benefit of children (see Chapter 12).

(i) Impact on children Children may suffer emotional trauma when their parents' relationship breaks up. They may suffer fear, anger, withdrawal, grief, depression and guilt. Research on children of divorced parents (by the Centre of Longitudinal Studies, based on the National Child Development Study, July 2008) found that divorce was not a single event in a child's life but a process which could begin years before the parents separated and which could have repercussions that reverberated through childhood and into adulthood. According to the report, children from separated families tended to do less well at school and in their subsequent careers. They were more likely to experience the break-up of their own partnerships; and more likely to have higher levels of alcohol consumption and problem drinking in adulthood. They were also likely to have poorer levels of general health, and a small minority of young adults developed serious mental health problems associated with parental divorce. (The report is available at: www.cls.ioe.ac.uk.)

(ii) Reaching agreement; keeping cases out of the court Because of the emotional impact that divorce and parental separation can have on children, it is better if parents make amicable arrangements for their children on family breakdown. Most parents make their own arrangements, but some fail to reach agreement and end up having to apply to the court for residence and/or contact orders. Going to court, however, can be costly, time-consuming, unpredictable and traumatic, and the judge may decide to refuse to make the order sought or make a different order. Also, having a court order does not necessarily guarantee that the other parent will comply with it.

Lawyers who deal with residence and contact disputes on family breakdown adopt a conciliatory, not a litigious approach, because of the benefits of reducing hostility and bitterness where children are involved. Mediation, a form of alternative dispute resolution, is increasingly promoted as a much better way of dealing with parental disputes (see 1.4). Collaborative law is also used to help parents reach agreement about their children in a non-confrontational way (see 1.4). The following words of Baroness Hale in a case about shared residence orders and housing (see 4.11 and 11.4) acknowledge the importance of agreement where children are concerned:

> ▶ **Baroness Hale of Richmond in** *Holmes-Moorhouse* v. *Richmond-Upon-Thames London Borough Council* **[2009] UKHL 7, [2009] 1 FLR 904**
>
> 'The reality is that every effort is made, both before and during any family proceedings, to encourage the parents to agree between themselves what will be best for their children. There are many good reasons for this. The parents know their own children better than anyone. They also know their own circumstances, what will suit them best, what resources are available and what they can afford. Agreed solutions tend to work much better and last much longer than solutions imposed by a court after contested proceedings. The contest is likely to entrench opposing viewpoints and inflame parental conflict. Conflict is well known to be bad for children. Not only that, the arrangements made when the couple separate are bound to have to change over time, as the children grow up and their own and their parents' circumstances change. Parents who have been able or helped, through mediation or in other ways, to agree a solution at the outset are more likely to be able to negotiate those changes for themselves, rather than to have to return to court for further orders.'

(iii) The role of Cafcass   Cafcass (the Child And Family Court Advisory and Support Service) and its equivalent in Wales (Cafcass Cymru) perform important functions in respect of children on family breakdown (see 1.6). One of its main functions is to provide officers for the court in children's cases. Of particular importance is the Children and Family Reporter who has a duty to provide a welfare report for the court (see below). Cafcass officers also perform an important conciliatory role in trying to help parents reach agreement about arrangements for their children. They also have to conduct risk assessments; and they have various obligations in respect of facilitating contact (see 11.6). A Children's Guardian, an officer of Cafcass, may be appointed by the court (under rule 9.5 Family Proceedings Rules 1991) to represent the interests of a child who has been made a party to family law proceedings (see 8.6).

(iv) Welfare reports   The court has the power to order a welfare report under s.7 of the Children Act 1989 by a Children and Family Reporter, an officer of Cafcass (see above), who has a duty to protect the child's best interests in the proceedings. The role of the Children and Family Reporter is to provide the court with advice and recommendations on matters relating to the welfare of the child who is the subject of the proceedings.

A welfare report is important as it provides an independent assessment of the case. The recommendations in the report are particularly important where a case is finely balanced. Judges must not depart from the recommendations in the report without giving reasons. Failure to do so may provide grounds for an appeal (as it did in *Re M (Residence)* [2004] EWCA Civ 1574, [2005] 1 FLR 656 where the Court of Appeal ordered a retrial). If the court decides to reject a clear conclusion and recommendation made in the report, it must allow the Cafcass officer to give oral evidence (see *Re R (Residence Order)* [2009] EWCA Civ 445 where the Court of Appeal held, by a majority, that the judge had erred in law in not hearing the Cafcass officer). However, where there is no clear recommendation in a report, it is not necessary for the court to adjourn proceedings to hear the officer (*Re C (Section 8 Order: Court Welfare Officer)* [1995] 1 FLR 617).

(v) The voice of the child in court proceedings   Children do not have automatic party status in residence and contact proceedings, but there has been a move towards giving more children rights of separate representation (see 8.6).

(vi) Enforcing residence and contact orders in other parts of the UK   Residence and contact orders made in England and Wales can be enforced in other parts of the UK under the Family Law Act 1986 (s.25). The order can be registered in the court in the other part of the UK, whereupon the court there has the same powers for the purpose of enforcing the order as if it had made the order (s.29), but the court can refuse to do so if enforcement is contrary to the child's best interests.

(vii) Family disputes involving parties from Member States of the European Union   Jurisdiction in respect of parental disputes between parents living in different Member States of the European Union is governed by Council Regulation (EC) (No. 2201/2003) Concerning Jurisdiction and the Recognition and Enforcement of Judgments in Matrimonial Matters and in Matters of Parental Responsibility (Brussels II Revised).

Art. 8(1) provides that: 'The courts of a Member State shall have jurisdiction in matters of parental responsibility over a child who is habitually resident in that Member State at the time the court is seised'. The aim of art. 8(1) is to ensure that in relation to matters of parental responsibility (including applications for residence and contact) that jurisdiction rests with the courts of the child's habitual residence; although art. 12 provides a limited opportunity for parents to elect for the jurisdiction of the court seised with the divorce proceedings if that is, *inter alia*, in the best interests of the child. In *Bush* v. *Bush* [2008] EWCA Civ, [2008] 2 FLR 1437, for example, the Court of Appeal held that the Spanish, not the English court, had jurisdiction in respect of orders relating to the arrangements for the children on divorce as, although the mother had instituted divorce proceedings in England, the father had begun children's proceedings in Spain.

In *Re I (A Child)* [2009] UKSC 10 the Supreme Court unanimously held that art. 12 of Brussels II (Revised) could apply to a child who was habitually resident outside the European Union, as nothing in art. 12 limited jurisdiction to children resident in the European Union. In this case the English mother wished to enforce contact with her son who was living with his paternal grandmother and aunt in Pakistan (after his father had removed him there in breach of an undertaking to return him to the UK).

11.2   Human rights and family breakdown

The Human Rights Act 1998 requires courts (including family courts) to comply with the European Convention for the Protection of Human Rights (ECHR) and to take into account the decisions of the European Court of Human Rights (ECtHR) (see 1.7). In *Hoppe* v. *Germany (Application No. 28422/95)* [2003] 1 FLR 384 the ECtHR identified the following general principles which courts must take into account when exercising their powers in the context of children on family breakdown:

- The mutual enjoyment by parent and child of each other's company constitutes a fundamental element of family life, even if the parents' relationship has broken down; and any measures which hinder such enjoyment amount to an interference with art. 8 (the right to family life).
- The task of the ECtHR is not to substitute itself for the domestic authorities in the exercise of their responsibilities regarding custody and access, but to review, in the light of the ECHR, their decisions in the exercise of their margin of appreciation.

- In determining whether the interference into family life was necessary in a democratic society for the purposes of art. 8(2) (see 1.7), consideration of what lies in the best interests of the child is of crucial importance. A fair balance must be struck between the child's interests and those of the parent, and, in striking such a balance, particular importance must be attached to the best interests of the child, which, depending on their nature and seriousness, may override those of the parent.
- In cases concerning a person's relationship with his or her child there is a duty to exercise exceptional diligence in view of the risk that the passage of time may result in a *de facto* determination of the matter.
- The manner in which art. 6 (the right to a fair and public hearing) applies to proceedings before courts of appeal depends on the special features of the proceedings viewed as a whole.
- It is not a breach of art. 6 if proceedings involving children are heard in private.
- The court must avoid delay in reaching a final decision.

In *Sahin* v. *Germany*; *Sommerfeld* v. *Germany (Application Nos. 30943/96 and 31871/96)* [2003] 2 FLR 671 the ECtHR held that, although national authorities enjoy a wide margin of appreciation when deciding on custody matters, a stricter scrutiny is called for regarding any further limitations, such as restrictions placed on parental rights of access. As regards hearing a child in court on the issue of access, the ECtHR held that domestic courts are not always required to hear the child. It depends on the facts of each case, having regard to the age and maturity of the child concerned.

11.3 The duty to children in divorce proceedings

An important policy objective of the law of divorce is to protect children. In furtherance of this objective, the petitioner must file with the divorce court a Statement of Arrangements for Children, which is a form setting out required information about any child of the family aged under 16, or over 16 if still receiving education or training (r.2.2 Family Proceedings Rules 1991). The Statement of Arrangements includes details, for instance, relating to the child's home, education and training, childcare, maintenance, contact, and health. The petitioner must sign the form and, where possible, the respondent must agree with the information on it. The petitioner must state on the form whether he or she intends to apply for any s.8 order under the Children Act 1989 (CA 1989). (The form is available on HM Courts' Service website).

The purpose of the Statement of Arrangements for Children is to enable the divorce court to fulfil its duty under s.41(1) of the Matrimonial Causes Act 1973 which requires it to consider, whether, in the light of the actual or proposed arrangements made for the children, it should exercise any of its powers under the Children Act 1989 with respect to any of the children (for these powers, see Chapter 10). If the court is satisfied with the arrangements, the district judge will certify to that effect. If not satisfied, he can direct that further evidence be filed, or order a welfare report, or order the parent(s) to attend court. If the child's interests require it, and the court is not able to exercise any of its powers under the Children Act 1989 without further consideration of the case, the district judge can direct that the decree of divorce should not be made absolute (s.41(2)). In practice, however, this rarely happens.

11.4   Residence disputes

An unresolveable dispute about residence arrangements for a child on family breakdown can be decided by making an application for a residence order, which the High Court, county courts and magistrates' family proceedings courts have jurisdiction to make under s.8 of the Children Act 1989 (CA 1989) (see also 10.5).

Residence disputes often go hand in hand with contact disputes, as the non-resident parent may wish to have contact with the child (see 11.5). Other parental disputes (for example about education, medical treatment, taking a child out of the UK and changing the child's name) can be decided by making an application for a prohibited steps or specific issue order (see 10.7 and 10.8). Some parents enter into disputes about financial provision for their children on family breakdown, in particular child support (see Chapter 12).

(a)   Residence orders

> **A residence order** is an order 'settling the arrangements to be made as to the person with whom a child is to live' (s.8(1) Children Act 1989).

Before the Children Act 1989 came into force unresolveable parental disputes about children on family breakdown were decided by way of custody proceedings. However, in discussions leading up to the Children Act the Law Commission was critical of the term 'custody' because it created a parental claim right and had the potential to increase hostility and bitterness between parents which was detrimental for children. Residence orders were therefore introduced by the Children Act 1989 to replace custody orders, with the aim of placing the emphasis on a child's living arrangements, not on which of the parents had a greater claim to the child. The idea was to encourage the view that parents have responsibilities for their children, not claims to them, an idea that was partly influenced by Lord Scarman's preference (in the *Gillick* case, see 8.4) for the term 'responsibility' rather than 'rights'.

Residence orders are often made, but not as often as contact orders. 38,080 applications for residence orders were made in England and Wales in 2008, compared to 40,900 applications for contact orders (*Judicial and Court Statistics 2008*, Ministry of Justice, Cm 7697, 2009).

Applicants   The child's parents (married or unmarried, and whether or not the father has parental responsibility) can apply. Other persons (including the child) can apply, but only with leave of the court (see further in Chapter 10).

Applicable principles   See below.

Other powers   The court can: attach a condition to a residence order (s.11(7)); order a welfare report (s.7); and direct that a local authority investigate the child's circumstances (s.37). It can also make a shared residence order under s.11(4) (see p. 296.)

Duration   The order can be made to last until the child reaches the age of 18 (s.91(10)).

(b) How the court exercises its powers in residence order proceedings

When exercising its powers to decide whether or not to make a residence order the court must apply the principles in s.1 Children Act 1989 (see 10.3). Thus, it must apply the welfare principle (s.1(1)), the no-delay principle (s.1(2)) and the minimum intervention principle (s.1(5)). In contested proceedings it must also apply the s.1(3) 'welfare checklist'.

The welfare checklist (s.1(3))

In addition to considering the paramountcy of the child's welfare (s.1(1)), the court in contested residence proceedings must apply the factors listed in s.1(3) of the Children Act 1989. The list is not exhaustive – other factors can be taken into account – and the factors are not in any hierarchy of importance. Under s.1(3) the court must take into account the following factors:

Section 1(3)(a) The child's wishes in the light of the child's age and understanding   If the child is intelligent and mature enough to make an informed decision, then the child's wishes may determine the matter, all other things being equal. The child's wishes are ascertained by a Cafcass Children and Family Reporter or a Welsh family proceedings officer, who has a duty to report to the court and to consider the best interests of the child; and who may be cross-examined on the report. The court also has the power to appoint a Children's Guardian to represent the child, and to permit the child to be represented by his or her own solicitor without a Children's Guardian (see 8.6). A failure to give any real effect to a child's wishes may provide grounds for an appeal as it did in *Re R (Residence Order)* [2009] EWCA Civ 445 where the Court of Appeal held by a majority that the judge had erred in not giving any real effect to the wishes of the child aged 9.

Section 1(3)(b) The child's physical and emotional needs   The child's physical and emotional needs are important, and might include, for instance, the emotional and psychological attachment a child has to a particular parent, and also housing needs. In earlier case-law the courts had stated that it was usually better for young children, particularly babies, to be brought up by their mother (an approach which was endorsed by the House of Lords in *Brixey* v. *Lynas* [1996] 2 FLR 499). Over the years, however, as the courts have given increasing recognition to the importance of fathers, the court is likely to consider the child's emotional and psychological attachment to *both* parents, not just the mother. In respect of the child's needs under s.1(3)(b), the fact that one parent is wealthier than the other is likely to count for little.

Section 1(3)(c) The likely effect on the child of a change of circumstances   This is similar to the 'continuity of care' or 'status quo' factor which was an important consideration in the case-law before the Children Act 1989, when there was no welfare checklist in the legislation. However, in *Re F (Shared Residence Order)* [2009] EWCA Civ 313 the Court of Appeal held that it was better, since the enactment of the Children Act 1989, to address the factors in the welfare checklist rather than to rely on any presumption of fact that might arise from status quo arguments. (For cases where the status quo prevailed, see *Re B (Residence Order: Status Quo)* [1998] 1 FLR 368 (as the father had cared for the 8-year-old child since the age of two); and *V* v. *T* [2007] EWHC 2312 (Fam), *sub nom Re C (Residence)* [2008] 1 FLR 826 (as the child had spent all his life in his mother's care and had a strong and beneficial bond with her)).

Under s.(1)(3)(c) the court may be unwilling to change existing residence arrangements if to do so will split up brothers and sisters, disrupt schooling arrangements, or result in the child losing contact with relatives and friends.

Section 1(3)(d) The age, sex, background and any of the child's characteristics which the court considers relevant   The child's religious preferences, racial and cultural background, health and disabilities can, for example, be considered under s.1(3)(d).

Section 1(3)(e) Any harm the child has suffered or is at risk of suffering   'Harm' has the same meaning as it has in s.31 of the CA 1989 (see p. 395) and also includes harm caused by 'hearing or seeing the ill treatment of another'. Thus, witnessing domestic violence can constitute harm.

Religious beliefs   Making a residence order in favour of a parent with extreme religious beliefs will not necessarily constitute harm. In *Re R (A Minor) (Residence: Religion)* [1993] 2 FLR 163, for example, a residence order was made in favour of the father, as the mother had died, even though he was a member of the Exclusive Brethren, an extreme religious sect in which members are not allowed to mix socially with anyone outside the fellowship (the court also made a supervision order in favour of the local authority to ensure the child's safety). In *M v. H (Education: Welfare)* [2008] EWHC 324 (Fam), [2008] 1 FLR 1400 Charles J held *inter alia* that the fact that one parent was a Catholic and the other a Jehovah's Witness was not of itself relevant in the circumstances of the case.

If the religion is deemed to be harmful, the court will take it into account, as it did in *Re B and G (Minors) (Custody)* [1985] FLR 493 where the court described the views held by members of the Church of Scientology as 'immoral and obnoxious' and denied the father and step-mother the care of the children in preference to the mother and step-father who had left the church.

A refusal to make a residence order in favour of a particular parent on the basis of his or her religious beliefs may constitute a breach of the European Convention for the Protection of Human Rights. But each case depends on its facts. In *Palau-Martinez v. France (Application No. 64927/01)* [2004] 2 FLR 810 the ECtHR held that an order granting residence to the child's father, not the mother, because of her religious convictions (she was a Jehovah's Witness), breached the mother's right to a private and family life under art. 8 and was discriminatory under art. 14. However, in *Ismailova v. Russia (Application No 37614/02)* [2008] 1 FLR 533 the ECtHR upheld the decision of the Russian courts to deprive the mother of custody because of the effect of her religion on the children.

Steps the court can take when there is a risk of harm   If the court is concerned about making a residence order because of a risk of harm, it can make an interim residence order, or back up the residence order with another order, such as a specific issue order, a prohibited steps order, a family assistance order, or a s.37 direction that the local authority investigate the case (see further in Chapter 10). Cafcass has a duty under s.16A of the Children Act 1989 to make risk assessments where it believes that a child might be at risk of significant harm (see p. 306 below).

Section 1(3)(f) How capable each parent is of meeting the child's needs   The court might consider, for example, whether a parent can provide accommodation, love, emotional security, intellectual stimulation, and also care during working hours.

Section 1(3)(g) The range of powers available to the court under the Children Act 1989   As proceedings for a residence order are themselves family proceedings (s.8(3)), the court can make other orders on application or of its own motion, for example: any other s.8 order; a s.16 family assessment order; an order appointing a guardian; or a s.37 direction that a local authority investigate the child's circumstances (for more on these orders, see Chapter 10).

(c)   Shared residence orders (s.11(4))

Under s.11(4) of the Children Act 1989 the court can make a 'shared' residence order, which is a residence order 'made in favour of two or more persons who do not themselves all live together', and which specifies 'the periods during which the child is to live in the different households concerned'. The phrase 'shared residence' must be distinguished from 'joint residence' which is the term used where a residence order is made in respect of two people who live together (see *Re K (Shared Residence Order)* [2008] EWCA Civ 526, [2008] 2 FLR 380).

In discussions leading up to the drafting of the Children Act 1989, the Law Commission had said that residence orders should be flexible enough to accommodate a wide range of situations, and that, although shared arrangements would rarely be practicable, evidence from the USA showed that they could work well in some circumstances. The Law Commission saw no reason why shared residence orders should be actively discouraged; and said that the aim in introducing shared residence was to 'lower the stakes' in disputes over children so that parents did not see themselves as having 'won or lost'. The aim was to reinforce the notion of shared parenting. The courts have adopted this approach. Thus, in *Re P (Shared Residence Order)* [2005] EWCA Civ 1639, [2006] 2 FLR 347 Wall LJ said that a shared order had the advantage of emphasising the fact 'that both parents are equal in the eyes of the law, and that they have equal duties and responsibilities as parents'.

In cases decided shortly after the Children Act 1989 came into force judges were reluctant to make shared residence orders because they felt they might create uncertainty and insecurity for children. In *Re H (A Minor) (Shared Residence)* [1994] 1 FLR 717 the Court of Appeal held that they should be made only in exceptional circumstances. Over the years, however, judges have become more willing to make shared residence orders, so that they are no longer unusual. In the following case the Court of Appeal held that there is no need for there to be exceptional circumstances before an order can be made:

▶ *D v. D (Shared Residence Order)* [2001] 1 FLR 495

A pattern had been established on marriage breakdown whereby the three children spent substantial periods of time with each parent, but where the arrangements were subject to a high degree of animosity between the parents and frequent legal proceedings had been brought to sort out the details. The father applied for a shared residence order, which was granted at first instance. The mother appealed. The Court of Appeal dismissed her appeal, and held that, contrary to earlier case-law, it was not necessary to show that exceptional circumstances existed before a shared order could be granted; and neither was it probably necessary to show a positive benefit to the child. What must be shown is that the order is in the child's best interests in accordance with the welfare principle in s.1 Children Act 1989. Here, on the facts, it was necessary to make the shared order to lessen the animosity between the parties.

How the court exercises its powers in shared residence order cases　When deciding whether or not to make a shared residence order, the court must apply the welfare principles in s.1(1) of the Children Act 1989 (see 10.3). There is no presumption of shared residence, however. Although the outcome of each case depends on its own facts, the following propositions about shared residence orders can be extracted from the case-law.

- It is not necessary to show exceptional or unusual circumstances before a shared order can be granted (*D* v. *D (Shared Residence Order*, above).
- There is no requirement that a child should be spending time evenly, or more or less evenly, in the two homes before a shared residence order can be made (*Re F (Shared Residence Order)* [2003] EWCA Civ 592, [2003] 2 FLR 397; and endorsed in *Re W (Shared Residence Order)* [2009] EWCA Civ 370, [2009] 2 FLR 436).
- The court will be alert to discern any malign intent on the part of a parent to use a shared residence application for the purpose of disrupting or interfering with the other parent's role in the management of the child's life (*Re K (Shared Residence Order)* [2008] EWCA Civ 526, [2008] 2 FLR 380).
- Although it may be appropriate to make a shared residence order in a case where there is likely to be a problem facilitating or enforcing contact, the court is unlikely to make an order where there is little contact between the parties (*A* v. *A (Shared Residence)* [2004] EWHC 142 (Fam), [2004] 1 FLR 1195).
- An order can be made even though there is a substantial geographical distance between the parents, as the order must reflect the underlying reality of where the children live their lives (*Re F (Shared Residence Order)* [2003] EWCA Civ 592, [2003] 2 FLR 397).
- Although the inability of the parents to work in harmony is not by itself a reason for making a shared residence order, a possible consequence of the parents' inability to work in harmony (namely a deliberate and sustained marginalisation of one parent by the other) may sometimes be so (*Re W (Shared Residence Order)* [2009] EWCA Civ 370, [2009] 2 FLR 436).
- It is wrong in law to make a contact order if a shared residence order has been made (*Re W (Shared Residence Order)* [2009] EWCA Civ 370, [2009] 2 FLR 436).

Examples from the law reports　There are many cases in the law reports where shared residence orders have been made:

▶ *A* v. *A (Shared Residence)* [2004] EWHC 142 (Fam), [2004] 1 FLR 1195

A shared residence order was made (even though the parents were not able to co-operate), as the children had been spending 50 per cent of their time with each parent. Wall J made a shared order partly to 'reflect that fact that the parents are equal in the eyes of the law, and have equal duties and responsibilities towards their children'.

> ▶ *Re C (A Child)* [2006] EWCA Civ 235
>
> The Court of Appeal described the case as 'a paradigm' case where a shared residence order should be granted. The child had a strong attachment to both parents and was happy and confident in both homes, which were proximate to each other and close to the child's school. The child had a real familiarity with both homes and a sense of belonging in each, and he had a clear perception that he had two homes. There was a post-separation history of the child's care being shared.
>
> ▶ *Re M (Residence Order)* [2008] EWCA Civ 66, [2008] 1 FLR 1087
>
> Wall LJ held that it was 'a paradigm case' for a shared residence order. The children needed to be kept together, they wished to spend time with each parent and needed to enjoy the benefits of being with both parents. The parents were clearly sufficiently co-operative and lived geographically close.

Shared residence order or defined contact?   The court may, depending on the circumstances, decide that it is sufficient to make an order for defined contact rather than a shared residence order. This was considered in *Re K (Shared Residence Order)* [2008] EWCA Civ 526, [2008] 2 FLR 380 where the father applied to have contact with the child increased from 40 per cent to 50 per cent and for a shared residence order. The Court of Appeal had to decide whether a shared residence order or an order for defined contact should be made. It held that the court should decide on the division of time the child is to spend with each parent and then determine whether that time should be effected by a shared residence order or a contact order. The Court of Appeal held that a shared residence order was more appropriate in the circumstances of the case. A shared residence order *or* a defined contact order should be made, as the Court of Appeal has held that it is a contradiction in terms to grant a contact order to a person who already has a shared residence order (*Re W (Shared Residence Order)* [2009] EWCA Civ 370, [2009] 2 FLR 436).

Making a shared residence order as a means of acquiring parental responsibility   A shared residence order can legitimately be made for the purpose of conferring parental responsibility on a person who does not possess it, and who is not otherwise able to apply for it (for instance, because he is not the child's biological father) (see *Re A (Shared Residence: Parental Responsibility)* [2008] EWCA Civ 867, [2008] 2 FLR 1503 where a shared residence order was made to confer parental responsibility on a man who was not the biological father of the child, but who had, with the mother, brought the child up for the first two years of the child's life on the assumption that he was the father).

Shared residence orders and housing   The House of Lords in *Holmes-Moorhouse* v. *London Borough of Richmond-upon-Thames London Borough Council* [2009] UKHL 7, [2009] 1 FLR 904 (see further at 4.11) held that, when deciding whether to make a shared residence order, the court must take into account the housing needs of the parties, and the fact that there is a shortage of local authority housing and that housing authorities have limited resources. The House of Lords held that a family court should not make a shared residence order unless it appeared reasonably likely that both parents would have accommodation in which the child could reside. Baroness Hale said that the family court 'should not use a residence order as a means of putting pressure upon a local housing authority to allocate their resources in a particular way'.

(d) Attaching a condition to an order and restricting residence

The court can attach a condition to a residence order (s.11(7)), but it usually only does this in exceptional circumstances. Placing a condition on a residence order which requires a person to live in a particular place is even more exceptional, as such a restriction is considered to be 'an unwarranted imposition upon the right of a parent to choose where he/she will live within the UK' (*per* Baroness Hale in *Re G (Children)* [2006] UKHL 43, [2006] 2 FLR 629). But each case depends on its facts; and in *B v. B (Residence: Condition Limiting Geographic Area)* [2004] 2 FLR 979 a condition was imposed that the mother and child live within a specified geographic area, as the mother had made two applications to remove the child to Australia and her prime motive in moving the child's residence from the south to the north of England was to get away from the child's father.

11.5 Contact disputes

Article 9(3) United Nations Convention on the Rights of the Child 1989

'States Parties shall respect the right of the child ... to maintain personal relations and direct contact with both parents on a regular basis, except if it is contrary to the child's best interests.'

(a) Introduction

Contact arrangements are best settled by the parents themselves, but if they cannot reach agreement, and mediation or collaborative law fail, then an application can be made to the court for a contact order under s.8 of the Children Act 1989.

According to *Judicial and Court Statistics 2008* (Ministry of Justice, Cm 7697, 2009), 40,900 applications for contact orders were made in England Wales in 2008 compared with 38,080 applications for residence orders in the same period. However, despite the number of contact orders, most parents make their own contact arrangements. Research by Hunt and Macleod of the Oxford Centre for Family Law and Policy found that less than one in 10 parents apply to the court for contact arrangements to be settled (*Outcomes of Applications to Court for Contact Orders After Parental Separation or Divorce*, 2008, available on the Ministry of Justice website). Their research also found that, even if cases did go to court, most parties reached agreement (it was rare for the court to have to make a final ruling). Also most cases ended with face-to-face contact; and contact typically involved overnight stays, at least fortnightly.

It is better if parents reach agreement about contact, because research has shown that parents who turn to the law to settle serious contact disputes risk making matters worse (see Trinder *et al, Making Contact: How Parents and Children Negotiate and Experience Contact After Divorce*, Joseph Rowntree Foundation, [2002] Fam Law 872). It has been recognised by the judiciary and by the Government that contact cases are best dealt with outside the courts. Wall J (as he was then), speaking at a conference on contact, said (see [2003] Fam Law 275):

'The law, which of necessity, operates within the discipline of defined orders is, in my judgment, ill-suited to deal with the complex family dynamics inherent in disputed contact applications.

Arrangements for contact stand more prospect of enduring if they are consensual. Wherever possible, contact disputes should be dealt with outside the courtroom.'

Amendments have been made to the Children Act 1989 to improve the facilitation and enforcement of contact (see 11.6 below).

(i) Human rights and contact The European Court of Human Rights (the ECtHR) recognises the importance of contact between parents and children as part of the right to family life under art. 8 ECHR (see, for example, *Johansen* v. *Norway* (1997) 23 EHRR 33). In *Kosmopolou* v. *Greece (Application No. 60457/00)* [2004] 1 FLR 800 the ECtHR held that:

'[T]he mutual enjoyment by parent and child of each other's company constitutes a fundamental element of family life, even if the relationship between the parents has broken down, and domestic measures hindering such enjoyment amount to an interference with the right protected by Art. 8 of the Convention.'

Thus the ECtHR takes the view that, unless the circumstances of the case are exceptional, the mutual enjoyment by parent and child of each other's company constitutes a right to family life under art. 8. In *Hansen* v. *Turkey (Application No. 36141/97)* [2004] 1 FLR 142, for example, the ECtHR held that the failure of the Turkish authorities to take realistic coercive measures against the father (who had custody) to allow the mother to have access to the child was a breach of her right to family life under art. 8. As the Human Rights Act 1998 requires courts in the UK to take account of the decisions of the ECtHR, they must ensure that they order contact and enforce it, unless it is contrary to the child's best interests.

However, the ECtHR has held that the duty on national authorities to enforce and facilitate contact is not absolute. The question to be asked is whether the national authorities concerned have taken all the necessary steps to enforce and facilitate contact as could reasonably be demanded in the circumstances (see, for example, *Zadwadka* v. *Poland (Application No. 48542/99)* [2005] 2 FLR 897). Each case depends on its facts, and in *Glaser* v. *UK* (2001) 33 EHRR 1, [2001] 1 FLR 153 the ECtHR rejected a complaint that the UK authorities were in breach of the ECHR in the circumstances by failing to take adequate steps to enforce contact against a mother.

Delay in the court process in respect of enforcing contact may constitute a breach of art. 6 (the right to a fair trial) as it did in *Adam* v. *Germany (No 44036/02)* [2009] 1 FLR 560 where the ECtHR held that the rights of the child's father and paternal grandparents had been breached under art. 6 due to the avoidable delays and protracted nature of the proceedings to enforce contact with the child (which had been going on for more than four years). However, the European Court of Human Rights has held that the obligation of national authorities to take measures to facilitate contact is not absolute (see *Kaleta* v. *Poland (Case No. 11375/02)*, [2009] 1 FLR 927 where it held that the key consideration is whether the authorities have taken all necessary steps as could reasonably be demanded in the special circumstances of each case. A balance had to be struck between the various interests involved).

(ii) Contact – difficult areas Contact disputes are 'among the most difficult and sensitive cases' which the courts have to deal with (*per* Wall LJ at [2005] Fam Law 26). Cases sometimes drag on for years, which not only takes up court time but is contrary to the best interests of children (see, for instance, *Re A-H (Contact Order)* [2008] EWCA Civ 630 where,

after five years, the contact question had not been resolved). There have also been problems with contact in the context of domestic violence (see p. 303); and in respect of the enforcement and facilitation of contact (see 11.6). There has also been increasing pressure by proponents of children's rights, including the UN Committee on the Rights of the Child (see 8.2), for children's views to be heard more in contact cases, and for children to have separate representation (but see *Re S (Contact: Children's Views)* [2002] EWHC 540 (Fam), [2002] 1 FLR 1156 where a contact order was refused because of the views of the two children aged 14 and 16).

Contact disputes are often lengthy and intractable. The *President's Direction (Representation of Children in Family Proceedings Pursuant to Family Proceedings Rules 1991, rule 9.5)* [2004] 1 FLR 1188 identified *inter alia* intractable contact disputes (as well as cases where the child may be suffering harm associated with the contact dispute) as suitable cases for the separate representation of children; but in practice separate representation in contact disputes is not common.

(b) Contact orders

A contact order is an order 'requiring the person with whom a child lives, or is to live, to allow the child to visit or stay with the person named in the order, or for that person and the child otherwise to have contact with each other' (s.8(1)).

Where a contact dispute cannot be settled by agreement, with or without the help of mediation or collaborative law, an application can be made for a contact order which the High Court, county courts and magistrates' family proceedings courts have jurisdiction to make under s.8 of the Children Act 1989. The term 'contact' was introduced by the Children Act to replace that of 'access', because 'contact' was considered to be a more child-centred term. A contact order allows a child to have contact rather that giving a parent a right to have access.

Applicants   The child's parents (married or unmarried, and whether or not the father has parental responsibility) can apply. Other persons (including the child) can apply, but only with leave of the court (see further at 10.6).

Other powers   The court can: attach a condition to a contact order (s.11(7)); order a welfare report on the child (s.7); and direct that a local authority investigate the child's circumstances (s.37).

Duration   A contact order cannot be made to last beyond the child's sixteenth birthday, unless there are exceptional circumstances (s.9(7)).

A welfare report   The court may require a welfare report from a Cafcass Children and Family Reporter or a Welsh family proceedings officer under s.7 Children Act 1989. The recommendations in the welfare report are an important consideration for the court when reaching its decision (see p. 290 above).

(c) How the court exercises its discretion in contact cases

When considering whether to make a contact order and, if so, in what manner, the court must apply the welfare principle (s.1(1)), the 'minimum intervention' principle (s.1(5)), the no-delay principle (s.1(2)) and, in a contested application, the s.1(3) welfare checklist (see further at 10.3).

(i) Contact as a right of the child Under the UN Convention on the Rights of the Child children have a right to contact with both parents on a regular basis, except when a court decides that contact is contrary to the child's best interests (art. 9) (see 8.2). The courts in England and Wales have also referred to contact as a right of the child. As Sir Stephen Brown P said in *Re W (A Minor) (Contact)* [1994] 2 FLR 441, it is 'quite clear that contact with a parent is a fundamental right of a child, save in wholly exceptional circumstances'. Cogent reasons will therefore be needed to deprive a child of contact (see *Re H (Contact Principles)* [1994] 2 FLR 969. In *Re R (A Minor) (Contact)* [1993] 2 FLR 762 Butler-Sloss LJ stated that it 'is a right of a child to have a relationship with both parents wherever possible' and that 'in general the parent with whom the child does not live has a continuing role to play, which is recognised by s.2(1) of the Children Act 1989'.

In most cases the court will therefore decide that it in the child's best interests for the non-resident parent to have contact. Because of the importance attached to a child knowing his or her natural parent, the court may decide to order contact even where the father is absent, for instance, because he is in prison (*A v. L (Contact)* [1998] 1 FLR 361). Because of the importance of contact for children the Court of Appeal has emphasised that the court should explore all options before contact is terminated (*Re W (Contact)* [2007] EWCA Civ 753, [2007] 2 FLR 1122).

The European Court of Human Rights has also recognised the importance of contact between parents and children (see p. 300 above).

Gilmore (2008) has challenged the assumption that contact is beneficial for children claiming that '[r]esearch suggests that it is not contact per se but the nature and quality of contact that are important to children's adjustment'.

(ii) A presumption or assumption in favour of contact? Although contact is considered to be a right of the child (see above), and is considered to be beneficial to a child, Thorpe LJ in *Re L, V, M and H* [2000] 2 FLR 334 (which involved contact and domestic violence, see p. 305 below) said that, although there was a 'universal judicial recognition of the importance of contact to a child's development', he was wary of talking of presumptions in the context of contact because it might 'inhibit or distort the rigorous search for the welfare solution'. For this reason, he preferred to talk about an 'assumption' in favour of contact or an assumption that contact is beneficial. Thorpe LJ was in no doubt, however, 'of the secure foundation for the assumption that contact benefits children'.

(d) Types of contact

Different types of contact can be ordered depending on the circumstances. Section 8(1) of the Children Act 1989 provides that the child can visit, stay or otherwise have contact with the parent or other named person. Direct contact (visiting or staying contact) will usually be ordered, unless there are cogent reasons to the contrary affecting the child's welfare (such as where there is violence). Instead of ordering direct contact, especially where it is of significant duration, it might be better to apply for a shared residence order (see p. 296).

Indirect and supervised contact   Sometimes the court will order indirect or supervised contact (the word 'otherwise' in s.8(1) allows this). The court may impose a condition on a contact order under s.11(7) to specify what arrangements are to take place (for instance indirect contact by letter, birthday cards, Christmas cards or telephone conversations). Indirect contact was ordered, for example in: *Re P (Contact: Indirect Contact)* [1999] 2 FLR 893 (the father was a former drug addict who had just been released from prison); *Re L (Contact: Genuine Fear)* [2002] 1 FLR 621 (the mother was genuinely and intensely frightened of the father, so that direct contact would cause the child emotional harm); and in *Re F (Indirect Contact)* [2006] EWCA Civ 1426, [2007] 1 FLR 1015 (the father had a history of serious and uncontrollable violence).

Where there is a risk that contact may harm the child, supervised contact can be ordered, whereby contact takes place in the presence of a third party. Supervised contact can take place in a contact centre run under the auspices of the National Association of Child Contact Centres, where children can enjoy contact with one or both parents (and other family members) in a comfortable and safe environment.

(e)   Parental hostility to contact

As contact is considered to be a right of a child and beneficial for a child, the courts are reluctant to allow contact to be thwarted because of parental hostility to it. In *Re H (A Minor) (Contact)* [1994] 2 FLR 776 Butler-Sloss LJ said that it was important that there should not be 'a selfish parents' charter' whereby a parent could make such a fuss about contact that it could prevent the court ordering it. Only in highly exceptional cases would contact be refused because of a parent's strong opposition and hostility to contact (see, for example, *Re J (A Minor) (Contact)* [1994] 1 FLR 729 where the mother's hostility to contact with the father caused the child stress).

Over the years the courts began to increasingly realise, however, that some parents had genuinely held reasons for being intractably hostile to contact, for instance because of fear that the child might suffer violence (see *Re H (Contact: Domestic Violence)* [1998] 2 FLR 42). Courts therefore began to take allegations of domestic violence and hostility to contact more seriously (see further below). On the other hand where hostility to contact is not genuinely held, then the court now has stronger powers to enforce and facilitate contact (see 11.6).

(f)   Contact and domestic violence

For many years allegations of domestic violence were not taken as seriously as they might have been in contact cases. Some of the reasons for this were that:

- Research on domestic violence had tended to concentrate on adult victims rather than children.
- The courts were of the view that, as children had a right to contact and contact was beneficial to them, then it should usually be ordered.
- The courts were distrustful of mothers who made allegations of violence by fathers, and considered that they were merely being hostile to contact.

▶ The courts were keen to ensure that children were brought up having a positive image of a father, even where there were allegations of domestic violence.
▶ There was nothing expressly about domestic violence in the Children Act 1989.

Increasing concern began to be voiced, however, that the courts had perhaps created too high a threshold for a denial of contact, and that contact was being ordered in cases even though there was a risk of violence. An important impetus for the courts changing their approach was research by psychiatrists which showed the harmful effects of domestic violence on children. Another impetus for change was a report by Radford (*Unreasonable Fears? Child Contact in the Context of Domestic Violence: A Survey of Mothers' Perception of Harm*, 1999, Women's Aid), which provided evidence of children being physically and sexually abused as a result of contact being ordered. The report stated that changes in court practice were overdue, and recommended the introduction of a rebuttable presumption against residence and direct or unsupervised contact in cases where there was a risk of violence.

In June 1999 a consultation paper by the Children Act Sub-Committee of the Advisory Board on Family Law (*Contact Between Children and Violent Parents: The Question of Parental Contact in Cases where there is Domestic Violence*) was published, proposing guidelines for good practice in contact cases where there were allegations of domestic violence. But the consultation paper was not in favour of introducing a legislative presumption against contact in domestic violence cases, which exists in some countries. The Government began to acknowledge that domestic violence had not been fully or appropriately handled by the courts in contact cases, and that something needed to be done. In a Report to the Lord Chancellor (*The Question of Parental Contact in Cases where there is Domestic Violence*, 2002) it was recommended that: guidelines for good practice should be drawn up; professionals involved should to be better informed and better trained; and there should be more research into contact and domestic violence.

As a result of the concerns voiced about contact and domestic violence, the courts began to take domestic violence more seriously in contact cases and would order indirect or supervised contact, or refuse contact, where there was violence (see, for example, *Re M (Contact: Violent Parent)* [1999] 2 FLR 321; and *Re K (Contact: Mother's Anxiety)* [1999] 2 FLR 703). The courts began to take the view that, where there was evidence of domestic violence, a father would have to show a future track record of proper behaviour, including taking up the offer of indirect contact, before successfully gaining direct contact (see dicta of Wall J in *Re O (Contact: Imposition of Conditions)* [1995] 2 FLR 124, approved by Cazalet J in *Re S (Violent Parent: Indirect Contact)* [2000] 1 FLR 481).

It was the following case, however, which was particularly important in the development of the law in contact cases in which there were allegations of domestic violence. In this case the Court of Appeal considered the Report by the Children Act Sub-Committee (see above) and a joint report by two child psychiatrists, Dr Sturge and Dr Glaser, in which they stated that domestic violence involved a significant failure in parenting and that, where it was proved, the balance should tip against contact with the abusive parent unless that parent: fully acknowledged the inappropriateness of the violence; recognised its likely ill-effects on the child; had a genuine interest in the child's welfare; and was fully committed to making reparation to the child.

> ▶ *Re L (Contact: Domestic Violence); Re V (Contact: Domestic Violence); Re M (Contact: Domestic Violence); Re H (Contact: Domestic Violence)* **[2000] 2 FLR 334**
>
> The fathers in the four conjoined appeals appealed against a judge's refusal to allow them direct contact with their children against a background of domestic violence. The violence or threats of violence had been proved, the fears of the resident parents were reasonable, and serious issues arose as to the risk of emotional harm to the children.
>
> The Court of Appeal, dismissing all four appeals, laid down the following principles which were to be applied in contact cases where there were allegations of domestic violence:
>
> ▶ Judges and magistrates need to have a heightened awareness of the existence, and consequences for children, of exposure to domestic violence.
> ▶ Allegations of domestic violence which might affect the outcome of a contact application must be adjudicated upon and found proved or not proved.
> ▶ Where domestic violence is proved, there is not, nor should there be, a presumption of no contact. As a matter of principle, domestic violence cannot of itself constitute a bar to contact.
> ▶ Domestic violence is a highly relevant and important factor, among others, which must be taken into account by the judge when carrying out the difficult and delicate balancing exercise of discretion, applying the welfare principle in s.1(1) Children Act 1989, and the welfare checklist in s.1(3).
> ▶ Where domestic violence is proved, the court should weigh in the balance the seriousness of the violence, the risks involved and the impact on the child against the positive factors, if any, of contact between the parent found to have been violent and the child.
> ▶ Where domestic violence is proved, the following factors, among others, are of particular significance: the extent of the violence; its effect upon the primary-carer; its effect upon the child; and, in particular, the ability of the offender to recognise his past behaviour, to be aware of the need for change, and to make genuine attempts to change it.
> ▶ In respect of art. 8 ECHR (the right to family life), where there is a conflict between the rights and interests of a child and those of a parent, the child's interests must prevail under art. 8(2).
> ▶ On an application for interim contact, when allegations of domestic violence have not been adjudicated upon, the court should give particular consideration to the likely risk of harm (physical or emotional) to the child if contact is granted or refused. The court should ensure, as far as it can, that any risk of harm to the child is minimised, and that the safety of the child and the residential parent is secured before, during and after any such contact.

The message which came out of *Re LVMH* was that courts and lawyers needed to be more aware of domestic violence and its effect on children. After *Re LVMH*, courts began to take allegations of violence in contact cases seriously, and, where violence was proved, would consider ordering indirect or supervised contact, or, in an extreme case, no contact. According to Kaganas ([2000] CFLQ 311, at 311), what *Re LVMH* did was 'to rein back, in domestic violence cases, what was a very strong trend to prioritise contact between children and non-resident parents and to downgrade the risks to which such contact might expose mothers and children'.

Other developments In response to concerns about children and domestic violence, the definition of 'harm' in the welfare checklist in s.1(3) of the Children Act 1998 (see 10.3) was redefined to include 'impairment suffered from seeing or hearing the ill-treatment of another'. Cafcass was also given an increased role to monitor domestic violence and conduct risk assessments (see over). Another development was the introduction of a new form (C1A) which must be completed in proceedings for *any* s.8 order under the Children Act 1989 in order to ensure that safety issues are prioritised throughout the proceedings and are brought to the attention of the court.

A practice direction was also issued (*Practice Direction: Residence and Contact Orders: Domestic Violence and Harm* [2008] 2 FLR 103) laying down rules of practice to be adopted in any family proceedings at any level of court where there is an application for a residence or contact order (under the CA 1989 or under the adoption legislation) and there is an allegation or other reason to suppose that a child or party has experienced domestic violence perpetrated by another party, or that there is a risk of domestic violence. 'Domestic violence' includes physical violence, threatening or intimidating behaviour and any other forms of abuse; and, in the case of a child, also includes impairment suffered from seeing or hearing the ill-treatment of another.

A failure to follow the fact-finding requirements of the *Practice Direction* may provide grounds for a successful appeal (as it did in *Re Z (Unsupervised Contact: Allegations of Domestic Violence)* [2009] EWCA Civ 430, [2009] 2 FLR 877 where, although the Cafcass officer had reported risks of violence, the judge decided that a fact-finding hearing should not go ahead).

Risk assessments (s.16A Children Act 1989)   Cafcass officers (or Welsh family proceedings officers) when exercising any of their functions in respect of any of the orders that can be made under Part II of the Children Act 1989 (see 10.2), and who suspect that the child concerned is at risk of harm, must make a risk assessment in relation to the child and make that assessment available for the court (ss.16A(1), (2)). The assessment must be presented to the court even if the officer concludes that there is no risk of harm to the child; as the fact that a risk assessment has been carried out is a material fact which should be placed before the court (*Practice Direction: Children Act 1989: Risk Assessments Under Section 16A* [2007] 2 FLR 625).

11.6   Enforcing and facilitating contact

> ▶ **Baroness Hale in *Re G (Children)* [2006] UKHL 43, [2006] 2 FLR 269**
>
> 'Making contact happen and, even more importantly, making contact work is one of the most difficult and contentious challenges in the whole of family law. It has recently received a great deal of public attention. Courts understandably regard the conventional methods of enforcing court orders as a last resort: fining the primary carer will only mean that she has even less to spend on the children; sending her to prison will deprive them of their primary carer and give them a reason to resent the other parent who invited this. Nor does punishment address the real sources of the problem, which may range from a simple failure to understand what the children need, to more complex fears resulting from the parents' own relationships.'

The courts in England and Wales must take effective steps to enforce contact, otherwise they risk being in breach of the European Convention for the Protection of Human Rights (see 1.7) and the UN Convention on the Rights of the Child (see 8.2).

Despite the obligation to enforce contact, enforcement has created (and continues to create) difficulties for the courts. Various steps to enforce and facilitate contact can be taken by the court.

(a)   The new provisions for enforcing and facilitating contact

In order to improve the enforcement and facilitation of contact, ss. 11A–P of the Children Act 1989 give the courts new powers to enforce and facilitate contact and resolve child contact disputes.

(i) The background to the new provisions   In 2002 the Children Act Sub-Committee of the Lord Chancellor's Advisory Board on Family Law, chaired by Wall J, published *Making Contact Work: A Report to the Lord Chancellor on the Facilitation of Arrangements for Contact Between Children and Their Non-Residential Parents and the Enforcement of Court Orders for Contact.* The Report made various recommendations, including: providing more information about contact; giving Contact Centres extra funding to facilitate contact; promoting mediation, conciliation and negotiation; amending the provisions governing family assistance orders; giving courts the power to refer a parent to a psychiatrist or psychologist, or to an education programme; imposing community service orders for breach of contact orders; and awarding financial compensation to parents who suffered financial loss as a result of loss of contact. Many of these recommendations were incorporated in the new law.

Two years later, in 2004, the Government published a consultation paper, *Parental Separation: Children's Needs and Parents' Responsibilities* (Cm 6273), in which it acknowledged that the current system for enforcing and facilitating contact was not working well. The consultation paper was followed in 2005 by the White Paper, *Parental Separation: Children's Needs and Parents' Responsibilities, Next Steps* (Cm 6452), which made the following proposals: to make changes in respect of the facilitation and enforcement of contact; to provide a wider range of services to support contact, including additional funding for Contact Centres, and advice and parenting support to help parents have meaningful contact with their children; to give Cafcass a greater role in the promotion and enforcement of contact; to give courts additional powers before making contact orders, to make family assistance orders more flexible so that they could be used effectively in difficult contact cases; to ensure that s.11(7) CA 1989 provides sufficient flexibility to the courts' power to attach conditions to contact orders; and to promote the increased use of mediation.

(ii) The new provisions   Many of the above recommendations were enacted in Part 1 of the Children and Adoption Act 2006, which inserted new sections (ss.11A–P) into the Children Act 1989. These came into force in December 2008. In addition to giving the courts additional powers when dealing with applications for contact orders, these provisions place a number of new duties on Cafcass officers and Welsh family proceedings officers, including monitoring compliance with contact orders, contact activities and enforcement, and reporting back to the court. The provisions give the courts more flexibility in dealing with breaches of contact orders and they exist alongside the courts' powers to deal with breach. Concern has been voiced (by Resolution and the Family Justice Council), however, that unless the new scheme is properly resourced, it will fail to fulfil its aims.

Under ss.11A–P of the Children Act 1989 the following steps can be taken to enforce and facilitate contact:

Contact activity directions and conditions   In order to facilitate contact, the court at the interim stage of a contact dispute can make a 'contact activity direction' (under s.11A) directing a party to the proceedings to take part in a specified activity which promotes contact with the child. Contact activities can include: classes; counselling; guidance; information and advice about contact; and information about mediation. However, there is no power to order a person to have a medical or psychiatric examination, assessment or treatment; or to take part in mediation. When considering whether to make a contact activity direction, the child's welfare is the court's paramount consideration.

When making or varying a contact order the court can include a 'contact activity condition' (under s.11C) in the order requiring the person with whom the child lives (or is to live) and/or a person with a right to contact under a contact order (or a condition under a contact order) to take part in an activity that will promote contact with the child. The condition will specify the activity and the activity provider.

Before making a contact activity direction or condition, the court must be satisfied that (s.11E): the activity is appropriate in the circumstances; the activity provider is suitable to provide the activity; and the proposed activity is in a place to which the person subject to the direction or condition can reasonably be expected to travel. Before making the direction or condition, the court must obtain and consider information about the person who is to be subject to the direction or condition; and consider the likely effect of the direction or condition on that person. This may include information about any conflict with the person's religious beliefs and any interference with that person's work or education arrangements. The court can ask a Cafcass officer (or a Welsh family proceedings officer) to provide this information.

The court can ask a Cafcass officer (or a Welsh family proceedings officer) to monitor a person's compliance with a contact activity direction or condition; and to report to the court on failure to comply (s.11G). Financial assistance may be available to assist persons who are required to undertake a contact activity (s.11F).

Monitoring contact orders (s.11H)   The court can ask a Cafcass officer (or a Welsh family proceedings officer) to monitor compliance with a contact order (or an order varying contact) and report to the court on such matters relating to compliance as the court may specify. The court can make the request when making or varying a contact order or in any subsequent contact proceedings. This monitoring role can only last for up to 12 months.

Warning notices (s.11I)   When a court makes a contact order (or varies a contact order), it must attach a warning notice to the order providing information about the consequences of failing to comply with the order.

Enforcement orders (ss.11J–N)   If the court is satisfied beyond reasonable doubt that a contact order has been breached without reasonable excuse, it may make an 'enforcement order' imposing an unpaid work requirement (community service) on the person in breach (see s.11J), unless that person proves on the balance of probabilities that he or she has a reasonable excuse for failing to comply with the contact order.

The following persons can apply for an enforcement order: the person who for the purpose of a contact order is the person with whom the child lives (or is to live); the person whose contact with the child is provided for in the contact order; any person subject to a condition in a contact order (made under s.11(7)(b)) or to a contact activity condition (made under s.11C); or the child concerned (but only with leave of the court, which it can grant if the child has sufficient understanding to make the application). Schedule A1 to the Children Act 1989 makes further provision in respect of enforcement orders.

An enforcement order cannot be made unless the person concerned has received a copy of a warning notice (see above); and it cannot be made against a person aged under 18 at the time of the breach (s.11K).

Before making an enforcement order the court must be satisfied that (s.11L): the order is necessary to secure compliance with the contact order; and that the likely effect of the order on the person in breach is proportionate to the seriousness of the breach. It must also be satisfied that the provision for the person to work under an unpaid work requirement can be made in the local justice area in which the person in breach resides, or will reside. The court must obtain and consider information about the person and the likely effect of the order on that person before making the order. The provisions about seeking information are the same as those for obtaining information before making a contact activity or direction. When making the order, the court must take into account the welfare of the child who is the subject of the contact order.

Compensation for financial loss (s.11O)   If certain persons suffer financial loss as a result of the breach of a contact order (for instance the loss of the cost of a holiday or outing which has been booked), the court can require the person in breach to compensate that person for the financial loss. The following can apply for compensation: the person who, for the purposes of the contact order, is the person with whom the child lives (or is to live); the person for whom contact is provided for in the contact order, or a person subject to a s.11(7)(b) contact condition or a s.11C contact activity condition; or the child concerned (but only with leave of the court, which it can grant if the child has sufficient understanding to make the application). The amount of compensation must not exceed the amount of the applicant's financial loss. In determining the amount payable, the court must take into account the financial circumstances of the person in breach. In exercising its powers, the court must take into account the welfare of the child. An order to pay compensation cannot be made against a person where the failure occurred before that person attained the age of 18 (see s.11P).

(h)   Other measures for enforcing and facilitating contact

The following powers are also available to the courts for the purpose of facilitating and enforcing contact, but the new provisions above will in some cases remove the need to use these options.

(i) Family assistance order (s.16)   A family assistance order (see further at 10.12) can be made under s.16 of the Children Act 1989 for the purpose of facilitating contact in difficult contact cases. Thus, a family assistance order can be made (when a contact order is in force) directing a Cafcass officer (or a Welsh family proceedings officer) or a local authority officer to give advice and assistance with regard to establishing, improving and maintaining contact to such persons as are specified in the family assistance order (s.16(4A)).

(ii) Contempt of court   Breach of a contact order is contempt of court, punishable by fine or imprisonment. However, contempt as a remedy for breach is a rather unsatisfactory

measure in family cases, as the imposition of a fine may reduce the amount of money available for maintaining the child; and sending a parent to prison may be emotionally damaging for the child. Despite these disadvantages, however, the courts have imposed fines and prison sentences for breaches of contact orders (see, for example, *Re S (Contact Dispute: Committal)* [2004] EWCA Civ 1790, [2005] 1 FLR 812). But the Court of Appeal has warned that a custodial sentence should not be imposed where a fine is appropriate (see *Re M (Contact Order)* [2005] EWCA Civ 615, [2005] 2 FLR 1006).

Contempt proceedings must comply with art. 6 (the right to a fair trial) and art. 8 (the right to family life) of the European Convention for the Protection of Human Rights. In *Re K (Contact: Committal Order)* [2002] EWCA Civ 1559, [2003] 1 FLR 277 a mother successfully appealed against her committal to prison for 42 days for breaching a contact order as the Court of Appeal held that her failure to have legal representation in the contempt proceedings breached art. 6; and the sentencing court had breached art. 8, as it should have considered the effect of art. 8 on the decision to separate her from her children.

(iii) Transfer residence to the other parent   Where there are difficulties enforcing contact the court may decide to order that the child's residence be transferred from the parent who is hostile to contact to the non-resident parent (as it did, for example, in *V v. V (Contact: Implacable Hostility)* [2004] EWHC 1215 (Fam), [2004] 2 FLR 851; and in *Re C (A Child)* [2007] EWCA Civ 866, [2008] 1 FLR 211). However, a transfer of residence will be ordered only in the last resort; and where it is not contrary to the child's best interests. In *Re A (Residence Order)* [2009] EWCA Civ 1141, for example, the transfer of residence from the mother to the father was held to be premature and too risky for the children in the circumstances of the case.

11.7   Changing a child's name on family breakdown

On family breakdown the parent with whom the child lives may decide to change the child's surname, perhaps because of a desire to sever ties with the other parent or for the child to acquire a step-parent's surname. However, there are restrictions on changing a child's surname, but these restrictions do not apply to a child's first name (see *Re H (Child's Name: First Name)* [2002] EWCA Civ 190, [2002] 1 FLR 973).

A child's surname can be changed by a person with parental responsibility for the child, provided every other person with parental responsibility consents. Oral consent is sufficient, except where a residence order is in force, when *written* consent is required (s.13(1)(b) CA 1989). Written consent is also required if the child is in local authority care (s.33(7) CA 1989). Where consent (oral or written) is not forthcoming, the court's consent will be needed.

A dispute about a child's surname can be settled by making an application for a s.8 specific issue order under the Children Act 1989 (see 10.8); or, if a residence order is in force, by applying under s.13. Where a change of name seems imminent, a s.8 prohibited steps order (see 10.9) may be necessary to stop the change of surname. When considering an application for a change of surname, the child's welfare is the court's paramount consideration (s.1(1)), and the s.1(3) welfare checklist applies if the application is by way of a specific issue or prohibited steps order (see s.1(4)). Although the provisions of the CA 1989 do not require the court to consider the welfare checklist in an application for a change of surname under s.13, the court is likely to perform the same sort of exercise.

The courts take the view that changing a child's surname is a serious matter (*Dawson* v. *Wearmouth* [1999] AC 308, [1999] 1 FLR 1167); and the child's wishes, not those of the parent, may prevail. In *Re C (Change of Surname)* [1998] 2 FLR 656 the Court of Appeal held that good reasons have to be shown before a judge will allow a change of name. In *Re W; Re A; Re B (Change of Name)* [1999] 2 FLR 930 Butler-Sloss LJ said that a desire to change a child's name, because the applicant parent did not have the same name as the child, will generally not carry much weight.

The court will take into account cultural and religious circumstances when deciding whether to permit a change of surname, but even then may be unwilling to permit a change (see, for example, *Re S (Change of Names: Cultural Factors)* [2001] 2 FLR 1005 where Wilson J refused to give the mother permission to change the child's Sikh names to Muslim names after she had moved back into a Muslim community on family breakdown). A change of surname may be permitted where there is a need to protect a child against the risk of abduction (see, for example, *Re F (Contact)* [2007] EWHC 2543 (Fam) where the father had made repeated threats to abduct the children).

In *Re R (Surname: Using Both Parents')* [2001] EWCA Civ 1344, [2001] 2 FLR 1358 it was suggested that parents should be encouraged to use the Spanish custom of combining the paternal and maternal surnames as a way of avoiding surname disputes.

11.8 Relocation on family breakdown

(a) Removing a child lawfully from the UK

On family breakdown, a parent may wish to take the child temporarily or permanently out of the UK. A parent can do this, provided he or she is not in breach of any statutory provision or court order and has obtained the necessary consents.

Obtaining the necessary consents   A parent who wishes to take a child out of the UK must obtain the consent of all those persons who have parental responsibility for the child, otherwise he or she may commit the criminal offence of child abduction or kidnapping (see 13.3) or be in contempt of court (if there is a court order prohibiting the child's removal). Oral consent to take the child abroad is usually sufficient, unless there is a court order to the contrary. If a residence order is in force, *written* consent is needed of all persons with parental responsibility, except where the holder of the residence order wishes to go abroad for a period of less than one month (s.13(1)(6) CA 1989). If written consent is not forthcoming then the court's permission to leave the UK will have to be obtained. Such applications are known as 'relocation applications'.

(b) Relocation applications

(i) Introduction   After family breakdown the parent who is the primary carer may wish to take the child out of the UK, perhaps to start a new relationship, or to take up a new job, or to move back to his or her country of origin. The other parent may refuse to agree to this, perhaps because of the difficulty of maintaining contact, or because of a fear that the child will not be returned. Where the necessary consents to taking the child out of the UK are not forthcoming, the court's permission must be sought in order to avoid committing a criminal offence or being in contempt of court (see above).

Permission to leave the UK (to relocate) can be sought by applying for a s.8 specific issue order (see 10.8), or, if a residence order is in force, by applying under s.13(1) CA 1989. The court will apply the welfare principle in s.1(1) and the other s.1 welfare principles in the CA 1989 (see 10.3).

The approach of the courts in relocation cases is to allow a reasonable and properly thought-out application, unless this is clearly incompatible with the child's welfare. This approach was laid down by the Court of Appeal in *Poel* v. *Poel* [1970] WLR 1469 and has been upheld by the courts in subsequent cases.

With the coming into force of the Human Rights Act 1998, however, parents (mostly fathers) began to argue that the rule in favour of permitting a reasonable relocation application breached their human rights (and those of the child) under the European Convention for the Protection of Human Rights. They also argued that the presumption was contrary to the welfare principle in s.1(1) of the Children Act 1989 because it failed to treat the child's welfare as the court's paramount consideration. Thus, for example, in *Re A (Permission to Remove Child from Jurisdiction: Human Rights)* [2000] 2 FLR 225 the father argued that, if permission was given to allow the mother to take their child to New York, it would breach his right to family life under art. 8 ECHR. However, the Court of Appeal, dismissing his appeal, held that art. 8(2) required the court to balance such rights where they were in conflict. It held that the test laid down in *Poel* v. *Poel* (see above) was not in conflict with the ECHR. In fact, Buxton LJ doubted whether difficult balancing questions of this nature fell within the purview of the ECHR at all.

(ii) **Payne v. Payne –** *the leading case*   In the following case (which is the leading case on relocation applications) the Court of Appeal reviewed the long line of authority on relocation applications in the light of the new obligations imposed on the courts by the Human Rights Act 1998:

> ▶ *Payne* v. *Payne* [2001] EWCA Civ 1166, [2001] 1 FLR 1052
>
> The mother (the primary-carer) applied for permission to remove the daughter (aged 4) permanently from the UK to live with her in New Zealand. The father opposed the application and applied for a residence order. The father and paternal grandmother had regular and exceptionally good staying contact with the child. The mother's application was granted at first instance, applying the principle in *Poel* (above). The father appealed arguing that: contact between children and non-residential parents had increased in importance since the decision in *Poel*; the principles in relocation applications were inconsistent with the Children Act (CA) 1989, as they created a presumption in favour of the applicant; and the court's approach was inconsistent with the Human Rights Act 1998.
>
>   The Court of Appeal dismissed his appeal, holding that there was no conflict between the case-law governing relocation applications and the European Convention for the Protection of Human Rights, and the Children Act 1989. It held that the proposition in *Poel* (that a reasonable application would be allowed) did not amount to a presumption in favour of the primary-carer. The child's welfare is always the court's paramount consideration, and the welfare checklist in s.1(3) CA 1989 (see 10.3) should be used by a judge when carrying out the welfare test.
>
>   Butler-Sloss P said that, although the reasonable proposals of the residential parent wishing to live abroad carried great weight, they had to be scrutinised carefully so that the court could be satisfied that there was a genuine motivation for the move and not an intention to terminate contact between the child and the other parent. Her Ladyship said that the effect on the child of a denial of contact with the non-resident parent and his family was an

important consideration, and that the opportunity for continuing contact between the child and the parent left behind in the UK might be a very significant factor.

Thorpe LJ agreed with Ward LJ in *Re A (Permission to Remove Child from Jurisdiction: Human Rights)* (see above) that the advent of the ECHR in domestic law by the HRA 1998 did not necessitate a revision of the fundamental approach to relocation applications formulated by the Court of Appeal and consistently applied over so many years. Thorpe LJ said that 'in a united family the right to family life is a shared right', but that 'once a family unit disintegrates the separating members' separate rights can only be to a fragmented family life'. In the present case the mother's right to mobility under art. 2 of Protocol 4 of the European Convention was another relevant right to be considered. Thorpe LJ said that he did not consider that a reasonable request by the primary carer created a legal presumption of permission to relocate. He also proposed a 'discipline' which the courts should use in relocation cases (see below).

The 'discipline' that courts should use   Thorpe LJ in *Payne* suggested that the following framework or 'discipline' should be used by the courts when deciding relocation applications:

'(a) Pose the question: is the mother's application genuine in the sense that it is not motivated by some selfish desire to exclude the father from the child's life? Then ask is the mother's application realistic, by which I mean founded on practical proposals both well researched and investigated? If the application fails either of these tests refusal will inevitably follow.

(b) If however the application passes these tests then there must be a careful appraisal of the father's opposition: is it motivated by genuine concern for the future of the child's welfare or is it driven by some ulterior motive? What would be the extent of the detriment to him and his future relationship with the child were the application granted? To what extent would that be offset by extension of the child's relationships with the maternal family and homeland?

(c) What would be the impact on the mother, either as the single parent or as a new wife, of a refusal of her realistic proposal?

(d) The outcome of the second and third appraisals must then be brought into an overriding review of the child's welfare as the paramount consideration, directed by the statutory checklist in so far as appropriate.'

The principles laid down in *Payne* were endorsed by the Court of Appeal in *Re G (Leave to Remove)* [2007] EWCA Civ 1497, [2008] 1 FLR 1587 where the father sought leave to appeal (against the trial judge's decision to grant the mother leave to relocate to Germany) arguing that some judges were misapplying *Payne* in that they were inappropriately prioritising the impact of refusal on the primary carer, and were disregarding modern views on the importance of co-parenting. The Court of Appeal refused permission to appeal. Thorpe LJ, giving judgment, held that it was not possible to argue that the principles in *Payne* were being widely misunderstood or misapplied by trial judges; but he said that he did recognise that relocation cases were very difficult for trial judges and that often the balance between grant and refusal was a very fine one.

In *Re H (A Child)* [2007] EWCA Civ 222, [2007] 2 FLR 317 Thorpe LJ said that a fundamentally important part of the judge's task in deciding a finely balanced relocation case was to assess the impact on the caring parent of a decision to refuse permission to relocate. He said that this was 'often the most important single task that confronts the judge'. In *Re B (Leave to Remove: Impact of Refusal)* [2004] EWCA Civ 956, [2005] 2 FLR 239 Thorpe LJ said that 'each case turned on its own facts, but that the applicant's explanation for fundamental relocation is the core of every case'.

(iii) Practical matters: While each relocation application turns on its own facts, practical matters (such as housing, education, contact arrangements and potential cultural difficulties for the child) will be important (see, for example, *Re F (Leave to Remove)* [2005] EWHC 2705 (Fam), [2006] 1 FLR 776, where the mother's application to remove the child to Jamaica was refused on the basis, *inter alia*, of her failure to make adequate plans in respect of supporting herself and the child and in respect of the child's schooling; and because there were insufficient funds available to pay for regular airfares for contact visits to the father).

However, where the primary carer is returning to a completely familiar home life after a brief absence, the Court of Appeal has held that the bar in respect of practical matters is set relatively low (see *Re F and H (Children: Relocation)* [2007] EWCA Civ 692, [2008] 2 FLR 1667 where the mother was granted permission to return to Texas with the children after a relatively brief absence from her home city, her family and all that was familiar). But, even if the caring parent is returning to his or her homeland, the application will not necessarily be allowed, as each case depends on its own facts (see *Re H (Removal from Jurisdiction)* [2007] EWCA Civ 222, [2007] 2 FLR 317 where the American mother's application to move back to the USA with the child (aged 5) and her new husband failed, as, although it was clear that if leave was refused the mother would be distressed and unhappy in the short term, there was no risk of her compromising the care of the child).

(iv) The psychological impact of relocation In *Re B (Leave to Remove: Impact of Refusal)* [2004] EWCA Civ 956, [2005] 2 FLR 239 Thorpe LJ, with whom May and Scott Baker LJJ agreed, said that it was important to give great weight to the emotional and psychological well-being of the primary carer, and not merely take note of the impact on the primary carer of refusing the application to relocate. However, in respect of possible mental harm to the applicant, it was held in *Re G (Removal from Jurisdiction)* [2005] EWCA Civ 170, [2005] 2 FLR 166 that an applicant is not required to prove that he or she will suffer psychiatric damage if permission to relocate is refused – all that is required is that a refusal will have an impact on the applicant's sense of well-being and that this will be transmitted to the children. In *R v. R (Leave to Remove)* [2004] EWHC 2572 (Fam), [2005] 1 FLR 687 Baron J refused the mother's application to remove the children to France on the basis, *inter alia*, that the mother (who had psychiatric problems) did not have the necessary emotional stability to establish a new life in another country.

The psychological impact on the children of relocation will be an important consideration under the welfare test. Thus, for example, in *Re B (Leave to Remove)* [2008] EWCA Civ 1034, [2008] 2 FLR 2059 the mother's application to remove the children of the marriage to Germany was refused as there was strong oral evidence from a psychologist that relocation to Germany would have a very negative effect on the children and would severely damage their relationship with their father.

(v) Cultural and religious objections to relocation Cultural and religious objections to a parent relocating outside the UK will not usually be allowed to prevail over the primary consideration of the child's welfare. In *Re A (Leave to Remove: Cultural and Religious Considerations)* [2006] EWHC 421 (Fam), [2007] 2 FLR 572 Hedley J allowed the child's mother to relocate with her son (aged 9) to The Netherlands where she lived with her new husband, despite the father's arguments that his son should remain in England for religious and cultural reasons (in particular, so that he could succeed to the mantle of head of the family group).

(vi) The voice of the child in relocation applications   The voice of the child can be taken into account in relocation applications and may be an important consideration in tilting the balance one way or the other. The children's voices were, for example, taken into account in the following case:

> ▶ *Re W (Leave to Remove)* [2008] EWCA Civ 538, [2008] 2 FLR 1170
>
> On divorce the Swedish mother, who had lived with her Swedish husband in London for 15 years, applied under s.13 CA 1989 to remove the children (aged 11, 13 and 15) with her to Sweden on the basis that the family's reduced financial circumstances and doubts over the father's future ability to generate income dictated return. The children supported the proposed move to Sweden. The father resisted the move. The Cafcass officer reported the children's positive views on the proposed move, but advised that the court should exercise a degree of caution in evaluating their views. The judge refused the mother's application, and so she appealed.
>
> The Court of Appeal allowed her appeal and granted her permission to take the children to Sweden. It did so, *inter alia*, on the basis that the judge had failed sufficiently to consider the wishes of the three children, who were particularly intelligent, mature and sophisticated for their different ages; and as the judge had not given sufficient weight to the family's financial situation if the mother and children were to remain in London, where they would have to find housing of a much lower standard.

(c) Is the approach in relocation cases the correct one?

Concern has been expressed by academics, lawyers and other persons (such as Sir Bob Geldof, see www.thecustodyminefield.com) that the approach in relocation cases is the wrong one. It has been argued, for instance, that the courts place too much emphasis on the reasonable wishes and proposals of the applicant parent, rather than looking at the best interests of the child from the point of view of having the benefit of maintaining a relationship with both parents. There is also concern that the courts are denying children their contact rights with the non-resident parent (usually the father).

Spon-Smith (2004) claims that the conventional approach to relocation applications is not supported by American research (by Braver *et al*, 2003) which shows that children do not necessarily benefit from moving to a new location which is distant from the other parent. Hayes (2006) argues that trial judges are being prevented by strong rulings from the Court of Appeal from exercising their discretion in relocation cases in a broad and principled manner. She claims that the 'discipline' recommended in *Payne*, and entrenched in subsequent Court of Appeal judgments, is misguided as it places a gloss on the welfare principle, it narrows the proper application of that principle and is biased in favour of the residential parent (who is almost invariably the mother). Herring and Taylor (2006) claim that principles adopted in relocation cases fail to take adequate account of the impact of human rights reasoning.

Geekie (2008) argues that the approach in relocation cases seems to be at odds with the approach adopted in shared residence cases where the approach has been to shake off 'the shackles of a dated approach to shared parenting'. Pressdee (2008) argues that Thorpe LJ's approach in *Payne* needs to be applied with greater flexibility.

(d) Temporary removals from the UK

Sometimes a parent may wish to take the child temporarily out of the UK (for instance for a holiday). In some cases the court's permission will be needed. Thus, if a residence order is in force and the primary carer wishes to take the child out of the UK temporarily for more than one month, then the written consent of all persons with parental responsibility is needed, or otherwise the consent of the court (see s.13(1)(b) CA 1989). In the following case, the Court of Appeal considered how the courts should deal with applications for temporary removal:

▶ *Re A (Temporary Removal from Jurisdiction)* [2004] EWCA Civ 1587, [2005] 1 FLR 639

The child (aged 4) spent five nights a week with the mother and two nights with the father under the terms of a shared residence order. The mother applied for permission to take the child to South Africa for two years to carry out research for her doctorate. The judge, applying the principles in *Payne* v. *Payne* (above), refused the application. The Court of Appeal allowed the mother's appeal, as the judge had erred in holding that the considerations which govern decisions about applications for permanent removal of the child should also apply, without modification, to applications for temporary removal. The considerations relevant to an application for permission to relocate permanently were not automatically applicable to applications for temporary removal. Thorpe LJ said: 'The more temporary the removal, the less regard should be paid to the principles stated in *Payne* v. *Payne*.'

Practical safeguards to ensure the child's return If there is a risk that a parent will not return after a temporary stay outside the UK, the court in England and Wales can impose certain safeguards. Thus, it may: impose a condition on a court order; require an undertaking to be given to the court; require the parties to enter into a notarised agreement containing provisions about returning the child; require 'mirror' orders (orders equivalent to English orders) to be applied for in the foreign court; order a parent to swear on the Holy Qur'an before a Shariah Court that the child will be returned; and/or order a parent to provide a sum of money as surety for the child's return (see, for example, *Re L (Removal from Jurisdiction: Holiday)* [2001] 1 FLR 241).

The following case provides an example of the court imposing a range of practical safeguards to ensure the children's return:

▶ *Re S (Leave to Remove from Jurisdiction: Securing Return from Holiday)* [2001] 2 FLR 507

The court wished to ensure that the mother would return the children after taking them to India on holiday. She was ordered: to return them by a certain date and not to return them to India without the father's written permission; to deposit the children's passports with her solicitors in India; to provide the father with copies of the airline tickets and the children's visas from the Indian High Commission; to seek only short tourist visas (that order to be served on the Indian High Commission); and not to seek Indian passports or Indian citizenship for the children while in India. The children were made wards of court, and the court made declarations that their habitual residence was England and Wales and that they were British citizens.

The approach in *Re S* above was followed in *Re DS (Removal from Jurisdiction)* [2009] EWHC 1594 (Fam) where a mother wished to take the child to India for a family wedding, but where the child was at risk because the mother had on a previous occasion been a month late in returning from India to the UK. She was granted leave to make the trip on the basis of a range of undertakings and a declaration as to the child's citizenship and habitual residence.

11.9   Relocation within the United Kingdom

Moving a child from England and Wales to another part of the UK (Scotland or Northern Ireland), unlike moving a child from the UK (see 11.8 above), does not require the oral or written consent of the other parent or anyone else with parental responsibility whether or not a residence order is in force. Neither is it a criminal offence under the Child Abduction Act 1984 (see 13.3), although it could constitute the offence of kidnapping.

(i) Steps to prevent removal   A parent (or other person with parental responsibility) who wishes to prevent the other parent (or person with parental responsibility) from moving the child from England and Wales to another part of the UK can apply under the Children Act 1989 for a s.8 prohibited steps order or residence order (with a condition attached to the residence order under s.11(7) (see 10.4)); or apply to make the child a ward of court (see 8.7).

(ii) Resolving a dispute about removal   A dispute between parents (and other persons with parental responsibility for a child), which cannot be settled by alternative means (such as mediation or collaborative law, see 1.4) can be settled by the court in an application under the Children Act 1989 for a s.8 residence order or specific issue order (see 10.5 and 10.8).

In such a case the court must apply the welfare principle and the welfare checklist and the other principles in s.1 of the Children Act 1989 (see 10.3). The Court of Appeal has held that a dispute about relocation within the UK must be decided by adopting a similar approach to that laid down in *Payne* v. *Payne* (see p. 312 above), but that the test is less stringent than that for external relocations (*per* Thorpe LJ in *Re H (Children: Residence Order: Condition)* [2001] EWCA Civ 1338, [2001] 2 FLR 1277 where a condition restricting relocation was upheld).

(iii) Restricting residence   The Court of Appeal has held that an order, or condition in an order, restricting a primary carer's right to choose where he or she lives should only be made in exceptional circumstances (see, for example, *Re E (Residence: Imposition of Conditions)* [1997] 2 FLR 638, and *Re B (Prohibited Steps Order)* [2007] EWCA Civ 1055, [2008] 1 FLR 613 (where the Court of Appeal allowed the mother's appeal against a prohibited steps order which had prohibited her from changing the child's residence from England and Wales to Northern Ireland). The House of Lords has also adopted the same approach (see *Re G (Children)* [2006] UKHL 43, [2006] 2 FLR 629, at 9.1)). Thus, the courts must acknowledge that the primary carer has reasonable freedom to choose where he or she resides with the child in the UK.

(iv) Relocation and shared residence   In *Re L (Shared Residence: Relocation)* [2009] EWCA Civ 20, [2009] 1 FLR 1157 the Court of Appeal held that a shared residence order is not an automatic bar to relocation, as it may well be in the child's best interests to relocate

notwithstanding the existence of such an order. It held that the correct approach to relocation in the context of shared residence is for the court to look at the underlying factual substratum in welfare terms bearing in mind the tension which may well exist between a parent's freedom to relocate and the welfare of the child which may militate against relocation. In *Re L* (where there was a shared residence order) the mother's application to move to Somerset from north London (where the parties lived separately) was refused at first instance, and dismissed by the Court of Appeal.

Summary

1 Many children experience parental relationship breakdown; and this can have an adverse effect on them.

2 Parents retain parental responsibility for their children on relationship breakdown.

3 Maintenance for children on family breakdown can be sought; and so can lump sum and property orders (see Chapter 12).

4 It is better for children if their parents reach agreement about arrangements for them on family breakdown rather than going to court.

5 Cafcass (see 1.6) plays an important role on family breakdown, which includes providing welfare reports (under s.7 CA 1989) and conducting risk assessments (under s.16A CA 1989).

6 In cases dealing with children's disputes on family breakdown (for instance in respect of residence and contact), the court must ensure that it complies with the European Convention for the Protection of Human Rights.

7 One of the aims of divorce law is to protect the best interests of children; and in furtherance of this aim, the petitioner must complete a form known as the Statement of Arrangements for the Children. This will be looked at by the district judge, who must consider whether he should exercise any of his powers under the Children Act 1989 (s.41 Matrimonial Causes Act 1973). In exceptional circumstances a decree absolute of divorce can be postponed.

8 Disputes about which parent the child should live with on family breakdown can be settled by making an application for a s.8 residence order under the Children Act 1989 (see also Chapter 10). The welfare of the child is the court's paramount consideration (s.1(1)) and the other welfare principles in s.1 apply. A shared residence order can be made (s.11(4)). Once a residence order is made, no person can change the child's surname or remove the child from the UK (except for up to one month) without the *written* consent of all persons with parental responsibility, or otherwise with permission of the court (ss.13(1), (2)).

9 Where a dispute about contact cannot be settled without litigation, an application can be made for a contact order under s.8 of the Children Act 1989. The court must apply the welfare principles in s.1 of the Act. Direct contact, indirect contact, supervised contact and an order of no contact are possible options for the court. Hostility to contact by residential parents has caused difficulties for the court. Domestic violence is a serious factor to be considered by the court, and various steps have been put in place to improve protection for children who may suffer domestic violence in the context of contact.

10 Difficulties in respect of facilitating and enforcing contact have led to the enactment of new provisions in the Children Act 1989 (ss.11A–P), which aim to improve and resolve contact difficulties on family breakdown.

11 Other disputes on family breakdown can be settled by an application for a s.8 specific issue or prohibited steps order under the Children Act 1989.

Summary cont'd

12 A dispute about a child's surname can be decided by making an application for a specific issue order, or, if a residence order is in force, by making an application under s.13 of the Children Act 1989. The child's welfare, not the parents' wishes, prevail.

13 There is increasing recognition that children should be allowed to participate in private law proceedings (such as for residence and contact) (see 8.6).

14 If a parent who wishes to take a child out of the UK cannot obtain the consent of the other parent and/or other persons with parental responsibility, then he or she will have to make a relocation application in order to avoid committing a criminal offence or being in contempt of court.

15 The framework for deciding relocation applications was laid down by the Court of Appeal in *Payne* v. *Payne* (2001) and this is still the leading case. However, there has been considerable concern voiced that the approach in *Payne* favours mothers, rather than fathers, and is out of line with modern views of shared parenting. It may also be in breach of the European Convention for the Protection of Human Rights.

Further reading and references

Bailey-Harris, 'Contact – challenging conventional wisdom' [2001] CFLQ 361.

Bainham *et al* (eds.), *Children and their Families: Contact, Rights and Welfare*, 2003, Hart Publishing.

Brasse, District Judge, 'The *Payne* threshold: leaving the jurisdiction' [2005] Fam Law 780.

Braver *et al*, 'Relocation of children after divorce and children's best interests: new evidence and legal considerations' (2003) 17(2) *Journal of Family Psychology* 206.

Butler *et al*, *Divorcing Children: Children's Experience of Their Parents' Divorce*, 2003, Jessica Kingsley.

Douglas and Ferguson, 'The role of grandparents in divorced families' (2003) *International Journal of Law, Policy and the Family* 41.

Fortin, Richie and Buchanan, 'Young adults' perceptions of court-ordered contact' [2007] CFLQ 211.

Geekie, 'Relocation and shared residence: one route or two?' [2008] Fam Law 446.

Gilmore, 'Contact/shared residence and child well-being: research evidence and its implications for legal decision-making' [2006] *International Journal of Law, Policy and the Family* 344.

Gilmore, 'Court decision-making in shared residence order cases: a critical examination' [2006] CFLQ 478.

Gilmore, 'Disputing contact: challenging some assumptions' [2008] CFLQ 285.

Gilmore, 'The assumption that contact is beneficial: challenging the "secure foundation"' [2008] Fam Law 1226.

Hayes, '*Dawson* v. *Wearmouth* – What's in a name? A child by any other name is surely just as sweet?' [1999] CFLQ 423.

Hayes, 'Relocation cases: is the Court of Appeal applying the correct principles?' [2006] CFLQ 351.

Herring and Taylor, 'Relocating relocation' [2006] CFLQ 517.

Humphreys and Harrison, 'Focusing on safety – domestic violence and the role of child contact centres' [2003] CFLQ 237.

Hunt, Masson and Trinder, 'Shared parenting: the law, the evidence and guidance from Families Need Fathers' [2009] Fam Law 831.

Johnson, 'Shared residence orders: for and against' [2009] Fam Law 131.

Kaganas and Diduck, 'Incomplete citizens: changing images of post-separation children' (2004) 67(6) *Modern Law Review* 959.

Further reading and references cont'd

Kaganas and Piper, 'Shared Parenting – A 70% solution?' [2002] CFLQ 365.

Kaganas, '*Re L (Contact: Domestic Violence); Re V (Contact: Domestic Violence); Re M (Contact: Domestic Violence); Re H (Contact: Domestic Violence)*: Contact and domestic violence' [2000] CFLQ 311.

Masson, 'Thinking about contact – A social or legal problem?' [2000] CFLQ 15.

Murch with Keehan, *The Voice of the Child in Private Family Law Proceedings*, 2003, Family Law.

Perry, '*Payne* v. *Payne* – leave to remove from the jurisdiction' [2001] CFLQ 455.

Pressdee, 'Relocation, relocation, relocation; rigorous scrutiny revisited' [2008] Fam Law 220.

Prest, 'The right to respect for family life: obligations of the state in private law children cases' [2005] Fam Law 124.

Reece, 'UK women's groups' child contact campaign: "so long as it is safe" ' [2006] CFLQ 538.

Relocation and Leave to Remove, A Report by Custody Minefield (www.thecustodyminefield.com) (with a Foreword by Sir Bob Geldof), December 2009.

Smart and May, 'Residence and contact disputes in court' [2004] Fam Law 36.

Spon-Smith, 'Relocation revisited' [2004] Fam Law 191.

Van Krieken, 'The "best interests of the child" and parental separation: on the "civilising of parents" ' (2005) 68(1) *Modern Law Review* 25.

Wall J, 'Making contact' [2003] Fam Law 275.

Wall LJ, 'Making contact work in 2009' [2009] Fam Law 590.

Wall, LJ, 'Enforcement of contact orders' [2005] Fam Law 26.

Worwood, 'International relocation – the debate' [2005] Fam Law 621.

Websites

Association for Shared Parenting: www.sharedparenting.org.uk

Cafcass: www.cafcass.gov.uk

Families Need Fathers: www.fnf.org.uk

Family and Parenting Institute: www.familyandparenting.org

HM Courts' Service: www.hmcourtsservice.gov.uk

National Association of Child Contact Centres: www.nacc.org.uk

National Youth Advocacy Service: www.nyas.net

Resolution: www.resolution.org.uk

Ministry of Justice: www.justice.gov.uk

Chapter 12

Child support and financial provision and property orders for children

All parents, whatever their status, have a duty to provide financial support for their children, and this obligation continues when parental relationships break down and when parents live apart.

Financial provision for children is usually in the form of maintenance (child support maintenance) (see below), but the family courts also have power to make lump sum and property orders for the benefit of a child (see 12.4 and 12.5).

12.1 Child maintenance

(a) Introduction

Parents have the following options available to them when considering child maintenance (see Child Maintenance Options, www.cmoptions.org):

(i) A private agreement about maintenance Parents can make their own private agreement about child maintenance whether or not they have arranged child support through the Child Maintenance and Enforcement Commission/Child Support Agency (CSA). The advantages of a private agreement are that it empowers the parties

and is quicker and cheaper than going to court; and is likely to lead to less bitterness between the parents. The disadvantage, however, is that, as the agreement is not legally binding, enforcement may be a problem and so may varying the agreement when circumstances change.

(ii) An application to the Child Maintenance and Enforcement Commission/CSA The advantages of this option (see further below) are that: the applicant does not have to be in contact with the other parent, or even know where he or she lives; the Commission/CSA can trace a parent who refuses to pay child maintenance; and, as a Commission/CSA maintenance arrangement is legally binding, the Commission/CSA can use its enforcement powers to enforce payment.

(iii) A consent order A parental agreement about child maintenance can be incorporated into a court order known as a consent order (see p. 183), whether or not parents have already arranged child maintenance through the Commission/CSA. The advantage of a consent order is that the court can, if needed, enforce payment (for example, by taking money directly from the payee's earnings or ordering the payee to sell property to make payment). If parents wish, they can, 12 months after the consent order has been made, apply to the Commission/CSA for a maintenance arrangement (which will have the effect of cancelling the consent order).

(iv) A court order for child maintenance In certain statutorily defined circumstances a parent can apply to the court for maintenance (for instance for school fees, or where the child is disabled) (see 12.4 and 12.5).

12.2 Child support maintenance – the Government's scheme

(a) Changes to the scheme

During 2008 radical changes were made to the child maintenance scheme by the Child Maintenance and Other Payments Act 2008 (which amended the Child Support Act 1991). Some of these changes are in force, but the new scheme is not expected to be fully implemented until 2013. Enhanced enforcement powers (see p. 329) are being introduced through 2009–10 and a new formula based on gross income (see p. 328) will be introduced from 2011. The Child Support Agency (the government's agency which deals with child maintenance) will eventually be replaced by the Child Maintenance and Enforcement Commission. To keep track of the changes reference should be made to the Child Maintenance and Enforcement Commission's website: www.childmaintenance.org.

Under the new scheme there is a greater emphasis on parents being encouraged to make their own private agreements about child maintenance and stronger enforcement measures have been introduced against parents who fail to pay.

Since October 2008, parents on benefit are no longer compulsorily required to seek child maintenance through the Commission/CSA. They can, if they wish, make their own private maintenance arrangements. The benefit disregard level has also been increased. Thus, parents with the main day-to-day care who are claiming benefits can now keep up to £20 per week of any child maintenance payments before it affects their benefits.

(b) The background to the child support scheme

Before 5 April 1993 (when the child maintenance scheme came into force) disputes about child maintenance were heard by the courts, which had wide discretionary powers to make maintenance orders for children according to the circumstances of each case. However, in 1990, as a result of dissatisfaction with the court-based system, the Government published a White Paper, *Children Come First* (Cm 1264), in which it made proposals for introducing a radically new child maintenance system which would be run by a Government agency (the Child Support Agency). The Government's case for reform was based on various arguments. One was that the discretion-based court system was causing arbitrary and unpredictable awards of child maintenance to be awarded. Another was that the court system was 'unnecessarily fragmented, uncertain in its results, slow and ineffective' (para. 2, *Children Come First*). A further argument in favour of reform was that many fathers were failing to fulfil their maintenance obligations to their children, and the cost of this was being thrown onto the State, and consequently onto the taxpayer. The Government also claimed that the welfare needs of children were not being sufficiently protected.

The Government therefore proposed to introduce a new child maintenance system based on those in Australia and the USA. It claimed that this new system would: enforce parental support obligations effectively, cheaply and quickly; introduce certainty and predictability; reduce the potential for inter-parental conflict; and reduce dependency on social security and reduce the cost to the taxpayer. The proposals were rapidly passed into law by the Child Support Act 1991, which was based, according to the Government, on a recognition that children have a right to be maintained, and that parents, not the State, have a responsibility to maintain them. The 1991 Act made three radical changes. It transferred the task of assessing, reviewing, collecting and enforcing child maintenance from the courts into a new Government body, the Child Support Agency. It prohibited the courts from making maintenance orders for children in any case where the Child Support Agency had jurisdiction to make a maintenance assessment; and it introduced a formula for calculating child maintenance.

(i) Reaction to the new scheme   Despite receiving all-party support, the scheme provoked immediate and intense hostility. The formula for calculating maintenance was considered to be too complex and too difficult to understand. The scheme was perceived by many fathers to be unjust and grossly unfair because they claimed they were being required to pay much higher levels of maintenance than under the court-based scheme. Step-fathers also felt aggrieved, as they claimed that the amounts of maintenance they were required to pay under the new scheme made it difficult for them to support their new families. Some fathers also thought the new system was unfair, because Agency assessments failed to take account of 'clean break' arrangements that had been made on divorce before the new scheme came into force.

(ii) Amendments to the scheme ('departures' or 'variations')   Because of dissatisfaction with the new scheme, minor changes were made to the formula for calculating maintenance (in February 1994); and, in April 1995, after the publication of a White Paper, *Improving Child Support* (Cm. 2745), a 'departures' system was introduced by the Child Support Act 1995 whereby the Agency was given power to depart from the formula where an

assessment had produced unfair results. (This later became known as 'variations', see p. 328 below.) These reforms, which modified rather than radically altered the scheme, did not, however, staunch the flow of criticism. Dissatisfaction with the formula continued to be voiced and there was also concern about delays, errors of calculation and difficulties enforcing payment.

(iii) Continuing dissatisfaction   Because of continuing dissatisfaction with the scheme, the Labour Government published a consultation paper in 1998 (*Children First: A New Approach to Child Support*, Cm 3992), followed by a White Paper in 1999 (*A New Contract for Welfare: Children's Rights and Parents' Responsibilities*, Cm 4349) in which it proposed to simplify and speed up the calculation of child support.

In the White Paper the Government acknowledged that the child support system had failed to improve the position of children. It acknowledged that parents found the system difficult to understand, that the scheme was prone to errors, and that it needed constant amendment to keep up with changes to welfare benefit levels. It therefore proposed that the system be replaced with 'a simple and more deliverable system focused on the needs of children and good, responsible parents' (Introduction, para. 9). These changes (which came into force in March 2003) were introduced by way of amendment to the Child Support Act 1991 by the Child Support, Pensions and Social Security Act 2000. The most radical change was the simplification of the formula in order to make it easier for parents to understand and easier and quicker for the Agency to administer.

(iv) Problems continue   Despite the changes which had been made over the years, the child support system continued to have problems (in particular in respect of enforcement and delays in making assessment) and it was the subject of much criticism, for instance by Resolution (the organisation of family lawyers) which recommended that the courts' jurisdiction should be re-established in cases where the court was already dealing with ancillary relief on divorce. In sum, it was recognised by judges, lawyers and politicians that there had been a catalogue of failures by the CSA and that the system had failed many children. Non-resident parents were refusing to pay maintenance and the CSA was failing to enforce payment. By July 2006, £3 billion was owed in unpaid child support. There had also been errors in maintenance calculations (in July 1997, the National Audit Office found that estimated bills sent to fathers were wrong in eight out of ten cases). In 2003, a new £456 million computer system was introduced but that also had major problems. There were also long delays in dealing with cases (by July 2006, the CSA had a backlog of 300,000 cases).

As a result of this catalogue of failings, the Government made proposals to completely reform the child support system; and in February 2006 it commissioned Sir David Henshaw to investigate the scheme and make suggestions for reform. In his report (*Recovering Child Support: Routes to Responsibility*, Cm 6894, Department for Work and Pensions, 2006) Sir David Henshaw identified major failings in the child support system and recommended that it should be replaced with a completely new system, where the emphasis would be on parents making private maintenance agreements and where difficult cases would be dealt with by a new body with tougher enforcement powers.

In July 2006 the Government's response to the Henshaw Report was presented to Parliament (*A Fresh Start: Child Support Redesign*, Cm 6895, Department for Work and Pensions). This was followed in December 2006 by a White Paper (*A New System of Child*

Maintenance, Cm 6979, Department for Work and Pensions) setting out a new child support system which would empower parents to take responsibility for making their own maintenance agreements but with radically strengthened enforcement powers in cases of non-compliance. It also proposed joint birth registration to encourage more fathers to pay maintenance, something which had been recommended in the *Henshaw Report*.

(c)   The Child Maintenance and Other Payments Act 2008

The above proposals resulted in the enactment of the Child Maintenance and Other Payments Act 2008 (CMOPA 2008), Parts 1–3 of which amended the Child Support Act 1991 to create a radically new scheme. The main aims of the new scheme are: to place a greater emphasis on encouraging parents to make their own child maintenance agreements; to strengthen collection and enforcement procedures; and to simplify the formula and improve the assessment process. The Commission's overarching objective is to increase the number of effective child maintenance arrangements and to reduce the maintenance owed by thousands of non-resident parents. The scheme is part of the Government's aim to reduce, and eventually eradicate, child poverty.

In respect of assessment, the new scheme places greater reliance on historic income tax data. The Act also introduces a new formula (based on the non-resident parent's gross income in the previous tax year), and which is due to come into force in 2011.

(i) The Child Maintenance and Enforcement Commission   The 2008 Act establishes a new body, the Child Maintenance and Enforcement Commission, which has statutory responsibility for the scheme currently operated by the CSA (see 12.3); but which will eventually take over the CSA completely. The Commission has three core functions: to promote the financial responsibility that parents have for their children; to provide information and support on the different child maintenance options available; and to provide an efficient statutory maintenance service, with effective enforcement.

The Commission's primary objective is to maximise the number of effective child maintenance arrangements (whether organised privately or through the statutory schemes) for children who live apart from one or both of their parents (s.2(1) CMOPA 2008). This main objective is supported by two subsidiary objectives (s.2(2)): to encourage and support parents in making and keeping appropriate voluntary maintenance arrangements for their children; and to support child support applications made under the Child Support Act 1991 and to secure compliance. The Commission has a duty to take such steps 'as it thinks appropriate' so as to 'raise awareness among parents' of the importance of taking responsibility for maintenance and making appropriate arrangements (s.4).It also has a duty to provide information and guidance services, with a view to encouraging parents to enter into effective maintenance arrangements (s. 5). The Commission can charge for its services (s.6).

(ii) The new system – what are the concerns?   A major concern relates to the new emphasis on encouraging parents to make their own maintenance agreements. Not only is it difficult to see why parents should suddenly start making agreements about child maintenance when one of the main reasons for establishing the CSA in the first place was because many parents were failing to make agreement, but there is concern about the enforceability and

adequacy of such agreements. Resolution (the organisation of family solicitors) has expressed concern (see [2007] Fam Law 762).

Another concern relates to the more stringent enforcement measures and penalties introduced under the new scheme. They may not be a proportionate response, and for that reason may not be human rights compliant. Also, the allocation of enforcement measures to the Commission, not the courts, may be a threat to the due process of law. The stronger enforcement measures may also act as a disincentive for some non-resident parents to seek work, or to continue to work.

12.3 The Child Support Agency (Child Maintenance and Enforcement Commission)

(a) Introduction

The Child Support Agency (CSA) is currently responsible for making child maintenance arrangements under the auspices of the Child Maintenance and Enforcement Commission (see above); but its powers are in the process of being changed and its functions will eventually be transferred to the Commission (in 2011, according to the Government). The CSA has powers and duties under the Child Support Act 1991 (as amended), and in regulations, to calculate and review child maintenance, and to collect and enforce payment.

(i) An outline of the scheme   An application to the CSA can be made by any parent (whether or not on welfare benefits), and certain other persons, provided:

- the child is under 16 (or over 16 but under 19 and in full-time education (not higher than A-level or its equivalent)) (see s.55);
- the applicant (parent or other person) has the main day-to-day care of the child and lives in the UK, and the parent without the main day-to-day care lives in the UK, or works in the civil service, the armed forces or for a UK-based company (see s.44); and
- no court order is in place from before April 2003, or there is a court order from after April 2003 but it was set up more than 12 months before the application.

The CSA calculates the amount of maintenance to be paid by using a formula (see over); and can take steps to enforce payment (see p. 328). The CSA does not charge for its services. Most CSA decisions are non-discretionary, but when exercising any discretionary power (such as whether to pursue child support against a parent on benefit), decision-makers must take account of the welfare of any child likely to be affected (s.2).

(ii) Applicants   The parent who has the main day-to-day care of the child (the parent with care, the PWC), or the non-resident parent (the NRP) can apply for a maintenance calculation and either party can apply for collection and enforcement (see s.4). Parents are free to make their own maintenance agreements or have their agreement incorporated into a consent order (see p. 183), but any provision in the agreement or order purporting to restrict an application to the CSA is void (s.9). The court has the power to direct a scientific test to establish parentage (see 9.2), and voluntary DNA testing is also available from the CSA.

(b)   Calculating child support maintenance – the formula

A maintenance calculation by the CSA is based on the non-resident parent's (NRP's) net income (income after National Insurance, tax and pension contributions have been deducted), or benefit status. The amount of child maintenance depends on: the number of children who qualify for child maintenance; the NRP's income and circumstances; and the number of any relevant 'other children' living with the NRP.

(i) Child support rates   Different rates are used for calculating child maintenance, which depend on the payer's income. In most cases the basic rate applies. Special rules apply in special cases (for example, if care of a child is shared). There is a maximum amount of net weekly income that can be taken into account when making an assessment; but the PWC can apply to the court (see 12.4 and 12.5) for 'top-up' maintenance if the NRP's net weekly income exceeds this amount. 'Top up' maintenance granted by the court can be collected by the CSA.

The four rates used for calculating child support maintenance are:

The Basic Rate applies if the NRP's net weekly income is at least £200. The NRP pays the following percentage of net weekly income as child support: 15 per cent for one child; 20 per cent for two children; and 25 per cent for three or more children.

The Reduced Rate applies if the NRP's net weekly income is more than £100 but less than £200. The NRP pays a flat rate of £5 a week on the first £100 of net income, plus a percentage of net weekly income over £100 of: 25 per cent for one child; 35 per cent for two children; and 45 per cent for three or more children.

The Flat Rate applies if the NRP's net weekly income is between £5 and £100 or he/she (or his/her partner) is in receipt of certain prescribed benefits. If the NRP has a partner, the NRP pays half the flat rate (£2.50 a week). If both members of a couple (in receipt of Income Support or Jobseeker's Allowance) are NRPs and both have a child, then they each pay child maintenance at a flat rate of £2.50.

The Nil Rate of liability applies to some NRPs, such as: persons with a net weekly income of less than £5; students in full-time education; persons under 16; persons in prison; and persons living in a care home or independent hospital and receiving help with the fees.

Where the information needed to calculate child maintenance cannot be obtained straight away, a *default rate* applies (currently £30 per week for one child, £40 for two children, and £50 for three or more children).

(ii) Deductions for relevant 'other children'   Less child maintenance is paid by the NRP where there are relevant 'other children' living with the NRP (for example, step-children or the NRP's children from a new relationship). In such cases, a lower amount of net weekly income is used for calculating maintenance. Thus, the NRP's income is reduced by: 15 per cent if there is one relevant other child; 20 per cent if there are two; and 25 per cent if there are three or more.

(iii) Shared care   Where the care of a child is shared by both parents for 52 or more nights a year, a discount is made when calculating the basic or reduced rate of maintenance.

(iv) Variations from the formula   Variations from the formula (upwards or downwards) are permitted in certain clearly defined circumstances (see Sched. 4B, Part 1), such as for special expenses incurred by a NRP (e.g. contact costs, looking after a disabled relevant other child, boarding school fees, and some prior debts). A variation upwards may be permitted on the application of a PWC if the amount of child maintenance does not property reflect the NRP's true circumstances (for instance, the NRP has a lifestyle which is inconsistent with the level of income which has been (or would be) used for the maintenance calculation). A variation application can be made at any time.

(v) Changes to the formula   The Child Maintenance and Other Payments Act 2008 makes important changes to the formula for calculating child support. This new formula is expected to come into force in 2011.

The new formula will be based on the NRP's gross, not net, income; and the Commission will have a new power to obtain income data from HM Revenue and Customs' tax records, instead of from the NRP (in order to obtain a more reliable figure and more quickly). As the formula will be based on gross income, under the basic rate (see above) the NRP will liable to pay 12 per cent of weekly gross income (for 1 child), 16 per cent (for 2 children) or 19 per cent (for 3 or more children). If the NRP's weekly gross income exceeds £800, then those rates will be applied only to the first £800 and the lower rates of 9, 12 or 15 per cent will be applied to the excess amount over that figure. The flat rate (see above) will be increased from £5 to £7 per week. In respect of shared care arrangements no changes are proposed, except that future shared care, not just past care, arrangements will be taken into account.

Another change will be the introduction of fixed annual awards of child maintenance, so that a change of circumstances (for example, a change in the NRP's income) will not take effect in the year in question, but prospectively, following an annual review. This will not apply, however, where, for example, there has been a major change in income or some other fundamental change of circumstance.

(c)   Child support maintenance: appeals, collection and enforcement

(i) Appeals   An appeal can be made to the Child Support Appeal Tribunal (s.20). Appeals on matters of law can be taken to the Child Support Commissioner (s.24), from whom there is a further right of appeal on a question of law to the Court of Appeal (s.25).

(ii) Collection of child support maintenance   The CSA provides a collection service for the payment of child maintenance. It will usually give the NRP the choice of paying by direct debit or standing order, or by a voluntary deduction from earnings order; and will stipulate the intervals when payment is to be made (s.29). The CSA can direct the NRP to try to open a bank or building society account for the purpose of making payment easier.

(iii) Enforcement   Enforcement of child maintenance has been one of the major difficulties of the child support system, and for this reason new more stringent enforcement

provisions are being introduced by the Child Maintenance and Other Payments Act 2008 (see below). The following enforcement measures are currently available when a NRP fails to pay child support, or sufficient child support:

- *A deduction from earnings order (s.31)* If a NRP is in employment or in receipt of an occupational pension, the CSA can make a deduction from earnings order whereby the NRP's employer is instructed to make deductions of maintenance from the payer's earnings or pension and send them to the CSA's bank; and when it has cleared it is sent to the PWC. There is a limited right of appeal to the magistrates' court (s.32). An employer who fails to comply with the duties laid down by the CSA 1991 commits a criminal offence (ss.14A and 15).

- *A deduction order (see ss.32A–32F)* Since August 2009 the Commission/CSA has had the power to make regular deduction orders and lump sum deduction orders where a liable person has failed to make payment. A regular deduction order (s.32A) orders the deduction of regular payments of child maintenance from a deposit or other account (held by the defaulter) (for example a bank or a building society account). The order may be made in relation to past and/or future liabilities. A lump sum deduction order (ss.32E and 32F) requires a deposit-taker of a deposit or savings account held by the defaulter to pay the Commission/CSA any outstanding arrears of child maintenance. This involves a two-stage process: an interim order (to enable representations to be made); followed by a final order. An appeal lies to a court against the order, but the court has no power to challenge the actual maintenance assessment (s.32J).

- *A liability order (s.33)* If it is inappropriate to make a deduction from earnings order, or if that order is ineffective, the Commission/CSA can apply to the magistrates' court for a liability order for the unpaid child maintenance. Once the order is made, the Commission/CSA can take various steps to ensure payment, for example: sale and seizure of the NRP's goods by a bailiff; obtaining a county court third-party debt order freezing the funds in the NRP's bank or building society; or by charging and selling the NPR's property to make payment. The Commission/CSA can enter a liability order on the Register of Judgments, Orders and Fines, which reference agencies can use when setting a person's credit rating (which can affect the NRP's ability to obtain finance, such as a loan, mortgage or credit card). The magistrates' court has no power to challenge the actual assessment (see s.33(4); and *Farley* v. *Secretary of State for Work and Pensions* [2006] UKHL 31, [2006] 2 FLR 1243; and *Child Support Agency* v. *Learad; Child Support Agency* v. *Buddles* [2008] EWHC 2193 (Admin), [2009] 1 FLR 31).

- *Other measures: removal of driving licences and imprisonment* If the above enforcement measures fail, more severe measures can be imposed. Thus the Commission/CSA can apply to the magistrates' court for an order removing the NRP's driving licence for up to two years (or preventing the NRP from obtaining one) where there is wilful refusal or culpable neglect in respect of paying child maintenance (ss.39A and 40B). In the last resort, a defaulting NRP may be committed to prison, on proof of wilful refusal or culpable neglect to make payment (s.40).

(iv) Proposed new enforcement provisions New provisions have been inserted into the Child Support Act 1991 (by the Child Maintenance and Other Payments Act 2008) to create new

more stringent enforcement provisions. These provisions are not currently in force. Thus, the Commission/CSA will have the following powers:

▷ To make a **deduction from earnings order** (s.28, as amended) as the standard collection method where a person liable to pay child maintenance is in employment or is in receipt of an occupational pension.
▷ To make an **administrative liability order** (s.32M) whenever it is satisfied that a person has failed to pay an amount of child support maintenance. This will replace the current system of liability orders which are made by the magistrates' court (see above).
▷ To apply to the High Court for an **avoidance prevention order** (s.32L), restraining a person who is liable to pay child support from disposing of his/her assets by transferring them out of the UK or otherwise dealing with them with the intention of avoiding paying child support. The Commission/CSA will also be able to apply for an order setting aside a disposition after it has been made if the intention in doing so was to avoid payment of child support. This provision will help reverse the position adopted in *Department of Social Security* v. *Butler* [1995] 1 WLR 1528, [1996] 1 FLR 65 where the Court of Appeal had held that it was not open to the CSA to apply for a 'freezing order' freezing a liable parent's assets.
▷ To seek **recovery from the estate of a deceased person** who has died owing arrears of child support (s.43A).
▷ To apply to the magistrates' court for a **travel authorisation disqualification order** (in other words to confiscate a UK passport) (ss.39B–39G). This application can be made only if all other enforcement actions have been taken, and failed, and only if there is wilful refusal or culpable neglect on the part of the defaulter.
▷ To apply to the magistrates' court for **a curfew order** (s.39H–39Q) against a defaulting NRP, provided the same conditions which apply to a travel authorisation disqualification order are satisfied (see above), and appropriate monitoring arrangements are in place.
▷ To apply to the magistrates' court for a **power to search** (s.39L).

The Government has reserved the right to revisit the new provisions above at a later date. Provisions in the Welfare Reform Act 2009 give the Commission/CSA the power, in the last resort, to bypass the courts and order defaulters to give up their driving licence and/or passport until they have met their obligation to pay child support. Resolution (the group of family lawyers) is strongly against this proposal. In November 2009 the Government announced that the Commission is to be given surveillance powers by the Home Office to track certain parents who fail to pay child support, in other words where there is criminal behaviour (such as fraud and deception) on the part of a parent.

(d) Actions by parents against the commission/child support agency

(i) Parents cannot institute court proceedings to enforce payment In the following case the House of Lords held that parents cannot take steps to enforce payment of child maintenance by seeking an order from the court:

▶ *R (On the Application of Kehoe)* v. *Secretary of State for Work and Pensions* **[2005] UKHL 48, [2005] 2 FLR 1249**

The NRP father failed to make payments of child maintenance to the mother. Various enforcement measures were taken by the CSA, but these failed. The mother brought judicial review proceedings seeking a declaration of incompatibility under s.4(2) of the Human Rights Act 1998 on the basis that the enforcement provisions of the CSA 1991 were incompatible with her right to a fair trial under art. 6 ECHR, as they precluded a parent from bringing enforcement proceedings in the court in her own name or on behalf of her children. She also sought a declaration that the delay by the Agency constituted a breach of her art. 6 rights; and she claimed damages under s.7 HRA 1998. Her claim failed at first instance and before the Court of Appeal; and so she appealed to the House of Lords.

The House of Lords dismissed her appeal (Baroness Hale dissenting) and held that the provisions in the CSA 1991 preventing her from enforcing her entitlement to child support were not incompatible with art. 6(1) ECHR. The claimant had no substantive right in domestic law which was capable in Convention law of engaging the guarantees that were afforded with regard to 'civil rights and obligations' by art. 6(1). Enforcement was exclusively a matter for the Agency. As art. 6(1) was not engaged, the Agency could not be said to have acted unlawfully within the meaning of s.7 HRA 1998; and accordingly the claimant had no remedy under that Act.

BARONESS HALE (dissenting): '[I]f I am right that the children's civil rights to be properly maintained by their parents are engaged, it follows that the public authority which is charged by Parliament with securing the determination and enforcement of their rights is under a duty to act compatibly with their art. 6 right to the speedy determination and effective enforcement of those rights. … Just as the courts, as public authorities, have to act compliantly with the Convention rights, so does the Agency.'

Note The mother took her case to the European Court of Human Rights (see *Kehoe* v. *United Kingdom (Application No 2010/06)* [2008] ECHR 528, [2008] 2 FLR 1014) but her claim was unanimously dismissed as there had been no breach of art. 6 ECHR (the right to a fair trial).

Sir David Henshaw in his report (see p. 324 above) suggested that the effects of *Kehoe* might be reversed, thereby ending the monopoly of the Agency in respect of enforcement, but this suggestion has not been implemented as part of the child support reforms.

(ii) Making a complaint Any person who is dissatisfied with the service provided by the Commission/CSA can make a complaint to the Commission/CSA. If still not satisfied, a complainant can write to the Independent Case Examiner, who has a duty to investigate the complaint (but not if it involves a matter of law). A complaint can also be made to the Ombudsman.

(iii) Bringing an action in negligence against the CSA A negligence claim is unlikely to succeed as the following case (the first negligence case to be brought against the CSA) shows:

▶ *R (Rowley)* v. *Secretary of State for Work and Pensions* **[2007] EWCA Civ 598, [2007] 2 FLR 945**

The mother and her three children sued the CSA in negligence for failure to enforce the child maintenance due. The Court of Appeal held that the action must fail as there was no assumption of responsibility on the part of the Secretary of State; and to impose a duty of care in negligence would not be an incremental development of the law but a massive extension of it. The CSA 1991 provided a set of remedies; and to impose a duty of care in negligence would be inconsistent with the statutory scheme.

Thus, in *Rowley* a similar approach was taken to that in *Kehoe* (above). In other words sufficient remedies were available within the framework of the CSA 1991 and that Act provided a complete code. However, in *Kehoe* Baroness Hale (dissenting) had stated that the case was in reality one about children's rights. The same could be said about the *Rowley* case. In other negligence claims involving children the courts have held that there is a duty of care (see 14.11); but *Rowley* is essentially a policy decision to stop a flood of claims being brought by aggrieved parents and children.

(iv) Bringing a human rights challenge A human rights claim against the Commission/ CSA for failing to enforce payment of child support is also unlikely to succeed as the following case shows:

> ▶ *Treharne* v. *Secretary of State for Work and Pensions* **[2008] EWHC 3222 (QB), [2009] 1 FLR 853**
>
> The applicants were adults who had been denied child maintenance owed to them during their minority, because of failures on the part of the CSA to take steps to enforce payment. They argued that the CSA's maladministration had violated their right to family life under art. 8 of the European Convention for the Protection of Human Rights (see 1.7); and they sought damages. Their claim failed.
>
> Cranston J, dismissing their appeal, held that the failure of the CSA to function effectively and to enforce the maintenance assessments could not found a claim for damages, as art. 8 ECHR did not include an economic right to reasonably regular maintenance from the State.

(e) The Child Support Act 1991 and the role of the courts

The court has jurisdiction to order child maintenance (see s.8) as follows: to 'top up' a maintenance assessment where a maximum assessment is in force (see p. 327 above); for school fees and fees for advanced education or training for a trade, profession or vocation; for a disabled child; for a child who is not a 'qualifying child' under the CSA 1991; when making, varying and enforcing a consent order which embodies child maintenance; when enforcing a parental agreement about child maintenance; where maintenance is required from the PWC; and where the Commission/CSA has no jurisdiction to make a maintenance calculation (for example because the parent is not habitually resident in the UK).

The courts have jurisdiction to make lump sum and property orders for children (see 12.4 and 12.5 below), whether or not an application for child support is made to the Commission/CSA.

12.4 Finance and property orders for children from the courts

(a) Introduction

Applications in respect of finance and property orders for a child can be made to the court under the Domestic Proceedings and Magistrates' Courts Act 1978, Part II of the Matrimonial Causes Act 1973, the Civil Partnership Act 2004 and Schedule 1 to the Children Act 1989.

Applications can only be made for child maintenance where the Commission/CSA has no jurisdiction to deal with such arrangements (see above). However, the new child maintenance provisions place greater emphasis on parents making their own private arrangements about child maintenance, including the right to apply to the court for a consent order containing an agreement about child maintenance provision.

Applications can also be made to the court for lump sum (capital) orders and property orders to or for the benefit of a child. However, because of the legal costs involved in bringing such claims, and the need for sufficient resources available against which orders can be made, such applications usually involve parties who have substantial sums of money available for distribution. For this reason, the reported case-law usually deals with 'big money' cases (see, for example, *Re C (Financial Provision)* [2007] 2 FLR 13, where capital provision of £2 million was ordered for a child).

(b) Orders for children on divorce and dissolution of a civil partnership

Under Part II of the Matrimonial Causes Act 1973 the divorce court can make periodical payments orders (maintenance) and lump sum orders to or for the benefit of a child of the family in proceedings for divorce (annulment or judicial separation) (s.23). A 'child of the family' includes the parents' own child, any step-child and a privately fostered child (but not a child in local authority care). The divorce court can also make the following property orders to or for the benefit of a child of the family (s.24): a transfer of property order; a settlement of property order; an order varying an ante-nuptial agreement; a post-nuptial settlement for the benefit of the child; and an order for the sale of property (s.24A). (For more on the divorce court's powers, see Chapter 7).

The above orders can be made to or for the benefit of (s.29): a child under 18; and a child over 18 who is, will be, or would be (if an order were made) receiving instruction at an educational establishment or undergoing training for a trade, profession or vocation, or where special circumstances justify an order being made.

When exercising its discretion the court must consider all the circumstances of the case, including in particular (s.25(3)): the child's financial needs, income, earning capacity (if any), property and other financial resources; any physical or mental disability of the child; and the manner in which the child is expected to be educated or trained. It must also take into account factors (a)–(d) of the statutory checklist in s.25(2) of the Matrimonial Causes Act 1973 (see 7.4).

Where the court is exercising its powers against a spouse in favour of a child of the family who is not that person's child (such as a step-child) the court must also consider (s.25(4)): whether that spouse assumed any responsibility for child maintenance, and, if so, the extent to which, and the basis upon which, he or she assumed such responsibility and the length of time for which that party discharged such responsibility; whether in assuming and discharging such responsibility that party did so knowing that the child was not his or her own; and the liability of any other person to maintain the child.

Similar provisions apply in respect of the dissolution (annulment or separation) of a civil partnership (see s.72(1) and Sched. 1 to the Civil Partnership Act 2004).

Consent orders   Spouses (and civil partners) can apply for a consent order in respect of financial arrangements for their children (including child support maintenance), which the court has jurisdiction to make under the legislation above. A consent order is a private agreement about financial provision and / or property arrangements for the parties and/or their children which is considered by the court and made into a court order (see further at p. 183). The advantage of a consent order is that (unlike a private arrangement about financial provision for a child) it can be enforced by the court if breached.

(c) Orders for children during a marriage or civil partnership

Orders can be sought from the magistrates' family proceedings court, or the county court. These provisions are rarely invoked, however, because child maintenance in most cases must be sought from the Commission/CSA (see 12.3 above), and, in any event, it is rare for married couples (and civil partners) to seek such orders during the subsistence of their relationship.

(i) In the family proceedings court   Under the Domestic Proceedings and Magistrates' Courts Act 1978 magistrates' family proceedings courts can make periodical payments orders and lump sum orders for parties to a marriage and children of the family. Lump sums are limited to a maximum sum (s.2(3)).

An application can be brought by either spouse on the grounds that the other spouse (s.1): (a) has failed to provide reasonable maintenance for the applicant; (b) has failed to provide, or to make a proper contribution towards, reasonable maintenance for any child of the family; (c) has behaved in such a way that the applicant cannot reasonably be expected to live with the applicant; or (d) has deserted the applicant.

The statutory criteria which the court must apply when exercising its discretion are similar to those in s.25 Matrimonial Causes Act 1973 which must be applied by the divorce court in proceedings for ancillary relief (see 7.4), but with the additional requirement that the magistrates must also consider whether to exercise any of their powers under the Children Act 1989 (s.8) (see Chapter 10).

Similar provisions apply to civil partnerships under s.72(3) and Sched. 6 to the Civil Partnership Act 2004.

(ii) In the county court   Under s.27 of the Matrimonial Causes Act 1973 either spouse can apply to the county court for reasonable maintenance (periodical payments and lump sums) on the ground that the other spouse has: (a) failed to provide reasonable maintenance for the applicant; or (b) has failed to provide, or to make a proper contribution towards, reasonable maintenance for any child of the family (s.27(1)). The statutory criteria under s.25 which apply to applications for ancillary relief on divorce must be applied (see 7.4).

Similar provisions apply to civil partnerships under s.72(1) and Sched. 5 to the Civil Partnership Act 2004.

12.5 Finance and property orders for children under the Children Act 1989

Under s.15 and paras. 1 and 2 of Schedule 1 to the Children Act 1989 magistrates' family proceedings courts, county courts and the High Court can make periodical payments orders, lump sum orders and property orders to or for the benefit of children aged under 18, and for some 'children' aged over 18. The court can make these orders only on an application, unless it is making, varying or discharging a residence order (para. 1(6)), or the child is a ward of court (para. 1(7)), when it can make any of these orders of its own motion.

Importance of Schedule 1 for cohabiting couples and their children   Schedule 1 is particularly important for cohabitants because, unlike married couples and civil partners, it is the only jurisdiction of the courts open to them if they wish to make applications about property and/or finance for the benefit of their children on family breakdown.

(a)   Orders under paragraph 1

On an application by a parent, guardian or special guardian of a child, or by any person in whose favour a residence order is in force with respect to a child, the court may make any of the following orders against either or both parents of a child (including a step-parent) (paras. 1(1), (2)):

- a periodical payments order;
- a lump sum order, provided that such an order may be made to enable expenses in connection with the birth or maintenance of the child, which were reasonably incurred before the making of the order, to be met (Sched. 1, para. 5(1));
- a settlement of property order;
- a transfer of property order.

These orders can be made in favour of the applicant for the benefit of the child, or in favour of the child – except for a settlement of property order, which can only be made for the benefit of the child. The High Court and the county court can make any of these orders (para. 1(1)(a)), but the powers of magistrates in the family proceedings court are limited (see over). The powers conferred under para. 1 may be exercised at any time (para. 1(3)). Periodical payment orders can be varied and discharged (see over). The court can make further periodical payments orders and lump sum orders with respect to a child who has not reached the age of 18, but it cannot make more than one settlement of property order and more than one transfer of property order (para. 1(5)). This is so, even though para. 1(3) provides that the power to make such orders can be 'exercised at any time' (see *Phillips* v. *Peace* [2004] EWHC 3180 (Fam), [2005] 2 FLR 1212).

(b)   Orders under paragraph 2

The court may make periodical payments orders and lump sum orders for a child aged over 18 against one or both parents (but not against a step-parent or foster-parent, para. 16). The court can make these orders on the application of a child aged over 18 who is, will be, or (if an order were made) would be receiving instruction at an educational establishment or undergoing training for a trade, profession or vocation (whether or not while in gainful employment). The court can also make an order where special circumstances exist. An application under para. 2 cannot be made by any person if immediately before the child reached the age of 16, a periodical payments order was in force with respect to the child (para. 2(3)). No order can be made under para. 2 if the applicant's parents are living with each other in the same household (para. 2(4)).

(c) Variation and discharge of periodical payments

Periodical payments orders made under Sched. 1 can be varied or discharged on the application of any person by or to whom payments were required to be made (paras. 1(4) and 2(5)). In exercising its powers of variation or discharge, the court must have regard to all the circumstances of the case, including any change in any of the matters to which the court was to have regard when making the order (para. 6(1)).

(d) Limits on the magistrates' jurisdiction

The magistrates in the family proceedings court cannot order the transfer and settlement of property and can make only unsecured, not secured, periodical payments orders. They can make lump sum orders up to a maximum of £1,000. County courts and the High Court, on the other hand, can make the whole range of orders.

(e) Agreements about maintenance

Under para. 10(3) of Schedule 1 the court has jurisdiction to alter the terms of an agreement about maintenance where it appears just to do so having regard to all the circumstances in cases: where there has been a change of circumstances; or where the agreement does not contain proper financial arrangements with respect to the child. In *Morgan* v. *Hill* [2006] EWCA Civ 1602, [2007] 1 FLR 1480 the Court of Appeal held that it was not necessary to demonstrate that such an agreement was massively inadequate in order to obtain a judicial award greater than the agreed settlement.

(f) The exercise of judicial discretion in Schedule 1 proceedings

Each case depends on it own facts, but when deciding whether to exercise its powers to make orders under paras. 1 and 2, and if so in what manner, the court must have regard to all the circumstances, including the following (see para. 4(1)):

'(a) the income, earning capacity, property and other financial resources which the applicant, parents and the person in whose favour the order would be made has, or is likely to have, in the foreseeable future;
(b) the financial needs, obligations and responsibilities which the persons named in (a) have or are likely to have in the foreseeable future;
(c) the financial needs of the child;
(d) the income, earning capacity (if any), property and other financial resources of the child;
(e) any physical or mental disability of the child; and
(f) the manner in which the child is being, or is expected to be, educated or trained.'

Where the court is exercising its powers under para. 1 against a person who is not the child's mother or father (such as in the case of a step-child), the court must also consider (para. 4(2)):

'(a) whether that person has assumed responsibility for the child's maintenance and, if so, the extent to which and the basis on which that responsibility was assumed and the length of the period during which he met that responsibility;
(b) whether he did so knowing that the child was not his child;
(c) the liability of any other person to maintain the child.'

(g)   The approach of the courts

The court adopts the following approach in applications under Schedule 1:

(i) The child's welfare   Although para. 4(1) of Sched. 1 does not expressly refer to the child's welfare, and the paramountcy principle in s.1(1) CA 1989 does not apply (see s.105(1) CA 1989), the child's welfare is nonetheless taken into account as part of the court's general duty to have regard to all the circumstances; and the child's welfare is 'a constant influence on the discretionary outcome' (*per* Thorpe LJ in *Re P (Child: Financial Provision)* [2003] EWCA Civ 837, [2003] 2 FLR 865, approving Hale J in *J v. C (Child: Financial Provision)* [1999] 1 FLR 152).

(ii) The 'minimum intervention' principle in s.1(5) Children Act 1989 (see 10.3)   This does not apply to applications under Sched. 1 (*K v. H (Child Maintenance)* [1993] 2 FLR 61).

(iii) The child's standard of living   Although para. 4 of Sched. 1 makes no mention of the child's standard of living as a factor to be taken into account, the court may take it into account in an appropriate case (see *Re P (Child: Financial Provision)* [2003] EWCA Civ 837, [2003] 2 FLR 865 where Thorpe LJ, approving Hale J in *J v. C (Child: Financial Provision)* (above), said that the child was entitled to be brought up in circumstances which bore some sort of relationship to the father's current resources and present standard of living). (See also *F v. G (Child: Financial Provision)* [2004] EWHC 1848 (Fam), [2005] 1 FLR 261).

(iv) The child's entitlement under Schedule 1   The entitlement to financial provision under Sched. 1 arises only during the child's dependency (or until the child has finished full-time education), unless the child's circumstances are special (for example if the child has a disability). For this reason, the court will usually make orders to last only during the child's dependency or until the child has finished full-time education (see, for example, *Kiely v. Kiely* [1988] 1 FLR 248, *T v. S (Financial Provision for Children)* [1994] 2 FLR 883, *A v. A (A Minor: Financial Provision)* [1994] 1 FLR 657, *Re P (Child: Financial Provision)* [2003] EWCA Civ 837, [2003] 2 FLR 865 and *Re S (Unmarried Parents: Financial Provision)* [2006] EWCA Civ 479, [2006] 2 FLR 950). This also applies to the provision of a home for the child (see below).

(v) A home for the child   In respect of the home, the court will usually make a settlement of property order (a '*Mesher* type' property adjustment order, see p. 180) settling the home on the primary carer for the benefit of the child, so that ownership reverts back to the owner at the end of the child's dependency or full-time education. Even if the parent who owns the home is incredibly wealthy, the court will not necessarily order an outright transfer of the home to the other parent (see *A v. A (Financial Provision)* [1994] 1 FLR 657; and *MT v. OT* (Financial Provision: Costs) [2007] EWHC 838 (Fam), [2008] 2 FLR 1311, where the father conceded that he was worth £40 million).

In *T v. S (Financial Provision for Children)* [1994] 2 FLR 883 an order was made that the property revert back to the father when the youngest child reached the age of 21. In *J v. C (Child: Financial Provision)* [1999] 1 FLR 152, where the father had won £1.4 million on the national lottery, Hale J made an order requiring the father to purchase a house for the child to live in with her mother, which would be held on trust for the child's benefit throughout her dependency and revert back to her father when she reached the age of 21 or finished full-time education, whichever was later.

In *Re N (Payments for Benefit of Child)* [2009] EWHC 11 (Fam), [2009] 1 FLR 1442 Munby J held *inter alia* that the district judge had erred in principle in ordering that the home be settled until the child reached 21 or completed tertiary education. Munby J said that the long-established general principle is that, absent special or exceptional circumstances such as disability, children are not entitled to provision under Schedule 1 except during their dependency or for their education. Special or exceptional circumstances apart, dependency ceased at majority.

(vi) Financial provision for the benefit of the child   The courts will guard against claims disguised as being for the benefit of a child when they are really for the benefit of the parent who is caring for the child (*per* Thorpe LJ in *Re P (Child: Financial Provision)*, above approving Hale J in *J v. C (Child: Financial Provision)* [1999] 1 FLR 152).

The word 'benefit' has been given a wide meaning by the courts. In *Re S (Child: Financial Provision)* [2004] EWCA Civ 1685, [2005] 2 FLR 94 the Court of Appeal held that the words 'for the benefit of the child' in Sched. 1 could include the cost of the mother travelling to the Sudan to see her child and to pursue legal proceedings there, even though this might be for the benefit of the mother as well as the child. In *MT v. T* [2006] EWHC 2494 (Fam), [2007] 2 FLR 925 Charles J held that, as the word 'benefit' should be given a wide interpretation, legal costs are not excluded as a matter of jurisdiction under Sched.1, although having that jurisdiction did not mean that is would always be exercised. Here the financial provision order made under Sched. 1 (which included an element for the mother's legal costs) was upheld by Charles J as being clearly for the benefit of the children so that the case could be put before the court fully and properly.

(vii) A broad-brush approach   In *Re P (Child: Financial Provision)* [2003] EWCA Civ 837, [2003] 2 FLR 865 the Court of Appeal held that a broad-brush assessment should be adopted in claims under Sched. 1, but that the starting point is to decide on the home that the respondent should provide for the child. It also held that a broad common-sense assessment of the amount of periodical payments should be taken, but that, in making that assessment, the judge should recognise the responsibility, and often the sacrifice, of the parent who was the primary, or perhaps the exclusive, carer of the child.

12.6   The voice of the child in financial proceedings

Children may be made parties to financial proceedings under Schedule 1 and other financial proceedings (such as under the Matrimonial Causes Act 1973).

In some cases the child can be separately represented by his or her own solicitors. In *Morgan v. Hill* [2006] EWCA Civ 1602, [2007] 1 FLR 1480 Thorpe LJ said that in exceptional cases brought under Schedule 1 the court should consider separate representation of the child. In *Re S (Unmarried Parents: Financial Provisions)* [2006] EWCA Civ 479, [2006] 2 FLR 950 Thorpe LJ said that the facts in *Re S* provided, in his opinion, 'a neat illustration of the advantages of ensuring separate representation for the child in some cases brought under s.15 of the Children Act 1989'. Here the child's father and mother were engaged in an intense and bitter battle and Thorpe LJ said that it was easy to see how in such circumstances 'the crux of the case can be lost to view unless there is some advocate there to urge constantly the needs and interests of the child' for whom the award is largely designed to satisfy.

In practice, however, children are rarely listened to or represented in financial proceedings, even though they may be significantly affected by the decision (for example, when the court is considering whether or not the family home should be transferred to a parent for the benefit of the child). Williams ([2008] Fam Law 135) has argued in favour of giving children a greater voice in proceedings under Sched 1 to the Children Act 1989 and in other financial proceedings. She states that: 'If we truly believe that our obligations under the UN Convention [on the Rights of the Child] require us to hear the voice of the child in matters in which they are directly affected, then we cannot ignore the huge impact on children of court decisions in financial proceedings'.

Summary

1 All parents have a duty to maintain their children, and all children have a right to be maintained.

2 If a parent fails to provide maintenance, an application can be made for child support from the Child Maintenance Enforcement Commission/Child Support Agency, which has the power under the Child Support Act 1991 to calculate, collect and enforce child support maintenance payments. The calculation is based on percentages of the non-resident parent's net weekly income and the number of qualifying and relevant other children. Deductions are made for shared care. Variations are permitted in certain limited and exceptional circumstances. The Commission/CSA is responsible for enforcing payments; and so parents cannot apply for enforcement in the court.

3 Because of criticisms of the CSA (for example, in respect of delays, errors and inadequate enforcement powers) new provisions have been introduced into the Child Support Act 1991 by the Child Maintenance and Other Payments Act 2008. This Act establishes the Child Maintenance and Enforcement Commission, a non-departmental Government body whose function is to oversee the workings of the CSA. The powers and duties will be eventually transferred from the CSA to the Commission. Reforms have also been made by the 2008 Act: to place a new emphasis on the importance of parents reaching private agreement; to introduce a new formula for calculating child support; and to introduce more stringent enforcement measures. As these reforms are being brought into force over a period of years, reference should be made to the websites at the end of this chapter.

4 Maintenance for children can be sought from the courts in certain cases (for example, in school fees cases, where a child is disabled, where the parents are wealthy, or where the Commission/CSA does not have jurisdiction). It is also open to parents to make applications for consent orders governing the payment of child maintenance.

5 Periodical payments orders, lump sum orders and property adjustment orders can be sought for children on divorce (and on nullity and judicial separation) under Part II of the Matrimonial Causes Act 1973. These orders can also be sought under s.72(1) and Sched. 5 to the Civil Partnership Act 2004 on the dissolution (annulment or separation) of a civil partnership.

6 During marriage, a parent may seek periodical payments (maintenance) and lump sums for a child from the magistrates' family proceedings courts under the Domestic Proceedings and Magistrates' Courts Act 1978. Civil partners can do the same under s.72(3) and Sched. 6 to the Civil Partnership Act 2004. The same orders for children (and also property adjustment orders) can be sought during marriage from the county court and the High Court under s.27 MCA 1973 (and also during a civil partnership under s.72(1) and Sched. 5 to the CPA 2004).

Summary cont'd

7 Orders for financial relief (periodical payments, lump sums, settlements and transfers of property) can be sought under s.15 and para. 1 of Sched. 1 to the Children Act 1989 by parents, guardians, special guardians and persons with a residence order in their favour. 'Children' aged over 18 can apply under para. 2 for periodical payments and lump sums against their parents.

Further reading and references

Gilmore, '*Re P (Child) (Financial Provision)* – shoeboxes and comical shopping trips – child support from the affluent to fabulously rich' [2004] CFLQ 103.

Tod, 'Schedule 1 and the need for reform: *N* v. *D'* [2008] Fam Law 751.

Wikeley, '*R (Kehoe)* v. *Secretary of State for Work and Pensions*: no redress when the Child Support Agency fails to deliver' [2005] CFLQ 113.

Wikeley, 'Child support reform – throwing the baby out with the bathwater?' [2007] CFLQ 434.

Williams, 'Voices in the wilderness: hearing children in financial applications' [2008] Fam Law 135.

Websites

Child Maintenance and Enforcement Commission: www.childmaintenance.org
Child Maintenance Options: www.cmoptions.org
Child Support Agency: www.csa.gov.uk

> **Article 11 United Nations Convention on the Rights of the Child 1989**
>
> '1. States Parties shall take measures to combat the illicit transfer and non-return of children abroad.
> 2. To this end, States Parties shall promote the conclusion of bilateral or multilateral agreements or accession to existing agreements.'
>
> **The legislation**
>
> **Child Abduction Act 1984** Creates a criminal offence of taking a child out of the UK without consent.
>
> **Child Abduction and Custody Act 1985** Ratifies the Hague Convention and the European Convention, two international conventions which make provision for facilitating the return of abducted children.
>
> **Family Law Act 1986** Provides legal mechanisms for returning children abducted within the different parts of the UK.
>
> **Children Act 1989** Provides a range of orders which can be used to prevent abduction, and to permit the lawful movement of children to countries outside the UK (and to other parts of the UK).

This chapter deals with international child abduction. For the law governing the relocation of children within and outside the UK, see 11.8 and 11.9.

13.1 Introduction

Child abduction is a distressing consequence of family breakdown. Abductions usually occur when relationships between parents break down and the parent who is not awarded custody (or residence) takes the child to another country and does not return. As a result of increasing numbers of international marriages and international cohabiting relationships (due in part to easier travel and to the use of the internet), abductions in the UK have increased. The enlargement of the European Union may also be responsible for the increasing incidence of child abduction. According to the *Guardian* newspaper (9 August 2009), in 2008 almost 500 children were abducted in the UK and taken abroad illegally. In the same year, 336 cases of child abduction were reported to the authorities in the UK, with 134 of those abductions involving children who were taken to countries which were not parties to the Hague Convention on Abduction.

The courts in England and Wales deal not only with international abduction cases where a child has been brought *into* the UK from abroad, but also hear applications by parents who wish to take a child permanently or temporarily out of the UK or to another part of the UK (see 11.8 and 11.9). The courts can make orders preventing parents (or other persons) from taking a child out of the UK (see 11.8) and orders declaring that the removal of a child from the UK is wrongful. They can also make orders asking for information about an abducted child to be disclosed to the court.

Advice about child abduction can be obtained from the International Child Abduction and Contact Unit (ICACU) (based within the office of the Official Solicitor) which is the central authority for England and Wales for Hague Convention cases and Brussels II Revised purposes. Advice is also available from the Foreign and Commonwealth Office, which deals with abductions to non-Convention countries. The UK Passport Office can provide information about issuing a passport for a child where there is a risk of child abduction. Reunite International Child Abduction Centre, a UK charity which specialises in international child abduction, provides advice to parents involved in international child abduction cases. (Website addresses for these sources of information can be found at the end of this chapter).

13.2 Preventing abduction

Where there is a risk of abduction, preventative measures should be urgently taken as, once a child has left the UK, finding and returning the child may be difficult. In addition to a parent being vigilant about an actual or potential risk of abduction, the following steps can be taken to prevent abduction:

(a) Police assistance

As child abduction is a criminal offence (see 13.3), a parent (or any other person) who believes that a child has been abducted (or may be about to be) can inform the police. The police have various powers. They can arrest any person who is abducting or is suspected of abducting a child. They can also bring into effect an 'all ports warning', whereby details of the child and the abductor are sent by the police national computer to ports and airports across the UK in order to prevent the child leaving the country. The application for a port alert must be *bona fide* and there must be a real and imminent danger of removal.

(b) A court order

Where there is a risk of abduction a court order may be useful. Not only is breach of a court order contempt of court (see *Re A (Abduction: Contempt)* [2008] EWCA Civ 1138, [2009] 1 FLR 1), but a court order may be useful if a parent wishes to institute court proceedings abroad or seek the help of various agencies abroad. Although an order is not needed to institute a port alert (above), it provides useful evidence of a genuine risk of abduction. An order is also useful for passport purposes (see p. 344 below).

(i) Orders under s.8 Children Act 1989   A useful range of orders is available under s.8 of the Children Act 1989 (see 10.4). For example, a prohibited steps order could be sought to prohibit a child being removed from the UK; or a specific issue order could be sought to decide a dispute about whether a child should be permitted to leave the UK. A residence order may be useful, because a child who is subject to a residence order may not be removed from the UK without the *written* consent of every person with parental responsibility (s.13(1)(b) CA 1989) – except for a period of up to one month by the holder of the residence order (s.13(2) CA 1989). If no such consent is forthcoming, the court will have to give its consent (see 11.8). Similar restrictions exist in respect of taking a child in local authority care out of the UK (s.33(7) CA 1989).

The court can make a s.8 order (see 10.4) even if the child has been abducted, but it may be reluctant to do so where there are likely to be problems enforcing the order abroad (*Re D (Child: Removal from Jurisdiction)* [1992] 1 WLR 315). Where urgent action is needed the court can make a s.8 order *ex parte* (without the respondent being given notice of the proceedings) (see, for example, *Re J (Abduction: Wrongful Removal)* [2000] 1 FLR 78).

In an exceptional case, where there is a danger that a parent may attempt to remove a child out of England and Wales, or the UK, the court can impose a direction on a residence order (under s.11(7) CA 1989). Where a contact order is in force and it is feared that the child may be abducted by the person exercising contact, an application may be made for a variation of the order to provide for the contact to be supervised.

Unmarried fathers who have no parental responsibility may find themselves in a vulnerable position where there is a risk of their child being abducted, and may have to take legal steps to prevent an abduction and to acquire parental responsibility (see p. 344 below).

(ii) Wardship   As an alternative to a s.8 order, an application can be made to the High Court for the child to be made a ward of court (see 8.7, and, for example, *Re B (Child Abduction: Wardship: Power to Detain)* [1994] 2 FLR 479). The advantage of wardship is that the situation is frozen immediately the application is made so that any attempt to remove the child from the UK without the court's consent may be contempt of court. The High Court continues to have a supervisory role over the ward, so that no major step in the child's life can be taken without its consent.

(iii) Other powers of the court   Under the inherent jurisdiction and under statute the court can order a person to disclose a child's whereabouts (s.33 Family Law Act 1986 and s.24A Child Abduction and Custody Act 1985; and see *Re H (Abduction: Whereabouts Order to Solicitors)* [2000] 1 FLR 766). The county court can authorise an officer of the court, or a police constable, to take charge of a child and deliver the child to a named person. The High Court can make: a 'seek and find' order requiring a court official to find the child and deliver the child as directed by the court; or a 'seek and locate' order requiring that the child be located. It can also make an order permitting media publicity about the child; or requiring any person to disclose information about the child to the court; or requesting the disclosure of an address from a Government department or agency. Under the Family Law Act 1986, the court can order: the surrender of a passport (s.37); the recovery of a child (s.34); and can restrict the removal of a child from the UK (s.35). The High Court can also make a declaration under s.8 of the Child Abduction and Custody Act 1985, on an application made for the purposes of art. 14 of the Hague Convention, that that removal of any child from, or his retention outside, the UK was wrongful under art. 3 of the Hague Convention.

(iv) Enforcing a court order in another part of the UK   Under the Family Law Act 1986 a court order relating to a child made in one part of the UK can be recognised and enforced in another. There is no need for the court in the other part of the UK to consider the merits of the case afresh. Once registered, the court in the other part of the UK has the same powers of enforcement as if it had made the original order. However, a parent and any other interested party can object to enforcement on the ground that the original order was made without jurisdiction; or that, because of a change of circumstances, the original order

should be varied. Although the court in the other part of the UK can stay proceedings or dismiss the application (ss.30 and 31), it is likely to enforce the order.

(c) Passport control

Children are required to have their own passport. To prevent abduction, a parent (or other person with parental responsibility) can contact the UK Passport Service and object to the child being issued with a passport. The Passport Service will require a court order as proof of a risk of abduction before it will respond to this request.

Where there is a risk of abduction, a restriction can be placed on the child's or the likely abductor's passport. The court can order a UK passport to be surrendered where an order restricting removal is in force (s.37 Family Law Act 1986; and see *Re A (Return of Passport)* [1997] 2 FLR 137). The court can order the surrender of a non-UK passport under its inherent jurisdiction (see 8.7, and *Re A-K (Foreign Passport: Jurisdiction)* [1997] 2 FLR 569). A s.8 order under the Children Act 1989 (see 10.4) can be made conditional on a suspected abductor depositing his passport with a solicitor or with the court.

(d) Curfews and electronic tagging

In an exceptional case the court may make a curfew order supported by electronic tagging. Thus, in *Re A (Family Proceedings: Electronic Tagging)* [2009] EWHC 710 (Fam), [2009] 2 FLR 891 the parents agreed that, when the child was with the mother, the mother should on an interim basis be subject to a curfew supported by electronic tagging. Here the mother had twice abducted the child to her country of origin and the child had been returned pursuant to proceedings under the Hague Convention. Parker J made an interim order giving effect to the parties' agreement and laid down guidelines in respect of electronic tagging.

(e) Unmarried fathers and child abduction

Unmarried fathers may find themselves in a vulnerable position if they have no parental responsibility (see 9.4) and their child has been, or is at risk of being, abducted. In such cases, it is important for the unmarried father to take immediate and urgent legal steps to protect himself and/or the child, for otherwise he may find himself deprived of any effective right of recourse to the Hague Convention on Abduction. Thus, he should consider obtaining a parental responsibility order (see 9.4), which can be obtained *ex parte* in an emergency; and he should also consider obtaining a declaration under s.8 of the Child Abduction and Custody Act 1985 that he has 'rights of custody' for the purposes of the Hague Convention (which is what the unmarried father did in *A v B (Abduction: Rights of Custody: Declaration of Wrongful Removal)* [2008] EWHC 2524 (Fam), [2009] 1 FLR 1253 when he discovered that the child's mother, a French national, was about to take their child to France). Other options for unmarried fathers are to apply for a residence order, prohibited steps order, or a specific issue order under s.8 of the Children Act 1989 (see 10.4).

The courts have taken a broad view of what constitutes 'custody rights' in the case of an unmarried father for the purpose of making a declaration under s.8 CACA 1985 (see *Re W; Re B (Child Abduction: Unmarried Father)* [1999] Fam 1, [1998] 2 FLR 146); and *Practice*

Note (Hague Convention – Application by Fathers without Parental Responsibility) 14 October 1997 [1998] 1 FLR 491). If, for instance, a father has been caring for the child, even though he has no parental responsibility in law, this may be sufficient for him to have 'custody rights' for the purpose of the Hague Convention on Abduction. Each case, however, depends on its facts. In *Re C (A Child) (Custody Rights: Unmarried Fathers)* [2002] EWHC 2219 (Fam), [2003] 1 FLR 252, where the unmarried father was concerned that the mother might take the child to Ireland, Munby J refused to make a declaration under s.8 CACA 1985 as there was nothing in the case-law to suggest that an unmarried father without parental responsibility could acquire rights of custody within the meaning of the Hague Convention in circumstances where a mother had remained the primary carer.

Thus, despite a purposive interpretation of 'rights of custody', the court will not necessarily hold that an unmarried father has rights of custody for Convention purposes, even if he has shared care of the child for a considerable length of time (see *Re J (Abduction: Acquiring Custody Rights by Caring for Child)* [2005] 2 FLR 791).

The European Court of Human Rights held in *B v. UK* [2000] 1 FLR 1 that it is not discriminatory (under art. 14 ECHR) in conjunction with the right to family life (under art. 8 ECHR) for the court to hold that an unmarried father without parental responsibility does not come within the scope of the Hague Convention on the ground that he has no right of custody. In this case an unmarried father without parental responsibility, whose child had been removed from the UK without his consent, argued that the UK Government was in breach of arts. 14 and 8 because he was treated differently from other fathers. His application failed. The ECtHR held that there was an objective and reasonable justification for the different treatment of the father in this case.

Beevers ([2006] CFLQ 499) has expressed the view that, had the father in *B v. UK* been more involved in sharing care of the child (rather than only being involved for the first few months of the child's life), then the outcome of the case might have been different.

13.3   Abduction – the criminal law

A person who abducts, or attempts to abduct, a child from the UK may commit a criminal offence under the Child Abduction Act 1984 or under the common law.

(a)   The Child Abduction Act 1984

Persons 'connected with a child' (s.1) and 'other persons' (s.2) can commit a criminal offence under the Child Abduction Act 1984.

(i) Persons 'connected with a child'   Under s.1 it is an offence for a person 'connected with a child' under 16 to take or send the child out of the UK without the 'appropriate consent'. A person 'connected with a child' is (s.1): a parent (including an unmarried father if there are reasonable grounds for believing he is the father); a guardian; a special guardian; any person with a residence order in their favour; and any person with custody of the child. 'Appropriate consent' means the consent of: the mother; the father (with parental responsibility); a guardian; a special guardian; any person with a residence order in force in their favour; and any person with custody of the child (s.1(2)(a)).

'Appropriate consent' can include the court's consent where it is required under Part II of the Children Act 1989 (ss.1(2)(b), (c)) (for example, where a residence order is in force, see s.13 CA 1989). However, a person with a residence order in force with respect to the child does not commit a criminal offence if he or she takes the child out of the UK for less than one month, unless this is in breach of another court order (s.1(4)).

It is a defence under the Act if the accused believed that the other person consented to the abduction, or would have consented had he or she been aware of all the circumstances; or the accused was unable to communicate with the other person despite taking reasonable steps to do so (s.1(5)). It is also a defence if the other person unreasonably refused consent to the child being taken out of the UK (but this defence does not apply if the person refusing consent has a residence order in his or her favour; or the person taking or sending the child out of the UK did so in breach of a court order) (s.1(5A)).

(ii) 'Other persons' Under s.2 a person who is not 'connected with a child' under s.1 (above) commits the offence of child abduction if, without lawful authority or reasonable excuse, he or she takes or detains a child under the age of 16 so as to remove the child from the lawful control of any person having lawful control of the child; or so as to keep the child out of the lawful control of any person entitled to lawful control (s.2(1)). An unmarried father without parental responsibility comes under s.2, unless he is the child's guardian, or has a residence order in his favour, or has custody of the child. An unmarried father, however, has a defence if he can prove that he is the child's father, or that at the time of the alleged offence he reasonably believed he was the child's father (s.2(3)(a)). It is also a defence if the accused believed that at the time of the alleged offence the child had reached the age of 16 (s.2(3)(b)). The mental state for an offence under s.2 is an intentional or reckless taking or detention of a child (see *Foster and Another* v. *Director of Public Prosecutions* [2004] EWHC 2955 (Admin)).

(b) The offence of kidnapping

A person who abducts a child unlawfully may commit the common law offence of kidnapping (see, for example, *R* v. *D* [1984] AC 778). Where the child is under 16 and the person removing the child is a person 'connected with' the child under s.1 of the Child Abduction Act 1984 (above), the consent of the Director of Public Prosecutions is needed to bring a prosecution (s.5 CAA 1984). The offence of kidnapping is rarely used, but may be relevant where an abduction involves a child aged over 16 – as such a child does not come within the scope of the 1984 Act above.

13.4 The Hague Convention on Abduction

(a) Introduction

The UK is a Contracting State to the Hague Convention on the Civil Aspects of International Child Abduction 1980 (the 'Hague Convention'), which has been implemented into UK law by Part I of the Child Abduction and Custody Act 1985. The text of the Convention and a list of Contracting States are available on Reunite's website (www.reunite.org).

> **Article 1 of the Hague Convention on the Civil Aspects of**
> **International Child Abduction 1980**
>
> 'The objects of the present Convention are –
>
> (a) to secure the prompt return of children wrongfully removed to or retained in any Contracting State; and
> (b) to ensure that rights of custody and of access under the law of one Contracting State are effectively respected in the other Contracting States.'

(i) The policy of the Convention The Hague Convention on Abduction is based on the policy that children should be swiftly returned to their country of habitual residence. It is also based on the principle of 'comity', a principle of international law which requires courts to respect the laws of foreign jurisdictions. Thus, the presumption lies in favour of returning a child, and it is generally assumed that, if a country is a party to the Hague Convention, then the child's case will be dealt with in a welfare-oriented way. Another policy objective of the Convention is to deter abductions. As Baroness Hale said, the 'message should go out to potential abductors that there are no safe havens among the Contracting States' (see *Re M (Abduction: Zimbabwe)* [2007] UKHL 55, *sub nom Re M and Another (Minors)* [2008] 1 FLR 251).

(ii) How the Convention works The scheme of the Hague Convention is to provide a speedy extradition-type remedy whereby Contracting States agree to return abducted children to their country of habitual residence so that the parental custody (or residence) dispute can be dealt with there. In this sense it is a provisional remedy, for Convention proceedings are not concerned with the merits of a custody issue (art. 19). That is a matter for the court in the child's country of habitual residence. In *C v. B (Abduction: Grave Risk)* [2005] EWHC 2988 (Fam), [2006] 1 FLR 1095 Sir Mark Potter P said that it was essential that the court hearing a return application did not usurp the function of the 'home' court by considering broader welfare considerations instead of confining itself to those matters which went to the establishment of the defence being relied upon under art. 13 of the Convention. The central question in Hague Convention proceedings is therefore whether the child should be returned to the *court* of his or her habitual residence, so that the custody issue can be considered there, not whether the child should be returned to a particular *person*.

As the Convention is concerned with breaches of custody *rights*, not custody orders, it is not necessary to have a court order to invoke it. Applications under the Convention in England and Wales are heard by the Family Division of the High Court which can also make declarations that a removal or retention of a child outside the UK is wrongful under art. 3.

(iii) Central Authorities The Convention works by establishing a network of Central Authorities which must co-operate with each other, and promote co-operation among the competent authorities in their respective States, in order to secure the prompt return of children and to achieve the other objects of the Convention (art. 7). Central Authorities have various duties under the Convention which include: discovering the child's whereabouts; preventing further harm to the child by taking provisional measures; securing the child's voluntary return; exchanging information; and providing

information. The Central Authority for England and Wales is the International Child Abduction and Contact Unit (based in the Office of the Official Solicitor at the Ministry of Justice), which is responsible for making administrative arrangements under the Convention, in order to secure the return of abducted children, and to enforce rights of access. It also provides advice and assistance.

(iv) Speed is of the essence   In abduction cases any delay is contrary to the child's best interests – because the longer the situation remains undecided the more difficult it will be to disturb the status quo. Because of the importance of speed, Convention proceedings are summary. The court will not, for example, investigate the parent's marital situation or examine the child's welfare (*per* Sir Stephen Brown P in *Re D (Abduction: Custody Rights)* [1999] 2 FLR 626). Cases are usually heard and decided upon on the basis of written evidence; oral evidence is only sparingly permitted (*per* Butler-Sloss LJ in *Re F (A Minor) (Child Abduction: Rights of Custody Abroad)* [1995] Fam 224, [1995] 2 FLR 31). In EU abductions (see over) art. 11(3) of Brussels II Revised provides that a return application under the Hague Convention must be completed within 6 weeks unless exceptional circumstances make this impossible.

(v) The welfare of the child   The welfare of the child is not paramount in Hague Convention cases because 'it is presumed under the Convention that the welfare of children who have been abducted is best met by return to their habitual residence' (*per* Butler-Sloss LJ in *Re M (A Minor) (Child Abduction)* [1994] 1 FLR 390). Nevertheless, as Baroness Hale emphasised in *Re M (Abduction: Zimbabwe)* [2007] UKHL 55 (see further at p. 359), the Convention is child-centred, as it is principally directed towards the protection of children, not adults. As Baroness Hale pointed out, the Preamble to the Convention states that the Contracting States are 'firmly convinced that the interests of *children* are of paramount importance in matters relating to the custody of children'.

(vi) Human rights and the Hague Convention   The European Court of Human Rights has held that a failure by a national authority (under domestic or international law) to secure the return of an abducted child may amount to a breach of the right to family life under art. 8 ECHR (see 1.7); and that national authorities must take positive measures to enable parents to be reunited with the child, unless contrary to the child's best interests. Breaches of art. 8 were found, for example, in *Gil and Aui v. Spain (Application No. 56673/00)* [2005] 1 FLR 190 and in *Maire v. Portugal (Application No. 48206/99)* [2004] 2 FLR 653, as the authorities had failed to take appropriate measures under the Hague Convention to secure the return of an abducted child.

(vii) Access (contact) rights   Although art. 21 of the Convention provides that access rights may be secured, it confers no power on the courts to determine access matters, or to recognise or enforce foreign access orders. It merely provides for executive co-operation between Central Authorities for the recognition and enforcement of such access rights as national laws allow. The International Child Abduction and Contact Unit (based in the Ministry of Justice) will provide assistance about finding a solicitor, legal aid and instituting s.8 proceedings under the Children Act 1989. If a foreign access order is in force, an application can be made to have it recognised and enforced in the courts in England and Wales under the European Convention on the Recognition and Enforcement of

Decisions Concerning Custody of Children 1980 (see *Re A (Foreign Access Order: Enforcement)* [1996] 1 FLR 561); or under Brussels II Revised if EU Member States are involved (see *Re S (Brussels II Revised: Enforcement of Contact Order)* [2008] 2 FLR 1358, where Wood J recognised a Polish contact order but refused to enforce it).

(viii) Breach of a return order   Breach of a return order made under the Hague Convention can be contempt of court provided there has been deliberate disobedience of the court order applying the criminal standard of proof. (But, see *Re A (Abduction: Contempt)* [2008] EWCA Civ 1138, [2009] 1 FLR 1 where the Court of Appeal allowed the father's appeal against committal for contempt of court on the basis that, at the time of the abduction, no order had been in existence forbidding removal of the child).

(b)   The Hague Convention and abductions within the EU

Where a child has been abducted within the European Union, it is also necessary to take into account the provisions of Council Regulation (EC) (No. 2201/2003) Concerning Jurisdiction and the Recognition and Enforcement of Judgments in Matrimonial Matters and in Matters of Parental Responsibility (Brussels II Revised, BIIR). Art. 11 of BIIR aims to harmonise the application of the Hague Convention in EU Member States by setting out details of procedure that are binding on the courts. As Schulz (2008) explains, while the Hague Convention contains provisions aimed at 'a quick clarification of the *factual* situation (return of the child)', BIIR contains provisions aimed at 'a quick clarification of the *legal* situation', in other words it enables a final decision about custody to be taken in the court of the State of the child's habitual residence even if the child is not being returned under the Hague Convention (see further below). The Central Authority in England and Wales for the purposes of Brussels II Revised is the International Child Abduction and Contact Unit.

The following regulations in Brussels II Revised apply in Hague Convention cases involving EU Member States:

- The court is required in every case to hear the views of the child unless this appears inappropriate having regard to the age or degree of maturity of the child (art. 11(2)).
- The court is required to hear the views of the applicant parent if it is considering not to return the child (art. 11(5)).
- Proceedings for the return of a child under the Hague Convention must be completed within 6 weeks unless 'exceptional circumstances make this impossible' (art. 11(3)). In *Re F (Abduction: Child's Wishes)* [2007] EWCA Civ 468, [2007] 2 FLR 697, which involved an abduction from Spain to the UK, the Court of Appeal held that the failure to hear the child's wishes and feelings (under art. 11(2)) did not override the obligation (under art. 11 (3)) to conclude the proceedings within 6 weeks.
- The court may not make a non-return order (if a defence of grave risk to the child has been made out under art. 13(b) of the Hague Convention, see p. 362) if it is established that adequate arrangements have been made to ensure the protection of the child after his or her return (art. 11(4)). (But, see *AF v. MB-F (Abduction: Rights of Custody)* [2008] EWHC 272 (Fam), [2008] 2 FLR 1239 where Sir Mark Potter P held that, despite this provision in BIIR, the child's objections to return can be heard under art. 13 of the Hague Convention, and may, in an appropriate case prevail, as they did in *AF v. MB-F*).

▶ Brussels II Revised allows a custody decision made in the child's home Member State to 'trump' a non-return order made in the Member State to which the child has been abducted (see below).

Brussels II Revised and non-return orders under the Hague Conventions Brussels II Revised provides protection for a parent whose child has been abducted in that arts. 11(6)–(8) allow the court in the child's home state to order the child's return even if the court in the country to which the child was abducted makes a non-return order under the Hague Convention (provided the non-return order was made on the basis of a successful art. 13 Hague Convention defence (see 13.8), not one based on art. 12 (see p. 363). (See *Re RC and BC (Child Abduction) (Brussels II Revised: Article 11(7)* [2009] 1 FLR 574; *Re RD (Child Abduction) (Brussels II Revised: Articles 11(7) and 19)* [2009] 1 FLR 586; and *Rinau (Case C-195/08)* [2008] 2 FLR 1495). Thus, Brussels II Revised 'accepts the parallel continuation of return and custody proceedings in two different Member States, regardless of the ultimate outcome of the Hague Convention return proceedings' (Schulz (2008).

As a result of Brussels II Revised, a custody decision made in another Member State of the EU can therefore take precedence over a decision made under the Hague Convention. Thus, for example, in *Re T and J (Abduction: Recognition of Foreign Judgment)* [2006] EWHC 1472 (Fam), [2006] 2 FLR 1290 the Spanish judgment (granting care and control of the children to the father, who was living in England) prevailed, with the result that the mother's application for the summary return of the children to Spain under the Hague Convention was refused in the English High Court. Custody decisions can therefore 'trump' Hague Convention orders. This also happened in *Vigreux* v. *Michel* [2006] EWCA Civ 630, [2006] 2 FLR 1180 where the English Court of Appeal held that McFarlane J had erred in law in refusing the mother's application for return of the child to France under the Hague Convention when she had already been granted sole parental responsibility for the child by a French court. Thorpe LJ held that the case was one in which the policy of the Hague Convention buttressed by the provisions of Brussels II Revised powerfully outweighed the art. 13 defence.

'Trumping cases' (those where a decision about the child's residence or custody can 'trump' a non-return order made under the Hague Convention) are heard in the High Court (see *Re A (Custody Order After Maltese Non-Return Order)* [2006] EWHC 3397 (Fam), [2007] 1 FLR 1923).

(c) The voice of the child in Hague Convention cases

As Hague Convention proceedings are summary and speed is of the essence, the usual way in which the voice of the child is heard is by means of a written report compiled by a Cafcass officer (see 1.6), or by another professional who has interviewed the child. There is no obligation on the judge to hear oral evidence even where an art. 13(b) defence (child's objection to return) is being argued (*per* Sir Mark Potter P in *Re M (Abduction: Child's Objections)* [2007] EWCA Civ 260, [2007] 2 FLR 72). In some cases the judge may wish to speak to the child, but this is not a common practice. In exceptional circumstances the child may have separate legal representation (see over).

Although the child's voice may be put before the court, it does not necessarily mean that the child's views will be taken into account. Thus, in *C* v. *B (Abduction: Grave Risk)* [2005] EWHC 2988 (Fam), [2006] 1 FLR 1095, for example, the views of the 9-year-old child, whose mother did not wish to return to Australia, were put before the court by means of a Cafcass report, but Sir Mark Potter P held that, while the child was of sufficient maturity to have his views taken into account, those views (anger with his father and concerns about his mother) did not provide a sufficient basis on which to withhold an order of return for him and his 5-year-old sister.

Separate representation of the child in Hague Convention proceedings Although the court has the power to allow children to intervene in Hague Convention proceedings, there is a long line of Court of Appeal authority which has emphasised that children will be allowed to intervene only in exceptional circumstances (see, for example, *Re F (Abduction: Joinder of Child as Party)* [2007] EWCA Civ 393, [2007] 2 FLR 313 below). Thus, despite the increasing importance of listening to children (see 8.6), separate representation remains the exception rather than the rule in Hague Convention proceedings. The test to be applied when deciding whether a child should be separately represented is whether separate representation will add enough to the court's understanding of the issues arising under the Hague Convention to justify the intrusion, expense and the delay that may result (*per* Baroness Hale in *Re M (Abduction: Zimbabwe)* [2007] UKHL 55, [2008] 1 FLR 251).

Although separate representation remains the exception rather than the rule, there has been an increasing trend to permit children to be separately represented. Thus, for example, in *Re C (Abduction: Separate Representation of Children)* [2008] EWHC 517 (Fam), [2008] 2 FLR 6 Ryder J directed that all four articulate siblings (aged 9, 11, 13 and 16), who vigorously objected to being returned to France, be joined as parties and that the three younger children be represented by a guardian *ad litem*. Ryder J (applying the test for separate representation laid down by Baroness Hale in *Re M* above and the approach taken by the Court of Appeal in *Mabon* v. *Mabon* (see p. 229)) held that there would be little additional delay and expense in allowing separate representation; and the younger three children were able to make submissions and defences distinct from those put forward by the mother. Ryder J said that it would be emotionally harmful for any one of the children to be refused permission to be separately represented where another was permitted to be so.

Re C (Abduction: Separate Representation of Children) (above) can be contrasted with *Re H (Abduction)* [2006] EWCA Civ 1247, [2007] 1 FLR 242 where the Court of Appeal refused permission to allow a girl (aged 15) to be made a party to proceedings, referring to Sir Thomas Bingham MR in *Re M (A Minor) (Child Abduction)* [1994] 1 FLR 390, who had stated that, while there is jurisdiction to permit a child to be joined as party, 'it would rarely be right to exercise it, and compelling grounds would be needed'. The argument based on *Mabon* (see p. 229) was rejected by the Court of Appeal in *Re H* on the ground that Hague Convention proceedings are summary proceedings where speed is of the essence. Wall LJ said that there were, in his judgment, 'material differences between the question of separate representation for a child in a welfare enquiry and separate representation in summary proceedings under an international convention, where the welfare enquiry is to take place elsewhere'.

Where a child has a distinctive point of view which needs to be heard separately from that of the defaulting parent, the court may decide to grant separate representation as it did to a 14-year-old boy in *Re L (Abduction: Child's Objections to Return)* [2002] EWHC 1864 (Fam), [2002] 2 FLR 1042. (For other cases where children were granted separate representation, see *Re S (Abduction: Children's Representation)* [2008] EWHC 1798 (Fam), [2008] 2 FLR 1918; and *Re B (Separate Representation)* [2007] EWCA Civ 1463).

Are children being heard enough in Hague Convention proceedings? There has been increasing concern that children are not being heard enough in Hague Convention cases, and that more children should be separately represented. Baroness Hale in *Re D (A Child) (Abduction: Rights of Custody)* [2006] UKHL 51, [2007] 1 FLR 961 said that, 'whenever it seems likely that the child's views and interests may not be properly presented to the court, and in particular where there are legal arguments which the adult parties are not putting forward, then the child should be separately represented'.

In respect of abductions within the European Union, a failure to hear a child may breach art. 11(2) of Brussels II Revised (see p. 349 above), which requires courts in Member States, when applying arts. 12 and 13 of the Hague Convention, to ensure that the child 'is given the opportunity to be heard during the proceedings unless this appears inappropriate having regard to his or her age or degree of maturity'. Although Brussels II Revised applies only to EU cases, Baroness Hale in *Re D* (above) held that, as the obligation to hear a child is a principle of universal application and consistent with the UK's obligations under art. 12 of the UN Convention on the Rights of the Child (see 8.2), the obligation to hear a child applies not just to EU cases but to all Hague Convention cases. Her Ladyship held that it created a presumption that a child would be heard unless this appeared inappropriate. She warned, however, that listening to a child does not mean that the court should necessarily give effect to those views.

However, in *Re F (Abduction: Joinder of Child as Party)* [2007] EWCA Civ 393, [2007] 2 FLR 313 Thorpe LJ said that *Re D* (above) was not to be interpreted as having the effect of lowering the bar with respect to granting party status to the child; and that there remained a need to demonstrate that a case was sufficiently exceptional. Thorpe LJ said that '[h]earing the child is one thing and giving the child party status is quite another'. In *Re F* the Court of Appeal refused leave for the child (aged 7) to be joined in the proceedings, despite the mother's argument that the judge had not observed her obligation to hear the child under art. 11 of Brussels II Revised. The Court of Appeal held that this refusal did not breach the child's human rights under arts. 6 (right to a fair hearing) and 8 (right to family life) of the European Convention for the Protection of Human Rights.

(d) Construing the Convention

As the Convention is an international legal instrument, the courts in England and Wales have stressed the importance of it being construed uniformly by courts in Contracting States (see, for example, *per* Lord Browne-Wilkinson in *Re H (Minors) (Abduction: Acquiescence)* [1998] AC 72). To promote uniformity of construction, the Hague Conference has an International Child Abduction Database (INCADAT) of leading Convention case-law from Hague Contracting States.

The courts in England and Wales adopt a purposive approach when construing the Convention. In *Re B (A Minor) (Abduction)* [1994] 2 FLR 249 Waite LJ said that the Convention was 'to be construed broadly as an international agreement according to its general tenor and purpose, without attributing to any of its terms a specialist meaning which the word or words in question would have acquired under the domestic law of England'. In *Hunter* v. *Murrow (Abduction: Rights of Custody)* [2005] EWCA Civ 976, [2005] 2 FLR 1119 the Court of Appeal held that the Convention was a living instrument to be interpreted and applied as necessary to keep pace with social and other trends. It also held that questions involving the construction or interpretation of the Convention were to be answered according to the international jurisprudence of the Contracting States, not simply according to the law of a particular jurisdiction.

In *Re M (Abduction: Zimbabwe)* [2007] UKHL 55, *sub nom Re M and Another (Minors)* [2008] 1 FLR 251 the House of Lords warned that the courts should not add additional words into the Convention (in that case, an additional test of 'exceptionality' to the circumstances under which a court should refuse to order the return of an abducted child). Baroness Hale, who gave the leading opinion, said:

'The Convention itself contains a simple, sensible and carefully thought out balance between various considerations, all aimed at serving the interests of children by deterring and, where appropriate, remedying international child abduction. Further elaboration with additional tests and checklists is not required.'

Baroness Hale said that, while the court is entitled to take into account the various policy aspects of the Convention (see p. 347 above), that was 'the furthest one should go in seeking to put a gloss on the terms of the Convention'. In *Re F (Abduction: Rights of Custody)* [2008] EWHC 272 (Fam), [2008] 2 FLR 1239 Sir Mark Potter P said that Baroness Hale's express disapproval of the 'exceptionality' test over and above the express requirements of the Hague Convention applied to all Hague Convention cases, including those brought under Brussels II Revised.

13.5   The Hague Convention – jurisdiction

To come within the jurisdiction of the Hague Convention, the child must be under 16 and have been habitually resident in one Contracting State and taken to another. If the child has reached the age of 16 by the time of the hearing, the High Court can consider the case under its inherent jurisdiction (see 8.7). The Convention does not apply to an unborn child (*Re F (Abduction: Unborn Child)* [2006] EWHC 2199 (Fam), [2007] 1 FLR 627). To come within the scope of the Convention, there must also have been a breach of a right of custody (see 13.6 below).

(a)   Habitual residence

Habitual residence, not domicile, is the connecting factor used in the Hague Convention. Thus, the child must have been habitually resident in one Contracting State and moved to another Contracting State. If the child is not, or has ceased to be, habitually resident in a Contracting State, there can be no wrongful removal or retention of the child for the purposes of art. 3(a), and the child will fall outside the scope of the Convention. 'Habitual residence' is not defined in the Convention – its meaning must be determined from the case-law. In the following case Lord Brandon laid down the principles which apply to the question of habitual residence:

▶ *Re J (A Minor) (Abduction: Custody Rights)* [1990] 2 AC 562, *sub nom C v. S (A Minor) (Abduction)* [1990] 2 FLR 442

The parents cohabited in Australia and had a son (aged about 2). The parents' relationship broke down, and, without informing the father, the mother left Australia and flew to England with the child, where it was her settled intention to remain and to make a long-term home for herself and the child. Five days after her departure the father applied to the Australian court for sole custody and guardianship of the child, which was granted. The Australian court later made a declaration that the child's removal from Australia was wrongful under art. 3 of the Hague Convention. A month after the mother's departure, the Australian authorities applied to the English High Court under the Hague Convention for the child's immediate return to Australia.

The House of Lords refused the application for return on the ground that there had been no wrongful removal or retention for the purposes of art. 3. There had been no wrongful removal because, under the law of Western Australia, the father possessed no custody rights capable of being breached at the time when the mother left Australia (as he was not married to the mother). There was no wrongful retention, as the child had ceased to be habitually resident in Australia before the Australian court had made the custody order, because the mother had a unilateral right to determine the child's place of habitual residence, and her settled intention to come to England had terminated the child's habitual residence in Australia.

In respect of habitual residence Lord Brandon said that:

▶ Habitual residence is to be understood according to its ordinary and natural meaning.
▶ Whether a person is or is not habitually resident in a particular country is a question of fact to be decided by reference to all the circumstances of the case.
▶ There is a significant difference between a person ceasing to be habitually resident in country A, and subsequently becoming resident in country B. A person may cease to be habitually resident in country A in a single day, if he leaves it with a settled intention not to return but to take up long-term residence in country B. But an appreciable period of time and a settled intention are needed for a person to become habitually resident in country B. During that 'appreciable period of time' the person will have ceased to be habitually resident in country A, but not yet have become habitually resident in country B.
▶ In the case of a child of the same age as the child in this case, and who is in the sole lawful custody of his mother, the child's habitual residence will be the same as hers.

In *R* v. *Barnet London Borough Council ex parte Shah* [1983] 2 AC 309 Lord Scarman said that habitual residence is the country adopted voluntarily and for a settled purpose as part of the regular order of a person's life, whether of short or long duration.

There have been many reported abduction cases involving the issue of habitual residence, from which the following propositions can be extracted:

Habitual residence

Habitual residence may be established even after a short period of residence, provided there is a settled intention to reside in that country (see, for example, *Re S (Habitual Residence)* [2009] EWCA Civ 1021 where seven to eight weeks' residence in London plus an intention to reside there was sufficient to establish habitual residence in England and Wales). In *Al Habtoor* v. *Fotheringham* [2001] EWCA Civ 186, [2001] 1 FLR 951 Thorpe LJ said that habitual residence could be acquired 'even if the person's move was intended to be fulfilled within a comparatively short duration, or was only on a trial basis'.

A short visit to a country does not necessarily start a period of habitual residence (see, for example, *Re A (Abduction: Habitual Residence)* [1998] 1 FLR 497 where a three-week visit to Greece for what was akin to a holiday was held not to be an 'appreciable period of time' to create a new habitual residence).

A child may have no habitual residence at all (see *W and B* v. *H (Child Abduction: Surrogacy)* [2002] 1 FLR 1008 where a Californian couple's application in England for the return of twins born of an English surrogacy arrangement was refused under the Hague Convention as the twins were not habitually resident in California or England).

A dependent child will not necessarily have the same habitual residence as a parent (see *Al Habtoor* v. *Fotheringham* (above) (a case brought in wardship, not under the Hague Convention) where the High Court refused jurisdiction as the applicant mother's nine-year-old child remained habitually resident in Dubai, even though the mother was habitually resident in England).

It is not necessary for a person to remain continuously present in a particular country in order for him or her to retain residence there (*per* Millet LJ in *Re M (Abduction: Habitual Residence)* [1996] 1 FLR 887).

Moving to another Contracting State for educational reasons may not constitute a change of habitual residence (see *TPC* v. *JMJ* [2009] EWHC 638 (Fam) where the children were held to be habitually resident in Spain even though they had come to England for 14 months, with the father's consent, in order to improve their English).

(b) Wrongful removal and retention

To come within the scope of the Convention, there must be wrongful removal from, or wrongful retention in, a Contracting State. Wrongful removal and wrongful retention are mutually exclusive concepts (*Re H; Re S (Minors) (Abduction: Custody Rights)* [1991] 2 FLR 262). Wrongful removal occurs when a child is wrongfully removed from his place of habitual residence in breach of a right of custody. Wrongful retention occurs when, at the end of a period of lawful removal, a parent refuses to return the child. Removal and retention are only wrongful if done in a breach of a right of custody (see below).

A declaration of wrongful removal   Under s.8 of the Child Abduction and Custody Act 1985 the High Court, on an application made for the purposes of art. 15 of the Hague Convention by any person appearing to the court to have an interest in the matter, may make a declaration that the removal of a child from, or his retention outside, the UK is wrongful within the meaning of art. 3 of the Hague Convention. In *Re C (Child Abduction) (Unmarried Father: Rights of Custody)* [2002] EWHC 2219 (Fam), [2003] 1 FLR 252 Munby J said that the grant of declaratory relief under art. 15 is always a matter of discretion, but in the normal case where an applicant succeeds in persuading the court that a child has been wrongfully removed, and seeks a declaration to assist his prospects of obtaining substantive relief in the requested State, he can normally expect to have the court's discretion exercised in his favour.

13.6   The Hague Convention – rights of custody

Article 3 of the Hague Convention on the Civil Aspects of International Child Abduction 1980

'The removal or retention of a child is to be considered wrongful where –

(a) it is in breach of rights of custody attributed to a person, an institution or any other body, either jointly or alone, under the law of the State in which the child was habitually resident immediately before the removal or retention; and

(b) at the time of removal or retention those rights were actually exercised, either jointly or alone, or would have been so exercised but for the removal or retention.'

The existence of a right of custody is crucial to establishing whether the Convention applies, as removal or retention are only wrongful if there has been breach of such a right.

The rights of custody mentioned in sub-para. (a) of art. 3 (above) may arise in particular by operation of law, or by reason of a judicial or administrative decision. Article 5(a) provides that for the purposes of the Convention 'rights of custody' 'shall include rights relating to the care of the person of the child and, in particular, the right to determine the child's place of residence'.

In *Re P (Abduction: Consent)* [2004] EWCA Civ 971, [2004] 2 FLR 1057 the Court of Appeal held that the court's task under art. 3 is to establish the custody rights of the parent under the law of the relevant State, and then to consider whether those rights are rights of custody for the purposes of the Hague Convention. In *Re T (Abduction: Rights of Custody)* [2008] EWHC 809 (Fam), [2008] 2 FLR 1794 Coleridge J held that it was particularly important that issues like rights of custody should be clearly settled by the foreign law, either directly by reference to statute or other written material, or by reference to the foreign court's previous decisions (see further at p. 357).

(a) A purposive construction of custody

In order to give effect to the overriding policy objective of the Hague Convention that children should be expeditiously returned to their country of habitual residence, the courts have adopted a purposive construction of 'rights of custody' and interpreted it broadly to include not just legal custody, but *de facto* (factual) custody. In other words, where a person has no custody rights in law, but is exercising rights of a parental or custodial nature, this can constitute custody. In this way, unmarried fathers without legal custody (or without parental responsibility) have been held to have custody rights. A broad view of custody was taken by the Court of Appeal in the following case:

> ▶ *Re B (A Minor) (Abduction)* [1994] 2 FLR 249
>
> The parents were cohabitants living in Australia. The mother, who was a heroin addict, left Australia and went to England, leaving the child with the father and maternal grandmother. Later, the grandmother took the child to England and failed to return the child to Australia, which was in breach of an agreement made between the mother and father that the child would be returned within six months. The father, who had been an exemplary parent (but who had no legal custody), applied to the English High Court for an immediate return order under art. 12. The judge ordered the child's immediate return to Australia. The mother appealed to the Court of Appeal.
>
> The Court of Appeal, by a majority, dismissed her appeal, and held that, as the purposes of the Convention were, in part, humanitarian, it had to be construed broadly as an international agreement according to its general tenor and purpose, without attributing to any of its terms a specialist meaning which the sort of words in question might have acquired under the domestic law of England. The expression 'rights of custody', in most cases, had to be interpreted to give it the widest sense possible in order to accord with the objective of returning children to their country of habitual residence. Rights of an inchoate nature were sufficient to create rights of custody. The removal and retention of the child were held to be wrongful, and the child was ordered to be returned to Australia.

Although the facts in *Re B* were similar to those in *Re J sub nom C v. S* (see p. 353 above), the majority of the Court of Appeal adopted a purposive construction and held that the father possessed *de facto* custody rights (he had cared for the child), which were sufficient to bring him within the scope of the Convention. Peter Gibson LJ, however, dissented as he considered that the Court of Appeal was bound by the decision of the House of Lords in *Re J sub nom C v. S*, as the facts of that case were indistinguishable other than for the fact that the mother in *Re B* had perpetuated a cruel deceit on the father.

The court can possess a right of custody Removal or retention of a child can be wrongful where it breaches a 'right of custody' possessed by the court. The House of Lords so held in *Re H (Abduction: Rights of Custody)* [2002] 2 AC 291, [2000] 1 FLR 374 where it overturned the trial judge's refusal to order that the mother return the child to Ireland (on the basis that the father had no custody rights), as the Irish court possessed custody rights in the child as an 'institution or other body' to which rights of custody could be attributed within the meaning of art. 3. It held that 'rights' should be given a wide interpretation and that the power to determine a child's place of residence could itself be characterised as a right. In *A v. B (Abduction: Rights of Custody: Declaration of Wrongful Removal)* [2008] EWHC 2524 (Fam), [2009] 1 FLR 1253 Bodey J confirmed that the courts can have rights of custody and made a declaration under s.8 of the Child Abduction and Custody Act 1985 to that effect. If a child is made a ward of court, the wardship court acquires rights of custody in the child, which enables it to invoke the Hague Convention if the child is abducted from England (*Re S (Brussels II Revised: Enforcement of Contact Order)* [2008] 2 FLR 1358).

(b) Seeking a determination about rights of custody

Under art. 15 of the Hague Convention the court in England and Wales can seek a determination from the authorities of the State of the child's habitual residence as to whether or not removal of the child was a breach of a right of custody under the law of that country. In *Re T (Abduction: Rights of Custody)* [2008] EWHC 809 (Fam), [2008] 2 FLR 1794 Coleridge J said that it was important that issues like rights of custody be very clearly settled by the foreign law; and that it would be highly invidious for the English court to trespass into such an area unless it was unavoidable. In *Re T* Coleridge J ordered that there should be a determination by the court in Oregon, USA, as to whether the father had rights of custody (as the mother had argued that he had no such rights).

The status of an art. 15 ruling The House of Lords held in *Re D (Abduction: Rights of Custody)* [2006] UKHL 51, [2007] 1 FLR 961 that an art. 15 ruling from a requesting State is conclusive as to the parties' rights under the law of the requesting State, unless the circumstances are exceptional (for example where a ruling was obtained by fraud or in breach of the rules of natural justice). It held that a foreign court was much better placed than the English court to understand the true meaning and effect of its own laws in Hague Convention terms; and only if its characterisation of the parent's rights was clearly out of line with international understanding of the Convention's terms should the court in the UK decline to follow it. In *Re D* the House of Lords held that the Court of Appeal had been wrong not to consider itself bound by a ruling of the Romanian court (which had held that the mother's removal of the child from Romania to the UK had not been wrongful, as the father had lost rights of custody on divorce under Romanian law).

13.7 The Hague Convention – return of children

Under the Hague Convention a person (institution or other body) claiming that a child has been removed or retained in breach of a right of custody can apply for assistance in securing the child's return from the Central Authority in the Contracting State of the child's habitual residence, or in any other Contracting State (art. 8). The Central Authority of the State where the child is present must take all appropriate measures to effect the voluntary return of the child (art. 10). But, if effecting a voluntary return is not possible, then court proceedings will have to be brought.

As the Convention is based on the presumption that an abducted child should be returned to his country of habitual residence, so that the court there can decide on his future, the court hearing a return application must order the child's return if the application is made during the first 12 months after the wrongful removal or retention (art. 12). After that 12-month period, the court must also order the child's return, unless the child is 'settled in its new environment' (art. 12) (see below). The duty to return a child is, however, subject to any defence being successful (see below). Because speed is of the essence in abduction cases, judicial and administrative authorities in a Contracting State are required to act expeditiously in return proceedings (art. 11, and see also Brussels II Revised, see p. 349 above).

13.8 The Hague Convention – defences to a return application

(a) Introduction

In addition to defences based on the court having no jurisdiction to hear the application (for example, because the child is not habitually resident in a Contracting State, or there is no custody right, see above), the following defences are expressly laid down in the Convention.

Defences under the Hague Convention

- ▶ The child is now settled in his new environment (art. 12).
- ▶ Consent (art. 13(a)).
- ▶ Acquiescence (art. 13(a)).
- ▶ Grave risk that the child's return will expose the child to physical or psychological harm or otherwise place him in an intolerable situation (art. 13(b)).
- ▶ The child objects to being returned and has attained an age and degree of maturity at which it is appropriate to take account of his views (art. 13).
- ▶ Where return of the child would not be permitted by the fundamental principles of the requested State relating to the protection of human rights and fundamental freedoms (art. 20).

In EU abductions these defences have to be considered in the light of Brussels II Revised (see p. 349 above).

A high threshold for defences   The courts in England and Wales have set a high threshold for defences in order not to frustrate the Convention's primary objective, which is to effect the return of abducted children and restore the factual situation which existed before the wrongful removal or retention. Thus, the courts are reluctant to refuse to order return, and constantly emphasise that the underlying thesis of the Convention is that the welfare of children is best determined by the court of the child's habitual residence. The alleged abductor therefore has a heavy burden to establish a defence; and, even if a defence is proved, the court retains an overriding discretion to order the child's return.

The overriding discretion of the court   A successful defence based on habitual residence or lack of a custody right will mean that the case does not come within the scope of the Convention, and that will be the end of the matter. In respect of the other defences, a successful defence will not necessarily result in the court refusing to order the child's return. This is because art. 18 of the Hague Convention gives the court an overriding discretion to decide whether or not to order return.

Before the decision of the House of Lords in *Re M (Abduction: Zimbabwe)* [2007] UKHL 55, *sub nom Re M and Another (Minors)* [2008] 1 FLR 251 (see below), a long line of Court of Appeal authorities had held that, even if a defence was established, the court should order return unless there was something special or exceptional about the case, but in *Re M* Baroness Hale said that it was neither necessary or desirable to import an additional gloss of 'exceptionality' into the plain wording of the Convention, as the circumstances in which return may be refused were themselves exceptions to the general rule.

(b)   The child is now settled in his or her new environment (art. 12)

Art 12 provides that a court hearing a return application must order the child's return if 12 months have passed since the wrongful removal or retention, unless it can be shown that the child is settled in his or her new environment. However, even if it is proved that the child is settled, the court has a discretion under art. 18 of the Hague Convention (see above) to order return, as the following case, the leading case on art. 12, shows:

▶ *Re M (Abduction: Zimbabwe)* [2007] UKHL 55, *sub nom Re M and Another (Minors)* [2008] 1 FLR 251

Two girls (aged 13 and 10 born in Zimbabwe to Zimbabwean parents), lived in Zimbabwe with their father after their parents separated. Four years later their mother wrongfully removed them secretly to the UK where she sought asylum. This was refused but the mother and the children remained in the UK where the two girls became well settled in their local church and school. The father discovered their whereabouts about six months later but did not seek their return under the Hague Convention until about two years later.

Despite finding that the two children were settled in the UK and that they objected to return (under art. 12), Wood J ordered their immediate return, applying the principle that only in exceptional cases should the court exercise its overriding discretion to refuse to order an immediate return once a defence was made out. The mother's appeal to the Court of Appeal (where she argued *inter alia* that Wood J had fallen into error by applying a test of 'exceptionality' at the discretion stage) was dismissed; and so she appealed to the House of Lords, where the children were joined as parties (having regard to the principles laid down in *Re D (Abduction: Rights of Custody)* (2006) (see p. 351 above). In addition to the arguments raised before the Court of Appeal, the mother raised the issue of whether the Court of Appeal had been right in *Cannon v. Cannon* [2004] EWCA Civ 1330, [2005] 1 FLR 169 to hold that, even if settlement was established under art. 12, the courts retained a discretion under art.18 to order return.

The House of Lords held (with Baroness Hale giving the leading opinion) that:

By a majority (Lord Rodger dissenting) that the courts have a discretion to order that a child be returned, even if the child is settled in his or her new environment for the purposes of art. 12. Baroness Hale said that such a construction recognised the flexibility in the concept of settlement, which might arise in a variety of circumstances and to very different degrees; and it acknowledged that late application may be the result of active concealment of where the child has gone. It also left the court with all options open.

Baroness Hale ruled that it was wrong to import any exceptionality into the exercise of discretion under the Hague Convention.

Baroness Hale said that the policy considerations of swift return and comity would carry less weight the longer the abducted child had been in the UK; but that in settlement cases 'the policy of the Convention would not necessarily point towards return'.

Applying the above approach to the facts of the case, the House of Lords allowed the mother's appeal and refused to order that the children be returned to Zimbabwe.

(For a case-commentary on *Re M*, see Schuz [2008] CFLQ 64).

(For a case where the discretion under art. 18 was exercised, see *F* v. *M and N (Abduction: Acquiescence: Settlement)* [2008] EWHC 1525 (Fam), [2008] 2 FLR 1270 where Black J, applying *Re M*, ordered the child's return to Poland even though it had been established that she was settled in England for the purposes of art. 12).

(c) Consent (art. 13(a))

The court can refuse to order return if it can be proved that the applicant consented to the child's removal or retention. Consent is a question of fact, but it must be clear, unequivocal and informed (*Re P (Abduction: Consent)* [2004] EWCA Civ 971, [2004] 2 FLR 1057). The principles that apply to acquiescence (see below) also apply to consent.

Consent can be valid if it is conditional on some future event occurring, provided that the happening of the event is of reasonable ascertainability (see *Re L (Abduction: Consent)* [2007] EWHC 2181 (Fam), [2008] 1 FLR 914 where consent was established as the parents had signed an agreement in which they had agreed that the mother could opt to reside in the UK on separation, but where Bodey J nonetheless ordered the children's return to the USA as that was the appropriate forum for decisions to be made about them).

Each case turns on its own facts. In *M* v. *M (Abduction: Consent)* [2007] EWHC 1404 (Fam), [2007] 2 FLR 1010 Sumner J refused to order the children's return to Greece as the mother had proved by clear and cogent evidence that the father had consented to her bringing the children to the UK.

(d) Acquiescence (art. 13(a))

Acquiescence is commonly argued as a defence. In the following case, the leading case on acquiescence, the House of Lords made it clear that an attempt to reach a voluntary agreement for a child's return does not necessarily of itself amount to acquiescence:

▶ *Re H (Abduction: Acquiescence)* [1998] AC 72, [1997] 1 FLR 87, HL

The parents were strict Orthodox Jews, who were married and lived in Israel. The mother took the children to England without the father's consent. The father contacted his local Beth Din (a religious court of law), and it entered its own summons for the children's return, which the mother ignored. The Beth Din later ordered the father to take whatever steps he saw fit, and six months after the children had been removed from Israel he invoked Hague Convention proceedings in the High Court in England. The mother argued that he had acquiesced in the children's removal by failing to make a prompt application. The High Court ordered the children's return, but the Court of Appeal allowed the mother's appeal, holding that the father had acquiesced, applying its earlier decision in *Re A (Minors) (Abduction: Custody Rights)* [1992] Fam 106, *sub nom Re A (Minors) (Abduction: Acquiescence)* [1992] 2 FLR 14 where by a majority it had applied an objective test to establish acquiescence, and had held that acquiescence could be signified by a single act or communication, even though that act or communication appeared to be at variance with the general course of a parent's conduct. The father appealed to the House of Lords.

The House of Lords held, allowing his appeal and ordering the children's return to Israel, that the objective test of acquiescence laid down by the Court of Appeal in *Re A* was wrong. The correct approach was that adopted by Balcombe LJ who had dissented in *Re A*. Applying this approach, it was clear that the father had not acquiesced in the children's retention in England.

Lord Browne-Wilkinson laid down the following principles on acquiescence:

▶ Whether the wronged parent has acquiesced in the removal or retention of a child depends on his or her actual state of mind. The test is subjective.
▶ The subjective intention of the wronged parent is a question of fact for the trial judge to determine in all the circumstances of the case, the burden of proof being on the abducting parent.
▶ But there is one exception, namely: where the wronged parent's words or actions clearly and unequivocally show and have led the other parent to believe that the wronged parent is not asserting or going to assert his right to the summary return of the child and are inconsistent with such return, justice requires that the wronged parent be held to have acquiesced.

Although each case depends on its own facts, the following approaches to acquiescence have been taken in the case-law:

A custody application made in the child's country of habitual residence is a strong indication that there is no acquiescence (*Re F (A Minor) (Child Abduction)* [1992] 1 FLR 548).

Making long-term plans for contact may indicate acquiescence (*Re S (Abduction: Acquiescence)* [1998] 2 FLR 115).

Bringing proceedings for contact in the English courts, even though brought in ignorance of the Convention, may indicate acquiescence (*Re B (Abduction: Acquiescence)* [1999] 2 FLR 818).

A willingness to be involved in negotiations to sort out what is best for a child and the parties does not necessarily amount to acquiescence, even if no agreement is reached (*Re I (Abduction: Acquiescence)* [1999] 1 FLR 778); *as negotiations at the early stage of a difficult broken relationship are to be encouraged* (*P v. P (Abduction: Acquiescence)* [1998] 2 FLR 835).

Consenting to full and final residence orders being made in England and Wales may constitute acquiescence (*Re D (Abduction: Acquiescence)* [1998] 1 FLR 686).

Mere inaction does not necessarily on its own amount to acquiescence (*AF* v. *MB-F* (*Abduction: Rights of Custody*) [2008] EWHC 272 (Fam), [2008] 2 FLR 1239).

It is not necessarily a prerequisite for establishing acquiescence that a parent has correct advice or detailed knowledge of his or her rights under the Convention; what is important that the applicant knew that he/she could bring a return application but chose to accept the situation as it was (*B-G* v. *B-G* [2008] EWHC 688 (Fam), [2008] 2 FLR 965).

(e)   Grave risk of physical or psychological harm, or otherwise placing the child in an intolerable situation (art. 13(b))

The art. 13(b) grave risk of harm defence was successful in the following cases:

▶ *Re D (Article 13b: Non-Return)* **[2006] EWCA Civ 146, [2006] 2 FLR 305**

The return of the children to Venezuela was refused as the mother had been shot at in the family home in Venezuela at close range by a hired gunman, whose attack the mother suspected had been initiated by the father. There was strong evidence of extreme violence and danger of physical harm to the children and emotional harm, and so the children should not be returned.

▶ *Klentzeris v. Klentzeris* **[2007] EWCA Civ 533, [2007] 2 FLR 996**

The return of the children to Greece was refused partly due to the fact that the Cafcass officer had reported that the youngest child had had a panic attack when recounting the incidents which had occurred in Greece; and because both children had expressed strong objections to being returned. A return order was refused even though it was an EU abduction and was therefore governed not only by the Hague Convention but by Brussels II Revised.

Separating siblings   Although the courts are alert to the fact that separating siblings may result in psychological or emotional harm, they have held that separating brothers and sisters will not necessarily be held to constitute psychological harm (see *Re C (Abduction: Grave Risk of Physical or Psychological Harm)* [1999] 2 FLR 478). The courts have recognised that some psychological harm to a child is inherent in any abduction case (see *E* v. *E (Child Abduction: Intolerable Situation)* [1998] 2 FLR 980).

Allegations of domestic violence   Whether allegations of domestic harm will constitute a grave risk of harm will depend on the circumstances of the case. Return may be ordered, even where serious domestic violence is alleged, as the court in England and Wales will presume that the courts in the foreign jurisdiction will be able to provide protection and support for a parent victim and for the child if return is ordered. (See *Re W (Abduction: Domestic Violence)* (2004) and *TB* v. *JB (Abduction: Grave Risk of Harm)* (2001), below).

Case-law examples where the Article 13(b) defence has been argued

▶ *Re S (Abduction: Intolerable Situation: Beth Din)* [2000] 1 FLR 454

The mother argued that, if the children were ordered to be returned to Israel, it would result in an intolerable situation under art. 13(b) (as women who were orthodox Jews were discriminated against under Israeli religious law), and this would result in her rights and those of the children being breached under art. 8 (the right to family life) of the European Convention for the Protection of Human Rights. Connell J refused to accept her argument and ordered their return.

▶ *Re S (Abduction: Custody Rights)* [2002] EWCA Civ 908, [2002] 2 FLR 815

The mother argued that if she was ordered to return the child to Israel, the child would suffer a grave risk of harm because of the political tension and terrorist attacks in Israel. The Court of Appeal held that, although this was a real risk of harm to the child, it was not a grave risk. The fact of terrorism in Israel was not sufficient to justify a refusal to return the child, which would defeat the predominant aim of the Convention to return children to their country of habitual residence.

▶ *Re W (Abduction: Domestic Violence)* [2004] EWHC 1247 (Fam), [2004] 2 FLR 499

The child's return to South Africa was ordered even though the mother's evidence showed that she had been subjected to regular abuse, which included violence, threats with a firearm and demeaning sexual practices. As there was no real evidence, however, that the child had suffered distress and no evidence about the psychological impact of the life that she had led, Baron J held that the grave hardship defence had not been made out.

▶ *TB v. JB (Abduction: Grave Risk of Harm)* [2001] 2 FLR 515

Despite the mother's claim that she was too frightened to return to New Zealand (because she claimed her husband had been physically and sexually violent towards her, and had physically abused the children), the Court of Appeal (Hale LJ dissenting) ordered return as Singer J in the High Court had erred (as his evaluation of the alleged risk to the children of returning home to New Zealand had not been carried out on the basis that the mother could take all reasonable steps to protect herself and the children if return was ordered).

Abductions in the European Union In an abduction involving two Contracting States to the Hague Convention which are also Member States of the European Union, art. 11(4) of Brussels II Revised provides that a court 'cannot refuse to return a child on the basis of the grave risk defence under art. 13(b) if it is established that adequate arrangements have been made to secure the protection of the child after his or her return' (see *F v. M (Abduction: Grave Risk of Harm)* [2008] EWHC 1467 (Fam), [2008] 2 FLR 1263).

(f) Child objects to being returned (art. 13)

The court may refuse to order return if it finds that the child objects to being returned; *and* the child has attained an age and degree of maturity at which it is appropriate to take account of the child's views. The court has a discretion as to the amount of weight to be given to the child's views, but will bear in mind the policy of the Convention that abducted children should be returned to their country of habitual residence. The weight to be attached to the child's objections will depend on the age and maturity of the child.

The usual way in which the child's objections are put before the court is by way of a report by the Children and Family Reporter (an officer of Cafcass, see 1.6), but in some cases the court may allow the child to be made a party to the proceedings and be separately represented, particularly if the child has an independent point of view which needs to be put before the court. (For more on the child's views, see p. 350 above).

In *AF* v. *MB-F (Abduction: Rights of Custody)* [2008] EWHC 272 (Fam), *sub nom* Re F *(Abduction: Acquiescence)* [2008] 2 FLR 1239 (see further below) Sir Mark Potter P, summarising the earlier case-law, said that the court must consider the following questions when considering the art. 13 defence:

▶ Are the objections made out?
▶ Has the child reached an age and degree of maturity at which it is appropriate to take account of his views?
▶ Have those views been shaped or coloured by undue influence or pressure directly or indirectly exerted by the abducting parent to an extent which requires such views to be disregarded or discounted?
▶ What weight should be placed on the child's objections in the light of any countervailing factors, and in particular the policy considerations of the Hague Convention (namely that deterrence of abductors and the welfare interests of children are generally best served by making of an order for prompt return; and the need to respect the judicial processes of the requesting State)?

(See also *JPC* v. *SLW and SMW (Abduction)* [2007] EWHC 1349 (Fam), [2007] 2 FLR 900 where Sir Mark Potter P ordered the immediate return of the child to Ireland as that was the appropriate forum for dealing with the welfare issues in accordance with the plain intention of the Hague Convention, as reinforced by Brussels II Revised, despite the fact that the child, who had been joined as defendant, objected to being returned).

The court will be vigilant to ascertain and assess the reasons for the child not wishing to return; and, although art. 12 requires the child to be returned to the *State* of habitual residence, not to the person requesting the child's return, the court can consider the fact that a child is objecting to returning to a parent rather than to a State (*per* Butler-Sloss LJ in *Re M (A Minor) (Child Abduction)* [1994] 1 FLR 390).

Although a child's views may be taken into account, those views are not necessarily decisive of the matter, because the court must decide what weight to give those objections when exercising its overriding discretion to decide whether or not to order return. The following cases are examples of cases where the child objected to being returned:

▶ *Re S (A Minor) (Abduction: Custody Rights)* [1993] Fam 242, *sub nom* S v. S *(Child Abduction) (Child's Views)* [1992] 2 FLR 492

A girl aged 10 with a severe stammer and associated behaviour problems was taken from France to England by her mother, where her stammer and behaviour problems disappeared. The father applied for the child's return, but the mother argued, *inter alia*, that the child objected to being returned and had reached an age and degree of maturity at which it was appropriate to take into account her views. The trial judge accepted this defence and refused to return the child. The father's appeal to the Court of Appeal was dismissed.

▶ *Re T (Abduction: Child's Objections to Return)* [2000] 2 FLR 192

The Court of Appeal refused to order the return of a girl (aged 11) and her brother (aged 6) to Spain, as the girl's objections to return had been made out. Although the girl's brother was held to be too young and immature for his views to be taken into account, the Court of Appeal refused to order his return, as there was a grave risk that if he were ordered to be returned to Spain without his sister it would place him in an intolerable position under art. 13(b).

▶ *Re G (Abduction)* [2008] EWHC 2558 (Fam), [2009] 1 FLR 760

Black J ordered the return of a girl (aged 11) to Lithuania (despite the fact that she was mature enough for her views to be taken into account and she had a strong objection to returning), as it could not be concluded from the evidence that she objected to a return to Lithuania *per se*. The reality of the girl's objection was that she vehemently did not want to return to live with the father and the father's wife. The Lithuanian court was the appropriate place for an investigation into the issues surrounding the child.

▶ *Re M (Abduction: Child's Objections)* [2007] EWCA Civ 260, [2007] 2 FLR 72

The Court of Appeal accepted the objections of the child (an intelligent girl aged 8) and refused to order her return to Serbia on the basis of her objections being exceptional in the context of the unusual circumstances of the case (the child had been traumatised by her personal experiences in Serbia where drugs had been planted on her mother (possibly by the father) in persistent attempts to incriminate her). Sir Mark Potter P, with whom Rix and Wilson LJJ agreed, held that the general welfare considerations in the case strongly militated in favour of refusing to order return.

▶ *Re S (Abduction: Children's Representation)* [2008] EWHC 1798 (Fam), [2008] 2 FLR 1918

Charles J refused to order the return of three children to Argentina, as the children (who were separately represented) objected to a return as their argument that their father would not take notice of their wishes outweighed the father's arguments based on the underlying purpose of the Convention.

▶ *AF v. MB-F (Abduction: Rights of Custody)* [2008] EWHC 272 (Fam), *sub nom* Re F *(Abduction: Acquiescence)* [2008] 2 FLR 1239

Sir Mark Potter P declined to order the return of two children to Poland because of their objections to return. He said that art. 13 does not inhibit the court from considering the objections of a child to returning to a particular carer; and that a court may consider objections to returning a child to a particular regime of contact with a feared parent. (*AF v. MB* also makes it clear that the provisions of Brussels II Revised (see p. 350), which are designed to make return to the State of habitual residence more frequent, do not override the test laid down in art. 13 of the Hague Convention).

13.9   The European Convention

The European Convention on the Recognition and Enforcement of Decisions Concerning Custody of Children 1980 (the 'European Convention') was implemented into UK law by Part II of the Child Abduction and Custody Act 1985. The text of the Convention is laid down in Sched. 2 to that Act.

Under the European Convention, a custody decision given in a Contracting State must be recognised and, where it is enforceable in the State of origin, made enforceable in every other Contracting State (art. 7). Like the Hague Convention, the European Convention creates an international network of Contracting States who must work together to effect the return of abducted children. Unlike the Hague Convention, however, it deals with the enforcement of custody (and access) *orders*, not custody rights.

A person wishing to have a custody or access decision recognised or enforced in another Contracting State must apply to the central authority in any Contracting State (art. 4), which must take various appropriate steps without delay. These steps include instituting proceedings, discovering the child's whereabouts, securing the recognition or enforcement of the decision, securing delivery of the child to the applicant where enforcement is granted, and informing the requesting authority of the measures taken and their results (art. 5). The Central Authority in England and Wales is the International Child Abduction and Contact Unit (ICACU) based in the Office of the Official Solicitor.

Before a custody decision made in another Contracting State can be recognised and enforced in England and Wales it must be registered (ss.15(2)(b) and 16 CACA 1985). An application for registration (which must be made in the High Court) can be made by any person who has rights under the custody decision. The High Court can refuse to register a decision, thereby refusing recognition and enforcement, on certain grounds (see below); or if a return application is pending under the Hague Convention (s.16(4) CACA 1985). In no circumstances may the original foreign custody decision be reviewed as to its substance (art. 9(3)).

Although the European Convention is rarely invoked, because it has largely been superseded by the Hague Convention and because cases involving Member States of the European Union (except Denmark) are dealt with under Brussels II Revised (see p. 350 above), it can be useful in access/contact cases as access/contact rights are not enforceable by Hague Convention proceedings (see p. 348 above). The European Convention may also be useful where the Hague Convention does not apply, for example, where the person who wrongly removed or retained the child has sole custody.

The European Convention deals with the recognition and enforcement of custody decisions where there has been 'improper removal of a child', by allowing any person who has obtained a custody decision in a Contracting State to apply to a central authority in another Contracting State to have that decision recognised or enforced in that State (art. 4). The Convention applies to custody decisions made before or after the child's wrongful removal across an international frontier from one Contracting State to another (art. 12). A 'custody decision' is a decision made by any judicial or administrative authority relating to the care of a child, including a right to determine the child's place of residence or a right of access to the child (art. 1(c)).

'Improper removal' is defined as 'the removal of a child across an international frontier in breach of a decision relating to his custody which has been given in a Contracting State and which is enforceable in such a State' and includes: (i) the failure to return a child across an international frontier at the end of a period of the exercise of the right of access to the child or at the end of any other temporary stay in a territory other than that where the custody is exercised; and (ii) a removal which is subsequently declared unlawful within the meaning of art. 12 (art. 1(d)).

Decisions on access, and custody decisions dealing with access, can also be recognised and enforced under the Convention subject to the same conditions which apply to custody decisions, but the competent authority of the State addressed may fix the conditions for the implementation and exercise of the right of access, taking into account, in particular, undertakings given by the parties on this matter (art. 11). Where there is no decision as to access, or where recognition or enforcement of a custody decision has been refused, the central authority of the State addressed may apply to its own competent authorities for a decision on the right of access if the person claiming a right of access so requests (art. 11(3)).

Grounds for refusal to register an order   The court can refuse to register an order, and thereby fail to recognise and enforce it (see art. 9 and 10). However, it is unlikely to do so, as the aim of the Convention, like the Hague Convention, is to foster international co-operation to effect the return of abducted children.

Article 9 lays down procedural grounds for refusing to register an order, which include, for instance: where the decision was made in the absence of the defendant or his lawyer; or there was lack of notice; or the decision is incompatible with another decision made in the State addressed before the child's removal. Article 10 lays down substantive grounds for refusing to recognise and enforce an order which include, for instance: where the effects of the decision are incompatible with the fundamental principles of family and child law in the State addressed; if the effects of the custody decision are no longer in accordance with the child's welfare because of a change of circumstances.

Where the court is considering whether to refuse to register an order on the basis that it is no longer in accordance with the child's welfare due to a change of circumstances, it must ascertain the child's views (unless it is impracticable to do so having regard to his age and understanding) (art. 15(1)).

There are few reported cases on the European Convention because it is rarely invoked in the courts in England and Wales, but it was invoked by: grandparents (unsuccessfully) who wished to enforce a French access order in *Re L (Abduction: European Convention: Access)* [1999] 2 FLR 1089); and by a father (unsuccessfully) who wished to enforce a Swedish custody order in *T v. T (Abduction: Forum Conveniens)* [2002] 2 FLR. In *Re A (Foreign Access Order: Enforcement)* [1996] 1 FLR 561 a French access order was recognised and enforced in England by the English courts.

13.10   Non-Convention cases

If a child is abducted out of the UK to a country which is not party to the Hague Convention (or the European Convention) (see above), the wronged parent is in a precarious position because there is no network of Contracting States which can work together to effect the child's return. A parent will therefore have to try to reach an amicable settlement with the abducting parent, or commence legal proceedings in the country to which the child has been taken. Bringing legal proceedings in a foreign country, however, can be difficult and expensive, and return of the child is not guaranteed, because in some countries fathers are favoured over mothers and the best interests of the child may not be the primary consideration. Bringing proceedings in countries with Islamic legal systems can be particularly difficult.

Where a child is brought *into* the UK from a non-Convention country, a return application can be made to the High Court in wardship proceedings or under the inherent jurisdiction (see 8.7, and, for example, *Re F (Abduction: Removal Outside Jurisdiction)* [2008] EWCA Civ 842, [2008] 2 FLR 1649 where the father successfully sought the return of the children to Mozambique under the inherent jurisdiction). An alternative to wardship is to seek a s.8 specific issue order under the Children Act 1989 (see 10.8). The court has a wide discretion in any of these proceedings, and, unlike Hague Convention proceedings, there is no presumption in favour of ordering return. The court can, if it wishes, investigate the merits of the case; or it may decide to exercise 'summary jurisdiction', in other words order the child's immediate return without conducting a full investigation of the merits of the case (see further below).

In some cases the High Court may not have jurisdiction to hear the case (see, for example, *Al Habtoor* v. *Fotheringham* [2001] EWCA Civ 186, [2001] 1 FLR 951 where the mother's application in wardship was refused as the child was resident in Dubai, not England, and because the child was not a British national).

The governing principles in non-convention cases The principles applicable in non-Convention cases were laid down by the House of Lords in the following case, which is the leading case:

▶ *Re J (A Child) (Child Returned Abroad: Convention Rights)* [2005] UKHL 40, [2005] 2 FLR 802

The mother took the child to England from Saudi Arabia. The father applied under s.8 of the Children Act 1989 for a specific issue order for the return of the child to Saudi Arabia, but the trial judge refused the application. The father appealed to the Court of Appeal which unanimously allowed his appeal. The mother appealed to the House of Lords, which allowed her appeal, and restored the orders made by the trial judge. The House of Lords held that the trial judge and the Court of Appeal had been wrong to leave out of account the absence of a jurisdiction in the home country to enable the mother to bring the child back to England without the father's consent.

Baroness Hale, who gave the leading opinion, laid down the following principles and approaches to be applied in non-Convention cases for the summary return of children:

▶ The child's welfare is paramount and the specialist rules and concepts of the Hague Convention are not to be applied by analogy in non-Convention cases.
▶ Each case depends on its facts. In some cases summary return will be in the child's best interests but in others it will not.
▶ In having to make a decision whether or not to order summary return, a judge might find it convenient to start from the proposition that it was likely to be better for a child to return to his home country for any dispute about his future to be decided there. Any case against his doing so had to be made.
▶ It should not be assumed that allowing a child to remain in the UK while his future was decided here inevitably means that he will remain here for ever.
▶ An important variable is the degree of connection of the child with each country. This does not involve applying the technical concept of habitual residence, but to ask in a common-sense way with which country the child has the closer connection. In determining this issue of the child's 'home country', the child's nationality, where he has lived for most of his life, first language, race or ethnicity, religion, culture and education are relevant matters. A closely related factor is the length of time that the child has spent in each country. Uprooting a child from one environment and bringing him to a completely unfamiliar one, especially if that has been done clandestinely, may well not be in the child's best interests. But, if the child is already familiar with the UK, and had been here for some time without objection, it might be less disruptive for him to remain a little longer while his medium- and longer-term future are decided.
▶ The relevance of the fact that the legal system of the other country is different from that in the UK depends on the facts of each case. It is wrong to say that the future of the child should be decided according to the conception of child welfare which exactly corresponds with that which is current in England and Wales. In a world which values difference, one culture is not inevitably to be preferred to another. For this reason, English law does not start from any *a priori* assumptions about what is best for any individual child. The court must consider the individual child and weigh in the balance the checklist of factors in s.1(3) of the Children Act 1989 (see 10.3). If there is a genuine issue between the parents as to whether it is in the best interests of the child to live in the UK or elsewhere, it is relevant whether that issue is capable of being tried in the courts of the country to which he is to be

returned. If those courts have no choice but to do what the father wishes, without hearing the mother, then the English courts must ask themselves whether it is in the child's best interests to enable the dispute to be heard. The absence of a 'relocation' jurisdiction in the other country may be a decisive factor, unless it appears that the mother may not be able to make a good case for relocation. There may be cases where the connection of the child and the family with the other country is so strong that any difference between the legal systems in the UK and the other country should carry little weight.

▶ These considerations above must not, however, stand in the way of a swift and unsentimental decision to return the child to his home country, even if that country is very different from the UK. The concept of welfare in the UK is capable of taking cultural and religious factors into account in deciding how a child should be brought up. It also gives great weight to the child's need for a meaningful relationship with both parents.

However, although the child's welfare is the paramount consideration in non-Convention cases, Baroness Hale stated *obiter* in *Re M (Abduction: Zimbabwe)* [2007] UKHL 55, *sub nom Re M and Another (Minors)* [2008] 1 FLR 251 (a Hague Convention case, see p. 359) that in non-Convention cases the court has 'the power to order the immediate return of the child to a foreign jurisdiction without conducting a full investigation of the merits'. Her Ladyship said:

'Thus there is always a choice to be made between summary return and a further investigation. There is also a choice to be made as to the depth into which the judge will go in investigating the merits of the case before making that choice. One size does not fit all. The judge may well find it convenient to start from the proposition that it is likely to be better for a child to return to his home country for any disputes about his future to be decided there. A case against his doing so has to be made. But the weight to be given to that factor and to all the other relevant factors, some of which are canvassed in *Re J* (see above), will vary enormously from case to case.'

Human rights, Sharia law and abductions   In the following case the mother abducted the child from the Lebanon and, when her application for asylum in England was refused, she claimed that deporting her and her son back to the Lebanon would infringe their human rights. Their claim before the House of Lords was successful, and the House also emphasised the importance of the separate representation of the child. Baroness Hale also considered that the child's human rights were of greater weight than those of his mother.

▶ *EM (Lebanon)* v. *Secretary of State for the Home Department* [2008] UKHL 64, [2008] 2 FLR 2067

The Lebanese mother had obtained a divorce in the Lebanon because of her husband's violence. Under Sharia law, which was applicable in Lebanon, the father (who had only seen their son on the day of his birth) retained custody of the child and would be entitled to physical custody once the child reached the age of 7, with contact to the mother entirely at the father's discretion. When the child reached 7, the authorities sought to enforce the transfer of the child to the father, whereupon the mother went into hiding and fled with the child to England where she sought asylum. Her application was rejected and she appealed, arguing in the House of Lords that deporting her and the child back to Lebanon would infringe their art. 8 right to respect for family life and her art. 14 right to non-discrimination under the European Convention for the Protection of Human Rights (ECHR). By the time of the hearing, the child was aged 12.

The House of Lords held, allowing the appeal that:

▶ The threshold test for determining whether returning a person to a State not bound by the ECHR will involve a breach of their art. 8 ECHR right is a stringent one. There must be a flagrant breach of the right, such as will completely deny or nullify it in the destination country. Serious or discriminatory interference with the right protected is insufficient.

▶ In no meaningful sense could occasional supervised visits by the mother to her child at a place other than her home, even if such visits could be ordered, be described as family life. The effect of return would thus be to destroy the family life of the mother and child as it was now lived.

▶ The lower courts had been disadvantaged by the absence of representations on behalf of the child. The hearing before the House of Lords had underscored the importance of ascertaining and communicating to the court the views of a child such as the child in this case. In the great majority of cases, the interests of the child, although calling for separate consideration, are unlikely to differ from those of the applicant parent. If there is a genuine conflict, separate representation may be called for, but advisers should not be astute to detect a conflict where the interests of parent and child are essentially congruent.

Per **BARONESS HALE**: The violation of the child's right was of greater weight than that of the mother's. The very essence of his right would be destroyed if he were returned and removed from her, with no justification possible under art. 8(2) since the reasons for its destruction were purely arbitrary and paid no regard to his interests. There had been no family life between the child and his father or paternal family in the Lebanon, and so the circumstances were quite different from the general run of child abduction cases where it is the abduction, rather than the return, that interferes with that family life.

Summary

1 Child abduction is a worldwide problem, caused by increasing family breakdown and increasing international mobility.

2 A child can be lawfully taken out of the UK provided there is no court order prohibiting removal and every person with parental responsibility consents. If consent is not forthcoming, a s.8 specific issue order can be sought under the Children Act 1989. Where a residence order is in force, there is an automatic prohibition against removing a child from the UK for more than one month unless all those with parental responsibility give written consent to the removal, or the court grants permission (s.13 Children Act 1989).

3 The following can be used to prevent abduction: a court order; passport control; and police assistance, including the 'All Ports Warning'.

4 Child abduction is a criminal offence under the Child Abduction Act 1984; and can also be a criminal offence of kidnapping.

5 The Family Law Act 1986 enables a court order made in one part of the UK to be enforced in another part.

6 The Hague Convention (to which the UK is a party) enables Contracting States to work together to return children wrongfully removed from their country of habitual residence or wrongfully retained in another Contracting State, subject to certain defences, but defences are rarely successful. Once a defence is made out, the court has an overriding discretion to decide whether or not it is in the child's best interests to order return.

Summary cont'd

7　With abductions within the European Union, in addition to the Hague Convention it is also necessary to take into account the provisions of Council Regulation (EC) (No. 2201/2003) Concerning Jurisdiction and the Recognition and Enforcement of Judgments in Matrimonial Matters and in Matters of Parental Responsibility (Brussels II Revised).

8　The European Convention (to which the UK is a party) enables custody and access orders made in one Contracting State to be recognised, registered and enforced in another when the child has been improperly removed. Certain defences are available. The Convention is rarely invoked.

9　Where a child is wrongfully brought into England and Wales from a non-Convention country, the court will decide whether the welfare of the child requires it to order the child's return. There is no presumption in favour of return, as there is in Hague Convention cases. The court has a discretion to decide whether or not to hear the case on its merits.

Further reading and references

Beevers, 'Child abduction: inchoate rights of custody and the unmarried father' [2006] CFLQ 499.

Freedman, 'International terrorism and the grave risk defence of the Hague Convention on International Child Abduction' [2002] IFLJ 60.

Lamont, 'The EU: protecting children's rights in child abduction' [2008] IFL 110.

McEleavy, 'Evaluating the views of abducted children: trends in appellate case-law' [2008] CFLQ 230.

Schuz, 'Habitual residence of children under the Hague Child Abduction Convention – theory and practice' [2001] CFLQ 1.

Schuz, 'In search of a settled interpretation of Article 12(2) of the Hague Child Abduction Convention' [2008] CFLQ 64.

Schulz, 'Guidance from Luxembourg: First ECJ judgment clarifying the relationship between the 1980 Hague Convention and Brussels II Revised' [2008] IFL 221.

Websites

Foreign and Commonwealth Office: www.fco.gov.uk/travel

Hague Conference Website: www.hcch.net

INCADAT (Hague Convention Child Abduction Database): www.incadat.com

International Child Abduction and Contact Unit (ICACU): www.officialsolicitor.gov.uk/os/icacu.htm

Reunite (the International Child Abduction Centre): www.reunite.org

UK Passport Service: www.ukpa.gov.uk

Article 19(1) UN Convention on the Rights of the Child 1989

'States Parties must take all appropriate legislative, administrative, social and educational measures to protect the child from all forms of physical or mental violence, injury or abuse, neglect or negligent treatment, maltreatment or exploitation, including sexual abuse, while in the care of parent(s), legal guardian(s) or any other person who has the care of the child.'

The key legislation

Children Act 1989 Lays down the powers and duties of local authorities in respect of certain child care functions, and the powers and duties of courts and local authorities in respect of protecting children from significant harm.

The Protection of Children: A Progress Report, **March 2009, DCSF, HC 330, by Lord Laming (para. 1.10).**

'[There are] 11 million children in England. Of these ...

▶ 200,000 children live in households where there is a known high risk case of domestic abuse and violence.
▶ 235,000 are 'children in need' and in receipt of support from a local authority.
▶ 60,000 are looked after by a local authority.
▶ 37,000 are the subject of a care order.
▶ 29,000 are the subject of a Child Protection Plan.
▶ 1,300 are privately fostered.
▶ 300 are in secure children's homes.'

Statistics

According to figures published by the Department for Children, Schools and Families for the year ending 31 March 2009 (see *Referrals, Assessment and Children and Young People Who Are the Subject of a Child Protection Plan*, 2009) there were 547,000 referrals to social services departments (compared to 538,500 in the previous year). The percentages for the categories of abuse were the same as those for 2008: neglect 45 per cent; emotional abuse 25 per cent; and physical abuse 15 per cent. Of the 2,800 children being looked after under a care plan, 85 per cent were placed in a foster-placement and 7 per cent were placed with their own parents.

14.1 The practice of child protection

(a) Personnel involved in child protection

In addition to lawyers, many other personnel are involved in the task of providing protection for children and services for children in need. The emphasis is on a multi-agency and inter-agency approach.

Local authority social workers have a statutory responsibility to work together with other agencies and relevant partners in order to protect children and to make provision for children in need. They work in departments headed by a Director of Social Services. Their responsibilities are laid down in the Children Acts 1989 and 2004, in rules of practice, regulations and in various guidances (in particular *Working Together to Safeguard Children* (2006); and *The Children Act 1989 Guidance and Regulations: Volume 1 – Court Orders* (2008)). Part I of *Working Together* and *The Children Act 1989 Guidance* must be complied with by local authorities when exercising their childcare functions unless local circumstances indicate exceptional reasons which justify a variation (s.7 of the Local Authority Social Services Act 1970).

Cafcass (the Children and Family Court Advisory and Support Service, see 1.5) performs an important function by providing children's guardians in public law proceedings under the Children Act 1989. Children's guardians are independent of the local authority and their role is to safeguard the welfare of the child in the proceedings. The court has a duty to appoint a children's guardian on behalf of the child in proceedings for care and supervision orders, emergency protection orders and child assessment orders, unless it is satisfied that it is not necessary to do so in order to safeguard the child's interests. The guardian is responsible for instructing the lawyer on the child's behalf, but in certain circumstances the child can instruct the lawyer without a guardian.

Voluntary agencies, such as the National Society for the Prevention of Cruelty to Children (NSPCC), also provide specialist services to protect and assist children and their families.

(b) The task of child protection – getting the balance right

Social workers engaged in the task of child protection have a difficult task as they must take adequate steps to protect children, but at the same time ensure that they are not too intrusive into family life. As social services departments are public authorities for the purposes of the Human Rights Act 1998 (see s.6 HRA 1998), they must exercise their duties and powers in line with the European Convention for the Protection of Human Rights (see over). They must respect the right of children and parents to enjoy a private and family life under art. 8, while at the same time ensuring that children do not suffer inhuman and degrading treatment under art. 3. Local authorities can have their acts or omissions challenged in the courts under the HRA 1998 and in other ways (see 14.11).

Social workers are sometimes criticised for not intervening enough to protect children; and there is considerable media coverage and concern when children are failed by the system. The Victoria Climbié case was such a case, and led to improvements being made to the child protection system by the Children Act 2004 (see over). Another case where social workers, and other persons working with children, were criticised was that of Baby Peter in 2007 who was seen 60 times in eight months by different agencies who were of the view (wrongly) that the child protection plan to which he was subject was working successfully. Baby Peter died at the age of 17 months from serious injuries inflicted by his mother, her boyfriend and the lodger. After his death, Lord Laming (who had conducted the Victoria Climbié Inquiry in 2003) was asked by the Government to conduct a further review of the child protection system, and prepare a progress report on how effectively children were being safeguarded after the reforms introduced following the Victoria Climbié Inquiry. Lord Laming's report, *The Protection of Children in England: A Progress Report*, March 2009, HC 330, made various recommendations including changes in the training and recruitment of social workers.

Social workers are sometimes criticised for being too interventionist into family, as they were in the 'Cleveland affair' in the 1980s, when more than 100 children suspected of being sexually abused were taken away from their homes on the evidence of two paediatricians without other agencies being consulted. The report of the public enquiry set up to investigate the matter (*Report of the Enquiry into Child Abuse in Cleveland 1987*, Cm 412, 1987) recommended, *inter alia*, better inter-agency co-operation to protect children and better safeguards for parents and children where emergency intervention was needed. The *Report* had a considerable impact on the drafting of the Children Act 1989, in particular in respect of achieving the right balance between family autonomy and State intervention.

The courts must also get the balance right. As Lady Hale said in *Re S-B (Children)* [2009] UKSC 17, 'on the one hand, children need to be protected from harm; but on the other hand, both they and their families need to be protected from the injustice and potential damage to their whole futures done by removing children from a parent who is not, in fact, responsible for causing any harm at all'.

Furthermore, as the courts, like other public authorities, have obligations under the Human Rights Act 1998 (see 1.7), they must ensure that they exercise their powers and duties under the Children Act 1989 in line with art. 8 ECHR (the right to family life) and art 6 ECHR (the right to a fair trial) (see further at p. 376). For example, removing a child from his or her family under a care order without good cause would be a breach of art. 8. In *Re S-B (Children)* [2009] UKSC 17, Lady Hale said:

> 'In this country we take the removal of a children from their families extremely seriously. The Children Act 1989 was passed almost a decade before the Human Rights Act 1998, but its provisions were informed by the United Kingdom's obligations under article 8 and article 6 of the European Convention on Human Rights. These affect both the test and the process for intervening in the family lives of children and their parents'.

(c) Child abuse

Local authorities are responsible for protecting children who have suffered, or who are at risk of suffering, child abuse. The Children Act 1989, the key statute governing the powers and duties of social workers (and other persons), does not use the term 'child abuse' for determining the legitimacy and appropriateness of State intervention to protect children, but uses that of 'significant harm'. Guidance on what constitutes child abuse, however, is provided in various documents governing social work practice, in particular in *Working Together to Safeguard Children* (2006). Child abuse is categorised as: physical abuse; sexual abuse; emotional abuse; and neglect. These categories are used by social workers for the purpose of reporting abuse in child abuse registers.

(d) Taking a child into care

Despite the need to respect the right to family life, it is sometimes necessary for a child to be removed from his home and placed in the care of a local authority. This may be with a foster-carer, or in a children's home, or with the child's own parent, relative, or a family friend. However, taking a child into care is a step of last resort, as removing a child from the care of his parents is a drastic measure and children in care usually fare less well socially and educationally than other children. Many turn to crime. Some children have even suffered abuse in the care system itself (see the Waterhouse Report, *Lost in Care*, 2000). In order for children to reap the benefits of living in a permanent family, the Government has adopted a policy of increasing the number of children in care who are placed for adoption (see Chapter 15).

14.2　The Children Act 2004

The Children Act 2004 was, in part, a response to the tragic death in February 2000 of Victoria Climbié, aged 8, who died from malnutrition and hypothermia after suffering months of torture and neglect, despite being in regular contact with social workers and other agencies. The inquiry into her death, chaired by Lord Laming, found grave errors on the part of social services and criticised social workers and other agencies for failing to intervene (*Laming Report on the Inquiry into the Death of Victoria Climbié*, Cm 5730, January 2003). Lord Laming found the legislation (the Children Act 1989) to be fundamentally sound, but there had been gaps in its implementation. The concerns related to lack of good practice; and organisational and management problems. There was poor co-ordination and a failure to share information, and no one with a strong sense of accountability.

After the publication of various Government papers in response to the *Laming Report* (including the White Paper *Every Child Matters: The Next Steps*; and *Keeping Children Safe*, 2003), reforms to improve the practice of child protection were implemented by the Children Act 2004, with the main aim of improving the life chances for all children by providing better integrated services, and improving multi-disciplinary practice. Under these changes, a greater emphasis has been placed on inter-agency work to fight child abuse.

Key developments under the Children Act 2004 included the creation of Children's Trusts and Local Safeguarding Children's Boards. Children Trusts were created in order to bring together all the services for children and young people in an area, with the aim of improving outcomes for children and young people by providing a better integrated and responsive service. Children's Trust partners include National Health Service Primary Care Trusts, Connexions, Youth Offending Teams and Sure Start local programmes. Local Safeguarding Children Boards (LSCBs) have been established by local authorities under the Children Act 2004 to replace area child protection committees (which were non-statutory bodies). These Boards have a duty to co-ordinate local arrangements and services to safeguard children and to ensure their effectiveness. The partners who must work together to safeguard children are prescribed by the CA 2004, and include local authorities, National Health Service bodies, the police, Cafcass and other agencies. LSCBs are responsible for co-ordinating the child death review process which must take place when a child dies in the local authority area.

The Children Act 2004 requires local authorities to promote inter-agency co-operation (s.10); and the various agency organisations and individuals involved must ensure that their functions are discharged with regard to the need to safeguard and promote the welfare of children (s.11). Section 12 of the Act makes provision for the creation of a nationwide information database of children to enable local authorities, the National Health Service and other agencies to share information on suspected abuse or neglect in families, with the aim of achieving early intervention. This database ('ContactPoint') contains the names, addresses, medical and school details of children and can be accessed online by certain authorised persons such as headteachers, doctors, and social workers.

14.3 The European Convention for the Protection of Human Rights and Child Protection

As local authorities and courts are public authorities under the Human Rights Act (HRA) 1998, they must exercise their powers and duties in compliance with the European Convention for the Protection of Human Rights and Fundamental Freedoms (ECHR) (see 1.7). The decisions of the European Court of Human Rights (ECtHR) must be taken into account by the courts in England and Wales (s.2(1) HRA 1998) and are also relevant to social work practice. A local authority social services department which is found to be in breach of the ECHR can be made to pay damages under the HRA 1998, although damages are not automatic as the court must be satisfied 'that the award is necessary to afford just satisfaction to the person in whose favour it is made' (s.8).

(i) The right to family life – the presumption in favour of parents Article 8 ECHR guarantees a right to respect for family life. The essential aim of art. 8 is to protect individuals against arbitrary action by public authorities. There are also positive obligations inherent in 'respect' for family life. In order to comply with art. 8, social services who work in the area of child protection must ensure that any interference into family life is lawful, proportionate and necessary.

The presumption in favour of keeping children in their families, unless contrary to their best interests, is recognised by the ECtHR under the right to family life in art. 8. In *Haase v. Germany (Application No. 11057/02)* [2004] 2 FLR 39 the ECtHR held that:

- authorities should make a careful assessment of the impact of proposed care measures on parents and children, and of the alternatives to taking children into public care;
- following a removal into care, a stricter scrutiny is called for in respect of any further limitations by the authorities, for example in respect of restrictions on parental rights and access;
- taking a child into care should normally be regarded as a temporary measure to be discontinued as soon as circumstances permit, and any measures of implementation of temporary care should be consistent with the ultimate aim of reuniting the natural parent;
- taking a newborn baby into public care at the moment of its birth is an extremely harsh measure, for which there must be extraordinarily compelling reasons.

In *Hokkanen* v. *Finland* (1995) 19 EHRR 139, [1996] 1 FLR 289 the ECtHR held that a 'fair balance has to be struck between the interests of the child in remaining in public care and those of the parent in being reunited with the child', but that in carrying out the balancing exercise 'the best interests of the child … may override those of the parent'. The ECtHR has held that public authorities must aim to seek to restore the child to his or her family as soon as is practicable; and that any measure which hinders this (such as prohibiting contact or placing the child a long way away) may violate art. 8 (see, for example, *KA* v. *Finland* [2003] 1 FLR 696).

However, each case depends on its facts. In *Johansen* v. *Norway* (1997) 23 EHRR 33 the ECtHR held that the mother's right to family life had been breached (because she had been deprived of her parental and access rights when her daughter had been taken into care and placed with foster-parents with a view to her adoption); but in *Söderbäck* v. *Sweden* [1999] 1 FLR 250 the ECtHR distinguished *Johansen* on its facts and found no breach of art. 8.

(ii) Newborn babies Taking a newborn baby into care may violate art. 8 (see *K and T* v. *Finland* (2001) 36 EHRR 255, [2001] 2 FLR 707; and *P, C and S* v. UK (2002) 35 EHRR 31, [2002] 2 FLR 631). But, as each case depends on its facts and the welfare of the child always prevails, in some circumstances the court may hold that such intervention is in the child's best interests. Thus, in *Re M (Care Proceedings: Judicial Review)* [2003] EWHC 850 (Admin), [2003] 2 FLR 171 (where the parents sought an injunction to restrain the local authority from commencing emergency protection or care proceedings in respect of their unborn child) Munby J held, dismissing the application, that although the ECtHR had made it clear that removing a child from his mother at or very shortly after birth was a draconian measure requiring exceptional justification, there are cases where the need for such highly intrusive intervention is imperatively demanded in a baby's interests.

In *Re D (Unborn Baby)* [2009] EWHC 446 (Fam), [2009] 2 FLR 313 Munby J held that the local authority would not be acting unlawfully by removing the unborn child from the mother at birth, despite the mother's right to family life under art. 8 ECHR. In the highly unusual circumstances of the case (the mother had attempted to kill the younger child), Munby J held that the very exceptional step of not engaging the parents fully and frankly in the pre-birth planning process was entirely justified. Munby J applied the approach adopted in *Venema* v. *Netherlands (Application No 35731/97)* [2003] 1 FLR 552 (and in *Haase* v. *Germany (Application No 11057/02)* [2004] 2 FLR 39), where the ECtHR held that it would not be a breach of the Convention if the public authority had considered all the circumstances of the case and there had been a careful assessment of the impact of the proposed care measure on the parents and child; and possible alternatives had been considered.

(iii) The right to family life – the principle of proportionality An important principle in respect of the right to family life in art. 8 ECHR is that of proportionality (see 1.7). Local authorities and the courts must ensure that any intervention into family life, by court order or otherwise, is a proportionate response to a legitimate aim, for otherwise they risk being in breach of art. 8. For example, it might be a disproportionate response for a local authority to decide to remove a child from his home under a care order before having exhausted its support functions; or to remove a baby shortly after birth without giving the mother an opportunity to improve her parenting skills.

The principle of proportionality was considered in the following cases:

▶ *Re C and B (Care Order: Future Harm)* [2001] 1 FLR 611

The Court of Appeal, allowing the appeal, held that full care orders in respect of two children (and permission for the local authority to refuse parental contact) was not a proportionate response in the circumstances. The local authority should have taken time to explore other options. There had been too much speed in the circumstances. Hale LJ, referring to the jurisprudence of the ECtHR on the need for interference to be necessary and proportionate to the legitimate aim, held that, while intervention in the family can be appropriate, cutting off contact and a relationship between a child and his family is only justified by the overriding necessity of the child's best interests.

> ▶ *Re B (Care: Interference with Family Life)* [2003] EWCA Civ 786, [2003] 2 FLR 813
>
> The Court of Appeal found that the threshold criteria for a care order had been satisfied, but that the interim care order was not a proportionate response under art. 8, as the children would have been sufficiently protected by an order adjourning the application for an interim care order with liberty to renew at short notice. Here the parents had been denied the opportunity of challenging or testing the evidence of a psychiatrist who had alleged that their daughter had been sexually abused by her grandfather.
>
> ▶ *Re W (Removal into Care)* [2005] EWCA Civ 642, [2005] 2 FLR 1022
>
> Care orders were made in respect of 5-year-old twins on the basis of a care plan whereby they would remain at home with their parents. As this did not work well, a decision was taken to remove them from their home, and the local authority applied to free them for adoption. The parents, in response, applied to discharge the care orders and sought an injunction under s.8 HRA 1998 to enable the twins to return. Their applications failed. The judge held that there had been no breach of s.8, as the local authority's response was a proportionate and legitimate response to the deterioration of the home situation. The decision was upheld by the Court of Appeal, but it held that parents must issue a HRA 1998 challenge prior to the removal of children and not as a reaction to their removal.

(iv) Procedural fairness and human rights   Procedural fairness is required at all stages of the child protection process, otherwise a local authority and/or the court may be in breach of the ECHR. In some cases parents have brought claims before the court arguing that there has been a breach of the requirement of procedural fairness. Thus, parents have sometimes claimed that they have not been sufficiently involved in the decision-making process, or that they have not been given reasons for a decision; and that this is a breach of their right to family life under art. 8 ECHR and their right to a fair hearing under art. 6 ECHR. Lack of procedural fairness can be a breach of art. 6 and art. 8. Parents must be fully involved in the decision-making process, otherwise local authorities risk being in breach of their obligations under the Human Rights Act 1998.

Local authorities engaged in care and supervision proceedings (see 14.7) may infringe the rights of parents (and children) under arts. 6 and 8 of the ECHR 'unless overall they conduct themselves with such integrity, transparency and inclusiveness as to satisfy the parents' rights, necessarily to be construed in a wide sense, to a fair hearing and to respect for their private and family life' (*per* Wilson LJ in *Re J (Care: Assessment: Fair Trial)* [2006] EWCA Civ 545, [2007] 1 FLR 77).

Procedural fairness was considered in the following cases:

> ▶ *Re L (Care: Assessment: Fair Trial)* [2002] EWHC 1379 (Fam), [2002] 2 FLR 730
>
> The mother, whose child was the subject of care proceedings, was not permitted to attend meetings between the local authority, the psychiatrist and the guardian when concerns about her parenting were expressed. No minutes of the meeting were taken and the mother was not informed of the outcome. Munby J held that the right to procedural fairness under art. 6 ECHR was not confined to the judicial process, but to all stages of the process, both in and out of court. Munby J emphasised certain principles of good social work practice. Social workers must notify parents of material criticisms, and advise them how to remedy their behaviour. All professionals involved should keep clear, accurate and full notes and the local authority should make full and frank disclosure of all key documents at an early stage of proceedings.

They should provide reports; and parents should be able to make representations, and have the right to attend meetings held by the professionals involved.

▶ *P, C and S v. United Kingdom* (2002) 35 EHRR 31, [2002] 2 FLR 631

The ECtHR held that the removal of the baby at birth under an emergency protection order breached the parents' right to family life under art. 8 ECHR and their right to a fair trial under art. 6 ECHR, as they did not have legal representation in the care and freeing for adoption proceedings. The child's right to family life was also held to be breached even though she was represented in the proceedings. The ECtHR stressed that emergency measures to remove a child from a situation of danger must be properly justified by the circumstances, and parents must have procedural protection, as part of the right to family life under art. 8, not just under art. 6.

▶ *Re J (Care: Assessment: Fair Trial)* [2006] EWCA Civ 545, [2007] 1 FLR 77

The Court of Appeal held that the way in which the local authority had reached its decision and communicated its care plan had fallen short of the proper standard of fairness and transparency expected of a local authority in care proceedings (because, *inter alia*, the mother had not been invited to comment on the concerns that were inclining the local authority towards adoption rather than a residential assessment). However, the Court of Appeal held that, while the local authority's conduct lacked fairness and transparency, it was not sufficiently substantial to constitute an infringement of the mother's rights under art. 6 or art. 8 ECHR.

▶ *G v. N County Council* [2009] 1 FLR 774

The local authority removed the child from the mother after a statutory review which the mother did not attend. She was successful in obtaining a declaration under the HRA 1998 that the local authority had acted unlawfully in breaching her substantive and procedural rights under art. 8 ECHR and also those of the child. McFarlane J held *inter alia* that the action taken by the local authority had not been proportionate or procedurally fair, and had failed to involve the mother in the process at all.

The European Court of Human Rights has held that parents must have access to the information which the local authority relies on for taking measures of protective care (*Venema v. The Netherlands (Application No. 35731/97)* [2003] 1 FLR 551). It has also held that a care order must be capable of convincing an objective observer that it is based on a careful and unprejudiced assessment of all the evidence with the distinct reasons for the care measures being explicitly stated, and with all the case material being available to the parents concerned, even if they have not requested it (*KA v. Finland* [2003] 1 FLR 696; and see also *K and T v. Finland* (2001) 36 EHRR 255, [2001] 2 FLR 707).

(v) Procedure for human rights claims A complaint arising under the HRA 1998 before a final care order is made should normally be made in the care proceedings by the court dealing with those proceedings (*per* Sir Mark Potter P in *Westminster City Council v. RA, B and S* [2005] EWHC 970 (Fam), [2005] 2 FLR 1309). In *Re S and W (Care Proceedings)* [2007] EWCA Civ 232, [2007] 2 FLR 275 Wall LJ endorsed this approach and said that 'it would be wholly undesirable to have separate proceedings for a care or supervision order under Part IV of the Children Act 1989 running concurrently with proceedings for judicial review'.

14.4　The UN Convention on the Rights of the Child 1989 and Child Protection

The UN Convention on the Rights of the Child 1989 (UNCRC) (see 8.2) contains various articles which are relevant to child protection. The courts in England and Wales and the European Court of Human Rights sometimes refer to the UNCRC when making decisions about children and families. Under the UNCRC, States Parties must:

- take all measures to protect children from all forms of abuse while in the care of their parents, guardians and any other person (art. 19);
- ensure the child such protection and care as are necessary for the child's well-being, taking into account the rights and duties of his or her parents or others with parental responsibility, and to this end take all appropriate legislative and administrative measures (art. 3(2));
- ensure that a child shall not be separated from his or her parents against their will, except when competent authorities subject to judicial review determine that such separation is necessary for the best interests of the child; and all interested parties must be given an opportunity to participate in the proceedings and make their views known (art. 9(1)).

Other articles are also relevant, for example art. 34 (right to be protected from sexual exploitation and abuse), and art. 40(4) (right to care, guidance, supervision, counselling and foster-care).

14.5　The Children Act 1989

Under the Children Act 1989 local authorities and the courts have various statutory powers and duties towards children in respect of making provision for them and providing them with protection. Local authorities have powers and duties to: provide support for children in need under Part III; to seek care and supervision orders under Part IV; and to apply for emergency protection orders and child assessment orders under Part V. Local authorities also have investigative powers and duties (under s.47).

(a)　The policy objectives of the Children Act 1989

The practice of child protection under the Children Act 1989 is based on the following policy objectives:

(i) Keeping children in their families　A major policy objective is that parents, not local authorities, have primary responsibility for children and that children should be kept in their families unless this is contrary to their best interests. Social services and the courts must carry out their functions on the basis of the presumption that intervention into family life is a serious matter and is only justified where it is a legitimate, necessary and proportionate response in the circumstances. The presumption in favour of keeping children in their families is also recognised by the European Court of Human Rights (see p. 376 above).

Wall LJ in *Re L and H (Residential Assessment)* [2007] EWCA Civ 213, [2007] 1 FLR 1370 held that the following words of Lord Templeman in *Re KD (A Minor)(Ward: Termination of Access)* [1988] AC 806, [1988] 2 FLR 139 underlie the Children Act 1989:

> 'The best person to bring up a child is the natural parent. It matters not whether the parent is wise or foolish, rich or poor, educated or illiterate, provided the child's moral and physical health are not endangered. Public authorities cannot improve on nature. Public authorities exercise a supervisory role and interfere to rescue a child when the parental tie is broken by abuse or separation.'

Thus, even if the parents have learning difficulties or intellectual deficits that of itself is unlikely to result in a child being removed from their care. In *Re L (Children) (Care Proceedings: Significant Harm)* [2006] EWCA Civ 1282, [2007] 1 FLR 1068 the Court of Appeal held that, although such cases were among the most difficult, the courts did not, nor ever should, remove children from biological parents on the basis that substitute parents would provide a greater intellectual stimulus. Such social engineering was wholly impermissible.

The parental presumption was considered in the following two cases:

▶ *Re D (Care: Natural Parent Presumption)* [1999] 1 FLR 134

On the basis of the presumption in favour of parents, the court held that the child, who was subject to a care order, should be placed with his father, rather than his grandmother (even though this would separate him from his siblings).

▶ *Re H (Care Order: Contact)* [2008] EWCA Civ 1245, [2009] 2 FLR 55

The Court of Appeal allowed the appeal against a care order in respect of a 10-year-old child because, not only had the trial judge failed to consider the child's wishes in the light of her age and understanding, but, more importantly, the judge had erred in failing to perpetuate the fundamental importance of a relationship and life with a parent if at all possible. The child had expressed a strong desire to be reunited with her mother with whom she had a strong relationship. The Court of Appeal ordered that the care order be replaced with a residence order in favour of the mother, but with a supervision order to last for 12 months.

The Children Act 1989 reinforces the policy of keeping children in their families, where possible, in the following ways:

- Under s.1(5) the court can make an order (for example, a care or supervision order) only if 'it considers that doing so would be better for the child than making no order at all'.
- Rules and regulations governing social work practice require local authorities to work in partnership with parents to promote and safeguard the welfare of children in order to prevent them being taken into care. Parents must be allowed to participate in decisions about their children, and so must children who are intelligent and mature enough to do so.
- Removing a child from his parents is a serious matter, which can only be effected by a court order and only on proof of certain grounds (that the child is suffering, or is likely to suffer, significant harm); and only after a thorough investigation and consideration of all the evidence. The only exception where no prior judicial authority

is needed is where a police officer can remove a child in certain circumstances (see p. 414).

The need for a court order before a child can lawfully be removed from a parent was shown in the following case:

▶ *R (G)* v. *Nottingham City Council* [2008] EWHC 152 (Admin), [2008] 1 FLR 1660

Two days after his birth the child had been removed from his mother (who was aged 18, had been in care and who had a history of alcohol and drug abuse and self-harm). No court orders had been passed to the medical team involved in the birth. In judicial review proceedings brought by the mother Munby J made an order that the baby be reunited with his mother, on the ground that removing a child requires prior judicial authorisation. Munby J held that the only time a social worker can intervene without a court order is where it is necessary to protect a baby from immediate violence at the hands of a parent or other person.

Note After the baby had been returned to the mother, an interim care order was made later that day (which was upheld by the Court of Appeal). The baby was placed in foster care with the mother having supervised contact; but, as this proved unsatisfactory, an order for no contact for a limited period was subsequently made.

(ii) Working in partnership with parents In order to promote the presumption that children should be kept in their families, local authorities are required to work in partnership with parents and to involve them as fully as possible. The guidance, *Working Together to Safeguard Children*, establishes two key policy objectives governing good social work practice: the importance of inter-agency co-operation; and the importance of encouraging partnership and participation with parents. Families are encouraged to participate in the decision-making process. A failure to involve parents and children sufficiently in the process, without good reason, may breach the European Convention for the Protection of Human Rights (see 14.3 above).

(iii) Inter-agency co-operation Another policy aim of the Children Act 1989, and of the Children Act 2004, is that of inter-agency co-operation, whereby the various agencies (for example, social services, local education authorities and health authorities) must consult with each other and be willing to provide help if this is in the best interests of a child (see ss.27 and 47 CA 2009). As part of this emphasis on inter-agency co-operation, s.27 CA 1989 provides that local authorities, local education authorities, local housing authorities and local health authorities (or National Health Service Trusts) have a right to request help from each other and have a reciprocal duty to provide it, except where this is incompatible with their own statutory obligations. Under s.27, for example, a social services department could ask a local housing department to provide accommodation for a child leaving care. The importance of communication and information-sharing about children was emphasised in the *Cleveland Report* (see p. 374 above). It was emphasised again in the *Laming Report on the Victoria Climbié Inquiry* (Cm 5730). The findings of the *Laming Report* led to the enactment of the Children Act 2004, in which an even greater emphasis is placed on inter-agency co-operation (see 14.2).

(b)   Local authority powers and duties under the Children Act 1989 – an overview

Local authorities have a wide range of powers and duties under the Children Act 1989. They have a duty to make such inquiries as are necessary to enable them to decide whether to take any action to safeguard or promote the welfare of the child (s.47(1)). This requires a local authority social worker to visit the child to make an assessment, unless there is already sufficient information available (s.47(4)). If access to the child is thwarted and the local authority is concerned about the child, it can consider applying for an emergency protection order under s.44 or invoking police powers under s.46. In respect of their s.47 investigative functions, local authorities are not required to make a finding on the balance of probabilities as to past conduct before assessing risk and taking any necessary protective steps (*Re S (Sexual Abuse Allegations: Local Authority Response)* [2001] EWHC Admin 334, [2001] 2 FLR 776). Under s.37 of the Children Act 1989 in any family proceedings (for example, in residence or contact proceedings) where a question arises with respect to the welfare of the child, and the court considers it may be appropriate for a care or supervision order to be made, the court can make a direction ordering that a local authority investigate the child's circumstances.

If, following initial inquiries, the child is assessed as not being at risk of harm, social services will consider whether the child and family need support under Part III of the Children Act 1989. If, however, it is established that the child is, or is at risk of, suffering significant harm, then a child protection conference will be convened. This takes the form of a multi-agency meeting at which information is assessed and plans are made to safeguard and promote the child's welfare. If the child is, or will be, at risk, the child's name will be placed on the child protection register. Following the decision to register the child, the conference must formulate a child protection plan, which may mean initiating care proceedings. A key worker for the child must be appointed. Regular reviews must be carried out, and, if the child is no longer at risk of significant harm, the child will be deregistered. If the initial assessment reveals a likelihood of serious immediate harm, emergency protection measures will have to be taken under Part V of the Children Act 1989 (see 14.9); and/or care and supervision proceedings under Part IV of the Act (see 14.7).

14.6   Part III of the Children Act 1989 – support for children in need

(a)   Introduction

Under Part III of the Children Act 1989 local authorities have a duty to provide support for children in need and their families. 'Family' for this purpose includes not just parents and children, but any person with parental responsibility or any other person with whom the child is living (s.17(10)). Services can only be provided, however, with a view to safeguarding or promoting the welfare of a child in need (s.17(3)). Part III duties include the provision of services (ss.17–19) and the provision of accommodation (ss.20 and 21). Local authorities have duties to children 'looked after' by them (ss.22 and 23) and must provide advice and assistance (s.24); and in some cases secure accommodation (s.25). Local authorities must hold case reviews, co-operate with each other and consult with and request help from other authorities within the local area (such as housing authorities, local education authorities, heath authorities and health service trusts), and provide advocacy services (see ss.26–30). Schedule 2 to the Children Act lists the services which local authorities can supply for children in need and their families.

The provision of support under Part III may obviate the need to bring care or supervision proceedings. Help and support for the child in his own home is the preferred option, with compulsory intervention by court order in the last resort. However, although the Children Act 1989 lays down a duty to safeguard and promote the welfare of children, the provision of services is only a discretionary matter. The provision of services also depends on the allocation and availability of resources, which are often limited. For this reason, it may be difficult to bring a successful challenge against a local authority.

Local authorities have various duties to children in need under Part III of the Children Act 1989, but these include the duty:

▶ to safeguard and promote the child's welfare (s.22(3));
▶ to consult the wishes and feelings of the child, his parents, any person who has parental responsibility for the child, and any other relevant person (s.22(4));
▶ to provide accommodation and maintenance for a child (s.23(2));
▶ to maintain the child in other respects apart from providing accommodation (s.23(1)(b));
▶ to promote contact (Sched. 2, para. 4);
▶ to provide 'after care' for children who leave care (s.24(1)).

(b) Who is a 'child in need'?

A child is a 'child in need' for the purposes of Part III if (s.17(10)):

'(a) he is unlikely to achieve or maintain, or to have the opportunity of achieving or maintaining, a reasonable standard of health or development without the provision of services by a local authority under [Part III];
(b) his health or development is likely to be significantly impaired, or further impaired, without the provision for him of such services; or
(c) he is disabled.'

A child is 'disabled' if he is blind, deaf or dumb or suffers from mental disorder of any kind or is substantially and permanently handicapped by illness, injury or congenital deformity or such other disability as may be prescribed; and 'development' means physical, intellectual, emotional, social or behavioural development; and 'health' means physical or mental health (s.17(11)).

(c) The Part III general duty

The general duty of local authorities in respect of children in need is laid down in s.17(1):

Section 17(1) Children Act 1989

'It shall be the general duty of every local authority, in addition to the other duties imposed on them by [Part III]:

(a) to safeguard and promote the welfare of children within their area who are in need; and

(b) so far as is consistent with that duty, to promote the upbringing of such children by their families,

by providing a range and level of services appropriate to those children's needs.'

The scope of the general duty in s.17(1) was considered by the House of Lords in the following case in which all three conjoined appeals raised the question of whether social services departments were obliged to provide accommodation for children in need and their families under the Children Act 1989 when local housing authorities were unable to house or rehouse them:

▶ *R (G)* v. *Barnet London Borough Council; R (W)* v. *Lambeth London Borough Council; R (A)* v. *Lambeth London Borough Council* [2003] UKHL 57, [2004] 1 FLR 454

In each appeal the mother argued that s.17(1) required a local authority to assess and meet the needs of a particular individual child in need. As one of the local authorities had adopted a policy of making accommodation available only for a child in need, but not his parents, the House of Lords had to consider two questions: did s.17(1) create a duty to consider and assess the needs of a particular child; and could a local authority meet a child's needs for accommodation by providing accommodation for the child alone, as distinct from providing accommodation for both mother and child, when it would cost no more to provide accommodation for them both.

The House of Lords held, dismissing all three appeals, that s.17(1) set out duties of a general character which are intended to be for the benefit of all the children in need in the local social services authority's area in general, and not for each and every individual child in need. Consequently, a local social services authority was not under a duty to provide residential accommodation for families so that children could be housed with their families. Although social services could provide accommodation for a child in need and his family, this was not the principal or primary purpose of the legislation. Housing was the function of the local housing authority. An obligation under s.17(1) to provide housing would turn social services departments into housing authorities and thereby subvert the powers and duties of housing authorities under the housing legislation.

(d)   Services for children in need

The general duty of local authorities laid down in s.17(1) (see above) is facilitated by the performance of specific duties and powers laid down in Part I of Sched. 2 to the Children Act 1989 (s.17(2)), such as: the identification and assessment of children in need; advertising available services; keeping a register of and providing services for disabled children; preventing neglect and abuse; providing accommodation for those who are ill-treating or are likely to ill-treat children in order to reduce the need for criminal or civil proceedings; reintegrating children in need with their families; and promoting contact between a child and his family. The services provided under s.17 may include the provision of accommodation and giving assistance in kind or in cash (s.17(10)). Local authorities also have a duty under s.20 (see below) to provide accommodation for children in need and their families; and a duty to provide day care for certain children (s.18).

Before determining what (if any) services to provide for a particular child in need, a local authority must, so far as is reasonably practicable and consistent with the child's welfare, ascertain the child's wishes and feelings regarding the provision of those services, and give due consideration to those wishes and feelings, having regard to the child's age and understanding (s.17(4A)).

(e) Children in need – the provision of accommodation

(i) The duty to provide accommodation As part of their general duty to safeguard and promote the welfare of children in their area, local authorities have a duty under the Children Act 1989 (ss.20–25) to provide accommodation for children in need and their families. Local Authority Circular (2003) 13, *Guidance on Accommodating Children in Need and their Families*, provides guidance for local authorities about this duty.

The duty to provide children in need with accommodation is laid down in s.20(1):

Section 20(1) Children Act 1989

'Every local authority shall provide accommodation for any child in need within their area who appears to them to require accommodation as a result of –

(a) there being no person who has parental responsibility for him ...;
(b) his being lost or having been abandoned; or
(c) the person who has been caring for him being prevented (whether or not permanently, and for whatever reason) from providing him with suitable accommodation or care.'

Before providing accommodation the local authority must, so far as is reasonably practicable and consistent with the child's welfare, ascertain the child's wishes and feelings regarding the provision of accommodation; and give due consideration to those wishes and feelings (having regard to the child's age and understanding) (s.20(6)). But the child's wishes, while relevant, are not necessarily determinative (*Liverpool City Council* v. *Hillingdon London Borough Council and AK* [2009] EWCA Civ 43, [2009] 1 FLR 1536). The local authority must also draw up a written care plan for the child. A child who is accommodated is described as being 'looked after' by the local authority, whereupon the local authority has certain statutory duties in respect of the child (ss.23–30). Children who are in care under a court order are also described as being 'looked after' and similar duties are owed to them under the same provisions.

Accommodation can be provided by the local authority by placing the child with another family, with a relative, with some other suitable person, or in a children's home (s.23(2)). Any family member, relative and any other person providing accommodation for a child is described as being a local authority foster-parent (s.23(3)).

Accommodation must also be provided for a child aged 16 or over if a local authority considers the child's welfare is likely to be seriously prejudiced without it (s.20(3)). Accommodation in a community home can be provided for someone aged 16 to 21 if it will safeguard or promote his or her welfare (s.20(5)) (see, for example, *Re T (Accommodation by Local Authority)* [1995] 1 FLR 159, where the court held that the local authority had erred in refusing a 17-year-old girl accommodation as it had failed to consider her future welfare).

A local authority has no duty, however, to provide accommodation if a person with parental responsibility objects, and is able to provide accommodation or arrange for it to be provided (s.20(7)). The only exception is where a person with a residence order or who has care of the child under a court order agrees to the child being accommodated by the local authority (s.20(9)). Any person with parental responsibility may remove the child from local authority accommodation at any time without giving notice (s.20(8)), except where the child is aged 16 or over and agrees to being provided with accommodation (s.20(1)). As the arrangement is voluntary the local authority must comply with the wishes of persons with parental responsibility, unless the child is suffering, or is likely to suffer, significant harm, in which case a care or supervision order or an emergency protection order will be applied for. The right to decide where the child lives remains with the parents; and so a local authority has no power to remove a child to different accommodation if this is contrary to parental wishes (see *R v. Tameside Metropolitan Borough Council ex parte J* [2000] 1 FLR 942 where it was held that the local authority had no power to move a seriously disabled 13-year-old girl from a residential home into foster-care, as this was contrary to her parents' wishes).

The extent of the duty to provide children in need with accommodation as part of the general duty under s.17 Children Act 1989 was considered by the House of Lords in *R (G) v. Barnet London Borough Council and Related Appeals* (2003) (see p. 385 above). However, a local authority cannot opt out of its duty to provide accommodation under s.20 by claiming that the duty is merely a general duty to act under s.17 or merely a power (Holman J in *H, Barhanu and B v. London Borough of Wandsworth, London Borough of Hackney, London Borough of Islington and Secretary of State for Education and Skills (Interested Party)* [2007] EWHC 1082 (Admin), [2007] 2 FLR 822).

(ii) Providing teenage children with accommodation

Local authority social services and local authority housing departments are required to co-operate with each other in respect of providing accommodation (see ss.27 and 47 CA 1989; and s.213A Housing Act 1996). However, the interface between the Children Act 1989 and the housing legislation can sometimes cause difficulties which may result in challenges by way of judicial review.

The *Homelessness Code of Guidance for Local Authorities* (2002) advises that, once it appears to a local housing department that a 16 or 17-year-old child may be homeless, then it must accommodate the child under s.188 HA 1996 pending clarification of whether the local children's services authority owes a duty to provide the child with accommodation under s.20 CA 1989. If the criteria in s. 20 are met, then the local authority social services department, not the local housing authority, is responsible for assessing the child (under the *Framework for the Assessment of Children in Need and their Families* (2000); and Local Authority Circular *Guidance on Accommodating Children in Need and Their Families* (2003)).

The House of Lords in *R(M) v. Hammersmith and Fulham London Borough Council* [2008] UKHL 14, [2008] 1 FLR 1384 held that a social services department cannot shirk its responsibility for a child under s.20 CA 1989 by passing that responsibility over to the local housing authority; and that, if the criteria in s.20 (see p. 386 above) are met, then social services, rather than the housing department, should take responsibility, because the young person would have needs over and above their housing needs that could be better met by social services. However, in *R(M)* the applicant (an 18-year-old girl) was unsuccessful in obtaining a declaration that the local authority owed her duties under the Children Act 1989, not the Housing Act 1996, as the House of Lords held that a 'looked after' child under s.22(1) CA 1989 did not include a child who had been provided with accommodation by the local housing authority, but who had not been drawn to the attention of the children's services department or provided with any accommodation or any other services by the social services authority.

R(M) was applied in *R(W)* v. *North Lincolnshire Council* [2008] EWHC 2299 (Admin) [2008] 2 FLR 2150 where a boy aged under 18 successfully challenged the local authority's decision that it would not accommodate him under s.20 CA 1989 on his release from a young offenders' institution. The judge held, referring to *R(M)* that he was an eligible child under s.20 as he had been accommodated and supported by the local authority's social services department at various times before he was 16.

The duty to provide accommodation under s.20 and the power to provide it under s.17(6) were also considered in *R (G)* v. *Southwark London Borough Council* [2009] UKHL 26 (see below) where the House of Lords held that a local authority's children's services unit cannot purport to have fulfilled its duties to a homeless child merely by referring the case to the local housing authority under Part VII of the Housing Act 1996 (see 4.11).

The background to the case is that the Homelessness (Priority Need for Accommodation) (England) Order 2002 expressly includes children aged 16 and 17 in the list of those who have priority need under the housing legislation, but expressly excludes those to whom a duty is owed under s 20 of the Children Act 1989 and 'relevant' children, previously looked after by a local authority. Local Authority Circular (2003) 13, *Guidance on Accommodating Children in Need and Their Families*, states that, although the power to provide accommodation under s. 17 CA 1989 almost always concerns children needing to be accommodated with their families, there may be cases where a lone child who needs help with accommodation might be appropriately assisted under s.17, even though he is not a child being 'looked after' by the local authority.

R (G) v. *Southwark* (below) dealt with the construction of s.20(1) CA 1989, in other words was the local authority entitled to distinguish between 'requiring accommodation' and requiring 'help with accommodation'? Baroness Hale stated that the question for the House of Lords was: if a child aged 16 or 17, who is thrown out of the family home, presents himself to a local children's services authority and asks to be accommodated under s.20 CA 1989, is it open to the authority to arrange instead for him to be accommodated by the local housing authority under the homelessness provisions of Part VII of the Housing Act 1996?

▶ *R (G)* v. *Southwark London Borough Council* **[2009] UKHL 26, [2009] 2 FLR 380**

A 17-year-old young man who could genuinely not continue living with his mother applied to the local authority's social services department requesting accommodation under s.20 and an assessment under s.17 CA 1989. Despite his claim that he should be accommodated under s.20(1)(c) (which would entitle him to the wide range of services available to him as a 'looked after child' until he was 21 (see s.22(1)), and would mean that he would thereafter qualify as a 'former relevant child'), the local authority said that he did not need accommodation under s.20 but only *'help* with accommodation' under s.17, as interpreted in Local Authority Circular (2003, 13), *Guidance on Accommodating Children in Need and Their Families*. The Court of Appeal dismissed his application (Rix LJ dissenting), holding that the distinction made in the *Circular* (between a child who required help with accommodation under s.17 rather than requiring accommodation under s.20) was lawful, even though the distinction was not expressly drawn in the Children Act 1989. The Court of Appeal held that the local authority had therefore been entitled to decide in the circumstances that the applicant only needed help with accommodation, and to refer him to the housing department. He appealed to the House of Lords.

The House of Lords held, allowing his appeal, that:

The key question was what the criteria in s.20(1) CA 1989 meant, and how, if at all, the application of the criteria was affected by the other duties of children's authorities, in particular under s.17 CA 1989. It held that he should have been provided with care by his local authority under the Children Act 1989 and not just provided with accommodation by the homeless persons unit under Part VII of the Housing Act 1996. Parliament had decided the circumstances in which the duty to accommodate arose, and then decided what the duty involved; it was not for the local authority to decide that, because they did not like what the duty to accommodate involved or did not think it appropriate, that they did not have to accommodate at all. The local authority was not entitled to 'side-step' the duty under s.20(1) CA 1989 by giving the accommodation a different label.

Section 27 CA 1989 Act empowered a children's authority to ask other authorities (including any local housing authority) for 'help in the exercise of any of their functions' under Part III; and the requested authority had to provide that help if it was compatible with its own statutory or other duties and did not unduly prejudice the discharge of any of its own functions. A local children's authority could not use s 27 to avoid its responsibilities by 'passing the buck' to another authority; but could ask another authority to use its powers to help the children's authority discharge theirs (for example a children's authority could ask a housing authority to make a certain amount of suitable accommodation available for it to use in discharging its responsibility to accommodate children under s. 20). The great flexibility provided by s.23(2) CA 1989 as to the ways in which accommodation could be provided for children being looked after by an authority, which included the power to make 'such other arrangements as ... seem appropriate to them', supported the court's construction of s.20(1).

(iii) Providing accommodation for persons leaving care   If a child has been looked after by a local authority for more than a prescribed period of 13 weeks when he or she attains the age of 18, then at that date that person becomes a 'former relevant child' in respect of whom the local authority has a range of powers and duties under the leaving care provisions, which include the provision of accommodation until the age of 21 or, in some cases, until the age of 24 or until that person has finished full-time further or higher education (see ss.24A and 24B CA 1989).

14.7   Part IV of the Children Act 1989 – care and supervision

(a)   Introduction

Voluntary arrangements provided under Part III of the Children Act 1989 may not work in some cases; or it may come to the notice of a local authority that a child is being, or is at risk of being, harmed. In such circumstances a local authority social services department may have to intervene by bringing proceedings for a care or supervision order under Part IV of the Act, and/or by taking emergency action under Part V (see 14.9). The court has jurisdiction to hear an application for a care or supervision order if the child is habitually resident, or resident, in England and Wales (ss.1 and 3 Family Law Act 1986), and the child is aged under 17 (s.31(3) CA 1989).

Best practice guidance for all professionals involved in care and supervision proceedings (*Preparing for Care and Supervision Proceedings*, Ministry of Justice) was published in 2009.

Although the National Society for the Prevention of Cruelty to Children (NSPCC) has standing to apply for a care or supervision order (s.31(9)), in practice applications are brought by local authority social workers who have a statutory responsibility to protect children and a duty to investigate cases where a child is suffering, or is at risk of suffering, significant harm (ss.37 and 47).

In 2008 there were 11,790 applications for care orders in the courts in England and Wales compared with 730 applications for supervision orders (*Judicial and Court Statistics 2008*, Cm 7697, Ministry of Justice, 2009).

(i) Care order or supervision order?　Although the same threshold criteria apply when the court is considering whether or not to make a care or a supervision order (see p. 393 below), the two orders are different. A care order places the child in the care of a designated local authority, whereas a supervision order places the child under the supervision of a designated local authority or a probation officer.

As a care order is a more severe order than a supervision order (because the child may be removed from his or her home and possibly placed for adoption), the court can make a care order, rather than a supervision order, only if a care order is really necessary for the child's protection. There must be cogent and strong reasons to make a care order rather than a supervision order, as a care order is a more draconian order (*per* Hale J in *Oxfordshire County Council v. L (Care or Supervision Order)* [1998] 1 FLR 70).

In *Re T (Care Order)* [2009] EWCA Civ 121, [2009] 2 FLR 574 the Court of Appeal said that the two principal reasons for making a care order rather than a supervision order were: that the local authority needed the power not only to remove the child instantly but also to plan for long-term placement outside the family without prior judicial sanction; or that it was necessary for the local authority to share parental responsibility with the parents. In *Re T* the Court of Appeal held that the fact that considerable help and advice might be necessary over a long period was not in itself a reason for making a care order; and it was wrong to impose an order simply to encourage a local authority to perform its statutory duties towards children in need. In *Re T* the Court of Appeal, allowing the local authority's appeal, held that there were no strong and cogent reasons for making a care order, the more draconian of the two orders. The Court of Appeal, applying human rights considerations, held that it was preferable in the circumstances to make a supervision order as this was a sufficient and proportionate response in the circumstance of the case. This order had been supported by all the parties in the case, including the children's guardian, and was in the best interests of the child. Cogent and strong reasons were required to force upon a local authority a more draconian order than that for which it had asked.

In *Re H (A Child)* [2008] EWCA Civ 1245, *sub nom Re H (Care Order: Contact)* [2009] 2 FLR 55 a care order was also substituted with a supervision order and residence order, as the trial judge had not sufficiently taken on board the child's understanding of her predicament and the depth of her feeling. She had consistently retained a wish to be with her mother and demonstrated her distress that she was not with her. The girl's wishes were a weighty factor and the judge had erred in failing to perpetuate the fundamental importance of a relationship with, and life with, a parent if that was at all possible.

As care and supervision proceedings under Part IV of the Children 1989 are 'family proceedings' for the purposes of the Children Act 1989 (s.8(3)), the court can make a s.8 order (see 10.4) instead of a care or supervision order, either on an application or of its own motion.

The court has no power to compel a local authority to institute care or supervision proceedings. All it can do is make a direction under s. 37 of the Children Act 1989 that the local authority investigate the child's circumstances.

(ii) Human rights and care and supervision orders   A care order must be a proportionate and legitimate response to the circumstances of the case, for otherwise a local authority may be in breach of the European Convention for the Protection of Human Rights and the Human Rights Act 1998. Thus, for example, making a care order where a supervision order would be adequate to protect the child might offend the principle of proportionality and be a breach of the right to family life under art. 8 ECHR (see 1.7 and 14.3).

In *Re W (Children) (Care: Interference With Family Life)* [2005] EWCA Civ 642, *sub nom Re W (Removal into Care)* [2005] 2 FLR 1022 Thorpe LJ stated that, whenever a local authority took any step as draconian as the removal of a child, the local authority must have 'due regard to the parents' European Convention rights and the Convention rights of the children' and removal 'was only lawful if it could be justified on both the heads of legality and proportionality'. In *Re T (Care Order)* [2009] EWCA Civ 121, [2009] 2 FLR 574 (see p. 390 above) the Court of Appeal again reiterated the rule that human rights' considerations required the court to make the less draconian supervision order rather than the more draconian care order, unless the child's welfare required a care order to be made and that order, rather than a supervision order, was a sufficient and proportionate response to the risk presented to the child.

The European Court of Human Rights has held as a guiding principle that a care order should be regarded as a temporary measure to be discontinued as soon as circumstances permit, and that any measures implementing temporary care should be consistent with the ultimate aim of reuniting the natural parent and the child (see *Olsson* v. *Sweden (No. 1)* (1988) 11 EHRR 259). However, this principle is subject to the best interests of the child.

The ECtHR has also held that, whereas authorities enjoy a wide 'margin of appreciation' (see p. 15), in assessing the necessity of taking a child into public care, a stricter scrutiny is required in respect of any further limitations, including restrictions placed on parental rights of access (*K and T* v. *Finland* (2001) 36 EHRR 255, [2001] 2 FLR 707; *R* v. *Finland (Application No. 34141/96)* [2006] 2 FLR 923).

(iii) The court cannot dictate how a care order is implemented   If the court makes a care order, it cannot dictate how the local authority should implement it, as to do so would circumscribe the wide discretionary powers entrusted to local authorities by Parliament. However, there are certain controls on local authorities. Thus the local authority must supply the court with a care plan containing proposals for future arrangements for the child; and the local authority must review the plan and amend or renew it accordingly (ss.31A(1), (2)). As the court is a public authority for the purposes of the Human Rights

Act 1998, it must ensure compliance with the European Convention for the Protection of Human Rights by considering a care plan carefully to make sure that care is the best solution for the child (see *Hokkanen* v. *Finland* (1995) EHRR 139, [1996] 1 FLR 289).

(b)　Care and supervision proceedings procedure

The *Public Law Outline* (see *Practice Direction: Guide to Case Management in Public Law Proceedings* [2008] 2 FLR 668) lays down rules for case preparation and case management in respect of care and supervision proceedings. Local authorities also have a statutory obligation to take into account *The Children Act 1989 Guidance and Regulations: Volume 1 – Court Orders*, 2008, which sets out the steps that local authorities must take before making an application for a care or supervision order. Care or supervision proceedings commence in the magistrates' family proceedings court, but can be transferred to a county court or the High Court, or to another family proceedings court. The local authority, the child and any person with parental responsibility are automatically parties to the proceedings, but other persons can be joined as parties with leave of the court. When considering whether to grant leave, the court exercises its powers in the same way as it does in leave applications for s.8 orders (see s.10(9), and see p. 282). In *Re W (Care Proceedings: Leave to Apply)* [2004] EWHC 3342 (Fam), [2005] 2 FLR 468 an aunt applied for leave to be a party to the care proceedings in relation to her niece, but was refused at first instance and by Sumner J on appeal.

An unmarried father without parental responsibility has no automatic right to be joined as a party to care or supervision proceedings, but is entitled to notice of the proceedings and is likely to be given leave by the court to take part. In *Re B (Care Proceedings: Notification of Father Without Parental Responsibility)* [1999] 2 FLR 408 Holman J said that an unmarried father should be permitted to participate in proceedings unless there was some justifiable reason to the contrary. A refusal to allow an unmarried father without parental responsibility to participate in care or supervision proceedings might breach his right to family life under art. 8 ECHR (see *McMichael* v. *United Kingdom (Application No. 16424/90)* (1995) 20 EHRR 205 where the ECtHR held that failure to allow an unmarried father without parental responsibility to participate in a Scottish children's hearing was a breach of art. 8).

The child will be represented by a children's guardian (see over) and a solicitor. Parties to the proceedings have a general duty of full and frank disclosure (*Re BR and C (Care: Duty of Disclosure: Appeals)* [2002] EWCA Civ 1925).

Pre-proceedings　Before care or supervision proceedings begin, local authority social workers must carry out various tasks, for example: conduct an initial assessment; conduct a core assessment; conduct (if necessary) a s.47 investigation; convene a child protection case conference; and hold various discussions and meetings involving the child and his or her family. Following the initial assessment the local authority must make a speedy decision as to whether the child is a 'child in need' under s.17 CA 1989. If so, then the child will be subject to a 'child in need' plan. If the local authority is concerned that a child is suffering, or is at risk of suffering, significant harm, then it must conduct an investigation (as required by s.47 CA 1989). This might lead to a child protection case conference being convened to which parents must be invited unless there are good reasons for excluding them (*Working Together to Safeguard Children*, 2006, para 5.84). A core assessment of the child (and his/her family) must be completed within 35 days of the commencement of the case conference. The local authority at, or immediately following, the case conference must formulate a plan for the family and child. The local authority will expect the parent to engage in, and comply with, the plan; and will keep it under review. If the plan goes well, then there will be no need to bring care or supervision proceedings, at least for the time being. The local authority has a duty to keep the parents informed, for otherwise it may breach the parents' human rights. As Munby J stated in *Re L (Care: Assessment: Fair Trial)* [2002] EWHC 1379 (Fam), [2002] 2 FLR 730, social workers must, as soon as is practicable, 'notify parents of material criticisms of and deficits in their parenting or behaviour and of the expectations of them'; and 'advise them how they might remedy or improve their parenting or behaviour'.

Where the child is in immediate or imminent danger, the local authority concerned must take emergency steps to protect the child by, for example, making an application for an emergency protection order (see 14.9).

The children's guardian   In care and supervision proceedings the court must appoint a Cafcass children's guardian (or a Welsh family proceedings officer), unless a guardian is not needed to safeguard the child's interests (s.41(1)). The role of the guardian is to protect and safeguard the best interests of the child in the proceedings. In *Re S and W (Care Proceedings)* [2007] EWCA Civ 232, [2007] 2 FLR 275 Wall LJ said that 'one of the guardian's functions is fearlessly to protect the children concerned against local authority incompetence and maladministration, as well as poor social work practice'.

The guardian must be independent of the parties, in order to prevent a conflict of interest arising. In addition to having a general duty to safeguard the child's interests in the manner prescribed by the rules of court (s.41(2)(b)), the guardian has specific duties which include duties: to ascertain the child's wishes and whether the child has sufficient understanding; to investigate all the circumstances; to interview people involved; to inspect records; and to appoint professional assistance. The rules of court provide that, in carrying out his or her duties, the guardian must have regard to the principle that delay should be avoided. The guardian has a right to examine and copy local authority records relating to a child, which can be admitted in evidence (s.42), such as minutes of a child protection conference or a report compiled by an area child protection committee (*Re R (Care Proceedings: Disclosure)* [2000] 2 FLR 75). When the investigation has been completed, the guardian must make a written report advising what should be done in the best interests of the child. The report (unless the court directs otherwise) must be filed at the court before the hearing date and copies served on all the parties. This report usually has a considerable influence on the court's decision.

Rules of court provide that the guardian must appoint a solicitor to act for the child (if not already appointed); and that the guardian must give instructions on the child's behalf, except where the child is capable of giving instructions and those instructions conflict with those of the guardian (in which case the solicitor must take instructions from the child).

(c)   The 'threshold criteria'

When exercising its power in care and supervision proceedings, the court must first be satisfied that the 'threshold criteria' in s.31(2) (see below) are established. If they are, then at the next stage, the second stage, the court must decide whether it is in the child's best interests to make a care or supervision order, a different order, or no order at all. When conducting the second part of the exercise, the court must apply the welfare principle (s.1(1)), the welfare checklist (s.1(3)), the 'minimum intervention principle' (s.1(5)) and the no-delay principle (s.1(2)) (see 10.3). The court must also apply the European Convention for the Protection of Human Rights as a result of its obligations under the Human Rights Act 1998 (see 1.7). Art. 6 (the right to a fair trial) and art. 8 (the right to family life) of the European Convention are particularly important as these two articles 'affect both the test and the process for intervening in the family lives of children and their parents' (*per* Lady Hale in *Re S-B (Children)* [2009] UKSC 17). Lady Hale said in *Re S-B*:

> '… it is not enough that the social workers, the experts or the court think that a child would be better off living with another family. That would be social engineering of a kind which is not permitted in a democratic society. The jurisprudence of the European Court of Human Rights requires that there be a "pressing social need" for intervention and that the intervention be proportionate to that need.'

In *Re B (Care Orders: Standard of Proof)* (2008) (see further at p. 347 below), Baroness Hale (now Lady Hale) held that, although the court has to ask two questions ('Has the threshold been crossed?' and 'If so, what will be best for the child?'), care proceedings are not a two-stage process, because threshold issues and welfare issues can be interconnected. Baroness Hale said that the purpose of a split hearing was not to split matters into a threshold stage and a welfare stage, but 'to separate out those factual issues which are capable of swift resolution so that the welfare professionals have a firm foundation of fact upon which to base their assessments of family relationships and parenting ability'.

If the threshold criteria are established, the court is under no obligation to make a care or supervision order. Whether it will do so or not depends on a detailed assessment of the child's welfare in all the circumstances of the case. Thus, for example, in *Re K; A Local Authority* v. *N and Others* [2005] EWHC 2956 (Fam), [2007] 1 FLR 399, although the threshold criteria were satisfied, Munby J refused to make a supervision order, applying the 'minimum intervention' principle in s.1(5) CA 1989. If the court decides to make a residence order, instead of a care or supervision order, it must also make an interim supervision order, unless the child's welfare is safeguarded without it (s.38(3)).

The court must also consider the arrangements that the local authority has made, or proposes to make, in respect of contact (see 14.8) and invite the parties to the proceedings to comment on those arrangements (s.34(11)). Expert evidence is important and the court will also consider the recommendations of the child's guardian.

The 'threshold criteria' (or 'threshold conditions') which must be satisfied before the court can consider whether or not to make a care or supervision order are laid down in s.31(2) of the Children Act 1989:

Section 31(2) Children Act 1989

'A court may only make a care order or a supervision order if it is satisfied –

(a) that the child concerned is suffering, or is likely to suffer, significant harm; and
(b) that the harm, or likelihood of harm, is attributable to –
    (i) the care given to the child, or likely to be given to him if the order were not made, not being what it would be reasonable to expect a parent to give him; or
    (ii) the child's being beyond parental control.'

'Harm' means ill-treatment or the impairment of health or development including impairment of the child's health or development as a result of seeing or hearing the ill-treatment of another person (s.31(9)). This could include, for example, seeing or hearing domestic violence. 'Development' means physical, intellectual, emotional, social or behavioural development. 'Health' means physical or mental health, and 'ill-treatment' includes sexual abuse and forms of ill-treatment which are not physical.

Section 31(10) provides that, where the question of whether harm suffered by a child is significant turns on the child's health or development, his health or development must be compared with that which could reasonably be expected of a similar child.

The leading case 'The leading case on the interpretation of [the threshold criteria] is the decision of the House of Lords *Re H and Others (Minors) (Sexual Abuse: Standard of Proof)* [1996] AC 563' (*per* Lady Hale in *Re S-B (Children)* UKSC [2009] 17). Lady Hale said in *Re S-B* that the decision in *Re H* (see further at p. 398 below) had established the following three propositions which had not been questioned since *Re H* was decided:

1. '[I]t is not enough that the court suspects that a child may have suffered significant harm or that there was a real possibility that he did. If the case is based on actual harm, the court must be satisfied on the balance of probabilities that the child was actually harmed.'
2. '[I]f the case is based on the likelihood of future harm, the court must be satisfied on the balance of probabilities that the facts upon which that prediction was based did actually happen. It is not enough that they may have done so or that there was a real possibility that they did.'
3. '[H]owever, if the case is based on the likelihood of future harm, the court does not have to be satisfied that such harm is more likely than not to happen. It is enough that there is "a real possibility, a possibility that cannot sensibly be ignored having regard to the nature and gravity of the feared harm in the particular case" (*per* Lord Nicholls [in *Re H*]).'

(For more on the balance of probability and the threshold criteria, see over.)

(i) 'Significant' harm The word 'significant' is not defined in the Children Act 1989. Whether harm is 'significant' will depend on the circumstances of the case. The guidance, *Working Together to Safeguard Children*, however, provides social workers with guidance on what constitutes 'significant harm'.

In *Re MA (Children) (Care Proceedings: Threshold Criteria)* [2009] EWCA Civ 853 the Court of Appeal considered the dividing line between harm and significant harm and held that, given the underlying philosophy of the Children Act 1989, the harm must be significant enough to justify the intervention of the state and disturb the autonomy of the parents to bring up their children by themselves in the way they choose. It must be significant enough to enable the court to make a care or supervision order if the welfare of the child so demanded. The Court of Appeal held that art. 8 of the European Convention for the Protection of Human Rights also informed the meaning of 'significant'. An evaluative judgment was essential. Wall LJ acknowledged that the line between significant harm and harm was a fine one, and referred to the dictionary definition of 'significant' as 'considerable, noteworthy or important'. The Court of Appeal held that the decision on its facts could have gone either way, but that, where the balance was a fine one (as it was in the case), then it was 'a classic case for trusting the judgment of the trial judge' (*per* Hallett LJ).

In *Re L (Care: Threshold Criteria)* [2007] 1 FLR 20 Hedley J held *inter alia*, dismissing the care application, that it was not the provenance of the state to spare children all the consequences of defective parenting; and that significant harm for the purposes of s.31(2) must be something unusual, and more than commonplace human failure or inadequacy.

(ii) Care and the reasonable parent (s.31(2)(b)(i))   Where the court has to consider whether the threshold criteria are satisfied by evaluating parental performance this requires an objective assessment applying the standard of the hypothetical 'reasonable' parent. In *Re K; A Local Authority* v. *N and Others* [2005] EWHC 2956 (Fam), [2007] 1 FLR 399 Munby J said that the court 'must always be sensitive to the cultural, social and religious circumstances of the particular child and family, particularly when the parents have recently, or comparatively recently, arrived from a foreign country with different standards and expectations from those in this country'. In this case the young girl (aged 16) and her family were Kurdish Muslims from Iraq.

(iii) When must the threshold criteria be satisfied?   The date on which the threshold criteria must be satisfied is the date of the application or, if temporary protective arrangements (such as an emergency protection order) have continuously been in place, the date on which those arrangements were initiated (see *Re M (A Minor) (Care Order: Threshold Conditions)* [1994] 2 AC 424). In other words, the date on which the threshold criteria must be established is the date when the local authority first took protective measures in relation to the child.

(d)   The standard of proof in care and supervision proceedings

The standard of proof is of considerable importance in care and supervision proceedings. If it is set too high, then there is a danger that a child will continue to suffer significant harm. If it is set too low, then there is a danger that a child will be removed from the care of his parents when he has not suffered, or is not at risk of suffering, significant harm. As Ryder J stated, the problem is 'how to balance the need to protect families from any disproportionate interference by the state with the imperative to protect children against harm' ([2008] Fam Law 30).

As care and supervision proceedings are civil proceedings, the local authority must prove the fact(s) alleged (the threshold criteria) on the basis of the civil standard of proof (the balance of probabilities). The test is whether, on the evidence, it is more likely than not that the event(s) took place.

As Lady Hale said in *Re S-B (Children)* [2009] UKSC 17, when establishing whether the criteria in s.31(2) are established, 'the law has drawn a clear distinction between probability as it applies to past facts and probability as it applies to future predictions'. In *Re S-B* her Ladyship stated:

> 'Past facts must be proved to have happened on the balance of probabilities, that is, that it is more likely than not that they did happen. Predictions about future facts need only be based upon the degree of likelihood that they will happen which is sufficient to justify preventive action. This will depend upon the nature and gravity of the harm: a lesser degree of likelihood that the child will be killed will justify immediate preventive action than the degree of likelihood that the child will not be sent to school.'

The leading case on the standard of proof of past facts is *Re B (Children) (Sexual Abuse: Standard of Proof)* [2008] UKHL 35, [2008] 2 FLR 141 where the House of Lords held that the standard of proof for establishing the threshold criteria under s 31(2) in respect of past facts is the simple balance of probabilities, no more and no less. In *Re B* the House of Lords refused to follow its earlier decision in *Re H and Others (Minors) (Sexual Abuse: Standard of Proof)* [1996] AC 563, *sub nom Re H and R (Child Sexual Abuse: Standard of Proof)* [1996] 1 FLR 80 (but refused to overrule it), in which it had held that there had to be a 'real possibility' of harm in order for the threshold criteria to be satisfied. In *Re B* the House of Lords held that there was no 'heightened civil standard' and no legal rule that 'the more serious the allegation, the more cogent the evidence needed to prove it'.

▶ *Re B (Children) (Sexual Abuse: Standard of Proof)* [2008] UKHL 35, [2008] 2 FLR 141

The mother had two children, aged 16 and 17, by a previous marriage, and two other children, aged 9 and 6, with her current husband (from whom she was separated). Allegations of sexual abuse and assault, some of which were certainly false, were made by the mother and the elder daughter (R) against the elder son, and by the elder daughter against her step-father (Mr B), and by the elder son against his mother. The two younger children were placed with foster-carers and care proceedings were instituted. These proceedings were transferred to the High Court by which time only the allegations against Mr B remained in issue. Charles J ruled that he was unable to make a finding as to whether Mr B had abused R. He said that he could not make a properly founded and reasoned conclusion that it was more likely than not that R was, or was not, sexually abused by Mr B. He said that his answer to which of these two possibilities was more likely would be a guess. On the basis, however, that he was unable to conclude that there was no real possibility that Mr B had sexually abused R, Charles J said that he had therefore come to the conclusion that there was a real possibility that he had done so. Charles J gave leave to appeal to the Court of Appeal. The Court of Appeal dismissed the appeal and gave leave to appeal to the House of Lords.

The House of Lords, dismissing the appeal, held in respect of the standard of proof in care proceedings that:

▶ The standard of proof in finding the facts necessary to establish the threshold under s.31(2) or the welfare considerations in s 1 of the 1989 Act is the simple balance of probabilities, neither more nor less. Neither the seriousness of the allegation nor the seriousness of the consequences should make any difference to the standard of proof to be applied in determining the facts. The inherent probabilities are simply something to be taken into account, where relevant, in deciding where the truth lies.

▶ There is no logical or necessary connection between seriousness and probability. In the context of care proceedings, this point applies with particular force to the identification of the perpetrator. It may be unlikely that any person looking after a baby would take him by the wrist and swing him against the wall, causing multiple fractures and other injuries. But once the evidence is clear that that is indeed what has happened to the child, it ceases to be improbable. Someone looking after the child at the relevant time must have done it. The inherent improbability of the event has no relevance to deciding whether the event actually took place.

BARONESS HALE 'I wish to announce loud and clear that the standard of proof in finding the facts necessary to establish the threshold under s 31(2) or the welfare considerations in section 1 of the 1989 Act is the simple balance of probabilities, neither more nor less. Neither the seriousness of the allegation nor the seriousness of the consequences should make any difference to the standard of proof to be applied in determining the facts. The inherent probabilities are simply something to be taken into account, where relevant, in deciding where the truth lies.'

> Baroness Hale rejected the approach taken to probability by Lord Nicholls in *Re H* (1996, see over) and said that there was no 'no logical or necessary connection between seriousness and probability'. She preferred the view of Lord Lloyd in *Re H*, who had said that he did not find helpful the reference to the cogency of the evidence needed to tip the balance. Baroness Hale also held that the 'simple balance of probabilities test should be applied' to identifying the perpetrator.
>
> **LORD HOFFMANN**: 'I think that the time has come to say, once and for all, that there is only one civil standard of proof and that is proof that the fact in issue more probably occurred than not.'

Re B *and the 'second stage' of the proceedings* In *Re B* the House of Lords held that the balance of probabilities test also applies to the second stage of proceedings, in other words where the threshold has been crossed and the court is deciding what order, if any, to make, applying the principle that the welfare of the child is the court's paramount consideration in s.1(1) and the welfare 'checklist' of factors in s.1(3) (see 10.3). Section 1(3)(e) in the checklist refers to 'any harm which he has suffered or is at risk of suffering'. In *Re M and R (Minors) (Sexual Abuse: Expert Evidence)* [1996] 4 All ER 239 the Court of Appeal held that s.1(3)(e) should be interpreted in the same way as s.31(2)(a) of the threshold criteria, in other words that the court must reach a decision based on facts, not on suspicions and doubts. In *Re B* the House of Lords agreed with this approach. In *Re O and N; Re B* [2003] UKHL 18, [2003] 1 FLR 1169 Lord Nicholls had also approved of this approach.

***In* Re B *the House of Lords refused to overrule* Re H** In *Re B* the House of Lords was asked by the children's guardian to overrule its earlier decision in *Re H* (see below) on the basis that, when taken in combination with *Lancashire County Council* v. *B* [2000] 1 FLR 583 and *Re O and N; Re B* [2003] UKHL 18, [2003] 1 FLR 1169 (see below), it produced illogical results. However, the House of Lords refused to do so because it considered the principle in *Re H* (that decisions should be made on facts, rather than on mere suspicions) remained 'thoroughly convincing' and provided an essential safeguard against unjustified intervention into family life. The House of Lords in *Re B* also rejected the argument that there was a conflict between *Re H* and the later authorities of *Lancashire* v. *B* and *Re O and N*, as it said courts can and must distinguish between cases where no significant harm has been proved (as in *Re H*) and those where significant harm has been proved but the actual perpetrator cannot be identified (as in *Lancashire* v. *B*; and *Re O and N*).

After the decision of the House of Lords in *Re B*, except for the removal of the 'cogent evidence' test, *Re H* therefore remains good law. In fact *Re B* affirms and reinforces the principle laid down in *Re H* by Lord Nicholls that 'unresolved judicial doubts and suspicions can no more form the basis of a conclusion that the second threshold condition in s 31(2)(a) has been established than they can form the basis that the first has been established'. It also leaves the test for likelihood of significant harm laid down by Lord Nicholls in *Re H* intact. As Lady Hale said in *Re S-B (Children)* [2009] UKSC 17:

> 'All are agreed that *Re B* reaffirmed the principles adopted in *Re H* while rejecting the nostrum, "the more serious the allegation, the more cogent the evidence needed to prove it", which had become a commonplace but was a misinterpretation of what Lord Nicholls had in fact said.'

▶ *Re H and Others (Minors) (Sexual Abuse: Standard of Proof)* [1996] AC 563, *sub nom Re H and R (Child Sexual Abuse: Standard of Proof)* [1996] 1 FLR 80

The local authority applied for care orders in respect of three girls (aged 13, 8 and 2) after the eldest daughter (aged 14) had alleged that she had been sexually abused by her mother's cohabitant. He had been charged with rape but acquitted. The applications for care orders were dismissed, as the threshold conditions in s.31(2) were not satisfied. It could not be established to the requisite high standard of proof that the 14-year-old daughter's allegations were true.

The House of Lords held by a majority that the standard of proof in care proceedings was the ordinary civil standard of balance of probability, but that the more improbable the event, the stronger the evidence had to be before, on the balance of probability, the occurrence of the event would be established. Lord Nicholls said that a conclusion that a child is suffering, or is likely to suffer, harm 'must be based on facts, not just suspicion'. The House of Lords unanimously rejected, however, a submission that 'likely' in the phrase 'likely to suffer harm' meant probable, but held that 'likely' meant likely in the sense of a real possibility, a possibility that could not sensibly be ignored having regard to the nature and gravity of the feared harm in the particular case.

Some commentators had criticised the decision of the majority in *Re H*. McCafferty (1999) said *inter alia* that it had created a complicated standard of proof for allegations of serious abuse. Hemingway and Williams (1997) described the reasoning as flawed, and said that the decision would create a real danger that some children would not be afforded the protection they deserved. These concerns should now have been appeased by the decision in *Re B (Children)(Sexual Abuse: Standard of Proof)* [2008] UKHL 35, [2008] 2 FLR 141, above.

(For a case commentary on *Re B* and the standard of proof, see Keating [2009] CFLQ 230).

(e)   Shared care, uncertain perpetrators and the threshold criteria

The threshold criteria (see above) do not require that a particular person (whether it be the parent, a person with parental responsibility, or any other person) should be found responsible for the harm which the child has suffered in the past or is likely to suffer in the future. All that is required is that 'the harm, or likelihood of harm, is attributable to ... the care given to the child, or likely to be given to him if the order were not made, not being what it would be reasonable to expect a parent to give to him'. The emphasis is on harm, not on identifying the perpetrator, or potential perpetrator, of the alleged harm.

In the following case the House of Lords held that uncertainty about the identity of the perpetrator of harm did not prevent the threshold criteria being proved:

▶ *Lancashire County Council v. B* [2000] 1 FLR 583

A young baby (child A) suffered harm as a result of being shaken, but it was impossible to prove whether A's parents or the child-minder, who also had a child (child B), was responsible. The Court of Appeal held that the threshold criteria in s.31(2)(b)(i) (lack of reasonable care) were satisfied in respect of child A, but not in respect of child B (because she had suffered no harm), even though it was unclear whether the parents or the child-minder were responsible for A's injuries. Child A's parents appealed to the House of Lords arguing that the harm suffered to their child had to be attributable to their care, and that the continuation of the care proceedings infringed their right to family life under art. 8 of the European Convention on Human Rights.

The House of Lord unanimously dismissed their appeal, as the threshold conditions had been met. A majority of the House of Lords said that, under s.31(2)(b)(i) the court had to be satisfied that the harm suffered by the child was attributable to 'the care given to the child', which normally referred to the care given by parents or other primary-carer. However, their Lordships said that different considerations applied in cases of shared care where the child suffers harm but the court is unable to identify which of the carers provided the deficient care. They held that the words 'care given to the child' in s.31(2)(b)(i) embraced the care given by *any* of the carers, and that the threshold conditions could be satisfied where there was no more than a possibility that the parents were responsible for inflicting the injuries. This interpretation, their Lordships said, was necessary to permit the court to intervene to protect a child at risk where the individual responsible for harming the child could not be identified. In other words, the interpretation was necessary to avoid the risk of a child remaining wholly unprotected.

The House of Lords stressed that in an uncertain perpetrator case the fact that it had not been proved that the parents had been responsible for the child's injuries could be taken into account at the 'welfare stage,' once the threshold conditions had been met. The House of Lords held that there had been no breach of art. 8 ECHR as the steps taken by the local authority had been those reasonably necessary to pursue the legitimate aim of protecting the child from injury.

The standard of proof and possible perpetrators In *Re S-B (Children)* [2009] UKSC 17 the Supreme Court, with Lady Hale giving the leading opinion, held that the test to be applied to the identification of perpetrators was that of the balance of probabilities as laid down in *Re B (Children) (Sexual Abuse: Standard of Proof)* [2008] UKHL 35, [2008] 2 FLR 141, even though *Re B* was not a case which was directly concerned with the identification of perpetrators. In *Re S-B* Lady Hale said the test is 'the balance of probabilities, nothing more and nothing less'. Although Lady Hale in *Re S-B* recognised that it might be difficult for a judge to decide, even on the balance of probabilities, who has caused the harm to the child, there was no obligation to do so, as the threshold criteria were concerned with a finding of harm, not who caused the harm.

Lady Hale in *Re S-B* agreed with Wall LJ's approach in *Re D (Care Proceedings: Preliminary Hearing)* [2009] EWCA Civ 472, [2009] 2 FLR 668 that judges should not strain to identify the perpetrator as a result of the decision in *Re B*. In *Re D* Wall LJ said that, although the House of Lords in *Re B* had established that the standard of proof to be applied to all findings of fact in care proceedings was the 'simple balance of probabilities' test, that rule did not require a court to come to a conclusion as to which of two people was more likely than not to be the perpetrator in order to satisfy the threshold criteria. Wall LJ said that two parents, could for example, be possible perpetrators. As the trial judge had been wrong in law to name the father as the perpetrator (applying the balance of probability test), when the mother could not be excluded, Wall LJ allowed the father's appeal.

However, in *Re S-B* Lady Hale stated that, even if it was not possible for the judge to identify a perpetrator or perpetrators, it was important for the judge to identify 'the pool of possible perpetrators', as this would sometimes be necessary in order to fulfil the 'attributability' criterion. Her Ladyship said that, if the harm had been caused by someone outside the home or family (for example at school or in hospital or by a stranger), then it was not attributable to parental care unless it would have been reasonable to expect a parent to have prevented it.

Lady Hale in *Re S-B* also addressed the question of what should be done about the risk that a judge might make a mistake and wrongly identify someone as the perpetrator. Lady Hale recognised that judges can make mistakes, but said that a judge 'must remain alive to the possibility of mistake and be prepared to think again if new evidence emerges which casts new light on the evidence which led to the earlier findings'. Her Ladyship said that it was 'well settled that a judge in care proceedings is entitled to revisit an earlier identification of the perpetrator if fresh evidence warrants this' (and she referred to *Re I (A Child)* [2009] UKSC 10 where the Supreme Court had witnessed an example of this).

The welfare stage and several possible perpetrators   In *Re O and N; Re B (Minors)* [2003] UKHL 18, [2003] 1 FLR 1169 the House of Lords unanimously held that in uncertain perpetrator cases, where the judge had found that the child had suffered significant harm at the hands of his parents or carer but was unable to identify which parent or carer had caused the harm, the preferred interpretation of the Children Act was that the court should proceed at the welfare stage of care proceedings on the footing that each of the possible perpetrators be treated as such (but see also *Re S-B* above).

(f)   The local authority's care plan

Where an application is made on which a final (not an interim) care order (see s.31A(5)) might be made, the local authority must, within such time as the court may direct, prepare a 'care plan' for the future care of the child (s.31A(1)). A care plan includes information, for example, about the child's needs, the placement, and the management and support to be provided by the local authority. It provides details about contact – as before making a care order the court must consider the arrangements, or proposed arrangements, for contact (see s.34(11)). In *Re J (Minors) (Care: Care Plan)* [1994] 1 FLR 253 Wall J said:

> 'A properly constructed care plan is not only essential to enable the court to make its decision based on all the known facts, it will or should have been compiled either in consultation with the parents and other interested parties, including where appropriate the child or children involved, or at the very least after taking their views and wishes into account. It will thus enable the other parties to focus on the relevant issues. Much court time and costs may thereby be saved.'

The court must carefully scrutinise the care plan in order to be satisfied that giving parental responsibility to the local authority will not do more harm than good for the child's welfare (see *per* Hale J in *Berkshire County Council v. B* [1997] 2 FLR 171).

If the court considers that the care plan is not in the child's best interests, or that more information is needed, it can make an interim care order even though it is not completely happy with the plan (*Re L (Sexual Abuse: Standard of Proof)* [1996] 1 FLR 116). The court can make a final order, even if it is not satisfied about the care plan. In *Re K (Care Proceedings: Care Plan)* [2007] EWHC 393 (Fam), [2008] 1 FLR 1 Munby J held that the court should have made a care order even though it was not satisfied about the contact proposed in the care plan. Munby J said that only in a rare case would the court's disapproval of a care plan prevent a care order being made when the threshold criteria had been satisfied and a care order was in the best interests of a child.

The duty to keep a care plan under review   While the application is pending the local authority must keep the care plan under review, and revise it or renew it if some change is required (s.31A(2)). Once a child is in care, the local authority must continue to keep the care plan under review and renew or revise the care plan if some change is required, and consider whether to apply for or discharge the care order (s.26(2)). A failure to keep a care plan up to date may provide grounds for an appeal (as it did in *Re A (Care Plan)* [2008] EWCA Civ 650, [2008] 2 FLR 1183 where the trial judge had made a care order on the basis of an outdated care plan).

If the child is in care, the local authority is not permitted to make significant changes to the care plan, or change the child's living arrangements, without properly involving the child's parents (and in some cases the child) in the decision-making process and without giving the parents a proper opportunity to make their case before a decision is made (see, for example, *Re G (Care: Challenge to Local Authority's Decision)* [2003] EWHC 551 (Fam), [2003] 2 FLR 42).

Involving parents   A failure to involve a parent in the decision-making process in respect of a care plan, or a change in a care plan, can constitute a breach of a parent's human rights, and may, depending on the circumstances of the case, result in a local authority having to pay compensation to the wronged parent in the form of damages (see *Re C (Breach of Human Rights: Damages)* [2007] EWCA Civ 2, [2007] 1 FLR 1957, but where damages were not awarded in the circumstances of the case).

Challenging a care plan   If the local authority fails to comply with its care plan, a parent (and/or child) can: apply to discharge the care order; make a complaint under the Complaints Procedure; bring a challenge under the Human Rights Act 1998; or bring a negligence claim (see 14.11). Independent Reviewing Officers can also provide assistance (see below).

In *R (CD)* v. *Isle of Anglesey County Council* [2004] EWHC 1635 (Admin), [2005] 1 FLR 59 a 15-year-old disabled girl successfully challenged a care plan on the ground that it had *inter alia* failed to give due consideration to her wishes in respect of the number of nights she should spend with her foster-carers. Wilson J held that it is generally preferable for issues relating to care plans to be resolved within an application for a care order, rather than by way of judicial review, as in family proceedings the emphasis is on the child's best interests whereas in judicial review proceedings the emphasis is on the lawfulness or otherwise of the local authority's action or inaction.

Independent reviewing officers and care plans   Before new provisions for the appointment of independent reviewing officers were introduced (see ss.24A and 24B CA 1989) there was judicial concern that, once a child was in care, a local authority could choose not to implement the proposals in its care plan, to the detriment of the child and with the court having no power to intervene. The judiciary was concerned that children could drift in care with no person, including the child, having the right to review the promises made by the local authority in its care plan. Young children with parents with no interest in them were in a particularly vulnerable position, even though local authorities were under a duty to conduct regular case reviews.

Concern about care plans was voiced by the House of Lords in *Re S (Care Order: Implementation of Care Plan); Re W (Minors) (Care Order: Adequacy of Care Plan)* [2002]

UKHL 10, [2002] 1 FLR 815 where in each appeal the local authority had failed to implement the proposed arrangements it had made for the child in its care plan. The House of Lords allowed the appeals, and held that, although the Children Act 1989 was not incompatible with the Human Rights Act 1998, there was a statutory gap in the Children Act 1989, as a child whose parents were not interested in the matter might be left without an effective remedy (as required by art. 6 ECHR) to challenge a local authority's failure to implement its proposals in its care plan.

The gaps in the Children Act 1989 identified by the House of Lords in *Re S; Re W* were subsequently filled by new provisions inserted into the Act requiring local authorities to appoint independent reviewing officers with various statutory functions (s.24B). Independent reviewing officers are responsible for participating in case reviews, for monitoring the local authority's functions in respect of case reviews, and for referring a case to a Cafcass or Welsh family proceedings officer where appropriate. That officer can then seek a court order against the local authority to put right its failings in relation to the care plan, for example by: applying to discharge the care order; applying for contact between the child and another person; or applying for a declaration under the Human Rights Act 1998 that the local authority's plans are contrary to the child's human rights. Before bringing court proceedings, the officer concerned will attempt to reach a negotiated settlement and will refer the case to mediation if appropriate.

(g) Effect of a care order – obligations of the local authority

If a care order is made, statutory responsibility for the child passes to the local authority and the court has no power (unless expressly provided by statute) to interfere with the local authority's powers (*A v. Liverpool City Council* [1982] AC 363). Because power passes to the local authority, the court has no power to impose conditions on a care order in respect of the child's accommodation arrangements; or to direct how the local authority should look after the child (*Re T (A Minor) (Care Order: Conditions)* [1994] 2 FLR 423; and *Re S and D (Children: Powers of Court)* [1995] 2 FLR 456).

If a care order is made, the child is described as being 'looked after' by the local authority, whereupon the local authority has various duties and powers in respect of the child. The court no longer monitors the administrative arrangements for the child and has no say in these arrangements unless there is an application before the court. The children's guardian's involvement in the case also terminates.

A care order imposes a duty on the local authority to receive and keep the child in its care (s.33(1)), and the local authority has a general duty to safeguard and promote the child's welfare (s.22). A care order discharges any s.8 order, a supervision order and a school attendance order, and terminates wardship (s.91). A care order, other than an interim care order, remains in force until the child reaches 18, unless brought to an end earlier (s.91(12)).

Care orders and parental responsibility A care order gives the local authority parental responsibility for the child and the power to determine the extent to which the child's parent(s) or guardian may meet their parental responsibility where it is needed to safeguard and promote the child's welfare (ss.33(3), (4)). A local authority must exercise its parental responsibility in a way which complies with the European Convention for the Protection of Human Rights, in particular with the substantive and procedural requirements of art. 8. Thus, it must inform parents of decisions it makes, give parents opportunities to be heard and make representations, and involve them in the decision-making process.

The parental responsibility acquired by a local authority is not absolute, for the child's parents do not lose parental responsibility while a care order is in force; and there is a presumption of reasonable contact between the child and his family (see 14.8). Thus, a parent remains entitled to do what is reasonable in all the circumstances for the purpose of safeguarding and promoting the child's welfare (s.33(5)), and retains any rights, duties, powers and responsibilities in relation to the child and his property under any other enactment (s.33(9)), for example to make decisions about education and medical treatment.

Furthermore, a local authority is not entitled to take decisions about the child without reference to, or over the heads of, the parents; and it is not entitled to make significant changes to its care plan (see p. 401 above). Neither is it entitled to make changes to the child's living arrangements without first discussing the matter with the parents, and, in some cases, the child. It has no power to give or refuse consent to the child's adoption, or to appoint a guardian, or to change the child's religion (s.33(6)).

Restrictions imposed by care orders   While a care order is in force no person can change the child's surname or remove the child from the UK without the *written* consent of every person who has parental responsibility for the child, or leave of the court (s.33(7)). However, a local authority can allow the child to be taken out of the UK for up to one month (s.33(8)(a)) and can under Sched. 2, para. 19 arrange (or assist in arranging) for the child to live outside England and Wales, subject to the court's approval.

Placement of the child   Most children who are the subject of a care order are not returned home to their parents. The court will instead approve a plan to place them outside the immediate family. The child may be placed with foster-parents, remain with existing short-term foster-carers, or be placed with members of the extended family (such as a grandparent or other relative). Placing the child can be implemented under the terms of the care order, or under a residence order (see 10.5) or under a special guardianship order (see 15.14). In some cases, the child may be placed for adoption (see Chapter 15).

(h)   Effect of a supervision order

A supervision order does not give the local authority parental responsibility, but places the child under the supervision of a designated local authority officer or a probation officer (s.31(1)(b)). With a supervision order, unlike a care order, safeguarding the child's interests remains the primary responsibility of the parents. Under a supervision order the local authority merely assists and befriends the child (ss.35(1)(a), (b)) and the operation of any conditions or undertakings depends on parental agreement (*Re B (Supervision Order: Parental Undertaking)* [1996] 1 FLR 676). A supervisor can, however, apply to have the supervision order varied or discharged where the order is not complied with or the supervisor considers the order is no longer necessary (s.35(1)(c)).

Parts I and II of Sched. 3 to the Children Act 1989 list specific powers in respect of supervision. For example the supervisor can give directions that the child live in a certain place, attend at a certain place and participate in certain activities. A supervision order can require a child to have a medical or psychiatric examination, but only with the child's consent if the child has sufficient understanding to make an informed decision, and only if satisfactory arrangements have been, or can be, made for the examination. A supervision order can be made in the first instance for up to one year, but the supervisor can apply to have the order extended for up to a maximum of three years (Sched. 3, para. 6). The court has no power to impose conditions on a supervision order (*Re S (Care or Supervision Order)* [1996] 1 FLR 753).

(i)   Interim care and supervision orders

The court has the power to make interim care and interim supervision orders (s.38). The purpose of interim orders is to enable the court to maintain the status quo pending the final hearing, and for it to obtain any information it needs before making a final decision. Although an interim care order is a 'holding' order, it is regarded as a form of care order, so that, once it is made, care of the child passes to the local authority and the manner in which the child is cared for passes out of the court's control.

The power to make interim orders can be exercised only where care and supervision proceedings are to be adjourned (such as for inquiries or reports to be made), or where the court makes an order under s.37(1) directing a local authority to investigate the child's circumstances (s.38(1)). An interim order cannot be made unless there are reasonable grounds for believing that the threshold criteria for making a care or supervision order are satisfied (s.38(2)) (see p. 393).

In *Re L (Care Proceedings: Removal of Child)* [2007] EWHC 3404 (Fam), [2008] 1 FLR 575 Ryder J had held that an interim care order could not be made unless there was 'an imminent risk of really serious harm', but this approach was refuted by Thorpe LJ in *Re L-A (Children) (Care Proceedings: Interim Care Order)* [2009] EWCA Civ 822 who said that the trial judge in *Re L-A* had been plainly wrong to think that 'the words of Ryder J that there should be an imminent risk of really serious harm prevented him from doing what he instinctively felt the welfare of the children required'. Thorpe LJ therefore allowed the local authority's appeal against the refusal by the trial judge to make an interim care order removing children from their home on the grounds of their alleged chronic neglect. Before the decision in *Re L-A*, Howe had expressed concern that the threshold set by Ryder J had been set too high, and that this had 'made it extremely difficult, particularly in long term neglect cases, to obtain the interim removal of children from the home' (see [2009] Fam Law 320).

If the court decides to make a residence order in care or supervision proceedings, an interim supervision order must also be made, unless the child's welfare is otherwise satisfactorily safeguarded (s.38(3)). There is no limit on the number of interim orders that can be made, but, as delay is detrimental to a child (s.1(2)) and it is important for a final decision to be made, interim orders are limited to a maximum of eight weeks in the first instance and four weeks subsequently (ss.38(4), (5)). However, there must be good reason for the continuation of an interim care order.

The court can include in an interim care order a requirement that the alleged abuser should leave the home, or be prevented from entering the home and/or an area round the home if it is satisfied that: there is reasonable cause to believe that by doing this the child will cease to suffer, or cease to be likely to suffer, significant harm; and there is a person living in the home who is able and willing to provide reasonable care for the child (see s.38A).

(i) Directing a medical or psychiatric examination or other assessment of the child

When the court makes an interim care or supervision order it can give such directions (if any) as it considers appropriate with regard to the medical or psychiatric examination or other assessment of the child (s.38(6)).

The aim of s.38(6) direction is to ensure that all the evidence is put before the court in order to assist it in its decision-making. Wall LJ in *Re L and H (Residential Assessment)* [2007] EWCA Civ 213, [2007] 1 FLR 137 held that, before moving children permanently from their families and placing them for adoption, the court must ensure that the case had been fully investigated and that all the relevant evidence necessary for the decision is in place. Art. 6 of the European Convention for the Protection of Human Rights (the right to a fair hearing) required it and so did the underlying policy of the CA 1989, which was that, wherever possible, children should be brought up by their parents or within their natural families. Wall LJ held that there were no general guidelines as to when the court should or should not order an assessment under s.38(6), but that the proceedings must be fair. If an expert brought in to advise the court strongly recommended a residential assessment, that was a powerful pointer to the propriety of such an order. (*Re L and H (Residential Assessment)* was considered by the Court of Appeal in *Re S (Residential Assessment)* [2008] EWCA Civ 1078, [2009] 2 FLR 397, where the mother's appeal against the circuit judge's refusal of her application for a residential assessment was dismissed).

A child can refuse the assessment or examination   A child with sufficient understanding to make an informed decision can refuse to submit to the medical or psychiatric examination or other assessment (see s.38(6)); but, as the child's welfare prevails, the court can override a child's refusal, even if the child has the required sufficiency of understanding (see *South Glamorgan County Council* v. *W and B* [1993] 1 FLR 574, see p. 221).

Directing a residential assessment   Under s.38(6) the court may decide that a *residential* assessment is needed in order to asses the child and/or parents. The court can do this even though the local authority objects (for example because of the cost), as the purpose of s.38(6) is to enable the court to obtain the information it needs so that it can decide what sort of final order to make (see *Re C (A Minor) (Interim Care Order: Residential Assessment)* [1997] AC 489, [1997] 1 FLR 1). But the court, when exercising its discretion to order a particular examination or assessment, will take into account 'the cost of the proposed assessment and the fact that local authorities' resources are notoriously limited' (*per* Lord Browne-Wilkinson in *Re C*, above). In *Local Authority* v. *M (Funding of Residential Assessments)* [2008] EWHC 162 (Fam), [2008] 1 FLR 1579, for example, Bodey J, having given careful consideration to the local authority's budget, made an order under s.38(6) even though the local authority, although agreeing in principle with the assessment, submitted that it could not afford to pay for it. Bodey J ordered that the local authority pay the entire cost of the residential assessment which the local authority had agreed was in the child's best interests.

A s.38(6) assessment is not restricted to residential assessments in institutional settings, as the scope and application of s.38(6) is wider than that. Thus, in *Re A (Residential Assessment)* [2009] EWHC 865 (Fam), [2009] 2 FLR 443 Munby J held that the justices had acted within their jurisdiction and in a perfectly lawful manner by making an interim care order on the basis that, before making a final order, they would require evidence of how the child had settled with her great grandmother and aunt for the purpose of an assessment under s.38(6).

Residential assessment for therapeutic purposes   The House of Lords has held that an assessment under s.38(6) does not include an assessment where the main focus of the assessment is to consider the parents' capacity to respond to therapeutic treatment, or to secure therapy for the child or the family (see *Re G (A Child) (Interim Care Order: Residential Assessment)* [2005] UKHL 68, [2006] 1 FLR 601).

(k)   Discharge and variation of care and supervision orders

A supervision order can be varied or discharged, but a care order can only be discharged, as variation would undermine a local authority's responsibility for a child.

(i) Discharge of a care order   An application for discharge of a care order can be made by: a person with parental responsibility for the child; the child; or the local authority (s.39(1)). A child does not need leave of the court to apply (*Re A (Care: Discharge Application by Child)* [1995] 1 FLR 599). Persons without parental responsibility cannot apply for discharge, but can, with the permission of the court, apply for a s.8 residence order, which (if granted) will automatically discharge the care order (s.91(1)). In practice, discharge applications are made by local authorities, which at every statutory case conference must consider whether to apply for discharge. As an alternative to discharge, the court can substitute the care order with a supervision order, without the need to satisfy the threshold criteria (ss.39(4), (5)).

In a discharge application the court must apply the s.1(1) welfare principle and the other s.1 provisions (see 10.3). There is no need to prove that the threshold conditions (see p. 393) no longer apply (*Re S (Discharge of Care Order)* [1995] 2 FLR 639). A further application to discharge the care order, or to substitute it with a supervision order, cannot be made for six months after the original application, except with leave of the court (s.91(15)).

(ii) Variation or discharge of a supervision order   A supervision order can be varied or discharged on the application of: a person with parental responsibility for the child; the child; or by the person supervising the child (s.39(2)). An order can also be varied on the application of a person with whom the child is living, if the original order imposes a requirement which affects that person (s.39(3)). When exercising its powers, the court must apply the s.1(1) welfare principle and the other s.1 provisions (see 10.3). A further application to discharge or vary the supervision order cannot be made for six months after the original application, except with leave of the court (s.91(15)).

(l)   Care and supervision orders – appeals

Any party to care or supervision proceedings can appeal against the making of, or refusal to make, a final or interim care or supervision order. The appeal court will not, however, interfere with a discretionary decision made by a lower court unless the judge has erred in law, or is under a misapprehension of fact, or the decision is outside a band of reasonable discretion within which reasonable disagreement is possible. As this is a high threshold, it is sometimes difficult for an appeal to succeed.

14.8 Contact in care

Article 9(3) United Nations Convention on the Rights of the Child 1989

'States Parties shall respect the right of the child who is separated from one or both parents to maintain personal relations and direct contact with those parents on a regular basis, except if it is contrary to the child's best interests.'

As contact between children and parents is considered to be mutually beneficial, and because children have a right to contact (see 11.5), the courts have held that cogent reasons are required for terminating contact (*per* Balcombe LJ in *Re J (A Minor) (Contact)* [1994] 1 FLR 729). The European Court of Human Rights has also recognised the importance of children in care having contact with their parents and family. Thus, in *K and T* v. *Finland* (2000) 31 EHRR 484, [2000] 2 FLR 793 it held that, while there is a wide margin of appreciation in care cases, it nevertheless remains important to scrutinise any restrictions placed by authorities on parental rights of contact. Contact is important for children in care, because it improves their chances of being rehabilitated with their families.

Section 34 of the Children Act 1989 makes provision in respect of contact in care. It lays down a duty of contact, and gives the court power to make orders in respect of contact (see below). It also requires the court, before making a care order, to consider the arrangements the local authority has made, or proposes to make, for contact; and it must invite the parties to the proceedings to comment on those arrangements (s.34(11)).

(i) The duty to provide contact Section 34(1) provides that a local authority must allow a child in care reasonable contact with: parents; a guardian or special guardian; a person with parental responsibility for him under s.4ZA and s.4A of the Children Act 1989; a person with a residence order in his or her favour in respect of the child; and a person who has care of the child under an order made by the High Court under its inherent jurisdiction. But a local authority can as a matter of urgency refuse contact for up to seven days without obtaining a court order where such action is needed to promote the child's welfare (s.34(6)). Regulations provide that in such a case written notice of the decision must be given to any child who has sufficient understanding, and to any person in respect of whom there is a presumption of reasonable contact.

(ii) Section 34 orders Under s.34 the court can make two sorts of order: an order in respect to contact; and an order authorising a local authority to refuse contact. These orders can be made on an application, or by the court of its own motion when making a care order, or in any family proceedings in connection with a child in care (s.34(5)). They can be made when a care order is made, or subsequently (s.34(10)). The court can impose conditions on an order (s.34(7)).

When exercising its powers, the court must apply the s.1(1) welfare principle and the other s.1 provisions in the Children Act 1989 (see 10.3); and it must also ensure that the order is human rights compliant (in other words that it complies, in particular, with art. 6 (the right to a fair trial) and art. 8 (the right to family life) of the European Convention for the Protection of Human Rights (see 1.7). The order must, for the purposes of art. 8, be lawful, necessary and proportionate.

As in private law (see 11.5) the courts are aware of the danger of authorising contact where there is a risk of the child witnessing domestic violence. In *Re G (Domestic Violence: Direct Contact)* [2000] 2 FLR 865 it was held that the reluctance of a child to see a parent in a case involving serious domestic violence requires careful consideration by the court, and the local authority was given permission to terminate direct contact.

Orders made under s.34 can be varied or discharged on the application of the local authority, the child, or any person named in the order (s.34(9)).

An order in respect to contact Under s.34(2) the court, on the application of the local authority or the child, can make such order as it considers appropriate in respect to the contact which is to be allowed between the child in care and any named person.

In 2008, 630 applications for such orders were made by the courts in England and Wales (*Judicial and Court Statistics 2008*, Cm 7697, 2009, Ministry of Justice).

Under s.34(3) the court may also make an order in respect of contact on the application of a person who has a right to reasonable contact under s.34(1) (see above), or a person who has been granted leave to apply. Although grandparents, relatives or friends of a child are not allowed contact with a child as of right (unless they have a residence order in their favour, or an order made under the High Court's inherent jurisdiction), they can apply for the court's leave to apply for an order in respect to contact with a child in care (s.34(3)(b)). Although the test which the court must apply when considering leave applications is the same as that laid down in s.10(9) which applies to leave applications for s.8 orders (see p. 282; and *Re M (Care: Contact: Grandmother's Application for Leave)* [1995] 2 FLR 86), the court is not restricted to considering only those matters set out in s.10(9), as it must conduct a full judicial inquiry into the application in accordance with arts. 6 and 8 of the European Convention for the Protection of Human Rights (*per* Sumner J in *Re W (Care Proceedings: Leave to Apply)* [2004] EWHC 3342 (Fam), [2005] 2 FLR 468). However, a frivolous or vexatious application, or one where the prospects of success are remote, will be dismissed. An applicant for leave to apply must prove that there is a serious issue to be tried and that he or she has a good arguable case.

An order authorising a local authority to refuse contact Under s.34(4) the court can make an order (on the application of the local authority or the child) authorising the local authority to refuse to allow contact between the child and any person entitled to reasonable contact under s.34(1) (see above). An interim order can be made. If the court refuses to make a s.34(4) order, a further application cannot be made for six months except with leave of the court (s.91(17)). The court can insert conditions into an order (s.34(7)).

In 2008, 560 applications for such orders were made in the courts in England and Wales (*Judicial and Court Statistics 2008*, Cm 7697, 2009, Ministry of Justice).

The courts have held that contact is only to be terminated where there is no likelihood of rehabilitation and where post-adoption contact is not considered to be in the child's best interests (see, for example, *Re H (Termination of Contact)* [2005] EWCA Civ 318, [2005] 2 FLR 408).

The court may be unwilling to make an order authorising a local authority to refuse contact between a newborn baby and its mother, particularly when the threshold for a care order have not been established, unless extraordinarily compelling reasons exist. Munby J so held in *Re K (Contact)* [2008] EWHC 540, [2008] 2 FLR 581, but on the facts a s.34(4) order was granted because the child's safety imperatively demanded that the court make the order. The supervised contact between the mother and child had been poor and during a contact session the parents had been involved in a fight and the mother had thrown the baby to the contact supervisor.

14.9 Part V of the Children Act 1989 – emergency protection

Part V of the Children Act 1989 provides the legal framework for dealing with children who need protection in an emergency by making provision, *inter alia*, for child assessment orders and emergency protection orders. These orders are subject to certain safeguards so as to prevent unjustifiable intrusion into family life. For example, they are of short duration and are open to challenge. In some cases, emergency action will be followed by an application for a care or supervision order (see 14.7).

Under Part V a local authority also has various investigative duties when it is informed that a child who lives, or is found in its area, is the subject of an emergency protection order or is in police protection, or if the local authority has reasonable cause to suspect that such child is suffering, or is likely to suffer, significant harm (see s.47(1)). Once a local authority has obtained an order under Part V, enquiries must be made to decide what action should be taken to safeguard or promote the child's welfare (s.47(2)).

As Part V proceedings are not 'family proceedings' for the purposes of the Children Act 1989 (s.8(4)), the court cannot make any s.8 order in the proceedings. When considering whether to make an order under Part V the child's welfare is the court's paramount consideration (s.1(1)) and the other s.1 principles apply (see 10.3), except the s.1(3) welfare checklist, as conducting the s.1(3) exercise is lengthy and would defeat the purpose of a Part V application which is for immediate short-term emergency protection.

The following are available for emergency protection under Part V of the Children Act: a child assessment order; an emergency protection order; and police protection. In practice, however, local authorities often prefer to make agreements with parents that a child be accommodated with the local authority under s.20 CA 1989 (see p. 386 above), instead of applying for an emergency protection order or requesting police protection (see research by Masson, 2005). In this way, they comply with the policy objective of the Children Act of local authorities working in partnership with parents.

(a) Child assessment orders

Under s.43 the court has jurisdiction to make a child assessment order (CAO), which is an order enabling a medical or psychiatric assessment of the child to take place in order to establish whether or not the child is suffering, or is likely to suffer, significant harm. A CAO allows a local authority to intervene to protect a child where the circumstances are not sufficiently urgent or serious to justify other intervention (for example an emergency protection order). With a CAO order the child can remain at home, and so it is less severe than an emergency protection order. CAOs are not commonly made. In 2008, only 44 applications for child assessment orders were made (*Judicial and Court Statistics 2008*, Cm 7697, 2007, Ministry of Justice).

Grounds The court can make a CAO on the application of a local authority (or the NSPCC) if it is satisfied that (s.43(1)): the applicant has reasonable cause to suspect that the child is suffering, or is likely to suffer, significant harm; and an assessment of the state of the child's health or development, or of the way in which he has been treated, is required to enable the applicant to determine whether or not the child is suffering, or is likely to suffer, significant harm; and it is unlikely that such an assessment will be made, or be satisfactory, in the absence of an order under this section.

The court can treat the application as one for an emergency protection order (s.43(3)). It cannot make a CAO if the grounds for an emergency protection order exist; and it considers an emergency protection order, rather than a CAO, ought to be made (s.43(4)). The CAO must specify when the assessment is to begin (which must not last longer than 7 days) (s.43(5)). The effect of a CAO is to order any person in a position to do so to produce the child to the person named in the order and to comply with any directions in the order (s.43(6)). The order authorises the person carrying out the assessment, or part of it, to do so in accordance with the terms of the order (s.43(7)). A child of sufficient understanding to make an informed decision may refuse to submit to a medical or psychiatric examination, or other assessment, regardless of any term in the order authorising assessment (s.43(8)), but the court can override the child's refusal if this is in the child's best interests (see *South Glamorgan County Council* v. *W and B* at p. 221).

A child can be kept away from home for the assessment, but only if this is necessary for the purposes of the assessment, and only in accordance with directions and for the period(s) of time specified in the order (s.43(9)). The CAO must contain directions about contact (s.43(10)). Before the application is heard, the local authority must take reasonably practicable steps to ensure that notice of the application is given to: the child's parents; any person with parental responsibility; any person caring for the child; any person who has contact with the child either under a s.8 contact order or a s.34 order; and the child (s.43(11)). This notice requirement is to ensure that, where possible, the hearing takes place between the parties in order to prevent unjustifiable intervention. A CAO can be varied and/or discharged (s.43(12)). The court is required to appoint a Cafcass officer for the child unless it is satisfied that it is not necessary to do so in order to safeguard the child's interests (ss.41(1) and (2)).

(b) Emergency protection orders

Under s.44 of the Children Act 1989 the court can make an emergency protection order (an EPO), which is an order providing an immediate but temporary remedy in a genuine emergency. In an emergency, an application can be heard by a single justice and may, with leave of the clerk of the court, be made without notice (*ex parte*), although, where possible, proceedings must be heard *inter partes*.

In 2008, 1,760 applications for EPOs were made (*Judicial and Court Statistics 2008*, Cm 7697, Ministry of Justice, 2009).

(i) Applicants   Section 44 provides that 'any person' may apply for an EPO, but in practice it is local authority social services departments who do so.

(ii) The grounds for making an EPO   The applicant must prove that there is reasonable cause to believe that the child is likely to suffer harm if: he is not removed to accommodation provided by or on behalf of the applicant; or he does not remain in the place in which he is being accommodated (s.44(1)(a)). The court can also make an EPO on the application of a local authority if enquiries in respect of the child are being made under s.47(1)(b) and

those enquiries are being frustrated by access to the child being unreasonably refused to a person authorised to seek access, and the applicant has reasonable cause to believe that access to the child is required as a matter of urgency (ss.44(1)(b), (c)). Local authorities must keep parents informed about what is happening at the hearing, and they have a continuing duty to keep the case under review (s.44).

(iii) The approach of the courts   The courts adopt the following approach when considering whether or not to make an EPO:

▷ As an EPO is a severe and extremely harsh measure requiring exceptional justification and extraordinarily compelling reasons, the court will not make an EPO unless it is necessary and proportionate and no other less radical form of order will promote the child's welfare. (See *P, C and S* v. *UK* (2002) 35 EHRR 31, [2002] 2 FLR 631, which involved the removal of a newborn baby).

▷ Separation of the child will be contemplated only if immediate separation is essential to secure the child's safety. Imminent danger must be established. (See *Re M (Care Proceedings: Judicial Review)* [2003] EWHC 850 (Admin), [2003] 2 FLR 171).

▷ An EPO should not be made for any longer than is absolutely necessary to protect a child.

▷ The evidence in support of an EPO must be full, detailed, precise and compelling.

▷ Save in wholly exceptional cases, parents must be given adequate prior notice of the date, time and place of the application for an EPO, and the evidence relied on.

▷ A without notice (*ex parte*) application will normally only be considered appropriate if the case involves a genuine emergency, great urgency or some other compelling reason to believe that the child's welfare will be compromised if the parents are alerted in advance (but even then some kind of informal notice to the parents may well be possible). As a result of their obligations under the Human Rights Act 1998, the courts must ensure that making an *ex parte* EPO does not breach art. 6 of the ECHR (the right to a fair trial), or is in breach of the principle of proportionality and therefore in breach of the right to family life under art. 8.

▷ A children's guardian (a Cafcass officer, see 1.6) must be appointed immediately upon the issue of proceedings for an EPO.

The rules above were described, and applied, by Munby J in the following case, where he described an EPO summarily removing a child from his parents as a 'terrible and drastic remedy':

▶ *X Council* v. *B (Emergency Protection Orders)* [2004] EWHC 2015 (Fam), [2005] 1 FLR 341

Three children were taken into foster-care under *ex parte* EPOs. Munby J held that, while child assessment orders, and possibly even very short-term EPOs, had been appropriate to enable medical tests and examinations to take place, it was not clear that there had been any justification for removing the children into foster-care. He said that the local authority had failed to address itself adequately to the requirements of ss.44(5) or (10) CA 1989; and it was not clear that it had exercised the exceptional diligence called for by art. 8 ECHR. The distress suffered by the children and parents due to their separation had been exacerbated by the unacceptably limited amount of contact permitted, and by the interventionist manner in which contact had been supervised. Munby J said that the Court of Appeal had repeatedly emphasised that any intervention under Parts V (and IV) of the Children Act should be proportionate to the legitimate aim of protecting the welfare and interests of the child. As Hale LJ had said in *Re O (Supervision Order)* [2001] EWCA Civ 16, [2001] 1 FLR 923, 'proportionality … is the key'.

In *Re X (Emergency Protection Order)* [2006] EWHC 510 (Fam), [2006] 2 FLR 701 McFarlane J emphasised that EPOs should be made only in a genuine emergency and only for the purpose of providing immediate short-term protection. He said lack of information or a need for assessment could not on their own justify the making of an EPO.

(iv) Duration of an EPO   An order can be made in the first instance to last for up to eight days, but can be extended for up to a further seven days on application if the court has reasonable cause to believe that the child is likely to suffer significant harm if the order is not extended (s.45).

(v) Effect of an EPO   While an EPO is in force it operates as a direction to any person who is in a position to do so to comply with any request to produce the child to the applicant (s.44(4)(a)). It authorises the child's removal to accommodation provided by or on behalf of the applicant and the child being kept there; or it prevents the child's removal from any hospital, or other place, in which the child was being accommodated immediately before the order was made (s.44(4)(b)). It is a criminal offence intentionally to obstruct a person authorised to remove the child, or to prevent the removal of the child (s.44(15)). An EPO gives the applicant limited parental responsibility (s.44(4)(c) and s.44(5)(b)). The applicant must comply with regulations made by the Secretary of State (s.44(5)).

While an EPO is in force, the local authority cannot remove the child from his home or retain him in a place for longer than is necessary to safeguard the child's welfare, and must return the child or allow him to be removed when safe to do so (s.44(10)). The child can be returned to the care of the person from whom he was removed or, if that is not reasonably practicable, then to a parent, a person with parental responsibility or to such other person as the applicant with the agreement of the court considers appropriate, although while the order is in force the applicant can exercise his powers with respect to the child where it is necessary to do so (ss.44(11), (12)). Local authorities must make arrangements (subject to directions in the order as to contact and medical assessment or examination) to allow the child reasonable contact with the following persons and any person acting on his or her behalf: parents; any other person with parental responsibility; any person with whom the child was living immediately before the order was made; and any person with a right to contact under a s.8 order or under a s.34 contact order (s.44(13)).

(vi) Imposing directions on an EPO   When an EPO is made, or while it is in force, the court can give directions and impose conditions as to contact and/or may give directions with respect to the medical or psychiatric examination or other assessment of the child, which can include a condition that no examination or assessment be carried out unless the court directs (ss.44(6), (8) and (9)). Where a direction as to medical or psychiatric examination or assessment is made, a child of sufficient understanding to make an informed decision

may refuse the examination or assessment (s.44(6)). Directions in an order can be varied at any time (s.44(9)(b)).

(vii) Challenging an EPO There is no right of appeal against making, or refusing to make, an EPO. However, an application for discharge can be heard 72 hours or more after the EPO was made (ss.45(9), (10)) on the application of: the child; his parent; any person who has parental responsibility for the child; or any person with whom the child was living immediately before the order was made (s.45(8)). An EPO can be challenged under the Human Rights Act 1998, and judicial review proceedings may provide a useful way of challenging an order. In *X Council* v. *B (Emergency Protection Orders)* (see p. 412 above), Munby J held that, while an application for judicial review is not normally an appropriate remedy for challenging an EPO, it is not necessarily precluded in an appropriate case in order to correct an error or injustice. He said that, as the effect of an EPO was to remove a child from a parent for up to 15 days without a statutory right of appeal, judicial review might provide a mechanism for review of an unreasonable decision by the family proceedings court.

(viii) An exclusion requirement The court can include in an EPO a requirement that the alleged abuser should leave the home or be prevented from entering the home and/or an area round the home if it is satisfied that: there is reasonable cause to believe that by doing this the child will cease to suffer, or cease to be likely to suffer, significant harm; and there is a person living in the home who is able and willing to provide reasonable care for the child (see s.44A).

(c) Police protection

Under s.46 of the Children Act 1989 the police have various powers in emergency cases involving children. Thus, any constable who has reasonable cause to believe that a child would otherwise be likely to suffer significant harm can remove the child to suitable accommodation, or take reasonable steps to prevent the child's removal (s.46(1)). This power lasts for up to 72 hours during which time the police must ensure that inquiries are conducted by a designated officer and that the child is accommodated by the local authority (ss.43(3)(e), (f)). The police must inform the local authority, the parents and the child of any steps it proposes to take. While the child is in police protection, the police do not have parental responsibility for the child but must do what is reasonable to safeguard or promote the child's welfare. While the child is accommodated under s.46, the parents cannot remove the child, but they are permitted to have contact.

According to research by Masson (2005) police protection is widely used, despite the lack of attention given to police protection in the literature on child protection.

14.10 Local authorities' duties towards 'looked after' children

Local authorities have duties under the Children Act 1989 towards children 'looked after' by them, whether accommodated under a voluntary arrangement or under a care order (s.22(1)). A local authority must safeguard and promote the child's welfare and make such use of services available for children cared for by their own parents as appears reasonable in the case of the particular child (s.22(3)). Before making a decision about a child being looked after, or proposed to be looked after, the local authority must ascertain the wishes and feelings of the child, his parents, any person with parental responsibility and any other relevant person (s.22(4)). It must also consider their wishes in respect of the child's religion, racial origin and cultural and linguistic background (s.22(5)). It must advise, assist and befriend the child with a view to promoting his welfare when he ceases to be looked after by it (s.24(1)). A local authority must encourage rehabilitation by allowing the child to live with his family, unless contrary to his welfare (s.23(6)), and ensure that the accommodation provided is near the child's home, and that brothers and sisters remain together (s.23(7)). A local authority's general duties to a child are facilitated by more specific duties, such as by the inspection of foster-parents, and children's homes. Local authorities also have a duty to promote contact (Sched. 2, para. 15, and see 14.8 above).

Children leaving care   The Children (Leaving Care) Act 2000 inserted new sections into ss.23–24 of the Children Act 1989, and into Schedule 2 (see paras. 19A–C) in order to impose certain duties on local authorities in respect of children who leave care. Each local authority is required to provide a comprehensive after-care service to ease the passage of looked after children into adulthood. A local authority looking after a child has a duty to advise, assist and befriend the child with a view to promoting his welfare when it has ceased to look after him (para. 19A). It must keep in touch with a care leaver and prepare 'needs assessments' and formulate 'pathway plans' in respect of education, training, careers and financial support until the person leaving care reaches the age of 21 (para. 19B). A local authority is required to appoint a personal adviser to keep in touch with the person leaving care (para. 19C). A local authority is also required to provide financial support, including the cost of education and training up to the age of 24.

   If a local authority fails to comply with these statutory requirements, a challenge can be made in judicial review proceedings (see, for example, *R (J)* v. *Caerphilly County Borough Council* [2005] EWHC 586 (Admin), [2005] 2 FLR 860 where Munby J held that a local authority has a duty to carry out its statutory obligations even if the person leaving care is unco-operative and unwilling to engage, or refuses to engage, with the local authority). In *R (Berhe and Others)* v. *Hillingdon London Borough Council* [2003] EWHC 2075 (Admin), [2004] 1 FLR 439 Sullivan J held that asylum-seeking minors who had been looked after by a local authority were entitled on reaching adulthood to benefit from the provisions of the Children (Leaving Care) Act 2000.

   In *R (G)* v. *Nottingham City Council and Nottingham University Hospitals NHS Trust* [2008] EWHC 400 (Admin), [2008] 1 FLR 1668 a mother (aged 18) successfully challenged in judicial review proceedings the pathway plan prepared for her by the local authority under ss.23A–23C and Sched. 2. Munby J held that there had been a serious failure by the local authority to comply with its statutory duties.

14.11   Challenging local authority decisions about children

Parents, relatives, children, foster-parents and others may sometimes be dissatisfied with action taken, or not taken, by a local authority. In such cases it may be possible to resolve a grievance informally, but if this is not possible the following procedures can be invoked.

(i) Using the Children Act 1989   One way of challenging a local authority is to appeal against a care or supervision order or apply to have it discharged (see p. 407 above). In

respect of an emergency protection order, a discharge application can be made, but there is no right of appeal. A decision about contact with a child may also be challenged (see 14.8 above). A care order can also be challenged by applying for a residence order, which, if granted, automatically discharges the care order (s.91(1)). However, the court is unlikely to grant a residence order, or grant leave to apply for one, where it interferes with a local authority's plans (see, for example, *Re A and W (Minors) (Residence Order: Leave to Apply)* [1992] Fam 182, [1992] 2 FLR 154 where a foster-mother's application for leave to apply for a residence order as a means of challenging a local authority decision forbidding her to foster children was refused).

Another option is to make a complaint to the Secretary of State, who has the power to declare a local authority to be in default, if it fails without reasonable cause to comply with a duty under the Children Act 1989, and who can require compliance within a specified period (s.84). It is not possible to apply to make a child a ward of court as a way of challenging a care order (ss.100(2)(c) and 91(4)).

(ii) The complaints procedure   The Children Act 1989 requires local authorities to establish a complaints procedure (see s.26). Complaints can be made in respect of the duties and powers of local authorities under Parts III, IV and V of the Act. The following persons can make a complaint: a 'looked after' child or a child in need; a parent; a person with parental responsibility; a foster-parent; any person whom the local authority considers has sufficient interest in the child's welfare to warrant representation being considered; a young person who considers he has been given inadequate preparation for leaving care or for after-care; and a child who is the subject of a placement order for the purposes of adoption.

(iii) Advocacy services for children   A child making a complaint can make use of an independent advocacy service (see s.24A). Local authorities must make arrangements to provide assistance (such as advocacy services and representation) for children and young persons who make, or intend to make, complaints under the Children Act procedures (s.26A(1)). This duty applies to the standard complaints procedure in s.26 (above) and to the procedure for young people leaving care under s.24D. The assistance which local authorities must put in place must include representation (s.26A(2)). Local authorities can choose whether to provide the assistance themselves or may come to an agreement with a national or local advocacy service provider.

(iv) A challenge under the Human Rights Act 1998   As local authorities are public authorities for the purposes of the Human Rights Act (HRA) 1998, they must act in a way which is compatible with the European Convention for the Protection of Human Rights (s.6 HRA 1998) (see 1.7). Any person who is a victim of an unlawful act (or proposed act) of a local authority may bring an application under s.7 HRA 1998 either by way of a free-standing application against a local authority or by relying on a Convention right in any legal proceedings (s.7). Damages can be awarded for a breach of a Convention right (s.8 HRA 1998). Human rights challenges can be made in proceedings under Parts III, IV and V of the Children Act 1989 or in judicial review proceedings (see over).

Human rights claims against local authorities are usually brought on the basis of a breach of art. 6 ECHR (the right to a fair trial) and/or art. 8 (the right to family life).

Case-law examples

▶ *Re G (Care: Challenge to Local Authority's Decision)* [2003] EWHC 551 (Fam), [2003] 2 FLR 42

The parents applied for discharge of care orders and an injunction under s.7 HRA 1998 to prevent their children's removal into care, as the local authority had delayed in making a decision about the children, and had kept no minutes or written records of meetings and decisions made. Munby J held that the local authority was in breach of the right to family life under art. 8.

▶ *Re M (Care: Challenging Decisions by Local Authority)* [2001] 2 FLR 1300

The child in care's parents had a long history of alcohol and drug abuse. At a planning meeting, to which the parents and their solicitors were not invited, the local authority finally ruled out any prospect of the child living with the father. Each parent commenced separate free-standing applications under s.7 HRA 1998 arguing that they were victims of an unlawful act of the public authority, and that the placement should be set aside. Holman J held that the local authority had acted unlawfully under s.6 HRA 1998 in respect of the way in which it had conducted the planning meeting, which was contrary to the parents' right to respect for their family life under art. 8. As the local authority had failed sufficiently to involve the parents at critical moments, Holman J quashed the decision made at the planning meeting.

▶ *Re W (Removal into Care)* [2005] EWCA Civ 642, [2005] 2 FLR 1022

The parents challenged the removal of twins from their care by means of an application to discharge the care orders and by way of injunction under s.8 HRA 1998. Thorpe LJ held that an application under the HRA 1998 was the right remedy, not the application to discharge the care orders, as what they were challenging was the lawfulness of the local authority's decision to remove the twins.

▶ *Re C (Breach of Human Rights: Damages)* [2007] EWCA Civ 2, [2007] 1 FLR 1957

The trial judge made a declaration under the HRA 1998 that there had been a significant breach of the mother's human rights caused by the local authority's decision to abandon the care plan without giving the mother an opportunity to participate in the decision-making process; but did not make an order for damages.

(See also *Re L (Care: Assessment: Fair Trial)* [2002] EWHC 1379 (Fam), [2002] 2 FLR 730; and *C v. Bury Metropolitan Borough Council* [2002] EWHC 1438 (Fam), [2002] 2 FLR 868).

(v) Judicial review   Judicial review is an administrative law remedy which may be made against a local authority (or other public body, such as a Government department, court or health authority) by an aggrieved person, including a child. The application is made in the Administrative Court. The court can grant the following remedies: a 'mandatory order' (directing the respondent to take a particular course of action); a 'prohibitory order' (prohibiting the respondent from taking a particular course of action); or a 'quashing order' (quashing the decision of the respondent). It can order damages in conjunction with one of these orders. The Administrative Court can also issue declarations and injunctions.

Strict rules govern judicial review applications. Thus, leave must be obtained from the court for the case to proceed to a full application on its merits, which will be granted only if the court considers that there is a reasonable chance of the court deciding that the local authority's decision was so unreasonable that no reasonable authority could have come to it. Leave to apply must be sought within three months from the date on which the grounds for the application arose. Leave will not be granted unless the applicant has a sufficient interest in the matter to which the application relates. The grounds on which judicial review may be granted are: illegality; procedural impropriety (breach of the rules of natural justice); and irrationality. To succeed on the ground of irrationality, a local authority must have taken into account irrelevant matters, or failed to have taken into account relevant matters, or have come to a conclusion that was so unreasonable that no authority would have come to it. However, as judicial review is a discretionary remedy, the court may refuse a remedy even if a ground is proved.

As local authorities are public authorities for the purposes of the Human Rights Act 1998, and as judicial review is a means of challenging local authority action or inaction, challenges by way of judicial review are often based on, or supported by, human rights arguments under the European Convention for the Protection of Human Rights:

> ▶ *The Queen on the Applications of L and Others* **v.** *Manchester City Council; The Queen on the Application of R and Another* **v.** *Manchester City Council* **[2001] EWHC 707 (Admin)**
>
> Children (by their litigation friend) successfully applied for judicial review of the local authority's policy whereby it paid substantially lower fostering payments to short-term foster-parents who were friends or relatives of children. Munby J held that the local authority's policy was irrational, and also breached art. 8 ECHR (right to family life), as under art. 8(2) it was neither a necessary nor proportionate response. The local authority had a positive obligation when exercising its duties under Part III of the Children Act to secure respect for family life under art. 8. The policy was also held to be discriminatory under art. 14 ECHR, as the reference in art. 14 to 'other status' included family status.

Where a local authority has wide discretion in a particular matter (as it has under the Children Act 1989) it is difficult to succeed in an action for judicial review, and, where there is another procedure for challenging a local authority, the court may not grant judicial review before that procedure has been pursued. Judicial review is therefore a remedy of last resort, and may be refused where there is another equally effective and convenient remedy (such as a bringing a complaint under the complaints procedure, see *R (On the Application of Appiatse and Another) v. Enfield Borough Council* [2008] EWHC 1886 (Admin), [2008] 2 FLR 1945).

A considerable disadvantage of judicial review is that, if a 'quashing order' is granted, the local authority's obligation is merely to reconsider its original decision, and, provided that decision is not illegal, procedurally improper or irrational, then it can come to the same decision as it did the first time.

The drawbacks of the court's powers in judicial review proceedings were referred to in *Re T (Judicial Review: Local Authority Decisions Concerning Child in Need)* [2003] EWHC 2515 (Admin), [2004] 1 FLR 601 where Wall J held that, while the court was in a position to direct the local authority to reconsider the question of the services it should provide under Part III Children Act 1989 for the child in question, it could not direct the local authority in respect of what to decide or direct that it make any special provision for the child.

There are many reported cases involving applications for judicial review in the context of local authorities' powers under the Children Act 1989, for example for: failing to allow a solicitor to attend a child protection conference and failing to supply the applicant with the minutes (*R* v. *Cornwall County Council ex parte LH* [2000] 1 FLR 236); failing to obtain parental permission to move a child from residential care to foster care (*R* v. *Tameside Metropolitan Borough Council ex parte J* [2000] 1 FLR 942); and refusing to carry out assessments of children in need (*R (On the Application of S)* v. *Wandsworth, Hammersmith and Lambeth London Borough Council* [2002] 1 FLR 469). Placing a child on the child protection register can be challenged by judicial review (see *R* v. *Harrow London Borough Council ex parte D* [1990] Fam 133), but the courts have held that the complaints procedure (see p. 416 above), rather than judicial review proceedings, should be followed (*R* v. *Hampshire County Council ex parte H* [1999] 2 FLR 359; and *A and S* v. *Enfield London Borough Council* [2008] EWHC 1886 (Admin), [2008] 2 FLR 1945).

(vi) Commissioner for Local Administration   A complaint can be made to the Commissioner for Local Administration (the Local Government Ombudsman), who has a duty to investigate complaints of maladministration by local authorities. This is a lengthy and limited remedy.

(vii) An application to the Children's Commissioner   A complaint can be made to the Children's Commissioner (see p. 216).

(viii) An application to the European Court of Human Rights   A parent, child or other aggrieved party, who has exhausted all the remedies available in the courts in the UK, can apply to the European Court of Human Rights (ECtHR) in Strasbourg, alleging that the UK is in breach of the European Convention for the Protection of Human Rights (see, for example, *X (Minors)* v. *Bedfordshire County Council and Related Appeals* [1995] 2 AC 633, [1995] 2 FLR 276; and *RK and AK* v. *United Kingdom* [2009] 1 FLR 274, below).

(ix) An action in negligence   Social workers and other persons working in the child protection system are not immune from liability in negligence, although the courts are aware of the difficult task social workers have and that local authorities have limited resources. A claim may therefore be struck out on the ground that there is no duty of care in negligence for reasons of public policy. There has, however, been a change of attitude in respect of negligence claims against local authorities working in the child protection area, and the courts are now more willing to allow claims to proceed to trial, particularly since the coming into force of the Human Rights Act 1998. The following cases are examples of claims brought in negligence:

▶ *X (Minors)* v. *Bedfordshire County Council and Related Appeals* [1995] 2 AC 633, [1995] 2 FLR 276

In the first appeal negligence claims were brought by five children against Bedfordshire County Council for failing to take steps to protect them from the years of neglect they had suffered, even though the defendant had been informed on several occasions that they were suffering harm. In the second appeal, the child and the mother sued the local authority (Newham London Borough Council) because the child had been mistakenly taken into care (for about one year) after a child psychologist employed by the local authority had wrongly identified the mother's cohabitant as having abused the child. The House of Lords held in respect of both appeals that the defendant local authorities owed the claimants no duty of care in negligence, and so the cases were struck out.

Note: Four of the children in 'the Bedfordshire case' subsequently took their case to the ECtHR in Strasbourg (see *Z and Others* v. *United Kingdom* [2001] 2 FLR 603), which held that the UK Government was in breach of art. 3 ECHR (as the children had suffered inhuman and degrading treatment) and art. 13 (because they had not had an effective remedy). The child and the mother in 'the Newham case' also took their case to the ECtHR which held that there had also been breaches of arts. 3 and 13 (see *TP and KM* v. *United Kingdom* [2001] 2 FLR 545). After these two decisions by the ECtHR, the courts in the UK became more willing to allow cases in negligence to proceed to trial and for negligence claims to succeed, particularly where the claimants were children, or adults who had suffered as children.

▶ *A v. Essex County Council* [2003] EWCA Civ 1848, [2004] 1 FLR 749

The parents were successful in claiming damages in negligence (including damages for psychiatric injury) against the defendant local authority for failing to give them sufficient information about a boy who had been placed with them for adoption and who subsequently attacked them and their own child.

▶ *D v. East Berkshire Community NHS Trust; MAK v. Dewsbury Healthcare NHS Trust; RK v. Oldham NHS Trust* [2005] UKHL 23, [2005] 2 FLR 284

The parents in the three appeals claimed that the medical professionals had negligently misdiagnosed child abuse of their children, when in fact the children had genuine health problems; and that this had disrupted their family life and caused them psychiatric injury. The House of Lords held by a majority (Lord Bingham dissenting) that the defendants owed no duty of care in negligence to the parents on grounds of public policy because doctors must be free to act in the best interests of children generally.

Note: The parents in the *RK* case successfully took their case to the European Court of Human Rights (see *RK and AK* v. *United Kingdom* [2009] 1 FLR 274) which awarded them substantial damages. The ECtHR held that there was had been no breach of art. 8 ECHR (the right to family life), as there had been relevant and sufficient reasons for the authorities to take protective measures and those measures had been proportionate to the aim of protecting the child. But it held that there had been a breach of art. 13 (the right to an effective remedy), as the parents (who had an arguable complaint concerning interference with their family life) should have had a means of claiming that the local authority's handling of the procedures was responsible for any damage they had suffered; and a means of obtaining compensation for such damage.

(See also *Pierce* v. *Doncaster Metropolitan Borough Council* [2007] EWCHC 2698 (QB), [2008] 1 FLR 922 where the adult claimant (who had suffered neglect and physical and emotional abuse as a child after being returned to the care of his parent by the local authority) was successful in claiming damages for negligence).

Summary

1 Local authorities have duties and powers under the Children Act 1989 to safeguard and promote the welfare of children. Local authorities must work in partnership with families and children, with compulsory intervention by court order in the last resort, as parents have primary responsibility for their children.

2 As local authorities are public authorities for the purposes of the Human Rights Act 1998, they must abide by the European Convention for the Protection of Human Rights.

3 Local authorities must co-operate with other professionals and other agencies in the task of child protection.

Summary cont'd

4   Under Part III of the Children Act 1989 local authorities have a duty to provide services for children in need and disabled children, including in particular the provision of day care and accommodation.

5   Under Part IV of the Children Act 1989 local authorities can apply for care and supervision orders, which may be granted by the court if the 'threshold criteria' in s.31(2) are satisfied, and the court considers the child's welfare requires such an order to be made. In assessing welfare, the court must apply the welfare principle (s.1(1)), the no-delay principle (s.1(2)), the welfare checklist (s.1(3)) and the no-order presumption (s.1(5)). A care order gives the local authority parental responsibility for the child, but a parent does not lose parental responsibility. A supervision order places the child under the supervision of a designated local authority officer or a probation officer. A care order can be discharged. A supervision order can be varied or discharged. There is a presumption of continuing reasonable contact between parents and others and the child in care, unless terminated or restricted by court order (s.34).

6   Under Part V of the Children Act 1989 a child assessment order (s.43) or an emergency protection order (s.44) can be made where children need emergency protection. The police have powers to provide protection for children where they have reasonable cause to believe that a child is likely to suffer significant harm (s.46).

7   Local authorities have certain duties to children 'looked after' by them whether under a voluntary arrangement or under a court order.

8   Local authorities can be challenged under the Children Act 1989 complaints procedure or under the general law by bringing a tort action or by seeking judicial review. An application may be made to the local ombudsman. Challenges can also be brought under the Human Rights Act 1998.

Further reading and references

Bailey-Harris and Harris, 'Local authorities and child protection – the mosaic of accountability' [2002] CFLQ 117.

Driscoll and Hollingsworth, 'Accommodating children in need: *R (M)* v. *Hammersmith and Fulham London Borough Council* [2008] CFLQ 522.

Hall, 'What price the logic of proof of evidence?' [2000] Fam Law 423.

Harwin and Owen, 'The implementation of care plans, and its relationship to children's welfare' [2003] CFLQ 71.

Hayes, 'Child protection – from principles and policies to practices' [1998] CFLQ 119.

Hayes, 'Farewell to the cogent evidence test: *Re B'* [2008] Fam Law 859.

Hollingsworth and Douglas, 'Creating a children's champion for Wales? The Care Standards Act 2000 (Part V) and the Children's Commissioner for Wales Act 2001' (2002) *Modern Law Review* 58.

Howe, 'Removal of children at interim hearings: is the test now set too high?' [2009] Fam Law 320.

Keating, 'Suspicions, sitting on the fence and standards of proof' [2009] CFLQ 230.

Masson, 'Emergency protection, good practice and human rights' [2004] Fam Law 882.

Masson, 'Emergency intervention to protect children: using and avoiding legal controls' [2005] CFLQ 75.

Masson, 'Reforming care proceedings – time for a review' (2007) CFLQ 411.

Masson *et al*, *Care Profiling Study*, 2008, Ministry of Justice (Research Series 4/08).

Masson *et al*, *Protecting Powers: Emergency Intervention for Children's Protection*, 2007, John Wiley & Sons.

Further reading and references cont'd

Murphy, 'Children in need: the limits of local authority accountability' (2003) *Legal Studies* 104.

Perry, '*Lancashire County Council* v. *B*: Section 31 – threshold or barrier?' [2000] CFLQ 301.

Ryder, The Honourable Mr Justice, 'The risk fallacy: a tale of two thresholds' [2008] Fam Law 30.

Williams, 'The practical operation of the Children Act complaints procedure' [2002] CFLQ 25.

Websites

Department for Children, Schools and Families: www.dcsf.gov.uk

Every Child Matters: www.everychildmatters.gov.uk

Ministry of Justice: www.justice.gov.uk

National Council of Voluntary Childcare Organisations: www.ncvcco.org

NSPCC (National Society for the Prevention of Cruelty to Children): www.nspcc.org.uk

Chapter 15

Adoption and special guardianship

This chapter deals with adoption and special guardianship. Although special guardianship is not part of the adoption legislation, it is dealt with in this chapter as it may provide a more suitable alternative for a child than adoption.

Article 21 of the UN Convention on the Rights of the Child 1989

'States Parties that recognise and/or permit the system of adoption shall ensure that the best interests of the child shall be the paramount consideration.'

The legislation

Adoption and Children Act 2002 Lays down the powers and duties of adoption agencies and the courts in respect of adoption.

Children Act 1989 Provides a range of alternatives to adoption including, in particular, special guardianship orders.

The Government website, Every Child Matters (www.everychildmatters.gov.uk) contains useful information on adoption; and so does that of the British Association for Adoption and Fostering (BAAF) (www.baaf.org.uk).

15.1 Adoption – Introduction

Adoption of a child is effected by an adoption order which extinguishes the parental responsibility of the child's birth parents, and other persons, and vests it in the adopters. Adoption therefore involves the complete legal transfer of parental responsibility and makes the child a full legal member of the new family.

The law of adoption is laid down in the Adoption and Children Act 2002, but the law on human rights is also relevant.

(i) Adoption and human rights   As adoption agencies and courts are public authorities for the purposes of the Human Rights Act 1998 they must exercise their powers and duties in compliance with the European Convention for the Protection of Human Rights (ECHR) (see 1.7). They must ensure, in particular, that adoption is in the best interests of the child; and that it does not breach the right to family life of the child and of the child's natural parents under art. 8 ECHR. Any interference with the right to family life must be legitimate, necessary and proportionate (art. 8(2)). Cases decided by the European Court of Human Rights (ECtHR) must be taken into account by the courts and other public authorities which have responsibility for adoption in England and Wales (see s.2(1) HRA 1998). In the following case the ECtHR emphasised the importance of the right to mutual enjoyment of the child and the biological parent(s):

> ▶ *Johansen v. Norway* **(1997) 23 EHRR 33**
>
> The child, who was in care, had been placed in a foster-home with a view to her adoption, and the mother had been deprived of contact. The ECtHR held that: 'the mutual enjoyment by parent and child of each other's company constitutes a fundamental element of family life and domestic measures hindering such enjoyment amount to an interference with the right protected by art. 8'. The ECtHR held that there had been a breach of the ECHR, as the far-reaching measures taken were inconsistent with the aim of reuniting the mother and child and should only have been taken in exceptional circumstances where they could be justified in the best interests of the child.

But each case depends on its facts. In *Söderbäck v. Sweden* [1999] 1 FLR 250 an adoption order was held not to breach art. 8 ECHR.

In *Keegan v. Ireland* (1994) 18 EHRR 342 the ECtHR has held that placing a child for adoption shortly after birth, without the natural father's knowledge or consent, may breach the right to family life guaranteed by art. 8 ECHR. However, in a similar case, *Eski v. Austria (Application No. 21949/03)* [2007] 1 FLR 1650, the father's art. 8 rights were not held to be breached, as the domestic court had carefully examined the case and given reasons; and the assessment of the interests of the child and the father's limited relationship with her lay within the 'margin of appreciation' (see p. 15) of the domestic court and justified a proportionate interference with the father's art. 8 rights.

A refusal by a court or a local authority or adoption agency to permit a person to adopt a child on the ground of that person's sexuality may breach the ECHR. In *EB v. France (Application No. 43546/02)* [2008] 1 FLR 850 the ECtHR held that the refusal of the French authorities to allow a lesbian woman in a stable and long-term relationship to adopt a child, on the basis *inter alia* of there being no paternal role model for the child, was a breach of art. 14 (the right not to suffer discrimination) taken in conjunction with art. 8 (the right to family life). The ECtHR held that the case differed in a number of respects from *Fretté v. France (Application No 36515/97)* [2003] 2 FLR 9 where a homosexual man was refused permission to adopt a child.

However, art. 8 ECHR does not create an absolute right to adopt as child, as the right to family life in art. 8 is not itself an absolute right (see 1.7).

The UN Convention on the Rights of the Child (see 8.2) is also relevant to the law and practice of adoption.

(ii) The role of Cafcass in adoptions   The role of Cafcass officers (or Welsh family proceedings officers) (see 1.6) in adoption depends on whether the child's birth-parents agree to the adoption. If they do, the court will appoint a Cafcass reporting officer who has a duty to make sure that consent to the adoption has been freely given. If the parents do not agree, or special circumstances exist, then the court will, if needed, appoint a Children's Guardian (also an officer of Cafcass). The case will then be investigated in more depth. Under s.22 of the Adoption and Children Act 2002 a Cafcass officer is responsible for witnessing pre-court consent to adoption and reporting back to the adoption agency prior to the court application for an adoption order.

(iii) Adoption procedure   Rules of procedure for adoption are laid down in the Family Procedure (Adoption) Rules 2005 and in Practice Directions (see in particular, *President's*

Guidance (Adoption: The New Law and Procedure) [2006] 1 FLR 1234). All three tiers of family courts (the High Court, county courts and magistrates' family proceedings courts) have jurisdiction to hear adoptions. Certain county courts are designated as adoption centres and any application for an adoption order to a county court must be commenced in such a centre. The overriding objective of the adoption procedure rules is to enable the court 'to deal with cases justly, having regard to the welfare issues involved' (r.1(1)).

(iv) Agency adoptions and non-agency adoptions   Agency adoptions are adoptions involving local authority adoption services or adoption agencies, which have statutory responsibilities for making arrangements for adoption and placing children for adoption (ss.2–17). Local authorities must maintain an adoption service and an adoption support service (which includes the provision of financial support); and they must advertise these services (ss.3–5 ACA 2002). Adoption agencies must also provide counselling, advice and information about adoption (s.2(6)).

Non-agency adoptions are those by relatives, step-parents, private foster-parents and by local authority foster-parents with whom the local authority has not placed a child with a view to adoption.

(v) Illegal arrangements, placements and transactions   It is a criminal offence for a person or body other than an adoption agency to make arrangements for adoption and for unauthorised persons to prepare adoption reports (ss.92–94). It is also unlawful for persons to advertise for adoption (ss.123, 124). Certain payments and rewards made in connection with adoption are also prohibited (s.95), although the court may retrospectively authorise certain payments. There are also prohibitions on bringing overseas children into the UK.

(vi) Adopters and the Independent Reviewing Mechanism   The Independent Reviewing Mechanism was established under the Adoption and Children Act 2002 with the aim of increasing public confidence in the adoption system. The function of the Review Panel is to offer prospective adopters a right of review if an adoption agency decides not to approve them. The Panel reviews the information that went before the original adoption panel and, if necessary, seeks further information. It will then make a recommendation as to whether or not the applicants are suitable to become adopters; but the final decision remains ultimately with the adoption agency.

(vii) Alternatives to adoption   An adoption order terminates the parental responsibility of the child's birth parents and gives it to the adopters. There are, however, other ways of obtaining parental responsibility, which may be preferable to an adoption order as they do not sever the child's legal relationship with the other half of his or her birth family. Special guardianship (see 15.14), residence orders (see 10.5) and parental responsibility agreements and orders (see 9.5) provide ways of obtaining parental responsibility which, depending on the circumstances, may provide a better alternative to adoption. The disadvantage of these alternatives, however, is that they lack the certainty and finality of an adoption order, which may create uncertainty and insecurity for the child and the carer(s). (For cases where a residence order, not an adoption order, was made, see, for example, *Re M (Adoption or Residence Order)* [1998] 1 FLR 570 (the 12-year-old girl did not wish to be adopted); and *Re B (Adoption Order)* [2001] EWCA Civ

347, [2001] 2 FLR 26 (the child maintained regular and good contact with the birth-father).)

Adoption trends

(i) Adoption statistics and the decline in adoption　In England and Wales about 5,000 children are adopted each year. In 2008 in England and Wales 4,939 children were entered into the Adoption Children Register following court orders made (207 more than in 2007); and 57 per cent of those children were aged between one and four (Office for National Statistics, www.statistics.gov.uk).

Adoptions were once much more common (for example, in 1971 there were 21,495 adoptions). However, during the 1970s the number of adoptions declined rapidly and continued to decline steadily in the 1980s and 1990s (Office for National Statistics). The decline in the number of adoptions over the years has been due in part to fewer babies being available for adoption, as a result of improved contraception, the legalisation of abortion, and the fact that single mothers are no longer stigmatised and put under pressure to give up their babies. Children who are available for adoption today are usually older children, some of whom are in local authority care.

(ii) Adoptions by step-parents and relatives　Some adoptions are 'in family' adoptions, in that they involve an adoption by a relative or step-parent. 'In family' adoptions can have drawbacks, as they can sever the child's legal and social relationship with the other birth-parent and the other side of the family. Because relationship breakdown is common, and many divorced parents re-marry, step-parent adoption is particularly common, accounting for nearly one-third of all adoptions (see www.baaf.org.uk). Before the Adoption and Children Act 2002 came into force, a step-parent had to make a joint application to adopt a step-child with the rather bizarre consequence that the birth-parent had to adopt his or her own child. However, this anomaly was removed by the 2002 Act so that a step-parent can now make a sole application to adopt his or her step-child. Step-parents also now have available a wider range of alternative ways of acquiring parental responsibility for a step-child. Thus, they can obtain parental responsibility by means of a parental responsibility agreement or parental responsibility order (see 9.5), a special guardianship order (see 15.14) or a residence order (see 10.5).

(The civil partner of the parent of the child can also make a sole application to adopt the child of his or her civil partner).

(iii) Adoption with contact – 'open' adoption　Attitudes to contact after adoption have changed over the years. At one time, adoption was 'closed' in the sense that contact after adoption was not considered a possibility – it was thought best if children permanently severed their links with their birth-family. However, it is now accepted that contact may be beneficial to some adopted children, particularly older ones. For this reason, the court has the power to order contact between an adopted child and a family member or other person (see 15.10). The importance of children maintaining links with their birth-family is also recognised in the welfare checklist in s.1(4) ACA 2002 (see p. 428 below).

15.3 Adoption – the development of the law

In the late 1980s and early 1990s the Conservative Government conducted an inter-departmental review of adoption, and various research and consultation documents were published including an Adoption Bill making fundamental changes to adoption law, but which was not presented to Parliament before the Conservative Government lost the election in 1997.

When the Labour Government came into power in 1997, it announced that it was committed to improving adoption (see para. 1.5, *Supporting Families*, Home Office, 1998). However, it began to realise, because of major failings in the child care system, that adoption could provide a better alternative for children in care. The '*Waterhouse Report*' (*Lost in Care – Report of the Tribunal of Inquiry into the Abuse of Children in Care in the Former County Council Areas of Gwynedd and Clwyd*, 2000) identified 'drift' in care as one of the major failings of the child protection system. Tony Blair, the Prime Minister, reacted to the *Waterhouse Report* by announcing that he would personally lead a thorough review of adoption policy in order to ensure that the Government was making the best use of adoption as an option to meet the needs of children looked after by local authorities. The *Prime Minister's Review: Adoption* (a study of the use of adoption for children in care by the Performance and Innovation Unit of the Cabinet Office, 2000) said that too many children were in care for too long and that they needed a family who could meet their needs on a permanent basis. It recommended that the Government should promote an increased use of adoption for children in care. The White Paper, *Adoption: A New Approach*, 2000, Cm 5017, set out the Government's plans to promote the greater use of adoption, to improve the performance of the adoption service and put children at the centre of the adoption process. These developments led to the enactment of the Adoption and Children Act 2002, which came fully into force on 30 December 2005.

The Adoption and Children Act 2002 replaced the Adoption Act 1976 and modernised the legal framework for adoption in England and Wales. It made important changes to adoption law, which included the following:

Changes to adoption law made by the Adoption and Children Act 2002

The Adoption and Children Act 2002:

- aligned adoption law with the Children Act 1989 by making the child's welfare the paramount consideration in all decisions relating to adoption;
- introduced a new welfare-based ground for dispensing with parental consent;
- abolished freeing for adoption orders and introduced new measures for placement for adoption (by parental consent or placement order);
- overhauled eligibility to apply for adoption by enabling single persons, married couples, civil partners, and, for the first time, unmarried couples (opposite-sex and same-sex) to apply; and introduced new provisions to enable step-parents to make sole applications for adoption;
- placed a duty on local authorities to maintain an Adoption Service, including new arrangements for the provision of Adoption Support Services;
- established an Independent Reviewing Mechanism to enable prospective adopters who had been turned down for adoption to be entitled to an independent review;
- established an Adoption and Children Act Register to suggest matches between children waiting to be adopted and approved prospective adopters;

> ▶ introduced new measures for tackling delay (courts are required to draw up timetables to prevent delay; and a 'no delay' principle like that in the Children Act 1989 was introduced); and
> ▶ introduced special guardianship to provide permanence for children who could not return to their birth families, but for whom adoption was not the most suitable option.

More adoptions for more children in care   A major aim of the Adoption and Children Act 2002 is to encourage the wider use of adoption for children in care. With a view to encouraging more adoptions of children in care, and to make them succeed, the 2002 Act places a duty on local authorities to provide comprehensive support services, including financial support. (For the year ending 31 March 2009, 3,300 children were adopted from care, see www.baaf.org.uk).

The Adoption and Children Act Register for England and Wales   To prevent delay in matching children with adoptive families, the Adoption and Children Act Register suggests matches between children waiting to be adopted and approved prospective adopters (ss.125–131). The British Association for Adoption and Fostering (BAAF) is responsible for operating the Register for England and Wales.

15.4   The welfare principles

Section 1 of the Adoption and Children Act 2002 lays down the welfare principles which must be applied by courts and adoption agencies when coming to a decision relating to the adoption of a child (s.1(1)). These new principles were introduced in order to bring the law of adoption into line with the welfare principles in the Children Act 1989 (see 10.3).

(i) The welfare principle (s.1(2))   The welfare principle is as follows:

> **Section 1(2)** The 'paramount consideration of the court or adoption agency must be the child's welfare, throughout his life.'

In contrast to the Children Act 1989 the welfare principle in adoption requires an analysis of the child's welfare through childhood into adulthood and for the rest of the child's life. The welfare principle also applies to the issue of dispensing with parental consent (see 15.9).

(ii) The no-delay principle (s.1(3))   The 'court or adoption agency must at all times bear in mind that, in general, any delay in coming to the decision is likely to prejudice the child's welfare'. This brings the law into line with the Children Act 1989 and the requirements of art. 6 of the European Convention for the Protection of Human Rights, which requires cases to be heard promptly.

(iii) The welfare checklist (s.1(4))   Courts and adoption agencies, when determining the best interests of the child in any decision relating to adoption, must have regard to the

factors laid down in the following 'welfare checklist'. This list is much more extensive than the checklist in s.1(3) of the Children Act 1989 (see p. 275).

'(a) the child's ascertainable wishes and feelings regarding the decision (considered in the light of the child's age and understanding);
(b) the child's particular needs;
(c) the likely effect on the child (throughout his life) of having ceased to be a member of the original family and become an adopted person;
(d) the child's age, sex, background and any of the child's characteristics which the court or agency considers relevant;
(e) any harm (within the meaning of the Children Act 1989) which the child has suffered or is at risk of suffering;
(f) the relationship which the child has with relatives, and with any other person in relation to whom the court or agency considers the relationship to be relevant, including –
   (i)   the likelihood of any such relationship continuing and the value to the child of its doing so;
   (ii) the ability and willingness of any of the child's relatives, or of any such person, to provide the child with a secure environment in which the child can develop, and otherwise to meet the child's needs;
   (iii) the wishes and feelings of any of the child's relatives, or of any such person, regarding the child.'

'Relationships' in s.1(4) are not confined to legal relationships (s.1(8)(a)), and 'relatives' includes *inter alia* the child's mother and father (s.1(8)(b)). 'Harm (within the meaning of the Children Act 1989)' (see s.1(4)(e) above) includes seeing or hearing the ill-treatment of another (such as witnessing domestic violence).

As s.1(4)(c) and s.1(2) require courts and adoption agencies to consider the child 'throughout his life', inheritance and succession interests may be relevant considerations.

(iv) The child's religious, racial, cultural and linguistic background (s.1(5))   When placing a child for adoption, 'the adoption agency must give due consideration to the child's religious persuasion, racial origin and cultural and linguistic background' (s.1(5)). However, the courts have held that, although religious beliefs must be taken into account, they are not necessarily determinative, but merely one of the factors that comprise welfare (*per* Ryder J in *Haringey London Borough Council* v. *C, E and Another Intervening* [2006] EWHC 1620 (Fam), [2007] 1 FLR 1035). Thus, however profound the religious belief may be, the child's welfare is the paramount consideration (see also *Re S; Newcastle City Council* v. *Z* [2005] EWHC 1490 (Fam), [2007] 1 FLR 861, where the mother wished to delay adoption for religious reasons until suitable adopters had been found).

(v) Duty to consider other powers; and the 'minimum intervention' principle (s.1(6))   Courts and adoption agencies must consider the whole range of powers available under the 2002 Act and the Children Act 1989 (see Chapter 10); and the court must not make any order unless doing so would be better for the child than not doing so (s.1(6)). Thus, if the court were to make an adoption order when another order would be sufficient to protect the child's welfare (for example, a special guardianship order), this might be in breach of s.1(6), and possibly the principle of proportionality which is part of the right to family life under art. 8 ECHR (see 1.7).

15.5 Eligibility for Adoption

(i) Who can be adopted? The child must be under 18 on the date of the adoption application (s.49(4)), but an adoption order can be made if the child reaches 18 before the conclusion of adoption proceedings (s.49(5)). However, an adoption order cannot be made in any case if the child is aged 19 or over or if the child is married (ss.47(8), (9)).

(ii) Who can adopt? Couples and sole persons can apply to adopt a child (s.49), provided they satisfy certain domicile and age limit requirements (ss.50, 51):

▷ *Couples* This includes married couples, civil partners, and cohabitants (opposite-sex and same-sex who are living as partners in an enduring family relationship) (s.144(4)). Each applicant must be at least 21 (s.50(1)), unless one of the couple is the child's mother or father, when she or he need be only be 18 (s.50(2)).
▷ *Sole applicants* A sole applicant must be at least 21, and must not be married (s.51(1)). A married person can, however, make a sole application if the court is satisfied that: the other spouse cannot be found; or that they are separated permanently and are living apart; or that the other spouse is incapacitated from applying because of physical or mental ill-health (s.51(3)).

(iii) Step-parent and civil partner applicants A step-parent (or a civil partner of the parent of the child) can make a sole application to adopt a step-child (or the child of his or her civil partner), provided the applicant is at least 21 (s.51(2)). As an alternative to adoption, a step-parent or civil partner can acquire parental responsibility for the child by means of a parental responsibility agreement or court order (see 9.5), or by becoming a special guardian (see 15.14) or by obtaining a residence order (see 10.5).

(iv) Foster-parent applicants A local authority foster-parent can apply to adopt a foster-child provided the child has had his or her home with the applicant at all times during the period of one year preceding the application (s.42(4)); or if the court grants leave for the application to be made (s.42(6)). The legal principles relevant to a leave application are the same as those for applications for leave to apply for revocation of a placement order under s.24(2) of the ACA 2002 (see p. 436 below; and see *Re A; Coventry County Council* v. *CC and A* [2007] EWCA Civ 1383, [2008] 1 FLR 959, where the Court of Appeal granted a foster-mother leave to apply for an adoption order).

(v) Domicile requirements At least one of the couple (or the sole applicant) must be domiciled in part of the British Islands; or both of the couple or the sole applicant must have been habitually resident in part of the British Islands for a period of not less than one year ending with the date of the application (s.49).

(vi) Baby adoptions Special provisions exist for the adoption of babies who are less than six weeks old. An adoption agency may place for adoption a baby who is less than six weeks old without the need for formal consent under s.19 or for a placement order (s.18(1)), but any consent by the birth-mother to a placement or to the making of an adoption order is ineffective if it is given less than six weeks after the child's birth (ss.52(3) and 47(4)). This six-week time limit is to enable the mother to recover from the child's birth

and for her to be sure that adoption is what she really desires. Contact orders can, however, be made under s.26, if the baby has been placed for adoption, because of the importance of allowing brothers and sisters and relatives to have contact with the child.

15.6 Preliminaries to making an adoption order or placement order

Before an adoption order or placement order can be made various procedures must be complied with as laid down in the Adoption and Children Act 2002 and in regulations. These requirements are strict: a failure to comply is likely to result in the order being set aside. Thus, for instance, in *Re B (Placement Order)* [2008] EWCA Civ 835, [2008] 2 FLR 1404 a placement order was set aside by the Court of Appeal on the basis that the trial judge had been plainly wrong to make the order, as the agency had failed to provide the Agency Adoption Panel with the required experts' reports and had misrepresented one expert. The Court of Appeal allowed the parents' appeal against the placement order as the Agency Adoption Panel's decision had been materially flawed. The due process laid down by Parliament had not been followed.

(i) Probationary residence requirements In an agency case the child must have had his home with the applicant(s) at all times during the 10 week period preceding the adoption application (s.42(2)). In a non-agency case the child must have lived with the applicant(s) as follows: step-parent or civil partner of the child's parent (a continuous period of at least six months preceding the application, s.42(3)); local authority foster-parents (a continuous period of at least one year preceding the application, s.42(4)). With other applications (such as by a relative), the child must have had his or her home with the applicant(s) for a cumulative period of at least three years (whether continuous or not) during a five-year period preceding the application, except where the court grants leave to apply, ss.42(5), (6)).

(ii) Agency adoptions – duty to provide a report (s.43) The adoption agency must submit to the court a report dealing with the suitability of the applicants and any relevant s.1 welfare issue in respect of the child, and must assist the court in any manner the court directs. A Cafcass officer or Welsh family proceedings officer (see 1.6) will be responsible for compiling the report.

(iii) Non-agency adoptions – notice of intention to adopt (s.44) The prospective adopter(s) must give notice to the appropriate local authority of their intention to apply for an adoption order, and this notice must not be more than two years, or less than three months, before the date on which the application for the adoption order is made. On receipt of notification, the local authority must arrange for the matter to be investigated; and it must submit a report to the court, in particular in respect of the prospective adopters' suitability for adoption and any relevant welfare issues under s.1 of the Act.

(iv) Suitability for adoption and the Independent Reviewing Mechanism Under the Adoption Agencies Regulations 2005, an adoption agency is required to take into account various matters for determining the suitability of the prospective adopter(s), and for reporting as to their suitability. If an adoption agency decides that a person is unsuitable to become an

adoptive parent, that person (or both persons in the case of a couple adoption) can challenge the refusal by applying for an independent review under the Independent Reviewing Mechanism (IRM).

In *R (AT, TT and S)* v. *Newham London Borough Council* [2008] EWHC 2640 (Admin), [2009] 1 FLR 311 the parents challenged by way of judicial review the local authority's decision to overturn the unanimous decision of the IRM panel which was that they were suitable persons to adopt a child. Bennett J granted their application on the ground of procedural unfairness, quashed the local authority's decision and ordered that the matter as to their suitability be considered afresh. Bennett J held, *inter alia*, that the welfare principle in s.1(2) ACA 2002 (see p. 428) does not to apply to cases of suitability to adopt under Part 4 of the Adoption Agencies Regulations 2005.

(v) The 'consent condition' or 'placement condition' must be satisfied (s.47)   In respect of adoption, the court must be satisfied that: each parent or guardian consents to the making of the adoption order or has given advance consent and does not oppose the making of the adoption order; or that the consent of each parent or guardian can be dispensed with. In respect of placement for adoption (whether by the consensual route or placement order), the court must be satisfied that the child has been placed for adoption with the prospective adopters with the consent of each parent or guardian; or has been placed under a placement order and that no parent or guardian opposes the making of the adoption order.

15.7   The adoption order

An adoption order (see s.46) is an order giving parental responsibility for the child to the adopter(s). It extinguishes the parental responsibility of the child's mother and father, and any other person with parental responsibility; and terminates any order made under the Children Act 1989. In the case of a step-parent adoption, however, the adoption order does not affect the parental responsibility or duties of the person who is the adopted child's natural parent. An adoption order extinguishes any duty to pay child maintenance (by agreement or court order), except where the maintenance duty arises under a trust or by an agreement which expressly provides that the maintenance duty is not to be extinguished.

(i) How the court exercises its powers in adoption proceedings   The welfare test (s.1(2)), and the 'welfare checklist' (s.1(4)), and the other s.1 principles must be applied by the court (see 15.4 above). Before making the adoption order, the court must also be satisfied that the consent conditions or placement conditions are satisfied (see above); and that the adoption agency or local authority has had sufficient opportunities to see the child with the applicant(s) in the home environment (s.47(2)). Before making the order, the court must also consider whether there should be arrangements for allowing any person to have contact with the child (s.46(6)). As the court has a duty under the welfare checklist to consider whether it should exercise any of its powers under the 2002 Act or under the Children Act 1989, it may make a contact order under the CA 1989 of its own motion. Parents also have a right at the final adoption hearing to apply for a contact order under s.26 (see p. 441 below).

(ii) Removal of the child   Where an application for an adoption order has been made, the child cannot be removed from accommodation, except with leave of the court (s.37(a)).

(iii) The status of the adopted child (s.67)   An adopted person is treated in law as if he or she were born as the child of the adopter(s). An adopted person is the legitimate child of the adopter(s), and, if the child is adopted by a couple or by one of a couple under a step-parent or civil partner adoption, the child is to be treated as the child of that relationship.

(iv) Restrictions on making a further application for an adoption order   Where a previous application for an adoption order has been refused by any court, a second application for an adoption order may not be heard unless it appears to the court that there is a change in circumstances, or other reason, which makes it proper to hear the application (s.48(1)).

(v) Revocation of an adoption order   An adoption order cannot be revoked, except where a child (who has been adopted by one natural parent as sole adoptive parent) subsequently becomes legitimised by his natural parents' marriage (s.55(1)).

(vi) Defending adoption proceedings   An application can be made to oppose the making of an adoption order on the ground of a change of circumstances (s.47(7)) provided the court has granted leave to make the application (s.47(5)). In an application for leave to defend adoption proceedings the court must first be satisfied that there has been a change of circumstances; and then, in the exercise of its discretion, applying the welfare test in s.1 (see p. 428), decide whether to permit the parent(s) to defend the adoption proceedings. In *Re P (Adoption: Leave Provisions)* [2007] EWCA Civ 616, [2007] 2 FLR 1069 (where the trial judge's decision to refuse the parents leave to defend adoption proceedings was upheld) the Court of Appeal said that the statutory criteria applicable to leave applications for a s.8 order under the Children Act 1989 (where the child's welfare is *not* the court's paramount consideration) are quite different from those that apply to leave to defend under the ACA 2002.

(vii) Setting aside an adoption order   Once an adoption order has been lawfully and properly made, it is only in highly exceptional circumstances that the court will permit the order to be set aside. Adoption orders validly and lawfully obtained will not be disturbed. In *Webster* v. *Norfolk County Council and the Children (By Their Children's Guardian)* [2009] EWCA Civ 59, [2009] 1 FLR 1378 the parents failed in their application to set aside adoption orders on the ground that three of their children had been taken into care and adopted on the basis of a wrong diagnosis of non-accidental injury. Only exceptional circumstances (such as procedural irregularity, mistake or fraud) are likely to be grounds for an adoption order to be set aside.

15.8   Placement for adoption

Sections 18–29 of the Adoption and Children Act 2002 contain provisions in respect of placement for adoption. The aim of placement is to enable consent to adoption to be sorted out at the placement stage and for subsequent leave for the child's natural parent(s) to oppose the adoption order to be granted only if there has been a change of circumstances after the placement order was made (s.47(7), and see further below). An adoption agency may place a child with prospective adopters or leave the child where he or she has already been placed, provided the child is at least six weeks old, and either the natural parents have consented to the child being placed (see 15.9) or a placement order (see below) has been made (s.18(1)). The adoption agency must be satisfied that the child should be placed for adoption with the prospective adopters (s.18(2)). Once a child is placed, or is authorised to be placed, for adoption by a local authority, the child is described as being 'looked after' by the local authority for the purposes of the Children Act 1989, whereupon the local authority has certain obligations to the child (s.18(3)) (see p. 14.10).

(a) Placement by consent of the birth-parents (s.19)

An adoption agency can place a child for adoption (except a baby aged under six weeks), provided it is satisfied that each parent or guardian has consented to the child being placed for adoption (with prospective adopters identified in the consent form and/or with any prospective adopters who may be chosen by the agency), and that consent has not been withdrawn (see s.19). 'Consent' is 'consent given unconditionally and with full understanding of what is involved, but a person may consent to adoption without knowing the identity of the persons in whose favour the order will be made' (s.52). A parent who consents to a child being placed for adoption may at the same time, or subsequently, give advance consent to the making of a future adoption order (s.20).

The child's parent(s) can withdraw consent at any time (s.20(3)); and the person giving consent can give notice to the adoption agency stating that he or she does not wish to be informed of any application for an adoption order, or withdraw such statement (s.20(4)). Where consent has not been withdrawn before an adoption application has been made, but the birth-parents do not wish the child to be adopted, they can defend the final adoption order but only with leave of the court (see p. 433 above).

(b) Placement by placement order (s.21)

A child can be placed for adoption by way of a placement order which is an order 'authorising a local authority to place a child for adoption with any prospective adopters who may be chosen by the authority' (s.21(1)).

(i) Preconditions   The court can make a placement order only if the child is subject to a care order; or the court is satisfied that the threshold conditions for making a care order are met (see p. 343); or the child has no parent or guardian (s.21(2)). The court must also be satisfied (see s.21(3)) that each of the child's parents or guardian has consented to the child being placed for adoption with any prospective adopters who may be chosen by the local authority and that that consent has not been withdrawn; or that their consent should be dispensed with (see 15.9).

(ii) A duty or a discretion to apply for a placement order   A local authority *must* apply for a placement order if (s.22(1)): the child has been placed for adoption by them or is being provided with accommodation by them; no adoption agency is authorised to place the child for adoption; the child has no parent or guardian, or the authority considers the threshold criteria for a care order (see p. 393) are met; and the authority is satisfied that the child ought to be placed for adoption.

A local authority *must* also apply for a placement order if it is satisfied that the child ought to be placed for adoption and (s.22(2)): an application has been made (and has not been disposed of) on which a care order might be made in respect of a child; or the child is subject to a care order and the appropriate local authority is not authorised to place the child for adoption.

A local authority *may* apply for a placement order if (s.22(3)): the child is subject to a care order; and the local authority is authorised to place the child for adoption by parental consent.

There is no duty or discretion to apply for a placement order if: there is notice of an intention to adopt (unless four months have passed since notification without an application having been made, or the application has been withdrawn or refused) (s.25(2)); or an application for an adoption order has been made but has not been disposed of (s.25(2)).

If a local authority is under a duty to apply for a placement order, or has made an application but it has not been disposed of, the child is described as being 'looked after by the authority' (s.22(4)).

A placement order can be varied on the joint application of two local authorities for the purpose of substituting one local authority for the other (s.23).

(iii) Making a placement order – the exercise of discretion When considering whether to make a placement order, the court must apply the welfare principle and the other principles in s.1 (see 15.4). Before making the order, the court has a duty to consider what arrangements for contact the adoption agency has made, or proposes to make, for the child, and must invite the parties to comment on those arrangements (s.27(7)). The court may, in an appropriate case, make an order as to contact (see 15.10). The court cannot make a placement order unless an effort has been made to notify the child's parent(s) or guardian(s) with parental responsibility about the application (s.141).

As a matter of law a placement order can be made even though the prospect of placing a child may prove difficult and it is uncertain whether an adoption will actually be achievable (see *Re T (Placement Order)* [2008] EWCA Civ 542, but where, on the facts, the Court of Appeal held that the two boys' best interests would be best served by long-term fostering rather than by adoption).

The court will not make a placement order merely on the basis that the long-term aim is for adoption; the child must be in a position to be adopted and is ready to be adopted, although the possibility of substantial difficulty and delay in finding a suitable adoptive placement, or even an ultimate failure to do so, does not prevent the from court making a placement order (see Re S-H (A Child) (Placement Order) [2008] EWCA Civ 493, [2008] 2 FLR 918 where Wilson LJ said that the 'necessary foundation for a placement order is that, broadly speaking, the child is presently in a condition to be adopted and is ready to be adopted').

Directions The court can direct a medical, psychiatric or other assessment of the child where an application for a placement order is pending or no interim care order has been made – but a child of sufficient understanding to make an informed decision can refuse to submit to the examination or assessment (s.22(6)). As this power is similar to that in s.38(6) Children Act 1989 (see p. 406), similar considerations are likely to apply.

(iv) Duration of the order   A placement order remains in force until revoked; or an adoption order is made; or the child marries or becomes a civil partner; or the child reaches the age of 18 (s.21(4)).

(v) Representation of the child   A child is party to placement order proceedings (see s.41 of the Children Act 1989, as amended); and the court has a duty to appoint a Children's Guardian (see 1.6) to safeguard the child's interests, unless it is not necessary to do so. Separate representation for the child is permitted in some circumstances (s.93 CA 1989, as amended).

(vi) Revocation of a placement order (s.24)   Any person (except the child and the local authority) can apply to revoke a placement order, provided leave to apply has been granted by the court and the child has not been placed for adoption by the local authority (ss.24(1), (2)). Leave can be granted only if there has been a change of circumstances since the placement order was made (s.24(3)). When considering whether to grant leave, the welfare of the child is not the court's *paramount* consideration (as s.1 of the ACA 2002 does not apply), but it is a *relevant* consideration. The court's approach to leave applications is similar to the approach in applications for leave to apply for s.8 orders under the Children Act 1989 (thus the applicant must have a real prospect of securing revocation of the placement order; and the court must take account of the delay that granting leave might cause).

Even where there has been a change of circumstances, the court has a discretion as to whether to grant leave to apply for revocation. Thus, for example, in *Re M (Children) (Placement Order)* [2007] EWCA Civ 1084, *sub nom M* v. *Warwickshire County Council* [2008] 1 FLR 1093 the mother applied for leave to apply for revocation of the placement orders (which had been made in respect of her two children) on the basis of a change of circumstances (that she had, *inter alia*, abstained from drugs, reduced her alcohol consumption and attended an HIV clinic), but her application for leave was refused by the Court of Appeal.

In *Re S-H (A Child) (Placement Order)* [2008] EWCA Civ 493, [2008] 2 FLR 918 the Court of Appeal held that it would occasionally be appropriate to grant leave, even though there was no real prospect that a court would find that it would be in the child's interests to return to live with the parents. Here the Court of Appeal held that it was in the child's interests to grant leave to revoke the placement order, in order to give the court an opportunity to examine the apparent change in the child's current suitability for adoption.

In addition to the leave requirement, revocation of a placement order is not possible if the child has already been placed for adoption (s.24(2)). The Court of Appeal has held that placement must be with a prospective, not a potential adopter (see *Re S (Placement Order: Revocation)* [2008] EWCA Civ 1333, [2009] 1 FLR 503). In *Re F (Placement Order)* [2008] EWCA Civ 439, [2008] 2 FLR 550 the Court of Appeal by a majority (Thorpe LJ dissenting) refused to grant leave (as the child had already been placed for adoption), even though the applicant for leave (the child's father) had not been involved in the proceedings for care and placement orders, as he had been hospitalised due to a heart attack. The father's arguments based on human rights failed as the Court of Appeal held that s.24 was human rights compliant.

(vii) Effect of a placement order　A placement order gives parental responsibility to the local authority (s.25(2)) or to the prospective adopters while the child is with them (s.25(3)). During the placement the parents' parental responsibility is not extinguished until the final adoption order is made. Parental responsibility is shared with the prospective adopters and the adoption agency, with the agency determining the extent to which the parental responsibility of the child's parents or of the prospective adopters is to be restricted (s.25(4)); and with the power to remove the child from the placement. If a placement with prospective adopters breaks down, and the local authority considers adoption is still in the child's best interests, there is no need for it to apply for another placement order before it makes a new adoption placement.

Once a placement order has been made, only the local authority can remove the child. The placement order remains in force until: it is revoked (see above), or an adoption order is made; or the child marries or becomes a civil partner; or attains the age of 18.

The adoption agency can remove the child from the placement (for example, where the placement is failing), whether or not the birth-parents have requested the child's return (s.30). Once placement for adoption has been authorised, contact provisions under s.8 and s.34 Children Act 1989 cease to have effect (ss.26(1), (6)), but this does not prevent an application for a contact order being made under s.26 of the 2002 Act (see 15.10).

While a placement order is in force:

▷ No one may cause the child to be known by a new surname or remove the child from the UK (except for a period of up to one month by the person who provides the child's home), unless the court has given permission or the child's parents or guardians have given *written* consent (ss.28(2), (3)).

▷ Any care order ceases to have effect (s.29(1)), and on the making of the placement order any s.8 order or supervision order under the Children Act 1989 ceases to have effect (s.29(2)). (A child subject to a placement order remains 'the subject of a care order' within s.100(2)(c) CA 1989 and, although the child cannot be made a ward of court, it remains open for a local authority to apply for leave to invoke the inherent jurisdiction in respect of the child, see *Re S-H (A Child) (Placement Order)* [2008] EWCA Civ 493, [2008] 2 FLR 918).

▷ The court has no power to make a s.8 order, a supervision order or a child assessment order under the Children Act 1989 (s.29(3)).

▷ A special guardianship order cannot be made until a final adoption order is made, but leave will be needed to apply for one. If a special guardianship order is made it does not automatically discharge the placement order. The court will have to consider whether to revoke the placement order, applying the welfare principle and the other s.1 principles.

There are also restrictions on making contact orders (see 15.10). Parents, guardians and other persons can, however, apply for a residence order if they have obtained the court's leave under s.47(3) or s.47(5) to oppose the making of a final adoption order.

(viii) Restrictions on removing the child pending a placement order　A child who is being accommodated pending a placement order cannot be removed from that accommodation except with leave of the court or the local authority (s.30(2)). Where a placement order has been made, only the local authority can remove the child (s.34). Thus, parents have no

automatic right to have their children returned to them. The only remedy they have is to apply for revocation of the placement order, which may be difficult (see p. 436 above).

(ix) Baby placements An adoption agency may place a baby who is less than six weeks old for adoption with the voluntary agreement of the parent or guardian, whereupon the baby becomes a 'looked after' child of the local authority. However, the placement provisions do not apply. Thus, the agency has no power to determine to what extent the parental responsibility of any parent, or of the prospective adopters, can be restricted under s.25(4) of the Act.

15.9 Consent to adoption and placement for adoption

Consent is relevant both to placement for adoption and to adoption. Consent is dealt with earlier in the adoption process than it was under the law prior to the Adoption and Children Act 2002 coming into force, in order to create certainty and stability for the child and to reduce uncertainty for the prospective adopters. Another aim is to reduce the extent to which birth-families are faced with a fait accompli at the final adoption hearing, as they sometimes were under the old law.

'Consent' for the purposes of placement and for adoption means (s.52(5)) consent given unconditionally and with full understanding of what is involved; but a person may consent to adoption without knowing the identity of the persons in whose favour the order will be made. The 2002 Act has introduced a new concept of 'advance' consent.

(i) Whose consent is required? The consent of each parent or guardian of the child (including a special guardian) is required before an adoption agency may place a child for adoption (s.19(1)) or the court can make an adoption order (s.47(2)). As 'parent' for the purposes of consent means a parent with parental responsibility (s.52(6)), the consent of the unmarried father without parental responsibility is not required. However, where an unmarried mother consents to adoption under s.19 (placement by parental consent), a father who subsequently acquires parental responsibility is to be treated as having at that time given consent in accordance with s.52 on the same terms as the mother (ss.52(9), (10)). Where a father acquires parental responsibility after an application for an adoption order has been made, he can, with leave of the court, oppose the adoption order on the basis that there has been a change of circumstances (s.46). Although the consent of the child's relatives is not needed, the court can take their wishes into account under the s.1(4) welfare checklist (see p. 428 above).

For more on consent of the unmarried father and notifying him of the adoption, see p. 439 below.

(ii) Mother's consent within six weeks of birth In respect of an adoption order, any consent given by a mother is ineffective if given less than six weeks after the child's birth (s.52(3)). In respect of a placement order, consent may be given at any time after the child's birth; there is no requirement that six weeks must have passed.

In *A Local Authority* v. *GC and Others* [2008] EWHC 2555 (Fam), [2009] 1 FLR 299 the parents had signed the consent to placement for adoption (under s.19) and to the making of a future adoption order (under s.20) when their child was only four weeks old, but, despite the error, Eleanor King J held that the adoption was lawful on the basis that the parents' consent could be dispensed with so that the six week requirement did not need to be satisfied.

(iii) Formalities   Consent to placement for adoption and to the making of an adoption order (including advance consent) must be given in the prescribed form (s.52(7)). Cafcass officers and Welsh family proceedings officers are responsible for advising parents on consent and for witnessing consent, and for reporting to the court on matters relating to the child (see s.102).

(iv) Withdrawal of consent   Once an application for an adoption order has been made, any consent given with respect to the placement for adoption or any advance consent cannot be withdrawn (s.52(4)). Parents who wish to oppose the adoption order after the cut-off point must obtain leave to do so, and the court can grant leave only if it is satisfied that there has been a change of circumstances since the consent was given or the placement order was made (s.47(7)).

(v) Advance consent (s.20)   A parent or guardian who consents to the child being placed for adoption by an adoption agency under s.19 may at the same time, or at any subsequent time, consent to the making of a future adoption order (s.20(1)). Advance consent can be withdrawn (s.20(3)), but any withdrawal is ineffective if made after an application for an adoption order has been made (s.52(4)). A parent who gives advance consent can at the same time, or subsequently, give notice to the adoption agency stating that he does not wish to be informed of any application for an adoption order (or can withdraw such statement) (s.20(4)). If a parent gives advance consent and chooses not to be notified of the application for the adoption order, placement and adoption can proceed without that parent being involved in any way. Parents are given some protection, however, as they have a right to be notified of the date and place of the adoption application (see s.143), whereupon they can apply for leave to oppose the making of the adoption order, which the court can grant if there has been a change of circumstances since consent was given (s.47(7)). Advance consent is subject to the provisions governing dispensing with consent (see p. 441 below).

(vi) The unmarried father without parental responsibility — consent to and involvement in adoption
Although there is no requirement in the Adoption and Children Act 2002 for unmarried fathers without parental responsibility to give their consent to placement for adoption or adoption, the courts have been increasingly willing to involve them in the adoption process, particularly with the coming into force of the Human Rights Act 1998 and the risk of breaching a father's human rights under art. 8 ECHR (right to family life) and art. 6 ECHR (right to a fair hearing) if he is not involved. In *Re R (Adoption: Father's Involvement)* [2001] 1 FLR 302 Thorpe LJ commented on the shift towards unmarried fathers without parental responsibility being accorded greater involvement in adoption proceedings, and held that the unmarried father might have been justified in raising a complaint under art. 6 ECHR if he had not been given notice of the adoption proceedings.

In most cases the unmarried father will be notified about the adoption. In fact, in *Re H; Re G (Adoption: Consultation of Unmarried Fathers)* [2001] 1 FLR 646 (decided under the 'old' adoption law) Butler-Sloss P held that, as a matter of good practice, judges would be expected to give directions so that unmarried fathers were informed of adoption proceedings, unless good reasons to the contrary existed (for instance, where there was no family life between the father and the child). In *Re C (Adoption: Disclosure to Father)* [2005] EWHC 3385 (Fam), [2006] 2 FLR 589 Hedley J, referring to Butler-Sloss P in *Re H: Re G*, directed that the father without parental responsibility and who was serving a prison sentence be informed about adoption proceedings despite the mother's wishes to the contrary. Hedley J said that both parents were entitled to be involved in decisions about their children, at least when the decision might have long-term implications for the child concerned. He said that, where family life was established as it has been here (they had parented other children together), then there had to be very compelling reasons indeed why a parent should be shut out from notice of the existence of the child or proposals for the future of the child.

Despite the shift towards recognising the importance of unmarried fathers and their involvement in bringing up their child, and the recognition of the importance of the child having a right to know his or her identity and origins, the court may in the exercise of its discretion decide that it is not in the best interests of the child for the father to be informed about pending adoption proceedings, as the Court of Appeal did in the following case:

▶ *Re C (A Child) (Adoption: Duty of Local Authority)* [2007] Civ 1206, *sub nom Re C (A Child)* v. *XYZ County Council* [2008] 1 FLR 1294

The child had been born as a result of a 'one-night stand' and the mother (aged 19) did not wish the child's father or her parents to know about the child's birth. The trial judge directed the local authority to disclose the existence and identity of the child to the extended maternal family and, if he could be identified, the putative father and any extended paternal family. The mother appealed.

The Court of Appeal allowed the appeal and gave directions pre-empting the guardian from taking further steps to identify the father. Arden LJ, applying ss.1(4)(c) and (f) of the welfare checklist (see p. 428), held that there is no duty of an absolute kind for inquiries to be made about the child's father when a decision needs to be made about the long-term care of a child. Such a duty only arises if it is in the child's best interests. There was no breach of the father's right to family life under art. 8 ECHR, as he had had no family life with the child. Neither was it a violation of the ECHR to deprive him of the possibility of obtaining a right to family life. The child's grandparents did have a right to family life under art.8, but they would be able to obtain the information by making their own application under the Children Act 1989.

(For a commentary on *Re C*, see Sloan [2009] CFLQ 87, who criticises the Court of Appeal for using 'an unnecessarily narrow conception of welfare' and for giving 'undue weight to the interests of the child's mother').

In order to clarify the situation, it may be advisable for a local authority to obtain the authority of the court if it decides not to contact the unmarried father and/or the extended family. In *Re L (Adoption: Contacting Natural Father* [2007] EWHC 1771 (Fam), [2008] 1 FLR 1079 the local authority under the inherent jurisdiction of the High Court (see 8.7) successfully did this.

(a) Grounds for dispensing with consent

Section 52(1) lays down two grounds on which the court can dispense with the consent of a parent or guardian to the child's adoption or placement for adoption:

- that a parent or guardian cannot be found or is incapable of giving consent (s.52(1)(a)); or
- that the welfare of the child requires the consent to be dispensed with (s.52(1)(b)).

The paramountcy of the child's welfare (s.1(2)) and the s.1(4) welfare checklist (see 15.4) apply to dispensing with consent.

Although the European Convention for the Protection of Human Rights, particularly art. 8 (the right to family life) is relevant to adoption and the question of consent, the Court of Appeal has held that the test for dispensing with consent in s.52(1)(b) does not, for this reason, demand an enhanced test beyond the welfare test set out in s.1(2); but that cogent justification must exist before consent can be dispensed with and adoption must be a proportionate and legitimate response (see *per* Wall LJ in *Re P (Children) (Adoption: Parental Consent)* [2008] EWCA Civ 535, [2008] 2 FLR 625).

15.10 Contact

The Adoption and Children Act 2002 makes provision in respect of contact in the context of placement for adoption. However, there is no presumption of contact as there is in the public law provisions of the Children Act 1989 (see 14.8).

Before making a placement order, the court must consider the arrangements which the adoption agency has made, or proposes to make, for allowing any person to have contact with the child; and must invite the parties to the proceedings to comment on them (s.24(7)). Once the adoption agency is authorised to place a child for adoption, it must consider what arrangements it should make for allowing any person to have contact with the child. The court will also have to consider contact between the child and his birth-parents and family when it conducts the welfare exercise.

(i) Children Act 1989 contact orders not effective and applications barred Where an adoption agency is authorised to place a child for adoption (whether by consent or under a placement order), any provision for contact under s.8 or s.34 CA 1989 ceases to have effect and any contact activity direction under s.11A CA 1989 relating to contact with the child (see p. 308) is discharged (ss.26(1), (6)). While an adoption agency is authorised to place a child for adoption, or the child is placed for adoption, an application for contact cannot be made under the Children Act 1989, but the court can make a contact order under s.26 ACA 2002 (see below).

(ii) A section 26 contact order Where an adoption agency is authorised to place a child for adoption (by parental consent or placement order), or the child is placed for adoption, the court can make a contact order under s.26 ACA 2002 requiring the person with whom the child lives, or is to live, to allow the child to visit or stay with the person named in the order, or for the person named in the order and the child otherwise to have contact with each other (s.26(2)). The following persons can apply for a s.26 contact order (s.26(3)): the

child; the adoption agency; parents, guardians or relatives; any person with a contact order which has ceased to be effective; any person with a residence order in force with respect to the child; any person who has care of the child under an order made by the High Court under its inherent jurisdiction; and any other person with leave of the court. The court of its own motion can make a s.26 contact order when making a placement order (s.26(4)).

The welfare principle and the other s.1 principles apply to the exercise of the court's discretion (see 15.4). The order may provide for contact on any conditions that the court considers appropriate (s.27(5)). The contact order is only effective while the adoption agency is authorised to place the child for adoption (or the child is less than six weeks old), but it may be varied or revoked by the court on the application of the child, the agency or the person named in the order (s.27(1)). The court may authorise the adoption agency to refuse to allow contact, if necessary to safeguard or promote the child's welfare, provided refusal is decided as a matter of urgency and does not last for more than seven days (s.27(2)).

The responsibility for determining contact, whether under s.26 or post-adoption (see below), rests firmly in the hands of judges, not in those of local authorities (see *Re P (Placement Orders: Parental Consent)* [2008] EWCA Civ 535, [2008] 2 FLR 625 where the Court of Appeal held that the trial judge had been right to make a s.26 order even though the psychiatrist had recommended that there should be no direct contact between the siblings (whom the local authority had planned were to be separately adopted) or between them and their birth family, and that placement orders should be sought).

(iii) Post-adoption contact As one of the main aims of the 2002 Act is to encourage adoptions of children in care, many adopted children will be older children. It may be contrary to the best interests of some children to sever their relationship with their birth-family. Contact can help children resolve feelings of separation and loss and give them a sense of their biological and social origins. However, the disadvantage of the courts making increased use of orders for post-adoption contact is that it may deter potential adopters from coming forward to adopt children.

Under the ACA 2002, before making an adoption order the court must consider whether any arrangements should be made for allowing any person contact with the child, and it must consider any existing or proposed arrangements and obtain the views of the parties to the proceedings (s.46(6)). As the welfare checklist in s.1(4) requires the court to have regard to the whole range of powers under the Children Act 1989, the court must also consider whether to make a s.8 contact order under that Act. An application for a s.8 contact order can be heard concurrently with an application for adoption (s.26(5)).

The court may be unwilling to make a contact order where there is any opposition by the adopters; for it would be contrary to the welfare of the adopted child if the adopters and the child's biological parent(s) were engaged in friction (see the decision of the House of Lords in *Re C (A Minor) (Adoption Order: Conditions)* [1989] AC 1 [1988] 2 FLR 159, decided under the 'old' law). The parties themselves can, if they wish, make their own arrangements about contact.

Once an adoption order is made, the birth-parents lose their automatic right to apply for a contact order (and other orders) under s.8 Children Act 1989; and must obtain leave of the court to apply (see p. 282), which the court may be unwilling to grant because of the possible disruption this may cause for the adopters and the child.

15.11 Adoption by step-parents, partners, relatives and foster-carers

(a) Step-parents and partner adoptions

A step-parent, or civil partner of a couple, can apply for an adoption order (see below), but an alternative way of acquiring parental responsibility is by making a parental responsibility agreement or obtaining a parental responsibility order (see 9.5), a residence order (see 10.5) or a special guardianship order (see 15.14). The disadvantage of these alternatives is that, unlike adoption, parental responsibility can be revoked.

If a step-parent or civil partner wishes to adopt a step-child, or a child of their civil partner, the child must have had his home with the applicant at all times during the six months preceding the application (s.42(3)). The step-parent or civil partner must give notice of his or her intention to adopt to the appropriate local authority not more than two years, or less than three months, before applying for the order (ss.44(2), (3)). This enables the local authority to investigate the case and submit a report to the court in respect of the applicant's suitability for adoption and any s.1 welfare issues (ss.44(5), (6)). The consent requirement must have been satisfied.

(b) Adoption by relatives

A person can adopt a child to whom he or she is related, provided the child has had his home with the relative for not less than three years (which need not be continuous) during the five years ending with the application (s.42(5)), or the court grants leave to apply for adoption (s.42(6)). The relative must have notified the local authority of his or her intention to apply for adoption not more than two years, or less then three months, before applying for the order (s.44(3)). The relative must be suitable for adoption (s.45), and consent must have been obtained (s.47(2)).

Although adoption by a relative may be in a child's best interests where the child's parents are dead or where a relative has been caring for a child and the parents are no longer involved, it may be better for a relative to obtain parental responsibility by means of a special guardianship order (see 15.14) or a residence order (see 10.5) in order not to sever the child's links with the other half of the child's birth family.

(c) Adoption by local authority foster-carers

Foster-carers can adopt a foster-child in their care, but the rules differ depending on whether the case is an agency case or a non-agency case. As an alternative to adoption, foster-parents can acquire parental responsibility by obtaining a residence order (see 10.5) or special guardianship order (see 15.14).

(i) Agency cases An agency case is one where the local authority decides to place a child with a foster-carer or to convert a foster placement into an adoption placement. A foster-carer can seek local authority approval to become a prospective adopter of a foster-child. If the local authority gives approval, the foster-child lives with the foster-carer as the

prospective adopter, provided the child's parent(s) or guardian have consented to adoption under s.19, or a placement order has been made. Once the child is placed with the foster-carer(s) as prospective adopter(s), only the local authority may remove the child (ss.30, 34). Preliminary requirements must be satisfied before an adoption order can be made. Thus, the child must have had his or her home with the foster-carer(s) at all times during the 10 weeks preceding the adoption application; and investigation and reports as to their suitability must have been made and satisfied.

(ii) Non-agency cases   A non-agency case is one where the local authority has not placed the child with the foster-carer for adoption and has refused to give its approval when the foster-carer sought it; but where the foster-carer wishes to apply for adoption. The child must have had his home with the foster-carer for a continuous period of not less than one year, although the court can give leave to waive this requirement (ss.42(4), (6)). The foster-carer must give notice to the local authority of his or her intention to adopt not more than two years, or less than three months, before the date on which the application is made under s.44. The consent condition in s.47(2) must also be satisfied.

15.12   Adopted persons – access to information

Adopted persons, once they reach 18, can investigate their origins and attempt to make contact with their birth-family. In this respect there has been a move towards greater 'openness' in adoption.

(a)   Access to birth certificates

An adopted child on reaching the age of 18 can obtain a copy of his or her original birth certificate. However, the Registrar-General has a discretion to refuse to provide a copy, for example on the ground of public policy (see *R* v. *Registrar-General ex parte Smith* [1991] 2 QB 393, [1991] 1 FLR 255 where the Registrar-General's refusal to supply a copy to an adopted person (who was serving a life sentence for murder) was held to be lawful).

(b)   The Adopted Children Register and the Adoption Contact Register

(i) The Adopted Children Register   The Registrar-General has a duty (under ss.77 and 78 ACA 2002) to maintain the Adopted Children Register, and an index of the register. The Register is not open to public inspection or search, but any person may search the index of the Register and have a certified copy of any entry in the Register (s.78(2)) and thereby trace the original birth registration of an adopted child. Where the adopted person is under 18, a person is not entitled to a certified copy of an entry in the Register, unless the applicant has provided the Registrar with certain prescribed particulars. Counselling is available for adopted adults before they decide to obtain information about their birth records. Local authorities are required to provide a counselling service.

The courts have no power to restrict the information placed in the Register, but the High Court may under its inherent jurisdiction prohibit the Registrar-General from providing details of the adoption to any applicant while the child is under 18 (see, for example, *Re W (Adoption Details: Disclosure)* [1998] 2 FLR 625). The court can also authorise the Registrar-General to disclose information (see *Re H (Adoption: Disclosure of Information)* [1995] 1 FLR 236 where it authorised the Registrar-General to provide information so that a 53-year-old adopted person with a treatable genetic disease could trace her brother so that he could be screened and treated if necessary).

(ii) The Adoption Contact Register   The Registrar-General has a duty to maintain this Register (under ss.80 and 81 ACA 2002), which allows an adopted person to register his or her interest in contacting birth relatives (in Part I of the Register); and relatives searching for an adopted person to register their interest in being contacted (in Part II). If there is a match, the Registrar-General gives the adopted person the relative's name and address, but no information is provided to the relative. Thus, the decision to initiate contact is left to the adopted person.

The Registrar-General has a duty (under s.79 ACA 2002) to make traceable the connections between the register of live births and any corresponding entry in the Adoption Contact Register, and to disclose that information, or any other information which might enable an adopted person to obtain a certified copy of his or her birth record. The Registrar-General is under a duty to give the connecting birth-record information to an adoption agency in respect of a person whose birth record is kept by the Registrar-General.

(c)   Disclosure of information

Sections 56–65 ACA 2002 lay down provisions governing the disclosure to adopted persons of information held by adoption agencies in connection with adoption, and for access to birth records. These provisions also cover the release of adoption agency information to birth-relatives and other persons. Under these provisions, adoption agencies act as a single point of access to identifying information (including information necessary to access birth records), as they are the bodies best placed to provide support and counselling for the sensitive task of disclosure.

15.13   Inter-country adoption

(a)   Taking a child out of the UK for an adoption abroad

It is unlawful to take a child out of the UK for the purposes of an adoption unless the prospective adopters have been granted parental responsibility for the child under s.84 ACA 2002, which the court has power to do if it is satisfied that the applicant(s) intend to adopt the child under the law of the country outside the UK, they are not domiciled in England and Wales and they have had the child living with them during the preceding 10 weeks (see s.84(4)). The order confers parental responsibility on the applicant(s) and extinguishes that of any other person (for example, that of the birth parent(s) and a local authority where a care order is in force). In *Re G (Adoption: Placement Outside Jurisdiction)* [2008] EWCA Civ 105, [2008] 1 FLR 1484 Sir Mark Potter P held that s.84(4) did not, however, require the physical presence of each adopter during the 10-week period in order to satisfy the proposition that the child's home was with the adopters throughout that period. In *Re G (Surrogacy: Foreign Domicile)* [2007] EWHC 2814 (Fam), [2008] 1 FLR 1047 an order was made under s.84 to facilitate the adoption of the child in Turkey in a case involving an English surrogacy arrangement (see p. 266).

(b) The Hague Convention on inter-country adoption

Inter-country adoptions have their own set of problems, for although adoption may give children from abroad a quality of life they did not have in their country of origin, there is a danger that such adoptions may exploit the needs of children by being too adult-centred. Inter-country adoptions may fail to take account of the importance of children remaining in touch with their own cultural roots and their birth-family, and they may have been arranged privately without the checks and safeguards which exist for adoptions under domestic law.

In response to concerns about inter-country adoption, there have been increasing numbers of safeguards put in place under international law and domestic law. The Hague Convention on the Protection of Children and Co-operation in Respect of Intercountry Adoption 1993 came into force in England and Wales on 1 June 2003, as a result of the Adoption (Intercountry Aspects) Act 1999. The Convention provides a framework for the regulation of inter-country adoption by setting out minimum standards for the control and regulation of the flow of children between the signatory States. The effect of the Convention is that any person in England and Wales who wishes to adopt a child from overseas must undergo the same procedures as he or she would if adopting a child under domestic law. Under these provisions there are restrictions on inter-country adoption, and stringent penalties, including imprisonment, for those who fail to comply with requirements. Any person who is habitually resident in the UK who wishes to adopt a child from abroad is required to be assessed and approved to be eligible and suitable to adopt.

The number of contracting parties to the Hague Convention on Inter-Country Adoption has grown over the years and there are now nearly 80 Contracting States. (For more on international adoption, see the guide published by the Permanent Bureau at The Hague, *The Implementation and Operation of the 1993 Hague Intercountry Adoption Convention: A Guide to Good Practice;* and the UK government's Every Child Matters website).

Article 1 of the Hague Convention on Adoption states that the aims of the Convention are:

'1. To establish safeguards to ensure that inter-country adoptions take place in the best interests of the child and with respect for the child's fundamental rights as recognised by international law;
2. To establish a system of co-operation amongst Contracting States to ensure that those safeguards are respected and thereby prevent the abduction, the sale of, or traffic in children;
3. To secure the recognition in Contracting States of adoptions made in accordance with the Convention.'

The underlying rationale of the Convention is for Contracting States to work together to ensure that adoption is in the best interests of the child, and only after possibilities for placement of the child within the State of origin have been given due consideration (art. 4(b)). The aim is for children to stay within their own communities where possible. Where this is not possible, the Convention makes provisions to regulate the adoption process. It does so by requiring Central Authorities to be established whose function is to work together to protect children during the adoption process and to monitor the operation of the Convention. Central Authorities are responsible, *inter alia*, for exchanging information about the child, ensuring that the child is adoptable, that the relevant consents have been given after appropriate counselling and that they have not been induced by payment or compensation, and that the prospective adopters are eligible and suitable to adopt the child. The Convention also provides for the automatic recognition in all Contracting States of adoptions certified by the Central Authority concerned as having been made in accordance with the Convention. Various regulations also govern inter-country adoption.

Part 2 of the Children and Adoption Act 2006 (which deals with adoptions with a foreign element) makes provision to suspend inter-country adoptions from countries where the Secretary of State has public policy concerns about the practices there in connection with the adoption of children (for example, child trafficking). These restrictions on adoptions from abroad came into force on 1 August 2008. The Act also amends s.83 ACA 2002 to make it more difficult for inter-country adopters to circumvent restrictions on bringing children into the UK.

15.14 Special guardianship

Sections 14A–G of the Children Act 1989 make provision in respect of special guardianship, which was introduced with the aim of giving children for whom adoption is not suitable the security and permanence of a legal secure family placement. Special guardianship orders are designed in part to provide a framework of permanency for 'children being cared for on a permanent basis by members of their wider birth family' (*Adoption: A New Approach*, Cm 5017, 2000). They are intended to fill the gap between residence orders and long-term fostering at one end of the spectrum of parental responsibility and adoption at the other. The aim is to provide a long-term care option similar to adoption but without the legal break with the birth family, and the finality associated with the making of an adoption order. Special guardianship may be appropriate, for instance, where it is not in a child's best interests to have his legal relationship with his birth-parents and birth-family severed by adoption, or where the child is an older child in foster-care who does not wish to be adopted, or where there are cultural and religious difficulties with adoption. However, the results of research on special guardianship conducted by Hall ([2008] Fam Law 148) showed that, while special guardianship was being used by 'kinship carers', there was no evidence that it was being used for children in other situations and it had not proved particularly attractive to foster-carers.

1,090 applications for special guardianship orders were made in 2008, an increase of 31 per cent on 2007 (see *Judicial and Court Statistics 2008*, Ministry of Justice, Cm 7697, 2009).

(a) Special guardianship distinguished from adoption

The following table shows the main differences between special guardianship and adoption:

	SPECIAL GUARDIANSHIP	ADOPTION
Status of the Child	The child lives with/is cared for by the special guardian but remains the child of the birth-parent(s).	The child is the child of the adopter(s). The adopters are the child's parents.
Parental Responsibility	Vests in the special guardian, but is retained by the birth-parent(s).	Vests in the adopters.
Restrictions on the Exercise of Parental Responsibility	Parental responsibility can be exercised by the special guardian to the exclusion of all other persons, but he/she will need the agreement of the birth parent(s) and anyone else with parental responsibility (or otherwise the court) to: take the child out of the UK for more than 3 months; change the child's surname; consent to the child's adoption; and consent to the child having serious medical treatment (such as sterilisation, circumcision, immunisation).	There are no restrictions on the exercise of the parental responsibility of the adopters.
Duration of Each Order	The order ceases automatically on the child reaching 18, if not revoked earlier by the court.	An adoption order is permanent.
Revocation or Discharge of the Order	Birth-parent(s) can apply for discharge of the special guardianship order, but leave of the court is needed, which it can grant only if there has been a significant change of circumstances. The court can discharge a special guardianship order of its own motion in any family proceedings.	An adoption order cannot be revoked (except in a wholly exceptional case, such as where there has been a serious procedural impropriety).
Maintenance of the Child	Birth-parent(s) continue to have a maintenance obligation to the child.	Any maintenance obligation owed by the child's birth-parent is extinguished on adoption, unless there is any such obligation in a trust deed.
Death of the Child	Special guardian must notify the child's parent(s) who have parental responsibility.	The adopters need not notify the birth-parents of the child's death.
Intestacy	The child has no right to inherit from a special guardian who dies intestate.	The child has a right to inherit from the adopters on the adopters' intestacy.

(b)   Making a special guardianship order

(i) Applicants   The following persons can apply for a special guardianship order (s.14A(5) CA 1989):

- a guardian of the child;
- a person with a residence order in force with respect to the child;
- a person who has the consent of all those persons who have a residence order in their favour with respect to the child;
- any person with whom the child has lived for three out of the previous five years, provided he or she has the consent of any person with parental responsibility, or any person with a residence order, or the local authority (if the child is in care);
- any other person who has the consent of all persons with parental responsibility for the child;
- a local authority foster-parent with whom the child has lived for a period of at least one year immediately preceding the application.

The applicant must be at least 18 years old and must not be a parent of the child (s.14A(2)). A joint application can be made (ss.14A(1), (3)).

Other persons can apply for a special guardianship order with leave of the court (s.14A(3)). When considering whether to grant leave, the court applies the same factors as those which apply to leave applications for s.8 orders under the Children Act 1989 (s.14A(12)) (see p. 282). A child can apply for a special guardianship order with leave of the court, which can be granted if the child has sufficient understanding to make the proposed application (s.14A(12)).

The court can also make a special guardianship order of its own motion in any family proceedings (see p. 281), which includes adoption proceedings (s.14A(6)).

(ii) Local authority duty to provide a report   In some circumstances, written notice of an intention to apply for a special guardianship order must be given to the relevant local authority (s.14A(7)). On receipt of this notice, the local authority has a duty to investigate the matter and prepare a report for the court about the suitability of the applicant(s) for special guardianship, and other matters (s.14A(9)). The court cannot make an order until it has received this report (s.14A(11)) dealing with the matters referred to in s.14A(8). The compulsory nature of these report provisions was emphasised in the following case:

> ▶ *Re S (Adoption Order or Special Guardianship Order) (No. 2)* [2007] EWCA Civ 90, [2007] 1 FLR 855
>
> The judge of her own motion made a special guardianship order in favour of the child's foster-parent (even though the foster-parent wished to adopt the child). She did so without a local authority report being available on the basis that the child's welfare was better served by a special guardianship order than an adoption order. The Court of Appeal held that the reporting requirement in s.14A(11) was unequivocal, and other reports containing relevant information (such as an adoption application report) could not be relied on in the absence of a s.14A(8) report. However, it held that the court should adopt a pragmatic approach, and in any case in which the court was minded to make a special guardianship order of its own

> motion, then, if much of the relevant information was already before the court, the local authority should be requested to fulfil the terms of s.14A(8) by providing missing information and by cross-referencing existing reports.

(iii) Making a special guardianship order – the exercise of discretion The rules governing the exercise of the court's discretion are laid down in s.14B(1). Thus, when considering whether or not to make a special guardianship order, the court must apply the welfare principle and other principles in s.1 Children Act (see 10.3); and before making an order must consider whether or not a contact order should be made in respect of contact between the child and his birth-family. The court must also consider whether to vary or discharge any existing s.8 order. On making the order, the court can permit the child to be known by a new surname or to leave the UK (s.14B(2)). To reduce delay, the court must draw up a timetable and give directions to ensure that the timetable is adhered to (s.14E).

An order is only appropriate if, in the particular circumstances of the case, it is best fitted to meet the needs of the child concerned (see *Re S (Adoption Order or Special Guardianship Order)* [2007] EWCA Civ 54, [2007] 1 FLR 819). Each case therefore depends on its own facts.

Sometimes the court will have to decide whether to make a special guardianship order or an adoption order (see further below).

(iv) Effects of a special guardianship order The effects of a special guardianship order are as follows:

▷ *Parental responsibility* The special guardian acquires parental responsibility for the child, which (subject to any other order in force with respect to the child) can be exercised *to the exclusion of any other person(s) with parental responsibility* (s.14C), apart from any other special guardian. This power to exercise parental responsibility to the exclusion of other persons with parental responsibility is the most significant effect of a special guardianship order and one which distinguishes it from a residence order. However, certain restrictions apply to parental responsibility. Thus, while a special guardianship order is in force, no one may change the child's surname or remove the child from the UK for more than three months without the *written* consent of every person with parental responsibility for the child, or with leave of the court (ss.14C(3), (4)); but these restrictions do not apply where a placement order is in force (s.29(7)(b) ACA 2002). A special guardian must take reasonable steps to inform the birth parent(s) of the child's death, should the child die (s.14C(5)).
▷ *A right to support services* Special guardians have a right to local authority support services, including financial support, similar to those available to adopters under the Adoption and Children Act 2002; and they have a right to make representations (including complaints) to the local authority about such support (ss.14F and G). They can also bring a challenge by judicial review (see *B* v. *Lewisham London Borough Council* [2008] EWHC 738 (Admin), [2008] 2 FLR 523 where the special guardian (a maternal grandmother) and the child were successful before Black J in having Lewisham's allowance scheme for special guardians quashed as being unlawful).

▶ *Effect on other orders* The making of a special guardianship order discharges any existing care order or related contact order (s.91(5A)), but it does not prevent a care order or a residence order being made while the special guardianship order is in force (s.10(7A) CA 1989), whereupon an application will have to be made to have the special guardianship varied or discharged (see below).

(v) *Where a placement order is in force* A special guardianship order cannot be made while a placement for adoption order (see p. 434) is in force (s.14A(13)), unless an application has been made for a final adoption order, and the person making the application for the special guardianship order has obtained leave under s.29(5) ACA 2002; or is the guardian of the child under s.47(5). Written notice of an intention to apply for a special guardianship order must be given to the local authority which is looking after the child or in whose area the applicant is ordinarily resident (s.14A(7) CA 1989, and s.29(6) ACA 2002).

(vi) *Variation and discharge* A special guardianship order can be varied or discharged by the court of its own motion during any family proceedings in which a question arises with respect to the child's welfare (s.14D(2)), or on an application by (ss.14D(1), (3)): the special guardian; a parent or guardian with leave of the court; the child with leave of the court; any person in whose favour a residence order is in force with respect to the child; and any person with leave of the court who has, or immediately before the making of the special guardianship order had, parental responsibility for the child. The court can grant leave to applicants (other than the child) if there has been a significant change in circumstances since the order was made (s.14(D)(5)). If a care order is in force with respect to the child, leave must be obtained from the local authority.

(c)　Special guardianship or adoption?

The court may have to decide whether the child's best interests are better promoted by making an adoption order or a special guardianship order. The decision will depend on the facts of the particular case.

The following case is the leading case on the principles to be applied when the court is considering whether to make an adoption order or a special guardianship order:

▶ *Re S (Adoption Order or Special Guardianship Order)* [2007] EWCA Civ 54, [2007] 1 FLR 819

The child (aged 6 and in care of the local authority) was placed with a foster-mother but the child's mother had regular contact, and the father had contact. The foster-mother applied to adopt the child but the judge concluded that adoption was not the best way of securing the child's welfare and made a special guardianship order of her own motion. The foster-mother appealed to the Court of Appeal.

The Court of Appeal held, dismissing her appeal, that:

▶ The key question which the court must ask itself when deciding whether to make a special guardianship order or an adoption order is which order would better serve the welfare of the child, applying the welfare checklists in s.1 CA 1989 and s.1 ACA 2002 (see p. 275 and p. 428).

▶ It is unlikely that the court will need to be concerned with the alternative of making 'no order' (see p. 276 and p. 429), as in most cases the issue will be not the actual placement of the child, but the form of order that should govern the future welfare of the child.

- Because of the importance of such cases to the parties and children concerned, judges must give full reasons and explain their decisions with care.
- Provided the judge has carefully examined the facts, made appropriate findings and applied the welfare checklists, it is unlikely that the court would be able to interfere with the exercise of judicial discretion, particularly in a finely balanced case.
- The risk of prejudice caused by delay is likely to be of less pivotal importance in this type of case; and in many cases it might be appropriate to pause and give time for reflection, particularly in cases where the order is being made of the court's own motion.
- The court must be satisfied that the order it decides to make is a proportionate response to the problem, having regard to the right to family life in art. 8 of the European Convention for the Protection of Human Rights (see 1.7). Special guardianship involves a less fundamental interference with existing legal relationships than adoption, and in some cases the fact that the welfare objective could be achieved with less disruption of existing family relationships could properly be regarded as tipping the balance. However, in most cases art. 8 ECHR is unlikely to add anything to the considerations contained in the welfare checklists.
- Special guardianship does not provide the same permanency as adoption (as the child's parents can apply for a residence order without leave and other s.8 orders with leave, and the leave threshold is set relatively low), although a court can make a s.91(14) order under the CA 1989 to prevent further applications to the court by the child's parents (see p. 285). The fact that special guardianship cannot give the same permanency as adoption might tip the scales in favour of adoption.
- When applying its own motion powers to make a special guardianship order the court can take into account the fact that the person concerned does not wish to be the child's special guardian. But if, applying the welfare checklist under the 1989 Act (including the potential consequences to the child of the refuser implementing the threat to refuse to be appointed a special guardian) the court came to the view that a special guardianship order would best serve the welfare interests of the child, that is the order the court should make.

Intra-familial cases – special guardianship or adoption?   Whether special guardianship instead of adoption will be the preferred option in an intra-family adoption will depend on the facts of the case, applying the principle that the welfare of the child is the court's paramount consideration. While special guardianship may be better than adoption in an intra-familial case (for example, in the case of an applicant grandparent or relative) because it has the benefit of not skewing family relationships, adoption may be better in other situations because of the security it provides for the child.

In *Re AJ (Adoption Order or Special Guardianship Order)* [2007] EWCA Civ 55, [2007] 1 FLR 507 (see over) the Court of Appeal stressed, however, that special guardianship orders had not necessarily replaced adoption orders in cases where a child had been permanently placed within the wider family. Thus, for example, adoption may be better than special guardianship where the relationship between the applicant family member and the child's birth parent is difficult (see *Re EN (A Child) (Special Guardianship Order)* [2007] EWCA Civ 264, [2008] FLR; and *Re M-J (Adoption Order or Special Guardianship Order)* [2007] EWCA Civ 56, [2007] 1 FLR 691, below).

In the following cases, the court had to decide whether to make a special guardianship order or an adoption order. They show the fact-based nature of the judicial decision-making process. They also show that appealing against a discretionary decision made at first instance is unlikely to succeed, unless the judge was plainly wrong or there was an error of law:

▶ **S v. B and Newport City Council; Re K [2007] FLR 1116**

Hedley J made a special guardianship order in favour of the grandparents with whom the child (aged 6) had been living under a care order since he was 6 months old. He did so, despite the grandparents' preference for an adoption order, because adoption would skew the family relationships. Hedley J also made an order under s.91(14) CA 1989 prohibiting any further applications to the court by the child's parents (see p. 285) and an order under s.14B(2)(a) giving leave for the child to be known by the grandparents' surname. Hedley J said that the case was 'one of those cases for which special guardianship was specifically designed' as it permitted familial carers, who were not the parents, 'to have all the practical authority and standing of parents, whilst leaving intact real and readily comprehensible relationships with the family'.

▶ **Re AJ (Adoption Order or Special Guardianship Order) [2007] EWCA Civ 55, [2007] 1 FLR 507**

The Court of Appeal upheld the adoption order in favour of the child's aunt and uncle, on the basis that the child, who had been living with the aunt and uncle since the age of 6 months, needed the assurance that the security of that placement would not be disturbed. A special guardianship order would not provide that assurance, whereas adoption would. The child's father had made aggressive telephone calls to the aunt, and the aunt was concerned that the parents were unpredictable and would litigate issues concerning the child's care. The Court of Appeal agreed with the judge that an adoption order would in the circumstances of the case not unduly distort the family dynamics.

▶ **Re M-J (Adoption Order or Special Guardianship Order) [2007] EWCA Civ 56, [2007] 1 FLR 691**

The child, who was subject to a care order, had been removed from his parents and looked after by his aunt since he was 6 months old (because of the mother's alcohol and drug dependency). The aunt applied to adopt the child but this was opposed by the child's mother. The recorder considered that, although many of the child's needs could be met by a special guardianship order combined with a s.91(14) CA 1989 order (restricting the child's mother from making further applications to the court), those orders did not provide total security. He found that no lesser order than adoption would meet the child's welfare; and that an adoption order was a proportionate order to make in the circumstances. The mother's appeal, on the basis that a special guardianship order was more appropriate in a family placement, was dismissed by the Court of Appeal, which held that there was no rule that a special guardianship order was to be preferred to adoption in family placement unless there were cogent reasons to the contrary.

▶ **Re EN (A Child) (Special Guardianship Order) [2007] EWCA Civ 264**

The paternal grandmother, who had cared for her grandson (aged 3) for most of his life, was refused a special guardianship order because of her fraught relationship with the child's mother. Despite the inevitable loss of the child's primary attachment to the grandmother and the potential for long-term attachment difficulties, the child psychiatrist recommended that child be removed from his grandmother because the 'deep rift' between the mother and grandmother would be a cause of ongoing emotional distress for the child. The child was placed with prospective adopters.

Summary

1 Adoption severs the legal link between the birth-parents and the child and creates a new legal link between the adopter(s) and the child.

2 The law on adoption is laid down in the Adoption and Children Act 2002 (ACA 2002).

3 A legal adoption can be effected only by an adoption order, which is irrevocable. It transfers parental responsibility from the birth-parents to the adopter(s).

4 In adoption cases the court and adoption agencies must apply the welfare principle which is that the 'paramount consideration of the court or adoption agency must be the child's welfare, throughout his life' (s.1(2) ACA 2002). Courts and adoption agencies must also apply the welfare checklist in s.1(4) ACA 2002.

5 A child under the age of 18 who is not, or has not been, married can be adopted.

6 Joint and sole applications for adoption can be made. Married couples can make a joint application, and so can cohabitants (opposite-sex and same-sex). A step-parent can make a sole application for adoption (which was not possible under the old law); and so can a civil partner in respect of the child of his or her civil partner.

7 Consent to adoption must be given but can be dispensed with under s.52 if: the parent or guardian cannot be found or is incapable of giving consent; or the welfare of the child requires consent to be dispensed with.

8 The Registrar-General is responsible for maintaining the Adopted Children Register, and the Adoption Contact Register.

9 Various provisions are in place to govern inter-country adoption, in particular the Hague Convention on the Protection of Children and Co-operation in Respect of Inter-Country Adoption 1993.

10 The ACA 2002 inserts new provisions into the Children Act 1989 which provide alternatives to adoption, in particular special guardianship orders (ss.14A–G CA 1989). Instead of adoption, a step-parent can acquire parental responsibility for a step-child by entering into a parental responsibility agreement or obtaining a parental responsibility order (s.4A CA 1989). A civil partner also has the same rights in respect of the child of his or her civil partner.

11 In some cases the court may have to decide whether to make a special guardianship order or an adoption order. The governing principle is that the welfare of the child is the court's paramount consideration (applying s.1 CA 1989 and s.1 ACA 2002), but the outcome of the case depends on its facts.

Further reading and references

Choudhry, 'The Adoption and Children Act 2002, the welfare principle and the Human Rights Act 1998 – a missed opportunity' [2003] CFLQ 119.

Cullen, 'Adoption – a (fairly) new approach' [2005] CFLQ 475.

Curry, '*EB* v. *France*: a missed opportunity?' [2009] CFLQ 365.

Hall, 'Special guardianship and permanency planning: unforeseen consequences and missed opportunities' [2008] CFLQ 359.

Hall, 'Special guardianship: a missed opportunity: findings from research' [2008] Fam Law 148.

Hayes, 'Giving due consideration to ethnicity in adoption placements – a principled approach?' [2003] CFLQ 255.

Further reading and references cont'd

Hitchings and Sagar, 'The Adoption and Children Act 2002: a level playing field for same-sex adopters?' [2007] CFLQ 60.

Implementing Special Guardianship (November 2009, Department for Children, Schools and Families, see website below).

Neil and Howe (eds.), *Contact in Adoption and Permanent Foster Care, Research, Theory and Practice*, 2004, BAAF.

Quinton and Selwyn, 'Adoption: research, policy and practice' [2006] CFLQ 459.

Sloan, '*Re C (A Child) (Adoption: Duty of Local Authority* – welfare and the rights of the birth family in "fast track" adoption cases' [2009] CFLQ 87.

Smith and Logan, 'Adoptive parenthood as a "legal fiction" – its consequences for direct post-adoption contact' [2002] CFLQ 281.

Thoburn, 'The risks and rewards of adoption for children in the public care' [2003] CFLQ 391.

Websites

British Association for Adoption and Fostering (BAAF): www.baaf.org.uk
Department for Children, Schools and Families: www.dcsf.gov.uk
Every Child Matters: www.everychildmatters.gov.uk

Index